AN IBSEN COMPANION

A DICTIONARY-GUIDE TO THE LIFE, WORKS, AND CRITICAL RECEPTION OF HENRIK IBSEN

George B. Bryan

Greenwood Press
Westport, Connecticut • London, England

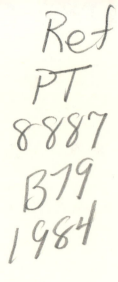

Library of Congress Cataloging in Publication Data

Bryan, George B.
  An Ibsen companion.

  Bibliography: p.
  Includes index.
  1. Ibsen, Henrik, 1828-1906—Dictionaries, indexes,
etc. 2. Ibsen, Henrik, 1828-1906—Handbooks, manuals,
etc. I Title.
PT8887.B79 1984   839.8'226   83-18551
ISBN 0-313-23506-6 (lib. bdg.)

Library of Congress Catalog Card Number: 83-18551
ISBN: 0-313-23506-6

First published in 1984

Greenwood Press
A division of Congressional Information Service, Inc.
88 Post Road West
Westport, Connecticut 06881

Printed in the United States of America

10 9 8 7 6 5 4 3 2 1

This book is affectionately dedicated to

WOLFGANG MIEDER

Professor of German in the University of Vermont,
who, in the words of John Henry Newman,
"displays his science in its most complete and winning form,
pouring it forth with the zeal of enthusiasm and lighting up
his own love of it in the breasts of his hearers,"
of whom I am an appreciative one.

Contents

Preface

Twenty-six years ago I worked on my first college theatrical production, an Expressionistic treatment of Henrik Ibsen's *Hedda Gabler*, directed by Orlin R. Corey and designed by Irene Corey, in which three actresses simultaneously represented different facets of Hedda's complex character. Years later I was enthralled by Maggie Smith's portrayal of the same character in Ingmar Bergman's more Realistic production mounted by the National Theatre of Great Britain. These experiences made me a devotee of Ibsen's works, a thorough chronological reading of which convinced me that the last word had not been said about Ibsen the dramatist. When still later the opportunity of offering a seminar dealing with Ibsen's life and works arose, I once again pored over the entire canon, this time in the company of students, Amy London and Andrew S. Ward, whose growing excitement at the Norwegian's accomplishments nearly matched my own. The teacher, as often happens, learned much from his students. For their insights and enthusiasm I herewith thank them.

F. E. Halliday's *A Shakespeare Companion 1564-1964* (1964) inspired the structure of this book, to which Professor Halliday's caveat is equally applicable: "The book is neither a glossary nor a concordance, nor does it make any claim to be complete; indeed, such a book could never be complete." My goal has been to note the major influences and events of Ibsen's life and dramas, identifying the characters of his plays and providing structural synopses of all his dramatic works. I have doubtless made injudicious omissions, improper assumptions, and an occasional misinterpretation of fact; such cannot be avoided in a book of this nature. Yet there are some entries that will seem novel to all except the most seasoned Ibsenian scholar. Such subjects as Charles Edmond Chojeçki's eyewitness account of an early performance of *The Feast at Solhoug*, the history of the Criterion Independent Theatre, particulars of the lives of Ibsen's brothers in America, the discussion of Ibsen's works on film, the criticism of Emma Goldman, additional biographical facts about William Lawrence, Ibsen's letter to Catherine M. Reignolds-Winslow, and the discussion of John Arctander fall into this category.

This book, which is organized to provide easy accessibility to its contents, will be useful to theatre artists, teachers, and students. The initial essay on "Ibsen the Dramatist" introduces his dramatic works, places them in their historical and critical context, and identifies his major thematic thrusts. A chronological account of Ibsen's life is then presented in outline form. The alphabetical format of the Dictionary-Guide includes entries on people connected with Ibsen's life and work; producing organizations, institutions, and locales; Ibsen's dramas (the names of which are given in italic capitals), their stage histories (which are as complete as available documentation allows), their major structural characteristics, and identification of all the speaking characters (the names of which appear in boldface capitals). With regard to the stage histories, numbers in parentheses indicate numbers of performances. The casting of leading performers, number of performances, and so on are given when such information is available. An asterisk (*) refers to a separate entry under the heading of the word that precedes it. Although the Dictionary-guide contains entries on all the speaking characters in Ibsen's plays, asterisks are not affixed to their names in the structural synopses of the dramas. To do so would prove unnecessarily cumbersome. Readers should also note that in the Norwegian language, "ae" and "ö" come at the end of the alphabet; that convention also applies to the Norwegian words in this work.

In describing Ibsen's dramas, I have not been content merely to tell the story of each play. In the attempt to provide what I call structural synopses, I have not written as an omniscient critic blessed with foresight but as a member of the audience viewing the incidents for the first time. I have, however, added structural comments on the unfolding plots. In the synopses and critical comments, I employ terms that perhaps require explanation.

I have assumed that every drama in production is comprised of six qualitative parts: Plot, Character, Thought, Diction, Melody, and Spectacle. Pantomimic dramatization, scenery, lighting, costumes, make-up—these constitute Spectacle. The sound of the actors speaking their roles with variations of pitch, rate, force, and quality constitutes the Melody of a drama. Diction, the playwright's major means of characterizing his agents, is the dialogue. If the sayings and doings of each character can be seen as a rhetorical argument, the Thought of the play is their aggregate viewed in terms of the ending of the drama. A dramatic Character is an agent of the action, a doer. The Plot is the overall structure of a drama; it is the formal cause of the other five elements. Complex plots contain action, discovery, and reversal; discovery (the passage from ignorance to knowledge) impels a dramatic action forward. Reversal is a peripety, a substantial alteration of the direction of a dramatic action.

To seem complete and satisfying, a drama must be unified. There are three types of dramatic unity, the most artistic of which is unity of action. In this type of formulation, each incident is the cause of the next in such a way that the beginning of the action is the direct cause of the ending; the ending, the result of the beginning. The greatest plays from Sophocles to Shakespeare to Ibsen exhibit this type of wholeness. Dramas may also be unified by Character and Thought. In the former, loosely related episodes illustrate a change in a protagonist; in the latter, episodic incidents depict various aspects of a principal idea.

Every drama has form (tragedy, melodrama, comedy, and so on), which is the result of the playwright's manipulation of the six qualitative parts, and style (Romanticism, Realism, Symbolism, and so forth), which is dependent upon the dramatist's view of reality. A complete analysis of the form and style of any play includes everything that may be said of the drama as a work of art. [For a discussion of form and style, see Oscar G. Brockett, *The Theatre: An Introduction*, 4th ed. (New York: Holt, Rinehart, and Winston, 1979).]

The perspicacious reader will have seen that these concepts have been derived from Aristotle's *Poetics*. They are, however, fully explicated by Hubert C. Heffner in *Modern Theatre Practice*, 5th ed. (New York: Appleton, Century, and Crofts, 1973).

Ibsen's dramas have been translated into nearly every European language. In an appendix I have listed the major early translators; an asterisk (*) following a translator's name directs the reader to a separate entry in the Dictionary-Guide.

Most of the entries in the Dictionary-Guide are followed by bibliographical references to material that is germane to that particular discussion. Except in a few cases, those citations are not repeated in the Selective Bibliography that appears at the end of the book. I have cited therein what I believe to be the most significant works that have yet appeared. Although most of the references are by design in English, I have included some works in other languages because of their special worth. By utilizing the references at the ends of the entries and consulting the Selective Bibliography, the reader will be equipped for intensive further study.

It is doubtful that any contemporary writer on Ibsen could neglect to acknowledge Michael Meyer for his *Ibsen: A Biography* (Garden City, N.Y.: Doubleday and Company, 1971) and James Walter McFarlane and Graham Orton, editors of *The Oxford Ibsen* (London: Oxford University Press, 1960-70). These men have made my task inexpressibly easier than it might have been, but they do not stand alone among those who ought to be thanked.

A research grant awarded by the Graduate College of the University of Vermont made it possible for me to work in the Scandinavian collections of the University of Minnesota and the Norwegian-American Historical Society, where Charlotte Jacobson was most obliging. Marian Lindkvist pursued nebulous leads in London's archives of public records. Raymond and Barbara Phillips of The Learning Center (Burlington, Vermont) providentially made their computer facilities available to me. Milton Ehre of the University of Chicago and Evert Sprinchorn of Vassar College have been generous with their advice, as have my colleagues at the University of Vermont: Veronica Richel and David Scrase of the Department of German and Russian; Edward J. Feidner of the Department of Theatre; and Sandra Gavett and her associates in the Interlibrary Loan Department of the Bailey-Howe Library. My special appreciation goes to Andrew S. Ward whose research help was indispensable and all the more valuable because it was given gratuitously.

Ibsen the Dramatist

Perhaps no other modern dramatist has been subjected to such damning criticism as Ibsen. William Archer* laboriously catalogued the canon of excoriation that greeted *Ghosts*,* its author, and its adherents (*Pall Mall Gazette,* April 8, 1891), but a similar wave of vituperation inundated each of Ibsen's dramas subsequent to *The League of Youth.** The American response was not appreciably different from the European. In 1899, for example, drama critic Amy Leslie, reacting to *A Doll's House*,* voiced the American anti-Ibsenite view:

In Ibsen's poignant sophistry there is always a dismal but touching relation to devout truth. That is all. There is no more honesty in Ibsen than there is in Wilde or Verlaine but the mighty Scandinavian has, through the average hysterical reasoning of his worshipers, come to be regarded in the light of a doleful but spurring prophet of brave ethics. [*Some Players: Personal Sketches* (Chicago: Herman S. Stone, 1899), p. 110.]

Yet Ibsen saw himself as a servant of truth and honesty. In view of the disparity between the playwright's intention and the reception of his dramas by his detractors, it is well to consider their responses as well as more positive ones.

When *Catiline** was published in 1850, two hundred fifty copies were printed, of which fewer than one-fifth were sold in the first year. (I had the pleasure of unearthing one of these in the Marsh Collection of the Bailey-Howe Library at the University of Vermont.) Eventually, the remainder was sold as waste paper to raise money. Yet, as first plays go, there was much to praise in *Catiline*, which received a few encouraging write-ups but was not accepted for production until 1880. As an unknown author writing in Norwegian at a time when there was no Norwegian theatre and no professional Norwegian actors, Ibsen suffered from lack of interest in his work.

Ibsen's second piece, *The Burial Mound*,* though structurally and thematically weaker than *Catiline*, was produced by the Christiania Theatre* in 1850 and was on the whole appreciated. Ibsen himself, however, was so dissatisfied with his simplistic play that he never allowed it to be published, although a revision was printed in a newspaper when the drama was produced in Bergen* in 1854.

The political satire of *Norma** (1851) was directed against Norway's Parliament, the Storthing. Although it was not intended for production, the drama contains some skillful verse and trenchant satire. Ibsen also declined to publish his next drama, *St. John's Night** (1853); yet it is not without charm. Its major fault is a too-close resemblance to the fairy scenes of *A Midsummer Night's Dream,* but its plot is skillfully manipulated in the current French fashion, the characters (particularly Julian Poulsen,* the quintessential Romantic poet), are interestingly drawn, and the prose dialogue is conversationally credible. As a Romantic fairy play, *St. John's Night* is commendable, but its production at Bergen was an abject failure.

*Lady Inger of Österaad** (1854) marked the end of the first phase of Ibsen's apprenticeship as a dramatist. If this play had succeeded with the Bergen public, perhaps Ibsen would have continued to write prose dramas, but once again his work went unappreciated. Despite its unrelieved gloom, complicated plot based on intercepted letters, confused identity, and lengthy asides, the drama is a powerful statement of internal conflict between duty and cowardice. For years Ibsen viewed *Lady Inger* as his best work.

Turning to the Norse family sagas for inspiration, Ibsen next produced *The Feast at Solhoug** (1856), written in both verse and prose, which brought him his first full measure of public acclaim. Ibsen's medieval drama was structurally flawed and looked toward old rather than new dramatic conventions, yet its authentic atmosphere and melodramatic revenge motif appealed to Scandinavian playgoers, who made it the second most popular play in the repertory of the Norwegian Theatre (Bergen).*

In *The Feast at Solhoug* Ibsen had employed medieval ballads as an expository, rhythmical, and atmospheric device, the response to which encouraged him to repeat the experiment in his next drama. He decided to rework his unfinished blank-verse script *The Grouse in Justedal*,* the result of which was *Olaf Liljekrans** (1857). Although contemporary audiences were lukewarm to the production and Ibsen virtually disowned it, the drama contains some good poetry and interesting characters. The storyline is rather conventional, however.

When Ibsen was engaged by the Norwegian Theatre (Christiania)* in 1857, he had already started work on *The Vikings in Helgeland*,* which proved to be a noble experiment as he tried to render in dramatic form certain epic characters and events of the Icelandic sagas. Although the result was not wholly successful, the play proved to be the most popular of all his dramas on the nineteenth-century Scandinavian stage. *The Vikings in Helgeland* was to be Ibsen's last play for five years.

Love's Comedy (1862) marked Ibsen's return as a dramatist. In it Ibsen freely expressed his advanced views about love and marriage in the contemporary age and received some of the blistering criticism that was to characterize his later work. For the first time, critics abused the philosophical content of an Ibsenian drama, but its form, especially the rhymed verse in which all the dialogue was cast, was cited as a weakness as well.

The second phase of Ibsen's dramatic apprenticeship ended with the appearance of *The Pretenders* (1863), a drama based on Norwegian history. In addition to three striking characterizations (Bishop Nikolas,* Haakon,* and Skule*), Ibsen demonstrated that he had at last managed to write colloquial speech reflective of a wide range of emotions. Ibsen's direction of his play on January 17, 1864, at the Christiania Theatre marked his retirement from active participation in theatrical production. Its success indicated that Ibsen had become a recognized man of the theatre and not simply a dilettante.

Brand was published in 1866. Since the work was not meant for production (Ibsen called it a dramatic poem), the playwright did not have to consider the practical limitations of the stage. As a consequence, *Brand* is of such poetic and descriptive magnitude that nearly all of Ibsen's previous dramas seem anemic by comparison. As a result of the popularity of the piece, Ibsen's countrymen came to see Ibsen as the spokesman for the new and progressive and the eulogist of everything moribund and retrospective. Naturally, there was some criticism of *Brand*, most of it in opposition to the unmistakable Romanticism of the piece, which became a *cause célèbre* and Ibsen's release from financial worry.

Ibsen's next work, *Peer Gynt* (1867), is in some ways complementary to *Brand*, each representing extreme views of life. Brand's motto was "All or Nothing," while Peer's was "Enough." Björnstjerne Björnson* admired Ibsen's audacity in creating such a dramatic poem, but others, led by critic Clemens Petersen,* reacted with a hostility that was incommensurate with the faults of the work. As a result, the book did not sell well, nor was there any interest in producing it until thirteen years after its publication. When viewed dispassionately, *Peer Gynt* stands as one of Ibsen's three most profound works (the others being *Brand* and *Emperor and Galilean*).

When *The League of Youth* appeared in 1869, Ibsen exhibited signs of having adopted a different dramatic technique from that of *Brand* and *Peer Gynt*. Its chief dissimilarity from its immediate predecessors lies in its colloquial Diction, which for the first time is realistic and contemporary. Ibsen saw the play as a comedy, but its satirical portraits of politicians convinced his detractors that Ibsen intended to pillory actual people. Numerous critics flailed *The League of Youth* principally for this reason, but the Norwegian people showed their delight in it by their attendance at the theatre and made it Ibsen's most popular drama in his native land.

Ibsen considered *Emperor and Galilean** (1873) to be his greatest work. If intellectual depth and dramatic scope (it is a drama in two five-act parts) constitute greatness, the playwright's opinion cannot be refuted. A drama of Faustian magnitude, *Emperor and Galilean* is a dramatization of the Hegelian dialectic (thesis-antithesis-synthesis) at work in the conflict between Christianty and paganism. Like *Brand* and *Peer Gynt, Emperor and Galilean* is a closet drama. When the play first appeared, it was generally admired, but as later readers embraced the contemporary social problem play, such a monumental treatise as *Emperor and Galilean* seemed increasingly remote. It is safe to say that most modern playgoers never heard of Ibsen's masterpiece.

With the publication of his three epic giants, Ibsen had explored the human condition from a distance; thereafter he was to examine life in proximity. *The Pillars of Society** (1877), similar in approach if not in dramatic skill to *The League of Youth*, is usually called the first of Ibsen's Realistic social problem plays. Although the book sold well and received good reviews throughout Scandinavia, on stage it has never been one of Ibsen's more popular dramas. From a practical standpoint, its nineteen characters and a crowd of townspeople present some problems. Structurally, the play has been criticized as an example of Ibsen's tenacious adheı ence to the well-made play* form, principally because of the contrived ending. His condemnation of unscrupulous capitalists was not wide of the mark.

Ibsen's manipulation of colloquial dialogue, psychological characterization, and organic structure made *The Pillars of Society* a harbinger of what was to come. His next play, *A Doll's House** (1879), demonstrated a noticeable advance in dramatic technique. This drama created a sensation wherever it was seen. Although some critics caviled at various structural weaknesses, their real focus was on the thematic content: the weakness of contemporary marriage, the double moral standard, the claims of motherhood, and the emancipation of women. For the rest of his creative life, Ibsen was to be subjected to scathing condemnation for his unconventional ideas.

In Nora Helmer* (*A Doll's House*) Ibsen depicted a woman seeking spiritual freedom by scrapping her marriage; in *Ghosts** (1881) he shows the disastrous consequences of a wife's adherence to a debilitating marriage. The catastrophe of *Ghosts* befalls Helene Alving,* the protagonist, but critics were so shocked by the onstage depiction of Oswald Alving's* syphilitic crisis that for many the true point of the play was obscured. *Ghosts* has remained Ibsen's most controversial play.

*An Enemy of the People** (1882) followed *Ghosts*. Ibsen's unsympathetic treatment of greedy politicians angered both liberals and conservatives. The critical reception of the play was mixed, but it has not been as successful the theatre as its merits warrant, perhaps because of the large crow required for the town meeting in Act IV.

With the appearance of *The Wild Duck** in 1884, the critics wailed of their bewilderment. Thereafter a chorus of complaint was to greet the canon as Ibsen increasingly utilized indirect suggestion and wove symbols into his plots. In those days before Freudian criticism existed, writers used symbols to express what could not otherwise be said. When Ibsen employed symbols such as the wild duck, it was because he was trying to communicate the inexpressible. The object of Symbolism has been warped by contemporary Freudian critics who think they can say precisely what symbols mean. Ibsen had the skill to express himself directly when his vision was expressible; he resorted to symbols when words would not do. Unfortunately, his public was not up to the task he set it.

Rosmersholm* (1886), one of Ibsen's most intriguing plays, caused almost as much furor as *Ghosts* had done. The old epithets of obscurity, unwholesomeness, and artificial characterization were resurrected and applied to *Rosmersholm*. In the play Ibsen implies incest, murder through hypnotism, and supernatural intervention in mundane affairs; he depicts a wayward clergyman in the toils of a female free-thinker. Once again some of his contemporaries were scandalized by his subject matter.

The happy ending of *The Lady from the Sea** (1888) caused that drama to fare a little better than its predecessor, but its complex psychological meanderings confused all but the most perceptive. The hypnotic effect of the sea upon the languid Ellida Wangel* produced the by-now typical bewilderment. *Hedda Gabler** (1890), perhaps Ibsen's most popular drama today, was roasted in the press. Hedda herself—an unwilling mother, undevoted wife, and a suicide—was viewed as unnatural and the play as Ibsen's most obscure piece to date. Ibsen's use of short speeches and discovery by implication was the major source of confusion to a public that demanded a clarification that was not forthcoming.

The Master Builder* (1892) was successful with the reading public but largely unappreciated on the stage. Its treatment of an aging man's morbid fear of the young did not threaten society's traditions, but the symbolism of the tower and the harps in the wind produced the usual imprecations of obscurity. By 1894 Ibsen's stature as a dramatist was almost universally recognized, so the publication of *Little Eyolf** was greeted by considerable interest. Indeed, it became quite a success, perhaps because those who preferred Realistic plays could view it with satisfaction on that level; for the more avant-garde, the symbolism was titillating. Despite its poetic excellence, *Little Eyolf* has not been popular in the theatre.

For some readers the Ibsenian obscurity was dissipated by *John Gabriel Borkman** (1896), and while a few critics condemned it as too pessimistic, the majority hailed it as a masterpiece. The denouement achieves a poetic magnitude nearly as great as that of *Brand*. The Scandinavian productions of *John Gabriel Borkman* were quite successful, but its stage history elsewhere has not been as distinguished. For a public now well-schooled in Realism, *When We Dead Awaken** (1899) proved to be problematical because of its poetic conception. Critics, however, were respectful of the aging dramatist, admired the lyricism of the piece, and were inclined to accept it as an arcane masterpiece. When first produced in European theatres, it invariably failed, perhaps because its scope exceeded that of its interpreters.

From the perspective of his entire career, Ibsen was initially criticized for inept craftmanship. In quick succession came censure for too much reliance on the well-made play technique, his subject matter, and finally his obscurity. In other words, once he mastered dramatic construction, he was denigrated because of his ideas; as the public came to accept his ideas, Ibsen's dramaturgy became more advanced. Ibsen's reputation outside Scandinavia was established by his social problem plays, but in the late twentieth century when Realism daily becomes more passé, his psychological/symbolic studies provide greater stimulation.

Although it is commonplace to divide the Ibsenian corpus of works into three groups (the nationalistic/historical pieces, the social problem plays, and the psychological/symbolic dramas), Ibsen's thought developed progressively, thus vitiating such easy generalizations. Perhaps this development may be suggested by a synoptical view of his dramatic writings.

Ibsen employed a number of quantitative forms. His only one-act drama to be produced was *The Burial Mound*. His three-act plays include *Catiline, St. John's Night, The Feast at Solhoug, Olaf Liljekrans, Love's Comedy, A Doll's House, Ghosts, The Master Builder, Little Eyolf*, and *When We Dead Awaken. The Vikings in Helgeland, The Pillars of Society, Rosmersholm, Hedda Gabler*, and *John Gabriel Borkman* are written in four acts. The five-act dramas are *Lady Inger of Österaad, The Pretenders, Brand, Peer Gynt, The League of Youth, An Enemy of the People, The Wild Duck*, and *The Lady from the Sea*. His only ten-act drama is *Emperor and Galilean*, written in two five-act parts.

The dramas vary in length as the following chart indicates. The numbers represent pages which the scripts occupy in *The Oxford Ibsen*.

The Burial Mound (24)	*Catiline* (73)
The Feast at Solhoug (53)	*Ghosts* (77)
St. John's Night (58)	*John Gabriel Borkman* (82)
When We Dead Awaken (62)	*Lady Inger of Österaad* (90)
The Vikings in Helgeland (66)	*The Master Builder* (92)
Little Eyolf (71)	*Rosmersholm* (92)

Ibsen described the forms of his plays in a number of ways, employing the terms *drama, dramatisk digtning* (dramatic composition), *eventyr komedie* (fairy tale comedy), *historisk drama* (historical drama), *skuespil* (play), *komedie* (comedy), *historisk skuespil* (historical play), *dramatisk digt* (dramatic poem), *lystspil* (comedy), *verdenshistorisk skuespil* (world-historical piay), *familjedrame* (domestic drama), and *dramatisk epilog* (dramatic epilog). In the following chart, more traditional formal designations are given as well as an indication of the dramatic styles of the plays: ROM-Romantic; RE-Relistic; SYM-Symbolistic; TRA-Tragedy; SD-Serious Drama; COM-Comedy.

DRAMA	*IBSEN'S FORM*	*TRADITIONAL FORM*	*STYLE*
Catiline	*drama*	SD	ROM
The Burial Mound	*dramatisk digtning*	SD	ROM
St. John's Night	*eventyr komedie*	COM	ROM
Lady Inger	*historisk drama*	SD	ROM
The Feast at Solhoug	*skuespil*	SD	ROM
Olaf Liljekrans	*skuespil*	SD	ROM
The Vikings in Helgeland	*skuespil*	SD	ROM
Love's Comedy	*komedie*	COM	ROM
The Pretenders	*historisk skuespil*	SD	ROM
Brand	*dramatisk digt*	TRA	ROM
Peer Gynt	*drmatisk digt*	SD	ROM
The League of Youth	*lystspil*	COM	ROM-RE
Emperor and Galilean	*verdenshistorisk skuespil*	SD	ROM-RE
The Pillars of Society	*skuespil*	SD	RE
A Doll's House	*skuespil*	SD	RE
Ghosts	*familjedrame*	SD	RE
An Enemy of the People	*skuespil*	SD	RE
The Wild Duck	*skuespil*	SD	RE-SYM
Rosmersholm	*skuespil*	SD	RE-SYM
The Lady from the Sea	*skuespil*	SD	RE-SYM
Hedda Gabler	*skuespil*	SD	RE-SYM

DRAMA	IBSEN'S FORM	TRADITIONAL FORM	STYLE
The Master Builder	skuespil	SD	RE-SYM
Little Eyolf	skuespil	SD	RE-SYM
John Gabriel Borkman	skuespil	SD	RE-SYM
When We Dead Awaken	dramatisk epilog	SD	RE-SYM

Certain types of character interested Ibsen throughout his career. Much has been written of his partiality to female protagonists—Lady Inger of Gyldenlöve, Margit,* Hjördis,* Nora Helmer,* Helene Alving,* Ellida Wangel,* and Hedda Gabler*—but it must be observed that most of his protagonists are male. The male protagonists with female antagonists are Catiline,* Gandalf,* Julian Poulsen,* Olaf Liljekrans,* Karsten Bernick,* Johannes Rosmer,* Halvard Solness,* Alfred Allmers,* John Gabriel Borkman,* and Arnold Rubek.* All the female protagonists, incidentally, conflict with male antagonists, but several of the male protagonists—Haakon,* Stensgaard,* Thomas Stockmann,* Gregers Werle*—are opposed by male antagonists. Three of his most significant protagonists contain their principal adversaries within themselves: Brand,* Peer Gynt,* and the Emperor Julian.* It cannot be denied, however, that Ibsen was unusually sensitive to the relationship between the sexes.

On the basis of his characterizations, Ibsen can be seen to have had little appreciation of the representatives of organized religion. His ministers from Pastor Straamand* to the Dean* (Brand) to Pastor Manders* are anything but attractive, and his depiction of Bishop Nikolas as the personification of of perpetual evil is one of Ibsen's strongest portraits. Other character types which appear in Ibsen's plays are poets, illegitimate children, doctors, and printers, all of which are psychologically linked with events and people in Ibsen's own life.

Since Ibsen was primarily a dramatist of ideas, his plays contain a variegated tapestry of numerous intellectual strands. Among his recurrent themes are the elusiveness of self-actualization, the moral bankruptcy of materialistic society, and the restrictive narrowness of traditional moral values. A thread of idealism, wholly expected in the Romantic and Symbolistic pieces, runs through even the most Realistic of his dramas. One of his favorite topics was the way in which geography affects temperament, an idea that first occurs in The Burial Mound. A fierce, cold, methodical Viking comes under the sway of a Christian girl from a southern locale. She is warm and emotional and in the end returns with him to Scandinavia to kindle the frozen hearts there. The climactic events of The Pretenders take place in the cold north, and an uncompromising Brand will not forsake the north for the south, even to protect the health of his dying son. In A Doll's House Nora takes Torvald from Norway to Italy to recuperate from his illness, and there she learns the tarantella, a sign of her adoption of the southern temperament. Thomas Stockmann has returned from the north to his southern home, where his principles create a crisis. The idealism of Gregers Werle was merely troublesome in the north; at home in the south, it produces a catastrophe. Old Ekdal* was happy and respected in the north; in the south he is a frustrated convict. Ellida Wangel, a denizen of the north, is like a fish out of water in the south. These are not all the examples of Ibsen's juxtaposition of the north and south, but they sufficiently indicate that to him the idea was compelling.

That mountains should figure in the compositions of a native Norwegian is not remarkable, but Ibsen's mountains assume a symbolic, brooding role in his plays. In *St. John's Night, Olaf Liljekrans*, and *Peer Gynt,* supernatural events are believed to occur on the heights. The mountains become a source of solace to the spurned lover in *Love's Comedy*, a place of mystical enlightenment in *Brand* and *Little Eyolf*, and the scene of spiritual rejuvenation in *John Gabriel Borkman* and *When We Dead Awaken*. In *The Master Builder* the mountain becomes a spire, but its application is the same.

Supernatural occurrences in such plays as *St. John's Night, Brand, Peer Gynt*, and *Emperor and Galilean* are predictable, but Ibsen's use of the irrational and inexplicable in *Rosmersholm, The Lady from the Sea, Little Eyolf, John Gabriel Borkman*, and *When We Dead Awaken* reveals his fascination with the parapsychological.

In terms of the Diction of his plays, Ibsen used prose, poetry, and various combinations of the two. His poetic dramas include *Catiline, The Burial Mound, Brand*, and *Peer Gynt*. The plays in both poetry and prose are *St. John's Night, The Feast at Solhoug, Olaf Liljekrans*, and *Love's Comedy*. All the rest are in prose, although at times the prose of the last four dramas is sufficiently rarified to be poetic.

Ibsen learned to be an expert manipulator of Spectacle. Details of setting and costume are rather vague in the early plays, but Ibsen grew more precise in his stage directions as Spectacle played an increasingly important role in his dramas. Spectacular transformations are required in *St. John's Night* and *Peer Gynt;* apparitions or magnificent atmospheric effects are demanded in *The Vikings, Brand, John Gabriel Borkman*, and *When We Dead Awaken*. A burning house is featured in *Olaf Liljekrans*. Six of the dramas are set out-of-doors: *The Burial Mound, St. John's Night, Olaf Liljekrans, Love's Comedy, The Lady from the Sea*, and *When We Dead Awaken*. Indoor/outdoor settings are depicted in *Catiline, The Vikings, The Pretenders, Brand, Peer Gynt, The League of Youth, Emperor and Galilean, Little Eyolf*, and *John Gabriel Borkman*. The settings of the remaining plays (which include the Realistic dramas) are indoors, which perhaps means that Ibsen thought that such enclosed arenas facilitated his stress on environment as a determinant of character.

Ibsen's dramas are far too complex to be encompassed by a brief introductory essay, but perhaps some of these suggestions considered in the context of the bibliographies that follow each play and the larger one at the end of the book will provide matter for intensive speculation. Here I have tried merely to hint at the richness of his work.

Chronology of Ibsen's Life

SKIEN (1828–43)

1828:	March 20	Henrik Ibsen is born in Skien.*
1830:		Johan Andreas Altenburg Ibsen* is born.
1831:		The Ibsen family moves to Altenburggaarden.*
1832:		Hedvig Ibsen* is born.
1834:	September 11	Nicolai Alexander Ibsen* is born.
1835:	June	Because of financial reversals, the Ibsen family moves to Venstöp.* Ole Paus Ibsen* is born.
1843:	Spring	Ibsen leaves school.
	October 1	Ibsen is confirmed in the parish of Gjerpen.
		The family moves to the outskirts of Skien.
	December 27?	Ibsen leaves his family to begin to support himself.

GRIMSTAD (1844–50)

1844:	January 3	Ibsen arrives in Grimstad* and assumes his duties as apprentice to apothecary J. A. Reimann.*
1846:	August	Reimann sells his business to Lars Nielsen,* who moves the shop to more commodious quarters and improves Ibsen's terms of employment.
	October 9	Ibsen and Else Sofie Jensdatter* produce an illegitimate son, Hans Jakob Henriksen.*
1848:		*Catiline** starts to occupy Ibsen's mind, perhaps as a result of his study of Latin. Ibsen is befriended by Christoffer Lorentz Due* and Ole Schulerud.*
1849:		Ibsen is introduced to Clara Ebbell* and becomes attached to her.
	September 28	His first publication, "In Autumn,"* appears.
	December 24	The Danish Christiania Theatre* refuses to stage *Catiline*.

1850:   January 2   The Norwegian Theatre (Bergen)* is opened.
         April 12   *Catiline's* publication is subsidized by Schulerud.
         April 13   Ibsen has a two-week holiday with his family in Skien.

CHRISTIANIA (1850–51)

1850:   May 16   In Christiania, Ibsen enters H.A.S. Heltberg's
                         "crammer" to prepare for his University entrance
                         examination. Ibsen writes the fragmentary *The
                         Grouse in Justedal.*
         September 3   Ibsen learns that he has scored a conditional pass on his
                         examination, although he failed Greek and arith-
                         metic.
         September 7   *The Burial Mound* is performed at the Christiania
                         Theatre.
         December 9   The Christiania Theatre awards Ibsen a free pass.
1851:   Student Ibsen contributes articles to *Samfundsbladet*
                         and *Andhrimner.*
         June 1, 8   *Norma** is published in *Manden*, the first incarnation of
                         the magazine *Andhrimner.*.
         September 15   His pass is renewed by the Christiania Theatre.
         October 15   Ibsen's prologue is read at the Students' Union Concert
                         in aid of the Norwegian Theatre (Bergen).
                         Ole Bull* notices Ibsen and subsequently hires him to
                         work in the theatre at Bergen.

BERGEN (1851–57)

1851:   October 26   Ibsen assumes his duties as stage director at Bergen.
         November 6   The governing board of the Norwegian Theatre appoints
                         Ibsen dramatic author.
1852:   January 2   Ibsen supplies a prologue for the Foundation Day of the
                         Norwegian Theatre.
         April 15-July   Ibsen studies theatrical practices in Copenhagen, Ham-
                         burg, and Dresden.
         October 6   Ibsen directs his first production.
1853:   January 2   *St. John's Night** is acted at Bergen. Ibsen becomes in-
                         fatuated with Rikke Holst, to whom he addresses
                         several poems.
1854:   January 2   The revised version of *The Burial Mound* is presented at
                         the Norwegian Theatre.
1855:   January 2   Ibsen stages *Lady Inger of Österaad** at Bergen.
         November 27   The Society of December 22 hears Ibsen's paper
                         "Shakespeare and His Influence upon Scandinavian
                         Literature."*
1856:   January 2   *The Feast at Solhoug** is presented at Bergen.
         January 7   Ibsen meets Suzannah Thoresen, his future wife.

	March 19	*The Feast at Solhoug* is published.
	Summer	Ibsen embarks upon a walking tour with Carl Johan Anker.*
1857:	January 2	Ibsen's last contractual play, *Olaf Liljekrans,** is performed at Bergen.
	February 2	Ibsen reads a paper, "On the Heroic Ballad,"* to the Society of December 22.
	April	The governors of the Norwegian Theatre renew Ibsen's contract for one year.
	July 9	Ibsen starts a vacation in Christiania that lasts until the end of August.
	July 23	The Norwegian Theatre (Christiania)* offers Ibsen a position.
		Ibsen asks to be released from his contract at Bergen.
	August 4	His release from Bergen becomes official.
	August 11	Ibsen signs a contract of employment as artistic director of the Norwegian Theatre (Christiania).

CHRISTIANIA (1857-64)

1858:		Ibsen becomes a founding member of The Learned Hollanders.*
	April 25	*The Vikings in Helgeland** is published after being refused for presentation by the Royal Theatre, Copenhagen.
	June 18	Ibsen marries Suzannah Thoresen.
	November 24	The Norwegian Theatre presents *The Vikings in Helgeland,* directed by Ibsen.
1859:	November	Ibsen and Björnstjerne Björson* form the Norwegian Society* to foster native culture.
	December 23	Sigurd Ibsen,* the dramatist's only legitimate child, is born.
1860:	August 6	Ibsen's request for a government subsidy of a tour of European capitals is refused.
		Things go poorly for the Norwegian Theatre, and Ibsen's leadership is questioned.
1861:		Some anti-Ibsenites call for Ibsen's resignation from the theatre, but he stays.
1862:	March 14	Ibsen applies to the Akademiske Kollegium* for a travel grant.
	May 24	He receives a smaller subsidy than requested.
	June 1	The Norwegian Theatre is bankrupted, so Ibsen is unemployed.
	June 24	Ibsen sets off for western Norway to collect folklore.
	December 31	*Love's Comedy** is published.
1863:	January 1	Ibsen is appointed temporary literary adviser to the newly reconstituted Christiania Theatre, now presenting dramas in Norwegian rather than Danish.

	March 6	Again Ibsen petitions the Akademiske Kollegium for funds to travel in northern Norway; again he receives a reduced sum.
	May 27	Ibsen asks the government for a travel grant after it has refused him an annual literary stipend; his petition is successful, but the amount is pared.
	October 31	*The Pretenders** is published.
1864:	January 17	*The Pretenders* is produced by the Christiania Theatre.

ITALY (1864-68)

1864:	April 5	Discouraged by conditions in his native land, Ibsen departs for Copenhagen, Lübeck, Berlin, Vienna, and Rome; he will not again live in Norway for twenty-seven years.
	Summer	The hot, humid months are spent in Rome and Genzano.
	Autumn	Suzannah and Sigurd join Ibsen in Rome.
1865:	March 25	Finding that continental living is expensive, Ibsen applies to the Royal Norwegian Society of Learning for a stipend; again his request is granted but diminished.
1866:	March 15	*Brand** is published by Frederik Hegel* in Copenhagen.
	May 12	The Norwegian government awards Ibsen an annual grant to subsidize his writing.
	June 28	The government grants Ibsen additional funds.
1867:	Summer	After traveling in Italy, Ibsen settles in Berchtesgaden.
	September	He moves to Munich.
	November 14	*Peer Gynt** is published.

DRESDEN (1868-75)

1868:	October	Ibsen takes up residence in Dresden.
1869:	June 3	Marichen Cornelia Martie Altenburg Ibsen,* the playwright's mother, dies.
	July 3	The Norwegian government subsidizes Ibsen's study in Sweden.
	July 27-30	Ibsen attends the Scandinavian Orthographical Conference in Stockholm, where he receives the first of many official decorations.
	September	Ibsen receives an invitation to be the Norwegian representative at the opening of the Suez Canal.
	September 30	*The League of Youth** is published.
	November	Ibsen visits Egypt for the first time.
	December	He returns to Dresden.
1870:	July 19	Ibsen leaves Germany for a period in Copenhagen.

	October	He again moves to Dresden.
1871:	February 13	Ibsen learns that he has been awarded the Order of Danneborg.
	May 3	His collected poems are published.
1872:	February	P. F. Siebold* publishes the first German translation of an Ibsenian work: *Brand*.
	July 15	Ibsen revisits Berchtesgaden.
	September	He returns to Dresden.
1873:	June 12	Ibsen travels to Vienna to serve as a judge at the International Art Exhibition.
	July	His own country at last pays Ibsen homage by creating him a knight of the Order of St. Olaf.
	October 16	*Emperor and Galilean** is published.
	November 24	*Love's Comedy* is staged at the Christiania Theatre.
1874:	January 23	Ibsen invites Edvard Grieg* to supply music for *Peer Gynt*.
	July 19	Ibsen arrives in Christiania for an extended visit.
	September 10	The students give Ibsen a torchlight procession.
1875:	April	Ibsen leaves Dresden and settles in Munich.

MUNICH (1875-79)

1875:	October 1	Ibsen returns to Munich after a summer in the Tyrol.
1876:	February	Catherine Ray* becomes Ibsen's first English translator when *Emperor and Galilean* is published.
	February 24	*Peer Gynt* is performed at the Christiania Theatre.
	April 10	*The Vikings in Helgeland* is seen at the Hoftheater, Munich.
	June 3	Ibsen witnesses a performance of *The Pretenders* staged by Georg II, duke of Saxe-Meiningen.*
1877:	May 1	Ibsen joins a literary society, the Crocodile,* in Munich.
	September 5	The University of Uppsala awards Ibsen an honorary doctorate.
	October 4	Knud Plesner Ibsen,* the dramatist's father, dies.
	October 11	*The Pillars of Society** is published.
1878:	Summer	Ibsen stays at Gossensass.
	July	He moves to Amalfi, where he finishes *A Doll's House.**
	Autumn	The early autumn is passed in Rome.
	October	Ibsen returns to Munich.
1879:	December 4	*A Doll's House* is published.

ITALY (1880-85)

1880:	November 2	The Ibsen family settles in Rome where Sigurd studies law.
	December 15	*Quicksands,** the first English production of an Ibsenian play, is seen in London.

1881:   December 12   *Ghosts** is published.
1882:   June 2   *The Child Wife** is staged in Milwaukee, the first pro-
                        duction in the United States of an Ibsenian drama in
                        English.

        November 28   *An Enemy of the People** is published.
1883:   Summer   Ibsen stops at Gossensass and Bolzano before returning
                        to Rome.

1884:   November 11   *The Wild Duck** is published.

1885:   Summer-Fall   Ibsen visits Norway, returns to Munich.

MUNICH (1885–91)

1886:   November 23   *Rosmersholm** is published.
        December 19   Ibsen journeys to Meiningen, where he is the guest of
                        Duke Georg.
        December 23   Ibsen sees the Meininger production of *Ghosts*.
1887:   Ibsen is also present when the Meininger stages *Ghosts*
                        in Berlin.
        Summer   Ibsen spends his vacation in Denmark and Sweden.
1888:   April 25   Nicolai Alexander Ibsen* dies in Iowa.
        November 28   *The Lady from the Sea** is published.
1889:   March 3-15   Ibsen sees productions of a number of his plays in Berlin
                        and Weimar.
        June 7   Janet Achurch's* *A Doll's House* becomes the first sig-
                        nificant production of any Ibsenian drama in English.
        Summer   Ibsen meets Emilie Bardach* and Helene Raff* at
                        Gossensass.
        September 29   *Ghosts* is the inaugural production of the Freie Bühne.*
1890:   May 29   The Théâtre Libre* presents *Ghosts*.
        December   *Hedda Gabler** is published.
1891:   March 13   *Ghosts* is staged by the Independent Theatre.*

NORWAY (1891–1906)

1891:   Summer   Ibsen takes his holiday in Norway.
        August   Ibsen meets Hildur Andersen.*
        October   Ibsen leases an apartment in Christiania.
1892:   June 5   Hans Jakob Henriksen, Ibsen's bastard, dies.
        October 11   Sigurd marries Bergliot Björnson.
        December 12   *The Master Builder** is published in Copenhagen.
        December 14   *The Master Builder* is published in Christiania.
1893:   July 11   Ibsen's first grandchild is born.
1894:   December   *Little Eyolf** is published.
1895:   July   The Ibsens take new lodgings in Christiania.
1896:   December 12   *John Gabriel Borkman** is published.

1898:	March 20	Ibsen is honored as a citizen of the world on his seventieth birthday.
1899:	February 19	The Moscow Art Theatre* produces *Hedda Gabler*.
	July 14	Sigurd becomes chief of the Norwegian Foreign Office.
	December 19	*When We Dead Awaken** is published.
1900:	March 15	Ibsen suffers his first stroke.
1901:	Summer	A second stroke leaves Ibsen scarcely able to walk.
	September 10	His second grandchild is born.
1902:	Spring	A third stroke debilitates Ibsen.
1906:	February	Eleonora Duse* attempts to see Ibsen, but his poor health prevents their meeting.
	May 16	Ibsen becomes comatose.
	May 23	Henrik Ibsen dies.

AN IBSEN
COMPANION

THE DICTIONARY-GUIDE

A

AALBERG, IDA (1857-1915): Aalberg was a Finnish actress who performed the role of Nora Helmer* (*A Doll's House**) in Russia in 1884. As it was played in Finnish, the production stirred little excitement.
Reference: Räsänen, Illmari. *Ida Aalberg*. Helsinki: n.p., 1925.

AASE (*Peer Gynt**): Aase is the mother of Peer Gynt.* Despite all her son's weaknesses, Aase remains a doting parent. Her death scene is one of the most moving moments in all of Ibsen's works.

ABILDGAARD, THEODOR F. S. (1826-84): One of Ibsen's roommates in 1851 in Christiania, Abildgaard was editor of *Arbejderforeningernes Blad* [*Labor Unions' Newspaper*], to which Ibsen contributed articles. When the police raided the newspaper shop on July 7, 1851, in search of seditious materials, an inspired shop foreman threw piles of articles and letters onto the floor, which was already littered with scrap paper. The ensuing search of the paper's records revealed little to incriminate Ibsen. Abildgaard, however, was arrested, imprisoned, and finally sentenced to four years' hard labor.
Reference: Norsk Biografisk Leksikon, I, 78-9.

ACHURCH, JANET (1862-1916): To this enterprising actress goes the credit for introducing Ibsen to the English stage in a fully professional manner. Going on the stage in 1883, she eventually became a member of Frank R. Benson's* company before leasing the Novelty Theatre (London) in 1889.

Achurch's interest in Ibsen surfaced when she and her husband, actor Charles Charrington,* produced *A Doll's House** at the Novelty Theatre on June 7, 1889. London had previously seen *Breaking a Butterfly** (1884) and an amateur production of *Nora* (1885) [the usual continental name of *A Doll's House**], but Achurch's Nora was the first professional enactment of the role as Ibsen wrote it. The redoubtable Clement William Scott* observed, "Not even Ibsen or Mr. [William] Archer* could have desired a better Nora than Miss Achurch, who entered into her difficult task body and soul." Another critic concluded, "Strong meat indeed and not fit for babes . . . is Henrik Ibsen. . . . [Achurch's] impersonation of the heroine is the finest thing I have seen on the boards for a long time." This production started a critical discussion that lasted for months. (See Egan, pp. 101-25.) After twenty-four performances, the Charringtons left for Australia and New Zealand, where they also presented *A Doll's House*, eventually playing in Egypt, India, and the United States. Achurch later repeated her impersonation of Nora in London on April 19, 1892, March 11, 1893, and May 10, 1897.

Achurch played Rita Allmers* to the Asta Allmers* of Elizabeth Robins* and the Rat-Wife* of Mrs. Patrick Campbell* in a production of *Little Eyolf** at the Avenue Theatre (London) on November 23, 1895. *The Pall Mall Gazette* thought that Achurch failed to convince in the lighter moments of the play but excelled in the tragic parts. Clement Scott reacted according to form: "If only Mrs. Achurch or somebody else could have screamed in every act, that scream would have been accepted as a godsend. But on it went, on, on, on, eternal, unbroken, never-ending talk."

After this production, which lasted only five performances, Achurch seldom appeared on the stage. On May 5, 1902, she opened as Ellida Wangel* in *The Lady from the Sea** at the Royalty Theatre (London), a presentation of the Incorporated Stage Society.* While voicing respect for Achurch's attempting the role, the critics generally believed that her Ellida was not sufficient, particularly in the difficult last act.

In April 1911 Achurch played the role of Kristine Linde* in a production of *A Doll's House* by the Ibsen Club, a group of amateurs dedicated to the presentation of all of Ibsen's plays. Her last performance on the stage occurred in 1913.

References: Egan, Michael, ed., *Ibsen: The Critical Heritage.* London: Routledge and Kegan Paul, 1972; "Nora Helmer off for the Antipodes," *Pall Mall Gazette*, July 5, 1889, pp. 1-2; *Who Was Who in the Theatre*, I, 6-7.

ADALGISA (*Norma*): Adalgisa represents the government in this satirical play about the Storthing. She is courted by the politician Severus,* who also woos Norma (the Opposition) and is jealous of Severus' love of Norma.

ADLER, LEOPOLD (1850-1919): German director and playwright Leopold Adler started his career in Leipzig, where he presented a shortened version of *Emperor and Galilean** at the Stadttheater in 1875. Although his decision to stage even an abbreviation of Ibsen's monumental play deserves credit for boldness, audiences were not supportive, and the production

failed. Adler, however, had a long and distinguished career afterwards.
Reference: Kosch, Wilhelm. *Deutsches Literatur-Lexikon* (Bern: Franche, 1953),
   I, col. 28.

ADLERSPARRE, KARIN SOPHIE (1823-95): A Swedish author and
editor, Baroness Adlersparre printed an article on *The League of Youth** in
her journal *Tidskrift för hemmet* [*Magazine for the Home*], Vol. XII
(1870), 190. Later, she presented a lecture on *Ghosts,* * part of which she
published under the title "What Are the Ethical Considerations of Marriage?" On June 24, 1882, Ibsen wrote to her from Rome in appreciation of
her part in clarifying his intentions in his controversial play. He admitted,
" . . . I dare not go further than *Ghosts.* . . . But *Ghosts* had to be written.
After Nora, Mrs. Alving had to come" (Sprinchorn, pp. 207-8).
Reference: Sprinchorn, Evert, ed. *Ibsen: Letters and Speeches.* New York: Hill and
   Wang, 1964.

AESTHETIC STUDIES (1868): In the autumn of 1868, Ibsen, residing in
Dresden, asked Frederik Hegel,* his publisher, to send him a copy of
Aesthetic Studies by Georg Morris Brandes* because he had heard that the
author spoke of comedy, about which he (Ibsen) was unclear. Perhaps this
was Ibsen's true motivation, but he could be forgiven for being eager to
read Brandes' long, complimentary essay on himself, which appeared in the
volume with discussions of tragedy, comedy, current Scandinavian authors,
and specific plays. On December 22, 1868, Ibsen told Hegel that "Georg
Brandes's *Aesthetic Studies* has been an absolute gold mine to me,
especially in regard to the study of the comic spirit" (Sprinchorn, pp. 76-7).
Reference: Sprinchorn, Evert, ed. *Ibsen: Letters and Speeches.* New York: Hill and
   Wang, 1964.

AGATHON (*Emperor and Galilean*): A boyhood friend of Julian,*
Agathon was converted by Julian to Christianity and later sent by God to
Constantinople to tell Julian that God wanted him to leave the capital. In
the second part of the play, Agathon is a leader of the opposition to Julian's
apostasy. Agathon defiles the temple of Venus and is drafted into the army
as punishment. He finally stabs Julian with the spear that had pierced
Christ's side as He hung on the cross.

AGNES (*Brand*): Brand* first sees Agnes, a young woman, on the
mountain with Ejnar,* her fiancé. Inspired by Brand's commitment to his
vocation, Agnes leaves Ejnar, accompanies Brand across the storm-tossed
lake, and marries Brand in order to share his vision. When their son dies
because of Brand's stubbornness, Agnes proves incapable of giving "All or
Nothing." Brand finally forces her to view their son's death as God's will,
after which Agnes dies.

AHLBERG, PAULINE: Ahlberg was among the first to comment in a French journal on Ibsen's social problem plays: "Une Poète du Nord—Henri Ibsen," *Nouvelle Revue*, 17 (July 1882), 139-77.

AKADEMISKE KOLLEGIUM: Ibsen addressed a request for a travel grant to this Norwegian governmental bureau in 1860 and was refused. In 1862 it awarded him a small sum of money to travel in Norway's hinterlands to collect folklore, a grant that was renewed the following year. In May 1863 Ibsen requested 600 specie-dollars to subsidize a year's study in Paris and Rome; he ultimately received 400 specie-dollars.

ALFHILD (*The Grouse in Justedal*): A mountain girl.

ALFHILD (*The Mountain Bird*): A mountain girl.

ALFHILD (*Olaf Liljekrans*): A mountain girl, Alfhild falls in love with Olaf* and plans to marry him. When she learns that her vacillating lover plans to marry Ingeborg,* Alfhild burns the wedding chapel with the bride and groom inside. Olaf escapes, finds Alfhild in the mountains, and marries her.

ALLMERS, ALFRED (*Little Eyolf*): A former schoolteacher, Alfred Allmers devotes his energies to the completion of a book called *Human Responsibility*. A trek in the mountains convinces him to live a responsible life rather than write about it. In the future he vows to devote himself to help-ing his crippled son Eyolf* to reach his potential. When Eyolf accidentally drowns, Allmers and his wife Rita* see that their marriage has not been a union of spirits. In the end they decide to build on the ruins of their lives by caring for local orphans in atonement for their previous neglect of Eyolf.

ALLMERS, ASTA (*Little Eyolf*): Orphaned at an early age and left with her half-brother Alfred,* Asta Allmers, a schoolteacher, continues to depend on Alfred into her adulthood. Since Alfred had always wanted a younger brother, in childhood Asta had dressed as a boy and pretended to be his Eyolf. After Alfred's marriage produces a child named Eyolf,* Asta takes a particular interest in him. The relationship between Alfred and Asta has always been close, its ineffable character protected by consanguinity. Asta learns, however, that she and Alfred are unrelated. Their affection for each other has become dangerous. After the death of Eyolf, Asta goes away with an engineer to escape the potentially dangerous consequences of prox-imity to Alfred.

ALLMERS, EYOLF (*Little Eyolf*): The nine-year-old, crippled son of Alfred* and Rita Allmers,* Eyolf has not been properly nurtured. His mother sees him as her rival for Alfred's attention, while his father is too preoccupied with his literary efforts to make time for the boy. Despite these conditions, Eyolf is a bright, courageous boy who dreams of a life of normal activity. Upon his death by drowning in Act I, his parents face the truth about themselves.

ALLMERS, RITA (*Little Eyolf*): Rita Allmers is wife of Alfred,* sister-in-law of Asta,* and mother of Eyolf.* Her principal motivations are jealousy and sexuality. She is incapable of sharing her husband with either his half-sister Asta or their son. Rita, suspecting that Alfred's fondness for Asta is more serious than mere familial love, becomes inimical not to Alfred but to Asta. Eyolf is lame because of a fall he sustained as a baby; Rita had left him unattended while she made love to Alfred. The child and his ever-present crutch are constant reminders that she must share Alfred and that she is partly responsible for Eyolf's condition. At the end of the play, Rita and Alfred try to atone for their mistakes toward Eyolf and each other, but the reader is left with the feeling that Rita will be unable to change her basic nature.

ALTENBURGGAARDEN: Ibsen's mother's house in Skien,* to which the family moved in 1831 when the dramatist was two years old.

ALVING, HELENE (*Ghosts*): The widow of Captain Alving, a dissolute philanderer, and the mother of Oswald,* Helene Alving is the living embodiment of the effects of serving social custom rather than individual needs. Soon after she married Alving, she learned of his sexual incontinence. Seeking solace from Pastor Manders,* for whom she developed more than a passing affection, she was sent back to Alving's home for the sake of maintaining appearances. When Oswald was old enough, she sent him away to protect him from his father's corrupting influence, little suspecting that he would inherit Alving's syphilitic condition. Helene's crisis comes when she must decide whether to administer enough poison to save Oswald from the final deterioration of the disease. The audience is left to imagine her decision.

ALVING, OSWALD (*Ghosts*): Oswald is the son of Helene* and Captain Alving, but he has been away from home for most of his life. After a stint as an artist in Paris, Oswald returns to Norway because his rapidly failing physical condition has rendered him useless as a painter. Aware that the syphilitic infection is rotting his brain, he is seeking someone to administer poison before his condition becomes unbearable. The maid Regine Engstrand* seems a likely candidate, but when she deserts him, Oswald must depend on his mother. In his last moment on stage, Oswald cries for the sun as Helene tries to decide if she can give him the drug.

AMBIORIX (*Catiline*): Ambiorix comes to Rome as an ambassador to ask the Roman conquerors to be merciful to his tribe, the vanquished Allobroges. He joins Catiline's* conspiracy against Rome.

AMMIAN (*Emperor and Galilean*): An army captain.

ANATOLUS (*Emperor and Galilean*): A captain of the Imperial Lifeguard.

ANDERSEN, HILDUR (1864-1956): Ibsen first encountered Hildur Andersen, the granddaughter of his old landlady Helene Sontum,* in Christiania* in 1874. She was a musically precocious child. When he met her again in 1891, an instant bond of sympathy was forged, Andersen becoming the dramatist's frequent companion when his wife was away and even helping him decorate his new apartment. Her career as a concert pianist necessitated her traveling both to study and perform, and during these periods, Ibsen wrote frequently to her. As gossip about the old man and the young woman intensified, some people, such as Magdalene Thoresen,* Suzannah's mother, thought that divorce was imminent and advised Suzannah Thoresen Ibsen* about the rumors. Then Ibsen had his first stroke in 1900 and saw little of Andersen afterward. As his debility advanced and he became housebound, Andersen did not visit him, possibly in deference to Suzannah's feelings. Although Andersen later burned all of Ibsen's letters to her, it is clear that she satisfied psychological needs that Ibsen did not meet elsewhere.

Reference: Bull, Francis. "Hildur Andersen og Henrik Ibsen," *Edda*, LVII (1957), 47-54.

ANDERSON, RASMUS BJÖRN (1846-1936): From 1869 Rasmus B. Anderson was a professor at the University of Wisconsin and held the first chair of Scandinavian languages in the United States from 1875. He was an early champion of Ibsen and Björnstjerne Björnson* and translated a number of Björnson's novels. William Moore Lawrence* of Milwaukee consulted Anderson in 1882 about Lawrence's translation of *The Child Wife*,* *The Pillars of Society*,* and *Ghosts*.* Anderson succeeded, moreover, in persuading Ibsen to name Lawrence as his authorized American translator, but he failed in getting A. M. Palmer of New York's Union Square Theatre to produce *The Child Wife* (Palmer had agreed to do so but did not live up to the bargain) and Lawrence Barrett to appear in *The Pillars of Society*. Barrett seemed most at home in Roman togas and could not face the prospect of appearing in contemporary garb in Ibsen's play.

In 1883 Anderson became an insurance salesman, turning his back on both academia and Ibsen. He came to despise all of Ibsen's plays after *The Pillars of Society*, about which he said, "Aside from the improprieties and offense against good morals that are found in them, they seem to me mere twaddle and all the symbolism which they are said to contain I regard as a mere opinion of his readers and admiring critics'' (Anderson, p. 487).

Between 1885 and 1889 Anderson represented the United States as ambassador to Denmark, meeting Ibsen in both Copenhagen and Munich. In the early years of the new century, Anderson worked to establish Norwegian Society* to promote Norwegian culture in America. He made it clear, however, that "devotees and admirers of the later works of Ibsen and Björnson would either have to be kept out . . . or at least take the back seat" (Anderson, p. 633). During these years Anderson also published his newspaper *Amerika*.

References: Anderson, Rasmus B. *Life Story of Rasmus B. Anderson*. Madison, Wis.:
    privately published, 1915; Hustvedt, Lloyd. *Rasmus B. Anderson: Pioneer
    Scholar*. Northfield, Minn.: Norwegian-American Historical Association, 1966.

ANDHRIMNER: In Teutonic mythology, the gods' cook in Valhalla. The name was chosen for a weekly literary journal published between January and September 1851 by Ibsen, Paul Botten-Hansen,* and Aasmund Olafsen Vinje.* The original title of the journal was *Manden* [*The Man*].

ANDREEVA, MARIE FEDOROVNA (1868-1953): Between 1898 and 1905 this actress, noted for her delicate and lyrical interpretations, was a member of the Moscow Art Theatre.* There she played Hedda Gabler* in 1899.

Reference: Great Soviet Encyclopedia (New York: Collier-Macmillan, 1973), II,
    91-2.

ANITRA (*Peer Gynt*): The fat and dirty daughter of a Bedouin chief, Anitra dances seductively for Peer Gynt* before robbing him and running away.

ANKER, CARL JOHAN (1835-1903): In the summer of 1856, Ibsen trekked from Bergen to Hardanger Mountain with Carl Anker, a soldier who became a gymnastics instructor and wrote *Ledetraad ved Underviisning i gymnastik* [*Guide for the Professor of Gymnastics*] (1864). While Anker was doing military service in Stockholm, Ibsen wrote him a uniquely self-revelatory letter (January 30, 1858) in which he apologized for his moodiness and inability to form convivial friendships. "Yet," added Ibsen, "I found it incomparably easier to make contact with you than with anyone else, for I found in you a spiritual youthfulness, a joy in life, a chivalry of outlook which warmed my heart" (Meyer, p. 154). Presumably, Anker passed out of Ibsen's life, but the dramatist profited by his brief friendship with Anker because the association provided the retiring Ibsen a chance to relate warmly to a kindred soul.

Reference: Meyer, Michael. *Ibsen: A Biography*. Garden City, N.Y.: Doubleday and
    Company, 1971.

ANNE MARIE (*A Doll's House*): Nurse of the Helmer* children.

ANNO, ANTON (1838-93): As manager of the Residenz Theater (Berlin) from 1884, Anton Anno staged Ibsen's *Ghosts** (January 8, 1887) and *Rosmersholm** (May 5, 1887), with his wife Charlotte Frohn* and Emanuel Reicher,* respectively, in the leading roles of each play. The *Rosmersholm* production was particularly successful, lasting twenty-three performances; *Ghosts*, though well-received by the avant-garde, was presented only once at a charity matinee. Ibsen himself witnessed the performance of *Ghosts*, and, according to Fritz Wallner, who played Oswald, "appeared repeatedly on the stage, tears of joy running down his face" (Quoted in Meyer, p. 575). *References:* Kosch, Wilhelm. *Deutsches Theater-Lexikon* (Klagenfurt: Ferd. Kleinmayr, 1953), I, 32; Meyer, Michael. *Ibsen: A Biography*. Garden City, N.Y.: Doubleday and Company, 1971.

ANTOINE, ANDRÉ (1858-1943): French actor/manager André Antoine was a key figure in the development of the modern French theatre. He was primarily associated with the initial Realistic and Naturalistic productions in Paris. Ibsen's works occupied a position of prominence in the career of André Antoine, whether he worked at the Théâtre Libre,* the Théâtre Antoine, or the Odéon. When Antoine staged *Ghosts** at the Théâtre Libre with himself in the role of Oswald Alving* (May 29, 1890), he and his troupe discovered that Norwegian Realism differed from French Realism in the demands it placed on actors, but despite all inadequacies, the presentation attracted admirers as well as detractors. While *Ghosts* was still a topic of controversy, the French Senate debated the legality of subscription theatres such as the Théâtre Libre, and later the idea of establishing a commission to strengthen censorship was bruited. Luckily, this did not come to pass, but the notoriety enabled Antoine to present about two hundred performances of *Ghosts* throughout France.

In the season of 1890-91, Antoine staged *The Wild Duck*,* which polarized audiences as *Ghosts* had done. One critic could not even follow the story, and some members of the audience vented their derision by cackling like birds during the performance. Others saw the drama as a happy blending of Realism and Symbolism. The production marked Antoine's last involvement with Ibsen at the Théâtre Libre.

The Théâtre Antoine was opened in 1897, and early in the next year Antoine added *Ghosts* to his repertory and restaged it in 1903. In May 1906, the month of Ibsen's death, Antoine presented *The Wild Duck* in continuous performances. When he assumed the directorship of the state-subsidized Théâtre de l'Odéon, Antoine revived his production of *The Wild Duck* (September 27, 1907) and soon added *Ghosts*. *References:* Carlson, Marvin. *The French Stage in the 19th Century*. Metuchen, N.J.: Scarecrow Press, 1972; Waxman, Samuel. *Antoine and the Théâtre Libre*. Cambridge: Harvard University Press, 1926.

APOLLINARIS (*Emperor and Galilean*): A hymnwriter.

ARCHER, CHARLES (1861-1941): The translator of *Lady Inger at Östraat* (1890) and *Rosmersholm* (1891) Charles Archer collaborated with his brother William Archer* in rendering *Peer Gynt** (1892) into English. All three translations appear in William Archer's *The Collected Works of Henrik Ibsen*. Charles was also his brother's biographer.

ARCHER, FRANCES ELIZABETH: William Archer's* family was indispensable to his goal of making all of Ibsen's dramas available in English. His wife Frances Elizabeth was responsible for the translation of *The Wild Duck** and *The Lady from the Sea.**

ARCHER, WILLIAM (1856-1924): British critic Edmund William Gosse* introduced Ibsen to readers of English, but William Archer led the skirmishes that won the acceptance of Ibsen's works for the stage. A Scot himself, Archer's grandmother had lived in Norway, and as a youth Archer spent many happy holidays there, soaking up the culture and learning *landsmaal.** In 1871, however, Archer began to study Norwegian literature, which necessitated mastering *riksmaal.** Although he had seen Ibsen's books in the shops, he took no notice of the dramatist until the controversy about *Love's Comedy.** Thereafter Archer enthusiastically read all of Ibsen's published works, especially enjoying *Emperor and Galilean.**

Archer received an M.A. degree from the University of Edinburgh in 1876, and the next year *The Pillars of Society** appeared. Since Archer believed it worthy of English notice, he made a hurried translation but proved unable to find a publisher. In the interval between entering the Middle Temple as a law student in 1878 and his "call to the Bar" in 1883, Archer was a practicing journalist, writing articles for *Figaro* and *The World* (London). His belief in Ibsen had not waned in the meantime, and his dream of seeing an Ibsenian work on the English stage was realized when W. H. Vernon* mounted a matinee performance of *The Pillars of Society* on December 15, 1880, at the Gaiety Theatre. Archer's translation was employed, but the venture brought neither Ibsen, nor Vernon, nor Archer any particular notice.

Archer spent much of 1881 in Europe trying to arrange a meeting with Ibsen; he succeeded grandly at last, meeting and talking with the Ibsens several times. By the end of his legal training, Archer was a regular contributor to the *Pall Mall Gazette*, which became his principal platform from which he waged the war for Ibsen's acceptance. By 1888 several translations of Ibsen's plays had been published, and Archer's own version of *The Pillars of Society* was included in Henry Havelock Ellis'* popular anthology. Archer had also strictly edited the translation of *Ghosts** that appeared in that volume.

Until that time there had been no significant presentation of any Ibsenian drama on the London stage. When Janet Achurch* and Charles Charrington* were planning their production of *A Doll's House** in 1889, they naturally turned to Archer, Ibsen's most outspoken champion, for advice. He not only provided the script but also attended rehearsals to advise the players about the deeper meaning of the lines and about Norwegian idiosyncrasies. For the most part, the production was well received, but there were enough dissidents that articles in defense of Ibsen poured from Archer's pen. When the Independent Theatre* presented *Ghosts* in 1891, the floodgates of criticism were opened; Ibsen's detractors came out in force, and Archer continued to be their chief gainsayer.

By then it was clear that Ibsen was an important figure in world theatre and deserved an edition of his collected works, a task which Archer set into motion. He eventually interested publisher William Heinemann in the project, and sixteen years later (1906), the first of the twelve volumes of *The Collected Works of Henrik Ibsen* appeared. Even in the 1920s it was fashionable to deplore Archer's own translations and those completed under his guidance as stilted and old-fashioned. Doubtless, this criticism is justified to a certain extent, but native Norwegians maintain that the Archer translations are closer in spirit to the originals than any other version. Despite this opinion, several successive generations of actors have sought other, less Victorian versions of the plays.

As a critic of Ibsen's works, Archer was a structuralist; that is, once Ibsen's English reputation was established, he rated the dramas as dramas without having to defend the content. In his excellent book *Play-Making: A Manual of Craftmanship* (Boston: Small, Maynard and Company, 1912), Archer cites many examples of successful playwriting drawn from the Ibsenian canon. About the dramatist's art, Archer says, "Rules there are none; but it does not follow that some of the thousands who are fascinated by the art of the playwright may not profit by having their attention called, in a plain and practical way, to some of its problems and possibilities" (pp. 6-7). He then launches into an amply illustrated study of dramatic form.

As Ibsen's polemicist, publicist, translator, and interpreter, Archer had no peer in the English-speaking world. In the midst of the Ibsenian struggle, it is all the more remarkable that he found the time to become a successful playwright, critic, and political activist.

Reference: Archer, Charles. *William Archer: Life, Work, and Friendships.* New Haven, Conn.: Yale University Press, 1931.

ARCTANDER, JOHN WILLIAM (1849-1920): John W. Arctander left his native Norway and settled in Chicago in 1869. Arctander was associated with the legal and journalistic professions and was a prominent member of the Norwegian-American colony. In 1870 he was named director of the Norske Dramatiske Forening [Norwegian Dramatic Society], and the following year his one-act play *Commotion in the House* was presented in the Aurora Turner Hall. In December 1871 he moved to New York but did not sever his relationship with the Norwegians in the Midwest. In 1893 the Waldm. Kriedt Company of Minneapolis published Arctander's translation of *The Master Builder*; by that time Arctander had settled in Minneapolis. His other dramas include *The Apostle of Alaska* (1909), *Guilty?* (1910), and *The Lady in Blue* (1911).

Reference: Wilt, Napier, and Henriette C. K. Naeseth, "Two Early Norwegian Dramatic Societies in Chicago," *Norwegian-American Studies and Records*, X (1938), 44-75.

ARIOVIST (*Norma*): Norma's* father, a Druid.

ARLISS, GEORGE (1868-1946): An exceptionally inventive English character actor, Arliss worked with Mrs. Patrick Campbell* in England and the United States and twice with Minnie Maddern Fiske* in America. He was also associated with David Belasco. Known primarily for his stage roles in *Disraeli* and *The Devil* and a distinguished film career, Arliss played Brack* to Mrs. Fiske's Hedda Gabler* in 1904 and Rosmer* to her Rebecca West* in 1907. In his autobiography Arliss is wholly reticent about his part in these productions.

References: Arliss, George. *Up the Years from Bloomsbury: An Autobiography.* New York: Blue Ribbon Books, 1927; *Who Was Who in the Theatre*, I, 69.

ARNE OF GULDVIK (*Olaf Liljekrans*): As head of a powerful clan, Arne of Guldvik comes to see the marriage of his daughter Ingeborg* to Olaf Liljekrans* as a means of laying to rest a chronic rivalry with Olaf's family.

ARNHOLM (*The Lady from the Sea*): A former suitor of Ellida Wangel,* schoolmaster Arnholm visits the Wangels and falls in love with Bolette Wangel,* the elder daughter.

ASGAUT (*The Burial Mound*): The only survivor of a fierce battle in the south, Asgaut, an old Viking, leads Gandalf* back to the place to avenge his father's death.

ASHCROFT, PEGGY (1907-   ): British actress Dame Peggy Ashcroft has essayed three of Ibsen's heroines: Hedda Gabler* (1954), Rebecca West* (1959), and Ella Rentheim* (1975). Her Hedda was first seen at the Lyric Theatre, Hammersmith, and then transferred to the Westminster Theatre. Of this performance the critic of *The Times* (London) wrote: "She delineates with minute sureness of touch all the actions through which Hedda becomes detestable, forces them to yield the maximum of overt drama, and at the same time enables them to laugh at the overweening pretentiousness of a creature whom fate over-reaches'' (Sept. 9, 1954, p. 11, col. 1). Dame Peggy's Hedda was also seen at the New Theatre in Oslo on November 16, 1955.

Her Rebecca was premiered at the tiny Royal Court Theatre and then moved to the Comedy Theatre. Both of these removals suggest that the productions were critical successes that demanded larger houses than those in which they were originally presented. As Rebecca, Dame Peggy made ''it clear that she is ready to die for Rosmer's belief that the guilt of murder must be expiated with blood'' (*The Times* (London), Nov. 19, 1959, p. 16, cols. 1-4). When Dame Peggy appeared as Ella Rentheim at the Old Vic in 1975, Ralph Richardson* was the John Gabriel Borkman.* The production and the stars were widely acclaimed.
Reference: Who's Who in the Theatre, 16th ed., pp. 362-3.

ASLAK (*Peer Gynt*): Aslak, a blacksmith, is Peer Gynt's* archenemy. He soundly thrashed Peer in a brawl before the play opens and so delights in tormenting him that he decides to beat him again at the wedding feast.

ASLAKSEN (*An Enemy of the People*): A printer by trade, Aslaksen is a political opportunist. When his selfish purposes are served by doing so, he supports Thomas Stockmann,* but he does an about-face when he sees that Stockmann has become a liability to him.

ASLAKSEN (*The League of Youth*): A printer by trade, Aslaksen is a chronic complainer as well as a frequent inebriate. He was sent to college by Daniel Hejre* and thus raised above his station, but local society, led by Chamberlain Brattsberg,* will not receive him. He attempts to blackmail Stensgaard* but is bested by him. Aslaksen is a mere toady.

ATWILL, LIONEL (1885-1946): British actor Lionel Atwill first appeared in an Ibsenian drama while on tour in England in support of H. V. Neilson in *An Enemy of the People* and Courtenay Thorpe in *A Doll's House.** As one of Alla Nazimova's* leading men in America, Atwill played Hjalmar Ekdal,* Jörgen Tesman,* and Torvald Helmer*—all in 1918.
Reference: Who Was Who in the Theatre, I, 91-2.

AUDUN (*The Burial Mound*): The real name of Bernhard* in the earlier version of the play.

AUNE (*The Pillars of Society*): The foreman of Karsten Bernick's* shipyard, Aune fears that modern construction techniques will displace workers from their jobs. He insists that more time is needed to make a ship seaworthy, but when Bernick threatens to fire him, he relents. Thinking better of his decision, Aune delays the sailing of the vessel, thus saving Bernick's reputation.

AURELIA (*Catiline*): The good angel in the Catilinian psychomachia, Aurelia is patient, long-suffering, and wholly forgiving. Even after she is spurned by Catiline,* she follows him into battle, is mortally wounded by him, and dies with him.

AXELSEN, N. F.: The printer of *Andhrimner*,* Axelsen was the source of the character Aslaksen* in both *The League of Youth** and *An Enemy of the People.**

B

BAARD BRATTE (*The Pretenders*): A chieftain from the Trondhejm district.

BADDELEY, ANGELA (1904-76): English actress Angela Baddeley's favorite stage role was Nora Helmer,* which she played in 1946 in London. If *The Times* (London) reviewer can be credited, her performance was flawed in precisely the same manner as those of numerous actors: "Miss Angela Baddeley gave the impression of being ill at ease in the several infatuations and general dollishness of Nora; it was only when she arrived at the didactic dignity of her dismissal of Torvald* that she really held the house and quelled the coughs. She played the early scenes as though she had just read the Elia essay on " 'the behaviour of married people' and was overacting that she might conceal her distaste for the uxoriousness of Torvald."
References: The Times (London) Jan. 18, 1946, p. 6, col. 5; *Who's Who in the Theatre*, 16th ed., pp. 372-3.

BAGGE, MAGNUS-THULSTRUP (1825-90?): A painter of *paysages*, Bagge gave Ibsen painting lessons around 1860 and eventually painted a portrait of the dramatist. He is thought to have been a model for Hjalmar Ekdal.*
Reference: "Bagge, Magnus-Thulstrup," *Dictionnaire des Peintres, Sculteurs, Dessinateurs et Graveurs* (Paris: Librairie Gründ, 1976), I, 374-5.

BAKER, LEE (1880-1948): Thirty-year-old Lee Baker made his debut in New York as a member of the repertory company of the ill-fated New Theatre in 1910. He was chosen to appear in the title role in the fourth act of *Brand,** which preceded the performance of Maurice Maeterlinck's *Sister Beatrice.*
References: New York Times, Mar. 15, 1910, p. 9, col. 1; *Who Was Who in the Theatre*, I, 112.

A BALDING GENTLEMAN (*The Wild Duck*): A chamberlain; one of the guests at Haakon Werle's* dinner party.

BALLESTAD (*The Lady from the Sea*): A jack-of-all-trades, Ballestad is a painter (his magnum opus is "The Dying Mermaid"*), a scene-painter, a hairdresser, a dancing-master, and a bandleader.

BALLON, MONS. (*Peer Gynt*): A rather disreputable Frenchman whom Peer Gynt* encounters on the southwest coast of Morocco. Ballon is a party to the theft of Peer's ship.

BANG, HERMANN JOACHIM (1857-1912): Danish novelist Hermann Bang introduced Ibsen to Aurélien-Marie Lugné-Poë,* actor and producer. When the Frenchman produced two of Ibsen's dramas in 1893, Bang served as Ibsen's representative at rehearsals, commenting particularly on details of Scandinavian atmosphere. He had considerable difficulty in getting the French actors to behave naturally rather than ritualistically on stage. Believing that he had failed Ibsen miserably, Bang left Paris to the French. In addition to his novels, Bang was the author of books of theatrical criticism, *Ti Aar* [*Ten Years*] (1891), and *Teatret* [*The Theatre*] (1892).

BANG, OLE (b. 1870): Minnie Maddern Fiske* sponsored Ole Bang, a Norwegian writer and playwright, in his public readings of Ibsen's works early in the twentieth century. He interpreted *Peer Gynt* at Fiske's Manhattan Theatre in 1905.
Reference: New York Dramatic Mirror, January 21, 1905, p. 17, cols. 1-2.

BARBARA (*Emperor and Galilean*): A procuress.

BARDACH, EMILIE (1871-1955): In July 1889, when he was sixty-one years old, Ibsen met eighteen-year-old Emilie Bardach at a concert in Gossensass. He subsequently cultivated her acquaintance, getting her to speak of herself in a highly personal manner. When Bardach fell ill, Ibsen was particularly solicitous. She confided to her diary the growing intensity of his attentions to her but early in the relationship concluded that because of his wife and son, the liaison could never be fully productive. Yet they continued to meet and declare passionate commitment. For two months they were inseparable; then on September 17, 1889, Bardach returned to her home in Vienna convinced that Ibsen would divorce his wife and spend the remainder of his life with her.

Ibsen went back to Munich, his ardor somewhat dampened. His letters to Bardach were at first affectionate but restrained. By November his thoughts seemed to be more on Helene Raff* in Munich than on Emilie Bardach in Vienna. In February 1890 Ibsen, who chafed at regular correspondence, told Bardach that he was ending his epistolary connection with her. He remained silent until Christmas, when he penned a short note, his last communication with her for seven years. On his seventieth birthday (1898), Ibsen received a congratulatory telegram from his young friend who was still devoted to him. He responded briefly, and this was their last contact.

Throughout the affair and afterward, Ibsen revealed that he felt very deeply for Bardach. Yet it is unlikely that the attachment ever had a physical consummation. Bardach claimed that he had not even kissed her. Psychologists, amateur and professional, have seen significance in this circumstance, but unquestionably the Bardach affair affected Ibsen's work from *Hedda Gabler** to the end.

References: King, Basil. "Ibsen and Emilie Bardach," *Century Magazine*, 106 (Oct. 1923), 803-15; 111 (Nov. 1925), 83-92; Lampl, Hans Erich. *Nova über Henrik Ibsen und sein Alterswerk*. Oslo: Edizione Alpha, 1977.

BARRYMORE, ETHEL (1879-1959): While on tour in 1905, Ethel Barrymore, then well on her way to becoming one of America's most distinguished actresses, was persuaded to portray Nora Helmer.* The production was rehearsed as she traveled and was eventually seen in a matinee performance in Boston. Her younger brother John played Doctor Rank,* giving a performance in which Ethel glimpsed the mastery that was to come. Her producer Charles Frohman decided to open the production in his Lyceum Theatre (New York) on May 2, 1905, with Bruce McRae* as Torvald Helmer.* It lasted fifteen performances, a respectable run in those days. Barrymore's performance was called "a fine achievement" (*New York Times*, May 3, 1905, p. 9, col. 3). Unfortunately she never again returned to Ibsen.

Reference: Barrymore, Ethel. *Memories: An Autobiography*. New York: Harper and Brothers, 1955.

BASIL OF CAESAREA (*Emperor and Galilean*): A boyhood friend of the Emperor Julian,* Basil is one of the last Christians to try to convince Julian to recant his apostasy. The Emperor's response is to draft Basil into his army as a nurse.

BASSERMANN, ALBERT (1867-1952): After training in the theatre of Georg II, Duke of Saxe-Meiningen,* Albert Bassermann spent fifteen years at Max Reinhardt's* Deutsches Theater in Berlin where he appeared in several Ibsenian dramas. In 1915 he performed in *A Doll's House** and *Ghosts** at the Munich Kammerspiele; both plays remained in his repertory for the rest of his life. In 1926 he undertook the role of Karsten Bernick* in *The Pillars of Society*,* also at the Chamber Theatre of Munich.

Reference: "Bassermann, Alfred," *Encyclopaedia Britannica* (1973), III, 259.

BATES, BLANCHE (1873)-1941): Blanche Bates was an established actress before she performed in New York, her career having started in San Francisco. Her portrayal of Nora Helmer* in *A Doll's House** caused a mild sensation when it was seen at Baldwin's Theatre (San Francisco) on November 6, 1898. In 1904 she added Hedda Gabler* to her repertory in Chicago. *Reference:* Philbrick, Norman. "Blanche Bates," *Dictionary of American Biography*, Supp. 3 (New York: Charles Scribner's Sons, 1973), pp. 39-40.

THE BEACON: Peter Mortensgaard's* radical newspaper in *Rosmersholm.**

THE BEARD HATER [*Misopogon*]: A tract written by Emperor Julian* (*Emperor and Galilean**) against the citizens of Antioch, who spurned his pagan religion and derided his philosopher's beard. The actual Julian wrote such a book.

BECKER, CARL FRIEDRICH: The author of *The World History* [*Die Weltgeschichte*] (Berlin: Duncker and Humblot, 1801-5). While still in Grimstad,* Ibsen acquired this book in a Danish translation. Peer Gynt* says (Act IV, Scene 9) that he intends to consult Becker's *World History* as a guide for his pilgrimage.

BEGRIFFENFELDT (*Peer Gynt*): Professor and director of the madhouse in Cairo.

BENGT GAUTESON (*The Feast at Solhoug*): The long-suffering but ineffectual husband of Margit*; the master of Solhoug.

BENGT OF BJERKEHOUG (*The Grouse of Justedal*): A rich yeoman.

BENSON, FRANK ROBERT (1858-1939): In 1891 there was considerable speculation as to whether F. R. Benson, known primarily as an athletic actor and director of Shakespeare, or Beerbohm Tree* was Henry Irving's heir-apparent in the realm of opulent Shakespearean production. Benson was decidedly out of his element when he allowed William Archer* to persuade him to appear as Rosmer* to the Rebecca West* of Florence Farr.* The production was to be directed by Archer himself, whose literary but amateur approach to directing conflicted with Benson's carelessness with the text of *Rosmersholm.** Benson indulgently recalls, "And if I, as Rosmer, did not set the Thames on fire, some of my adherents were very favourably impressed by the passion and sincerity of my performance" (Benson, p. 297). Most of the critics, however, were mystified by the production, one of them remarking that Benson played Rosmer "like a curate with cholera" (*Sunday Times*, Mar. 1, 1891, p. 7). Opening at the Vaude-

ville Theatre (London) on February 23, 1891, the presentation lasted but two performances.
Reference: Benson, Frank R. *My Memories.* London: Ernest Benn, 1930.

BERG (*St. John's Night*): A former estate-owner; Mrs. Berg's* father-in-law. He is an old man with a defective memory and an inordinate love of folk traditions.

BERG, ANNE (*St. John's Night*): Mrs. Berg's* stepdaughter. A fey child whose grandfather Berg's* tales keep her in touch with the supernatural world, Anne finally marries Johannes Birk.*

BERG, MRS. (*St. John's Night*): A widowed mother in straitened circumstances who hopes to recoup her finances by marrying her daughter Juliane Kvist* to Johannes Birk.*

BERGEN: The town in which Ibsen resided between 1851 and 1857. It was here that Ole Bull's* Norwegian Theatre* was located and here that Ibsen first worked in the theatre.

BERGHOF, HERBERT (1909-   ): Principally known as a teacher at the Actors' Studio (New York) and the H. B. Studio (New York), Herbert Berghof acted in Europe before coming to the United States. In 1948 he was Pastor Manders* in *Ghosts** and Judge Brack* in *Hedda Gabler.** Berghof appeared as Doctor Wangel* in *The Lady from the Sea** in 1950.
Reference: Who's Who in the Theatre, 16th ed., pp. 408-9.

BERGSÖE, JÖRGEN WILHELM (1835-1911): A Danish novelist, Bergsöe was Ibsen's companion on the island of Ischia for three months in 1867. Years later he published his reminiscences of that time: *Henrik Ibsen paa Ischia: og "Fra Piazza del Popolo."* Copenhagen: n.p., 1907.

BERNHARD (*The Burial Mound*): An old recluse, Bernhard is really a Viking king thought to have been killed.

BERNHARDT, SARAH (1844-1923): That Sarah Bernhardt as one of the best Romantic actresses of the modern theatre never attempted Ibsen's Lady Inger of Gyldenlöve,* Margit,* or Hjördis* is regrettable. Her impassioned demeanor, her expressive gestures, and her unforgettable voice brought to bear on these roles might have made stage history, but until late in her career, the actress was scornful of Ibsen's accomplishments.
    In the early twentieth century, however, when Bernhardt's fame was already legendary, she altered her opinion of Ibsen and actually mounted a production of *The Lady from the Sea,** the details of which are confusing.

Michael Meyer (p. 570, n. 44), referring to the *Aftenposten* of September 22, 1904, says that Bernhardt played Ellida Wangel* at Sens in 1904. Actually, the newspaper records that the teenaged Hilde Wangel* was Bernhardt's role, but Meyer thinks this is a preposterous error. One of Bernhardt's many biographers, Gerda Taranow, places the production in Geneva in the spring of 1906 (Taranow, p. 209). It is certain, nevertheless, that the actress was not successful in her attempt to play an Ibsenian heroine, and *The Lady from the Sea* was not retained in her repertory.

Despite this experience, Bernhardt wanted to essay Nora Helmer,* largely because the character resembled one of her favorite roles in Henri Meilhac and Ludovic Halévy's *Frou-Frou*, the subject of which is similar to that of *A Doll's House*.* She never played Nora, however, perhaps because she finally realized that her style of acting was incompatible with Ibsen's demands. When speaking of George Bernard Shaw,* Bernhardt as an old woman said, "I admire him tremendously, but my style of acting would never suit either his plays or Mr. Ibsen's" (Noble, p. 180).

References: Meyer, Michael. *Ibsen: A Biography.* Garden City, N.Y.: Doubleday and Company, 1971; Noble, Iris. *Great Lady of the Theatre: Sarah Bernhardt.* New York: Julian Messner, 1960; Taranow, Gerda. *Sarah Bernhardt: The Art Within the Legend.* Princeton, N.J.: Princeton University Press, 1972.

BERNHOFT, THEODOR CHRISTIAN (1833-85): Bernhoft, the son of a poet and bookseller, was a student in Christiania* with Ibsen. According to Ibsen, Bernhoft was the source of the idea of *St. John's Night*.* Bernhoft also wrote a vaudeville called *My Daughter*, which was produced in 1854 by the Christiania Theatre.* He eventually became a clergyman.

Reference: Norsk Biografisk Leksikon, I, 489.

BERNICK, BETTY (*The Pillars of Society*): As the wife of Karsten Bernick,* Betty shoulders great responsibility in maintaining the family's appearance of respectability. Bernick married her in order to acquire her large dowry for his business speculations. Hers has not been a marriage of love.

BERNICK, KARSTEN (*The Pillars of Society*): Bernick is an entrepreneur who realizes that his success in business depends upon maintaining his image as a pillar of society; yet he has no scruples about entering into deals that skirt the spirit of the law. He has, moreover, built his shipyard and his reputation on lies. The near-death of his son causes him to admit his faults and to promise to become a true pillar of society, father, and husband.

BERNICK, MARTHA (*The Pillars of Society*): Karsten Bernick's* unmarried sister.

BERNICK, OLAF (*The Pillars of Society*): Karsten Bernick's* willful son. His attempt to stow away on an unseaworthy ship precipitates his father's reformation.

BERTE (*Hedda Gabler*): The maid in the Tesman* household.

BIE, EMIL: A theological student in Grimstad* with whom Ibsen read Latin and Greek.

BILLING (*An Enemy of the People*): Hovstad's* colleague in the newspaper office.

BIRK, JOHANNES (*St. John's Night*): A student who visits the Berg home as fiancé to Juliane Kvist.* He falls in love with Anne Berg,* disappointing Mrs. Berg's* plans for his money.

BIRKELAND, MICHAEL (1830-96): As a member of Ibsen's literary circle, The Learned Hollanders,* Birkeland supported Ibsen's request for a governmental writer's pension. From 1863 Birkeland was national archivist of Norway.
Reference: Norsk Biografisk Leksikon, I, 540-7.

BJARME, BRYNJOLF: For reasons that are not clear, Ibsen employed this pseudonym when he published *Catiline*,* *The Burial Mound*,* and various poems until July 1851.

BJELKE, JENS (*Lady Inger of* Österaad): A Danish military commander.

BJÖRN (*The Grouse in Justedal*): The son of Bengt of Bjerkehoug.*

BJÖRN (*Lady Inger of Österaad*): Lady Inger of Gyldenlöve's* retainer.

BJÖRNSON, BJÖRN (1859-1942): The son of Björnstjerne Björnson,* this man had a distinguished career as an actor and director, being named head of Norway's National Theatre (Christiania)* in 1899. As a member of the company of the Christiania Theatre,* Björnson was widely admired for his performance as Peer Gynt* in 1892.
Reference: Norsk Biografisk Leksikon, I, 605-7.

BJÖRNSON, BJÖRNSTJERNE (1832-1910): Ibsen and Björnson stand almost alone among Norwegian dramatists of the nineteenth century. During his first weeks in Christiania,* Ibsen met the man who would become one of the most important influences on his life. Their subsequent relationship was volatile and highly mercurial, which is not surprising in view of the differences in their temperaments, approaches to writing, and political strategies. Björnson sometimes praised Ibsen's work but felt free to criticize it. Four years younger than Ibsen, he followed the older man as director of the Norwegian Theatre (Bergen)* and the Christiania Theatre.* Yet success and recognition came easily to Björnson and only with difficulty to Ibsen. Perhaps Ibsen reacted to their uneasy rivalry by depicting Björnson as Haakon* and himself as Skule* in *The Pretenders.** Björnson stood as godfather to Sigurd Ibsen* and in 1892 approved of his marriage to his daughter Bergliot. In the intervening years Björnson's friendship with Ibsen had been very strained. Although Björnson won the Nobel Prize for Literature in 1903, he was still annoyed that Ibsen had become a wealthy man.

Reference: Brandes, Georg. *Henrik Ibsen, Björnstjerne Björnson: Critical Studies.* Trans. Jesse Muir and Mary Morison. London: William Heinemann, 1899.

BLANKA (*The Burial Mound*): In the first version of the play, Blanka is the foster-daughter of Bernhard*; in the second, of Roderik.* In both versions she is the warm-hearted, Christian girl who warms the bellicose, Viking heart of Gandalf* and returns with him to convert the paganistic Scandinavians.

A BLIND BEGGAR (*Emperor and Galilean*): A plebeian.

BLINN, HOLBROOK (1872-1928): American actor Holbrook Blinn's sole Ibsenian characterization was that of Karsten Bernick* in Minnie Maddern Fiske's* production of *The Pillars of Society** in 1910.

Reference: Who Was Who in the American Theatre, I, 229-30

BLOOM, CLAIRE (1931-   ): During the 1970s Claire Bloom was a conspicuous impersonator of Ibsen's heroines. While still a student at London's Central School, she played Dina Dorf* in *The Pillars of Society** as an examination piece. Nurturing her fondness of Ibsen, she at last appeared as Nora* (*A Doll's House*)* for 111 performances in New York commencing on January 3, 1971. After touring and filming the play, she opened as Nora at London's Criterion Theatre on February 20, 1973, which lasted six months. The actress writes: "It was my part and I'd always known it. . . . I'd been trying to convince producers for years. . . . I knew that it was about practically every woman I'd known who wanted something more from her life" (Bloom, pp. 146-7).

On February 17, 1971, Bloom started alternating her Nora with Hedda Gabler,* which she believes is the best woman's role in the modern theatre. This production was seen in New York fifty-six times. In 1977 Bloom added another Ibsenian character to her repertory: Rebecca West* in *Rosmersholm.** From the actress's perspective, however, the production was a disaster. "But *Rosmersholm*," she says, "was a non-event. It didn't happen. It was a mistake even to try it in the commercial theatre. . . . The odds were against it all the way, and I knew when I went into it that it wasn't at all what I wanted" (Bloom, pp. 157-58).

Claire Bloom is still in her prime as an actress, and she has not lost her respect for Ibsen's mastery of characterization. Doubtless she will take him up again and illuminate several other roles.

Reference: Bloom, Claire. *Limelight and After: The Education of an Actress.* New York: Harper and Row, 1982.

BLUHME, HELGA VON: In 1882 Helga von Bluhme, a Danish actress, performed *Hedda Gabler** in Dano-Norwegian in Chicago and other Midwestern cities. She was, therefore, the first Helene Alving* in the United States.

BLYTT, PETER: A lumber merchant, Peter Blytt became chairman of the governing board of the Norwegian Theatre (Bergen)* and thus Ibsen's superior. His memoirs are a valuable source of information on Ibsen's early career: *Minder fra den förste norske scene i Bergen.* Bergen, n.p., 1894.

BODDE, IVAR (*The Pretenders*): Haakon's* chaplain.

BORCHGREVINK, ANDREAS: Borchgrevink, a poet, delivered a paper called "A Visit to the National Theatre at Bergen" before the University Literary Society in Christiania* in September 1851. Student Ibsen, who rarely spoke in public, was so angered by what he saw as Borchgrevink's attack on the new theatre that he arose and replied in defense of Ole Bull.* This speech brought Ibsen to Bull's notice and won for him his appointment to the Norwegian Theatre (Bergen).*

BORGAARD, CARL PETER (1801-68): A sometime playwright and head of the Danish Christiania Theatre (1851-62), Borgaard angered Ibsen by accepting and then indefinitely postponing a production of *The Vikings in Helgeland** in 1858.

Reference: Norsk Biografisk Leksikon, I, 101.

BORGHEJM (*Little Eyolf*): Borghejm, a road-builder, is a healthy outdoorsman whose invitation to share his adventures is accepted by Asta Allmers.*

BORKMAN, ERHART (*John Gabriel Borkman*): Erhart is the son of John Gabriel* and Gunhild Borkman* and the nephew of Ella Rentheim.* His loyalty is a matter of bitter dispute between the two women, but Erhart opts for freedom and goes away with Mrs. Fanny Wilton.*

BORKMAN, GUNHILD (*John Gabriel Borkman*): When her husband John Gabriel Borkman* was imprisoned for dubious financial dealings, Gunhild felt that her entire social position was eradicated. She locked herself up in her apartment, seldom received visitors, ostracized her husband when he was released, doted on her son, and grew daily more embittered. Her crisis is precipitated by the appearance of Ella Rentheim,* her sister, who vies for Erhart's loyalty and gets John Gabriel to emerge from his self-imposed exile. At the end of the play, Gunhild is left with neither husband nor son but the possibility of an accommodation with her sister.

BORKMAN, JOHN GABRIEL (*John Gabriel Borkman*): Former bank president Borkman is a true creature of the Industrial Revolution, seeing business, industry, and automation as the apothesis of human society. When he makes some unwise financial decisions, he is prosecuted and sentenced to a term of imprisonment. Upon his release, he waits for death in the upstairs apartment of a house provided by his wealthy sister-in-law Ella Rentheim.* His wife declines to see him and keeps his son away; his sole visitor is a friend with whom he dreams of the days that might have been. The appearance of Ella and the elopement of Erhart* change all that. Borkman goes out into the wintry elements and dreams of his return as a titan of industry. He wanders excitedly into a storm and expires as a result, but not before his sense of vision is resurrected.

BOTTEN-HANSEN, PAUL (1824-69): When Paul Botten-Hansen, the editor of the handwritten student newspaper at Christiania,* *Samfundsbladet* [*Union News*],* published an appreciative review of *Catiline*,* he came to Ibsen's notice and continued as one of the dramatist's friends until his untimely death. With Ibsen and Aasmund Olafsen Vinje,* Botten-Hansen founded the political newspaper *Andhrimner*.* He was also the central figure of the nationalistic coterie The Learned Hollanders* of which Ibsen was a member.
Reference: Norsk Biografisk Leksikon, II, 112-21.

BOYESEN, HJALMAR HJORTH (1848-95): A professor of German at Cornell University (1874-80) and Columbia University (1880-95), H. H. Boyesen was a critic, poet, and novelist. Boyesen had lived in Christiania* between 1864 and 1869, and his description of life in that overgrown village makes Ibsen's decision to abandon his native land wholly creditable. In 1869 Boyesen emigrated to the United States where his *A Commentary on the Works of Henrik Ibsen* was published in 1894.

As a critic, Boyesen was a Spencerian evolutionist whose basic assumptions prompted him to praise Ibsen's Realistic works and to disparage, though respectfully, his Romantic plays. He admired Ibsen's passionate commitment to evolutionism but was unsympathetic to the author's lack of patience with the slowness of societal change. Boyesen writes, "The great charm of Ibsen is that he always deals with vital things. He is strong and virile, and opens to his reader long vistas of thought in unsuspected directions. He is a cosmopolitan spirit, betraying only the faintest perceptible trace of the limitations of nationality" (Boyesen, pp. 14-5).

In a lengthy introduction Boyesen pays homage to Ibsen, traces the salient details of his life, and speaks briefly of all the dramas through *The Pretenders*.* Individual chapters are devoted to the plays from *Love's Comedy** through *The Master Builder*.* Writing of Brand's* sacrifice of all who love him, Boyesen concludes, "Well . . . I am inclined to think that he regards this as the inexorable law of nature, which it is futile to endeavor to evade. The lesser creature is always being sacrificed to the higher creature" (Boyesen, p. 101). Here is natural selection at work.

When explicating the Third Empire envisioned in *Emperor and Galilean*,* Boyesen again reveals his scientific bias: "What I take it to mean is that in the gradual enfranchisement of humanity which the deeper acquaintance with nature's laws, revealed by science, is to accomplish the rights of the flesh will be more freely recognized and the antagonism between spirit and flesh . . . will be obliterated in a loving and harmonious union" (Boyesen, p. 177). According to Boyesen, *The Master Builder* "shows what damage a man's character suffers, and must suffer, under the pitiless law of competition called the survival of the fittest" (Boyesen, p. 305). These examples are sufficient to indicate the trend of Boyesen's critical thought. His insights are keen, and he had the advantage of knowing personally the milieux about which Ibsen wrote. Boyesen's work comprises some of the earliest and most important Ibsenian criticism in America.

References: Boyesen, Hjalmar H. *A Commentary on the Works of Henrik Ibsen.* New York: Russell and Russell, 1973 [1894]; Glasrud, Clarence A. *Hjalmar Hjorth Boyesen.* Northfield, Minn.: Norwegian-American Historical Society, 1968.

BRACK, JUDGE (*Hedda Gabler*): Judge Brack is an amoral, pivotal character. It is he who encourages Hedda Gabler* to slake her boredom by manipulating the lives of those about her. It is he, furthermore, who kills Hedda's will to live by manipulating her. Brack is urbane, seemingly generous, and ostensibly helpful, but his influence on Hedda is debilitating.

BRAHM, OTTO (1856-1912): Teacher, director, and man of the theatre, Otto Brahm was one of Ibsen's early German advocates. His delight in Anton Anno's* productions of *Ghosts** and *Rosmersholm** in 1887 prompted Brahm's publication of *Henrik Ibsen: Ein Essay* (1887). Also in 1887 Brahm directed Emanuel Reicher* in *The Wild Duck** at the Residenz Theater in Berlin.

With Brahm as its first president, the Freie Bühne* opened with *Ghosts* on September 29, 1889, and under Brahm's regime at the Deutsches Theater (1894-1904), Ibsen's dramas were often staged.

References: Claus, Horst. *The Theatre Director Otto Brahm.* Ann Arbor, Mich.: UMI Research Press, 1982; Newmark, Maxim. *Otto Brahm.* New York: G. E. Stechert, 1938.

BRAND: A poetic tragedy in five acts.

Composition: Started in the summer of 1865; finished in November; published on March 15, 1866.

Stage history:

June 26, 1867	Christiania Theatre* (3 perfs.) [Act IV only]
Mar. 24, 1885	Nya Theatre, Stockholm
1885	Christiania*
1885	Norwegian Theatre, Bergen*
1885	Trondhjem
June 2, 1893	Opera Comique, London (4) [Act IV only]
June 22, 1895	Théâtre de l'Oeuvre, Paris, Aurélien-Marie Lugné-Poë* as Brand
Oct. 21, 1895	Eldorado Theatre, Christiania,* dir. August Lindberg*
1895	Bergen, dir. August Lindberg
1895	Trondhjem, dir. August Lindberg
Mar. 17, 1898	Schiller Theater, Berlin
Apr. 3, 1898	Dagmars Theatre, Copenhagen
1900	Vienna
Sept. 14, 1904	National Theatre, Christiania*
Dec. 20, 1906	Art Theatre, Moscow,* dir. Vladimir Nemirovich-Danchenko*
Mar. 14, 1910	New Theatre, New York [Act IV only], Lee Baker* as Brand
Nov. 11, 1912	Court Theatre, London
Apr. 2, 1942	National Theatre, Christiania,* Johanne Dybwad* as Brand's Mother
Apr. 8, 1959	Lyric Theatre, Hammersmith (London), Patrick McGoohan* as Brand
Apr. 25, 1978	Olivier Theatre, London, National Theatre of Great Britain. Michael Bryant* as Brand

Synopsis: Brand, dressed entirely in black, is discovered struggling across a snowbound mountain pass in the company of a guide and his son. Brand outstrips his companions, who warn him to be careful of the glacial ice and crevasses which lead to an underground river. Despite the admonitions of the guide, Brand insists that he must press on because he is in God's service. The guide remonstrates that a frozen lake must be crossed, but Brand is undaunted by the danger. He is willing to sacrifice his life and discovers that the guide draws the line there, even though he is eager to join his ailing daughter on the other side. When Brand sees that the man will not risk everything, he sends him home. An avalanche fortuitously intervenes, separating Brand from the guide who is bent on retreating with Brand in tow; Brand is left to make his way alone. Brand, standing on a high ledge, soliloquizes on men's disinclination to sacrifice their lives; he is fascinated by the dichotomy between what is and what should be, a true Kierkegaardian paradox. Then, as the mists lift and the sun appears, Brand hears singing in the distance; he sees a crowd of people at the crest, two of whom break from the group and approach him. Ejnar and Agnes dance happily along the edge of the precipice and speak flirtatiously. Brand shouts to them to beware of the abyss and an overhang of heavy snow. The young people are unconcerned about the danger because they are young; when their lives have run their courses, they say, they will return to Heaven, their origin. Ejnar, a painter, was hiking through the mountains, saw Agnes, fell in love with her, and asked her to marry him; they are now bound for the city to celebrate their wedding feast, after which they will live in the south and be eternally happy. Brand wishes them well and starts to go, but Ejnar recognizes him as a friend from school, one who was always shy and withdrawn. Brand explains that he is a product of the frozen north and could never feel at home among the southerners. Now, Brand explains, he is a mission preacher and plans to catch a ship that will take him to a burial feast to celebrate the interment of the traditional conception of God. He faults the young people for frittering their lives away without total commitment. "Be wholly what you are, not half and half," he advises. He counsels them to live their faith to the fullest, not the faith of churches and sects but that of God's eternal spirit. Having delivered his injunctions, Brand decides to take the northern trail to the fjord while Ejnar takes the westward. Brand then starts down the path, leaving Agnes to her thoughts.

Now Agnes misses the light of the sun and feels cold blasts of wind; her joy has departed, and Ejnar cannot cheer her. Agnes can only remember how Brand's stature seemed to grow as he spoke. Then the two begin to descend the path as the scene changes to a narrow trail high in the lofty mountains. Brand makes his way to an abyss and, looking out, recollects the scene of his childhood spent near this place. In the distance he can make out a red cottage that was his boyhood home, but the memory of it only increases his sense of isolation in the world. Then he catches a glimpse of people walking toward the church where, in his estimation, they will utter inane prayers of cloying selfishness. At that point, a stone rolls past him in its path from above. Brand looks up and sees Gerd, a mountain girl of fifteen, who is delighted that her stone hit its target; she throws another stone at an unseen adversary and shrieks. When Brand goes to her aid, Gerd speaks of an ugly hawk that was harassing her. In response to Brand's query as to her destination, Gerd replies, "To church," but not the tiny one in the valley below but to a chapel of ice in the high mountains. Brand remembers such a place—a frozen lake for a floor, a great snowdrift for a roof—from his youth and warns her not to go there as any loud noise may cause it to tumble down. Gerd, in turn, advises Brand not to go to the valley because it is ugly. She invites him to accompany her to the Ice Church where nature is reverent and the hawk cannot menace her. Again she thinks she sees the hawk, so she runs off up the mountainside. In the people he has now encountered, Brand sees examples of different types of faith: the light of heart, the dull of heart, and the wild of heart. He sees them all as enemies whom he must vanquish. He then recognizes his mission as doing battle with these types of people for the glory of heaven. Brand starts to walk toward the valley.

The first scene of Act II is laid in the village beside a lake. A storm is brewing as the Mayor and the Sexton distribute corn and other comestibles to the assembled people. Brand emerges from the mountain beside a derelict church. He watches the people behaving almost like animals in their mad dash for food. The place has been racked by drought, famine, and flood; many have died, and supplies are running out. Ejnar contributes all his money for the relief of the poor and accuses Brand of standing aloof from their suffering. Brand comes down and tells the crowd that they should count themselves fortunate because, through death, God is teaching them the value of life. They will, he says, derive strength from their suffering. As he speaks, the storm breaks over the fjord and is interpreted as a sign of God's wrath against Brand. The people start to threaten him and drive him from the village, but everyone is distracted by the sudden appearance of a greatly agitated woman who shouts for a priest. Her family lives across the lake, where three of her children have died; their crazed father killed the youngest and tried to do away with himself. Now, as her husband stands on the brink of eternity, she wants a priest to save his soul. Brand orders someone to row him across the lake, but no one will brave the storm and risk his life. Not even the distraught woman will go in the boat with him. As the storm mounts, Agnes, mesmerized by Brand's strength, tells Ejnar to accompany Brand, but the young man is too fond of his life to take the chance. Agnes sees that everything is over between her and Ejnar. She says that she will go with Brand and so rushes into the boat. Ejnar and the crowd try to call her back, but the boat moves away from shore. The people gather on the brow of a hill to watch the fate of the intrepid two. On the mountain Gerd is seen laughing, throwing stones, and blowing a buck's horn. As the people watch Brand sail into the eye of the storm, they decide that he is indeed a holy man who should be their priest.

Scene 2 takes place in front of a hut on the far side of the fjord. It is hours later, and the water is calm. Brand emerges from the hut and tells Agnes that the father is dead and at peace but that the two children must always carry the vision of his crime. Their story is mankind's: guilt inherited from generation to generation. Some of the villagers come into view, bearing some necessities for the family of the dead man. They ask Brand to be their priest, but he is reluctant to accept because he thinks that his is a wider mission than an isolated community can afford. Boldly, they tell him to sacrifice his will to their necessity, but he will not relent. The delegation sadly departs. Brand sees Agnes sitting quietly and asks what she is looking at. She feels that she is at a pivotal time as she has been called to take up her burden of populating the world with creatures attuned to the urges of the eternal. Brand exults in her vision and reflects on the meaning of being wholly oneself. Then he sees an aged body in the distance; as it draws nearer, Brand sees his mother. She shields her eyes and complains of the sun's brightness as Brand remembers that the sun never shone in her home. The mother warns him to take care of his life because he will someday inherit all her money if he provides male heirs. Brand asks what she would do if he decided to scatter her wealth to the winds after she was stretched out in death. She asks what put such an idea into his head, and Brand tells her how as a boy he had been quietly looking at his father's corpse when a woman slipped into the room, groped in the bedclothes around the body, and drew out caches of money. As she had greedily laid hands on the treasure, she had alternately prayed, keened, and cursed. Then she had crept out of the room. The woman was, of course, Brand's mother, and her avaricious deed had resulted in the loss of her son. From her point of view, she had also lost the ability to love. Brand reminds her that she had also abandoned her soul, but she is confident that her son the priest will be able to save her soul when death comes. That will be the price he pays for his inheritance. Brand replies that a son must also assume his parents' debts. Since she has lost her soul, the son must pay that price as well. By his own life he will answer for her soul-debt, but she must answer for her sins by either repentance or damnation. This discussion makes the mother giddy, so she decides to return to her home in the shadow of the glacier with Brand's assurance that he will come should she feel attracted to God when death rings in her ears. Then he adds a disquieting stipulation: he will minister to her as a son and a priest if she renounces all her worldly possessions. Brand demands the sacrifice of everything she holds dear. The mother, uncertain as to her future action, goes away determined to enjoy her riches for as long as she can.

Brand goes to Agnes, and together they agree that their lives have been drastically altered since the morning. She renounces her empty pursuit of pleasure, and he sees that his work is here, not in the wide world. He will strive to bury the old, ineffectual concept of God in each individual heart by giving in its place the will to transform human life. Brand turns toward the village, which he apostrophizes as his mission field. As he starts to move away, however, Ejnar enters and demands that Brand surrender Agnes to him. The young woman is not at all interested in Ejnar's promise of joy, bliss, happiness; she casts her lot with Brand. The priest cautions her to consider her decision carefully because life with him will not be easy, for he will demand All or Nothing, perhaps even her life. Like psychomachic angels, Brand and Ejnar offer Agnes conflicting roles in life. She chooses

Brand and follows him off the stage, leaving Ejnar staring after her as the act ends.

Three years have passed as Act III, set in the garden of Brand's parsonage, starts. Brand stands on the steps of the porch and gazes into the distance. At Agnes' question, he explains that he is waiting for a message from his mother because he has heard that she is dying. Agnes urges him to go to her, but he will not go unless his mother repents. Brand and Agnes speak of their life together, Brand reminding her that he had warned that it would be difficult and Agnes saying that it has not been so. He observes that the bloom has gone from her cheek as a result of living in a house never warmed by the sun. She asks what secret fear haunts him and learns that he is anxious about the health of their son Ulf. Brand's belief in a good God assures him that his very pale child will be well and not be taken from him; yet he trembles at the possibility that Ulf may die. Because Agnes has given him light and peace and Ulf has provided strength, Brand believes that his ministry has been successful. Love has been a potent factor in his life with Agnes and Ulf. By learning to love one, Brand says, he has learned to love all. Still, Agnes reminds him, his unrelenting demand for All or Nothing has repelled people. Brand answers that he cares nothing for others' opinions; his salvation lies in his willingness to suffer everything for his beliefs. Agnes agrees that the goal is commendable but acknowledges her weakness in the attainment of it, which prompts Brand to express his great law for everyone: no cowardly compromise. Once again she takes courage in his strength and commitment and vows to follow him. As they embrace, the Doctor enters, takes pleasure in their relationship, and comments on the unwholesomeness of the place. He is on his way to visit Brand's mother and invites the priest to join him, but Brand will not come, asserting that he will pay his mother's debts. The Doctor angrily says that Brand may have great strength of will but an absolute deficiency of love. He then exits.

Brand tells Agnes that love is merely a word used to mask weakness, that will is what matters. Agnes begs that he will give her strength when her will falters. After one masters one's will, Brand says, love is possible, but in this place he can best show his love by hating the laxity and lack of commitment of the people. He rushes madly into the house, leaving Agnes to describe his kneeling and weeping at the baby's bed. She rejoices that he is capable of loving a small child. Then he emerges from the house to ask if there has been a message from his mother. Brand reports that Ulf's condition is not good. As the distraught parents comfort each other, a messenger enters with the news that Brand's mother has agreed to give half her wealth for the sacrament. Brand will not go to her. The man is amazed that a son will not attend his dying parent. He leaves to carry Brand's message and observes that luckily God is not as hard as Brand. Brand derides the idea that the old God can be appeased by deathbed confessions. The first man returns with a second whom he has met on the path; the second man reports that the old woman will give away nine-tenths of her fortune if he will come. Angrily, Brand dismisses them both with the injunction All or Nothing. Agnes asks if any man of this generation could live up to his hard terms; Brand despairs of humanity. He sends Agnes into the house to make Ulf as comfortable as possible. Agnes leaves Brand fully confident that God will not demand the sacrifice of their child, but Brand wonders if God will test him as he did Abraham.

The Mayor enters, expresses his condolence at the illness of Brand's mother, and suggests that as a rich man, Brand probably would prefer to live elsewhere. He is, in fact, inviting Brand to leave the community; if he insists on staying, he must not overstep the limits of his calling. Brand's response is to declare war on the Mayor and everything he stands for. The Mayor tries to convince Brand that he will lose everything if he loses this particular war. When Brand says that he will win with the aid of his best men, the Mayor reminds him that he has the most men. Having said this, the Mayor exits, followed by Brand's pitying comments about the danger caused by such men of the people.

Then the Doctor enters with the news that Brand's mother died mumbling that God is not as cruel as her son. Brand collapses on a bench and buries his face in his hands. The Doctor counsels that Brand's Old Testament religion has been replaced in this age by a gentler commandment: be humane. Brand retorts that God was not humane to Jesus Christ. A frightened Agnes comes out of the house and asks the Doctor to go in to Ulf, leaving Brand to his thoughts. He concludes that his behavior at his mother's death will give him the strength of will to remain true to his mission. The Doctor comes out of the house and tells Brand that he must move from this place if he wishes to save his son's life; another winter in this cold, sunless, damp place will kill the child. The Doctor advises their getting out the next day, but moved by his son's danger, Brand tells Agnes to prepare to leave that very night. As Brand stares distractedly, the Doctor observes that the man who demanded that others sacrifice everything is sacrificing his mission to expediency. Brand becomes quite confused, wondering whether he was correct before or now. The Doctor says that Brand is doing the right thing and is now a more likable person than he was before. Then the Doctor leaves.

Brand again gives voice to his quandary. As the sun sets, Agnes comes out with the baby in her arms; a man rushes in to report that the Mayor is telling people that Brand will desert them now that he has inherited his mother's fortune. The man has difficulty believing that Brand would leave because he had always preached that people must live up to their callings. The man is so confident in Brand and in the salvation he has received through Brand that he knows the pastor will not desert his flock. For him to do so would be to destroy the souls of the faithful parishioners. He departs, leaving Brand to ponder his own words pronounced against him.

As they prepare to go, Gerd comes down the path singing gleefully about the flight of the parson which has unleashed the mountain trolls. Brand reminds her that he has not left, but she says that he is not her priest. As the ugly village church is now empty and locked, her church, the one of ice, has come into its time. Brand upbraids her for speaking of idols in the ice, but she responds by calling Ulf Brand's idol. Brand tells Agnes that God has sent Gerd to him. Continuing to babble about the return of the trolls, Gerd disappears up the mountain. Agnes tells Brand it is time to go, but he wavers between the choice of the house and the gate. At last he chooses to remain. Agnes lifts the child toward heaven and accepts Ulf as a sacrifice. Brand watches silently as Agnes takes the child into the house; then he falls onto the steps weeping copiously and imploring Jesus to give him light.

Act IV occurs inside the parsonage on Christmas Eve. Agnes, garbed in deep mourning clothes, waits anxiously at the window for Brand's arrival. The sound of his steps is soon heard, and when Brand comes in, she begs him not to leave her again for so long. Brand lights one candle by the light of which he notices her pallor. Agnes says she is tired from the effort of making a few decorations for the Christmas tree from the same branches used for the wreath that now hangs over Ulf's grave. Brand asks if her tears are the means by which she celebrates the Lord's birthday; he is uncompromising in his insistence that she face the fact of Ulf's death. Yet even Brand is desolated by the loss of the child. Brand admits that he feels nearer to God now that he is able to weep, which he was unable to do prior to his decision to forfeit his son's life. When Agnes tells of feeling that Ulf visited her room last night, Brand tells her that his body is in the ground under the snow but his soul is with God. Agnes replies that she cannot separate the two; she begs Brand to be gentle with her because she trembles to approach her warrior God with her small sorrow. She longs to be somewhere where it is light and everything is not of such magnitude as it is in Brand's world; only the church is too small. Brand agrees that the edifice is too confining, and at that moment he decides to rebuild it if only she will put down her sorrow and help him. Agnes enthusiastically agrees and starts to resume her household duties for the first time since Ulf's death, even to the point of celebrating Christmas by putting a candle in each of the windows. As Agnes goes about her jobs, Brand prays that she may be given strength and that he may be allowed to shoulder part of her burden in doing God's will.

The Mayor's entrance is announced by a knock at the door; he has come to concede that Brand has won the war for the villagers' hearts. Now, in order to assure his reelection, he has come to ask Brand what he should build to relieve his people—a poorhouse, jail, meeting hall? Whatever the project, he will require Brand's financial support. Brand tells him that he plans to rebuild the church. At first the Mayor is suspicious, but when Brand says he will spend his whole fortune on the new edifice, the Mayor relents and agrees to give up his plan. Brand's only stipulation is that the old church must be razed, so the Mayor says that he personally will tear it down if the people should want to save it for historical and sentimental associations. Before leaving, the Mayor speaks of having arrested some gypsies, and in passing he tells Brand about a young gypsy man who had fallen in love with Brand's mother. She had sent him away, and in the heat of his passion, he had married a gypsy woman and sired none other than Gerd. The Mayor wryly observes that Brand's mother was the cause of both the priest and the mountain girl. Left alone, Brand muses that his mother was also the cause of Ulf's death because Gerd had convinced him to stay in the mountains. He wonders about the efficacy of prayers and sees himself again plunged into darkness. Brand shouts for Agnes to bring him light, and when she appears with the Christmas candles, the room is bathed in light. Agnes wipes the windowpane clean so that Ulf from the graveyard can see the brightness of their Christmas celebration. Brand peremptorily orders her to close the shutters because she must sacrifice her grief; resignation to Ulf's death is not enough. All or Nothing. Once again she is frightened by Brand's demands, but his arms give her courage to follow wherever he leads. He exits to start planning his new church but admonishes her not to open the shutters even a tiny crack.

Cloistered in the Christmas room, Agnes feels stifled, yet she knows that God's eyes will follow her everywhere. Brand is too absorbed in his own plans to comfort her. She starts to believe that Ulf may be standing outside the door but cannot come in because Brand has closed the house to him. Agnes draws various objects from a chest—a veil, Ulf's christening shawl, his shirt—and takes comfort from them. Unseen by her, Brand has come into the room and silently watches her. Brand, moved to pity, prays God to send him another idol to destroy. Suddenly the door flies open, admitting an unkempt gypsy woman with a child in her arms. She asks that Agnes share her treasures with her poor child; she wants Ulf's baby clothes but spurns Brand's preaching and the offer of warmth and light. Brand tells Agnes to do her duty, but she refuses; he says that Ulf will have died in vain if she does not comply. Agnes agrees to share the clothes with the woman, but Brand reminds her that she must give all. In the end, the woman takes everything and leaves. Agnes asks Brand if she has not given enough now, but he concludes that the gift was worthless because she did not surrender willingly. Then she tells him that she has kept back Ulf's cap. When he shows his displeasure, Agnes gives up the cap, which Brand takes to the woman who is still outside. When Brand returns, Agnes rushes into his arms exclaiming that at last she is free, and he agrees that she has conquered. Agnes reminds him that now he will be put to the test because she believes that whoever has seen God will die. Is he prepared to lose her? Remaining true to his old principles, Brand realizes that they cannot go back to living in the former manner. Agnes goes to bed, leaving Brand to steel himself to losing everything and through that to achieving ultimate victory.

Six months have passed. In Act V, Scene 1, the Sexton is hanging decorations on the new church which is ready to be consecrated. The Schoolmaster enters and discusses with the Sexton the many changes that have taken place in the valley. The sound of an organ is heard, and the Sexton comments that the priest often plays to assuage his insomnia which followed the death of his wife. The Schoolmaster observes that the new church has not gladdened the priest or the parishioners, who feel that an alien God must inhabit the new church. Then the two men exit to their official responsibilities. Brand appears and laments the inutility of the organ to express his thoughts. He says that Agnes' presence would have given meaning to the church, but now all he wants to do is hide. The Mayor enters in full municipal regalia and exuberantly compliments Brand and the church. Brand is already dissatisfied with the structure, but the Mayor wants to report that Brand is to receive a royal decoration this morning. Brand dismisses the Mayor and continues to wallow in his misery, which is interrupted by the entrance of the Dean. After discoursing about Brand's exalted status among his fellow ministers and anticipating the sumptuous feast that will follow the consecration, the Dean tells Brand that he hopes he will stop treating each member of his congregation as an individual with respect to specific spiritual problems. The church's job, he says, is to serve the state, and by raising the moral tone of the village at large, Brand will aid in the state's progress. Treating people as individuals will merely ruin them and do a disservice to the state. Brand sees this as contrary to his vocation and tells the Dean that he has sold his principles for worldly rewards. The Dean merely reminds Brand that individualism is dangerous and goes off to eat a bit before preaching his sermon. Brand cries out for only one person to share his faith, to stand at his side as he battles his worldly foes. Ejnar comes down the road, haggard, pallid, and decked in black. Ejnar rejects Brand's attempt at camaraderie because he needs no priest. He has found peace and salvation after falling into drunkenness and gambling, loss of health, talent, and love of fun. Now he is a missionary en route to Africa. He expresses very little interest in hearing what happened to Agnes. He dismisses her marriage, her child, her life as trivial; the only important thing is how she died. When Brand says that she died secure in her faith in God, Ejnar responds that she was then damned, implying that Brand's interpretation of God is of Satan. He quickly exits. At last Brand sees that it is his destiny to stand alone.

When the crowd comes in demanding to be allowed into the church, Brand addresses the villagers with inspired frenzy, concluding that the new church is a monstrous lie and must be done away with. The Dean tries to intercede, but the crowd is electrified by Brand's inspiration. He urges the people to follow him into the great Church of Life, and when the Mayor orders the door of the church to be unlocked, the people clamor not for that church but for the Church of Life. Brand eloquently speaks of the natural world as the ideal church. Then he relocks the church and appeals for the people to follow him into the true church. The Mayor and Dean feel that they will lose their congregation and constituency, but they decide not to interfere. Brand throws the keys of the church into the fjord and bids the people to follow him in a pilgrimage throughout the land as they make the earth their church. The crowd energetically agrees and hoists him aloft as a visionary hero. The protestations of the Mayor and Dean cannot now deter them as they start up the mountain. Although the Dean is desolated, the Mayor senses that the victory of his kind of materialism is imminent. Slowly, they walk after the multitude.

In Scene 2, set beside a farmhouse high in the mountains, Brand walks before the host of his supporters. He urges them to climb onward. The people are tired, disgruntled, some sick, but Brand exhorts them to cross the mountain. They cavil, they fear, they scruple, but Brand assures them that victory will be theirs if only they are willing to gamble All or Nothing. The throng feels betrayed. Believing themselves unable to go back and afraid to go on, the mob attacks Brand with the intention of killing him. Their interest is arrested by the appearance of the Mayor and Dean who promise them spiritual security and material plenty. Brand tells the people that their choice is between the world and God. They choose the world and drive Brand up the mountain. As they lead their flock back to the village, the Dean excuses the Mayor's lie about communal riches as expedient and forgivable.

Scene 3 finds Brand among the highest peaks as a storm is gathering. He soliloquizes about the meaning of Christ's sacrifice, but voices from the storm taunt him with his inability to be Christlike, and they enjoin him to do God's will. As the voices tell him that he is lost, Brand weeps for the return of Agnes and Ulf. An apparition of Agnes appears in the mist and tells him that he merely dreamed that she is dead, that Ulf is alive too, that everything in the valley is as it was before he returned. She entreats him to follow her to happiness which can be done if he forgets three words: All or Nothing. Now Brand sees this ghostly confrontation as identical with that which he has lived previously. He makes the same decisions, thus driving away the vision of Agnes. Brand sees its disappearance as the flight of a great hawk. Gerd enters, and Brand tells her that he too has seen the hawk. As Brand tells his story to Gerd, she comes to see him as the Biggest Man of all, one with nail marks in his hands, blood in his hair. He is, in her estimation, the Savior of Man, but when she tries to worship him, Brand is horrified. The mists lift as Gerd tells Brand that he is actually standing in the Ice Church. He weeps, calls upon Jesus, and this time he believes his prayers are heard. As Brand sinks to his knees, Gerd sees the hawk above and fires her silver bullet, which produces a vast rumble from the mountain overhead. Gerd exults in her shooting of the hawk whose white feathers are floating down the mountainside. Brand asks if every man must die to atone for human sin. As cascades of snow bury Brand and Gerd, he asks how can man be redeemed if not by will, and the voice answers through the thunder: "He is the God of Love."

Structural analysis: In the Aristotelian sense, *Brand* is a tragedy because it depicts in dramatic form with elevated language the enlightening downfall of a protagonist with human virtues and faults through an error of judgment based on ethical considerations. In a plot unified by Thought, Ibsen episodically reveals stages in the development of Brand's character. When first seen, Brand has a worldwide vision of his vocation, but as he sees the villagers' spiritual hunger in general and his mother's need in particular, he reduces his field of endeavor to a narrow valley, Gudbrandsdalen.* In a series of episodes illustrative of the application of Brand's All or Nothing theology, Brand loses his mother, his child, his wife, and eventually his congregation. Only when he has been stripped of every tie to this world is he capable of concluding that to die is to be most Christlike, a conclusion voiced by Sören Aabye Kierkegaard.* In his death throes Brand hears the counterproposal: to love is to be most Christlike; but for Brand it is too late.

References: Anderson, Marilyn A. "Norse Trolls and Ghosts in Ibsen," *Journal of Popular Culture*, 5 (1971), 349-67; Dalstrom, E.W.L. "Brand—Ibsen's Bigot?" *Scandinavian Studies*, 22 (1956), 1-13; Saari, Sandra E. "Ibsen's *Brand:* The 19th-Century Play and the 1978 British National Theatre Production," *Scandinavian Studies*, 51 (1979), 413-27; Wood, Forrest, Jr. "Kierkegaardian Light on Ibsen's *Brand*," *Personalist*, 51 (1970), 393-400.

BRAND (*Brand*): Brand is a minister for whom the claims of Christianity are unrelenting. Compromise with worldly philosophies is an impossibility for him. He believes that what one most cherishes must be surrendered, even if it be one's child, one's wife, or one's life. Brand is strong, a dutiful but stern husband and father, and a charismatic priest, but he remains blind to the injunctions of *agape*-love until the moment of his death.

BRANDES, CARL EDVARD (1847-1931): Edvard Brandes was an influential Danish writer and politician. With his brother Georg* he founded a journal called *The Nineteenth Century*, the pages of which included numerous references to Ibsen's works. Edvard also wrote theatrical criticisms for *Politiken*, of which he was editor from 1888. He was an avid supporter of Ibsen the revolutionary dramatist, but that did not deter him from pointing out what he saw as the weaknesses of Ibsen's plays. Deeply moved by a performance of *A Doll's House*,* Brandes became a playwright, penning about eleven dramas in the Ibsenian mold. His theatrical reviews are the subject of his *Om Teater* [*About Theatre*] (1947).

BRANDES, GEORG MORRIS (1842-1927): The publication of *Brand** (1866) called Ibsen to the attention of the young literary critic Georg Brandes who recognized the power of the poem but could not reconcile himself with the Romanticism of the piece. When *Peer Gynt** appeared, he criticized Ibsen's view of human nature—Brandes always judged plays not as theatrical works but by their social utility or philosophical content. Yet in *Peer Gynt* he admired Ibsen's mastery of language, and doubtless Ibsen respected Brandes' growing critical acumen because Ibsen enthusiastically read the Dane's *Aesthetic Studies.** Soon after the rift in Ibsen's relationship with Björnstjerne Björnson,* Ibsen turned to Brandes as his principal ally, a strange association because Brandes was wholly unacquainted with the practical demands of the theatre. Brandes, for his part, valued Ibsen's counsel in a series of domestic crises, but their friendship was interrupted for four years in 1877 when Brandes was piqued by an imaginary slight. The controversy over *Ghosts** in 1881 brought the men back into contact. Brandes admired *An Enemy of the People** and in 1883 wrote an adulatory essay about Ibsen which greatly pleased the dramatist. After its publication in German, the article reappeared in Brandes' *Henrik Ibsen* (1898). The critic, however, was not enthusiastic about *The Wild Duck** and *Rosmersholm,** which perhaps explained why Ibsen remarked that Brandes was ignorant of Norwegian literature. Since Brandes extolled all the plays after *The Master Builder,** their friendship remained intact until Ibsen's death. At the end of 1902 Brandes saw the afflicted Ibsen for the last time, noting his lucidity but his pathetic creative inertia.

References: Brandes, Georg. "Henrik Ibsen: Personal Reminiscences and Remarks about His Plays," *Century Magazine*, 93, 4 (Feb. 1917), 539-46; Laurvik, John, trans. "Letters of Henrik Ibsen to Georg Brandes," *The Critic*, 46, 2 (Feb. 1905), 157-62.

BRAND'S MOTHER (*Brand*): A type rather than a fully drawn dramatic portrait, Brand's Mother is a tenacious materialist. She was unable to wait until Brand's father's corpse was buried before appropriating his money; she afterward lived a life of comfort, ease, and pleasure in her fortune. As she sickens and nears death, she proves incapable of parting with her money, even for the sake of her soul and her son's blessing.

BRATTSBERG, CHAMBERLAIN (*The League of Youth*): As owner of the local ironworks and the richest man in town, Chamberlain Brattsberg is a very powerful political figure whose patronage of office-holders is unattractive to those who covet his position. Brattsberg and his associates become the target of the new political machine called the League of Youth.

BRATTSBERG, ERIK (*The League of Youth*): The ineffectual son of the elder Brattsberg*; the husband of Selma*; a merchant who contracts serious debts.

BRATTSBERG, SELMA (*The League of Youth*): The wife of Erik Brattsberg,* Selma is wise enough to realize that her husband's business practices have jeopardized their marriage. By the end of the play, when Erik seems to have learned a lesson, Selma agrees to try to make a success of their life together.

BRATTSBERG, THORA (*The League of Youth*): Thora, the daughter of Chamberlain Brattsberg,* provides romantic interest in the play. She is secretly engaged to marry Dr. Fjeldbo.*

BRAUSEWETTER, ERNST (1863-1904): A prolific German writer, Ernst Brausewetter was an accomplished translator of Scandinavian works, particularly those of August Strindberg* and Ibsen. He translated *The Wild Duck** (1887), *Emperor and Galilean** (1888), and *Rosmersholm** (1889).
Reference: Deutsches Literatur-Lexikon (Berlin, 1968), I, col. 941.

BRAVO, JOHAN (1797-1876): Danish-born Johan Bravo lived in Rome after 1827 and served as Norwegian consul there. A convivial man noted for his atrocious Danish, Bravo was Ibsen's sponsor in Rome, introducing him in cultural circles and proposing him for membership in the Scandinavian Club.
Reference: Dansk Biografisk Leksikon, IV, 33-4.

BREAKING A BUTTERFLY (1884): Upon the advice of Helena Modjeska,* Henry Arthur Jones* and Henry Herman adapted *A Doll's House** under the title of *Breaking a Butterfly*. It was presented at London's Prince's Theatre for a month beginning on March 3, 1884, becoming only the second professional production in England of an Ibsenian drama. The cast-list follows:

Humphrey Goddard	Kyrle Bellew
Philip Dunkley	H. Beerbohm Tree*
Martin Grittle	John Maclean
Dan Bradbury	G. W. Anson
Flora Goddard	Miss Lingard
Agnes Goddard	Helen Matthews
Mrs. Goddard	Mrs. Leigh Murray
Maid	Annie Maclean

Harley Granville-Barker was a member of the audience and formulated this synopsis of the story:

The scene is laid in some English town. Nora becomes Flora and, to her husband, rather terribly, Flossie. He is Humphrey Goddard and we find him gifted with a mother (quite unnecessarily) and a sister (wanted for the piano-playing, *vice* Mrs. Linde, who disappears). The morbid Dr. Rank is replaced by a Charles-his-friend, called, as if to wipe out every trace of his original, Ben Birdseye! He is not in love with Nora-Flora, of course; that would never do. But Dunkley, alias Krogstad, had loved her as a girl, when Humphrey Goddard stole her young heart from him; so love has turned to hate and revenge is sweet. Observe the certainty with which our operators in the English market fasten on the flawed streak in Ibsen's play and cheapen it still further. The tarantella episode, of course, will be the making of the whole affair (such was many people's judgement then, and now we find it rather marring), and this is left intact. But the third act sees the parent play stood deliberately on its head, and every ounce of Ibsen emptied out of it. Burlesque could do no more. Torvald-Humphrey behaves like the pasteboard hero of Nora's doll's-house dream; he *does* strike his chest and say: "I am the guilty one!" And Nora-Flora cries that she is a poor weak foolish girl, " . . . no wife for a man like you. You are a thousand times too good for me," and never wakes up and walks out of her doll's house at all (De la Mare, pp. 167-8).

William Archer* also witnessed the production: "Take a piece of music, omit all the harmonies, break and rearrange the melodic phrases, and then play them with your forefinger on the pianoforte—do this, and you will have some idea of the process to which Messrs. Jones and Herman have subjected *A Doll's House*" (Archer, p. 209). Fortunately for Ibsen, the stage life of *Breaking a Butterfly* was mercifully short.

References: Archer, William. *"Breaking a Butterfly,"* *The Theatre*, III (Apr. 1, 1884), 209-14; "The Coming of Ibsen," *The Eighteen-Eighties*, ed. Walter de la Mare. Cambridge: Cambridge University Press, 1930.

BRECHER, EGON (1880-1946): Bohemian-born Egon Brecher emigrated to the United States in 1921 and soon found employment at New York's Civic Repertory Theatre. He appeared with Eva Le Gallienne* in *The Master Builder** (1925) and *John Gabriel Borkman** (1926), playing the title roles in both dramas.

Reference: Who Was Who in the Theatre, I, 274-5.

BRENDEL, ULRIK (*Rosmersholm*): Brendel, remembered variously as scoundrel, writer, and revolutionary, was the teacher of Johannes Rosmer.* His unexpected return to Rosmersholm* considerably abashes his former pupil who must lend him a shirt to make Brendel presentable enough to show his face in the village. Brendel wants to rent a hall in which to espouse his remarkable plans for improving human life. In some respects he resembles Julian Poulsen* of *St. John's Night** forty years later in that he is almost a stereotypical Romantic poet. Expansive gestures, picturesque language, and impossible dreams characterize both poets.

BRETT, JEREMY (1935-   ): One of the best of the current generation of British actors, Jeremy Brett was Jörgen Tesman* to Maggie Smith's* Hedda Gabler* (1970) and Johannes Rosmer* to Joan Plowright's* Rebecca West* (1973). Both performances were seen in London.

Reference: Who's Who in the Theatre, 16th ed., pp. 436-7.

THE BRIDEGROOM (*Peer Gynt*): The young man whose bride was abducted by Peer Gynt.*

BROVIK, KNUT (*The Master Builder*): Brovik, an ailing man who was once an architect, is in the employ of Halvard Solness.* His dying wish is to see his son Ragnar* be given the chance independently to design a house. Solness cruelly rejects his suggestion. Brovik dies early in the play.

BROVIK, RAGNAR (*The Master Builder*): Although he is only a drafts-man in Halvard Solness's* company, Ragnar is a gifted architectural designer, but because he is young, Solness fears Ragnar.

BRUN, JOHANNES FINNE (1831-90): In 1851 Ibsen met Johannes Brun, a popular comic actor, when both were employed at the Norwegian Theatre (Bergen).* Brun accompanied Ibsen on his first European trip to observe theatrical practice. Later, he created a number of Ibsenian roles, including Daniel Hejre* in *The League of Youth** and Ulrik Brendel* in *Ros-mersholm.**
Reference: Almquist, Olaf. *Johannes Brun: En skildring av hans liv og samtidige* Christiania: Alb. Cammermeyer, 1898.

BRUN, LUISE GULBRANDSEN (1831-66): Luise Brun completed the trio when her husband Johannes* and Ibsen were sent to observe continental production techniques in the spring and summer of 1852. She was a gifted actress and created the role of Lady Inger of Gyldenlöve.*
Reference: *Norsk Biografisk Leksikon*, II, 238-40.

BRUNA, EDA (fl. 1905): After playing small roles for the Progressive Stage Society (New York) in *An Enemy of the People** and *The League of Youth*,* Eda Bruna graduated to portraying Hilde Wangel* in *The Master Builder** in 1905.
Reference: Briscoe, Johnson. *The Actors' Birthday Book*, 2d ser. New York: Moffat, Yard, 1908.

BRUUN, CHRISTOPHER ARNT (1839-1924): Ibsen knew Bruun as a theological student, clergyman, and lifelong friend. Coming from Gud-brandsdalen,* Bruun is believed to have inspired some aspects of Brand.* When Germany annexed parts of Denmark, Bruun fought for the Danes and disquieted Ibsen by asking why he too did not fight. Ibsen preferred his battles in books and on the stage: *Brand** was the result of his uneasiness at Bruun's suggestion.
Reference: *Norsk Biografisk Leksikon*, II, 256-63.

BRYANT, MICHAEL (1928-   ): Michael Bryant, an Englishman, has recently played two major Ibsenian roles in London: Brand* (1978) and

Gregers Werle* (1979). Both productions were presented by the National Theatre of Great Britain.

References: The Times (London), Mar. 3, 1978, p. 15, col. 4; Dec. 14, 1979, p. 13, col. 7; *Who's Who in the Theatre*, 17th ed., I, 93.

BRYCELAND, YVONNE: When the National Theatre of Great Britain presented *The Wild Duck** in 1979, Yvonne Bryceland, a South African, was Gina Ekdal* to Michael Bryant's* Gregers Werle.*

Reference: Who's Who in the Theatre, 17th ed., I, 93-94.

BÜLOW-SCHANZER, MARIE VON (1856-1941): A member of Berlin's Freie Bühne* as well as Berlin's National Theater, Marie Bülow-Schanzer played Helene Alving* in the inaugural production of *Ghosts** (1889). Her performance, however, was eclipsed by the controversy over the implied references in the play to venereal disease.

Reference: Kosch, Wilhelm. *Deutsches Theater-Lexikon* (Klagenfurt: Ferd. Kleinmayr, 1953), I, 232.

BULL, OLE BORNEMANN (1810-80): An internationally discussed virtuoso violinist, Ole Bull was an ardent Norwegian nationalist. His concert programs included selections by Norwegian composers (himself included) and his own improvisations on Norwegian folk songs. Bull's fervent patriotism led him into at least two notable undertakings, one of which had important ramifications for the development of dramatic art. The first was the Norwegian Theatre and the second a Norwegian commune in America.

A native of Bergen,* Bull returned to Norway in 1848 after an extensive tour in the United States and Europe and discovered there a rampant nationalistic spirit, led in part by Aasmund Olafson Vinje.* A visit to his home town in 1849 prompted Bull to actualize what had been only a dream: the establishment of a theatre in which Norwegian actors would present Norwegian dramas in a pure Norwegian tongue. (Professional theatre in Norway was then conducted by Danish actors in Danish.) Bull converted Fritz Jensen,* a multi-talented man, to his scheme, and together they proceeded to create a national theatre, Bull providing the enthusiasm and contacts and Jensen doing most of the work.

Bull aroused Bergen's interest by playing several concerts, the principal content of which was Norwegian folk music. Afterward, crowds followed him to his rooming house and demanded encores. Ever obliging, Bull played for a bit and then exhorted his auditors to express their patriotism by supporting every aspect of Norwegian art. In July Bull published an advertisement in the newspapers inviting singers, instrumentalists, dancers, and actors to attend auditions for a Norwegian Theatre company. Then he left town. Jensen spent weeks auditioning the applicants and finally chose five men and eight women for the original company, none of whom had any professional experience. Johannes Finne Brun,* destined to become a theatrical legend in Norway, was one of them.

When Bull returned to Bergen, he assembled an orchestra, leaving the dramatic considerations to Jensen. Bull gave private lessons, rehearsed orchestral sections, and eventually put together a musical ensemble. In the midst of this formidable task, he frequently spoke in support of the theatre and presented concerts by which to finance it. On November 21, 1849, a public rehearsal signaled the birth of the Norwegian Theatre. Four hundred invited guests gathered in the unheated theatre with red walls. Despite the many obstacles, the performance of Ludvig Holberg's* *Henrik and Pesille*, of Mozart's "Jupiter Symphony," and of a dialectical monologue "Hans Peter," was an unqualified success. Afterward, Bull delighted the audience by a rendition of his own composition, "A Visit to a Saeter." The theatre officially opened on January 2, 1850, and fared surprisingly well for a new organization.

Numerous problems, however, plagued Bull. He imported a peasant-fiddler, but audiences did not appreciate his playing. Bull was dismayed that patrons ate picnic lunches while he conducted and played serious music. The violinist went to court over his attempt to deny complimentary tickets to the police force and later endured harassment by the police for his efforts. Guided by his mercurial temperament, Bull was so depressed by these events that he was unable to remain long in Bergen. After arranging the season of 1850-51, he relinquished active control of the theatre to Jensen and spent his time in Christiania* in a vain effort to win a governmental subsidy for the Norwegian Theatre.

The students of the University of Christiania, however, made Bull's exertions a rallying point for their own nationalistic aspirations. The theatre was the subject of a discussion at the Literary Society (see Borchgrevink, Andreas*) where Student Ibsen spoke in favor of the Norwegian Theatre, thus coming to Bull's notice. On October 11, 1851, the students presented a musical evening to benefit the Norwegian Theatre at which Poet Ibsen's prologue was spoken. Bull then met Ibsen and soon offered him the post of dramatic author at the theatre in Bergen. Bull then left Norway for America where he entered into the second significant undertaking mentioned above.

In America, Bull established a "New Norway," a commune for Norwegian immigrants at Oleana, Pennsylvania, in 1852. There he planned to build mills, shops, homes, schools, and churches for the Norwegians. The plan failed within the year. Ibsen was aware of this project, which he utilized in his conception of Gyntiana* in *Peer Gynt*.* The virtuoso returned to the concert stage in Europe and America. Bull died in Norway honored for his accomplishments.

Reference: Smith, Mortimer B. *The Life of Ole Bull*. Westport, Conn.: Greenwood Press, 1973 [1943].

THE BURIAL MOUND: A one-act Romantic serious drama.
Composition: Written in 1850; revised and published in 1854.
Stage history:

Sept. 26, 1850	Christiania Theatre,* (3 perfs.), Laura Svendsen (Gundersen)* as Blanka
Jan. 2, 1854	Norwegian Theatre, Bergen,* (1)
1900	Vienna
May 30, 1912	Clavier Hall, London, pro. Ibsen Club

Synopsis: At a time prior to the Christianization of Scandinavia, a recluse named Bernhard sits writing on a scroll before a warrior's tomb on the coast of Normandy. In the evening light can be discerned a simple altar topped by a cross. Blanka, a young girl, seems preoccupied as Bernhard inscribes another stanza of a Viking saga. Noticing her distraction, Bernhard recalls the days when he sang the Northmen's songs as he fared the frozen seas. Blanka's thoughts have been on the contrasts between northern and southern life, her preference being for the heroic north. She asks why Bernhard is reluctant to consider his youth, and in reply he explains how he found Blanka abandoned after a Viking raid. Her father was killed in defense of his now-ruined castle. She wonders if he harbors any dream of returning to his native land, only to be silenced as Bernhard embarks on his nightly stroll. Blanka accompanies him with the intention of entwining the cross on the burial mound with a new circlet of flowers. While there, she will pray for the dead man's soul.

As they depart, Gandalf enters with his band of Vikings and recollects that his father perished in this land. He states that he has come for vengeance and to take his father's ashes back to his home land. In a passionate prayer to the Viking gods, Gandalf vows that if he fails, he will kill every person in sight or take his own life. Hemming the skald,* harp in hand, advises Gandalf not to swear by the gods, and Asgaut, an old warrior, suggests that they camp there in view of a distant cottage. Gandalf sends his men toward the cottage to pillage and kill. Hemming remains, and Gandalf realizes that in such a place Hemming had said that his father had fallen. Then he sees the burial mound and the altar and wonders if it is his father's tomb. Blanka approaches as Gandalf remembers his oath to kill everyone he meets. While Asgaut summons his men, he watches Blanka praying and decorating the altar. As she speaks to the buried Viking, Blanka becomes aware that she is not alone.

Gandalf reveals himself, and Blanka recognizes him as the Viking of her imagination. Hemming, seeing Blanka, warns Gandalf that Blanka is no ordinary woman, but he is silenced by his chief. The man and woman fall easily into conversation, as Blanka suggests that Gandalf lie down and rest while she provides refreshment. Gandalf, however, sees her invitation as veiled treachery. Although he storms at her, Blanka knows that a Viking warrior would never harm a defenseless woman. Mollified, Gandalf asks who is interred in the mound. Blanka knows only that it is a Viking. He then inquires who erected the mound and is amazed to learn that Blanka herself did the deed. As a Christian she is required to love even those who ravaged her land and killed her people; she is obliged to offer the hand of reconciliation. Gandalf asserts that Viking reconciliation comes by the sword, in both this world and the next. Obviously, they represent opposite views of the nature of life, but he is mysteriously attracted to her faith. The woman with passionate eloquence scorns his rapacious way of life and challenges him to carry the Christian faith to his home land. Gandalf is agitated and confused: on the one hand he revels in the Viking bloodlust, and on the other he is enticed by the world of peace and serenity represented by Blanka.

A decision is postponed as the Vikings come back with Bernhard as captive. After establishing that Gandalf is the son of the entombed Viking, Bernhard pleads for Blanka's life and reveals that Gandalf's father was the one who killed Blanka's father. Startled at first, Blanka breathes a prayer for the murderer's soul. Gandalf is wholly perplexed by her behavior, which divides the camp. Asgaut urges vengeance, Hemming, forgiveness. When Gandalf decides not to kill them, Bernhard admits that he killed Gandalf's father. The Vikings lunge at Bernhard with drawn swords, but Gandalf intervenes, commanding them to spare his father's killer. Asgaut reminds Gandalf of his oath, and as the younger man suffers remorse, Blanka declares her love of him, which convinces him that honor demands his death. He orders his ship to be prepared and says farewell to Blanka, who declares that they will meet in heaven. He retorts that his soul will go to Valhalla where it will be in eternal conflict, while hers will go to heaven and sweet rest. When he is dead, Blanka declares, she will travel north to evangelize his people. During this interchange, Bernhard has been struggling with himself, and finally the pain of the young people forces him to tell Blanka that she has been misled. Bernhard reveals himself as Gandalf's father, displaying a scar that can be identified by Asgaut. It is clear, then, that Bernhard is Audun, former chief of the Vikings, Gandalf's sire, who then tells his story.

He had lain wounded and bleeding when his men departed after the terrible carnage, but when he awoke the next day, he saw a five-year-old Blanka who nursed him back to health while speaking of Christ's love. After becoming a Christian, he erected the burial mound to cover his armor and sword. As Blanka had prayed for the soul of the dead Viking, he had grown more resigned to the life of a hermit far away from his home. Asgaut asks Blanka's forgiveness for his rough treatment of her, but Gandalf, although he loves her, cannot desert his old gods. He does promise, however, that he will forsake his marauding life, and his followers agree to abide by his decision. They plan to embark for the north, which pleases Blanka, but

Audun announces his intention to remain where he has found contentment. He blesses Blanka and Gandalf, sending them off on their mission, while Hemming too, having accepted Christianity, lays his harp on the altar and says that he will remain with Audun. As a final gesture, Audun marries the young couple, who set off to purify the northern lands with Blanka's prophecy ringing clearly: "The North shall also rise from out of the tomb to purer strife on silver seas of thought," surely a reference to the Norway of 1850.

The Version of 1854: A ruined temple dominates the background of the scene, while in the center of the stage there is a large burial mound and a monument. While Roderik writes, Blanka lyrically soliloquizes about the decayed life in southern locales (the scene is an island near Sicily) and the heroic tales she once heard about the denizens of the north. Roderik pauses and utters a few lines of the saga which he has been inditing; he remarks on Blanka's distraction. If she were a swan, she says, then she could wing her way to the frozen north, but her love of Roderik binds her to the south. Yet she dreams of a Viking warrior who will enter her life bringing heroism, adventure, and love. Roderik chides her for living in a dream world, but Blanka replies that it is he who filled her head with the old sagas. When Blanka starts to talk about a certain night ten years ago when pillagers landed on her shore, Roderik becomes agitated and urges her to stop. Before they go, Blanka realizes that she has forgotten to place a fresh wreath of flowers on the monument but decides to see Roderik to their cottage before going in search of violets and roses.

Gandalf and the Vikings enter in search of a particular place known only to Asgaut, an old warrior. Jostejn and Hrolloug remind Gandalf that their interest is in booty, to which he replies that Viking law requires vengeance when a fallen comrade lies buried in the enemy's domain. Their purpose in being there is to avenge their former king's death, Gandalf's father, the story of which is unknown to the younger warriors. Gandalf tells of the events of twelve years ago when his father sailed off on an expedition that ended on this island where the local chieftain was rumored to own a vast treasure. There was a terrible battle in which the king and a hundred others fell; only Asgaut and a few others escaped to tell the tale. After ten years of searching, Asgaut located Gandalf and told of the king's slaughter, the news of which brought him to this place to wreak vengeance. Gandalf vows that he will be avenged on this night or die. Hemming the skald* advises the king not to swear because the Norse gods cannot hear his words in this alien place which the Christian faith has penetrated. Gandalf chides him for his susceptibility and challenges Hemming to become a monk if he wishes. Lamenting the decline of the old ways, Asgaut reminds the king that it is his responsibility to maintain the old religion; then he withdraws with the other Vikings.

In a long soliloquy Gandalf considers Asgaut's admonition and vows to go home to prevent the passing of the old ways; then he notices the monument and recalls stories of such tombs and the Norse gods. At the sound of approaching footsteps, Gandalf hides in the bushes. Blanka has returned to place a new garland on the monument. When she throws the old wreath to the ground, Gandalf catches it and shows himself. Astonished but not frightened, Blanka recognizes Gandalf as the man of her imagination, so she speaks freely of herself and Roderik. Gandalf learns from her that the island had been heavily populated three years ago, but at that time, a band of looters slew everyone but her. As she wandered later among the devastation, she found Roderik, hurt and weakened. She nursed him back to health, and they have lived as father and daughter ever since. When asked why she does not fear him, Blanka answers that the fierce Vikings would not stain their bravery by harming women. She recognizes that Gandalf has come for vengeance and calls it a hideous custom. Before leaving, Gandalf asks who is buried beneath the mound and learns that she does not know. Roderik had shown it to her and asked her to pray daily for the Vikings. Gandalf scoffs at the weak faith that demands such foolish things as praying for the enemy, but Blanka asks him to consider what would happen if her simple faith were transplanted in Norway. She begs him to take her there, even if she must become his skald. When Gandalf seems on the verge of agreeing, Blanka relents and admits that the journey is but a dream, that she could never leave Roderik. In an interchange of innuendo and indirection, each of the young people suggests the love that is growing. When they seem on the verge of openly speaking of it, Blanka says she must go, but not before she places a garland of oak leaves in Gandalf's hair. The Viking king hurries away, leaving Blanka to ponder the outcome of this stirring meeting.

The tender mood is broken when Gandalf hurriedly enters and tells Blanka to flee and to hide because the Vikings are coming and will surely do her harm. He tells her that his father was king of the Vikings and fell on this shore; she, in turn, sees that the Viking troop is bent on revenge. When it occurs to her that these men killed her father, she says, "Killer be gone!" while Gandalf places himself between her and his men who have just come into view with Roderik in tow. Blanka rushes into Roderik's arms. When the moment comes for Gandalf to strike them down, he cannot. Asgaut reminds him of his oath and his responsibility to maintain the faith. Asgaut prepares to kill them, but Hrolloug suggests that they take Blanka aboard the ship for the entertainment of the men. Gandalf intervenes, and Roderik bargains for Blanka's life by promising to produce the man who slew the old king. With Blanka's safety guaranteed, Roderik confesses to the deed and says that the king lies buried in the mound. That news of proper Viking burial convinces Gandalf that vengeance is not required, but the Vikings demand blood. Gandalf frees Roderik and declares that he will redeem his oath: he himself will die. Ordering his men to prepare his ship and funeral pyre, Gandalf bemoans his inability to maintain the old religion in the sapping atmosphere of the south. Blanka implies that she will commit suicide if he carries out his plan; at least they will meet in heaven. As they sorrowfully take leave of each other, Roderik confesses that he is King Rörek, the supposedly slain Viking. His identity is established by a scar. Rörek explains how he symbolically buried his armor as a sign that he had surrendered the old ways. Asgaut, in despair over the abasement of the traditional customs, leaves to settle in Iceland, which is still primitive. He gives Blanka his place at Gandalf's side. Gandalf and Blanka will return to Norway to establish the reign of peace, while Rörek and Hemming remain in the south. The Vikings of the new era embark for Norway, while those of the old Norway, Rörek and Hemming, mount the burial mound and wait for death.

Structural Analysis: A comparison of the two versions of the play shows that Ibsen learned much about dramaturgy between 1850 and 1854. Despite several problems of chronology, the second version is the more theatrically sound. The 1854 characterizations, particularly those of Gandalf and Asgaut, are more strongly motivated and thus are rendered more probable than those in the script of 1850. By moving the action from Normandy to the Mediterranean, Ibsen intensified the contrast between the northern and southern temperaments, an idea which he injected into most of the plays that followed. The drama is unified by action:

Gandalf comes to the island to seek revenge for his father's death;

(as a result of which)

Gandalf discovers Blanka's presence and starts to fall in love with her;

(as a result of which)

Gandalf decides to satisfy his honor by killing himself rather than harming Blanka;

(as a result of which)

Gandalf discovers that his father is alive, which eliminates the necessity of Gandalf's suicide;

(as a result of which)

Gandalf marries Blanka, adopts Christianity, and sails north to evangelize Norway.

A BUTTON-MOLDER (*Peer Gynt*): The Button-Molder melts down men's lives and molds the raw material in other forms. He is, thus, the emissary of death who is twice put off when he comes to claim Peer Gynt.*

BYGMESTER SOLNESS: The Norwegian title of *The Master Builder*.*

C

CAESARIUS OF NAZIANZUS (*Emperor and Galilean*): A court physician.

CAMERON, BEATRICE (1868-1940): Successful in amateur productions in her native Troy, New York, Beatrice Cameron played several minor roles in professional productions before joining Richard Mansfield's* company in 1886. She married Mansfield in 1892 and retired from the stage in 1898 after having performed a notable service for Ibsen—introducing American audiences to their first English version of an Ibsenian drama. She had avidly read every available translation of Ibsen's plays, and when *A Doll's House** appeared, she prevailed upon Mansfield to stage it. The actor/manager was already deeply in love with her and could refuse her nothing. Accordingly, Mansfield's company presented Beatrice Cameron as Nora Helmer* in Boston on October 30, 1889, and in New York on December 21. Ibsen's drama was subsequently performed in Philadelphia, Washington, Baltimore, and Chicago, the greatest crowds attending in Philadelphia. The matinee audience was composed mostly of children and their nurses while "the sidewalk outside the theatre was lined with perambulators" (Wilstach, p. 194). The cast included Atkins Lawrence as Torvald Helmer,* Merwyn Dallas as Nils Krogstad,* Herbert Druce as Doctor Rank,* and Helen Glidden as Kristine Linde.*

The *New York Dramatic Mirror* roundly criticized Cameron's interpretation of Nora as containing "more energy than intelligence. Her performance was marked by artificiality and over-elaboration." The *New York Times*, however, noted the same traits and decided that Cameron's calculated nervousness, while distracting in the first act, was fully justified in the ensuing parts.

Since Ibsen's reputation preceded Mansfield's production, audiences and critics alike knew what to expect. The production attracted only a moderate-sized house in New York, and, according to the *New York Times*, many of those in attendance failed to understand Ibsen's point. Those who had read the play beforehand were prepared to interpret the nuances. The critic of the *Dramatic Mirror*, on the other hand, called the production "a dose that will even make the Ibsen cranks quail," the character of Nora a freak, and the dialogue "an arid desert without oases." He further concluded, "However profitable the study of the piece is to the sociologist it is by no manner of means pleasurable from the playgoer's standpoint."

References: "At the Theatre," *New York Dramatic Mirror*, Dec. 28, 1889, p. 4, col. 1; "Ibsen's 'Doll's House' at Palmer's," *The Critic*, XV, 313 (Dec. 28, 1889), 329; "A Play by Ibsen," *New York Times*, Dec. 22, 1889, p. 11, col. 1; Wilstach, Paul. *Richard Mansfield: The Man and the Actor.* New York: Charles Scribner's Sons, 1909.

CAMERON, DONALD (1889-1955): After studying at the American Academy of Dramatic Art in 1912-13, Donald Cameron became a member of Eva Le Gallienne's* Civic Repertory Company. He supported that actress as Ejlert Lövborg* in 1934 and Johannes Rosmer* in 1935.

Reference: Who Was Who in the Theatre, I, 367-8.

CAMPBELL, MRS. PATRICK (1865-1940): One of England's leading emotional actresses, Mrs. Campbell first allied herself with Ibsen when she played one performance as Helene Alving* in the Independent Theatre's* production of *Ghosts** on January 26, 1893, a role to which she did not return until March 27, 1928.

Mrs. Campbell was engaged to play the Rat-Wife* in *Little Eyolf,** starring Janet Achurch* as Rita Allmers* and Elizabeth Robins* as Asta Allmers,* at London's Avenue Theatre, opening on November 23, 1896. During the run of the play, Achurch fell ill, and Campbell with only a day's notice was asked to replace her. Unable to master the words, Campbell acted with a script, to which she frequently referred, tied to her waist by a ribbon.

On March 5, 1907, Mrs. Campbell commenced a successful limited engagement (seven matinees) as Hedda Gabler* at the Court Theatre (London). She stressed Hedda's pregnancy by a ridiculous husband whose presence made her neurotic, but the actress did not believe that Hedda and Lövborg had experienced a physical liaison. To Campbell, Hedda was "a vital creature, suffocated by the commonplace" (Campbell, p. 274). She was so greatly acclaimed in this role that it became the nucleus of her American tour later that year.

*Hedda Gabler** opened at New York's Lyric Theatre during the week of November 11, 1907, eliciting the following review from the critic of the *Evening World*:

It was a merciless, cold performance. The smoldering fire in the gloomy eyes flamed brightly only once, when, with figure drawn up and head thrown back, in a pose of magnificent challenge, Mrs. Campbell held out the pistol that was to make an end of the disgraced and drunken Lövborg. Mrs. Campbell's Hedda seemed to have nothing in common with the stage. (Quoted in Campbell, p. 286.)

That is, her acting was so natural that it did not seem theatrical. The production was seen afterwards in several American cities. Campbell subsequently returned to *Hedda Gabler* in a revival in London on May 22, 1922.

Ella Rentheim* in *John Gabriel Borkman** was the last of Ibsen's characters undertaken by Mrs. Campbell. It was staged at London's "Q" Theatre on October 15, 1928.
Reference: Campbell, Mrs. Patrick. *My Life and Some Letters.* New York: Dodd, Mead and Company, 1922.

CAPTAIN ALVING'S MEMORIAL ORPHANS' HOME: The name of the orphanage in *Ghosts.** It was built by Helene Alving* with the last of her husband's money and burned down at the end of Act II.

CAPTAIN OF THE WATCH (*Emperor and Galilean*): One of the many military characters of the drama.

CAPUANA, LUIGI (1839-1915): Italian critic and theatre historian Luigi Capuana was Eleonora Duse's* choice as translator of her version of *A Doll's House** (1892). Capuana became a champion of *verismo* and Luigi Pirandello's mentor.

CARRÉ, ALBERT (1852-1938): Between 1885 and 1895, Albert Carré managed the Vaudeville Theatre in Paris where he stressed plays of social commentary. At one of his special matinees in 1891, Carré produced *Hedda Gabler,** which was the first commercial production of an Ibsenian drama in the French capital.
References: Carlson, Marvin. *The French Stage in the 19th Century.* Metuchen, N.J.: Scarecrow Press, 1972; Carré, Albert. *Souvenirs de Théâtre.* Ed. Robert Favart. Paris: Plon, 1950.

CARSON, CHARLES (b. 1885- ?): Charles Carson, a British actor, was a devoted Ibsenian during the period between the world wars. He played Karsten Bernick* (1926), Johannes Rosmer* (1926), Halvard Solness* (1928), and Pastor Manders* (1933).
Reference: Who's Who in the Theatre, 11th ed., pp. 422-3.

CATILINE: A Romantic serious drama in three acts.
Composition: Written during the first three months of 1849; published in April 1850.
Stage history:

Dec. 3, 1881   Nya Teatern, Stockholm, pro. Ludvig Oscar Josephson.*
Jan. 27, 1936   Croyden Repertory Theatre, Donald Wolfit* as Catiline.
Feb. 18, 1936   Royalty Theatre, London, Donald Wolfit as Catiline.

Synopsis: Lucius Catiline is discovered in the evening on a road near Rome, the lofty towers of which form the backdrop of the action. Leaning against a tree, Catiline soliloquizes on the need to reform his dissipated life, to recapture his youthful goals. Despite his innate goodness, Catiline's debauchery is equaled by that of Rome. His deliberations are interrupted by the entrance of Ambiorix and Ollovico, envoys of the Allobroges, who do not see the Roman. They have arrived at Rome to sue for peace and humane treatment for their tribe, but Ambiorix is not optimistic as to the outcome because of the corruption of the Roman rulers. Sensing kindred spirits, Catiline reveals himself and in passionate language catalogues the taints of the Roman body politic. After predicting the appearance of one who will restore Roman freedom, Catiline exits with his new allies.

Inside the city young Roman noblemen Lentulus, Statilius, Coeparius, and Cethegus also agitatedly speak of the desperate state of the republic. When an old soldier Manlius appears, the young men learn of the gratitude of the state to its faithful defenders: the government has commandeered Manlius' farm, land it had bestowed as the soldier's pension. Manlius inflames them with zeal to topple the government, but Statilius realizes that a forceful leader will be necessary. Lentulus suggests Catiline, who is known to be plotting against the state. The band of conspirators leaves in search of its putative captain.

Catiline and Curius, a relation, slip into the temple of Vesta, where the sacred hearth fire is burning. Curius is concerned about the growing severity of Cicero's denunciation of Catiline as well as about his kinsman's seeming heedlessness of it. Catiline boasts of his infatuation with Furia, a Vestal Virgin, who is so different from Aurelia, his gentle wife. Furia then storms in, raging about the fate that consecrated her to religious service and denied her the freedom to satisfy her passionate nature. Seeing Catiline but not recognizing him, Furia expresses her longing for danger and adventure, the pursuit of which is impossible for a priestess. She learns that Catiline is similarly repressed and suggests that they escape from Rome together. Catiline is at first tempted by her suggestion but finally decides that Rome itself offers the scope for such grandiose deeds as they both desire. Furia's excitement is abated by Catiline's reluctance to elope with her, but before she leaves, Furia secures Catiline's promise that her mortal enemy will be his as well. Like Oedipus, Catiline swears that he will pursue and punish the malefactor; only then does he ask the identity and crime of Furia's nemesis. She tells him that this man had seduced her sister, prompting her suicide, and that the man was Catiline himself. He immediately senses the horror of his position, and only then does Furia recognize that her paramour is her sister's defiler. She calls down the wrath of Nemesis on Catiline, who leaves in confusion at the transformation that has occurred in her. Hearing the frenzy of the priestess, the other vestals enter and discover that Furia has committed the sacrilege of letting the sacred flame go out. Curius, who has watched these events with great interest, discovers a strange fascination with

Furia, which he quickly identifies as love. He is now in a moral dilemma: he loves the woman who has sworn dire vengeance on the man who has been a second father to him. Can he love her? Must he remain loyal to Catiline? Curius decides to save Furia and depend on Catiline's ability to protect himself from her vengeance.

At his house Catiline considers the implications of what has just occurred, recognizing his oath to punish himself as a possible omen of his ruination. Aurelia silently steals into his chamber and tries to comfort him. Catiline is attracted to the quiet domestic life she represents, but his ardent wish to accomplish great deeds is equally compelling. In explaining his situation to Aurelia, Catiline provides an exposition of previous events. He is so desirous of the consulship that he has squandered his fortune to suborn votes, a conspiracy eloquently denounced by Cicero. The orations have been so effective that Catiline's name is blackened in both the present and future. Aurelia suggests going away, but Catiline cannot because he has sold their very home to raise money for bribes. At that climactic moment, an old soldier approaches Catiline with the sad tale that he is about to lose his farm because his son is in debtors' prison. Catiline hands over the purse that contains the price of his house and says, "It may be pleasant bringing tyrants down . . . but simple kindness has its own reward!"

Clad in somber black, Furia awaits death in a subterranean prison, but still she calumniates Catiline. Then the door of her cell is quietly opened, and Curius leads her from captivity.

Act II opens with Catiline in frenzied discussion with the young conspirators who have come to enlist him as their leader. When Catiline scruples against treason, Lentulus reminds him that public sentiment will be strong against one who has sent a Vestal Virgin to her death. Cethegus affirms that Furia is indeed dead. Then Lentulus appeals to Catiline's love of power, and Cethegus to his fondness of sensual pleasure. Catiline says that his goal in seeking the consulship was the common good despite his questionable tactics. Then Cethegus asks his cooperation as a means of saving his friends from ruin and disgrace. All persuasion is in vain, for Catiline intends to settle in rural Gaul with Aurelia. Convinced of his resolution, the conspirators depart, as Aurelia enters. She has packed their belongings, gathered what money she could find, and prepared to depart that very night. Sending Aurelia to rest until their midnight departure, Catiline douses the light and soliloquizes by moonlight: this, then, is to be his fate—to disappear without a trace from the active life. Furia steals in. Catiline at first thinks she is a ghost but soon sees that she is all too real. Furia assures him that her wrath against him subsided as she waited in the dark dungeon on the brink of execution. Instead of anger, she feels that their mutual dream of power and adventure must become a reality. Catiline tells her that he is no longer impelled by ambition, but Furia knows better, forcing him to choose between a life of power and action and one of solitude and uncelebrity. As he wavers, Furia describes the future as she sees it. Catiline relents and admits that he "shall be a light to abject Rome." When they clasp hands to seal their alliance, an almost magical reaction transforms Catiline, who dashes out with the battle cry "Blood and Flames" on his lips.

In a tavern the young conspirators meet. Lentulus and Cethegus bring the news that Catiline will not join the cabal, that he plans to leave Rome. Lentulus proposes himself as captain of the conspiracy. At that moment Catiline rushes in and assumes the mantle of responsibility, thereby alienating Lentulus. Catiline then outlines his plans for restoring the republican freedom formerly enjoyed in Rome, but his supporters are interested only in affluence and power. Turning on Catiline, they draw their daggers, but he merely bares his breast to them. Since no one can lift a hand to harm Catiline, he regains their support. Catiline realizes, however, that with such adherents, the glories of old Rome can never be recaptured. Lentulus and the others swear allegiance to Catiline with the clear intention of ousting him once Rome lies in ruins. When the others leave to gather weapons, Lentulus remains behind to suggest to Catiline that the Allobroges be enlisted to bring the forces of all Gaul against the Roman government.

In a garden behind Catiline's house, Curius learns from Cethegus that Catiline has joined the conspiracy. Catiline then enters and tells Curius that a plan is in the offing and that he realizes it may end disastrously for him. For that reason, Curius is to remain in Rome and not become involved. Left alone, Curius cannot free his mind of thoughts of Furia, who, he begins to suspect, is mad. When Furia approaches, he tries to take her away to safety, but she merely speaks as if she were already dead. When Furia inquires about Catiline, Curius jealously declares his love of her. Unmoved, she asks if Catiline has joined the plot and if Curius will support his relative. Violently jealous now, Curius declares that he could murder Catiline to win Furia's favor. She asks not for murder but for treachery: Curius is to betray the plot. In his mad desire for the enchantress, Curius agrees to betray Catiline and leaves immediately to do so. Gloating over her imminent revenge, Furia is left alone on the stage.

Ambiorix and Ollovico emerge from Catiline's house in conversation about their recent decision to join the conspiracy. Standing in the shadows, Furia eerily says, "Alas, alas for you!" Then she warns them against siding with Catiline, and the Allobroges leave vowing to heed her words. Catiline comes outside when he hears this muffled interchange, and his distress at the exigency of utilizing such assistance is obvious. Armed conspirators dash out to the capitol. Then Aurelia appears, sees the plotters and her husband armed, and realizes that Catiline has changed his mind. Catiline quells her complaint and takes his place at the head of his troop.

Catiline's forest camp is shown at the beginning of Act III. Manlius nervously paces before Catiline's tent while Statilius slumbers by the fire. When he awakes, the old campaigner speaks of the day's battle and the undependable reinforcements of slaves and gladiators. Manlius sends Statilius to see that all is ready to repel a night attack. In a soliloquy Manlius eloquently talks of the oppressive weather and his commitment to guard Catiline from his own scurrilous supporters. The commander himself joins Manlius around the fire. Sleep has eluded both men. Afraid to sleep because of troublesome dreams the meaning of which he cannot understand, Catiline describes one dream to old Manlius. In it he has seen a murky, vaulted chamber at the top of which thunder clouds roll, and out of the tempest, two figures at times emerge, one tall and dark, the other fair and serene. They bend over a table and seem to play some sort of game, but the fair one loses and disappears, leaving only the dark figure with flame-darting eyes. After that, Catiline cannot remember what happened. Determined to put the dream out of mind, Catiline dismisses Manlius and walks up and down in silence.

A phantom enters and asks if Catiline recollects its voice; Catiline says he does. The phantom recalls that he too, like Catiline, was mad for power, riches, and renown, but through death he lost it all. Uttering a statement of Catiline's fate, "Though thou shalt fall by thine own hand yet shall another force strike thee down," the spirit disappears. Then Catiline recognizes the apparition as the old dictator Sulla. Beleaguered by the influences of Aurelia, Furia, and Sulla, Catiline declares his unwavering devotion to the path he has chosen. Curius rushes in, and when Catiline tries to embrace him for support, Curius pushes him away and warns that Catiline has been betrayed. Curius pleads with Catiline to flee for his own safety, but when he demurs, Curius confesses that he himself is the betrayer and offers Catiline his dagger with which to slay him. Simply but magnanimously Catiline forgives him, but Curius warns that Roman soldiers are in pursuit and that Catiline's friends in the city have been taken. Curius begs to be executed, but Catiline brushes him away and concludes that his own death should be that of a hero. To this end, he leaves. Curius follows him, determined to die at his kinsman's side.

Then Lentulus and two gladiators enter. Lentulus plans to murder Catiline so that he himself will become the conspirators' leader. They hide, and soon Catiline enters. The assassins rush at him, but when the gladiators see that their prey is none other than Catiline, they flee, leaving Lentulus to face his enemy. In a fight Catiline disarms Lentulus, who confesses that he planned to seize the leadership. Catiline says that he will resign in favor of Lentulus, who should be aware, however, that the conspiracy has been betrayed. Sniveling, Lentulus shows his cowardice by refusing the captaincy; he prefers to escape, which Catiline allows. In an aside, Lentulus says that he will get even by leading the Roman army directly to Catiline's camp. Catiline then hears the clash of swords and knows that his pursuers are near. His friends enter and vow to support him to the death, and Catiline vows to lead them to glorious heroes' deaths in battle. Furia appears and says that she must accompany him toward his goal. Aurelia comes in, sees that Catiline is prepared for battle, and vows to stand by his side too. Furia goads Catiline to savagery, so he thrusts Aurelia aside as the sound of fighting comes nearer. At the head of his troop, Catiline rushes out to meet his foes. Left alone, Furia and Aurelia comfort each other, as a result of which Aurelia goes to the battlefield to die at Catiline's side even though he spurned her love. Furia remains and graphically describes the battle, gloating over the imminence of Catiline's death. Greatly to her surprise, a weary warrior stumbles into view. It is Catiline, mumbling the prediction of his fate to die by his own hand. Furia weaves Catiline a wreath of flowers as she learns that all his friends perished on the battlefield. Furia suggests suicide, but the memory of Aurelia's love prevents Catiline from taking that final step. Catiline decides that Aurelia's continued life is the only thing preventing him from embracing death. He vows that Aurelia must die, and as he does so, the heavens thunder and roil in witness of his oath. Aurelia then comes into view and runs into Catiline's arms, but he repels her again. Drawing his dagger, Catiline prepares to murder Aurelia to the accompaniment of thunder, but she breaks away and flees. Catiline pursues her, and Furia remains behind to narrate the bloody slaughter. Catiline stumbles back onto the stage and realizes that life is nothing but the struggle between opposing forces in the soul and that his life is pointless because his good angel is now dead. Furia thrusts the dagger into Catiline's breast, and, as his life seeps away, Catiline prepares to tread the path to Tartarus, an eternity of hell. Suddenly, a pale but bloody Aurelia staggers in and urges him to take the road to Elysium, heaven, instead. Day dawns as Catiline sees that he has lived through the dark night of Furia's evil schemes. As Aurelia's life ebbs before his eyes, Catiline tears the knife from his breast and reconciles himself with the gods. Furia steals away, as Catiline dies with his head on Aurelia's moribund chest.

Structural analysis: Act I, in which Catiline swears to Furia that he will punish the man who wronged her sister, suggests the structure of Sophocles' *Oedipus the King.* One might expect Catiline to slay himself when he discovers that he himself is the culprit. Ibsen was not that derivative, however, even in his first play. Catiline dies, not by his own hand, but by Furia's. Rather than follow the usual Greek pattern of unity of action, Ibsen constructed a plot unified by Character. Catiline's character is revealed episodically, and Catiline's enlightenment comes, not as one might expect from his oath to Furia or even from his engineering the conspiracy. It comes from his realization that the forces of Good (Aurelia) and Evil (Furia) have used his soul as a battleground.

References: Anderson, Andrew R. "Ibsen and the Classical World," *Classical Journal,* 11 (1916), 216-25; Pearce, John C. "Hegelian Ideas in Three Tragedies by Ibsen," *Scandinavian Studies,* 34 (1964), 245-57.

CATILINE (1875): In November 1874 Ibsen suggested to Frederik Hegel* that a revised version of *Catiline** might win favor with the public that had shown interest in *Lady Inger of Östraat** and *The League of Youth.** Hegel agreed, and Ibsen immediately set to work. James W. McFarlane and Graham Orton in Vol. 1 of *The Oxford Ibsen* (p. 581) have set forth the major differences between the two versions of the drama:

(1) While the story remains substantially the same, the revision is longer than the original by over 100 lines.

(2) Most of the alterations are linguistic—attempts to vary the vocabulary and strengthen the syntax.

(3) In the revision, "The Phantom" is identified as "Sulla's ghost."

(4) The names of some of the characters are altered.

(5) Instead of merely being imprisoned as she is in the original, Furia is immured.

(6) In the revision the probability of Curius' betrayal of Catiline is increased by Furia's promise of her favors.

(7) In the revision the probability of the Allobroges' collusion with the plot is strengthened by the Senate's rejection of their suit.

(8) Lentulus' villainy is enhanced in several ways.

(9) Some prosodic infelicities are corrected.

CATILINE (*Catiline*): Lucius Catiline, a disaffected Roman nobleman, is the protagonist of the drama. His conspiracy against the Rome of Julius Caesar provides the context of the action, but his soul is the scene of the psychomachy waged by Furia,* his paramour, and Aurelia,* his wife. Although his indignation and ambition lead him to treason, Catiline has the redeeming features of forgiveness, loyalty to friends, and bravery.

CETHEGUS (*Catiline*): One of the young Roman noblemen who recruit Catiline* into their treasonous conspiracy.

CHARRINGTON, CHARLES (? -1926): Charles Charrington's contributions to Ibsen's success on the English stage have been obscured by the attention focused on his actress/wife, Janet Achurch.* Yet his cooperation was an essential element of all her Ibsenian undertakings; Charrington always served as her director or fellow actor—sometimes as both. In the historic production of *A Doll's House** in 1889, Charrington directed and played Doctor Rank.* In quick succession he acted the roles of Torvald Helmer,* Doctor Wangel,* Doctor Relling,* Aslaksen,* and Ejlert Lövberg.* When in October 1892 Charrington stumbled through the Lövberg role like a sleepwalker, it was because his wife had administered an overdose of morphia for his neuralgia (*James*, p. 74).
Reference: Theatre and Friendship: Letters from Henry James to Elizabeth Robins.
    New York: G. P. Putnam's Sons, 1932.

THE CHILD WIFE (1882): William Moore Lawrence* of Milwaukee, Wisconsin, translated this version of *A Doll's House,** which was used in the earliest production in the United States of an Ibsenian drama in English.

Its date was June 2-3, 1882, three performances being given in Milwaukee's Grand Opera House. Lawrence made his translation from the German version of Wilhelm Lange, which was not a precise rendition of Ibsen's script. As Lange Germanized the characters and locale, Lawrence Anglicized them. The *dramatis personae* are:

Robert Harmon, a bank officer	Mr. Henry Aveling
Eva, his wife	Miss Minerva Guernsey
Mrs. Linton, Eva's old schoolmate	Miss Tillie Stephany
Dr. Rankin, a devoted friend	Mr. Jos. J. Dowling
Mr. Fullerton, a bank employee	Mr. J. H. Ferris
Mary Ann, an old servant	Mrs. Emily Stowe
Bob	Master Harry
Emma	Miss Bella

Very little of Ibsen's drama remained, as a notice in *Dagbladet* (Christiania) reveals: "Thus the ending was changed according to the German model so that Nora at the sight of her children suddenly decides to remain. The nurse Ann Marie had been changed into a rather coarse Irish girl. . . . As the actress who played Nora was unable to dance the tarantela, this highly exciting and characteristic scene was omitted and the play suffered greatly on this account."

The newspaper reviewers complimented Lawrence's efforts and those of all the adult actors, who were professionals, except Minerva Guernsey,* but they had very little to say about the play itself. The translator had been encouraged at the beginning of the project by Rasmus Björn Anderson,* a professor of Scandinavian Literature. After the performances of *The Child Wife*, Anderson himself worked on the translation, which was accepted for presentation by A. M. Palmer of New York's Union Square Theatre. Apparently, the production never materialized. Presumably that marked the demise of *The Child Wife*, but Lawrence turned his hand to translating *The Pillars of Society** and *Ghosts.**

Reference: Haugen, Einar I. "Ibsen in America: A Forgotten Performance and an Unpublished Letter," *Journal of English and Germanic Philology*, 33 (1934), 396-420.

CHLAPOWSKI, KAROL BOZENTA (1832-1916): Count Chlapowski joined his actress/wife Helena Modjeska* as an immigrant to America from their native Poland in 1876. In 1883, aided by his wife's secretary, he translated *A Doll's House** from Polish and German versions. Modjeska then presented an ill-fated performance of the drama, now called *Thora,** in Louisville, Kentucky (December 7, 1883).

CHOJEÇKI, CHARLES EDMOND (1822-99): Chojeçki, who wrote under the name Charles Edmond, traveled on the corvette *The Queen Hortense* when Prince Napoléon (Napoléon Joseph Charles Paul Bonaparte, 1822-91) embarked on an excursion to Scotland, Greenland, and other locales of the North Sea. Their peregrinations took them to Bergen* where Chojeçki and the prince witnessed a performance of *The Feast at Solhoug** at the Norwegian Theatre (Bergen).* Chojeçki's description of the theatre and the production constitutes perhaps the earliest mention of Ibsen in French. The relevant passage translated below [by G.B.B.] is interesting because it represents Chojeçki's response solely to the pantomimic dramatization and the vocal patterns of the actors. Since he could not understand Norwegian, his perceptions of the story are somewhat skewed:

After a day's excursion in the vicinity of Bergen, a true holiday for the enthusiastic glances of the landscape painter, if, toward evening, one is surprised by rain, which happens too often, one has the resources of the Norwegian theatre, a rare occasion to observe native habits. The auditorium, made of wood, forms a simple rectangle. It has been in existence for only five years; the town council directs and stages the productions. For a long time, the puritans of the town had resisted the introduction of this profane entertainment, but the tolerant party won out. The municipality itself chose the actors from the poor young people of the town; it provides their training by delegating some of its members to fulfill the tasks of declamation teacher, song teacher, orchestra conductor, and director. The bigots have continued to overwhelm this dangerous innovation with their mistrust and disdain. In order to remove all pretexts from their adversaries, the tolerant party has resolved to supervise the artists not only on the stage but also in the principal endeavors of their everyday lives. As soon as any actress reaches marriageable age, the town council approves plans for a marriage settlement and even abridges the engagement period which the fashion of the country delights ordinarily to prolong beyond measure. In order to obtain the grand annual prize awarded by the town, it does not suffice to be first in declamation, it is also necessary to be first in good conduct.

The performance of August 25, 1856, at Bergen, included a drama entitled *The Master of Solhug [sic]*. It is the work of a young native author, Mr. Ibsen, who has drawn his subject from an old Scandinavian saga. The action takes place in the seventeenth century in Norway. A girl is engaged to a young man who on the next day is condemned to banishment. One year later, she receives news of the death of her fiancé. She acts precipitately in accepting as true the gloomy news, and she marries an old, rich booby. The young exile returns, however, which is as well, one feels, for the sake of the saga and of the play. Finding his fiancée married to another, he adjusts quickly and falls in love with her younger sister, a young blonde in the flower of youth, as blonde and as white as her elder sister is dark and somber. This sudden passion enrages the wife of the old man. The sight of the object of her first love rekindles in her the old fires. As she can no longer marry her warrior, she intends to worship him to distraction. That was acceptable in the time of the old sagas; it sometimes is in our own time. Rejected by the younger man, jealous of her sister whom she loves and hates at the same time, indifferent to the hostility of her old husband, she experiences all the world's punishment through not revealing the agony of her soul. At the moment where, in the presence of family and friends, the exile asks for the young blonde in marriage, the unfaithful lover no longer has the strength to master the emotions that distract her. She is on the verge of bursting, despite the presence of her husband. But what to do without causing a scandal? She rises in an inspired manner and narrates a saga which she improvises. The tale is full of devious and transparent allusions destined to agonize the soul of her sister and to cloud the heart of the young man. During this time, the husband empties his tankard full of hydromel (mead) and listens to the story without suspecting anything. She seems no longer sad. All at once the girl collapses in a heap, like a pythoness, exhausted by the violence of her recitation, fatigued by her improvisation. The curtain falls on the tableau, which ends the second act. This ending is of a savage beauty. The situation of the characters, especially that of the husband, is most dramatic and inspires impassioned and moving interest. As for the conclusion, it is a little brusque, and the author is in no wise preoccupied with scenic art. The woman dies in the manner of Phaedra. Her old husband disappears, one knows not how nor why. The rest for another time.

Despite the inexperience of the actors in their debut, the drama is played with intelligence. The woman who filled the leading role, with her severe profile, her black hair and her impassioned speech, has truly the air of one inspired. Her solemn gesture, her vocal inflections, her natural poses and her expressive countenance would be worthy of one of our Parisian stages. The Norwegian language is sweet to hear (pp. 436-8).

The writer's ingenuous comment on the availability of a theatre in which to pass a rainy evening is quite misleading. Peter Blytt* tells the whole story. When Prince Napoléon asked to see a performance, he learned that the theatre was closed for the summer, and all the actors were on holiday. The prince remained adamant, and Ibsen was summoned and told to solve the problem. He was reluctant to do so until he learned that Blytt wanted to present *The Feast at Solhoug*. So Ibsen recalled the actors and set about preparing the production.

On the night of the performance, Blytt provided a running synopsis of the story in German since the prince could not understand Norwegian. When Ibsen was presented to the royal visitor, he gave the prince a bound, handwritten copy of the script. The prince, in turn, promised that a French version of the play would be given in the court theatre at St. Cloud. This did not come to pass.

Apparently, Chojeçki was not within earshot of Blytt's German commentary because he confused the old husband's drinking the flagon, which occurs in the third act, not the second. In the third act the husband is killed, and Margit,* the thwarted lover, goes into a convent; Chojeçki was incorrect on both counts.

If Chojeçki was impressed by Luise Gulbrandsen Brun's* acting, Prince Napoléon liked her costume (designed by Ibsen). The prince ordered a copy of it to be made for the Empress Eugénie. At the prince's departure, he entertained Ibsen and some of his troupe aboard *The Queen Hortense*.

References: *Dictionnaire de Biographie Française* (Paris: Letouzey et Ané, 1959), VIII, cols. 1231-2; Edmond, Charles. *Voyage dans les Mers du Nord à Bord la Corvette La Reine Hortense*. Paris: Michel Lévy Frères, 1857.

CHRISTIANIA: The Norwegian capital, now Oslo, was named Christiania from 1624 to 1925. Ibsen was a resident of the city in 1850-51, 1857-64, and 1891-1906. The youthful Ibsen was not comfortable in the atmosphere of the capital, the reasons for which are made plain by Hjalmar Hjorth Boyesen* who lived there in the 1860s:

One hundred thousand village souls do not make a city. In Christiania the standards of judgment were mean, petty, provincial. What the Germans call *Brodneid*, that is, professional envy, the desire to destroy every possible rival, was rampant in the upper as in the lower social strata. There was, indeed, no lack of superficial culture; and some few highly refined families were to be found, among whom life had a certain gloss, and the manners were good enough to pass muster anywhere. But outside of University circles there were no intellectual interests; and even in University circles these had a wholly professional flavour and betrayed none of that charming hospitality of mind and generous flow of enthusiasm for all that is beautiful in the domain of thought. Of course the Philistine is in the majority there as everywhere. . . . In Christiania there was during the years of Ibsen's residence no escape from the Philistine. He was ubiquitous and all pervasive (Boyesen, pp. 42-3).

Reference: Boyesen, Hjalmar Hjorth. *A Commentary on the Works of Henrik Ibsen.* New York: Russell and Russell, 1973 [1894].

CHRISTIANIA THEATRE: From its founding in 1827 until 1863, the Christiania Theatre was the principal playhouse in Norway's capital; its repertory and acting company were Danish. It was announced in 1859 that performances would be given in Norwegian, but that did not actually occur until 1863. Ibsen served the theatre as aesthetic adviser for just over a year starting in 1863. The Christiania Theatre was closed on June 15, 1899, and reopened as the National Theatre.* This organization was inextricably linked with Ibsen's career.

References: Anker, Öyvind. *Christiania Theaters Repertoire 1827-99.* Oslo: Gyldendal, 1956; Huitfelt, H. J. *Christiania Theaterhistorie.* Köbenhavn: Gyldendal, 1876.

COEPARIUS (*Catiline*): A particularly hedonistic conspirator against Rome.

COLLETT, CAMILLA (1813-95): Nearly as peripatetic as Ibsen, Camilla Collett, Norway's first important advocate of women's rights and author of the nation's first Realistic novel, *The Governor's Daughters*, was in Dresden with Ibsen in 1871, Munich in 1877, and Rome in 1881. Whenever the dramatist and novelist met, enthusiastic conversation about art and life, particularly the place of women in society, ensued. Their discussions sporadically continued by letter when their travels separated them.

That Collett's advanced views about women influenced Ibsen cannot be doubted. She had objected to his description of Solveig* in *Peer Gynt** as a denigration of women in general, but when Ibsen was besieged on every side because of *Ghosts*,* Collett defended him in speeches and in print. In her old age, Collett liked to think that she had inspired Ellida Wangel.*

References: Encyclopaedia Britannica (Chicago: William Benton, 1973), VI, 56; Wergeland, Agnes M. "Collett on Ibsen's *Ghosts*," *Leaders in Norway and Other Essays* (New York: Books for Libraries, 1966 [1916]), pp. 189-90.

COLLEVILLE, LUDOVIC DE (1855-1918): In addition to writing a book on Danish folklore and a biography of Ibsen, the Vicomte de Colleville translated into French *Love's Comedy** (1896), *Lady Inger of Östraat** (1903), *Catiline** (1903), *The Feast at Solhoug** (1904), and *Olaf Liljekrans** (1904).

Reference: Dictionnaire de Biographie Française (Paris: Letouzey et Ané, 1961), IX, col. 275.

COLLIER, PATIENCE (1910-): When the National Theatre of Great Britain presented *Peer Gynt** on April 25, 1978, Patience Collier was Aase.*

Reference: Who's Who in the Theatre, 17th ed., I, 135.

COMPTON, FAY (1894-1978): As a young actress Fay Compton gravitated toward roles in musicals and light comedies, but in her middle years she exhibited considerable skill in emotional roles such as Gina Ekdal,* which she played in 1948. *The Times* (London) reviewer observed that Compton "loyally transforms herself into a Gina in whom domestic drudgery and the practical care of a blatant yet, to her, lovable egotist has almost destroyed the memory of early romance. In the scene of the confession, memory stirs again and comes and goes, as the actress wills, in perverted and horrifying forms."

References: Compton, Fay. *Rosemary: Some Remembrances.* London: Alston Rivers, 1926; *The Times* (London), Nov. 4, 1948, p. 6, col. 4.

CONQUEST, IDA (1876-1937): American actress Ida Conquest's experience in Ibsen's plays was brief — a sole appearance as Rita Allmers* in 1910. In that production she supported the Asta Allmers* of Alla Nazimova* and therefore received only brief critical notice.

Reference: Storms, A. D. *The Players' Blue Book.* Worcester, Mass.: Sutherland and Storms, 1901.

CONSTANTIUS (*Emperor and Galilean*): Emperor of the Eastern Roman Empire whose mantle, after Byzantine machinations, falls on Julian.*

COTTON, MASTER (*Peer Gynt*): One of the characters encountered by Peer Gynt* in Morocco. Cotton is almost a personification of the materialistic man of commerce. He is party to the theft of Peer's ship.

COUNTY NEWS: Kroll's* newspaper in *Rosmersholm*,* the editorship of which Johannes Rosmer* refuses.

COWIE, LAURA (1892-1969): Scottish actress Laura Cowie's career encompassed only one Ibsenian role, that of Hedda Gabler,* which she undertook in 1928 and played as "intolerably evil," which was "scarcely relevant to Ibsen's play" (*The Times* [London], Mar. 13, 1928, p. 14, col. 3.) *Reference: Who Was Who in the Theatre*, I, 546-7.

CRAIG, EDWARD GORDON (1872-1966): After serving an actor's apprenticeship with Henry Irving and rising sufficiently to play Hamlet in 1897, Craig pursued his growing commitment to stage design. He planned costumes and scenery for a number of plays (including *Peer Gynt** and *The Lady from the Sea**), but only twelve of his productions actually reached the stage. Three of them were by Ibsen.

His first foray into Ibsen's world was his mother Ellen Terry's* presentation of *The Vikings in Helgeland** (1903), for which he designed scenery, lighting, and costumes. His first-act setting created an ominous environment with purple light, sinister shadows, and a billowing ground fog. The second act, set in the banqueting hall, suggested "an extraordinary atmosphere of gloomy radiance" (Craig, p. 173). The third tableau gleamed with a hard, clear light which flooded the spacious setting.

In 1906 Craig staged Eleonora Duse's* version of *Rosmersholm** at Florence's Pergola Theatre. Rosmer's green and blue drawing room was monumental, containing a thirty-foot square window through which shafts of light transfixed the actors. Outside was a landscape painted with vivid primary colors. By this time Craig's anti-illusionistic approach to stage design was burgeoning. This setting was intended to represent a state of mind rather than a realistic scene.

Finally, Craig designed a revival of *The Pretenders** at the Royal Theatre, Copenhagen, in 1926. A memorable moment occurred when the ghost of Bishop Nikolas,* a skeletal figure with a fleshless arm waving lifelessly, entered to the effect of a spiraling, projected snowstorm. In all of these productions, Craig developed his theories of idealized stage beauty devoid of Realistic detail and historical accuracy.

References: Craig, Edward. *Gordon Craig: The Story of His Life.* New York: Alfred
    A. Knopf, 1968; Marker, Frederick J. and Marker, Lise-Lone. *Edward
    Gordon Craig and The Pretenders: A Production Revisited.* Carbondale, Ill.:
    Southern Illinois Press, 1981; Rose, Enid. *Gordon Craig and the Theatre.*
    London: Sampson, Low, Marston, 1931.

CRAWFURD, GEORGIANA (c. 1778-1865): Ibsen met Georgiana Crawfurd, a spinster, when he lived in Grimstad.* She had a large private library which she placed at Ibsen's disposal. Her copy of Sören Aabye Kierkegaard's* *Either-Or* might have provided Ibsen's introduction to the works of the Danish theologian.

CRITERION INDEPENDENT THEATRE (New York): Although the history of the Criterion Independent Theatre, modeled on the Théâtre Libre* and the other European independent theatres, is obscure, its relationship to Ibsen is quite clear. The enterprise was undertaken in 1897 by Henri Dumay (1867-1935), a Frenchman who was educated in the United States, taught at St. Louis University, and became the editor of *The Criterion*, an avant-garde literary journal published by Grace L. Davidson of St. Louis. Although *The Criterion* attracted favorable comment, its circulation never equaled its prestige. Dumay, Rupert Hughes, Charles Henry Meltzer, and, later, Joseph I.C. Clarke, therefore, propagated the Criterion Independent Theatre to bolster circulation by presenting dramas by playwrights avoided by commercial theatre managers. The announcement of their plans was greeted by a good deal of criticism, but the *New York Dramatic News* argued for a fair reception (Nov. 13, 1897, p. 15, col. 2).

Dumay projected a series of ten matinee performances, the first of which was Ibsen's *John Gabriel Borkman*,* presented at Hoyt's Theatre on November 18, 1897. The audience, each member of which received a copy of the current *Criterion* at the door, was large and receptive, although the reporter of the *New York Times* caviled that most of the auditors had not paid the price of admission. That same critic, while mildly complimenting the leading players E. J. Henley,* who directed the performance, and Maude Banks (Gunhild Borkman*), damned the production and the play, the first act of which he called "uncommonly tedious and the last preposterous" (Nov. 19, 1897, p. 7, col. 5). Not surprisingly, the *New York Dramatic Mirror*, published by the husband of the Ibsenian champion Minnie Maddern Fiske,* appreciated the acting, regretted the production, and lauded the drama as a "matchless work of dramatic construction." The last act was unfortunately marred by a backstage fire, the odor of which made the audience understandably restless (Nov. 27, 1897, p. 16, col. 1).

In addition to this initial production of *John Gabriel Borkman* in the United States, the Criterion mounted José Echegaray's* *The Great Galeoto* (Feb. 28, 1898) and Joseph Clarke's *The Rights of the Soul*.

Reference: Clarke, Joseph I.C. *My Life and Memories*. New York: Dodd, Mead and Company, 1925.

CROCODILE: A Munich-based literary group with which Ibsen was associated in 1876. Largely a social organization, the Crocodile included poets, novelists, and dramatists in its membership. Ibsen's association with Franz Grandaur, dramaturge of the Hoftheater (Munich), resulted in the production of *The Vikings in Helgeland** at that theatre (April 10, 1876).

CRONBERG, JENS (fl. 1850-57): Cronberg, a Danish actor, had to be removed as director of the Norwegian Theatre (Christiana)* prior to Ibsen's appointment to that post on September 3, 1857.

CROWDEN, GRAHAM (1922-): Graham Crowden played Doctor Wangel* in the production of *The Lady from the Sea** which opened in London on May 16, 1979.

Reference: Who's Who in the Theatre, 17th ed., I, 154.

CUPID'S SPORTING NEWS: A journal jokingly proposed by Falk* in *Love's Comedy** in which he could advertise his belief in unfettered love and debunk the traditional concept of marriage.

CURIUS (*Catiline*): As Catiline's* ward, Curius is devoted to the older man. When Curius becomes infatuated with Furia,* however, she prompts him to betray Catiline's conspiracy. In the last act, Curius repents, is forgiven by Catiline, and dies nobly in battle.

CYRILLUS (*Emperor and Galilean*): A teacher.

D

DAGFINN THE PEASANT (*The Pretenders*): King Haakon's* marshal and faithful retainer.

DAGNY (*The Vikings in Helgeland*): Dagny is Örnulf's* daughter, Hjördis'* sister, and Sigurd's* wife. Her principal function is as confidante to Sigurd and as contrast to Hjördis.

DARRAGH, LETITIA MARION (d. 1917): Miss Darragh, as the British actress was known on the stage, played Helene Alving* in London in 1917 and "beautifully played" it according to *The Times* (London) reviewer. "You cannot help thinking of Miss Darragh as clever, cynical, *blasée*, the sort of woman for whom the Manders type would be simply beneath contempt."
Reference: The Times (London), Apr. 30, 1917, p. 11, col. 4.

DARZENS, RODOLPHE (1865-1938): In addition to serving as secretary of Paris' Théâtre Libre,* Darzens translated *Ghosts** for André Antoine's* production. A Frenchman born in Moscow, he was also a playwright and director.
Reference: Dictionnaire de Biographie Française (Paris: Letouzey et Ané, 1965), X, col. 231.

A DEACONESS (*When We Dead Awaken*): The shadowy, almost spectral attendant of Irene de Satow.* The deaconess may be symbolic of the dark, irrational forces that govern the life of her mistress.

THE DEAN (*Brand*): As Brand's* ecclesiastical superior, the Dean becomes a chief opponent when Brand refuses to open the new church and wants to lead his parishioners away from traditional beliefs.

DECENTIUS (*Emperor and Galilean*): A tribune.

DENCH, JUDI (1934-   ): Lona Hessel* (August 1, 1977) is Judi Dench's only Ibsenian characterization. She was a member of Great Britain's Royal Shakespeare Company when she undertook the role.
Reference: Who's Who in the Theatre, 17th ed., I, 174.

DIANA, MLLE. (*Hedda Gabler*): The keeper of the bordello frequented by Ejlert Lövberg,* Mlle. Diana is mentioned but never appears.

DIETRICHSON, LORENTZ HENRIK (1834-1917): Like all of Ibsen's friends, Dietrichson was sometimes in favor, sometimes out. He was the librarian of the Scandinavian Club in Rome when Ibsen lived there and so was in a position to introduce Ibsen to interesting people and sights. Dietrichson was often Ibsen's traveling companion, and he was instrumental in securing Ibsen's honorary doctorate from the University of Uppsala. Dietrichson himself was a professor of history at the University of Christiania.
Reference: Norsk Biografisk Leksikon, III, 322-30.

DIGGES, DUDLEY (1879-1947): Irish actor Dudley Digges worked at Dublin's Abbey Theatre before emigrating to the United States in 1904. In 1919 he became associated with the Theatre Guild and was the Troll-King (See Old Man of the Dovrë) in its production of *Peer Gynt* in 1923. He also played Jörgen Tesman* twice, once in 1924 and again in 1926.
Reference: Who Was Who in the Theatre, II, 667-8.

DITRICHSTEIN, LEO (1865-1928): After leaving his native Hungary, actor and dramatist Leo Ditrichstein settled in the United States in 1890. Eight years later he supported Elizabeth Robins* as Jörgen Tesman* to her Hedda Gabler.*
Reference: Who Was Who in the Theatre, II, 671-2.

DOCTOR (*Brand*): The most forthright character in the play, the Doctor tries to convince Brand* to visit his dying mother, and when Brand will not, the Doctor prays deliverance from Brand's sort of religion. The Doctor also advises Brand to move elsewhere to save Ulf's* life. When Brand agrees, the Doctor points out that by compromising his principles, Brand has become more human.

A DOLL'S HOUSE: A Realistic serious drama in three acts.
Composition: Conceived in December 1878; written during May-August 1879; published on December 4, 1879.

Stage history:

Dec. 21, 1879	Royal Theatre, Copenhagen
Jan. 8, 1880	Royal Theatre, Stockholm
Jan. 20, 1880	Christiania Theatre* (28 perfs.)
Jan. 30, 1880	Norwegian Theatre, Bergen*
Feb. 28, 1880	Suomalainen Theatre, Helsingfors
Mar. 3, 1880	Residenz Theater, Munich, dir. Ernst von Possart,* Marie Ramlo* as Nora
Mar. 3, 1880	Residenz Theater, Berlin
Nov. 22, 1880	Residenz Theater, Berlin, Hedwig Niemann-Raabe* as Nora
1880	Stadttheater, Gothenburg
1880	Residenz Theater, Hannover
1880	Thalia Theater, Hamburg
1880	Royal Theatre, Dresden
Sept. 8, 1881	Stadttheater, Vienna, dir. Heinrich Laube
1881	Hoftheater, Munich
1881	Thalia Theater, Hamburg
Mar. 10, 1882	Imperial Theatre, Warsaw, Helena Modjeska* as Nora
1882	Korsh Theatre, Moscow, dir. F. A. Korsh*
June 2, 1882	Grand Opera House, Milwaukee (3), (as *The Child Wife**)
Jan. 25, 1883	St. Petersburg, Gabriela Zapolska* as Nora
June 17, 1883	Christiania Theatre*
Dec. 7, 1883	Macauley's Theatre, Louisville (1), (as *Thora**), Helena Modjeska* as Nora
Feb. 8, 1884	Alexandrinsky Theatre, St. Petersburg, Maria Savina* as Nora
Mar. 3, 1884	Prince's Theatre, London (as *Breaking a Butterfly**), Herbert Beerbohm Tree* as Dunkley (Krogstad)
Mar. 25, 1885	School of Dramatic Art, London, pro. Scribblers
1887	Residenz Theater, Munich
1887	Hoftheater, Munich
Sept. 24, 1887	Imperial Theatre, Warsaw, Gabriela Zapolska as Nora
Nov. 25, 1888	Lessing Theater, Berlin
Mar. 3, 1889	Théâtre du Parc, Brussels, pro. Léon Vanderkindere
Mar. 7, 1889	Lessing Theater, Berlin
Apr. 13, 1889	Imperial Theatre, Warsaw (3), Gabriela Zapolska as Nora
June 7, 1889	Novelty Theatre, London (24), Janet Achurch* as Nora
Sept. 26, 1889	Amberg Theatre, New York (2), (in German), T. Leithner* as Nora
Oct. 30, 1889	Globe Theatre, Boston, Beatrice Cameron* as Nora
1889	Stadttheater, Gothenburg
Dec. 21, 1889	Palmer's Theatre, New York (2), (as *A Doll's Home*), Beatrice Cameron* as Nora
1890	Royal Theatre, Stockholm (2)
Sept. 26, 1890	Christiania Theatre (16), Johanne Dybwad* as Nora
Jan. 27, 1891	Terry's Theatre, London (1), Marie Fraser* as Nora
Feb. 9, 1891	Teatro di Filodrammatici, Milan, Eleonora Duse* as Nora
Apr. 20, 1891	National Theatre, Budapest
June 2, 1891	Criterion Theatre, London (1), Rose Norreys* as Nora

Nov. 21, 1891   Korsh Theatre, Moscow (2)
Mar. 25, 1892   Christiania Theatre (8)
Apr. 19, 1892   Avenue Theatre, London (30), Janet Achurch as Nora
        1893   Hoftheater, Munich
Mar. 11, 1893   Royalty Theatre, London (14), Janet Achurch as Nora
June 9, 1893   Lyric Theatre, London (3), Eleonora Duse as Nora
        1893   Teatro de la Calle de las Cortes, Barcelona
Feb. 15, 1894   Empire Theatre, New York, Minnie Maddern Fiske* as Nora
Apr. 20, 1894   Théâtre du Vaudeville, Paris, Gabrielle Réjane* as Nora
Sept. 1894   Deutsches Theater, Berlin, Agnes Sorma* as Nora
Apr. 1894   Abbey's Theatre, New York (2), Gabrielle Réjane as Nora
Sept. 18, 1895 Suvorin Theatre, St. Petersburg, Lydia Yavorska* as Nora
Sept. 25, 1895 Christiania Theatre (4)
Mar. 19, 1896   Garden Theatre, New York (3), Minnie Maddern Fiske as Nora
Apr. 12, 1897   Irving Place Theatre, New York, Agnes Sorma as Nora
May 10, 1897   Globe Theatre, London (5), Janet Achurch as Nora
Mar. 20, 1899   Gärtner Theater, Munich, Agnes Sorma as Nora
Oct. 20, 1899   Hoftheater, Braunschweig
Nov. 4, 1900   Alexandrinsky Theatre, St. Petersburg, Maria H. Potocka* as
                Nora
May 21, 1902   Manhattan Theatre, New York (1), Minnie Maddern Fiske as
                Nora
May 30, 1902   Manhattan Theatre, New York (1), Minnie Maddern Fiske as
                Nora
Sept. 17, 1904 St. Petersburg, Vera Kommisarzhevskaya* as Nora
May 2, 1905   New Lyceum Theatre, New York (15), Ethel Barrymore* as Nora
Nov. 29, 1906   National Theatre, Christiania,* Johanne Dybwad as Nora
Dec. 18, 1906   Kommisarzhevskaya Theatre, St. Petersburg, dir. Vsevelod
                Meyerhold*
Jan. 14, 1907   Princess Theatre, New York, Alla Nazimova* as Nora
Mar. 1908   Daly's Theatre, New York, Vera Kommisarzhevskaya as Nora
Apr. 17, 1909   Hoftheater, Braunschweig
Feb. 14, 1911   Royalty Theatre, London, Lydia Yavorska as Nora
Apr. 22, 1911   Kingsway Theatre, London, Janet Achurch as Nora
May 7, 1911   Maly Theatre, Moscow, V. A. Suchmina as Nora
Dec. 12, 1912   Hoftheater, Braunschweig
Jan. 28, 1914   Vaudeville Theatre, London, Mrs. J. H. Sinclair as Nora
June 1, 1915   Kammerspiele, Munich, Albert Bassermann*
Nov. 23, 1917   Kammerspiele, Berlin, dir. Max Reinhardt*
Apr. 29, 1918   Plymouth Theatre, New York (32), Alla Nazimova as Nora
June 7, 1918   Workers' Club, Petrograd, dir. Vsevelod Meyerhold
Aug. 6, 1920   Lenin Theatre, Novorossisk, dir. Vsevelod Meyerhold
Jul. 11, 1921   Everyman Theatre, London
Nov. 20, 1925   Playhouse Theatre, London, Madge Titheradge* as Nora
Mar. 20, 1928   Kingsway Theatre, London, Gillian Scaife* as Nora
Mar. 20, 1930   Arts Theatre, London, Gwen ffrangcon-Davies* as Nora
Apr. 14, 1930   Criterion Theatre, London, Gwen ffrangcon-Davies as Nora
Feb. 22, 1933   Arts Theatre, London

Mar. 4, 1934 Arts Theatre, London, Lydia Lopokova* as Nora
Mar. 2, 1936 Criterion Theatre, London, pro. Leon M. Lion,* Lydia Lopokova
              as Nora
        1937 National Theatre, Oslo, Johanne Dybwad as Nora
Dec. 27, 1937 Morosco Theatre, New York (144), Ruth Gordon* as Nora
Feb. 3, 1939 Duke of York's Theatre, London, Lucie Mannheim* as Nora
July 11, 1945 Arts Theatre, London, Jenny Laird* as Nora
Jan. 17, 1946 Winter Garden Theatre, London, Angela Baddeley* as Nora
Mar. 22, 1950 Brunnenhof Theater, Munich, Joana Maria Gorvin* as Nora
Sept. 18, 1953 Lyric Theatre, Hammersmith (London), Mai Zetterling* as Nora
Feb. 2, 1963 Theatre 4, New York (66), Astrid Wilsrud as Nora
Jan. 13, 1971 Playhouse Theatre, New York (111), Claire Bloom* as Nora
Nov. 1, 1972 Greenwich Theatre, London, Susan Hampshire* as Nora
Feb. 20, 1973 Criterion Theatre, London, Claire Bloom as Nora
Mar. 5, 1975 Vivian Beaumont Theatre, New York (66), Liv Ullman* as Nora

Synopsis: Holiday festivities reign at the Helmer home as Nora Helmer, her arms laden with Christmas packages, returns from shopping. She generously tips the delivery boy who has carried the Christmas tree and tells the maid Helene to hide it until it is decorated later in the evening. Torvald Helmer emerges from his study, greets Nora affectionately as his lark and squirrel, and soon chastises her for spending so much money. Nora has spent extravagantly because her husband has been named manager of the bank, a position commanding a handsome salary. He tries to convince her of the seriousness of financial matters, but Nora maintains a bland nonchalance. She starts to sulk as Helmer continues his lecture, and soon he begins to call her pet names and finally bribes her with money to cover additional Christmas expenses. Quickly regaining her cheer, Nora seems extraordinarily glad to have extra money. Excitedly, Nora shows Helmer the gifts she has just bought but cannily keeps him from seeing his present. When he asks what she wants, Nora asks for money. Helmer is reluctant to give her money because in the past she has spent it on household expenses and later asked for more. In response to a lecture on being a spendthrift, Nora tells him that he has no idea what expenses a lark or a squirrel might incur. Helmer merely concludes that she has inherited from her father her loose ways with money. Then he gently chides her for eating pastries and macaroons, which she roundly denies having done. Then they remember past Christmases when they were poor and rejoice that now their expectations are quite optimistic.

The doorbell rings, and soon Helene shows in Kristine Linde, a friend whom Nora has not seen for ten years. They sit down and start to catch up on old news. Kristine has arrived by ship; she has been a widow for three years; Nora had intended to write but never did; Kristine was left with no children and no sense of loss. After establishing that Kristine must be miserable, Nora expatiates on her joy in her own children, Helmer's new job and large salary, and her happiness. When Kristine brings her back to reality,

Nora says that life has not been simple for her either. The Helmers were quite poor when they first married; Nora had supplemented their small income by taking in sewing; Helmer had done so many extra chores that the doctor recommended a stay in southern, warmer climates. The year in Italy had cost 4,800 crowns, which she was lucky enough to get from her father who died about the same time. Kristine asks about Helmer's present health because a doctor had entered the house when she came in. Nora explains that Doctor Rank is a close friend who visits every day; Helmer and the entire family are conspicuously healthy. Finally, Nora ends the paean to her own happiness and asks about Kristine's loveless marriage. Kristine married Linde because his wealth would support her sick mother and two young brothers; then he died, leaving her penniless and forced to drudge unceasingly to keep her little family alive. Then her mother died and the brother became old enough to work, thus eradicating the sense of necessity that had kept her going for so many years. She has come to town in search of interesting work and a new life. She was particularly interested in hearing of Helmer's good fortune because he might find a position for her at the bank. Nora agrees to maneuver him into doing so. Kristine compliments Nora on her empathy and kindness which seem all the more remarkable because she has never had to bear any serious burdens. Goaded by the accusation and her desire to boast, Nora reveals that she saved Torvald's life by raising the money for the Italian trip. Kristine is suitably impressed but quite unable to imagine how Nora achieved her coup; Nora merely tantalizes but never reveals her strategy. She does tell how she threw tantrums to convince Helmer that she needed to travel abroad like other young wives. His masculine pride would destroy their marriage if he ever learned that she had provided the money, although she might use the information to rekindle his ardor when he tires of her dancing and baby tricks. It has been exceedingly difficult to meet the payments, but she has done so by using gift money, manipulating household accounts, and economizing in personal expenses. She had even taken in copying work which she did after everyone else had gone to bed. Despite all her efforts, Nora is unable to say precisely how much she has paid on her debt. Her despair at her heavy burden has now vanished, however, because she has Helmer's large income to which to look forward. The bell rings, and Helene admits Krogstad.

Nora is stunned by his visit, but she shows him toward Helmer's study because he says he has come on bank business. After he has entered the study, Kristine, upon hearing his name, remembers that Krogstad had been a law clerk in her village. Together the women note that he had an unhappy marriage, is now a widower with several children, and is engaged in all sorts of businesses. Nora professes utter disinterest in this last observation. Then Rank emerges from Helmer's study and is introduced to Kristine. Rank, drawn into a discussion of health by Kristine's overexertion, admits that he would like to live indefinitely despite his physical torment. He assumes that moral invalids, among them Krogstad, feel the same way. Rank proclaims Krogstad rotten because he is an extortionist. Krogstad's presence and Rank's comment greatly disturb Nora, who breaks out into a nervous laugh at the realization that Krogstad, because he works at the bank, is now in Helmer's power. In celebration she takes a bag of macaroons from her pocket and offers one to Rank, claiming all the time that Kristine had given them to her. Her excitement mounts as she concludes that her greatest desire is to say "hell and damnation" in front of Helmer, who enters at that moment. Nora immediately curbs her jollity. Krogstad has left through the study door, and Nora introduces Helmer to Kristine and immediately asks him to give her a job at the bank. Helmer quickly agrees. Helmer has to leave the house on business, so Rank and Kristine agree to walk with him. As they put on their coats, old Anne Marie the nurse brings in the chattering children. The adults leave Nora with her offspring. She natters gaily with them and eventually starts to play games, hiding under the table while the children try to find her. Eventually, she reveals herself to gleeful shouts while, unknown to Nora, Krogstad opens the hall door and quietly looks on. Finally, he speaks to her, and she sends the children from the room. Nora is disturbed by his presence and blurts out that it is not the first of the month. He had been in a restaurant across the street when he saw the party emerge from the Helmer house. He thought he recognized Kristine and wants to know if she has gotten a job at the bank. Krogstad asks if Nora will use her influence to see that he keeps his position at the bank, as he thinks that Kristine will be given his job. Earlier, Nora had boasted of her influence over Helmer; now she claims that she has none. Krogstad explains his position: years ago he did something that might have landed him in court. Although the case was never pursued, his reputation was ruined, and honorable positions were denied to him. As a result, he has had to support himself in whatever manner possible. Now he wants to redeem himself in the community's eyes for the sake of his children. The bank position is absolutely necessary to his rehabilitation, and Helmer wants to fire him. If Nora wants him to maintain his silence about her loan from Krogstad, she will have to intervene to save his job. When Nora threatens to tell Helmer herself, Krogstad shows his unscrupulousness: he observes that Nora's father was supposed to have co-signed her loan note, yet his signature was dated three days after his death. Realizing that her secret has been penetrated, Nora admits that she forged her father's signature. Her dilemma had been that on the one hand she thought that an explanation of the loan would precipitate her father's death, while on the other hand she knew that her husband's health depended on his taking the European trip. Krogstad's ultimatum is simple: if he loses his position, he will talk about her forgery. Having said this, Krogstad exits as the children pour into the room to continue their game. The mother, however, is in no mood for playing.

First, she starts to sew, and then she decides to trim the tree. Meanwhile, Helmer returns and reports that he has seen Krogstad leaving and suspects that he has asked Nora to intercede for him, to which Nora replies he is correct. He cautions her always to tell him the truth. Nora starts to talk expectantly about a holiday costume party and asks her husband to decide what she should wear as fancy dress. He gives his opinion. She obliquely asks what Krogstad's crime had been. Forgery is the response. Helmer admits that anyone could make a mistake and ought to be forgiven if he admits his error and takes his punishment; Krogstad's real ignominy rests in the fact that he has never paid his debt to society. Helmer commiserates with Krogstad's wife and children because Krogstad's evil, degenerate nature must have infected their whole environment. He further observes that most criminals had mothers who were chronic liars, the mothers' influence being dominant. He concludes that he must fire Krogstad because he could never work with such an evil man, and Nora must say no more about it. He then goes back into his study, leaving Nora to wonder if her crime is poisoning her children. In a moment of strength, Nora asserts that that could never be the case. The curtain falls.

Act II has the same setting as the previous act. The Christmas celebration is over, and Nora moves restlessly about the room listening for a knock or a rattle of the letterbox. She is filled with dread that Krogstad will make good his threat to expose her. Anne Marie enters with the box of masquerade costumes, but Nora cannot show much interest in them. She asks about the children but expresses her determination not to spend as much time with them as she has done. She asks for Anne Marie's reassurance that her children would not forget her if she were gone forever; she is calmed by the knowledge that they would be entrusted to Anne Marie as she had been when her mother died. Desultorily she opens the costume box and then throws it aside. She is considerably relieved to see that Kristine has called. Helmer has decided that Nora should go to the party as a Neopolitan peasant girl and dance the tarantella; but the costume needs appreciable repair. Kristine begins repairing the dress while they chat; Rank's name is brought up, and Nora explains that he suffers excruciating pain from tuberculosis of the spine. Nora concludes that Rank's condition is inherited from a reprobate father. Kristine asks if Rank was exaggerating when he said yesterday that her name was often heard in this house. After all, Helmer seemed never to have heard of her. Nora tells her friend that Helmer is so jealous that he never wants to hear about her friends. Thus it was that she kept quiet to him and talked often of Kristine to her friend Rank. Kristine, thinking Rank to be the source of Nora's loan, cautions Nora to stop Rank's daily visits. Of course, Nora denies the suggestion but becomes visibly agitated as the matter of the loan becomes uppermost in her mind. They hear Helmer approaching, so Nora rushes Kristine out of the room because he cannot bear to see people sewing.

Nora puts on her most ingenuous guise, prancing like the little squirrel and fawning over Helmer, and asks if Helmer would give in to a request that was really important to his little squirrel. She asks him to let Krogstad keep his job, but Helmer has already planned to give it to Kristine. Nora, fears that Krogstad will write something nasty about Helmer and send it to the newspapers, but Helmer feels secure in his probity. Then he says that the bank staff already knows his intention of firing Krogstad, and he would be ruined in their eyes if they learned that he had capitulated to his wife. He then reveals that he and Krogstad had been boyhood friends, and it would be embarrassing for Krogstad to play on that association now that their roles are so different. Nora calls this petty reasoning, and Helmer storms out of the room in search of the maid, to whom he entrusts an envelope to be delivered immediately. As Nora feared, it is Krogstad's notice of termination. Helmer feels that his masculine ego has been vindicated and so quickly gets over his pique with Nora. He tells her to practice her tarantella while he does some more work. Desperate and stunned, Nora tries to find a means of escape, but her thoughts are interrupted by the entrance of Rank. He reports that his death is imminent and that he will die a bankrupt. Rank, knowing that Helmer is so repelled by anything ugly, is prepared to keep him from his bedside. When the final breakdown starts, he will send Nora a card with a black cross as a sign to keep Helmer away. His attitude is particularly grim because he believes that his illness is an inheritance from his father. Nora tries hard to cheer him a bit and appears to do so. Rank's moroseness returns when he says that he will be replaced in the Helmers' affection by Kristine. Nora disabuses him of that notion and decides to ask a large favor of him; Rank answers tellingly that he would be glad to lay down his life for her. For the first time she realizes that his visits have been prompted by more than mere friendship, the knowledge of which now prevents her asking for his help. Helene enters and gives a calling card to Nora, who sends Rank into Helmer's room. Krogstad appears and hits Nora with the news that the situation has changed now that he has been sacked, that for the moment he plans to do nothing about her forgery. He tells her not to consider suicide or running away from home, both of which had occurred to her. He then shows her a letter addressed to Helmer in which he has written the details of her crime. She offers to buy it from him, but he will be satisfied by nothing but a more prestigious position at the bank from which he can quickly rise to eminence. Now, she says, she has the courage to kill herself, but Krogstad deters her by saying that even so, he has power over her posthumous reputation. He then leaves, depositing the letter in the mailbox to which, Nora knows, Helmer has the only key.

Kristine enters and is shown the letter in the box; she sees that Krogstad was the source of Nora's loan. Nora, still considering suicide, admits the forgery so that Kristine can testify if necessary that Nora's death is a consequence of her own guilt and that no one else is involved in her shame. Kristine, referring darkly to a past relationship with Krogstad, determines to have a talk with him. She urges Nora to delay Helmer's examining the mail while Kristine convinces Krogstad to ask for his letter back. Kristine exits, and Rank and Helmer come into the living room expecting to see

Nora in her peasant costume. Nora extracts a promise that Helmer will devote the night to her; business affairs must wait. Helmer decides to check the mail, but Nora strikes the first chords of the tarantella and urges him to play the piano so she can practice her dance. As Nora dances to the playing of Helmer and then of Rank, she becomes more and more frenetic; then she sees that Kristine has returned. Helmer makes her stop dancing as she seems entirely to have forgotten the steps. When she again asks him to conduct no business, to read no letters, he realizes that a letter from Krogstad must be in the box. After Rank urges him to accede to Nora's plea, he reluctantly agrees to postpone reading the letter. The maid announces dinner, to which the men adjourn, leaving Nora to hear from Kristine that Krogstad has left town to return on the evening of the next day. Nora seems resigned to the inevitable, and after Kristine goes in to dinner, Nora muses that she has only thirty-one hours to live.

Act III takes place in the Helmers' living room where Kristine sits thumbing through a book and waiting anxiously for a sound that will indicate that Krogstad has responded to the note she left for him on the previous day. Soon he appears, and they commence to talk about the past. He thinks that Kristine spurned him because she had found a richer man, but she very practically says that her marriage had been necessary to preserve her family. Kristine tells him that she has just learned that she is to replace him at the bank. She then offers to resume their former relationship because she needs someone on whom to focus her life; she could be a good wife to him and mother to his children. Krogstad agrees to her plan as the sound of the tarantella is heard from the dance upstairs. He wishes he could take back his letter to Helmer and learns that she thinks it is still possible. Momentarily, he questions the sincerity of her marriage proposal, but Kristine quietly reassures him. Krogstad says he will demand his letter back, but Kristine convinces him that Helmer needs to face the truth about his life. She sends him out to wait for her downstairs as the end of the tarantella signifies the return of the Helmers. Nora's dance has been a spectacular success, and she is quite reluctant to leave the party. Helmer has insisted, however, and he must be obeyed. When Helmer exits to get some more candles, Nora asks Kristine what happened with Krogstad. Her friend tells her that she must explain the entire situation to her husband. Nora refuses, and Kristine taunts that the letter will make everything clear. Nora thanks Krogstad and says that she now knows what must be done. Helmer returns, and Kristine goes home.

Left alone with his wife, Helmer starts to get romantic, but she repels his advances. A knock is heard. Rank appears and asks if he may come in. He merely wants to talk about the party and congratulate Nora for her charming appearance and Helmer for leading such a charmed life. He mentions that he will be invisible at the next party; he asks for a cigar and goes. Helmer takes out his keyring to open the letterbox and discovers that someone has tampered with the lock with a hairpin. In the box he finds two calling cards from Rank, one with a black cross on it. Nora tells Helmer that their old friend plans to shut himself up to die. The man laments the passing of his comrade but rejoices that he will have Nora to himself in the future; he wishes that something dire would happen to cause him to stake everything for his love of her. Nora urges him to read his mail, but he is more interested in satisfying his romantic urges. Nora again spurns him by reminding Helmer that their best friend is dying. He agrees that they should stay apart until Rank's end has come. He exits into his study, leaving Nora to imagine the icy waters in which she will kill herself. Helmer reenters reading Krogstad's letter. Learning that the accusations are true, Helmer makes no attempt to understand Nora's motives but merely brands her a criminal and an object of disgust. She fears that he will try to take the blame, but Helmer gives no sign of intending to do so. He merely raves about the ruination of his life and happiness; at last his practical nature takes over as he plans to buy Krogstad's silence and maintain the appearance of marital felicity. On no account will Nora be allowed access to the children. While Helmer hatches this plan, the doorbell rings and the maid delivers a note from Krogstad, who says that he will not make use of his knowledge of Nora's crime. Helmer's mood changes mercurially. Now he is saved. To reassure Nora, he shreds the letter and burns the pieces in the stove. Finally, he realizes how terribly Nora must have suffered during the past three days; he magnanimously forgives her for making a stupid error of feminine judgment. She thanks him for his forgiveness and leaves the room to get out of her costume. Helmer rambles on at length about his great heart which is capable of overlooking Nora's little mistake. Nora soon enters in her regular clothes, determined not to sleep but to have a frank discussion with her husband.

For the first time in the eight years of their marriage, she says, they are going to have a serious conversation. She says that both her father and Helmer have wronged her by never taking her seriously. Both treated her like a plaything living in a playpen, and she in turn has made dolls of her own children. She now sees that she is not fit to rear children, and before she can ever be so, she must educate herself. To accomplish this, she plans to leave him. Helmer forbids her to leave, but the new Nora will not listen. He brings up the matter of her sacred vow only to hear her say that her responsibility toward herself must take precedence. She has some serious doubts about religion, morals, and the rightness of the law which can condemn a woman for sparing her dying father or saving her husband's life. He claims that she could not love him and act this way, and Nora responds that she realized she did not love him when he failed to justify her behavior to the world in the teeth of Krogstad's accusations. Then he let her down further by not offering to take the blame himself. Had he done that, she would have spared him the shame by commiting suicide. Helmer replies that no one gives up honor for the sake of love. She tersely says that numerous women have done so. Nora admits that he disappointed her greatly by failing to realize her great strength once Krogstad's threat was gone; instead, he started treating her like a fragile doll again. Now she must go. Her coat and suitcase are waiting in the hall. Nora tells him that she will not see the children because she is of no use to them as she now is. Before leaving, she releases Helmer from all legal responsibility for her upkeep; both must be absolutely free. She insists that they return their wedding rings. Helmer asks to be allowed to write to her, but Nora insists that he must not. She will accept nothing from him because she must take nothing from a stranger. Only a miracle could stop her from seeing him as a stranger, and she has stopped believing in miracles. Such a miracle would enable them to live together in a true marriage. Helmer is left puzzling over this announcement as the door slams shut, and the curtain falls.

Structural analysis: Ibsen employs his characteristic manner of exposition in this play—the encounter of people who have been separated by time and distance and the concomitant necessity of exchanging information. Through the agency of Kristine, Ibsen tells almost all that is necessary about Krogstad's unwholesome past. The remainder comes out as a result of the fortuitous fact that Helmer and Krogstad had been boyhood companions.

The drama is full of allusions to heredity and environment as determinants of character, although Helmer's pronouncements on genetic inheritance are highly dubious. Krogstad's criminal nature is explained by the poisonous atmosphere of his home; Nora questions if her deeds have created a noxious environment for her children. Nora's father and husband have limited her personal growth by keeping her in the doll-house environment. Rank believes he inherited his disease from his father, while Helmer thinks Nora inherited her spendthrift nature form her father.

As in most of his Realistic plays, Ibsen favored unity of action:

Nora discovers that Krogstad plans to blackmail her;

(as a result of which)

Nora tries unsuccessfully to convince Helmer not to dismiss him;

(as a result of which)

Nora discovers that Krogstad has been fired and has written Helmer a letter inculpating her;

(as a result of which)

Nora confesses her guilt to Kristine and promises to keep Helmer from reading the letter until Kristine deals with Krogstad;

(as a result of which)

Nora discovers that Kristine insists that Nora tell Helmer the truth;

(as a result of which)

Nora agrees that Helmer must hear the truth even if it results in her suicide;

(as a result of which)

Nora discovers that Helmer has Krogstad's letter;

(as a result of which)

Nora urges him to read it;

(as a result of which)

Nora discovers that at last Helmer knows her secret;

(as a result of which)

Nora admits that Krogstad's accusations are true, believing that Helmer will defend her actions;

(as a result of which)

Nora discovers that Helmer is accusatory and ungrateful, that he is, in fact, a stranger to her;

(as a result of which)

Nora sacrifices marriage, home, and children and goes off in search of her own self-actualization.

References: Pearce, Richard. ''The Limits of Realism,'' *College English*, 31 (1970), 335-43; Richardson, Jack. ''Ibsen's Nora and Ours,'' *Commentary*, 52, 1 (1971), 77-80.

A DOLL'S LIFE (1982): This musical, based on *A Doll's House,** tells what happened to Nora Helmer* after she walked out on her marriage. With book and lyrics by Betty Comden and Adolph Green and music by Larry Grossman, *A Doll's Life* lasted only five performances at New York's Mark Hellinger Theatre. It was directed by Hal Prince and starred Betsy Joslyn, whose performance in this ''hyper-elaborate'' show was described as ''shrill and unvaried.'' The character of Nora lacked magnitude, and the script was improbable.

Reference: Kerr, Walter. ''In 'A Doll's Life' It's the Same Old Nora,'' *New York Times*, Oct. 2, 1982, Sect. H, p. 3, cols. 1-4; p. 23, cols. 1-3.

DOMESTIC HANDICRAFTS OF BRABANT IN THE MIDDLE AGES: Jörgen Tesman's* book, the research for which he completed while on his wedding trip with Hedda Gabler.*

DORF, DINA (*The Pillars of Society*): Dina Dorf has lived in the Bernick household as a ward of the family, but she is really the illegitimate daughter of Karsten Bernick* and serves as but another example of the dichotomy between his appearance as an upright pillar of society and the reality of his dishonorable dealings. Dina eventually sails to America with Johan Tönnesen.*

DOUGLAS, MARION BOOTH (1856-1932): A minor member of America's fabled theatrical dynasty, Douglas was the daughter of Junius Brutus Booth II. In 1882 she wrote a version of *A Doll's House* called *Nora*, but whether it was produced remains unclear.

DRESDEL, SONIA (1909-76): After studying at England's Royal Academy of Dramatic Art, English-born Sonia Dresdel twice (1942 and 1943) played Hedda Gabler* in London.

DRESDEN: The capital of the German state of Saxony, where Ibsen resided between 1868 and 1875.

DUE, CHRISTOFFER LORENTZ (1827-1923): As a member of the staff of the customshouse at Grimstad* after 1845, Due became a friend of Ibsen and in 1909 published *Erindringer fra Henrik Ibsens Ungdomsaar* [*Reminiscences of Henrik Ibsen's Youth*].

ET DUKKEHJEM: The Norwegian title of *A Doll's House.**

DUMONT, LOUISE (1862-1932): Several of Ibsen's characters—Rebecca West,* Hedda Gabler,* Irene de Satow*—were in German actress Louise Dumont's repertory, but she was especially praised for her performance as Helene Alving* in the production of *Ghosts** mounted by the Deutsches Theater (Berlin) on November 27, 1894.
Reference: Enciclopedia della Spettacolo, IV, cols. 1118-20.

DUNNOCK, MILDRED (1900-   ): Mildred Dunnock was a member of the company at New York's Civic Center in 1951. In that year she played Aase* and Gina Ekdal,* which was called "genuine and illuminating" in a production that "treats *The Wild Duck** as if it were a show and not a play."
References: Atkinson, Brooks. "At the Play," *New York Times*, Dec. 27, 1951, p. 17, cols. 1-2; *Who's Who in the Theatre*, 16th ed., pp. 567-8.

DUSE, ELEONORA (1858-1924): In 1879, the year of the publication of *A Doll's House,** twenty-one-year-old Eleonora Duse, Italian-born heiress of a long family theatrical association, startled audiences with her truthful impersonation of Thérèse Raquin, the heroine of Emile Zola's Naturalistic play. At the time, she had already been on the stage fourteen years. Duse thereafter built her reputation on the works of Dumas *fils*, Gabrielle d'Annunzio, and Ibsen. In the 1880s she formed her own company and became an international star.

While playing in Milan in 1891, Duse first essayed Nora Helmer,* a role that was never afterwards absent from her repertory. When George Bernard Shaw* saw her performance in 1893, he observed that Duse knew Nora more intimately than Nora herself did. A bit of characteristic stage business occurred in the third act when Nora decides that she can no longer live with Helmer: when she made the decision, she accidentally dropped her wedding band.

Duse's Ellida Wangel* was one of her most celebrated roles. A reviewer noted that "It was not necessary for us to understand what she was saying,

because we understood what she was feeling." Rebecca West* and Helene
Alving* were also undertaken by the Italian actress.

In 1906 Duse visited Norway for the first time and desired to do homage
to Ibsen whose works had helped to shape her career. He was so near death,
however, that he could not see her. Duse stood for some time in the snow
hoping in vain for a chance to spy him at the window.

References: Harding, Bertita. *Age Cannot Wither: The Story of Duse and
d'Annunzio.* Philadelphia: J. B. Lippincott, 1947; Rohe, Alice. "Duse
Breaks Her Silence," *Theatre*, 36 (1922), 137.

DYBWAD, JOHANNE (1867-1950): One of Norway's most distinguished
actresses, Johanne Dybwad's name is inextricably linked with Ibsen's.
Between her first appearance as Nora Helmer* in 1887 and her impersonation of Brand's Mother* in 1942, Dybwad portrayed twenty other Ibsenian
women: Hilde Wangel* (both roles), Hedvig Ekdal,* Thea Elvsted,* Solveig,* Selma Brattsberg,* Asta Allmers,* Frida Foldal,* Signe,* Maja
Rubek,* Eline,* Gerd,* Rebecca West,* Helene Alving,* Hjördis,* Lady
Inger of Gyldenlöve,* and Aase.* In addition to establishing herself as an
Ibsenian actress, Dybwad directed a number of productions of his plays.

References: Elster, Kristian. *Skuespillerinden Johanne Dybwad: Til belysning av
realismen i skuespillkunsten.* Oslo: H. Aschehoug, 1931; Sklavan, Einar.
"Johanne Dybwad," *American Scandinavian Review*, 20, 6-7 (1932), 327-38;
Waal, Carla R. "Johanne Dybwad, Norwegian Actress." Unpublished
doctoral dissertation, Indiana University, 1964.

"THE DYING MERMAID": A painting undertaken by Ballestad* in *The
Lady from the Sea.* * Its content is a metaphor of Ellida Wangel's* position.

E

EAMES, CLARE (1896-1930): After leaving the American Academy of Dramatic Art, Clara Eames appeared in *Hedda Gabler** in 1922 and 1924 and in *Little Eyolf** in 1926.
Reference: Who Was Who in the Theatre, II, 732-3.

EBBELL, CLARA: Young Clara Ebbell, a resident of Grimstad,* was the object of Ibsen's infatuation during the summer of 1849. He dedicated his poem "To the Star" to her, but her response to Ibsen's effusion presumably was not positive.

EBERKOPF, HERR VON (*Peer Gynt*): One of the men encountered in Africa by Peer Gynt.*

ECHEGARAY, JOSÉ (1832-1916): A contemporary of Ibsen, José Echegaray was a pioneer Realist and thus indebted to Ibsen. His play *The Son of Don Juan* (1892) is suggestive of *Ghosts** in that it deals with a promiscuous father, inherited disease, and a young man's dying while calling for the sun.
Reference: Gregersen, H. "Ibsen and Echegaray," *Hispanic Review*, 1 (1933), 338-40.

ECKSTROM, CARL: A reporter of the *New York Dramatic Mirror* called Carl Eckstrom's performance as Gregers Werle* in March 1907 in Chicago "a fine Ibsenian accomplishment" (Mar. 23, 1907, p. 10, col. 1).

EGIL (*The Vikings in Helgeland*): The four-year-old son of Gunnar,* whose supposed murder precipitates the crisis of the drama.

EINAR (*The Grouse in Justedal*): A young yeoman.

EINAR (*Lady Inger of Österaad*): Lady Inger's* faithful retainer.

EJNAR (*Brand*): A young painter who represents to Brand* a feckless, fun-loving type of person. When he is first seen, Ejnar is engaged to Agnes,* who deserts him to go with Brand.

EKDAL, GINA (*The Wild Duck*): As the wife of Hjalmar* and the mother of Hedvig,* Gina is the mainstay of the Ekdal household. She had been a servant in the home of Haakon Werle,* who is the real father of Hedvig. Gina's happy world is destroyed when Gregers Werle* moves into the apartment and forces everyone to face the truth about Hedvig's parentage.

EKDAL, HEDVIG (*The Wild Duck*): Teenaged Hedvig leads a limited sort of existence because of her failing eyesight and the necessity of her aiding her mother Gina* in cosseting Hjalmar.* When Hjalmar discovers that Hedvig is not his natural daughter, he spurns her, which leads Hedvig to commit suicide as a sacrifice to regain his love.

EKDAL, HJALMAR (*The Wild Duck*): A photographer by profession, Hjalmar Ekdal is a dreamer. He fantasizes about creating a great invention but actually does nothing except bask in the attention of his wife, daughter, and limited circle of friends. Gregers Werle* evinces Hjalmar's crisis by revealing that Hedvig* is not Hjalmar's natural daughter. After Hedvig's suicide, there is no suggestion that Hjalmar has learned anything at all from his bitter experience with facing the truth about himself and his relationships.

OLD EKDAL (*The Wild Duck*): The father of Hjalmar,* Old Lieutenant Ekdal lives on the boundary between reality and fantasy since he was wrongly implicated in illegal activities by Haakon Werle,* who now pays old Ekdal to do meaningless work as an expiation of his guilt. Old Ekdal, once a hunter, is the keeper of the fowl in the Ekdal attic.

ELIAS, JULIUS (1861-1927): Julius Elias, a German art and literary historian, was Ibsen's German editor and literary executor. He published *Letters of Henrik Ibsen*, 2 vols. Copenhagen, n.p., 1904.
Reference: Uhde-Bernays, Hermann. "Julius Elias," *Neue Deutsche Biographie* (Berlin, 1957), IV, 439-40.

ELINE (*Lady Inger of Österaad*): The daughter of Lady Inger of Gyldenlöve,* Eline is a young, romantic woman. Her idealism causes Eline to censure her mother for failing to take action to win Norway's independence. She becomes a pawn in a political game by becoming engaged to Nils Lykke,* the seducer of her sister, against whom she had sworn to wreak vengeance.

ELLIS, HENRY HAVELOCK (1859-1939): Havelock Ellis is best known for his seven-volume *Studies in the Psychology of Sex* (1897-1928), but before he started that work he was editor of the Camelot Series of cheap editions of important dramatic pieces. In 1888 he published *The Pillars of Society and Other Plays*, which included his own introduction, William Archer's* translations of *Ghosts** and *The Pillars of Society*,* and Eleanor Marx's* rendition of *An Enemy of the People.** It was through Marx that Ellis' interest in Ibsen was aroused.

In January 1885 Ellis was invited to hear a reading of *Nora* (a translation of *A Doll's House** by Henrietta Frances Lord*) at the house shared by Eleanor Marx and Dr. Edward Aveling, who was married to someone else. The cast included Marx and Aveling as the Helmers* and George Bernard Shaw* as Nils Krogstad.* Ellis was unable to attend, but his friends' enthusiasm for Ibsen was contagious. Soon he found himself searching for a publisher for *Ghosts*, which he considered Ibsen's greatest drama. As it eventuated, Ellis himself published the drama in the Camelot volume, the inexpensive price of which attracted over fourteen thousand purchasers within four years.

Ellis contributed to Ibsen's growing reputation by including an essay on the Norwegian in his *The New Spirit* (1890), in which he depicts Ibsen as a "man with that little diamond wedge of sincerity and the mighty Thor's hammer of his art." Unfortunately, Ellis says very little about Ibsen's dramatic art. To appreciate Ibsen's skill, he says, one should consider the environment of Norway. Avidly interested in ethnic influences on the development of personality, Ellis dwells upon Ibsen's German, Danish, and Scottish ancestry. As a literary critic, Ellis closely resembles John Aldington Symonds whom he praised for having no discernible critical method. Ellis is, in fact, not a critic of Ibsen's dramas but a champion of his ideas, many of which coincided with his own. As a Fabian socialist, Ellis viewed *The League of Youth** as an anti-government tract. As a defender of women's rights, he saw *A Doll's House* as a condemnation of traditional roles in marriage. When Ellis married Edith Lees in 1891, he too contracted an unconventional marriage, for the bride was a lesbian and the groom of dubious sexual appetites. Perhaps Ibsen's unique marital arrangement served as a model for Ellis.

Ellis ignores the subject of dramatic construction, merely nods in the direction of characterization, and expends his charming prose in describing the Thought of Ibsen's dramas. Writing of the canon from *Catiline** through *The Lady from the Sea*,* Ellis sees a common thread: ". . . an eager insistence that the social environment shall not cramp the reasonable freedom of the individual, together with a passionately intense hatred of all those conventional lies which are commonly regarded as 'the pillars of society' " (Ellis, p. 148). Ellis was useful, then, in publicizing Ibsen's ideas and making some of the dramas available at affordable prices.

References: Brome, Vincent. *Havelock Ellis, Philosopher of Sex: A Biography*. London: Routledge and Kegan Paul, 1979; Ellis, Havelock. *The New Spirit*. Washington, D.C.: National Home Library Foundation, 1935; Grosskurth, Phyllis. *Havelock Ellis: A Biography*. New York: Alfred A. Knopf, 1980.

ELLMENREICH, AUGUST (1851-1928): After playing Arnold Rubek* in Munich in 1900, German actor August Ellmenreich appeared in *The Pillars of Society,* *Rosmersholm,* and *John Gabriel Borkman.* He acted in the United States under the name of August Lauber.

ELVSTED, THEA RYSING (*Hedda Gabler*): A schoolgirl acquaintance of Hedda Gabler,* Thea Elvsted has followed Ejlert Lövberg* to the city, where she enlists Hedda's assistance in keeping him sober. As a young girl, Hedda had been jealous of Thea's abundant hair; as a matron, Hedda is jealous of Thea's influence over Lövberg. When Thea and Jörgen Tesman* devote themselves to reconstructing Lövberg's destroyed manuscript, Hedda becomes jealous of Thea's collaboration with Hedda's husband. Thea Elvsted, then, is a metaphor for Hedda's frustrations. She is also a useful expository device to reveal Lövberg's activities during Hedda's separation from him.

EMPEROR AND GALILEAN: A ten-act Romantic serious drama in two parts.
Composition: Idea conceived in 1864; intermittently written from spring 1865; finished in February 1873; published on October 16, 1873.
Stage history:

  Dec. 5, 1896   Stadttheater, Leipzig, pro. Leopold Adler*
  Feb. 27, 1896   Stadttheater, Leipzig
  Mar. 17, 1898   Belle-Alliance Theater, Berlin
  Mar. 20, 1903   National Theatre, Christiania* (1st part only)

Structural synopsis: Part 1: *Caesar's Apostasy.* On Easter night A.D. 351, a great crowd gathers in the gardens near the Imperial Palace in Constantinople. A liturgical service is in progress in the Imperial Chapel, which is guarded by soldiers and fringed by beggars, cripples, and blind men. The aura of a marketplace is inescapable as fruitsellers and water-carriers ply their wares. As a Christian anthem is heard from within, Potamon the Goldsmith asks a soldier when the Emperor will come. Phocion the Dyer overhears and says that he is expected at midnight. Eunapius the Barber, a Christian, enters quickly and knocks down a heathen fruitseller; Phocion joins him in kicking and deriding that fallen man. Phocion says for the benefit of the Captain of the Guard that someone should report this scene to the Emperor who has expressed his concern about Christians' consorting with heathen. Soon these three men are brawling because of their religious beliefs: Eunapius is a Donatist; Potamon, a Manichean; Phocion, a Cainite. The melée is soon dispelled by the call that the Emperor is coming in regal procession. Preceded by thurifers, Emperor Constantius and Empress Eusebia enter, followed by nineteen-year-old Prince Julian. Then come the Emperor's sister Princess Helena and her retinue, after which marches the rest of the court, including Memnon, the Emperor's Ethiopian body-slave. Constantius quickly turns and asks Julian where Gallus is. The youth pales and asks what Constantius could want with Gallus, which the suspicious Constantius interprets as Julian's collusion in a plot against him. The more Constantius talks, the more obvious it is that he is ill. Memnon is sent to fetch the doctor. Julian asks Constantius for permission to go to Egypt to seek eremitical solitude because in the capital he cannot escape evil thoughts even though he wears hair shirts and flagellates himself. Constantius equivocates and then is drawn into the chapel by Memnon. Eusebia tells Julian to fear nothing, but Constantius bars him from the church because of his evil thoughts. Memnon scatters silver coins to the ailing rabble outside the chapel. Julian is left outside to wonder why Constantius wants to see Julian's old friend Gallus. As Julian leaves the scene, he encounters Agathon, a childhood friend from Cappadocia. They sit and talk of their boyhood, their old teacher Mardonius, and the uncompleted church which Gallus and Julian started over the grave of the false prophet Mamas. Julian confesses that now God will have none of him, which Agathon finds difficult to believe because it was Julian who had converted him. Now, says Agathon, he has come to Constantinople at the bidding of God. Julian tells him to go home because the capital has become a Babylon of blasphemy since Libanius has come. This philosopher has spellbound all sorts of people with his arguments and jests, and, worst of all, Constantius has been misled into thinking that Julian had personally conversed with Libanius. Julian believes that Libanius has poisoned the very air with his heresy, but the Emperor is so concerned with his war with the Persians that he fails to recognize the danger at home. Agathon says that a vision has sent him to Constantinople, but before he can describe it, a philosopher and his school appear.

Julian learns that they are bound for Athens where the church does not limit free discussion; he asks the philosopher if truth is not to be found where Libanius is. The answer is that Libanius is weary of strife and will soon be silent as he is also tired of waiting for his peer, Constantius' successor. Julian is immediately frightened that some word of this will get back to the Emperor; he sends Agathon away. The philosopher knows Julian's reputation—how in a debate with Gallus he had defended the old gods against the Galilean, how he has been prepared by two great teachers Mardonius and Hecebolius, how his eloquence has been matchless since his boyhood. The philosopher decribes a glowing world of intellectual honesty of which Julian may be king, and even then Julian realizes that that sort of kingdom must be won at the cost of his salvation. The philosopher and his group descend the steps to a waiting boat and depart, leaving behind a greatly excited Julian. Agathon emerges from the shadows and says that this encounter was the work of Satan, but Julian can only see that he is an alien in this place. He is flattered to believe that the great Libanius sees him as his equal. Agathon insists on telling of his vision which occurred after a bloody persecution of Christians in Cappadocia: an angel had appeared to him and told him to command the one who will inherit the empire to go into the lions' den and do battle with the lions. Julian interprets this as meaning that he should confront Libanius, but Agathon adds to his vision by saying that Julian should leave Constantinople and never return. Prince Gallus, a martial man of twenty-five, enters and hears from Julian that an angry emperor wants to see him. Gallus sees that death or banishment awaits him because he has addressed a question to the oracle at Abydos. Julian sees that consulting a heathen priest is an offense, but he senses that Gallus has done something more suspicious; he rightly guesses that Gallus asked the oracle when and how Constantius would die. Gallus becomes so exercised that he loses all caution and calls Constantius the murderer of his father, stepmother, eldest brother, and eleven members of his family. Then Gallus turns on Julian, accusing him of spying on him for Constantius, but Julian denies that he has done so or that he will succeed Constantius.

The church door is opened, and as the congregation streams out, Hecebolius approaches Julian to tell him of his concern for Julian's soul. Julian accuses him of circulating his own verses against Julian and attributing them to Libanius. Hecebolius admits that he did so for Julian's soul. Constantius emerges from the chapel and surprises everyone by naming Gallus Caesar, the designation of the heir to the throne. He sends Gallus away to prosecute the Persian war and tells Julian that he can settle down because Libanius has been banished to Athens and has already sailed. Julian then realizes that he had unwittingly conversed with Libanius. Julian asks to be allowed to go to study in Pergamus. Eusebia, Gallus, and Hecebolius entreat Constantius to accede, so he allows Julian to go. As the procession starts towards a banquet, Gallus speaks quietly with Helena, his beloved. At last Julian and Agathon are left alone. Julian says that he plans to go first to Pergamus and then to Athens and invites his friend to accompany him, but Agathon must return to Cappadocia.

Act II takes place in a *porticus* in Athens where various students of philosophy, including Basil of Caesarea and Gregory of Nazianzus, exchange ideas. When a shout announces the arrival of a ship from Ephesus bearing new scholars, Gregory and Basil start to leave, but the movement is arrested by the appearance of a red-faced Julian reeling from an all-night carousal. As Basil exits, Julian enters in the company of reveling students, among them Libanius' friend, Sallust of Perusia. The students decide to amuse themselves by staging a mock trial with Julian as judge, but he defers to the wiser Gregory and decides to play the defendant. At the urging of the crowd, Julian pretends to be a Christian who refuses to pay tribute to the Emperor. After quoting the injunction to render to Caesar and to God what is due to each, Julian traps Gregory into pronouncing a judgment on how much of God's property the Emperor has a right to demand. Gregory tries to evade the judgment as unseemly toward both God and the Emperor, but Julian turns the judgment against Gregory and then in a bit of sophistry makes a hero of him, thus showing his rhetorical skill. Libanius and his school enter to be asked by Julian if he is going to the port to enlist students from the ship that has just docked. Libanius lengthily says that it is beneath the dignity of a true philosopher to try to ensnare pupils, but when Julian tells him that two sons of a very rich man are aboard, Libanius and the other teachers rush to the port. Julian is left alone with the thoughtful Gregory, who mildly rebukes him for his dissolute life. Julian attributes his behavior to his princely upbringing but primarily to his uneasiness that he has heard nothing from Constantius who must know that Julian has gone from Pergamus to Nicomedia to Athens. By associating with Libanius, he is violating the Emperor's express command. Gregory asks why Julian has been participating in the mystery religion and hears that it is merely because Julian is bored at the University and is disappointed that Libanius is not the great man he had imagined him to be. Julian had thought that as equals he and Libanius would debate the relative merits of Christianity and paganism, but Libanius has not seriously desired any sort of contact. To make matters worse, Julian says, Libanius is an opportunist, stooping so low as to send flattering letters to Gallus for his middling victories against the Persians.

Basil comes in bearing letters from Cappadocia, one of which describes Gallus' bloody tyranny in Antioch. Julian interprets Gallus' deeds as a necessary concomitant of princely power and thanks God that he was not named Constantius' successor. Gregory, however, says that as a Christian, it is Julian's responsibility to face Gallus with his crimes and bring about retribution. This battle between Christianity and the world is to occur in life, not in the lecture room. When Julian admits the truth of the proposition but seems afraid to act on it, Gregory accuses him of being just like Libanius. Julian asks if Gregory will accompany him into danger, but Gregory is evasive. Julian's answer is to start off to another bacchanal. Gregory exits, but Basil detains Julian as a crowd of teachers and new students noisily fills the square. Night falls as the host subsides into drinking, roistering, ogling dancing girls, and reveling. In an effort to erase the events at Antioch from his mind Julian rhapsodizes about the beauty of pagan sin. He and Basil speak of the presence of Maximus the Mystic in Ephesus, who, according to Basil's sister Makrina, is confounding the world with his strange deeds. Julian is dismayed to learn that Makrina too sees him as Christ's weapon against pagan evil. He describes his indecision which is the result of his splintered universe—the conflicting claims of church and state, of the old and the new, of the many sects and heresies. When Basil counsels him to find his answers in books, Julian insists that he requires concrete answers, nothing short of a new revelation. If that occurred, even a martyr's death would seem sweet. According to Julian, Athens has taught him that the old is no longer beautiful and the new no longer true. Libanius excitedly enters and explains that Maximus has convicted himself by admitting that he has power over spirits and the dead. As Libanius reads of Maximus' exploits from a letter sent from Ephesus, Basil is scandalized, but Julian is tantalized. To the amazement of Libanius and the horror of Basil, Julian announces that he is going to Maximus, for he is the one whom Julian has been seeking.

Act III is set in Julian's home in Ephesus. The prince's chamberlain Eutherius conducts Gregory and Basil into the hall. Soon Julian, clothed in Oriental garb and very animated, comes in to greet them. He claims that he knew of his friends' coming because their spirits had visited him, his description of which convinces Basil and Gregory that the rumors of Julian's practice of the black arts are true. Julian claims to be extremely happy because of the teachings of Maximus, who is himself the new revelation. As he describes his mystical experiences, Julian's friends are shocked by his ungodliness. Julian encapsulates his wisdom for them: that which is, is not; that which is not, is. He believes that he and Gallus will soon control the earth, but his precise role is not yet clear. Julian speaks at length of the glory that awaits him once he has mated with the perfect bride, the pure woman, and produced a race of pure, beautiful people (See Nietzsche, Friedrick Wilhelm.*) Basil and Gregory are scandalized by Julian's frenzied, blasphemous talk and refuse to remain in town for the night in order to see what revelations Maximus will produce. They sever their bond of friendship with Julian and leave.

Curtains are drawn aside to reveal a tall, veiled object; then Maximus, dressed in a pointed hat and long black robe, enters carrying a white wand. He removes the drape from a bronze lamp on a high tripod and pours oil into the lamp; the fire lights itself and burns with a red glare. Julian expectantly asks if the time for revelation has come. At Maximus' bidding, the room beyond becomes alive with music and dancing girls. Maximus gives Julian some doctored wine, and in a hallucination he sees a face in the now blue lamplight. A voice in the flame enigmatically answers Julian's questions about his mission: he is to establish the empire. The magical spell is broken. Julian asks Maximus about the empire, only to be told that there are three: that founded on knowledge, that based on the Cross, and that which is to come, derived from both. In answer to Julian's further questions, Maximus produces a vision of Cain, one of Judas Iscariot, and a third which will not materialize because it is not yet dead. Julian interprets the apparitions to mean that he will found the third empire, but he resists violently. The tension of this scene is broken by the news that a guard has been placed around Julian's house.

Leontes enters to say that Julian has been appointed Caesar because Gallus and his wife have been killed. Gregory bursts in to tell Julian that Gallus has been murdered, implying that Constantius is the indirect culprit. Julian avoids the implication and takes the purple robe. Gregory is joined by Basil, who also urges him not to don the purple. As Julian vacillates, Leontes produces a letter from Constantius in which Julian reads that Constantius has given him Helena as his wife. Since Julian sees the unattainable Helena as the pure woman of his dreams, he is convinced. Leontes drapes him in the royal purple and leads him to be acclaimed by the people. Maximus, Basil, and Gregory are left with their thoughts as to the outcome of this event.

Caesar's palace in Lutetia in Gaul is the scene of Act IV. A pregnant Helena with her slave Myrrha awaits Julian's return from a military campaign. A dusty Julian enters, quickly embraces Helena, and tells Eutherius to bar all the doors. Helena thinks he has lost the battle, but actually he has not. After many questions as to his peremptory uneasiness, Julian tells Helena that spies in his army have misconstrued all his actions in their secret reports to Constantius, as a result of which he has been stripped of everything except the outward show of power. Despite these insults, he was victorious in battle; yet an accident may ruin him. When he spared the life of the enemy leader, the man was so relieved that he shouted his thanks to the Emperor Julian. The cry was picked up and echoed by thousands, causing his enemies to report that he was seizing the throne. Weary of such strife, Julian asks if Helena will follow him. She agrees, thinking he truly means to become Emperor. He, in fact, was speaking of returning to the quiet life of a scholar. When Helena sees his purpose, she goads him to take the throne so she can be Empress. Helena's temptation is interrupted by the news that Constantius' emissary has arrived. After greeting Decentius, Helena leaves the room. Julian reads the letter from Rome and is surprised to discover that no umbrage had been taken at his being called Emperor. Decentius explains that a barbarian could easily confuse the meanings of Caesar and Emperor. Julian had earlier summoned Florentius and his other captains, all of whom now appear.

When Julian introduces Decentius and says that he brings Rome's favor, Florentius and Severus are clearly disappointed that Julian has escaped the Emperor's wrath. Julian again shows his skill as a disputant by claiming that he has accomplished nothing in Gaul, which causes Severus and Florentius to wax eloquent in his praise. Then Julian produces the Roman letter in which Constantius claims credit for all that has been done in Gaul. Florentius and Severus are now in the unhappy position of having detracted from the Emperor's glory, which Julian points out to Decentius. He has, in fact, disarmed the spies in his camp. Decentius reveals another document, and while Julian reads it, the two spies corner Decentius and try to talk their way out of the treasonous utterances into which Julian had trapped them. Having completed the document, Julian lays down his command of the army, and Decentius goes out to a conference with the generals. Only Sintula remains behind to hear Julian say that Constantius has disbanded the army of Gaul, the troops of which are to be sent to the Asian battlefields. Sintula reminds Julian that he had promised the barbarian soldiers that they would never have to fight beyond the Alps. By his order Constantius will dishonor Julian and turn the army against him. To make matters worse, Sintula is named to head the troops in their return to Rome. Julian had thought that Sintula was loyal to him, but the man hastens to curry favor with the Emperor by doing his will. Myrrha rushes in to say that

Helena is ill, and soon a distraught princess enters. She has been poisoned by edible gifts from the capital; she faints proclaiming her sexual infidelity to Julian, who is not the father of her child. Decentius comes in full of false, abject contrition about what has felled Helena. Sintula reports that he cannot take command of the soldiers because they have become an undisciplined mob at hearing Julian's promise dishonored. The courtyard is now filled with angry warriors. When Julian decides to face the belligerent army, Decentius arrests him and orders Sintula to transport Caesar to Rome. Julian shouts through the window for help, but the soldiers break into the room demanding his death. They are surprised when he begs them to prevent his being murdered like Gallus. In a masterpiece of persuasion, Julian slowly turns the tide of opinion in his favor so that eventually the army proclaims him Emperor. Julian emerges victorious from a situation that might have ended in his death. In the moment of his triumph, Helena dies.

Vienna in Gaul is the locale of Act V. Julian paces anxiously in the catacombs where he has retreated to bury Helena. Psalms are being sung in the adjacent church. Sallust reports that the army is growing impatient because Julian spends all his time underground and will not show himself. Julian claims that he is mourning his wife, but he shows that he has actually lost his courage when Sallust says that an angry Constantius is in Antioch with an army that he plans to lead to Gaul. When Julian says that he would rather parley with the Emperor than fight him, Sallust admits that he has been an unwilling spy and asks Julian to kill him because Constantius will certainly do so for his coming over to Julian's side. Julian magnanimously excuses Sallust, who must now tell him that the Emperor is remarrying; any heirs would keep Julian from the throne. He further admits that Helena was killed lest she should produce a worthy claimant to the throne. Julian must act now or lose everything. At the moment that Julian decides to face his army again as Emperor, a mysterious voice hails him. Sallust begs Julian to dismiss himself from any participation in such arcane practices; he fears that any delay will cause the troops to mutiny. Julian tells him to go.

Then Julian sees Maximus, with a sacrificial fillet around his head and a bloody knife in his hands, ascending from the crypt. Julian has conjured the appearance of his old tutor whose arguments he uses to justify his actions. Maximus interprets Julian's position as the confrontation between Emperor and Galilean; he shows Julian that Christianity has been debased. Eutherius breaks in to report that miracles are being performed at Helena's tomb. Oribases the physician says that Julian must choose between life and the lie. Oribases tells Julian that the soldiers are blaming Julian for killing Helena and that he must divert them somehow. Julian decides to opt for the empire, but before he faces the troops, he takes the sacrificial implements from Maximus and descends into the crypt. Meanwhile, Sallust comes into the catacomb at the head of a throng of soldiers whom he is trying to convince not to kill Julian. Julian is heard from below calling on the name of Helios, the sun god; then he emerges from the depths with blood on his head, chest, and hands, having sacrificed to the pagan god. One sight of him and again the soldiers are his partisans. Julian throws open the doors of the church and proclaims that his is the kingdom. Maximus rejoices at his forensic success.

Part 2: *The Emperor Julian.* Ten years have passed, and at the beginning of Act I, Emperor Julian stands surrounded by his retinue on a landing stage in Constantinople; a multitude of people has gathered on the beach. It awaits the ship that will return Constantius' body to the capital. The plebeians exchange gossip about their new Emperor. Julian, however, listens to the flattery of his advisers and says he hopes he will prove worthy of his high office. A regal procession bearing Constantius' coffin wends its way toward Julian, who lays his hand upon it; some in the crowd notice that he does not make the sign of the cross or bow to the sacred icons. He then amazes some of his counselors by reinstating the heathen gods while vowing that Christianity may be practiced without any hindrance. He himself will lead in the celebration of the rites of Apollo, Dionysus, and Fortuna, which he commences to do at a newly unveiled altar. As Julian follows the ritual, only a few onlookers remain—to his great chagrin.

Scene 2 occurs in the great hall of the Imperial Palace, where Julian declares that he will remain patient with those who do not appreciate his reforms. After he has received a delegation from the eastern territories, Julian's ego grows perceptibly to the point that he tells one of his men to spread the rumor that Alexander the Great has been reincarnated in him. When Ursulus, his adviser, tells Julian that the fawning delegation had been enroute while Constantius was alive and that their flowery tribute was for the Emperor but not necessarily for Julian, all of Julian's protestations that there will be no dissembling in his court are exposed as groundless. He roundly censures Ursulus, who is a Christian; Julian makes it clear that Christians will find it hard to survive under his sway. Then the Emperor retires all his old counselors and puts his creatures in their places.

In Scene 3, which takes place in a narrow street, Eunapius tells old Hecebolius about the strict changes in the palace. Julian is seen with vine-leaves in his hair; he is leading a Dionysian procession on a white ass. Half-naked dancers, musicians, and revelers complete the picture. A Christian citizen takes him to task, but the Emperor brushes him away as deluded.

Scene 4 depicts Julian in the palace after the Dionysian festival. He is quite dejected because the celebration was not as beautiful as it should have been. Hecebolius, ruing his influence in making Julian a Christian, is shown into the Emperor's presence; now Hecebolius has come to the conclusion that the old religion is the correct one. Julian is delighted to have the support of his old teacher. Caesarius, brother of Gregory of Nazianzus, enters to tell Julian that his new court officials are imprisoning good men and persecuting Christians in the Emperor's name, but Julian merely says that such measures are necessary if error is to be rooted out. Caesarius, a Christian, asks to be allowed to leave the capital if Julian's reign is to be characterized in this way. Even the Emperor's bribes cannot buy his loyalty. Julian and Hecebolius plan to journey to Antioch which has not been corrupted by Christianity.

In Act II, Scene 1, Julian harangues his court in Antioch for being so slow to reinstate the old religion. His old friend Gregory of Nazianzus emerges from the crowd to warn Julian about going to battle with God and to plead for the life of Ursulus, his brother, whom Julian's officials have doomed. Gregory tells Julian of severe anti-Christian persecutions in Cappadocia, in response to which he warns Julian that he personally will supervise the razing of the temple of Fortuna in Caesarea. Julian forbids him to do so. Eunapius rushes in to say that Christians have violated the temple of Venus in Antioch. In anger Julian orders all the perpetrators to be killed and makes certain the example is not lost on Gregory. He then departs.

Scene 2 occurs on a street of Antioch where citizens discuss the latest imprisonments. Julian enters as the priest of Apollo while the fickle crowd loudly acclaims him and his gods. Guards with Christian prisoners appear. The procession of prisoners cuts across that of the Apollonians, and from the group of condemned people emerges Agathon, Julian's boyhood friend. He had been the ringleader in the defilement of Venus' temple. Julian gives the prisoners a chance to recant, but they remain faithful to their beliefs and march out to death.

At the temple of Apollo, Scene 3 depicts an earthquake which Julian interprets as a sign of the gods' approbation of his policies. Blind Bishop Maris comes in and calls Julian to repentance, and when Julian merely scoffs, Maris pronounces him apostate, after which another earth tremor demolishes Apollo's shrine. Julian tries to calm his supporters by saying that Apollo destroyed the temple because it had been defiled by a Christian, but they remain pale and terrified.

In Act III, Scene 1, a group of ragged, hungry citizens assembles near the Emperor's home in Antioch and talks of the famine abroad in the land. Julian enters unnoticed by them and listens with exasperation as Heraclius mocks many of the old gods for their impotence. Julian chastises Heraclius, and then a richly dressed Libanius comes in to see Julian. Libanius is now the chief magistrate of Antioch. Libanius' mission is to complain about the imposition of a ruffian as governor of Antioch, but Julian explains that the governor is the city's punishment for countenancing the likes of Gregory and a poet named Apollinaris who foment rebellion. Despite all of Libanius' arguments, Julian remains vindictive toward the city. As a mark of special favor, he commissions Libanius to write a panegyric on Julian's favor toward Antioch and Caesarea.

On the outskirts of the city (Scene 2), Gregory of Nazianzus comforts the suffering Christians who complain that Julian has ordered the Scriptures to be burned. Julian enters at the head of a band of soldiers, sees Gregory, and warns him to get out of town if he values his life, but Gregory will accept martyrdom if it comes. Julian enters into a debate with the Christians and in a rage orders Cyrillus to be scourged until he admits that Julian, not Jesus, is the supreme power.

In Scene 3 Julian is sacrificing at a roadside shrine of Cybele. As he commits great quantities of food to the statue, the poor, starved people mutter about their gnawing hunger. Guards bring in a tortured, bloody Cyrillus who thanks Julian for bringing him closer to God. He tears bits of flayed skin from his wounds, throws them at Julian's feet, and prophesies that Julian will soon be as powerless as his gods. A group of Christian women enters and taunts Julian to his face, one of them cutting her breast with a knife and probing it while she sings hymns. In the face of these examples of staunch faith, the crowd concludes that God is stronger than Julian's deities. Julian had planned to erect a pagan temple over the ruins of the Jewish temple in Jerusalem, but a messenger brings a report that all sorts of supernatural occurrences have prevented any progress in the building. Julian postpones his sacrifice and storms off.

In the next scene Julian and Maximus the Mystic converse in the ruins of Apollo's temple. A dispirited Julian admits that the Galilean seems to murder everything that comes from Augustus (himself). He asks Maximus to predict the outcome of the struggle and is surprised to hear that both Emperor and Galilean will succumb when the right man comes, the one who will be the God-Emperor and the Emperor-God, the true ruler of the third empire.

At the beginning of Act IV, Julian appears at the head of his troops in defense of the eastern frontiers. From his advisers Julian receives conflicting advice about the pursuit of the war; Maximus always encourages him to boldness and excess. Julian is dismayed, however, to learn that one of his most trusted aides, Jovian, has become a Christian. Left alone with Maximus, Julian speaks of his dread of showing himself to his army, although he has circulated a declaration of his own divinity. Maximus tries to bolster his courage by telling of a prophecy that Christ's empire would last only until A.D. 365, two years from then. In that time, Julian declares, he will bring the earth under his sway.

In a hilly, wooded area (Scene 2), Basil of Caesarea and his sister Makrina, dressed as hermits, offer refreshments to the haggard soldiers who pass them. Basil concludes that Julian hopes to disguise his oppressive policies by a spectacular victory in the east. One of the soldiers falls from exhaustion; it is Agathon who has paid for defiling the temple of Venus by being impressed into the army. As he is beaten to get him to his feet, Agathon rejoices in suffering and predicts the downfall of Julian. The Emperor enters; he recognizes Basil and meets Makrina. The three discuss their conflicting theologies, Makrina accusing Julian of realizing that Christ still lives in him. Julian counters by drafting them into service as nurses to his army.

Scene 3 takes place in Julian's camp beyond the Tigris and Euphrates. A letter is brought to Julian from which he learns that the Christians at the rear of his army are using his absence to preach, teach, and pray, thus cementing their gains. Some of his satraps have converted, and formidable Christian leaders have arisen. A Persian defector appears and reveals that Julian's strategy has been discovered by the Persians, who have blockaded the river to forestall the use of his boats in the siege of Ctesiphon. In exchange for riches, the Persian tells Julian of an alternative way by which he may capture the city. Because of the progress of Persian reinforcements, Julian must make his bold move within three days. At the Persian's urging, Julian decides to burn his boats rather than leave behind a large force to guard them. While some of his people counsel caution, Maximus tells him that he will be invulnerable. Some Christian soldiers come into Julian's view beating their breasts and lamenting wildly because Julian has tricked them into honoring his statue as if it were a god; they desert his army. In the flames of his boats, Julian sees the funeral pyre of the old religion and Christianity; he is certain that the third empire has been born and that he is its ruler. Word is brought to him that the Persian defector, who was a spy, has disappeared. Julian orders the fire to be extinguished, but it is too late. Retreat is thus cut off; battle lies ahead.

Act V, Scene 1 occurs outside the Emperor's tent on a bare desert. The military situation is dangerous. The Persians have set the very grass afire, making it impossible for the Roman to progress until the ground cools. Retreat is impossible because the boats have been burned. A war council is being conducted inside Julian's tent, out of which comes Nevita wondering whether Julian's mind is impaired. Oribases says that the night before Julian was prevented from suicide. Julian emerges and announces that the army will try to move northward; some of his men had counted on moving westward—to retreat, that is. Julian's troubled mind cannot escape from thoughts of Christian duplicity. He consults Maximus for omens to support his plans, but for once Maximus reports that the auguries have said nothing, concluding that everything rests on Julian alone. Julian gives the order to break camp.

In Scene 2 soldiers gossip about the situation as Agathon appears with a spear with which he intends to kill the beast with seven heads. The soldiers lead him away. Julian and Maximus enter talking about the battle, the decisive one, that is about to be enjoined. Julian is morose because he feels that the Galilean may have vanquished him. A friend brings word that the fighting has already started, and Julian rushes off to don his armor.

The battle rages in Scene 3. Julian runs in, his horse having been killed beneath him. By now his mind is confused by dreams, visions, and a sense of defeat. The battle is ranged about the stage, and Julian jumps into the fray. Agathon appears with his spear, which he throws; it finds its mark in the Emperor's side. When Julian falls, Agathon identifies it as the spear that pierced Christ's side at Golgotha. Julian tries to rise but falls back saying, "Thou hast conquered, Galilean!" As Julian is carried off, Jovian, a Christian, rallies the troops and beats back the Persians.

In Scene 4 Makrina tends to the wounds of the unconscious Julian. When the Emperor awakens, he is told that victory has been won over the Persians. In his frenzy to crush the Persians, Julian moves about on his bed, disturbs his wound, and starts to bleed profusely. When he hears that he was wounded at a place called Phrygia, he remembers Maximus' prophecy that he would fall there; thus, Julian resigns himself to death. Basil comes in to comfort him. As his mind starts to wander, Julian sees visions of the beautiful kingdom. With his last breath, he asks why Helios has betrayed him. So Julian dies, not a tragic figure because recognition of his error is denied him. As Basil tries to make sense of all that has happened, he sees Julian's apostasy as a God-given force that impelled Christians to unite to advance the kingdom. Julian would have been pleased, Basil thinks, to realize that he had changed the course of history.

Structural analysis: As Ibsen's most intellectual play, the Thought of *Emperor and Galilean* is its most provocative element. Not only is the play filled with nuances descriptive of the tenets of various Christian sects and heresies, but also it shows familiarity with ancient mystery religions as well. Most of the characters are one-dimensional and merely representative of theological postures. Only Julian and Maximus stand out in full relief. Ibsen's interest in the philosophies of Nietzsche* and Georg Wilhelm Friedrich Hegel* is clearly evident. In his early years, Julian is an Apollonian—in the Nietzschean sense; after his apostasy he becomes Dionysian. The third empire is the Hegelian synthesis of the conflict between Christianity (thesis) and paganism (antithesis).

The drama is unified by Character in that it depicts a completed change in the protagonist who passes from a sort of humanistic Christianity to paganism to self-deification in his pursuit of the ideal. Yet even in his downfall and death, Julian does not experience a moment of truth in which he recognizes his mistakes. He dies a defeated and uncomprehending man. Tragic stature is thus denied him, at least in the Aristotelian sense.

References: Arestad, Sverre. "Ibsen's Concept of Tragedy," *PMLA*, 74, 3 (1959), 288-9; Johnston, Brian. "The Mythic Foundation of Ibsen's Realism," *Comparative Drama*, 3 (1969), 27-41.

AN ENEMY OF THE PEOPLE: A five-act Realistic serious drama.
Composition: Perhaps planned as early as 1881; finished on June 20, 1882; published on November 28, 1882.

Stage history:

Jan. 13, 1883	Christiania Theatre* (27 perfs.)
Jan. 24, 1883	Norwegian Theatre, Bergen*
Feb. 1883	Stadttheater, Gothenburg
Feb. 1883	Helsinki
Mar. 1883	Royal Theatre, Stockholm (13)
Mar. 4, 1883	Royal Theatre, Copenhagen (9) pro. Edvard Fallesen*
1884	Royal Theatre, Stockholm (1)

Mar. 5, 1887   Ostend Theater, Berlin (1)
    May 1888   Hoftheater, dir. Georg II, Duke of Saxe-Meiningen*
        1888   Bern
        1888   Royal Theatre, Stockholm (1)
Sept. 7, 1889   Residenz Theater, Munich
Aug. 16, 1890   Lessing Theater, Berlin
Oct. 23, 1890   Hoftheater, Vienna
Apr. 16, 1891   Burgtheater, Vienna
        1891   Hoftheater, Munich
        1891   Korsh Theatre, Moscow
        1893   Burgtheater, Vienna
Apr. 14, 1893   Teatro de Novedads, Barcelona
June 14, 1893   Haymarket Theatre, London (7), Herbert Beerbohm Tree* as Dr.
                 Stockmann
July 20, 1894   Haymarket Theatre, London (1), Herbert Beerbohm Tree as Dr.
                 Stockmann
 Mar. 8, 1895   Grand Opera House, Chicago, Herbert Beerbohm Tree as Dr.
                 Stockmann
 May 6, 1895   Hoftheater, Braunschweig
June 14, 1895   Abbey's Theatre, New York, Herbert Beerbohm Tree as
                 Dr. Stockmann
 Mar. 5, 1896   Theatro de la Comedia, Madrid
Sept. 2, 1899   National Theatre, Christiania*
Oct. 24, 1900   Art Theatre, Moscow, Konstantin Stanislavsky* as Dr. Stockmann
May 12, 1901   Deutsches Theater, Berlin
 Jan. 1, 1905   Berkeley Lyceum Theatre, New York, Charles James as
                 Dr. Stockmann
Apr. 30, 1909   His Majesty's Theatre, London, Herbert Beerbohm Tree as
                 Dr. Stockmann
Mar. 31, 1918   Hoftheater, Braunschweig
June 20, 1921   Comédie Française, Paris
 Oct. 3, 1927   Hampden's Theatre, New York (113), Walter Hampden* as Dr.
                 Stockmann
Mar. 26, 1928   Wyndham's Theatre, London, Rupert Harvey as Dr. Stockmann
 Nov. 5, 1928   Hampden's Theatre, New York (16), Walter Hampden as
                 Dr. Stockmann
 Oct. 1, 1934   Embassy Theatre, London, Ronald Adam as Dr. Stockmann
Feb. 15, 1937   Hudson Theatre, New York (16), Walter Hampden as
                 Dr. Stockmann
Feb. 21, 1939   Old Vic, London, Roger Livesey as Dr. Stockmann
Dec. 28, 1950   Broadhurst Theatre, New York (36), Fredric March* as
                 Dr. Stockmann
Mar. 11, 1971   Vivian Beaumont Theatre, New York (54), Stephen Elliott as
                 Dr. Stockmann
Apr. 18, 1975   Aldwych Theatre, London, pro. Compagnia di Prosa Tina
                 Buazelli

Synopsis: The first two acts take place in the living room of Dr. Thomas
Stockmann, resident physician of the city baths of a coastal town of

southern Norway. Although a cluttered dining-room table suggests that a meal has been finished, Mrs. Katherine Stockmann is passing food to Billing, an editorial assistant at the local newspaper, the *People's Herald*. Hovstad the editor is expected, but a knock at the door precedes not his entrance but that of Peter Stockmann, the mayor and Thomas' brother. He is an overly fastidious, mildly carping man. Hovstad's arrival creates a tense situation because the mayor does not approve of the newspaper's liberal leaning. Nevertheless, in orotund words he praises the town's toleration of all views, a magnanimity produced by the citizens' joint pride in their handsome spa facilities. The mayor attributes the town's resuscitated economy to the opening of the baths, the revenues of which are expected to grow substantially. Hovstad says that he has come to talk to the doctor about an article on the baths that he had submitted to the *People's Herald*. When Hovstad asserts that Doctor Stockmann first conceived of the idea of municipal baths, the mayor bridles and claims the credit for himself. The editor admits that the practical impetus did, in fact, originate with the mayor. Ever caviling, the mayor condemns his brother as merely a man of ideas and praises himself as a man of action. Seeing that her brother-in-law and the editor are heading towards an argument, Mrs. Stockmann steers Hovstad toward the dining table while she calms the mayor's ruffled pride. Thomas, who has been walking with his two sons, has brought Captain Horster home with him. He directs his guest and the children toward the dining table and then greets his brother profusely. Thomas' spirits are soaring with energy and optimism, and his every word is an occasion for misunderstanding and misinterpretation by his brother. Thomas explains his positive view of life by remembering his years in a village of the far north; life in this southern town is quite exciting by comparison. Thomas interrupts his effusions by asking if the mail has come. Hearing that it has not, Thomas praises his newly acquired solvency by admiring the roast beef, the new tablecloth, and the new lampshade, luxuries that he would not be enjoying if the position at the baths had not materialized. He further maintains that entertaining his friends, friends such as Hovstad, is a vital necessity. Peter mentions the article about which Hovstad has come, but Thomas dismisses that article as irrelevant in view of a possible new development. Seeing that Thomas is reluctant to explain his statement, Peter berates him for his deep-seated desire to go his way alone and warns that individualism is not tolerated in a well-ordered society in which the one must be subordinated to the whole. Having said this, the mayor pompously leaves the house. Stockmann is more concerned that the post has not come than by his brother's abrasive behavior.

When his other guests come in from the dining room, Thomas becomes the genial host and offers everyone hot drinks and cigars. For the first time, Horster, a sea captain, is drawn into conversation. He is not concerned that his next week's sailing will cause him to miss the local elections since he takes no interest in public affairs. The liberal Billing and Hovstad are particularly distressed by his stance. When Hovstad tells Thomas that he plans to print his article on the baths, the doctor says that he must wait. The Stockmanns' daughter Petra comes in with an armful of books and a letter for her father, who snatches it from her hand and rushes into the study to read it. In the conversation that ensues, Petra emerges as a hardworking teacher who yearns for the freedom to teach truth as she sees it, not as the establishment requires. Thomas excitedly enters and reveals that the water of the baths is tainted because of pollution and represents a serious hazard to health. He has sent samples of the water to a laboratory which has confirmed his suspicions, the knowledge of which will require the whole water system to be dug up and pipes relaid. He had originally protested about the way in which the system had been installed, but no one had listened. Now everyone will hear and proclaim him a hero for detecting the problem. He will immediately dispatch a report to the board of directors of the baths. Hovstad asks and receives permission to run the story in his newspaper. In his naiveté Thomas expects that the city fathers will congratulate him for his vigilance, a conclusion which his family and liberal friends share. The act ends with laughter and celebration of his great accomplishment.

Thomas' receipt of his brother's response to his report marks the commencement of Act II: the mayor has returned the manuscript with a note that he will visit Thomas at noon. The doctor is convinced that his brother will wish to take the credit for finding the pestilence in the baths. Katherine's father, Morten Kiil, enters to ask if the story about the spa is true; when Thomas corroborates it, the older man concludes that it is an elaborate trick on the mayor and council. Since he had been dismissed as old-fashioned by the city fathers, Kiil is delighted that Stockmann may manage to discomfit them. He is so delighted in fact that he promises the doctor a large sum of money if he is successful. Before Thomas can convince Kiil that his charge is serious, Hovstad enters and old Kiil departs. Hovstad has come to see the situation at the baths as merely another example of the corruption of the wealthy establishment of the town; he has decided, therefore, to use his newspaper and the issue of the polluted water as a means of exposing the ruling class as immoral opportunists. Committed to truth, Thomas accepts Hovstad's position, but he is nonetheless shocked by imagining the repercussions such a course would involve. Then Aslaksen the printer comes in to show his support of Thomas and to propose arranging a demonstration by small businessmen as well as a small public tribute to the doctor. Thomas graciously accepts Aslaksen's support; then the printer leaves. Hovstad the radical questions Aslaksen's motives and ignores his urging of moderation. Thomas insists that Hovstad make no move until the doctor has consulted the mayor; the editor plans to have an editorial on hand—just in case. If Peter Stockmann refuses to act on Stockmann's advice, then Hovstad will be free to print the report on the water in its entirety. Hovstad leaves with the manuscript in his hand.

Petra and Katherine enter and learn from a gleeful Thomas that his position has won the support of the solid majority. The women join him in his delight but are cut short by the appearance of the mayor, who is reluctant to talk business until the women exit. Peter wants to know if his brother plans to submit the report to the directors as an official recommendation. Thomas says that this is his plan because expedition is necessary. Peter demurs because of the cost of making the required repairs over a period of two years; the loss of revenue and the attendant bad publicity would allow other spas to benefit from the closure, thereby causing inevitable financial ruin to the town. The mayor urges the doctor to treat the water as it stands; then in time the directors will find a way of alleviating the contamination completely. Thomas brands this suggestion as nothing but trickery and asserts that the mayor's intransigence is the result of his inability to admit that he had erred in recommending the faulty manner of constructing the spa. At any rate, the mayor insists that the matter receive no publicity; the directors will hold private discussions. Thomas answers that the newspaper and others already know about the problem, and soon everyone will be made aware. Seeing the full import of this revelation, Peter obliquely tells his brother that Thomas' constantly precipitate behavior will have dire consequences for him and his family. He must repudiate his claims and publicly avow his confidence in the directors. Thomas hotly asserts his right to tell the truth about anything, but Peter forbids him to do so about the baths. When Thomas asks what consequences will follow if he refuses, the mayor says that Thomas will lose his position at the baths and be recognized as an enemy of society. Having delivered his ultimatum, Peter departs. The Stockmann women, first listening at the keyhole and then entering the room near the end of the confrontation, address Thomas individually, Katherine urging caution and Petra counseling immediate action. Katherine's appeal for him to consider his family steels Thomas' resolution to stand up for the truth. He dashes into his study flinging defiance to the establishment as the act ends.

The locale of Act III is the office of the *People's Herald*. Billing comes in to remark to Hovstad the daring of Stockmann's article. Billing sees in the situation the seeds of revolution, and Hovstad delights in noting that Mayor Stockmann will suffer no matter what course of action he follows. If he gives in to the doctor, the wealthy investors in the spa will desert him; if he remains obdurate, he will lose the support of the small businessmen and homeowners led by Aslaksen. The situation is ripe for radical opportunism. Thomas enters and tells Hovstad to start his presses; the mayor has refused to take action. Thomas, fired up to do battle, says he has four or five additional, equally damning pieces for publication. Aslaksen agrees that the article should be published and that it will receive his personal attention. When Thomas threatens to assault his enemies by a new article each day, the moderate Aslaksen becomes alarmed, but the revolutionary Hovstad and Billing cheer the doctor, who plans to decontaminate the whole society, not just the baths. Carried away by his own rhetoric and the manipulative support of the radicals, Thomas leaves. Aslaksen tries once again to convince Hovstad and Billing that their goals would be better served by moderation than by radical deeds, but he is not successful. Billing leaves to write a scalding article as Petra enters to tell Hovstad that she cannot translate an English story for him because it is sentimental and untrue. Hovstad tells her that Billing planned to use such a simplistic story as a means of duping the public into believing that the other views expressed in the *Herald* are equally acceptable. The conversation turns to the baths issue, and Hovstad lets slip that his involvement with Thomas stems from his romantic interest in Petra. She says that she will never trust him again and leaves. Aslaksen nervously reports that the mayor has called.

Peter has come to reclaim Thomas' manuscript, but at that moment Aslaksen comes in from the pressroom to fetch it. Peter forestalls Aslaksen by noting that Thomas' improvements would cost a great deal of money, the expenditure of which would result in raised taxes harming mainly the poor people. As head of the small businessmen and homeowners' group, Aslaksen sees the danger of supporting the doctor. Although he has been relatively silent, Hovstad also realizes how this situation would affect the workers. The mayor then suggests that Hovstad print his own statement outlining stopgap measures rather than his brother's. With the announcement that Thomas is approaching, the mayor slips into an adjoining room. Thomas has returned to see the proofs of his article but is not unduly surprised to learn that the article has not yet been printed. As he leaves, he asks Hovstad to quash any sort of laudatory celebration that may be planned for him once the working classes read his article. Hovstad starts to tell Thomas the truth, but before he can begin, Katherine enters to renew her plea that Thomas consider his family before releasing his article. The doctor maintains that he will not lose his position at the baths because he is supported by the solid majority, and as he gloats in his picture of himself as the savior of society, he sees the mayor's official hat on a chair. He opens the door leading to the next room and invites his embarrassed brother to join them. Thomas has so convinced himself of his ultimate success that he assumes that he can dismiss the mayor from office with the aid of Hovstad and Aslaksen. The printer and the editor tell Thomas that they will not support him. Realizing the reversal of his fortunes, Thomas surrenders the official hat to his brother as the radicals desert him. Hovstad refuses to print the doctor's article while accepting the mayor's. Aslaksen refuses to issue the doctor's article as a pamphlet. Thomas then declares that he will read his report at a mass meeting, but the mayor retorts that no one will rent him a hall. Katherine is so disgusted by the behavior of these men that for the first time she sides with her husband regardless of the consequences. Thomas threatens to shout his message from the streetcorners accompanied by his children. The Stockmanns exit determined and united in their efforts to cleanse society.

Act IV is located in a great room of Horster's house where a large group of townspeople has gathered to hear Doctor Stockmann denounce his brother, although he does not have the support of the *People's Herald*. Horster escorts the Stockmann family to chairs near the door. Silently, the mayor enters and takes a place by the wall; then the doctor makes his entrance as some of the people hiss. As Thomas moves to begin the meeting, Aslaksen insists that a chairman be elected. Peter also suggests the naming of a moderator, a sentiment echoed by the crowd. Aslaksen nominates Peter as chairman, but the mayor declines in favor of Aslaksen, who is elected by acclamation. As he takes the chair, the printer urges Thomas to use moderation in his remarks. Peter then moves that his brother not be allowed to discuss the sanitary conditions of the baths as to do so would run counter to the interests of the town. He is upheld in this motion. Then Peter explains that he has already presented a plan to remedy the situation at the baths and that to follow the doctor's advice would cost a great sum of money that would have to be recouped in the form of taxes on the working classes. Then Aslaksen seconds Peter's motion and adds that Thomas' real motive is to create a social revolution rather than purify the baths. Hovstad rises to say that he cannot support Thomas because he seems at odds with the wishes of the *Herald's* readers. Aslaksen calls for a vote, but Thomas agrees not to talk about the baths. He finally wins the floor. He starts by saying that his basic right to free speech is not at issue, but his discovery that their lives are polluted and their community founded on lies is the real cause of concern. Believing that his duty is to do what is best for his home town, Thomas accuses the local authorities of depredating the town, the worst culprit being his own brother. He concludes that corrupt officials are not the greatest enemies of society, but that it is the solid majority. Pandemonium breaks out in the room.

The chairman calls for order, while Hovstad and Billing talk loudly at the same time. Then order is reestablished. Aslaksen asks Thomas to withdraw his comments, but the doctor refuses and compounds his error by proclaiming that the majority is never right largely because it is composed of the most stupid citizens. Again the audience tries to shout him down. Then Thomas maintains that the minority is always right, that he is fighting for those individuals who advance society's goals by speaking the truth in defiance of the majority. He favors new truths over old, established ones. Then Thomas repudiates Hovstad's tenet that the ill-educated, uninformed multitudes have the right to govern "the few spiritually accomplished personalities." Once again the room erupts as the crowd voices its displeasure. He proves the relative value of the crowd and the elite by comparing them with purebred and hybrid animals, the purebred being meaty and productive and the hybrid being scrawny and relatively useless. Then he extends the analogy to the street cur and the pampered, pedigreed poodle. Hovstad in the *Herald*, he says, asserts that the mongrels are the core of society. The common strain is traceable in the upper classes too, as witnessed by his brother Peter whose ideas are those of his social betters. Finally, Thomas equates broadmindedness with morality. Someone moves that Thomas be ruled out of order, but the doctor threatens to speak on streetcorners and to write articles for out-of-town newspapers. He then says that he would rather destroy his town than allow it to grow rich on lies. Hovstad starts the cry that is soon taken up by the people: Stockmann is a public enemy. Aslaksen offers a resolution to that effect; it is quickly adopted. As a secret ballot is prepared, Morten Kiil asks Thomas if he intends to assert publicly that his tannery is a major source of contamination of the water supply. Hearing Thomas' affirmative answer, Kiil exits muttering a threat. A man upbraids Horster for making his house available to Stockmann and threatens to get even with him; the man is the owner of Horster's ship. Aslaksen announces a unanimous vote in favor of proclaiming Thomas an enemy of the people. The meeting is adjourned. Thomas says that he will not be Christlike and forgiving, that these people will hear from him. As the Stockmanns leave the hall, cries of "Enemy! Enemy!" are heard. The act ends.

Act V is set in Thomas' study, strewn with rocks and broken window panes. The glazier has been summoned, but he reports that he may be unable to stop by. Katherine delivers a letter to Thomas that turns out to be their eviction notice. Thomas is undaunted by the news because he intends to take his family to America. His wife asks if leaving town will really solve the problem, and Thomas admits that the common herd is much the same everywhere. Petra enters and reports that she has lost her position as schoolmistress. Captain Horster drops by to see how the family is faring and to report that he has lost his captain's berth. The next caller is the mayor, at whose entry the women and Horster withdraw to an inner room. Peter delivers the notice of Thomas' dismissal from his position at the baths. He further states that the homeowners' group is circulating a resolution urging all citizens to dispense with Thomas' medical services. Peter counsels Thomas to leave for a few months and then to reinstate himself by offering the town an apology. The mayor almost guarantees that the doctor can take up his old job if he signs a repudiation of his claims. When Thomas vehemently refuses to comply, Peter accuses him of arrogantly basing his stubbornness on his expectations from Morten Kiil's will. This is news to Thomas, who feels greatly relieved that his wife and children will be provided for. Peter cautions that Kiil may alter his will, but Thomas replies that the old man has been supportive in his war against the town. The mayor sees all of Stockmann's actions as services rendered for a portion of Kiil's fortune. He revokes the option of Thomas' written apology and eventual reinstatement as he exits. By then Kiil has arrived at the house and desires to speak with the doctor.

The elder man produces a sheaf of papers which turns out to be as many shares in the baths as Kiil could purchase. His conscience aches that people may know that his tannery has been poisoning the water supply; he has therefore used Katherine's inheritance for the purchase of stock in the baths. If Thomas continues his campaign to shut down the spa, he will make the stocks worthless and disinherit his wife and children. The inheritance is to be the price of Thomas' silence. The doctor now faces a true dilemma, one that causes him to waver. Kiil increases the pressure by saying that Thomas must decide by two o'clock; if he does not comply, the stocks will be willed to charity and Katherine will get nothing. Hovstad and Aslaksen enter as Kiil leaves.

Peremptorily Thomas asks the reasons for their visit. His old allies believe that Thomas has created the panic just so he could acquire a controlling stock of the baths; they wish he had confided in them and made use of their assistance. Thomas is dumbfounded. They continue by offering him the use of the *Herald* to continue his attack; they also guarantee the cooperation of the homeowners' association and small businessmen. All they ask in exchange is that Thomas finance the *People's Herald*. If he does not cooperate, they will use their influence to put the worst possible construction on his actions and destroy him entirely. Thomas, enraged, drives them from his house with an umbrella. The doctor then writes "no" three times on a visiting card and tells Petra to deliver it to her grandfather. He has made his decision to remain in town (Horster offers a place to live) and face the solid majority. His boys enter having had a fight with other boys; Petra and Thomas will teach them at home in the company of other poor children. Thomas is exuberant because he has made another discovery: the strongest man is the one who stands most alone. The family is united as it braves the world. The curtain falls.

Structural analysis: This drama features a complex plot; that is, the incidents are arranged causally and include a major reversal:

Stockmann discovers that the bath waters are polluted;

(as a result of which)

Stockmann takes steps to publicize his discovery in the expectation of being viewed as a public benefactor;

(as a result of which)

Stockmann discovers that he will be punished by his brother and the directors if he follows through;

(as a result of which)

Stockmann decides to air his views because he is convinced that the people will support him against the materialists;

(as a result of which)

Stockmann discovers that Hovstad and Aslaksen withdraw their support of him;

(as a result of which)

Stockmann holds a public meeting to discuss his views;

(as a result of which)

Stockmann discovers that he is branded an enemy of the people rather than a savior of the people [REVERSAL];

(as a result of which)

Stockmann decides to fight the misguided majority;

(as a result of which)

Stockmann discovers that his wife's inheritance depends on his silence; he will be extorted by Hovstad and Aslaksen; his livelihood is threatened; his family is in physical danger;

(as a result of which)

Stockmann refuses to comply with Kiil's ultimatum and decides to remain and fight the establishment.

Thomas Stockmann is a Kierkegaardian idealist in his decision that no man is stronger than when he stands alone; he is somewhat reminiscent of Brand* in his dogged determination to uphold his principles, whatever the consequences to himself and his family.

References: Johnston, Brian. "The Poetry of *An Enemy of the People*," *Scandinavia*, 18 (1979), 109-22; Rönning, Helge. "Individualism and the Liberal Dilemma: Notes toward a Sociological Interpretation of *An Enemy of the People* by Henrik Ibsen," *Ibsen Aarbok*, 3 (1975-76), 101-21.

ENGESTRÖM, LARS VON: A Pole of Swedish ancestry, Engeström published the first entire book on Ibsen: *Henryk Ibsen, Poeta Norwegski.* Warsaw: n.p., 1875.

ENGLUND, HILDA: When Hilda Englund attempted to portray Helene Alving* in New York in 1933, she committed the gravest fault in acting: "Hilda Englund, who has had considerable experience in the works of the master, found difficulty in adapting her voice to the auditorium, with the consequent distraction from her reading."

Reference: *New York Times*, May 24, 1933, p. 24, col. 5.

ENGSTRAND, JACOB (*Ghosts*): Engstrand is the supposed father of Regine Engstrand,* who in the end joins him in establishing a home for sailors. By trade he is a carpenter who was employed in building the orphanage. His principal function is to be the means of destroying the orphanage, which was burned by a fire resulting from sparks from his pipe.

ENGSTRAND, REGINE (*Ghosts*): The natural child of Captain Alving and his maid, Regine has lived as the dutiful ward of Helene Alving,* the experience of which has considerably raised her social expectations. She interprets Oswald Alving's* interest in her as a means of rising socially, but when Regine discovers that he wants her as a nurse and a means of suicide, Regine leaves him flat and joins her stepfather in the management of a sailors' home.

ERIC OF HAEGGE (*The Feast at Solhoug*): As a friend of Margit* and Bengt Gauteson,* Eric proposes that Signe* should marry Knut Gjaesling.* Eric is Knut's confidant.

ERVINE, ST. JOHN (1883-1971): St. John Ervine, Irish man of letters, dramatist, and theatre manager, expressed his evaluation of Ibsen's cultural contributions in a clever analogy:

Great institutions do not die easily, and the theatre had been great. Just as it was on the point of expiring, a poet who had turned sociologist, Henrik Ibsen, came and restored its mind to activity. Indeed, he overworked its mind. He forgot that the creature had been half-starved for nearly a century, and he set himself to improving its mind before he had improved its body. It is doubtful whether he ever thought of its body at all. He filled its head with arguments and taught it to ask questions and to discuss policies and points of view, but he did not fill its stomach with nourishing meat. The result was that the theatre, except in France, was thrown into a fever of the mind, and became slightly neurotic. In France, it remained in a fever of the body, and became nauseous. (Ervine, pp. 113-4.)

Reference: Ervine, St. John. *The Organised Theatre: A Plea in Civics.* New York: Macmillan, 1924.

EUNAPIUS (*Emperor and Galilean*): A hairdresser.

EUSEBIA (*Emperor and Galilean*): Empress of Rome, wife of Constantius.*

EUTHERIUS (*Emperor and Galilean*): Julian's* chamberlain.

EVANS, EDITH (1888-1976): That the finest English actress of the current generation should have had such limited experience with Ibsen's dramas is regrettable. Under the direction of Barry Jackson, Edith Evans appeared as Rebecca West* at London's Kingsway Theatre, commencing on September 30, 1926, with Charles Carson* as Johannes Rosmer.* Jackson sought stark Naturalism in the production, but critic Ivor Brown observed that Evans "kept wrenching the play up to a different theatrical level" (Forbes, p. 125). George Bernard Shaw* saw the production and wrote: "Rebecca very memorable; but the rest mostly ill chosen" (Forbes, p. 125).

Near the end of her illustrious career, the mature actress appeared as Anne Marie,* the Helmers'* nurse, in the film of *A Doll's House,* which starred Claire Bloom* and Ralph Richardson.*

Reference: Forbes, Bryan. *Dame Edith Evans: Ned's Girl.* Boston: Little, Brown and Company, 1977.

EVANS, MAURICE (1901-   ): Shakespearean actor Maurice Evans' only Ibsenian role was that of Hjalmar Ekdal* in *The Wild Duck** in 1951. Brooks Atkinson thought that Evans resorted to too much trickery "in an elaborate, exterior and expansive style that never touches the soul of the character" (*New York Times*, Dec. 27, 1951, p. 17, cols. 1-2).

Reference: Who's Who in the Theatre, 16th ed., pp. 590-1.

F

FALK (*Love's Comedy*): As a young author and the protagonist of the drama, Falk is the principal spokesman for the view of love and marriage that shocked Ibsen's contemporaries: that marriage is a certain means of killing love. Unfortunately for him, Falk convinces Svanhild Halm* of the truth of his position, so she decides to marry another man rather than face the possibility of Falk's love of her ending. Falk himself faces the situation romantically and joins a group of students in a mountain hike.

FALLESEN, EDVARD (1817-94): As head of the Royal Theatre, Copenhagen, Edvard Fallesen fostered Ibsen's Scandinavian reputation by presenting his dramas.
Reference: Dansk Biografisk Leksikon, VI, 574-6.

FARMER AT HAEGSTAG (*Peer Gynt*): The father of Ingrid,* the bride carried off by Peer Gynt* at her wedding feast.

FARR, FLORENCE (1860-1917): Playing Rebecca West* to Frank Benson's* Johannes Rosmer* in London in 1891, Florence Farr did not generate much critical response. The reviewers chose to spend their vituperation on Ibsen instead.
Reference: Who Was Who in the Theatre, II, 803.

FARRAND, JANE (1925-   ): Few actresses have had the opportunity to play both sisters in *John Gabriel Borkman.* Jane Farrand portrayed Ella Rentheim* in New York in 1977 and Gunhild Borkman* in New York in 1980.
Reference: Who's Who in the Theatre, 17th ed. I, 216.

A FAT GENTLEMAN (*The Wild Duck*): One of the guests at Haakon Werle's* dinner party; a chamberlain.

FAWCETT, GEORGE (1860-1939): For one performance in New York in
1891, George Fawcett played Karsten Bernick* in a production of *The
Pillars of Society.** He had no subsequent experience in Ibsen's plays.
Reference: Briscoe, Johnson. *The Actors' Birthday Book*, 3d ser. New York:
     Moffat, Yard and Company, 1909.

THE FEAST AT SOLHOUG: A three-act Romantic serious drama.
Composition: Written in the summer of 1855; published in 1856; revised
and reissued in 1883.
Stage history:

Jan. 2, 1856	Norwegian Theatre, Bergen* (6 perfs.), dir. Henrik Ibsen
Mar. 13, 1856	Norwegian Theatre, Christiania* (5)
May 1856	Trondhjem, dir. Henrik Ibsen
Jan. 6, 1857	Christiania Theatre* (3)
Nov. 4, 1857	Royal Theatre, Stockholm
Nov. 12, 1861	Christiania Theatre (3)
1861	Royal Theatre, Copenhagen
May 17, 1866	Christiania Theatre
1886	Dagmars Theatre, Copenhagen
1889	Norwegian Theatre, Bergen
Nov. 22, 1891	Burgtheater, Vienna
Feb. 3, 1895	Alexandra Theatre, St. Petersburg, Maria G. Savina* as Margit
Apr. 18, 1897	Deutsches Theater, Munich
Dec. 6, 1897	Christiania Theatre (22), Johanne Dybwad* as Signe
Sep. 12, 1924	Kammerspiele, Munich

Synopsis: The scene is a medieval hall named Solhoug. A rugged fjord is
seen through doors that open onto a gallery. The master of the hall, Bengt
Gauteson, and his wife Margit are speaking with Eric of Haegge, a friend
who has proposed the marriage of Knut Gjaesling to Margit's younger sister
Signe. Knut is also present and becomes agitated when Margit suggests that
in view of his reputation as a carouser, it may be difficult to secure Signe's
favor. Eric suggests that a faithful wife will settle Knut's irregular habits,
but Knut says that he has vowed to marry Signe within the year. This he
intends to do with or without their approval. Margit capitulates enough to
stipulate that he may marry Signe within the year if he mends his manners
and adopts a regular style of life. Reluctantly, Knut agrees to Margit's
conditions, and in return she invites him to come to the feast in celebration
of her third wedding anniversary. Knut then informs Margit and Bengt that
he has come to Solhoug to meet Margit's kinsman Gudmund Alfson. She is
surprised at this news because she thought Gudmund was in Bergen. In view
of Eric's and Knut's whispered comments, Gudmund is nearer than she
thinks. At that point Knut withdraws with his retinue to prepare for the
feast.
    When Bengt speaks affectionately of their years of marriage, Margit
barely manages to conceal her bitterness at the remembrance. Bengt leaves

to attend to details of the banquet, and Margit is left alone to soliloquize about her revulsion at the man she married. At age twenty-three she feels doomed to a lifetime of boredom with Bengt. Almost compulsively Margit starts to sing a song about the bride of the Mountain King, a song that Gudmund had sung in the hall of her father. It is clear that the source of her frustration is her unrequited love of Gudmund.

Signe enters with the news that Gudmund is coming to Solhoug, which surprises Margit, who asks for details. In a lyrical description of how she heard Gudmund's song ring out magically across the fjords that morning as she rode to church, Signe is convinced that Gudmund is in the vicinity. She will therefore polish his harp so that it is ready to accompany his songs to delight Margit's heart. Signe is certain that Gudmund's presence would cure Margit of her chronic melancholia; her elder sister suggests that a suitor may be coming to claim Signe's hand, but the girl says that she is too young and happy for love.

Bengt enters and says there is no possibility that they will be visited by Gudmund. At that moment, Gudmund appears in the distance. A great bustle ensues as servants are dispatched to prepare things for Gudmund's visit, his first in seven years. Margit is again left alone. She muses about fortune that could change a penniless lad into a rich man with a squire and armed escort. If he has come to observe her grief over him, Margit decides, he will be disappointed. She commands her servants to dress her in her finest clothes and jewels so that she can present her best appearance to Gudmund.

Gudmund enters with Bengt, who delights in playing the host. Gudmund particularly wants to know if Margit is happy. Even Bengt has noticed that she seemed happier before she became his wife, which confirms Gudmund's suspicions. Margit, splendidly appareled, enters and greets Gudmund as if she hardly recognizes him. Through the ensuing conversation, she makes every effort to seem particularly disinterested in his presence. She is in command of the situation until Bengt announces his intention of withdrawing; Margit clearly does not want to be left alone with Gudmund, who inquires of Signe and seems incapable of speaking of anything but her. They descend to the charade of describing their lives in the most glowing terms, which leads to a dropping of all pretense. Gudmund tells Margit that he is now an outlaw; his very life is imperiled. He has come to Solhoug expecting to be harbored, but Margit's once-friendly attitude toward him has changed. He is determined to leave her to her happy, opulent life. At last she greets him honestly and reveals that she sacrificed youthful happiness for the riches that attended Bengt Gauteson's wife. She married because Gudmund stayed away so long, but her yearning for his return has carried her through each dull day. Margit admits that she never loved her bumbling husband. Now, finally, both have heard the truth. Gudmund explains that he is being pursued by the chancellor, whom he had overheard in a romantic liaison with the queen-to-be whom he was escorting to Norway. When he surprised the lovers, they fled, leaving behind a phial of poison that was intended for the king. Now it is vital that the chancellor destroy Gudmund lest his treason be unearthed. After telling this story, Gudmund's thoughts return to Signe. He goes out to greet her, leaving Margit alone.

Margit speaks lovingly to herself of Gudmund, happy in the recollection of the goblet from which they had drunk when he first went away. For the first time, she notices that the day is sunny and that the weather has not been so fine for three years. Signe enters with Gudmund, happy in their reunion. He had left her as a little girl and now he sees her as a hulder,* an enchantress. He has fallen in love with her. Signe takes down Gudmund's harp, and as his song begins, the guests start to arrive for the feast. Gudmund's song rouses feelings of love in the hearts of both Margit and Signe. Then the celebration starts in earnest.

Act II is set in a copse beyond Solhoug. With sounds of the feast emanating from the hall, Eric and Knut appear, talking animatedly about Knut's problem. He is the king's sheriff and ought to apprehend Gudmund the outlaw, but he dares not to do so if he is to win Signe's hand. Tonight their former friendship will protect Gudmund, who tomorrow must protect himself.

Signe and Gudmund enter and soon declare their mutual love. Signe wanders off when Gudmund goes in to tell Margit of their commitment. Meanwhile, Margit appears and expresses her disappointment that Gudmund is not inside celebrating with the others. She is unable to dismiss the phial of poison from her thoughts, which represents a way to free herself of Bengt, but she must be sure of Gudmund's intentions. He comes out of the house at that point and is soon agitated by Margit's thinly veiled romantic talk. Her passion for Gudmund has made her consider dire deeds, but, unlike the foreign princess he told her about, she has not been sufficiently brave to use poison to alter her situation. Remembering the phial, Gudmund prepares to cast it away, but Margit asks to have it; she pretends to throw it into the water. Now Margit feels bold enough to speak openly of her love of Gudmund, but she approaches the subject through a legend about a man who loved a woman who loved another. When his lover died, he killed himself so they could be together beneath the churchyard. Margit's interpretation of the story is that the church cannot separate two people who are really in love. Gudmund senses the drift of her abandoned talk and starts to tell her about himself and Signe but is interrupted by the entrance of Knut, Eric, Signe, and others.

A scene of convoluted dramatic irony follows. Margit thinks that Gudmund is about to declare his love of her and believes that Knut will speak to Signe. Knut intends to ask Gudmund to speak in behalf of his suit for Signe, and Gudmund plans to ask Knut to help him and Signe to elope. At last both men indicate the object of their attention—Signe—the news of which is overheard by Margit, who is stunned by the turn of events. Knut demands that Margit pledge Signe to him, and when she refuses, he vows to return after midnight and function as sheriff with respect to Gudmund. With his rival out of the way, he will still have Signe. Knut and his men leave, uttering menacing maledictions on all who have opposed him. Gudmund and Signe speak of fleeing, while Margit concludes that he would have loved her if she had only been free of Bengt.

The party spills out of doors with Bengt greatly enjoying his role as host. They decide to play the game of making up entertaining verses, despite the reluctance of some to participate because in the past violence has resulted from it. Margit is asked to start, but she defers to Gudmund, whom in whispers she threatens. He decides to sing a verse designed to make it clear to Margit that he could never love her; all this is, of course, disguised in the verse. Margit understands and agrees to "stitch a stave" in response. Her verse describes a maiden who marries the Mountain King, lives in his hall, and dreams of the life that might have been. Into her gaze rides a knightly singer who awakened love in her bosom, then sailed off across the sea, leaving her more miserable than she had ever been. As Margit tells this tale, she becomes increasingly more frantic and cries out, "Let me out! Let me out to where valleys are green! Here in my mountain halls I shall die!" She collapses in a faint, as Signe and Gudmund rush to her fearing that Margit has died. The act ends in general confusion.

Several hours have passed as Act III begins. Bengt says farewell to the last of the guests as servants tidy up the hall. Offstage voices sing goodbye as they fade into the distance. Margit enters and learns from a servant that some of the guests have departed, while others have remained to sleep overnight, among them Gudmund. Left alone, Margit soliloquizes on the desolation of her life with Bengt after Gudmund leaves with Signe. The prospect is so grim that she considers following Gudmund; for a moment she even imagines herself as his wife. Then she considers the poison, starts to toss it through the window, but stops.

Bengt enters, asks for a filled goblet, and talks of Knut. He plans to kill him because of his insults. Bengt's empty posturing further sickens Margit. Bengt asks for more mead and tries to pull her down on his knee. She pulls away, but Bengt praises the good fortune that gave him Margit before Gudmund appeared; even he has deduced that Gudmund had been in love with Margit, but he will have to be content with Signe. As Bengt rambles on and on about killing Knut and possessing Margit, she struggles heroically with herself and then empties the poison into his goblet and throws the phial from the window. Margit sets the goblet before him, wavers once, and then leaves Bengt to his fate.

Before Bengt can drink, however, a servant brings news that Knut and his warriors are returning. Bengt rushes out, leaving the goblet on the table. Signe and Gudmund come in discussing his plans for their flight to Denmark. Signe takes up the goblet to drink to Margit's health, but Gudmund stops her when he recognizes it as the goblet from which Margit had drunk to her reunion with him. As he explains, Gudmund pours the poisoned wine out the window. Sounds of fierce fighting are heard. It is Knut and his men. Margit enters and sees Gudmund holding the empty goblet; concluding that they have taken the poison, she starts to scream dementedly. Servants break in with the news that the overnight guests have prevailed and captured Knut's marauders.

Knut, Eric, and several others are brought in bound. Knut is almost prostrate for killing Bengt, which Margit countenances if he will give up his designs on Signe. Gudmund still feels that he must flee. Margit gives her blessing to Gudmund and Signe as horses are heard outside. The King's Messenger and his men enter in search of Gudmund, who proclaims his innocence. He is surprised when the Messenger confirms his innocence and invites him to join the king at the palace. The evil chancellor has been overthrown. Now that Gudmund and Signe's future is assured, Margit heaves a sigh of relief that she escaped without blood on her hands; she announces her intention of going into a convent. The play ends with a prayerful song of God's praise.

Structural analysis: Ibsen was much under the influence of the well-made play* when he wrote this drama. It is marred by numerous inconsistencies of Character and Plot, yet the drama is solidly unified by action:

Margit discovers that Gudmund has returned;

(as a result of which)

Margit declares her continuing passion for him;

(as a result of which)

Margit decides to poison Bengt and considers following Gudmund;

(as a result of which)

Margit discovers (falsely) that Gudmund and Signe have taken the poison and that Bengt has been killed;

(as a result of which)

Margit, seeing that Gudmund and Signe will not die, blesses them and goes into a convent.

THE FEAST AT SOLHAUG (1883): Ibsen's revisions of his youthful drama were minimal. McFarlane and Orton [*The Oxford Ibsen* (London, 1970), I, 699] have summarized his alterations:

(1) The fourteenth century is cited as the time of the action.
(2) There are no scene divisions.
(3) After placing the poisoned goblet before Bengt, Margit begs him to stop drinking for the night, thus softening her murderous nature.
(4) Knut's killing of Bengt is attributed to self-defense.
(5) Margit leaves the stage after her last line; then the sunrise brightens the room.

FELLAH WITH A ROYAL MUMMY (*Peer Gynt*): A peasant encountered by Peer Gynt* in his African travels.

FERGUSON, ELSIE (1883-1961): American actress Elsie Ferguson appeared primarily in musicals and comedies before she left the stage for films. In 1918 this competent actress played Nora Helmer* in a filmed version of *A Doll's House** with a happy ending.

References: Anthony, Luther B. "A Doll's House Filmed," *The Dramatist*, 9 (1918), 922-3; Meyer, Annie N. "The Bare Bones of Ibsen," *Drama*, 8 (1918), 369-75.

FFRANGCON-DAVIES, GWEN (1896-   ): After playing Hilde Wangel* in *The Master Builder** at the Birmingham Repertory Theatre in 1924, English actress Gwen ffrangcon-Davies successfully portrayed Nora Helmer* in London in 1930. A critic observed that her performance was "one that will be memorable in the history of the part. . . . Miss ffrangcon-Davies's work is the melody of the play. . . . " [*The Times* (London), Mar. 21, 1930, p. 12, col. 3].

Reference: Who's Who in the Theatre, 16th ed., pp. 603-4.

A FIDDLER (*Peer Gynt*): One of the wedding guests.

FILM, IBSEN ON: Filmmakers in Great Britain and the United States have not to any significant extent seen cinematic potentiality in Ibsen's dramas. Only three of his scripts were adapted for silent movies:

Peer Gynt (U.S., 1915). Oliver Morosco Photoplay Company.

A Doll's House (U.S., 1917). Bluebird Photoplays.

A Doll's House (U.S., 1918). Famous Players-Lasky. Elsie Ferguson* played Nora Helmer.*

The Pillars of Society (G.B., 1920). R. W. Productions. Ellen Terry* starred as Widow Bernick in this Anglicized version by Walter C. Rowden.

A Doll's House (U.S., 1922). United Artists. This seven-reel version was adapted by Charles Ryan and starred Alla Nazimova.*

*Hedda Gabler** was also filmed in the 1920s, but particulars cannot be located. Floyd Dell [*Looking at Life* (New York: Alfred A. Knopf, 1924), pp. 34-35] writes of this bowdlerized adaptation:

Instead of being a normal pleasure-loving young man who is wrecked by an unsatisfactory marriage, Oswald's father is shown as a scoundrel who marries knowing that he has a transmissible venereal disease; and he teaches his innocent boy to drink beer, which leaves no doubt that he is a very bad man. The wife is a saint and martyr, and no one would ever guess that Ibsen thought *she* was to blame. The great scene in the play is that which shows the doctor hurrying up hill and down dale breathlessly to the church in which Oswald and Regina are to be wedded, arriving just in time to hold up his hand and say impressively, "I forbid this marriage!". . . . So in the movies Oswald wriggles across the floor, making faces, toward the bottle of rat poison, while his mother and pastor are hurrying—up hill and down dale, of course—to save him. Finding the dead body, his mother swoons in the good man's comforting arms, pitied—and respected—by everybody. . . . Thus art is robbed of its sting, truth of its victory.

Once sound was added to moving pictures, Ibsen was ignored for generations before being rediscovered by filmmakers:

Peer Gynt (U.S., 1965). Willow Corporation. Charlton Heston starred in this eighty-five-minute film directed by David Bradley.

A Doll's House (G.B., 1973). Claire Bloom,* Ralph Richardson,* and Edith Evans* appeared in this version.

A Doll's House (G.B., 1973). Jane Fonda and David Warner headed the cast of this film.

Hedda [Gabler] (G.B., 1975). This is a filmed version of the production of the Royal Shakespeare Company starring Glenda Jackson.*

References: Gifford, Denis. *The British Film Catalogue, 1895-1970.* New York: McGraw-Hill, 1973; U.S. Copyright Office, *Catalogue of Copyright Entries: Motion Pictures, 1912-39.* Washington, D.C.: Library of Congress, 1951; *Catalogue of Copyright Entries: Motion Pictures, 1960-69.* Washington D.C.: Library of Congress, 1971. For a discussion of Ibsen in non-English films, see Alnaes, Karsten. "Footlights to Film," *Scandinavian Review*, 66, 4 (1978), 67-71.

FINN (*Lady Inger of Österaad*): Lady Inger of Gyldenlöve's* retainer.

FISCHER, ALICE (1869-1947): On March 6, 1891, the New York audience was twice introduced to *The Pillars of Society*.* In one of those productions, Alice Fischer was Lona Hessel.* This American actress had previously performed mostly in comedies, so she was ill-equipped to assume a major Ibsenian role.
Reference: Who Was Who in the Theatre, II, 840.

FISKE, MINNIE MADDERN (1863-1932): One of the principal stars of the American theatre, Minnie Maddern turned down veteran classical actor Lawrence Barrett's suggestion in 1880 that she play Nora Helmer*; the young actress thought the role was untheatrical. Barrett repeated his advice in 1888 and received an identical response. Six years later on February 15, 1894, Mrs. Fiske appeared as Nora in a charity performance, which marked the second time Nora was acted in New York. Ibsen was so delighted that Mrs. Fiske appeared in his drama that he sent her a wreath entwined with Norway's colors and a congratulatory letter to be presented at the curtain call. Since Ibsen's plays already had a reputation as gloomy, Mrs. Fiske played the first act in her most winsome manner, eliciting sympathy for Nora and laughter at her childlike antics. In the ensuing scenes she brought the audience's attraction to her into sharp focus as the serious content of the play emerged. A critic observed, "Ibsen has been cold-shouldered in America for twenty years—yet all his plays needed to make them popular was an actress like Mrs. Fiske." Her first experience with an Ibsenian drama turned Mrs. Fiske into an ardent devotee who suffered only one aberration of faith. Under the influence of a drama with strict Christian overtones, she contributed an article to the Christmas 1902 *Theatre Magazine* in which she said that Ibsen had "all but banished beauty, nobility, picturesqueness, and poetry from the stage." A few months later her study of *Hedda Gabler** caused her to repent of her temporary apostasy.

On a European journey in the summer of 1903, she closeted herself in Meiningen with *Hedda Gabler* and emerged fully committed to producing it. Some purists were disappointed that her characterization of Hedda did not admit Hedda's pregnancy, but Mrs. Fiske believed that motherhood diluted Hedda's frigidity. After opening in New York on October 3, 1903, the production was taken on tour and generally attracted capacity audiences. It was so popular that *Hedda* was revived for the 1904-5 season and featured George Arliss* as Brack.*

Mrs. Fiske presented *Rosmersholm** in New York on December 30, 1907, after having planned the production for five years and rehearsed parts of it while on tour. As Rebecca West* her most powerful scene was the interview with Kroll* in which her incest is implied. The actress played the scene with economical precision, never rising from her chair and employing minimal gestures. The production ran for three weeks in New York before being taken on the road. The audience at the Grand Opera House in Chicago was the largest in the history of that theatre. After six months *Rosmersholm* paid off its investment and made a clear profit of $40,000.

In 1910 Mrs. Fiske again rehearsed the production of another Ibsenian drama. This time it was *The Pillars of Society.** As Lona Hessel,* Mrs. Fiske moved a critic to tears by her playing of the scene of Karsten Bernick's* confession: "Mrs. Fiske, as Lona, sat quiet, one of the crowd; but gradually, as she saw the man she loved throwing off his yoke of hypocrisy, the light of a great joy radiated from her face, ending in a stifled cry, half-sob, half-laugh of triumph, of indescribable poignance." By 1910 Mrs. Fiske's reputation as an interpreter of Ibsen was so well established that when she purposely excluded *The Pillars of Society* from her schedule for San Francisco, the public outcry was so great that the play was hurriedly announced.

When the actress appeared as Helene Alving* in *Ghosts** on January 10, 1927, her battle in behalf of Ibsen was won. Largely through her efforts, the works of the Norwegian dramatist came to be regarded as modern classics.

References: Binns, Archie, and Olive Kooken. *Mrs. Fiske and the American Theatre.* New York: Crown Publishers, 1955; Woollcott, Alexander, ed. *Mrs. Fiske: Her Views on Actors, Acting, and the Problems of Production.* New York: Century Company, 1917.

FITINGHOFF, ROSA (1873-1949): At his seventieth birthday celebration in Stockholm, Ibsen met twenty-six-year-old Rosa Fitinghoff, daughter of a well-known Swedish novelist, who, with others, performed folk dances for his entertainment. He managed to disentangle himself from his hostesses and converse with the young woman, whom he invited to see him off on the next day, April 17, 1898. After his return to Christiania,* Fitinghoff sent Ibsen a postcard, and he asked her to write more frequently, as apparently she did.

With her mother as chaperone, Fitinghoff visited Ibsen in Christiania in July 1899. After entertaining them at the Grand Hotel, Ibsen took the women to his home where they conversed at length. The visit must have inspired Ibsen because a few days after Fitinghoff's departure on July 26, he completed the first act of *When We Dead Awaken.** Soon after he finished the play, Ibsen had his first stroke (1900), which diminished his social contacts, even by letter. On January 15, 1901, he penned a short note thanking Fitinghoff for a Christmas gift and asking her to write again. His growing debility, however, abbreviated the relationship.

FJELDBO, DOCTOR (*The League of Youth*): As the company physician of the local ironworks, Fjeldbo has free entry into the home and society of the owner, Chamberlain Brattsberg.* Although his primary function is that of *raisonneur*, Fjeldbo provides romantic complication and at the end of the play announces his engagement to Thora Brattsberg.*

FLIDA, PAUL (*The Pretenders*): As a partisan of Earl Skule,* Paul Flida's role is chiefly that of a messenger.

FLORENTIUS (*Emperor and Galilean*): A general; one of Constantius* spies in Julian's* camp.

FOLDAL, FRIDA (*John Gabriel Borkman*): The daughter of Vilhelm Foldal,* Frida amuses Borkman* by playing the piano for him. Her running away with Borkman's son and Fanny Wilton* places her father and Borkman in analogous positions.

FOLDAL, VILHELM (*John Gabriel Borkman*): A subordinate clerk in a governmental office, Foldal is Borkman's* only friend during his years of isolation after his release from prison. He is Borkman's confidant and foil. Foldal's dreams of being a writer are as unlikely of fulfillment as are Borkman's of re-establishing his financial empire.

EN FOLKEFIENDE: The Norwegian title of *An Enemy of the People.**

FORBES-ROBERTSON, JEAN (1905-62): The career of London-born Jean Forbes-Robertson as an Ibsenian actress spanned twenty-one years.

She appeared first as Rita Allmers* in 1930 and in the following year as Hedda Gabler.* Her Hedda was repeated in 1936 and 1951. In the interim she essayed Rebecca West* in 1936. All these appearances were on the London stage. Forbes-Robertson appeared in contemporary dramas, but she was known primarily for her roles in the English classics.
Reference: Who Was Who in the Theatre, II, 858-60.

A FOREIGN LADY (*When We Dead Awaken*): See Satow, Irene de.*

FOSLI, KAJA (*The Master Builder*): Knut Brovik's* niece and fiancée of Ragnar,* Kaja, an ambitious young woman, falls in love with Halvard Solness,* who uses her infatuation with him to ascertain that Ragnar remains in his subservient position in the business.

FRASER, MARIE (fl. 1886-91): Although Marie Fraser had frequently played Nora Helmer* in the provinces, she was severely criticized for her portrayal when she played in London (January 27, 1891). Perhaps bias against provincial players accounts for some of the criticism, but Fraser was counted inferior to Janet Achurch* who had introduced the role in London.

FREEMAN (*The Lady from the Sea*): The real name of Ellida Wangel's* seafaring fiancé.

FREIE BÜHNE (Berlin): Inspired by the Théâtre Libre,* a group of German literary and theatrical personalities formed the Freie Bühne [Free Stage] principally to encourage the work of new dramatists. State censorship was avoided by enrolling a subscription audience. The enterprise was governed by a director, the literary critic Dr. Otto Brahm,* and a board of ten members. Since professional actors were employed in the productions, the presentations of the organization were given on Sunday afternoons when theatre people were free. A number of theatres, dark on Sundays, housed the presentations of the Freie Bühne, the first of which was Ibsen's *Ghosts** on September 29, 1889.

Ibsen's controversial play had already been seen in 1887 at the Residenz Theater in Berlin, but Brahm and the governors believed that such a play would best indicate the tone of ensuing productions of the Freie Bühne. By 1891 the group had ceased to mount productions according to a fixed schedule but chose to sponsor presentations intermittently in the future. When Brahm assumed the directorship of the Deutsches Theater in 1894, the work of the Freie Bühne had been completed, although the organization gave its last performance in 1901. As a result, Realistic drama had found a forum, and a number of playwrights, notably Gerhart Hauptmann, had been discovered.

The Freie Bühne gave way to a number of similar organizations, the most significant of which was the Freie Volksbühne [Free People's Stage], which presented *Ghosts* and *The Pillars of Society.**

References: Miller, Anna Irene. *The Independent Theatre in Europe.* New York: Benjamin Blom, 1966 [1931]; Newmark, Maxim. *Otto Brahm: The Man and the Critic.* New York: G. E. Stechert, 1938.

FREUD, SIGMUND (1856-1939): The year 1899 was a momentous one in the history of ideas: in that year Ibsen published his last play and Viennese psychoanalyst Sigmund Freud published his first non-collaborative work, *The Interpretation of Dreams.* Although one significant career was finished when another was commencing, the two men had much in common as each in his own way explored and interpreted human motivations. They never met, but Freud was a great admirer of Ibsen. In 1916 Freud published *Einige Charaktertypen aus der psychoanalytischen Arbeit* [*Some Character Types from Psychoanalytical Work*], a précis of which follows:

Frustration can precipitate a neurosis that causes illness; this occurs when one's basic urges conflict with his ideals and no way of satisfying the ideal can be found. Some people, moreover, become ill when the means of satisfying some deep-seated wish is at hand. Shakespeare's Lady Macbeth is an example of one who strove to reach a goal (Macbeth's elevation to the throne of Scotland) yet found little joy and great disillusionment in the attainment of it.

Rebecca West* presents another opportunity of observing this kind of behavior. At the precise moment when all her schemes to be mistress of Rosmersholm come to fruition, when Rosmer* proposes marriage to her, her immediate joy turns to a firm resolution that she cannot marry him; if he should continue to press her, suicide will be her only recourse. Her seemingly inexplicable behavior is explained by the fact that her conscience has been awakened and produced a sense of guilt. After goading Beata [Rosmer]* to her death, Rebecca learned from Kroll* that the man with whom she had previously had sexual relations was her father, a discovery that produced crippling guilt. This explains Rebecca's second refusal of Rosmer's proposal, but what of the first?

Even before the action of the drama begins, Rebecca must have had some notion of her mother's liaison with Doctor West, so, moving under the influence of the Electra complex, she plotted to take her mother's place in the bed of her lover, a pattern of behavior repeated when she joined the Rosmer household. Thus her fantasy about becoming mistress of Rosmersholm had its basis in adolescent reality. *Rosmersholm** is a cogent demonstration of this behavioral pattern and masterfully shows how neurotic frustration kept Rebecca from enjoying the spoils of her plot.

In this penetrating essay Freud calls attention to a critical error which some believe to be a major failing of Freudian criticism: viewing a dramatic character as if it were a real person. Freud says, "So far we have treated Rebecca West as if she were a living person and not a creation of Ibsen's imagination, which is always directed by the most critical intelligence" (Freud, p. 263). Although he realizes that a dramatic character is an artificial entity that possesses only the traits necessitated by the dramatic situation, Freud thinks that Ibsen supplied enough veiled hints about Rebecca's motivations to enable him to psychoanalyze her behavior.

References: Freud, Sigmund. "Some Character Types Met with in Psychoanalytic Work: Those Wrecked by Success," *Modern Continental Literary Criticism*, ed. O. B. Hardison, Jr. (New York: Appleton-Century-Crofts, 1962), pp. 249-65; MacIntyre, Alasdair. "Sigmund Freud," *Encyclopedia of Philosophy*, ed. Paul Edwards (New York: Macmillan, 1967), III, 249-53.

FROHN, CHARLOTTE (1844-88): A gifted actress in her own right, Charlotte Frohn was the first wife of director Anton Anno,* under whose supervision she undertook the roles of Helene Alving* (January 1887) and Rebecca West* (May 5, 1887) at the Residenz Theater in Berlin.
Reference: Kosch, Wilhelm. *Deutsches Theater-Lexikon*, I, 33.

FROMENTIUS (*Emperor and Galilean*): A captain.

FRUEN FRA HAVET: The Norwegian title of *The Lady from the Sea.**

FRU INGER TIL ÖSTRAAT: The Norwegian title of *Lady Inger of Östraat.**

A FRUIT-SELLER (*Emperor and Galilean*): A member of the Roman mob.

FULTON, CHARLES J. (1857-1938): As an Ibsenian actor Charles J. Fulton's success was conspicuous, yet for some reason he failed to list his roles in *A Doll's House** (1891) and *The Wild Duck** (1904) in his biographical sketch. When he performed in London, Fulton's Krogstad* was highly praised and his Gregers Werle* was hailed as strong and boldly conceived. Perhaps his reticence was prompted by the fact that his reputation was founded on his enactment of Romantic heroes quite unlike Ibsen's characters.
Reference: Who Was Who in the Theatre, II, 894-5.

FURIA (*Catiline*): Furia is a passionate creature who chafes at the restrictive life of a Vestal Virgin. She desires action, adventure, and especially revenge on the man who raped her sister—Catiline.* Furia vows his destruction and accomplishes it, but her evil influence is thwarted by the love of Aurelia.*

G

GABINIUS (*Catiline*): A young Roman nobleman; a member of Catiline's* conspiracy.

GABLER, HEDDA (*Hedda Gabler*): As the attractive wife of an unimaginative professor, Jörgen Tesman,* Hedda Gabler is perhaps the most fascinating of Ibsen's protagonists. When she first appears, she is already Mrs. Tesman, but she still sees herself and others refer to her as Hedda Gabler. The daughter of General Gabler (no mother is mentioned), Hedda inherited an innate urge to command people's lives; from the general she inherited a brace of pistols with which she terrifies the neighborhood. These weapons become the engines of the destruction of both Hedda and Eylert Lövborg.* It goes without saying that Freudian critics have seen Hedda, like Aeschylus' Clytemnestra, as a "man-hearted" woman and the pistols as her phallic parts.

Hedda married Jörgen Tesman* because she feared he was the best she could do; she inhabits a house that is loathsome to her, a house that became hers because in a moment of boredom she had admired it; her doting husband mortgaged his aunts' pension to acquire the house which is nothing less than a prison for Hedda. Hedda's boredom is her motivating factor, and when she discovers that she can manipulate Lövborg like a puppet, she seizes on this game as a means of alleviating her ennui. By doing so, she unknowingly places herself under the control of Judge Brack.* Hedda's realization that life for her means being bored by her husband and controlled by Brack prompts her eventual suicide.

The most intriguing aspect of Hedda's character is the matter of her pregnancy, about which Ibsen is quite cryptic. Most interpreters believe that she was pregnant by Tesman, but others that she merely led him to believe that she had conceived as a means of further manipulating him.

GALLATIN, ALBERTA (1871-1948): Alberta Gallatin was a traveling star in the United States after 1900 and in the early years of the century added *Ghosts** to her repertory. She was practiced in the role of Helene Alving* when she introduced it in New York in 1915, but, even so, her portrayal did not elicit general approval.

References: Briscoe, Johnson. *The Actors' Birthday Book*, 2d ser. New York: Moffat, Yard, 1908; *New York Dramatic Mirror*, Apr. 21, 1915, p. 8, cols. 2-3.

GALLUS (*Emperor and Galilean*): A Roman prince, Gallus is Constantius'* cousin and heir to the throne. As young men Gallus and Julian* had become Christians in Cappadocia, but when Gallus was named Caesar, thus heir-apparent, he started to persecute the Christians. After Gallus is deposed, Julian becomes Caesar.

GANDALF (*The Burial Mound*): A chief of a Viking band bent on revenge, Gandalf is the protagonist of the drama and the representative of the northern temperament. When he encounters Blanka,* the Christian of southern temperament, Gandalf experiences a change of heart and returns to Norway to Christianize the land.

GARFIELD, JOHN (1913-52): John Garfield studied with Maria Ouspenskaya, one of Konstantin Stanislavsky's* pupils, and acted at the Civic Repertory Theatre with Eva Le Gallienne.* His exposure to the requirements of Realistic acting and Ibsen was, therefore, profound. With that background, it is odd that in 1951 he should have undertaken to act Peer Gynt.* Not surprisingly, the reviewer of the *New York Times* called his performance "literal and casual" but "completely lacking in poetic animation" (Jan. 29, 1951, p. 15, cols.2-3).
Reference: Who Was Who in the Theatre, II, 908.

GARRETT, FYDELL EDMUND (1865-1907): F. E. Garrett's translation of *Brand** was published in London in 1894, and his *Lyrics and Poems from Ibsen* appeared in 1912.

GENGANGERE: The Norwegian title of *Ghosts.**

GERD (*Brand*): Gerd is a wild girl of the mountains who exerts great influence over Brand.* She causes him to remember the church of ice early in the play and leads him to his death there at its end. Gerd's taunting causes Brand to remain in Gudbrandsdalen* even at the cost of his son's life. Brand discovers that his spiritual affinity with Gerd is the result of Brand's mother's* rejection of a gypsy suitor; the gypsy precipitately entered into a loveless union and fathered Gerd.

GHOSTS: A three-act Realistic serious drama.
Composition: Started in June 1881; finished on September 23, 1881; published on December 13, 1881.
Stage history:

May 20, 1882   Aurora Turner Hall, Chicago, (in Dano-Norwegian), Helga von Bluhme* as Helene Alving

Aug. 22, 1883	Hälsingborg, dir. August Lindberg*
Aug. 28, 1883	Folk Theatre, Copenhagen, dir. August Lindberg
Sept. 27, 1883	Royal Theatre, Stockholm, dir. Ludvig Josephson*
Oct. 17, 1883	Norwegian Theatre, Christiania,* dir. August Lindberg
1883	Royal Theatre, Copenhagen
1884	Helsinki
Apr. 14, 1886	Augsburg, dir. Georg II, Duke of Saxe-Meiningen*
Dec. 22, 1886	Hoftheater, Saxe-Meiningen
Jan. 2, 1887	Berlin (1 perf.), Berlin Dramatic Society
Jan. 9, 1887	Residenz Theater, Berlin (1), Charlotte Frohn* as Helene Alving
1887	Columbia Theatre, Chicago, Friedrich Mitterwurzer* as Oswald
Sept. 29, 1889	Freie Bühne, Berlin*
May 29, 1890	Théâtre des Menus Plaisirs, Paris (2), pro. Théâtre Libre,* André Antoine* as Oswald
Dec. 3, 1890	Norwegian Theatre, Bergen*
Mar. 13, 1891	Royalty Theatre, London (1), pro. Independent Theatre,* Alice Austin (Mrs. Theodore) Wright* as Helene Alving
Nov. 21, 1891	Volkstheater, Vienna
Feb. 22, 1892	Milan, pro. Zacconi
Jan. 26, 1893	Athenaeum, London, pro. Independent Theatre,* Mrs. Patrick Campbell* as Helene Alving
Jan. 27, 1893	Royalty Theatre, London, pro. Independent Theatre,* Mrs. Patrick Campbell as Helene Alving
Mar. 8, 1893	Gärtner Theater, Munich, pro. Karl Werckmeister
Jan. 5, 1894	Berkeley Lyceum, New York, Ida Jeffreys Goodfriend* as Helene Alving
Jan. 25, 1894	Garden Theatre, New York, Ida Jeffreys Goodfriend as Helene Alving
June 18, 1894	Gärtner Theater, Munich, pro. Emil Messthaler*
Nov. 27, 1894	Lessing Theater, Berlin (3)
1894	Deutsches Theater, Berlin
Apr. 16, 1896	Teatro Independent, Barcelona
June 24, 1897	London, pro. Independent Theatre, Alice Austin (Mrs. Theodore) Wright* as Helene Alving
Feb. 6, 1898	Théâtre Antoine, Paris, pro. André Antoine
Mar. 20, 1898	Central Theatre, Christiania
1898	Royal Theatre, Stockholm (1)
May 29, 1899	Carnegie Lyceum, New York, pro. Emanuel Reicher,* Mary Shaw* as Helene Alving (also on a thirty-seven-week tour)
Mar. 20, 1900	Teatro Intim, Barcelona
Jan. 26, 1903	Manhattan Theatre, New York, Mary Shaw as Helene Alving
1903	Royal Theatre, Copenhagen
Mar. 3, 1903	Mrs. Osborn's Theatre, New York (16), Mary Shaw as Helene Alving
Jan. 7, 1904	Nemetti Theatre, St. Petersburg, dir. Pavel Orlenev
Oct. 24, 1904	Kommisarzhevskaya Theatre, St. Petersburg, dir. Vsevelod Meyerhold*
Mar. 31, 1905	Art Theatre, Moscow, pro. Konstantin Stanislavsky* and Vladimir Nemirovich-Danchenko*

Oct. 20, 1906	Madrid, pro. José Tallavi
Nov. 8, 1906	Kammerspiele, Berlin, dir. Max Reinhardt*
Mar. 13, 1907	Michail Theatre, St. Petersburg, Maria Savina* as Helene Alving
May 26, 1910	Hoftheater, Braunschweig
June 4, 1910	Residenz Theater, Munich, Bernhard von Jacobi as Oswald
1910	Budapest, dir. Max Reinhardt
May 10, 1911	Volkstheater, Munich, Alexander Moissi* as Oswald
Mar. 14, 1912	Garrick Theatre, New York (4), Ludmilla N. Liarova* as Helene Alving (performed in Russian)
Sept. 1913	Dresden, dir. Max Reinhardt
Apr. 26, 1914	Court Theatre, London, pro. New Constitutional Society for Women's Suffrage, dir. Leon M. Lion*
Jul. 14, 1914	Haymarket Theatre, London, dir. Leon M. Lion (first licensed production)
Apr. 20, 1915	Longacre Theatre, New York (2), Alberta Gallatin* as Helene Alving
June 1, 1915	Kammerspiele, Munich, Albert Bassermann* as Oswald
Apr. 28, 1917	Kingsway Theatre, London, Letitia Darragh* as Helene Alving
May 7, 1917	Comedy Theatre, New York, pro. Washington Square Players, Mary Shaw as Helene Alving
Nov. 6, 1917	St. James' Theatre, London
Feb. 7, 1919	Longacre Theatre, New York (1), Maud Hilyard* as Helene Alving
Feb. 6, 1922	Punch and Judy Theatre, New York, Mary Shaw as Helene Alving
June 12, 1923	New Oxford Theatre, London, as *Spettri*, Eleonora Duse* as Helene Alving
June 1923	Pavilion Theatre, London, pro. People's Theatre,* Ernest Milton* as Oswald
Oct. 13, 1925	Everyman Theatre, London, Irene Rooke* as Helene Alving.
Oct. 30, 1925	National Theatre, Christiania,* Johanne Dybwad* as Helene Alving
Mar. 16, 1926	Comedy Theatre, New York (34), Lucile Watson as Helene Alving
Jan. 10, 1927	Mansfield Theatre, New York (24), Minnie Maddern Fiske* as Helene Alving
Feb. 7, 1928	Deutsches Theater, New York (3), Alexander Moissi as Oswald (performed in German)
Mar. 27, 1928	Wyndham's Theatre, London (9), Mrs. Patrick Campbell as Helene Alving
Apr. 19, 1930	Everyman Theatre, London, Sybil Thorndike* as Helene Alving
Mar. 20, 1933	Arts Theatre, London, Louise Hampton* as Helene Alving
May 23, 1933	Sutton Theatre, New York, Hilda Englund* as Helene Alving
July 19, 1935	Little Theatre, London, Nancy Price* as Helene Alving
July 30, 1935	Duke of York's Theatre, London
Dec. 12, 1935	Empire Theatre, New York, Alla Nazimova* as Helene Alving
Nov. 8, 1937	Vaudeville Theatre, London, Marie Ney* as Helene Alving
May 30, 1940	Duchess Theatre, London, Katina Paxinou* as Helene Alving
June 25, 1943	Duke of York's Theatre, London, Beatrix Lehmann* as Helene Alving
Feb. 16, 1947	Cort Theatre, New York, Eva Le Gallienne* as Helene Alving

Feb. 24, 1948   Cort Theatre, New York (10), Eva Le Gallienne as Helene Alving
Jan. 3, 1950   Staatsschauspiel, Munich, Albert Bassermann as Oswald
June 12, 1951   Embassy Theatre, London, Beatrix Lehmann as Helene Alving
Nov. 12, 1958   Old Vic Theatre, London, Flora Robson* as Helene Alving
Apr. 6, 1959   Prince's Theatre, London, Flora Robson as Helene Alving
Sept. 21, 1961   4th Street Theatre, New York (216), Leueen McGrath* as Helene
            Alving
Apr. 4, 1965   Theatre Royal, Stratford East (London), Catherine Lacey as
            Helene Alving
Apr. 3, 1973   Roundabout Theatre, New York (89), Beatrice Straight* as
            Helene Alving
Jan. 17, 1974   Greenwich Theatre, London, Irene Worth* as Helene Alving
Aug. 30, 1982   Brooks Atkinson Theatre, New York, Liv Ullman* as Helene
            Alving

Synopsis: A dismal rain darkens a handsome garden-room in a spacious house situated on one of Norway's western fjords. Regine Engstrand, a member of the household, and Jakob Engstrand, her father, engage in a none-too-friendly conversation centering on his fondness of alcohol and her concern that his loud voice will awaken the young master who is asleep upstairs. Then they speak of tomorrow's opening of the orphanage, which will draw a number of important guests, including Pastor Manders whom Engstrand has gulled on a number of occasions. With his carpentry work on the orphanage finished, Engstrand plans to return to the town and wants his daughter to accompany him. Regine will not even consider such a move since Mrs. Alving, the mistress of the house, has treated her almost like a member of the family, while her own father, in his cups, has called her a bastard on numerous occasions. Engstrand attributes such derision to his drinking to escape the cavils of his wife who had taunted him with recollections of her years of service in Chamberlain Alving's house. Now Engstrand reveals his great plan to Regine: he wants to open a tavern for seamen with Regine as hostess and principal entertainer. That, he reasons, should be preferable to her remaining here and working at the orphanage. Cryptically Regine says that she has hopes of something better. Engstrand reminds Regine that with her looks she could snare a rich man as her mother had once done. Infuriated, Regine drives him from the room while warning him not to disturb Mr. Alving. Her solicitude is so obvious that even Engstrand deduces that Alving is the object of her machinations, but he is unable to pursue this because Pastor Manders, long a friend of the Alvings, arrives. Engstrand exits as Manders enters and chats with Regine.

Manders mentions Oswald Alving's unexpected return; Regine observes that he had looked unduly exhausted after his trip from Paris. Manders notes the fullness of Regine's maturing body before steering the conversation toward his belief that Engstrand needs to be under the supervision of a caring person; indeed, he thinks that Regine should return to town with her father. She is dismayed by the suggestion but counters that she would enjoy living in town under the protection of a respectable bachelor, leaving no doubt that she refers to the minister himself. The pastor declines and quickly asks her to announce his presence to Mrs. Alving. Left alone for a moment, Manders desultorily picks up a book from the table, notes its title, and gives a start of agitation, which is repeated as he considers several others.

Helene Alving enters and greets her old friend, glad that he has arrived early so that certain items of business may be disposed of. When she discovers that he plans to stay at the inn, she invites him to remain at the house. Manders makes excuses about the convenience of the inn's proximity to the landing pier, but Mrs. Alving knows that he is studiously avoiding staying under her roof. He changes the subject to her son Oswald, learning that he has been away for two years but intends to remain at home during the whole winter. She is delighted that Oswald is still affectionate toward her; Manders, too, seems pleased that Oswald's addiction to art has not dulled his natural affections. Manders extracts some papers from his briefcase, but he cannot begin to discuss business before he asks about Mrs. Alving's reading materials. She openly says that she has been reading the books that lie on the table and that they have confirmed many of her own suspicions about herself and life in general; she is pleased to have the freedom to devote to such studies. Manders, on the other hand, is scandalized that she should undertake personally to investigate such subjects rather than merely accepting authoritarian pronouncements on them. He believes that the survival of "Society" depends on not asking too many questions. He continues to berate her, but she merely turns the talk to the orphanage. Manders produces the legal papers connected with the endowment of the orphanage and then asks Mrs. Alving if she wants to insure the buildings. When she answers affirmatively, he tries to dissuade her on the grounds that public opinion would interpret such a move as indicating a lack of faith in the Almighty's providence toward an institution functioning in His name. Manders also fears that his reputation as Mrs. Alving's adviser might suffer. Finally, she is persuaded not to insure Captain Alving's Orphanage. Manders asks if she would be able to restore the structures if an accident happened, and Mrs. Alving replies that it would be out of the question. She then tells him of a coincidence that happened only yesterday: there had been a fire in Engstrand's carpentry shop, perhaps because the man is so careless with matches. The subject of Engstrand having been introduced, Manders asks how Mrs. Alving would react to Regine's returning to town to live with Engstrand. She emphatically declines to allow it. Their further discussion of the issue is interrupted by the appearance of Oswald.

When Oswald comes into the room, he looks so like his father that Manders is momentarily speechless. Despite his knowledge that Manders disapproves of his artistic calling, Oswald greets the pastor warmly. Manders says that he has read several favorable notices of Oswald in the papers but has not seen much about his work. The younger man admits that he has not painted much lately. When Manders observes that Oswald favors his father, Mrs. Alving retorts that he takes after her. Oswald remarks that he plans to stay at home indefinitely. His mother states her belief that it was good for Oswald to go away from home at an early age, but Oswald and Manders believe there is no substitute for the environment of home and family. Manders is surprised to hear from Oswald that many of his artistic friends have set up housekeeping, although not all of them have been married. Manders is shocked and pontificates that no circumstances would make such unions valid, that people should resist temptation. When Oswald maintains that he has met more true morality in such homes than he has in "respectable" society, Manders becomes outraged. Mrs. Alving intervenes to quell Oswald's excitement. He admits that such agitation is bad for him in view of his unusual tiredness, so he apologizes to Manders and goes off for a walk.

Manders remains angry at Oswald's opinions and is further annoyed when Mrs. Alving maintains that Oswald was absolutely right. Manders, speaking as her spiritual adviser, reminds her of when she had deserted her husband and refused to return until Manders convinced her that it was her duty to return regardless of her husband's gross immorality. She had, moreover, compromised Manders' reputation by coming to him, but he rejoices that he was able to send her back to Alving's home. Not content to remind her of this terrible time, Manders tells Mrs. Alving that she failed not only as a wife but also as a mother by sending Oswald away from home when he was a mere boy. He concludes that she is atoning for her first lapse by endowing the orphanage; he asks what she will do to atone for her treatment of Oswald. Mrs. Alving listens rather patiently to this harangue, but afterward she speaks equally brutally to Manders. She reminds him that he ceased to visit the Alvings after she had returned to the captain; he had not, in fact, known anything about her marriage except by hearsay. Now he will hear the truth: Alving continued to the very end to be profligate. In the words of his own doctor, Alving was "depraved." She recounts how she had overheard Alving seducing the chambermaid, who eventually became Regine's mother. After that, she had determined to send seven-year-old Oswald away so that his life would not become poisoned in such a "sordid, depraved home." Manders is aghast at these revelations. Mrs. Alving states that she created the orphanage for two reasons: to whitewash Alving's reputation in case the truth about him should ever emerge and to rid herself of the precise amount of money which Alving brought to the marriage so that Oswald would inherit nothing from his father. Her son's inheritance is to come entirely from her. At that moment Oswald returns from his walk. Regine brings in a parcel and then retires to lay the dinner, followed by Oswald. As Mrs. Alving lingers over her package, the sound of an overturning chair is heard from the dining room. Regine's voice is raised in a plea for Oswald to release her. Mrs. Alving identifies the situation immediately as ghosts from the past; this is, in fact, the initiation of the subsequent action. The curtain falls.

Act II occurs in the same room just after dinner. Oswald has gone for another walk, and Regine is attending to her chores, so Manders and Mrs. Alving are left alone to discuss what plan of action to follow. Mrs. Alving concludes that Regine must leave the house before matters become more serious. Manders says that she must go to her father and then sees that Engstrand is not her natural parent. Mrs. Alving tells him that when Regine's mother left her job, she had been given a large sum of money. With it she had attracted Jacob Engstrand and married him, the service being conducted, she reminds him, by none other than the estimable Pastor Manders. Manders censures Engstrand for marrying a deflowered woman, but Mrs. Alving counters that she had married a dissolute man. Manders sees them as two entirely different matters: Mrs. Alving had married on the advice of family and friends as well as the dictates of her heart. She answers that her heart was devoted to Manders, yet she allowed her family to dictate her marriage to another. Now, she says, she must be rid of such false restrictions so that she can work her way toward freedom. Mrs. Alving blames herself for being a moral coward; she should have made her husband's behavior public as well as told Oswald what sort of man his father was. Whatever her previous failings, she will not allow Oswald to get Regine in trouble. If she felt that he really loves her, she would countenance their marriage. Naturally, Manders is shocked by such brazenness, but Mrs. Alving notes that numerous such liaisons exist in the countryside. She says that she lives in fear of the ghosts of the past, that she wishes she had the courage to shine the light of truth upon them all. Manders sees this merely as the result of her free-thinkers' books. She responds that his insistence upon her return to a marriage of pretense and horror is what actually prompted her to analyze his beliefs; it was then that she saw that his principles were lifeless and artificial. He softens enough to say that this is his reward for living up to his principles, although his feelings for her tempted him to return her love. He sees his behavior as a victory; she views it as a crime and realizes that they can never come to an understanding. They turn from the past and conclude that a suitable match must be found for Regine.

Engstrand enters and asks to speak with Manders. He has come to ask Manders to lead a prayer meeting for all the workers who have completed the orphanage; he seems the soul of piety. Manders is still affronted that Engstrand lied to him about Regine's parentage, so he now asks the carpenter for the truth about the girl. Faced by the facts and Mrs. Alving's presence, Engstrand must tell the truth, which causes Manders to vow to have nothing further to do with him. Then in a clever bit of sophistry, Engstrand gets Manders to admit that it is a man's duty to help those in trouble as well as to keep his word, both of which he had done. The carpenter so limns himself that he soon convinces Manders that he has been perfectly upright and Christlike in his dealings with Regine and her mother. Manders eventually asks Engstrand's pardon for doubting his motives. The man presses his point by telling Manders that he needs some help in founding a home for wayward seamen. Manders agrees to think about it and sends Engstrand away to prepare for the prayer service. Manders is so proud of what he sees as his good influence on Engstrand that he positively gloats. Mrs. Alving says that he is and always will be a big baby, laying her hands on his shoulders as she does so. He draws back from her, packs up his papers, and leaves with the promise of returning later.

Mrs. Alving walks about the room tidying up a bit when she hears someone in the dining room. It is Oswald. He did not go for a walk and has poured himself a drink, which elicits a motherly warning. His excuse is his irremediable chilliness. Oswald proves unable to concentrate as he asks a second time where Manders went. Although he is glad to be back in his mother's house, Oswald is depressed by the constantly gloomy weather. Mrs. Alving suggests that he might have been happier if he had not come home; to which he responds by asking if his presence means so very much to her in view of the fact that she had sent him away so long ago. Twilight has fallen, and Oswald decides to tell his mother the truth about his physical condition: a form of mental breakdown that has doomed him never to be able to work again. Having said this, he dissolves into convulsive sobbing. She comforts him and asks how such a thing could have happened to him, but Oswald is mystified because he claims not to have led a dissipated life. He first noticed the signs of the illness in Paris when devastating headaches racked him. Then he lost strength and the ability to concentrate. At last he had gone to a doctor who attributed his condition to inherited factors: "the sins of the fathers. . . ." Oswald had been unable to believe this diagnosis because of the fictions about his father's probity. He finally convinced the doctor—and himself—that his style of living had merely been too much for his strength. Now Oswald believes that inherited illness would be preferable to the knowledge that he has destroyed himself. When Oswald complains of the darkness, Mrs. Alving summons Regine and asks her to bring in a lamp. When he asks for a drink, Mrs. Alving says that she could not refuse him anything. He asks if she really means that. Then Oswald begins to talk of Regine and says that she is the only thing that can save him from his agony. To spare his mother the horrifying sight of his imminent decline, he must go away and then Regine would prove useful. He says that on his previous visit at home, he had playfully talked with Regine about life in Paris, and now she is eager to go there. Perhaps her joy of life would prove to be his salvation. He is so committed to this plan that he asks Regine to join them for a drink. Oswald further explains that his delight in life would degenerate into ugliness if he remained in this environment. Manders comes in, sees Regine, and says that she must go to help her father. She immediately says no to that plan. Mrs. Alving is unaffected by this bickering because, in light of Oswald's reasoning, she has decided to tell him the truth. Her revelation, however, is cut short by shouts announcing that the orphanage is on fire. Manders calls it a judgment of God, to which Mrs. Alving agrees. In the general confusion, the curtain falls.

The outer darkness of Act III is relieved only by the glow of the smoldering remains of the orphanage, which are being scrutinized through the window by Mrs. Alving and Regine. Mrs. Alving exits to take Oswald's hat to him, leaving Regine to encounter Manders a moment later. Engstrand comes in and in an aside to Regine indicates his intention of twitting Manders again. He says openly that he saw Manders snuff a candle with his fingers and throw the wick into a pile of wood shavings. Despite Manders' contrary protestations, Engstrand then reminds the pastor that there was no insurance on the orphanage. Both men see what the newspapers will make of the situation. Mrs. Alving enters and surprises them all by noting that no good could have come from the orphanage. She instructs Manders to take all the papers relating to the institution when he leaves by the next boat; she also gives him the power to deal as he sees fit with the trust fund and the remnant of Alving's estate. Engstrand suggests that Manders might use some of the Alving money to support his seamen's home, to which Manders assents. Thus, Engstrand's blackmail is accomplished. Engstrand and Manders leave together, but Regine enthusiastically declines to accompany them.

Oswald comes in from fighting the fire and asks what sort of home Engstrand was referring to as they passed. Upon hearing the explanation, he concludes that it would only be burned up as will everything associated with his father, including Oswald himself. When his mother begins to pamper him and urge him to get some rest, he replies that he will sleep soon enough; for the present he wants all the doors closed. Oswald says that Regine must be there to help him when the time comes, but his mother says that she can be trusted to do what is right. For the present she intends to tell him that he did not cause his sickness. She now sees that Alving had had Oswald's joy of life and that the environment and her firm adherence to duty had left him no recourse except dissipation. She also tells Regine that she stands on an equal footing with Oswald, since she is also Captain Alving's child. Now that she knows the truth, Regine wants to leave as she cannot spend her young life nursing invalids. Regine goes off in search of Manders so that she can acquire her part of her mother's pay-off money. If Manders will not take her in, she can always go to the seamen's hostel.

Oswald and his mother are left alone. The son admits that he feels sorry that his father was so unhappy but that his feelings go no further than that. Filial love in his circumstances can be only a superstition. Mrs. Alving sees that she must win his love, but Oswald is too concerned about his own death to worry about her feelings. He says that she has freed him of self-reproach and asks who will rid him of the terror of an ugly, painful death. Night has passed, and the morning is dawning, which alleviates some of Oswald's horror. He asks his mother if she had seriously meant that she would do anything in the world for him. Again she affirms it. He explains that he is terrorized by the realization that his illness will result in the loss of his mind, a gradual deterioration the thought of which he cannot bear. He has a box of morphine tablets which his mother must administer when the next seizure is upon him. Mrs. Alving recoils in horror, rushes out to summon a doctor, but Oswald locks the door before she can exit. He asks how she can bear to see him suffer if she really loves him. After a painful moment of deliberation, she promises that she will administer the tablets if it becomes necessary, all the while maintaining that the necessity will never arise. Reassured, Oswald concludes that they will live together as long as they can. The sun rises in all its glory as Oswald settles into a chair. Mrs. Alving natters about their future together, but Oswald quietly asks her to give him the sun. Again he asks for the sun and then crumples into his chair; his eyes lose their animation. The fit is upon him. She screams, shakes him, calls his name, but Oswald can only tonelessly ask for the sun. She tears her hair, refuses to consider the tablets, and then looks for them, wavers, deciding to administer them, concluding that she will not. She stares blankly at her son as he again asks for the sun. The curtain falls.

Structural analysis: Ghosts is the shortest of the social problem plays and so economical of incident that it almost has the compactness of a Greek tragedy. Its five characters, isolated in a gloomy rural environment, play out their stories with inexorable desperation. Ibsen chose to unify his Plot by action:

Mrs. Alving discovers that Oswald is trying to seduce Regine and sees this as the reappearance of ghosts from the past;

(as a result of which)

Mrs. Alving decides that a suitable marriage for Regine must be found;

(as a result of which)

Mrs. Alving discovers that Oswald needs Regine to help him face his illness;

(as a result of which)

Mrs. Alving decides to tell Oswald the truth about his father;

(as a result of which)

Mrs. Alving discovers that Oswald thinks he has caused his disease;

(as a result of which)

Mrs. Alving tells Oswald about his father's profligacy, thereby ridding him of his self-reproach;

(as a result of which)

Mrs. Alving discovers that Oswald fears the loss of his mental faculties and requires her to administer a lethal drug;

(as a result of which)

Mrs. Alving conditionally agrees to help him;

(as a result of which)

Mrs. Alving discovers that Oswald is having a seizure and requires the morphine;

(as a result of which)

Mrs. Alving must make a choice.

The Thought of the drama deserves a comment. Ibsen's contemporaries were so absorbed by Ibsen's controversial treatment of venereal disease that all but the most astute interpreted the play as a tract against social illnesses. Surely that is not Ibsen's primary point. Helene Alving is the protagonist, and her situation is the result of her conceding to societal pressure to enter into a loveless marriage and to continue to preserve the appearance of normalcy, although she lived with a depraved monster. The pathetic aspect of her situation is that her concession to a wife's duty created a child doomed to destruction through no fault of his own. Not only was her life sacrificed to societal expedience but that of Oswald was as well. Ibsen wisely ended the play without revealing whether Mrs. Alving could at last function as a feeling, thinking entity entirely released from the presssures of society's expectations.

References: Corrigan, Robert W. "The Sun Always Rises: Ibsen's *Ghosts* as Tragedy?" *Educational Theatre Journal*, 11 (1959), 172-80; Swanson, C. A. "Ibsen's *Ghosts* at the Théâtre Libre," *Scandinavian Studies*, 16, 8 (1941), 281-90; Wergeland, Agnes M. "Collett on Ibsen's *Ghosts*," *Leaders in Norway and Other Essays* (New York: Books for Libraries, 1966 [1916]), pp. 189-90; Zucker, A. E. "Southern Critics of 1903 on Ibsen's *Ghosts*," *Philological Quarterly*, 19 (Oct. 1940), 392-9.

GIELGUD, JOHN (1904-   ): British actor John Gielgud's participation in Ibsenian productions has been limited. As a mere youth, he played a walk-on part in an Old Vic production of *Peer Gynt** (1922), and in 1928 he was Oswald Alving* to Mrs. Patrick Campbell's* Helene Alving.* His memoirs reveal very little about his performance but provide several insights into his leading lady's approach to her role.

Reference: Gielgud, John. *Early Stages.* New York: Macmillan, 1939.

GILDET PAA SOLHOUG: The Norwegian title of *The Feast at Solhoug.**

GINSBURY, NORMAN (1902-   ): British actor Norman Ginsbury has translated *Peer Gynt,** *Ghosts,** *An Enemy of the People,** and *A Doll's House.**

A GOBLIN (*St. John's Night*): A supernatural creature that lives in the attic of old Birk's* cottage. His prank of putting a drug in the punchbowl occasions the fantastic events on the mountain on midsummer night.

GOLDMAN, EMMA (1869-1940): Anarchist, lecturer, and author, Emma Goldman saw in Ibsen's works a stance similar to her own with regard to contemporary social issues. She wrote, "Above all did he thunder his fiery indictment against the four cardinal sins of modern society: the lie inherent in our social arrangements; Sacrifice and Duty, the twin curses that fetter the spirit of man; the narrow-mindedness and pettiness of Provincialism, that stifles all growth; and the Lack of Joy and Purpose in Work which turns life into a vale of misery and tears" (p. 12).

Goldman was the daughter of a Lithuanian theatre manager. Since her youth paralleled the growth of theatrical Realism, it is natural that the young political activist would see in Ibsen's plays, particularly the social problem plays, the same iconoclasm that impelled her. Goldman's critical insight was in some cases more profound than that of professional critics. In her view, people like Karsten Bernick* "must learn that society is rotten to the core; that patching up or reforming one sore spot [as Bernick attempted to patch up *The Indian Girl*] merely drives the social poison deeper into the system." (p. 18).

Goldman saw that *Ghosts* * is not about venereal disease but about "the paralyzing effect of Duty" and "the uselessness and evil of Sacrifice." Ibsen's voice, she wrote, "sounds like the trumpets before the walls of Jericho. Into the remotest nooks and corners reaches his voice, with its thundering indictment of our moral cancers, our social positions, our hideous crimes against unborn and born victims" (p. 33).

Although Goldman's passion aggrandizes her rhetoric somewhat, her conclusion is undeniable: "His dramatic art, without his glorious rebellion against every authoritative institution, against every social and moral lie, against every vestige of bondage, were inconceivable. Just as his art would lose human significance, were his love of truth and freedom lacking" (p. 42).

Although Ibsen occupied the dominant position in Goldman's pantheon of modern dramatists, she also spoke and wrote penetratingly of August Strindberg,* Hermann Sudermann, Gerhart Hauptmann, Frank Wedekind, Maurice Maeterlinck, Edmond Rostand, Eugène Brieux, George Bernard Shaw,* John Galsworthy, William S. Houghton, Leo Sowerby, William Butler Yeats, Lennox Robinson, Thomas C. Murray, Leo Tolstoy, Anton Chekhov, Maxim Gorky, and Leonid Andreyev.

References: Goldman, Emma. *The Social Significance of the Modern Drama.* Boston: Richard G. Badger, 1914; Ishill, Joseph. *Emma Goldman, a Challenging Rebel.* Berkeley Heights, N.J.: Oriole Press, 1957.

GOODFRIEND, IDA JEFFREYS (1856-1926): Already an established star when she was associated with Beatrice Cameron's* *A Doll's House* * (1889), Ida Jeffreys Goodfriend entered the ranks of Ibsenian pioneers by presenting the first production of *Ghosts* * in New York, initially at the Berkeley Lyceum Theatre (January 5, 1894) and then at the Garden Theatre (January 25, 1894). Courtenay Thorpe supported her Helene Alving* before "an exceedingly small but select band of Ibsenites." The reviewer of *The Critic* ignored the production, choosing to spew his bile at the play which he condemned for a surfeit of talk and an absence of action. He admitted that Ibsen had chosen a tragic theme, but his formulation of the plot fell far short of tragedy. Other reviewers were appreciative of Goodfriend's efforts. Just prior to this presentation, Ida Jeffreys had married Si Goodfriend and slowed down her theatrical activities, appearing rarely afterward. On May 12, 1905, she played Aline Solness* in a single matinee performance of *The Master Builder** with William Hazeltine* as Halvard Solness.*

References: Briscoe, Johnson. *The Actors' Birthday Book*, 2d ser. New York: Moffat, Yard, 1908; "Ghosts," *The Critic*, XXIV, 621 (Jan. 13, 1894), 31.

GORDON, RUTH (1896-   ): Thornton Wilder* convinced actress Ruth Gordon that she should attempt a classical role. On the basis of Wilder's agreement to modernize the script of *A Doll's House*,* Gordon persuaded Jed Harris to stage the production which opened at the Morosco Theatre (New York) on December 27, 1937, and eventually took its place as one of Ibsen's longest running productions—144 performances.

The fate of this presentation might have been significantly different had not Alexander Woollcott chosen to recommend it on his *Town Crier* radio broadcast. After two weeks, *A Doll's House* was in danger of closing from lack of interest, but Woollcott proclaimed, "Here . . . is a night in the theatre which many people throughout the country would remember all their lives. It is so right, so true, so devastating that it knocks at the door of every human heart. . . . It is part of the music of the spheres that such a thing should come into its own" (Gordon, p. 27). As a result of Woollcott's broadcast, the show was moved from the Morosco to the Broadhurst Theatre and enjoyed a record-setting run.

Commenting on "the extraordinary industry" of Gordon's performance, Brooks Atkinson wrote that after the flippancies of the first act, Gordon went "straight to the heart" of the role. She "completely mastered" the serious scenes and "concluded the play with force and her own touch of modest glory."

References: Gordon, Ruth. *Myself among Others*. New York: Dell Publishing Company, 1972; *New York Times*, Dec. 28, 1937, p. 28, col. 6.

GORING, MARIUS (1912-   ): Marius Goring acted with Alan Napier as Gregers Werle* and Hjalmar Ekdal* in 1936 and supported Jean Forbes-Robertson* as Johannes Rosmer* in 1948.

Reference: Who's Who in the Theatre, 16th ed., pp. 664-5.

GORVIN, JOANA MARIA (1922-   ): Only seven years after her debut at Berlin's National Theatre in 1943, Joana Maria Gorvin portrayed the role of Nora Helmer* in Munich under the direction of Jürgen Fehling.

Reference: Encyclopedia of World Theatre, ed. Martin Esslin. New York: Charles Scribner's Sons, 1977.

GOSSE, EDMUND WILLIAM (1849-1928): Edmund Gosse, literary critic and poet, introduced Ibsen's work to the English-reading public. In 1871, while on the staff of the British Museum, Gosse journeyed to Norway as a journalist and discovered Ibsen on the lips of his literary acquaintance. Gosse, marveling that such celebrity could remain so obscure in England, set about the task of establishing Ibsen's English reputation. His efforts as Ibsen's champion can best be summarized by listing the major items on Ibsen among the twenty-odd that he published between 1872 and 1878:

"Ibsen's New Poems," *Spectator*, XLV (Mar. 16, 1872), 344-5.

"A Norwegian Drama [*Peer Gynt*]," *Spectator*, XLV (July 20, 1872), 922-3.

"Kongs-emnerne," *Academy*, III, 53 (Aug. 1, 1872), 281.

"Norwegian Poetry since 1814," *Fraser's Magazine*, n.s. VI (Oct. 1872), 435-50.

"Ibsen, the Norwegian Satirist," *Fortnightly Review*, XIX (Jan. 1, 1873), 74-88.

"Ibsen's Julian the Apostate," *Spectator*, No. 2374 (Dec. 27, 1873), 1655-6.

"Ibsen's Jubilee," *Spectator*, No. 2439 (Mar. 27, 1875), 401-2.

The opinions expressed in these articles were repeated in the chapter on Ibsen in Gosse's *Studies in the Literature of Northern Europe* (London: Kegan Paul, 1879).

While Gosse's efforts did not bring Ibsen immediate acceptance in England, at least the literary population had been made aware of the dramatist's existence and the merit of his work. For reasons that are not entirely clear, Gosse's interest in Ibsen waned for several years after the 1870s. His next important statement was an article called "Ibsen's Social Dramas" in *Fortnightly Review*, XLV (Jan. 1, 1889), 107-21.

The critic Gosse stressed the milieu out of which Ibsen had arisen. He was very sensitive to the Norwegian cultural environment and its effect on the writer. As a poet himself, Gosse favored Ibsen's dramatic poems, especially *Peer Gynt*.* He was decidedly cool toward the social problem plays, seeing *Ghosts** as a tract on venereal disease and censuring *The Pillars of Society** as a farrago of the tricks of the well-made play.* *The Wild Duck** was "difficult to comprehend," but Gosse saw *The Lady from the Sea** as "a glamour of romance, of mystery, and landscape beauty," a picture of society that induced health.

The absence of acceptable translations of his plays retarded Ibsen's progress in England. Between 1872 and 1878, several pieces were rendered in English, but they were ineffective. In 1888 William Archer's* translation of *The Pillars of Society* appeared, inaugurating a new era for Ibsen in England. Gosse had translated *Love's Comedy** but could not find a publisher; he had also received Ibsen's permission to try his hand at *A Doll's House*,* but nothing came of it. In 1891 Gosse's version of *Hedda Gabler** was published and created a break with Archer, who disputed Gosse's publication rights. Whatever their personal feelings, the Gosse-Archer rendition of *The Master Builder** came off the presses in 1893.

Gosse's last major effort in Ibsen's behalf was his biography *Henrik Ibsen* (1907), which became Vol. XIII of Archer's *The Collected Works of Henrik Ibsen*. Ibsen and Gosse maintained a correspondence over the years, but the Englishman did not meet the Norwegian until 1899 and came away with a number of mistaken notions about the old dramatist. He concluded that Ibsen owned no book, but a Bible and that Ibsen reviled Leo Tolstoy. Gosse erred on both of these points.

References: Bredsdorff, Elias, ed. *Sir Edmund Gosse's Correspondence with Scandinavian Writers.* Copenhagen: Gyldendal, 1960; Charteris, Evan. *The Life and Letters of Sir Edmund Gosse.* London: Heinemann, 1931.

GRAABERG (*The Wild Duck*): As Haakon Werle's* bookkeeper, Graaberg serves as the emissary between his employer and the Ekdal* family.

GRAN, ALBERT (1862-1932): Actor Albert Gran was Johan Tönnesen* in the Incorporated Stage Society's* production of *The Pillars of Society** in London in 1901. The critics noted his intense passion. He also traveled throughout the English-speaking countries in 1907 and gave readings from Ibsen's dramas. His interpretation of Aase's* death in *Peer Gynt** and the fourth act of *Brand** was seen in Chicago (March 31, 1907) as well as in England.

A GREEN-CLAD WOMAN (*Peer Gynt*): This woman with whom Peer Gynt* becomes infatuated is the daughter of the Troll King (See Old Man of the Dovrë). It is upon her that Peer fathers the Ugly Brat.*

GREENE, J. H.: Apparently, this undistinguished actor's performance in the Progressive Stage Society's production of *The Master Builder** in New York in 1905 was not inspired. The *New York Times* wrote: "Of the acting in the present production the best that can be said is that the women were generally better than the men, although there was not especial evidence of fitness for the task on the part of any of those engaged" (May 1, 1905, p. 9, col. 1).

GREENWOOD, JOAN (1920-   ): Joan Greenwood twice played in Ibsenian dramas at the Oxford Playhouse: Nora Helmer* in 1945 and Hedda Gabler* in 1960. In 1964 Greenwood's Hedda Gabler was seen in London's West End.

Reference: Who's Who in the Theatre, 16th ed., p. 676.

GREGORI, FERDINAND (1870-1928): As a Romantic leading man, Ferdinand Gregori appeared as Brand* at Berlin's Schiller Theater on March 17, 1898. Johannes Rosmer* was also in his repertory.

Reference: Kosch, Wilhelm. *Deutsches Theater-Lexikon*, I, 607.

GREGORIUS JONSSON (*The Pretenders*): A nobleman; adherent of Earl Skule.*

GREGORY OF NAZIANZUS (*Emperor and Galilean*): A friend of Julian*
who tries to prevent his apostasy. Gregory eventually becomes a major
opponent of Emperor Julian.

GREIN, JACOB THOMAS (1862-1935): J. T. Grein was a Dutch journalist who lived and worked in London. His continental theatrical connections
made him aware of Ibsen's dramas, and as the head of the Independent
Theatre,* Grein inaugurated his enterprise with a production of *Ghosts**
(1891). In 1894 he produced *The Wild Duck.** As dramatic critic of the
Sunday Times, Grein continued to champion Ibsenian productions.
Reference: Orme, Michael. *J. T. Grein: The Story of a Pioneer, 1862-1935*. London:
    John Murray, 1936.

GREINZ, HUGO (1873-1946): German novelist Hugo Greinz made an
authorized translation of *Catiline** in 1896.
Reference: Deutsches Literatur-Lexikon (Bern: Francke, 1978), VI, 762-3.

GRIEG, EDVARD (1843-1907): Norwegian composer Edvard Grieg was
asked to furnish incidental music for *Peer Gynt** when the musical manu-
scripts of another composer were lost. He was unenthusiastic about the
project, which was completed in July 1875. Grieg's music is largely responsible for creating in the public mind a saccharine impression of the drama.
While Grieg's score is pleasant, it is wholly inappropriate to the drama.
Reference: Johansen, David M. *Edvard Grieg*. Trans. Madge Robertson. Princeton,
    N.J.: Princeton University Press, 1938.

GRIMSTAD: An isolated Norwegian village in which Ibsen lived between
1844 and 1850. At age sixteen he left his family and moved to Grimstad as
an apprentice to apothecary J. A. Reimann.* Young Ibsen was little better
than a servant in Reimann's shop; his days were filled with work and his
nights with loneliness. He turned to Elsie Sofie Jensdatter,* a maid, for
consolation, and the birth of Hans Jakob Henrikson* out of wedlock was
the result of their liaison. While in Grimstad, however, Ibsen determined to
take the matriculation examinations for the University of Oslo, so the
formation of a goal helped to brighten his final days there. It was during his
time in Grimstad that Ibsen wrote his first poems and the drama *Catiline.**
Reference: Eitrem, Hans. *Ibsen og Grimstad*. Oslo: Aschehoug, 1940.

THE GROUSE IN JUSTEDAL: A projected four-act serious drama of
which only two acts were completed.
Composition: Started and left unfinished in 1850.
Stage history: None.
Synopsis: As evening falls in the rugged Norwegian mountains, Paal, a
veteran hunter, and Björn, the son of his master, are returning from a hunting expedition. En route to Bjerkehoug, Björn wishes to tarry in the
mountains that are the home of the elfin folk. Fascinated by such beliefs,

Björn is warned by Paal that speaking of the fairy world as the sun goes down is likely to precipitate a visitation by them. Paal relates how he had met a hulder* while hunting grouse in this very region. The experience convinced him that the grouse was a troll-bird. At that time he had run away, for he knew that the hulder had wanted to tempt him to go away with her, as she had lured Eivind Bolt, kept him hidden in the recesses of the mountain for many years, and finally released him. Björn thinks this is an exciting fate and admits that he has roamed the mountainside at dusk in the expectation of encountering the hulder. His zeal has taken him as far as Justedal, a haunted region shunned by everyone. When Paal questions him about what he saw in Justedal, Björn becomes quite tight-lipped, admitting only that he *saw* nothing unusual. Paal believes that the hulder owns Justedal because the local farmgirls have heard her blowing her lur, a wooden shepherd's horn. At the mention of the hulder's music, Björn leaps up and wants to know whence the sound emanated. Paal believes the sound came from this very hilltop, at the base of which lies a derelict cottage. Björn quickly decides that they should spend the night in the hut. Paal enters the cottage to prepare it for their night's rest while Björn remains to soliloquize.

Björn says that he has heard the hulder's lur, which mesmerized him into returning to the mountain each day in pursuit of the enchantress. Hearing footsteps, he discovers a man with a fiddle in his hand. The man is apparently bound for the village. Harald is a minstrel, and the world is his home. He has surprisingly youthful ideas and intends to seek a warm hearth in Justedal, which he has not visited for many years. He walks off reminding Björn that the forest is full of life and activities that may be perceived only by those who have special keenness. While musing about the strange traveler, Björn hears the notes of the hulder's lur. As the mysterious music resounds, Alfhild appears in the heights and sings a pastoral lyric about the thrush's love song. As she finishes her song, Alfhild notices Björn and disappears into a copse. Björn recognizes her as the hulder and vows to elicit more information from Harald, so he rouses Paal and together they set out for Bjerkehoug.

The second locale is the great hall of Bjerkehoug, with a fireplace and seat of honor. Mereta, the young mistress of the house, and Ingeborg, a servant, enter and prepare for a feast. As Ingeborg exits, Einar comes in determined to say something important to Mereta, but the girl playfully speaks of his urban life and loss of country interests as if to forestall what she believes he will say. Before he can speak his mind, Mereta leaves the room, while a confused Einar is unable to interpret her contradictory behavior: sometimes she seems to jeer at him, but at other times, she encourages his attentions.

Einar's ruminations are interrupted by the entrance of Mogens, a priest who seeks Bengt, the master of the house and guardian of Mereta. Over a potation of mead, Mogens remarks that for some unknown reason, Bengt has been rather moody and depressed of late. The priest thinks that Bengt's youthful follies lie at the base of his unsettled humor. Einar, who has been away at court since his childhood, asks for clarification, which impels Mogens to expound ancient history. Bengt had had a sweet-tempered brother, Alf, who, as the elder son, was to inherit the family property. Bengt, like his son Björn, was a rash, worldly man who tried to poison his father's mind against Alf. When Alf had married, Bengt was at last successful in turning the father against him; as a consequence, Alf and his wife disappeared without a trace, probably into the high mountains. It was assumed that they had succumbed to the Black Death, as had all the inhabitants of that region. Later, the father had died, Bengt inherited, and the atmosphere of Bjerkehoug had become increasingly dismal. Despite his guilty conscience, Bengt is a powerful man, and his son will exceed him in greatness if he marries Mereta, an idea wholly acceptable to her. Hearing this, Einar realizes the reasons for Bengt's coldness toward him. Bengt's approach is heard, and Einar withdraws.

Bengt sees Mogens and asks for papers that prove Mereta to be her father's only heir. When Mogens assures him that this is so and that he now sees nothing in the way of the wedding, Bengt explodes, especially when Mogens suggests that the village people have been gossiping about his motivations. Bengt is now disposed to announce the wedding of Björn and Mereta, neither of whom is privy to his plan. Hearing delighted laughter from the hearthside, Bengt finds Einar and Mereta telling fairy tales. When they invite him to add a tale, Bengt refuses because such stories interfere with his sleep. Mereta recalls how Grandpapa used to tell them stories of Singer Knud, a wandering minstrel, who, according to old Paal, is still alive and singing. Finally, Bengt relents and starts to tell the story of the nomadic minstrel whose stories of the hulder never failed to please. As he speaks, Knud enters and sings of his travels, but not of the elfin folk, for this would, he learns, annoy Bengt. He mentions his kinsmen, Alf and Ingierd, the very names of whom hurl Bengt into a rage. Knud says he means no harm and asks permission to sing his song. Before the issue can be resolved, Björn and Paal come in from their hunting trip and Björn recognizes Knud as the Harald whom he saw on the mountain. Knud, prophesying woe to the house in which the minstrel's songs are unwelcome, leaves with the warning that Bengt will hear further of him. Paal notices the golden strings of the minstrel's fiddle and identifies the stranger as the Singer Knud, which causes a furor of reaction. Paal explains that good luck comes to those who listen to Knud's songs and evil fortune to those who turn him away. Bengt dismisses this warning and sends Mereta to prepare the meal; then he withdraws with Mogens.

Björn, perplexed by the events of the day, tells Einar about seeing Alfhild on the mountainside; Einar immediately sees that this girl might be the hulder. Whatever her identity, Björn is set on meeting her again. He is deeply chagrined when Einar tells him of Bengt's intention of marrying

Björn to Mereta; Björn is interested only in the hulder, and he rushes out in pursuit of her.

Act II takes place in Justedal, a rugged but luxuriant valley. Björn comes in, wearied by his pursuit of the hulder, the sound of whose lur he at last hears. Then he sees Alfhild, who is speaking to herself of her unhappiness at not finding the man whom she had previously encountered. She then notices Björn and rushes into his arms, begging him not to leave her again as he had done last night. When Björn expresses ignorance of this, Alfhild offers to explain. Last night, it seems, the elves did not come to bring her flowers and cavort about her bed as they normally do. She concluded that they had been frightened by the presence of a mortal, none other than Björn. When Björn attributes these feelings to a dream, Alfhild does not comprehend, but she urges him to remain with her. Björn questions her about her origins and learns that she had once lived here with her mother and father, a man whom Björn greatly resembles. Through the entire conversation, Alfhild refers to herself in the third person or by her name. Now she lives alone, she says, in the company of the elves, but occasionally she sees her aged father and a minstrel. Björn speaks of his home and asks Alfhild to live with him there. She agrees, but their happy mood is interrupted by the appearance of Knud, whom Alfhild addresses as father. Joyously, Alfhild tells Knud that Björn has sworn never to leave her and wishes to live in his own house with her. Knud promises to visit her in Bjerkehoug, for his mission is to protect her. When Knud departs, Alfhild reaffirms her decision to go away with Björn. Björn declares that he will love her forever, and Alfhild asks the meaning of the word "love." When he explains, Alfhild tells him that she would die without his love. A chorus of elves commences to serenade the lovers, but in their song they predict that she will rejoin them on the mountain some day. As the elfin music fades, the lovers depart for Bjerkehoug.

In a green near the house at Bjerkehoug, Paal greets Mereta with news of the gloom spread by Bengt on this otherwise festive Midsummer Night. Mereta observes that even Björn is so afraid of Bengt that he spends all his time hunting in the mountains. Paal is on the verge of telling her of Björn's pursuit of the hulder, but Bengt's entrance prompts Mereta to withdraw, a fact noticed by Bengt who complains that his presence adversely affects all women. Bengt dispatches Paal to summon Mogens to a business conference. When he is alone, Bengt cannot dismiss the recollection of his wronged brother, but these thoughts are chased away by his glimpse of something among the trees. Bengt crosses himself and goes into the house.

Einar reproaches Mereta for not taking his affection seriously, but she taunts him and causes him to withdraw once again without declaring his intentions toward her. Before he can get far, she calls him back to offer him her hand — and heart — as he embarks upon his path. Surprised but delighted, Einar embraces her joyfully; Bengt and Mogens, however, enter in time to apprehend them. Bengt chastises Mereta, who slips away; then he tells Einar that he has disposed of Mereta in a way that will thwart Einar's plans.

So Einar realizes that Mogens was right in saying that Bengt planned to marry Mereta to Björn. Music is heard as Paal, musicians, and several peasants enter. [The manuscript ends at this point.]

GUDBRANDSDALEN: A valley through which Ibsen passed in his search for folklore, Gudbrandsdalen is the locale of *Brand*.*

GUDMUND ALFSON (*The Feast at Solhoug*): Cousin of Margit* and Signe* and the object of their romantic interest. As a minstrel and state counselor, Gudmund has led an adventurous life and is a fugitive when he first appears in the drama.

GUERNSEY, MINERVA: Minerva Guernsey was the first English-language Nora Helmer* in the United States, appearing in *The Child Wife** in Milwaukee in 1882. Little is known of her, and much of that is contradictory. Guernsey was a native of Janesville, Wisconsin, and spent five years training for the theatre. Her performance in *The Child Wife* marked her professional debut, a not very auspicious beginning if the newspaper reviewers are to be believed. They said that she lacked power, seemed nervous, and habitually forgot her lines—conditions under which a creditable performance was impossible. Nothing is known about her subsequent career.
References: (Milwaukee) *Republican-Sentinel*, June 3, 1882, p. 5, col. 1; (Milwaukee) *Evening Wisconsin*, June 3, 1882, p. 4, col. 2.

GUIDE'S SON (*Brand*): A minor character in Act I. He and his father try to convince Brand* to turn back rather than cross the snowbound mountain pass. When they are unsuccessful, they leave him.

GULDSTAD (*Love's Comedy*): A wholesale merchant, Guldstad is Falk's* competitor for the affection of Svanhild Halm.* He is ultimately successful.

GUNDERSEN, LAURA SVENDSEN (1832-98): As a youthful member of the first company at the Norwegian Theatre, Bergen,* Laura Svendsen originated the role of Blanka.* She also played Lady Inger of Gyldenlöve,* Hjördis,* Selma Brattsberg,* Ellida Wangel,* and Gunhild Borkman.* Gundersen was one of Norway's major actresses at the time of her death.
Reference: Norsk Biografisk Leksikon, V, 94-5.

GUNDERSEN, SIGVARD EMIL (1842-1903): Norwegian actor Sigvard Gundersen appeared in a number of Ibsenian roles, among them Haakon,* Dr. Fjeldbo,* Karsten Bernick,* Peter Stockmann* (Ibsen advised him to look as thin as possible for this role), Haakon Werle,* and Falk.*
Reference: Norsk Biografisk Leksikon,, V, 94-5.

GUNNAR HEADMAN (*The Vikings in Helgeland*): A rich yeoman of Helgeland, Gunnar was the boyhood friend and rival of Sigurd.* He is married to Hjördis,* whom he had abducted from her father's home. At the start of the play, the Vikings have come to avenge this deed.

GUTHORM INGESSON (*The Pretenders*): A disappointed pretender.

GYNT, JON (*Peer Gynt*): The father of Peer Gynt.* He is mentioned but does not appear. As a lovable wastrel, Jon Gynt may have been suggested by Ibsen's father, Knud.*

GYNT, PEER (*Peer Gynt*): One of Ibsen's most compelling characters, Peer Gynt is the epitome of the Romantic protagonist. He is a teller of tall tales, a daydreamer, and an impulsive activist. He seeks happiness and self-satisfaction but has to undergo rigorous adventures to discover that love and commitment are the essential ingredients. He must be brought to the brink of destruction before he sees that contentment and fulfillment are to be found at home at the side of Solveig.*

GYNTIANA: After watching his ship explode on the seacoast of Morocco (IV, 5), Peer Gynt* soliloquizes about colonizing Africa with Scandinavian stock. There he will erect Peeropolis in a "virginal" spot called Gyntiana. Peer's dream of a New Norway is quite similar to that of Ole Bull* at Oleana.

A GYPSY WOMAN (*Brand*): Brand* forces Agnes* to give her All or Nothing through the Gypsy Woman. When the gypsy appears at their door begging clothes for her baby, Brand insists that Agnes surrender the clothes of their dead child.

H

HAAKON HAAKONSSON (*The Pretenders*): As leader of the Birkebeiner party (the Birchlegs), Haakon first appears as the rightful claimant of the Norwegian throne. Through a series of ordeals and political maneuvers, he is proclaimed king, but his rule is complicated by the rival ambitions of Earl Skule* and the satanic machinations of Nikolas Arnesson, Bishop of Oslo.* He is strong, certain of his legitimate right to the throne, fearless in battle, generous to his vanquished foes, and a loving husband—the complete opposite, in fact, of his antagonist Skule.

HAAKONSSON, JULIA (1853-1940): As one of Sweden's chief actor/managers, Julia Haakonsson first appeared as Nora Helmer* in 1886 at the Royal Theatre in Stockholm. After working with several directors, Haakonsson formed her own company and toured Sweden between 1898 and 1905, playing Lady Inger of Gyldenlöve,* Hedda Gabler,* Helene Alving,* Rebecca West,* Hilde Wangel* (in *The Master Builder*), Rita Allmers,* Gunhild Borkman,* Ella Rentheim,* and Gina Ekdal,* among other, non-Ibsenian roles. Her acting was characterized by "natural intimacy" and "aristocratic elegance" (*Enciclopedia della Spettacolo*, VI, 105). Near the end of her active career, Haakonsson forsook acting in favor of directing.
Reference: Svenskt Biografiskt Handlexikon, I, 528-9.

HALM, ANNA (*Love's Comedy*): Younger daughter of Mrs. Halm*; fiancée of Lind.*

HALM, MRS. (*Love's Comedy*): Mrs. Halm, the mother of Svanhild,* is a widow of a government official. Falk* has rooms in her house, which is the scene of the drama. Mrs. Halm is representative of traditional values in marriage.

HALM, SVANHILD (*Love's Comedy*): Mrs. Halm's* elder daughter, Svanhild is the object of Falk's* romantic inclinations. It is to Svanhild that Falk outlines his theory that marriage kills love. Svanhild loves Falk but decides to marry Guldstad* in order to preserve her love of Falk.

HAMMER, BORGNY (1878-1947): An important Norwegian-American interpreter of Ibsen's heroines, Borgny Hammer acted in the Norwegian theatres in her native Bergen* and in Christiania.* With her family she emigrated to the United States in 1910 and was associated with the Norwegian Theatre in Chicago. Beginning in 1918, Hammer took Ibsen's plays to schools and universities across America, performing in Norwegian when there was an audience and in English when necessary. Her family thereafter settled in the East, where she established the Norwegian Theatre of Brooklyn in 1924. Her last American tour in a repertory of Norwegian plays occurred in 1935. By this time she had appeared as Hedda Gabler,* Nora Helmer,* Helene Alving,* Hilde Wangel,* Rebecca West,* and Rita Allmers.*
References: American Scandinavian Review, 35 (Dec. 1947), 364; *New York Times*, Aug. 12, 1947, p. 23, col. 3.

HAMPDEN, WALTER (1879-1955): Walter Hampden's Ibsenian involvement spanned thirty years, although he performed only three roles. In 1907 he played Torvald Helmer* to the Nora* of Alla Nazimova,* and in the same year he appeared as Halvard Solness.* In 1927 and again in 1937 Hampden portrayed Thomas Stockmann* in *An Enemy of the People*,* the first time being in his own theatre. The play achieved a long run of 113 performances. On the occasion of the centenary of Ibsen's birth, Hampden wrote:

Ibsen's place in the theatre is assured for many years to come, possibly for centuries. He is one of the few modern dramatists who will survive. While it has become the habit of some critics who go into ecstasies over "new" methods in playwriting to pronounce Ibsen hopelessly old-fashioned, his work has certain eternal qualities which will keep them [sic] from perishing. . . . While my keenest personal satisfaction is in acting the great Shakespearean roles, there is much mental exhilaration in acting and staging Ibsen. . . . The very contrast between Ibsen and Shakespeare in subject matter, characterization, and structure is a stimulus to the actor and director. (Quoted in R. H. Fife and Ansten Anstensen, "Henrik Ibsen on the American Stage," *American Scandinavian Review*, XVI, 4 [Apr. 1928], 228.)
Reference: Who Was Who in the Theatre, II, 1069-71.

HAMPSHIRE, SUSAN (1942-   ): British actress Susan Hampshire's only Ibsenian role was that of Nora Helmer* in London in 1972.
Reference: Who's Who in the Theatre, 17th ed., I, 292.

HAMPTON, LOUISE (1876-1954): Long on the British stage, Louise Hampton brought maturity and experience to the role of Helene Alving* in

1933. In 1950 she again turned to Ibsen and played Gunhild Borkman* to the John Gabriel Borkman* of Frederick Valk.*
Reference: Who Was Who in the Theatre, II, 1071-2.

HANSEN, JOHAN (d. 1865): Ibsen studied at Johan Hansen's school at Skien* from 1841 to 1843. Hansen's theological studies had given him enough Latin with which to tutor Ibsen in the classics. The kindly teacher is one of the few residents of Skien* whom the adult Ibsen was to remember with kindness, as Ibsen's childhood there was marked by poverty, strict pietism, and loneliness.

HANSTEEN, ASTA (1824-1908): Radical feminist Asta Hansteen was much in the public's view while Ibsen was writing *The Pillars of Society*.* In 1876 Hansteen gave a series of lectures that so inflamed the male-dominated establishment that Hansteen emigrated to the United States in 1880 to escape constant harassment. Ibsen's Lona Hessel* (originally named Hassel) is based on this "clever, plain, little woman, fanatical and tactless, a forerunner of militant suffragism, who wrote violent pamphlets, held violent meetings, and excited discussion by brandishing a riding whip about the streets to keep off blackguard males" (Lucas, p. 125). Hansteen was the author of *Aabent Breve [An Open Letter]* (1875) and *Kvinden, skabt i Guds billede [The Woman, Made in God's Image]* (1878).
Reference: Lucas, F. L. *The Drama of Ibsen and Strindberg*. New York: Macmillan, 1962.

HARRING, HARRO PAUL (1798-1870): Harro Harring, a German, was resident dramatist of the Theater am der Wien, and his plays reflect the breadth of his interests. Among them are *Tragicomical Adventure of a Lover of Greece* (1823); *The Student of Salamanca* (1825); *The Gamehunter* (1825); *Theokla, the Armenian* (1827); *Faust in the Dress of the Time* (1831). His early plays are included in *Harro Harrings Werke* (1844-46). Harring used his literary talents in support of radical politics. He fought for the liberation of both the Greeks and Poles.

Harring emigrated to Norway in 1849. In that same year his radical principles spurred him to publish a politically inflammatory newspaper called *The Voice of the People*. Then he wrote a play called *Testament from America* (1850), which urged Norwegians to abandon their home land and settle in America. The authorities forcibly arranged for him to leave Norway for good, holding him in custody on the ship until it sailed. Ibsen was but one of over a hundred people who signed a petition of protest and marched to the quay in Harring's support. There a deputation was allowed to speak with the prisoner, who later appeared on deck to receive the cheers of the crowd. This was Student Ibsen's first and last political demonstration.

HARRIS, ROBERT (1900-): Robert Harris appeared as Johannes Rosmer* in support of Signe Hasso's* Rebecca West* in London in 1950.
Reference: Who's Who in the Theatre, 16th ed., pp. 704-6.

HARRISON'S *HISTORY OF LONDON:* In *The Wild Duck* * (Act III) Hedvig Ekdal* enthusiastically talks of one of the many books left in her garret by the previous owner, a sea captain known as "The Flying Dutchman." "There's one very large book," she says, "—Harrison's *History of London* it's called—it must be a hundred years old, I should think. That has lots of pictures in it. On the front page there's a picture of death holding an hourglass—and he has a lady with him."
    She is, in fact, referring to an actual book by Walter Harrison, published in London in 1775: *A New and Universal History, Description and Survey of the Cities of London and Westminster, the Borough of Southwark and Their Adjacent Parts. . . .*
    Harrison's book figured in Ibsen's life as well as Hedvig's, for when his family moved into the house at Venstöp,* it inherited a number of books belonging to the previous owner, a sailor affectionately called "The Flying Dutchman." One of the "Dutchman's" books was *Harrison's History of London.*

HASSO, SIGNE (1910-): After a varied career on continental stages and films, Swedish actress Signe Hasso settled in the United States and England. She had already played Nora Helmer* and Hilde Wangel* in Swedish when she essayed Rebecca West* in 1950 in English. In 1964 she toured America as Hedda Gabler* with the National Repertory Theatre.
Reference: Who's Who in the Theatre, 16th ed., pp. 709-10.

HAZELTINE, WILLIAM (1866-1912): William Hazeltine's Ibsenian experience was limited to one performance in New York in 1905 as Halvard Solness* to Ida Jeffreys Goodfriend's* Hilde Wangel.*
Reference: Browne, Walter, and E. D. Koch. *Who's Who on the Stage 1908.* New York: B. W. Dodge, 1908.

HECEBOLIUS (*Emperor and Galilean*): A theologian, Hecebolius was tutor to the young Julian.* When his charge became Emperor and a persecutor of Christians, Hecebolius again rallied to his cause and became Julian's ally.

HEDDA GABLER: A four-act Realistic-Symbolistic serious drama.
Composition: Started in the fall of 1890; finished on November 16; published on December 16, 1890.
Stage history:

Jan. 31, 1891   Residenz Theater, Munich, Clara Heese* as Hedda
 Feb. 6, 1891   Helsinki

Feb. 10, 1891	Lessing Theater, Berlin
Feb. 19, 1891	Stockholm
Feb. 25, 1891	Royal Theatre, Copenhagen, Betty Hennings* as Hedda
Feb. 26, 1891	Christiania Theatre* (21 perfs.)
Feb. 1891	Norwegian Theatre, Bergen*
Mar. 31, 1891	Stadttheater, Gothenburg, Julia Haakonsson* as Hedda
Apr. 20, 1891	Vaudeville Theatre, London (37), Elizabeth Robins* as Hedda
Dec. 17, 1891	Théâtre du Vaudeville, Paris (5), Mme Brandes as Hedda
1891	Hoftheater, Munich
1891	Swedish Theatre, Stockholm
May 18, 1893	Christiania Theatre (8)
May 29, 1893	Opera Comique, London (4), Janet Achurch* as Hedda
Mar. 19, 1898	Deutsches Theater, Berlin
Mar. 30, 1898	5th Avenue Theatre, New York (1), Elizabeth Robins as Hedda
Feb. 19, 1899	Art Theatre, Moscow (11), Maria F. Andreeva* as Hedda
Oct. 5, 1901	National Theatre, Christiania*
Oct. 5, 1903	Adelphi Theatre, London, Eleonora Duse* as Hedda
Oct. 5, 1903	Manhattan Theatre, New York (5), Minnie Maddern Fiske* as Hedda
Nov. 19, 1904	Manhattan Theatre, New York (24), Minnie Maddern Fiske as Hedda
May 29, 1905	Waldorf Theatre, London, Eleonora Duse as Hedda
Nov. 24, 1905	Daly's Theatre, New York (4), Nance O'Neil* as Hedda
Nov. 10, 1906	Kommisarzhevskaya Theatre, St. Petersburg, Vera Kommisarzhevskaya* as Hedda
Nov. 13, 1906	Princess Theatre, New York (40), Alla Nazimova* as Hedda
Mar. 5, 1907	Court Theatre, London (7), Mrs. Patrick Campbell* as Hedda
Mar. 11, 1907	Bijou Theatre, New York (32), Alla Nazimova as Hedda
Mar. 11, 1907	Kammerspiele, Berlin, dir. Max Reinhardt*
Nov. 11, 1907	Lyric Theatre, New York, Mrs. Patrick Campbell as Hedda
Feb. 21, 1908	Kharkov Theatre, St. Petersburg, dir. Vsevelod Meyerhold*
Dec. 10, 1909	His Majesty's Theatre, London, Lydia Yavorska* as Hedda
May 27, 1911	Kingsway Theatre, London, Lydia Yavorska as Hedda
July 6, 1911	Hoftheater, Braunschweig
Apr. 8, 1918	Plymouth Theatre, New York (24), Alla Nazimova as Hedda
May 22, 1922	Everyman Theatre, London, Mrs. Patrick Campbell as Hedda
May 16, 1924	48th Street Theatre, New York (8), Clara Eames* as Hedda
Mar. 9, 1925	Comédie Française, Paris, Mme Piérat as Hedda
Jan. 26, 1926	Comedy Theatre, New York (59), Emily Stevens* as Hedda
Mar. 12, 1928	Everyman Theatre, London, Laura Cowie* as Hedda
Mar. 26, 1928	Civic Repertory Theatre, New York (15), Eva Le Gallienne* as Hedda
Feb. 2, 1919	49th Street Theatre, New York (25), Blanche Yurka* as Hedda
Mar. 17, 1931	Arts Theatre, London, Jean Forbes-Robertson* as Hedda
Dec. 8, 1934	Broadhurst Theatre, New York (4), Eva Le Gallienne as Hedda
Mar. 9, 1936	Criterion Theatre, London, Jean Forbes-Robertson as Hedda
Jan. 29, 1942	Longacre Theatre, New York (12), Katina Paxinou* as Hedda
Sept. 30, 1942	Mercury Theatre, London, Sonia Dresdel* as Hedda
Mar. 16, 1943	Westminster Theatre, London, Sonia Dresdel as Hedda

Feb. 24, 1948   Cort Theatre, New York (15), Eva Le Gallienne as Hedda
Jan. 17, 1951   Arts Theatre, London, Jean Forbes-Robertson as Hedda
Sept. 8, 1954   Lyric Theatre, Hammersmith (London), (154), Peggy Ashcroft*
                 as Hedda
Nov. 9, 1960   4th Street Theatre, New York (340), Anne Meacham* as Hedda
Feb. 12, 1964   New Arts Theatre, London, Joan Greenwood* as Hedda
Mar. 2, 1964   St. Martin's Theatre, London, Joan Greenwood as Hedda
June 8, 1970   Cambridge Theatre, London, Maggie Smith* as Hedda
June 16, 1970   Actors' Playhouse, New York (81), Rebecca Thompson as Hedda
Feb. 17, 1971   Playhouse Theatre, New York (56), Claire Bloom* as Hedda
June 28, 1972   Royal Court Theatre, London, Jill Bennett as Hedda
July 17, 1975   Aldwych Theatre, London, Glenda Jackson* as Hedda
June 15, 1977   Duke of York's Theatre, London, Janet Suzman* as Hedda

Synopsis: The entire action takes place in the attractive but somber drawing room of Jörgen and Hedda Gabler Tesman, who have just returned from their wedding trip. The room is dominated by a portrait of General Gabler, Hedda's father. A warm, autumnal sun brightens the room as Berte, the maid, and Miss Juliane Tesman, Tesman's aunt, enter discussing the late arrival of the couple on last night's steamer. Juliane makes a point of opening a glass door to admit fresh air. As the women chat, Juliane remarks that she and her invalid sister Rina will miss Berte, who was their longtime servant; yet, she says, Berte will continue to look after Jörgen as she has done since his boyhood. In effect, Jörgen's youthful environment will simply be transferred to the new house. Berte, on the other hand, is concerned that she may not be able to satisfy her new mistress. Juliane agrees that the General's daughter is used to being spoiled. She then reminds Berte that Jörgen is no longer her young master; he is now Doctor Tesman, having won his degree while abroad. Juliane archly confides that soon Berte may have to call Jörgen by an even grander name, implying that he may soon be a father. Hedda, says Berte, in her brief time in the house has already asserted her control as mistress of the establishment by ordering the dust covers to be taken off the furniture of the drawing room; she intends, it seems, to use this chamber as a living room.

Jörgen Tesman, a studious man of thirty-three, enters, greets his aunt warmly, and compliments her for having the stamina to visit so early in the morning after his late-night arrival. She responds that she is used to getting very little rest at night. Her mien of patient suffering prompts Tesman to offer Hedda's many boxes and valises as a reason for not escorting his aunt to her own house. Luckily, a friend of the family, Judge Brack, was available. Tesman sends Berte out with a suitcase which he has emptied of research notes gathered during his journey. Juliane observes that Tesman wasted no time while he was away. As he takes her hat, Tesman notes its elegance and learns that Juliane bought it to please Hedda. When they settle down for a chat, the subject of Aunt Rina arises. Juliane hopes that her ailing sister may live for some time because Juliane needs someone in whom to invest her life now that Tesman has left her home to marry the beautiful, sought-after Hedda Gabler, with whom he has spent nearly six months abroad. When his aunt obliquely turns the conversation toward his expectations, he assumes that she means a professorship, whereas her concern is for his putative fatherhood. Juliane mentions the expense of the trip, which, Tesman confirms, was great, but Hedda simply had to have it. In his absence this house had been procured and furnished for the Tesmans. He is delighted by it, although he is unsure as to what use to put the two rooms between the back parlor and *Hedda's* bedroom. Juliane implies that they will become the children's rooms, but Tesman sees them absorbing the overflow from his library. As they discuss the house, it becomes clear that it is too expensive for Tesman to afford, that Hedda had insisted on inhabiting it, that Brack, in consultation with Hedda, made the deal, and that Juliane had mortgaged the aunts' pension to raise funds. Tesman praises his aunt for her spirit of sacrifice, but she merely remarks that helping him is her only pleasure. Basking in the happy promise of the future, Juliane tells Tesman that his principal rival Ejlert Lövborg, has published a new book but that it will be inferior to Tesman's forthcoming volume. He plans to write on the domestic handicrafts of Brabant in the Middle Ages. They exult in his prospects, his erudition, his house, and, mainly, his good fortune in marrying Hedda Gabler, who then enters.

A distinguished-looking woman of twenty-nine, Hedda first appears in a loose-fitting dressing gown. After desultorily greeting Juliane, Hedda objects to the open door that admits so much sunlight. Hedda affects great disinterest in the old bedroom slippers that Juliane has brought to her nephew and then castigates the maid for having left her ugly hat in the drawing room. When Juliane claims it as her own, Hedda makes a feeble apology. For Tesman's sake, Juliane makes little of the affront, and she is genuinely pleased when Tesman observes how plump Hedda has become on the trip. Hedda immediately silences him when he speaks of his opportunity to see her without her voluminous robe; she reminds him that he has no such opportunity. Juliane goes up to kiss Hedda, but the new wife pulls away in disgust; the aunt leaves with a promise to visit every day.

As Tesman accompanies his aunt to the door, Hedda frenetically paces the room, clinches her fists, raises her arms, and finally stares out the glass door into the garden. Tesman returns and asks what she is looking at. Her eyes have alighted on the yellow, withered leaves, a certain sign of September, the realization of which makes her restless again. She then tells Tesman that she will make amends with Juliane about the hat, for which he is grateful, but when he asks her to call his aunt by her Christian name, Hedda says that she might manage "Aunt" but never "Juliane." Hedda decides that her old piano should be moved to another room and a new one bought for the drawing room. Noticing some flowers, Hedda discovers that the card says that Thea Elvsted, an old school rival, intends to call that day. Thin-haired herself, Hedda chiefly remembers that Thea had flaunted her abundant hair in an irritating manner. Then it occurs to them that Thea has been living near Ejlert Lövborg. This line of discussion is interrupted by Berte's announcement that Mrs. Elvsted has returned.

Thea Elvsted looks distraught upon her entrance and wastes no time in explaining that there was no one else to whom she could turn in view of the fact that Ejlert Lövberg is also in town. Her concern is that he has been in Christiania for a week and may have fallen in with bad companions. In response to Hedda's questions, Thea tells them that Lövberg had been tutor to her husband's children and had acquitted himself without a hint of erratic behavior. When Lövborg's book was published, however, he was unable to remain peacefully in the country in view of its great success. Lövborg's treatise on the history of civilization was written entirely while he resided near the Elvsteds, but now that he is in town, he will certainly visit his old friend Tesman. Thea extracts from Tesman a promise to look after Lövborg if he should appear. Hedda tells Tesman to write to Lövborg to invite him to visit. After getting the address from Thea, Tesman exits to write the letter, leaving Hedda and Thea alone.

At first Thea is wary of Hedda, not only because Hedda had taunted her as a schoolgirl, but also because she believes her social position inferior to Hedda's. Hedda acts very sympathetic toward Thea in order to get her to tell the truth about the Lövborg situation. Thea admits that she had gone to the Elvsted house as a servant to its invalid mistress and at her death had risen to be mistress herself. Since her husband was often away, she had found herself more and more in the company of Ejlert Lövborg, the children's tutor. When Lövborg departed three years later, Thea had left her home, husband, and foster-children to follow him. Hedda goads Thea to speak of her intimacy with Lövborg. While admitting that she had helped him to cure some of his bad habits, Thea concludes that he improved her too through intelligent conversation and allowing her to help him with his writing. She admits, however, that a woman's shadow stands between her and Lövborg. The woman's identity is unknown, but Lövborg had said that she once had threatened him with a pistol. Hedda scarcely credits that, remarking that no one around there would behave that way. These confidences are interrupted by the reappearance of Tesman who has the letter in his hand. Hedda, planning to ask Berte to mail the letter, starts to accompany Thea to the gate but is deterred by the arrival of Judge Brack.

After being introduced to Brack, Thea is conducted out by Hedda. Left alone with Tesman, Brack observes that buying and furnishing the house for Tesman proved to be costly, but Tesman replies that Hedda could not be expected to do with less. Brack also bears the news that Lövborg is in town and that the success of his book has placed him in competition with Tesman for the university professorship. When Hedda returns, Brack urges that she reconsider some expenditures on the house in view of Tesman's uncertain future. Then he leaves. Hedda reminds Tesman that their marriage bargain demands that they move in society and maintain a great house, but he despairingly tells her that she may not have a butler or a horse at the moment. Hedda then responds that she has General Gabler's pistols, twin weapons in a handsome case, with which to amuse herself.

Act II is set in the drawing room of the Tesman house; the piano has been removed. It is afternoon of the same day. Hedda stands by the door and loads one of her pistols. Brack enters from the garden as Hedda fires in his direction. After putting her firearms away, Brack learns from Hedda that Tesman is out of the house; he laments that he did not arrive sooner because he misses their intimate chats. Hedda bemoans the boredom of her marriage trip and her continual exposure to Tesman's company. When Brack asks how she and Tesman ever formed a liaison, Hedda replies that she had danced herself out, so when Tesman, who seemed to have good prospects, begged to be allowed to take care of her, she capitulated. What else was there to do, she wonders, since her other male friends, particularly Brack, were disinclined to propose marriage? The judge says that he prefers to come and go as a "trusted friend" inside an intimate circle. Hedda sees that a triangular arrangement would be welcome, and so they agree. Tesman then enters with an armload of new books, including Lövborg's. Before exiting to cut the pages and dress for the stag party he plans to attend at Brack's house, Tesman tells Hedda that Juliane will not visit because Aunt Rina's condition has deteriorated. Finally, Tesman reminds Hedda how pleased Juliane was to see how Hedda had "filled out," which infuriates Hedda.

Hedda tells Brack that she had pretended that Juliane's hat was Berte's because such uncontrollable urges sometime seize her. For example, at a loss for conversation she once mentioned to Tesman that she had always wanted to live in this house. Actually, she hates the house which, she says, has the odor of death. Brack suggests that having a goal in life would help alleviate her boredom. She considers pushing Tesman into politics just to demonstrate that she can make him do something for which he is wholly unsuited. Brack intimates that pregnancy might provide direction to her existence, but she retorts that he will never see her in that condition. Her only talent, Hedda believes, is boring herself to death.

Tesman, now dressed for the party, comes in as if expecting Lövborg already to have arrived. If Lövborg should come after Brack and Tesman have left, Hedda would be faced with entertaining him alone with Thea Elvsted. Before that can happen, however, Berte announces Lövborg's visit.

A gaunt Lövborg enters the room and thanks Tesman profusely for the invitation before greeting Hedda and Brack. The conversation turns to Lövborg's book which, he says, he wrote only to win popular approval so that he could work on a really important book, the manuscript of which he produces. This work deals with the future of civilization; its two parts are about the determinant forces of civilization and contain a projection as to the future direction of society. Lövborg has brought the manuscript in anticipation of reading it aloud, but when he is invited to Brack's party instead, he demurs. Brack tempts him by saying that he could provide a private room where Lövborg could read to Tesman, who seconds the idea. Hedda invites him to supper with herself and Thea; this invitation he accepts. Tesman asks Lövborg about a series of talks he projects for the autumn; Lövborg responds that he intends to wait until after Tesman's appointment as professor to begin his lectures. Lövborg, it seems, does not plan to compete with Tesman. Hedda offers the men a cold punch as refreshment, but Lövborg declines. He remains to talk with Hedda while the other men retire to an inner room to drink and smoke.

Hedda produces a photograph album which will mask the private conversation she wants to have with Lövborg. Lövborg asks Hedda how she could waste herself with Tesman. She replies that she does not love him but does not intend to be unfaithful despite her previous relationship with Lövborg. Lövborg says that in their past relationship Hedda had strange power over him to make him do things he never intended to do. When he asks why she has engaged him in such intimate conversation, Hedda says it is in order to enter into a world generally denied to women. She finally broke off the relationship when it seemed in danger of becoming more than mere friendship. They agree that she could not have shot Lövborg as she once threatened in anger because she is fundamentally a coward. Hedda then admits that her failure to shoot him was not her biggest act of cowardice that night, implying an unconsummated physical relationship. This conversation is interrupted by Thea's entrance.

Thea learns that Tesman and Brack are about to go to a drinking party but is relieved to hear that Lövborg does not intend to accompany them. Hedda sits on the sofa with Thea on one side and Lövborg on the other. As Hedda strokes Thea's hair, Lövborg boasts of their perfectly honest relationship and Thea's courage. Again Hedda laments her own lack of courage. Hedda offers drinks, but both of her guests refuse. When Hedda asks Lövborg what he would do if she insisted he have a drink, he responds that he would still decline. She taunts him by saying that his refusal to drink a mere fruit punch would convince people that he lacked strength of character; she says that Brack sneered when Lövborg refused both a drink and the invitation to attend the party. Congratulating Lövborg on remaining true to his principles, Hedda turns to Thea and tells her that she had no reason to have been so distraught this morning when she thought that Lövborg was on the town with his disreputable friends. This announcement rattles Lövborg and embarrasses Thea, who sees how her lack of trust has angered Lövborg. He picks up a glass of punch and toasts Thea's health; then he drinks to Hedda, who claims innocence with regard to Lövborg's resumption of drinking. He begins to taunt Thea about her husband's collusion in her coming to spy on him; a toast is then drunk to Mr. Elvsted, after which Lövborg begins to settle down. He apologizes to Thea, who is visibly relieved. Brack and Tesman come back into the room to depart for the party, and Lövborg asks to go along, saying that he will come back to the Tesmans' to escort Thea home. The three men depart as Berte sets a lighted lamp on a table in the drawing room.

In response to Thea's apprehension, Hedda prophesies that Lövborg will return at ten o'clock "with vine leaves in his hair," a clear Dionysian allusion. Thea asks why Hedda has engineered this situation; her answer is that for once she wanted to have power over someone. Then Hedda throws her arms around Thea and threatens to burn off her hair just as she had done when they were schoolgirls. Thea, struggling to be free, cries that she is frightened of Hedda and wishes to go home, but Hedda almost bodily propels her toward the dining room where they will eat and wait for Lövborg to return with vine leaves in his hair.

The time of Act III is daybreak the next morning. Hedda and Thea nervously await the return of the men as Berte enters to deliver a message from Juliane. Seeming to gloat over the evening's outcome, Hedda makes a pretense of allaying Thea's fears and sends her to bed with the promise to awaken her as soon as news of Lövborg should come. Hedda calls Berte to stoke the fire, but the servant is summoned by the doorbell. Tesman shuffles into the room and starts to tell Hedda about his evening, the high point of which occurred when Lövborg read from his remarkable book, a book that caused Tesman to feel quite jealous. Then, says Tesman, Lövborg became so inebriated that he delivered a drunken oration on the woman who inspired his book. Hedda inquires if he had vine leaves in his hair, but the allusion escapes Tesman. After the party had wound down, he and Brack decided to take Lövborg home, and on the way Tesman had found a parcel lying in the road — Lövborg's manuscript. Feeling that Lövborg was in no condition to guard the irreplaceable document, Tesman had retained it with the intention of returning it later. Hedda ascertains that no one knows that Tesman has the manuscript and then discovers that Lövborg had met some roistering friends and gone off with them. Hedda asks to read Lövborg's book before its return, but he is eager to restore it to Lövborg as soon as possible. She asks whether it could be rewritten if it should be lost, but Tesman doubts the possibility because Lövborg no longer has the same inspiration. She then remembers Juliane's note which contains the news that Rina is dying. A frantic Tesman implores Hedda to go to the deathbed with him, but she refuses, saying that she wants to avoid everything ugly. Before Tesman can leave, Berte announces that Brack has called. Hedda quickly picks up the manuscript and hides it in the writing desk before Brack comes in. Tesman explains his rush and dashes out.

Brack has come to describe last night's events from his perspective. Lövborg had left Brack's party to visit a brothel run by his old paramour Mademoiselle Diana, a red-haired singer. Once there, Lövborg had discovered the loss of his manuscript, accused Diana and her friends of having robbed him, and started an imbroglio that finally brought the police. After resisting arrest and assaulting an officer, Lövborg had been carted off to the police station. Hedda, fascinated by the narration, asked if Lövborg had had vine leaves in his hair. Brack, too, is mystified by the question. His concern, however, is that Lövborg will henceforth be denied the hospitality of every respectable home; as a result, he will wish to use the Tesman residence as a place of assignation with Mrs. Elvsted. That, according to Brack, would irritate him immensely as it would disrupt his triangular relationship with Hedda and Tesman. He intends to fight with every means at his command to retain his position as "cock of the walk." For the first time Hedda sees how formidable Brack can be and rejoices that he has no hold over her. Brack wonders aloud what she would do if he had some sort of sway over her, which Hedda interprets as a threat. Having said this, Brack pointedly exits through the garden doors, the back way.

Left alone, Hedda starts to examine Lövborg's manuscript when she hears voices in the hall. Quickly, she locks the document in the writing desk. Lövborg bursts in looking for Thea, who quickly appears. Highly agitated, Lövborg tells Thea that they must separate because he has no more use for her. Hedda is triumphant, but Thea is incredulous that they will no longer work together. Lövborg says that he does not intend to do any more work. The reason for his despair is, of course, the loss of his book of which Thea was the inspiration. He claims that he destroyed the book as he destroyed his life. Thea sees this wanton act as the destruction of their child, a comparison that is not lost on Hedda. Stunned and dispirited, Thea leaves the room.

Lövborg will not take Thea home because he has concluded that she has killed "the courage and daring for life" in him. Hedda is angered by the realization that an insignificant person like Thea could control a man's destiny. Lövborg then confesses to Hedda that he has lost the manuscript and nothing remains but to take his own life. Intrigued by the possibility, Hedda asks if he will do it beautifully. He smiles and asks if she wants vine leaves in his hair, but she will forego the vine leaves if he will die artistically. She tells him never to return, but before he goes, she gives him one of General Gabler's pistols. After Lövborg leaves, she takes the manuscript from the desk, rifles the pages, and tosses them into the stove while whispering that she is burning Thea's child.

It is evening of the same day as Act IV begins. Hedda is pacing in the darkened drawing room. When a sobbing Berte enters to bring a lamp, it is seen that Hedda is dressed in black. Juliane, also clad in mourning, enters to thank Hedda for her note of condolence at Rina's death, which was quiet and painless. As Juliane speaks of sewing a shroud at her house, she cannot resist alluding to sewing baby clothes. Before Hedda can angrily respond, Tesman comes in.

Juliane tells him that in a few days she intends to install in Rina's room some other invalid who requires care because she needs someone for whom to live. Tesman seems on the verge of inviting Juliane to live with him and

Hedda, but his wife's icy manner forestalls the suggestion. Then Juliane exits.

Tesman is concerned not only with his aunt's death but also with Löv-borg. He had stopped at Lövborg's lodging to tell him about finding the manuscript, but Lövborg was not at home. Thea had told him that Lövborg had claimed to have shredded the book. Tesman now wants to know if Hedda had returned the book or told Lövborg where it was. When she replies in the negative, he asks for the document so he can return it before Lövborg in desperation does himself harm. Without emotion, Hedda responds that she no longer has the manuscript, that she burned it. Tesman is shocked into a frenzy, but Hedda warns him not to mention her deed to anyone because she acted in his behalf. His shock changes to jubilation that she would do such a terrible thing out of concern for him. She intimates that she is about to show her love in a more tangible way — pregnancy. He is so delighted that he shouts and wants to dash out and tell Berte immediately. Rather than share his joy, Hedda clinches her fists and exclaims that she will die because of all this. For the first time, she uses his Christian name. Now that Tesman believes that Hedda is to bear his child, he will keep her destruction of the book to himself.

This strange scene is interrupted by the entrance of Thea Elvsted, who agitatedly announces that she believes Lövborg has had an accident. Rumors have linked Lövborg's name and the hospital, but she was unable to learn anything definite. Tesman offers to make inquiries, but Hedda tells him not to get involved.

Brack comes in with the news that Lövborg is dying in the hospital. He says that Lövborg had shot himself in the chest. Hedda would have preferred the temple, but she sees the beauty in such a death as Lövborg's because he had the courage to act. Thea claims that he was desperate at having torn up his book, a fact that seems significant to Brack. Tesman and Thea decide that a fitting memorial would be the reconstruction of Löv-borg's book, a deed made possible because Thea has all his notes. Tesman dedicates his whole life to the re-creation of Thea and Lövborg's "child." Hedda is mortified, but after Thea and Tesman exit to start work, she quietly rejoices to Brack that Lövborg's courageous end was truly beautiful. Brack feels he must disillusion her as to that.

The facts are that Lövborg died in Mademoiselle Diana's boudoir where he went demanding the restitution of his lost child. The pistol was discharged accidentally while still in his breast pocket, fatally wounding him in "the lower body." Hedda is sickened to discover that her elaborate plan has gone awry in such a distasteful manner. Furthermore, Brack recognized the pistol as Hedda's.

At that point Tesman and Thea come back to work by the better light of the drawing room. Hedda and Brack continue to discuss the pistol, which, according to Brack, must have been stolen. A series of persistent questions establishes that the pistol is indeed Hedda's, but she says it will never be identified as long as he keeps quiet. Hedda sees that Brack now has her in his power as the discovery of the pistol's owner would create a scandal. She is no longer free, the thought of which she cannot bear. Hedda's fortunes have now been reversed. Looking up from his work, Tesman tells Brack that he will have to keep Hedda company in the future. Hedda goes into the inner room, ostensibly to rest on the sofa, but she is heard playing a frenetic tune on the piano. Tesman calls out that she should consider Aunt Rina and Lövborg. Hedda's head appears between the curtains; she says that she will also think of Aunt Juliane and all the others; she will, in the future, be quiet. Hedda closes the curtains, and momentarily a shot is heard. Tesman dashes into the room and shouts that Hedda has shot herself in the temple. Brack sinks into a chair and utters perhaps Ibsen's most famous line: "But good God! People don't *do* that sort of thing!"

Structural analysis: For this play Ibsen favored the tightly knit, complex plot that moves inexorably from initiation to crisis to reversal to denouement:

Hedda learns from Thea that Lövborg is back in town;

(as a result of which)

Hedda tells Tesman to invite Lövborg to the house;

(as a result of which)

Hedda discovers that Lövborg and Thea have an honest, happy relationship;

(as a result of which)

Hedda goads Lövborg to drink, to attend the party, thereby jeopardizing his and Thea's happiness;

(as a result of which)

Hedda discovers that Brack does not want his relationship with the Tesmans to be altered by Lövborg's presence;

(as a result of which)

Hedda encourages Lövborg to commit suicide and burns the manuscript;

(as a result of which)

Hedda discovers that Brack has her in his power [REVERSAL];

(as a result of which)

Hedda commits suicide.

Ibsen's employment of the Nietzschean concept of the Apollonian and the Dionysian approaches to life is clearer in this play than in any of the others. Tesman is the Apollonian force — logical, sane, rational (if a bit scatty). Lövborg, on the other hand, is the irrational, insane, emotional Dionysian. It is not mere whimsy that led Ibsen to characterize Hedda as wishing to see Lövborg "with vine leaves in his hair," a trait associated with Dionysus, the deity of wine and fertility. In Lövborg's case, the Dionysian fertility produced a book rather than a baby; yet Thea convinces the others that the book is a child sired by Lövborg and borne by herself. One needs only to consider Euripides' *Bacchae* to be reminded of the violence that can attend Dionysian frenzy.

References: Durbach, E. "Apotheosis of Hedda Gabler," *Scandinavian Studies,* 43 (1971), 143-59; Gosse, Edmund. "Ibsen's New Drama: with Excerpts," *Fortnightly Review,* 55 (Jan. 1891), 4-13; Kildahl, Erling E. "The Social Conditions and Principles of *Hedda Gabler,*" *Educational Theatre Journal,* 13 (1961), 207-13; Swanson, Carl A. "Ibsen and the Comédie Française," *Scandinavian Studies,* 19 (1946), 70-8.

HEESE, CLARA (1851-1921): Heese enacted Hedda Gabler* (1891) and Ella Rentheim.*

HEGEL, FREDERIK (1817-87): Hegel, the head of the Gyldendal publishing house since 1850, was Ibsen's Danish publisher until 1887. As their relationship ripened, Hegel became Ibsen's literary adviser and financial consultant.

Reference: Nielsen, L. C. *Frederik V. Hegel: Et Mindeskrift.* Copenhagen: Bagges Kgl. hof-bogtrykkeri, 1909.

HEGEL, GEORG WILHELM FRIEDRICH (1770-1831): Although Hegel was one of the most influential philosophers of the nineteenth century, there is no evidence that Ibsen ever read a line of his works. Instead, Ibsen absorbed Hegelian thought through Sören Aabye Kierkegaard,* Johan Ludvig Heiberg,* and Marcus Jacob Monrad.*

Hegel interprets human history in terms of the conflict of a thesis and an antithesis that results in a synthesis. He sees progress as the product of conflicting forces. In discussing historical drama, Hegel says that protagonists should embody opposing theories of life and that tragic heroes should come to misfortune as they bring about the collapse of the original conditions (the thesis).

The slightest consideration of these Hegelian ideas brings to mind Ibsen's *Catiline,* * *The Pretenders,* * and *Emperor and Galilean.* * Ibsen's masterpiece, *Emperor and Galilean,* is the clearest example of his use of the Hegelian dialectic. In this case, the thesis is Christianity, the antithesis is paganism, and the synthesis is the Third Empire. Julian* advocates a return to paganism and precipitates his personal catastrophe in an attempt to replace Christianity as the official religion of the Roman Empire.

Reference: Pearce, John C. "Hegelian Ideas in Three Tragedies by Ibsen," *Scandinavian Studies,* 34 (1962-63), 245-57.

HEIBERG, JOHAN LUDVIG (1791-1860): Ibsen encountered J. L. Heiberg both as a critic and a practical man of the theatre. As a young playwright, Ibsen read and digested Heiberg's *Om Vaudevillen som dramatisk digtart* [*On the Vaudeville as Dramatic Composition*] (1826). Heiberg was a practitioner of the technique of the well-made play* and was the originator of Danish vaudevilles in the French manner.

When Ibsen went abroad in 1852 to study continental theatrical practices, he met Heiberg who between 1848 and 1856 was director of the Royal Theatre, Copenhagen. Heiberg was a deeply thoughtful man and a confessed disciple of Georg Wilhelm Friedrich Hegel.* Doubtless he transmitted his modified Hegelianism to the young Norwegian playwright and director.

Heiberg's *Autobiographical Fragments* has been published in many editions.

HEIBERG, JOHANNE LUISE (1812-90): Considered the finest Danish actress of her time, Johanne Luise Heiberg went on the stage as a young girl and retired as an actress in 1864. She was Sören Aabye Kierkegaard's* favorite performer during the years she acted at the Royal Theatre, Copenhagen, under the direction of her husband, J. L. Heiberg.* She favored psychologically complex characters. After Heiberg gave up acting, she continued to serve the theatre as a director and reformer. She was responsible for the production of *The Pretenders** on January 11, 1871, at Copenhagen's Royal Theatre.

References: Bergsöe, Clara. *Johanne Luise Heiberg.* Copenhagen: Gyldendal, 1896; Heiberg, Johanne L. *Et Liv: Gjenoplevet i Erindringen,* 4 vols. Copenhagen: Gyldendal, 1891-92; Kierkegaard, Sören. *Crisis in the Life of an Actress and Other Essays on the Drama.* Trans. Stephen Crites. London: Collins, 1967.

HEJRE, DANIEL (*The League of Youth*): Daniel Hejre (whose name means "stork") joins the League of Youth because he nurses a grudge against Chamberlain Brattsberg.* Once wealthy and now bankrupt, Hejre claims that Brattsberg legally robbed him of a parcel of land that had been sold to Hejre's father. Hejre's major function is to be a gadfly to the principal participants in the dramatic action.

HELENA (*Emperor and Galilean*): Princess Helena, sister of Emperor Constantius,* is given in marriage to Julian* when he is appointed Caesar. Her outstanding trait is ambition. Helena urges Julian to let the army proclaim him Emperor, but Helena's influence is obviated when Constantius has her poisoned. At the moment of her death, Helena tells Julian that the child she is bearing is not his.

HELENE (*A Doll's House*): The Helmers' maid.

LITTLE HELGA (*Peer Gynt*): A newcomer to the district; Solveig's* sister.

HELLE (*The League of Youth*): A theological student and tutor. As the eventual fiancé of Ragna Monsen,* Helle is one of the romantic interests of the play.

HELMER, NORA (*A Doll's House*): Nora is the wife of Torvald Helmer.* She has proven to be one of the most difficult roles for actresses because of the requisite breadth of effect. On the one hand, the player must be convincing as the capering, fawning, childlike bride who inhabits her husband's doll's house. On the other hand, the actress must persuade the audience that such a person is capable of altering a check, dealing with an extortioner, keeping the secret, and finally leaving her marriage to seek self-knowledge. Perhaps because of this complexity, Nora has been a favorite role in the Ibsenian canon.

HELMER, TORVALD (*A Doll's House*): A lawyer who has become a bank president, Torvald Helmer is the husband of Nora.* There is no doubt that he loves his wife, but his Victorian ideals have limited his appreciation of the nature of true marriage. He wants Nora to be his plaything, the keeper of his house, and the mother of his children. When Torvald learns of the sacrifices Nora made for the sake of his health, he censures her. Even when she is on the verge of deserting him, Torvald cannot see why Nora acts as she does.

HELSETH, MRS. (*Rosmersholm*): As the housekeeper at Rosmersholm,* Mrs. Helseth provides an exposition of previous events and helps to establish the probability of the supernatural appearance of the white horses of Death. She is superstitious and passes along the folklore of the area to Rebecca West.*

HELTBERG, HENRIK A. S. (1806-73): Beginning in 1843 H.A.S. Heltberg operated a school in Christiania* that prepared students to pass matriculation examinations at the University of Christiania. Ibsen and several of his friends studied there.
Reference: Norsk Biografisk Leksikon, VI, 17-8.

HEMMING (*The Burial Mound*): Gandalf's* skald,* or minstrel, who opts to remain and pass his final days with the old king rather than accompany the Vikings in their return to Norway.

HEMMING (*Olaf Liljekrans*): Arne's* page; marries Ingeborg.*

HENLEY, EDWARD J. (1862-98): After establishing himself as an actor in the British theatre, E. J. Henley came to America where he was known as a thorough and painstaking craftsman. He played John Gabriel Borkman* in the Criterion Independent Theatre's* production of *John Gabriel Borkman* in 1897.
Reference: The Marie Burroughs Art Portfolio of Stage Celebrities. Chicago: A. N. Marquis, 1894.

HENNINGS, BETTY (1850-1939): Danish actress Betty Hennings created the role of Nora Helmer* at the Royal Theatre, Copenhagen, in 1879, She also played Hedda Gabler,* Hedvig Ekdal,* Helene Alving,* and Aase* numerous times throughout her career.

References: Moritzen, Julius. "Ibsen's First Nora," Theatre, 3 (1903), 70-1; Neiiendam, Robert. "Betty Hennings, the Great Danish Ibsen Actress," American Scandinavian Review, 10 (1922), 102-7.

HENRIKSEN, HANS JAKOB (1846-1916): H. J. Henriksen was Ibsen's illegitimate son by Else Sofie Jensdatter,* who was a servant of Apothecary J. A. Reimann.* Ibsen supported his son until he reached age fourteen. At that time Henriksen moved to Börkedalen with his mother and worked as a blacksmith. He became an alcoholic and married three times. Six of his seven children died young. He met Ibsen only once, near the end of his father's life.

HERACLIUS (Emperor and Galilean): A poet.

HERDAL, DOCTOR (The Master Builder): Family physician to the Solnesses. He acts as confidant to both Halvard* and Aline,* doing his best to reconcile their misunderstandings. Herdal is the raisonneur.

HERFORD, CHARLES HAROLD (1853-1931): As professor of English at the University of Aberystwyth (1887-1901), C. H. Herford translated Brand* and Love's Comedy* into English in 1894.

"THE HEROIC BALLAD AND ITS SIGNIFICANCE TO MODERN POETRY": An address delivered by Ibsen to the Society of December 22 (an exclusive discussion group in Bergen*) on February 2, 1857. In it he gives his rationale for using the folk ballad as a dramatic device in his works for the theatre. It was published in Illustreret Nyhedsblad on May 10 and 17, 1857.

HERRMANN, PAUL (1866-1930): German writer Paul Herrmann translated Emperor and Galilean* (1888) and The Master Builder* (1893). He was also the author of Nordische Mythologie (1903).

Reference: Deutsches Literatur-Lexikon (Berlin, 1953), II, 950.

HERTZ, HENRIK (1798-1870): The Danish author of plays, lyrics, and poetry, Hertz wrote Svend Dyring's House, which some believe Ibsen plagiarized for The Feast at Solhoug.*

HESSEL, LONA (The Pillars of Society): Betty Bernick's* elder stepsister, Lona Hessel emigrated to America to take care of Johan Tönnesen.* Her return precipitates a crisis for Karsten Bernick* because she threatens to tell the truth about his nefarious past if he refuses to do so. She is, in fact, the antagonist of the drama.

HETMAN, ULRIK (*Rosmersholm*): The *nom de plume* of Ulrik Brendel.*

HETTNER, HERMANN (1821-82): As a German literary historian, Hettner published *The Modern Drama* in 1852, a book eagerly read by Ibsen. Hettner's discussion of fairy-tale comedy and historical drama formed the basis of Ibsen's thought on those matters. Hettner believed that historical drama should have contemporary psychological application and that in fairy plays, fantasy can demonstrate what reality sometimes cannot.
Reference: Hettner, Hermann. *Das moderne Drama.* Braunschweig: Bieway and
    Cohn, 1852.

HILARION (*Emperor and Galilean*): Son of Publia.*

HILLBERG, EMIL (b. 1852): Swedish actor Emil Hillberg played Haakon* in a production of *The Pretenders** at the Vasa Theatre in Stockholm in 1898. He also played Brand,* Thomas Stockmann,* Ulrik Brendel,* Nils Krogstad,* and Nikolas Arnesson, Bishop of Oslo.*
Reference: Svenskt Biografiskt Handlexikon, I, 498-9.

HJÖRDIS (*The Vikings in Helgeland*): Örnulf's* foster-daughter who was abducted by Gunnar Headman* and taken to Helgeland. Bored by her dull existence and infatuated by Sigurd the Strong,* she does everything she can to precipitate a bloody conflict between Gunnar's retainers and the Vikings. Once she is successful, she attempts to persuade Sigurd to join her in suicide so they can be together in Valhalla. When he tells her he is a Christian and cannot go to Valhalla, she tosses herself into the sea.

HÖFER, EMIL (1864-1949): Emil Höfer offered a praiseworthy performance of Nikolas Arnesson, Bishop of Oslo* in Munich in 1907; he also played Peter Mortensgaard.*

HÖRBIGER, ATTILA (1896-   ): As Doctor Wangel* in *The Lady from the Sea,** performed in Munich in 1949, Austrian actor Attila Hörbiger created a favorable impression. He had previously worked with Max Reinhardt* for twenty-one years and several times played the title role in the Salzburg *Everyman.*
Reference: Brockhaus Enzyklopaedie, 8, 674.

HOFFORY, JULIUS (1855-97): Julius Hoffory, a Dane, was professor of Nordic philology at the University of Berlin in the 1880s. He edited Ludvig Holberg's* dramas in German (1885-88) and translated *The Lady from the Sea** in 1888. Hoffory widely advertised the notion that he was the inspira-

tion of Ejlert Lövborg.* He eventually lost his sanity and left his entire estate to Ibsen.
Reference: Dansk Biografisk Leksikon, X, 306-7.

HOFMEISTER, OSKAR (b. 1869): Oskar Hofmeister played Guldstad* in *Love's Comedy* in Berlin in 1900.
Reference: Kosch, Wilhelm. Deutsches Theater-Lexikon, I, 826.

HOLBERG, LUDVIG (1684-1754): A native of Bergen,* Holberg wrote in Danish and established himself as the only important Scandinavian dramatist of his time. Ibsen admitted reading Holberg's plays before he began to write *Catiline*,* which constituted his only documented exposure to drama before he wrote his own first play.
Reference: Hammer, Simon C. Ludvig Holberg: The Founder of Norwegian Literature and an Oxford Student. Oxford: Blackwell, 1920.

HOLT, NETTA (*The Pillars of Society*): Daughter of Mrs. Postmaster Holt* and a member of Betty Bernick's* charitable group.

HOLT, MRS. POSTMASTER (*The Pillars of Society*): One of the members of Betty Bernick's* charitable circle, Mrs. Holt functions much as a Greek chorus.

HONE, MARY (1904-   ): When Mary Hone, a graduate of London's Royal Academy of Dramatic Art, essay Ellida Wangel* in 1934, critic Brooks Atkinson called her performance "neither magnetic nor imaginative" (*New York Times*, May 2, 1934, p. 25, cols. 2-3).
Reference: Who Was Who in the Theatre, II, 1205-6.

HORMISDAS (*Emperor and Galilean*): An exiled Persian prince.

HORSTER, CAPTAIN (*An Enemy of the People*): A sea captain who braves the wrath of the solid majority by allowing Thomas Stockmann* to hold his public meeting on his property. As a result, he loses his position but remains a friend to the Stockmanns.

HOVSTAD (*An Enemy of the People*): Editor of the *People's Herald*,* a radical newspaper. Hovstad first offers his support to Thomas Stockmann* and then retracts it in the face of contrary public opinion. He eventually becomes an extortioner when he threatens to use his paper against Stockmann if Stockmann decides not to subsidize the journal.

HROLLOUG (*The Burial Mound*): A belligerent Viking.

HUHU (*Peer Gynt*): A language reformer encountered by Peer Gynt.*

HULDER: In Scandinavian folklore, a female creature of the forest whose siren music enslaves unwary men.

HUMAN RESPONSIBILITY: The title of Alfred Allmers'* unfinished book.

HUNEKER, JAMES GIBBONS (1860-1921): J. G. Huneker was an influential critic of music and drama in New York after 1891. His treatment of Ibsen in his book *Iconoclasts: A Book of Dramatists* (1905) did much to win Ibsen acceptance in America.

HUSSEIN (*Peer Gynt*): An eastern minister.

HAERMAENDENE PAA HELGELAND: The Norwegian title of *The Vikings in Helgeland.**

I

IBSEN, BERGLIOT (1869-1953): The daughter of Björnstjerne Björnson,*
Bergliot was the wife of Ibsen's son, Sigurd.* Her reminiscences of the
family are a valuable research tool: *The Three Ibsens: Henrik Ibsen, Suzannah Ibsen and Sigurd Ibsen*. Trans. Gerik Schjelderup. London:
Hutchinson, 1951.

IBSEN, HEDVIG (b. 1832): Ibsen was three years older than his sister
Hedvig; yet they were very close as children, and their intimacy continued
until the dramatist's death. Like Henrik, Hedvig was a retiring child, quite
unlike the other Ibsen siblings. While quite young, Hedvig was converted to
the highly emotional, evangelical religion of Pastor Gustav Adolph
Lammers.* Ibsen was so alienated from this kind of pietistic fervor that he
was for a time annoyed by his sister's adoption of it. After Ibsen left home,
Hedvig's letters provided his sole means of contact with his family; periodically he promised to be a more faithful correspondent, but he seldom
followed through. Eventually Hedvig married a ship's captain, Hans Jacob
Stousland, and afterwards enrolled in a religious sect similar to the Quakers.
Her paternal relatives were so embarrassed by this affiliation that they
threatened to deprive Captain Stousland of his position. The threat became
reality, and Stousland's fate was depicted as Captain Horster's* in *An
Enemy of the People*.* Perhaps it is not mere coincidence that Hedvig
Ekdal* helped a long-suffering mother to cosset a dreamy father in *The
Wild Duck*,* for Hedvig Ibsen fulfilled a similar responsibility both before
and after her mother's death in 1869.

IBSEN, HENRIK PETERSEN (c. 1765-97): H. P. Ibsen, the playwright's
grandfather, was a sea captain who went down with his ship at Hesnaes near
Grimstad.*

IBSEN, JOHAN ANDREAS ALTENBURG (b. 1830): Ibsen's younger brother emigrated to the United States in 1850 and temporarily settled in Wisconsin. He took odd jobs, which were scarce, while trying to get a foothold in the new land. On May 28, 1850, he wrote a letter to his father in which he described the difficulties faced in America by the Norwegian immigrants who could speak no English. Johan Andreas wrote passionately about the local disease, "gold fever." His letter closes with the injunction, "When any of you write to my dear brother Henrik, greet him from me and ask him to write me also." [The letter, translated by Theodore Jorgenson, is owned by the Norwegian-American Historical Association and is catalogued as Box NAHA/MSS/821.] Perhaps the contents of this letter were communicated to Ibsen because there are echoes of it in Johan Tönnessen's* adventures in America. After May 1850 Johan Andreas disappears from history. It is presumed that he died while crossing the desert in search of California's gold.

IBSEN, JOHAN PAUS (1826-28): Ibsen's elder brother died three weeks after the dramatist's birth.

IBSEN, KNUD PLESNER (1797-1877): Ibsen's father, Knud, seems to have been what we would today call an entrepreneur. At various times he was a merchant, lumber-trader, and investor. For a time he was successful, but a financial reversal destroyed the family's security. Ibsen may have used his father as the model for Jon Gynt.*

IBSEN, LILLEBIL: The wife of Ibsen's grandson Tancred, Lillebil Ibsen was a dancer and actress. She played Anitra* in Norway and New York (1923) and Ellida Wangel* in London in 1925.
References: Ibsen, Lillebil. "Grandfather Ibsen and *Peer Gynt*," *New York Times*, Feb. 4, 1923, Sect. III, pp. 10, 15; *The Times*, Feb. 3,1925, p. 10, col. 5.

IBSEN, MARICHEN CORNELIA MARTIE ALTENBURG (1799-1869): Ibsen's mother Marichen, the beautiful daughter of wealthy parents of Danish, German, and Norwegian stock, was probably the source of his artistic temperament. As a small boy, Ibsen was exposed to her accomplished watercolors and her avid enjoyment of the theatre. He must also have noticed that even as an adult, she doted upon dolls, which perhaps is the source of his inspiration for *A Doll's House.** Marichen was gay, effervescent, and sociable until her husband's financial position collapsed; thereafter she hid her embarrassment in sullenness and reclusiveness. When Marichen adopted the pietistic religion of Gustav Adolph Lammers,* Ibsen was so alienated that he never again felt close to his mother. By that time Ibsen had heard the rumors that he was the illegitimate son of Marichen and Tormod Knudsen,* which compounded his sense of rejection. When Marichen died, Ibsen did not attend the funeral.

IBSEN, NICOLAI ALEXANDER (1834-88): Ibsen's younger brother Nicolai, the victim of an accident that caused brain damage, emigrated to the United States as a young man after having twice failed in business in Norway. He gravitated toward Chicago, moved to Rock County, Wisconsin, and finally walked to Hardin County, Iowa. There he became a rough herdsman, acquired a small parcel of land, and ensconced himself. Though a hunchback and of a retiring nature, Nicolai made a few friends. When he died on April 25, 1888, his acquaintances helped to pay the funeral expenses. His headstone in Esterville, Iowa, bears the epitaph: Nicolai A. Ibsen, By Strangers Honored and by Strangers Mourned.''

Nicolai's life was celebrated by Mrs. C. M. Gronstal in a poem called "The Wanderer." Ibsen's relationship with his brother is indicated in the lines:

> Born brother of the great Henrik Ibsen beneath Norwegian skies.
> Two brothers, one a wanderer, one a genius rare.

Reference: Crumrine, Marjorie. "Simple Epitaph Marks Grave of Nicholai Ibsen, Buried Here," *Esterville (Iowa) Daily News*, an unpaginated clipping in the files of the Norwegian-American Historical Association, Box NAHA/MSS/P822.

IBSEN, OLE PAUS (1836-1917): Ibsen's brother, Ole Paus, became a sailor.

IBSEN, PETER: Ibsen's ancestor, his great-great-grandfather Peter Ibsen, a Danish sea captain, moved from Möen to Bergen* in the early eighteenth century.

IBSEN, SIGURD (1859-1930): Ibsen's only legitimate child, Sigurd received an extensive education throughout Ibsen's self-imposed exile in Europe. He studied law and worked for a time in the Swedish foreign service. He was a successful journalist, politician, novelist, and playwright. He also translated *The Master Builder** (1893) and *John Gabriel Borkman** (1897) into German.

IBSEN, SUZANNAH THORESEN (1836-1914): Ibsen married Suzannah Thoresen, the daughter of Magdalene Thoresen,* in 1858. Their union was in some ways rather strange, but it seemed to accommodate their unique personalities. One wonders if Falk's* ideas about how marriage destroys love were not Ibsen's own. Although their marriage lasted nearly fifty years, it was not without pain on both sides. Suzannah often traveled alone or with Sigurd* as companion, leaving Ibsen to his work or increasingly frequent liaisons with young women. Despite his dalliance, Ibsen too must have suffered because of Suzannah's independence of spirit and doting rearing of Sigurd.*

"IN AUTUMN": This poem was Ibsen's first work to appear in print. It was published on September 28, 1849, in the *Christiania Post* under the Brynjolf Bjarme* pseudonym.

INCORPORATED STAGE SOCIETY (London): Founded in 1899 as a
successor of the Independent Theatre,* the Incorporated Stage Society
concentrated on producing modern plays disallowed by the Lord Chamberlain or ignored by commercial managers. The Incorporated Stage
Society, which was financed by banker Frederick Whelan, nourished the
reputation of George Bernard Shaw,* in particular. Its productions, staged
by professionals, were first shown on Sunday afternoons, but as
membership increased (1,500 by 1914), Monday afternoon performances
were added. By 1939 the Society had presented about two hundred dramas
and had helped to establish numerous dramatists, among them Ibsen. Five
Ibsenian dramas were staged, the dates and directors of which follow:

*The League of Youth** (February 25, 1900), directed by Charles Charington*;

*The Pillars of Society** (May 12-13, 1901), directed by Oscar Asche;

*The Lady from the Sea** (May 4-5, 1902), directed by Charles Charrington;

*When We Dead Awaken** (January 25-26, 1903), directed by G. R. Foss;

*Lady Inger of Östraat** (January 28-29, 1906), directed by Herbert Jarman.

Reference: Franc, Miriam Alice. *Ibsen in England.* Boston: Four Seas, 1919.

INDEPENDENT THEATRE (London): The Théâtre Libre* served
as a model for the dependent Theatre, which was founded by Jacob
Thomas Grein* and others as a showcase for the new continental drama.
Ibsen's *Ghosts,** its first offering on March 13, 1891, caused a storm
of protest that was finally resolved by Ibsen's acceptance in England thirty
years later. The original cast for the single performance at the Royalty
Theatre included Alice Austin (Mrs. Theodore) Wright* (Helene Alving*),
Frank Lindo (Oswald*), Leonard Outram (Pastor Manders*), Sydney
Howard (Jacob Engstrand*), and Edith Kenward (Regine Engstrand*). In
1893 the Independent Theatre restaged *Ghosts* with Mrs. Patrick Campbell*
in the leading role. *Ghosts* was again mounted on June 24, 1897, with Mrs.
Theodore Wright as Helene Alving.

Grein himself directed three performances of *The Wild Duck** on May
4-5, 1894, at the Royalty Theatre; Charles Charrington* prepared another
version of the play with Laurence Irving* as Hjalmar Ekdal* for production
on May 17-21, 1897, at the Globe Theatre. Charrington, assisted by Dorothy
Leighton, presented Janet Achurch* as Nora Helmer* at the Globe Theatre
on May 10, 1897.

Since the Independent Theatre's performances were usually matinees, it
stressed the introduction of promising dramatists rather than production
values. Between 1891 and 1897 the organization staged over twenty plays.
Its most important accomplishment was persuading George Bernard Shaw*
to write for the stage.

Reference: Franc, Miriam Alice. *Ibsen in England.* Boston: Four Seas, 1919.

THE INDIAN GIRL: The American ship that was slated to be repaired negligently in *The Pillars of Society.**

INGA OF VARTEIG (*The Pretenders*): Inga, mother of Haakon,* has such faith in his rightful claim to the Norwegian throne that she submits to the ordeal of grasping red-hot irons. Miraculously, she is not harmed, her son is elected king, and Inga is sent away for her safety.

INGEBORG (*The Grouse in Justedal*): A servant at Bjerkehoug.

INGEBORG (*The Mountain Bird*): Ivar's* daughter.

INGEBORG (*Olaf Liljekrans*): Arne's* daughter, betrothed to Olaf Liljekrans.*

INGEBORG (*The Pretenders*): Although Ingeborg is the wife of Anders Skialdarband, she is the mother of Peter,* who is Haakon's* natural son.

INGER OF GYLDENLÖVE (*Lady Inger of Österaad*). See Lady Inger of Gyldenlöve.

INGER OF ÖSTRAAT. See Lady Inger of Östraat.

INGRID (*Peer Gynt*): The daughter of the farmer at Haegstag, Ingrid is abducted on her wedding day by Peer Gynt.*

INSPECTOR AT THE WATERING PLACE (*When We Dead Awaken*): This character is used as an expository device through which Arnold Rubek* learns of the rumors surrounding the mysterious Irene de Satow.*

IRVING, LAURENCE (1871-1914): The younger son of actor/manager Henry Irving, Laurence Irving first became acquainted with Ibsen's works in two productions of *The Wild Duck** (1894 and 1897) staged by the Independent Theatre.* In the earlier production, Irving played Doctor Relling,* and in the later, Hjalmar Ekdal.* Clement William Scott* wrote in the *Daily Telegraph* (May 5, 1894, p. 7): "The young man made the character tell by sheer force of will and accentuated comedy power. . . . His Ibsenite doctor, with all its shrewdness, character, observation, and common sense, is an earnest of still better things to come." Irving's comedic gifts were employed in the later production to soften Hjalmar's ineptitude.

Irving's name is hardly mentioned in most of the reviews of the Incorporated Stage Society's* production of *When We Dead Awaken** (January 1903) beyond the bare statement that he played Ulfhejm* the bearhunter. The critics were so occupied with deprecating the play that the actors escaped crippling critical barbs.

By the time Irving played Earl Skule* in the Frederick Harrison-William Archer* version of *The Pretenders** (February 13, 1913), the actor was a veteran Ibsenian performer. According to his biographer, as Skule "Laurence Irving proved himself a worthy successor of his father as an actor" (Brereton, p. 198). "Unhappily, few people saw it, and the most notable performance of all that he ever gave passed out of mind." *The Pretenders* was presented thirty-five times, which was a respectable run.

Reference: Brereton, Austin. *"H.B." and Laurence Irving.* London: Grant Richards, 1922; *Who Was Who in the Theatre*, III, 1272.

ISACHSEN, ANDREAS HORNBECH (1829-1903): Isachsen was the first student to join the newly formed Norwegian Theatre, Bergen.* He was Roderik* in the first production of *The Burial Mound.** Because of Isachsen's abrasive personality, Ibsen was continually at odds with him at Bergen, and in 1873, when Isachsen gave an unauthorized public reading of *Emperor and Galilean,** Ibsen wrote him a furious letter of censure.

Reference: Norsk Biografisk Leksikon, VI, 540-1.

IVAR (*The Mountain Bird*): A rich, old farmer.

IVERSLIE, PETER P. (1844-1921): Iverslie was born in Gudbrandsdalen,* the locale of *Brand.** Coming to the United States in 1847, the Iverslie family settled in Wisconsin and Minnesota. Young Iverslie farmed in the summer and taught school in the winter. He was an inveterate writer and contributed numerous articles, both in English and Norwegian, to the journals of the day; eventually, he published four books.

Iverslie was the earliest reviewer in America of Ibsen's works. His appreciative review of *The Pillars of Society** appeared in the pages of *Norden*, a weekly newspaper published in Chicago for Norwegian immigrants on January 2, 1879.

Twenty months after his favorable reception of *The Pillars of Society*, Iverslie submitted a blistering letter to *Norden* (August 25, 1880) in which he condemned *A Doll's House** as a "sad witness of moral degeneration" (Paulson and Björk, p. 6). He concluded that Ibsen, then fifty-two years old, had entered his second childhood. Iverslie's opinions were read by O. S. Hervin (1852-1923), a former Norwegian soldier and occasional writer who had emigrated to the United States in 1880. Under the pseudonym "Herm. Wang," Hervin suggested to the editor of *Norden* (September 1, 1880) that Iverslie must be aged about ninety, thereby inaugurating a critical "war" that was to last for several months.

On September 15, 1880, Iverslie rejoined that the moral of Ibsen's play was un-Christian, that Christianity required marriage partners to endure each other's faults rather than evade them. This prompted Hervin to answer (September 29, 1880) that he too found the moral tone of the drama untenable, but such a lapse did not make Ibsen a fool. Then with considerable humor he suggested that if this "war" were to continue, might the disputants limit themselves to discussing Ibsen's work without indulging in mutual characterization?

Iverslie's response (October 20, 1880) was to return to his assessment of Hervin's moral laxity. He then reasserted that when such poets as Ibsen professed themselves to be wise, they became merely foolish, especially when their wisdom deviated from Christian precepts. Iverslie admitted, however, that Christian principles might be misunderstood even by sincere believers.

On November 3, 1880, Hervin replied that he viewed *A Doll's House* as a true picture of how cultivated contemporaries live, not as a lesson in morality. Since he despaired of correcting Iverslie's narrow view, Hervin withdrew from the contest.

This interchange between Norwegian-Americans is instructive as it reflects the effect of Ibsen's writings on his countrymen far away from their native land. Iverslie was representative of those very Norwegians who received the brunt of Ibsen's satirical volleys.

References: Paulson, Arthur C. *The Norwegian-American Reaction to Ibsen and Björnson 1850-1900.* Northfield, Minn.: St. Olaf College Press, 1937; Paulson, Arthur C., and Kenneth Björk, "*A Doll's House* on the Prairie: The First Ibsen Controversy in America," *Norwegian-American Studies and Records*, XI (1940), 1-16.

J

JACKSON, GLENDA (1936-): The Royal Shakespeare Company (London) presented Glenda Jackson as Hedda Gabler* in 1975. Possessed of great skill, Jackson made a memorable Hedda, concerning which J. C. Trewin wrote, "No Hedda, seeking an object she cannot determine, has been more infinitely bored, or more dangerous" ("Things People Do," *Illustrated London News*, 263, 6926 [Sept. 1975], 81).
Reference: Who's Who in the Theatre, 16th ed., p. 772.

JAMES, HENRY (1843-1916): James, the author of twenty novels, 112 stories, twelve dramas, voluminous letters, and frequent newspaper criticisms, was an early detractor of Ibsen and a later champion. The means of his conversion was, it seems, the experience of seeing three performances of Elizabeth Robins'* Hedda Gabler* in April and May of 1891. He had attended *A Doll's House** earlier that year and disliked it; nor did he appreciate *Rosmersholm** or *Ghosts,** both of which were staged in 1891. About this trio of productions, James said, "Must I think these things works of skill?" To him, Ibsen's plays seemed merely "moral tales in dialogue—without the objectivity, the visibility of the drama" (Edel, p. 23). Elizabeth Robins' portrayal of Hedda Gabler changed James' opinion, and thereafter he wrote about 150 letters to the actress, many of them chronicling his growing appreciation of Ibsen. (In 1932 she published them under the title *Theatre and Friendship: Some Henry James Letters*.) For public consumption James penned a long essay entitled "On the Occasion of Hedda Gabler," which appeared in the *New Review* (June 1891).

In the article James identifies Ibsen's particular talent as "his habit of dealing essentially with the individual caught in the fact" (James, p. 255). In another section James writes that "Ibsen kneads the soul of man like a paste, and often with a rude and indelicate hand to which the soul of man objects'' (James, p. 252). Despite such quotable judgments, however, James' appreciation of Ibsen was still reserved, particularly in view of what he saw as Ibsen's disregard of social niceties.

James was sufficiently committed to Ibsen's interests to publish in the *Pall Mall Gazette* (February 17, 1893) an article which called for a judicious reception of *The Master Builder*,* which was to be produced three days later. In "On the Occasion of *The Master Builder*," James referred to "the hard compulsion of [Ibsen's] strangely inscrutable art" (James, p. 258). Of the play itself he remarked, "The mingled reality and symbolism of it all give us an Ibsen within an Ibsen" (James, p. 259).

After reading an advance copy of *Little Eyolf*,* James prophesied success, but he despaired of the third act as too simplistic. He conceded, however, that this weakness could be obviated by a good production. When he wrote publicly about the play (*Harper's Weekly*, January 23, 1897), he blatantly said that he preferred Ibsen on stage to Shakespeare. Ibsen produces a "click" in the aesthetic sense of the spectator. "It is simply the acceptance of the small Ibsen *spell*, the surrender of the imagination to his microcosm, his confined but completely constituted world, in which, in every case, the tissue of relations between the parts and the whole is of a closeness so fascinating" (James, p. 289).

When James read *John Gabriel Borkman** in 1897, his conclusion was: "Every time [Ibsen] sounds his note, the miracle, to my perception, is renewed" (James, p. 292). *When We Dead Awaken** was not produced in London until 1903, by which time James' failures as a dramatist had soured him on the theatre. His opinion of Ibsen's last drama would be valuable, but its absence notwithstanding, Henry James was an astute commentator on Ibsen's works.

References: Edel, Leon. *Henry James: The Treacherous Years, 1895-1901*. London: Rupert Hart-Davis, 1969; James, Henry. *The Scenic Art*. Ed. Allan Wade. New York: Hill and Wang, 1957.

JATGEIR (*The Pretenders*): An Icelandic poet.

JENSDATTER, ELSE SOFIE (1818-92): When young Ibsen was an apothecary's assistant of J. A. Reimann* in Grimstad,* he came into contact with Else Jensdatter, a maid whose duties included seeing to Ibsen's mending. She came from a respectable family that had lost its financial footing through seeking Norway's independence from Denmark. On October 9, 1846, in her native town of Börkedalen, she gave birth to a son sired by sixteen-year-old Henrik Ibsen: Hans Jakob Henriksen.* The mother and son remained in Börkedalen for twenty-nine years sinking deeper and deeper into unrelieved poverty. She died penniless in 1892 in her shanty on a hillside.

JENSEN (*The Wild Duck*): A hired waiter at Haakon Werle's* dinner party.

JENSEN, FRITZ (1818-70): A man of many interests—theology, landscape painting, and theatre—Fritz Jensen, a native of Bergen,* was the first director of the Norwegian Theatre, Bergen.*
Reference: C. W. "Frederick (Fritz) Nicolai Jensen," *Allgemeines Lexikon Bildenden Künstler* (Leipzig, 1925), XVIII, 515.

JENSEN, H. J.: Jensen, the Norwegian publisher of *Illustreret Nyhedsblad*, published *Lady Inger of Österaad** and *The Vikings in Helgeland** in his journal. When Jensen later pirated the script of *The Vikings* as a book, Ibsen successfully sued him.

JESSEN, COLLA (b. 1869): Colla Jessen played two Ibsenian roles in Munich: Peer Gynt* in 1902 and Halvard Solness* in 1905.

JOHN GABRIEL BORKMAN: A four-act Realistic-Symbolistic serious drama.
Composition: Begun on July 11, 1896; finished on October 18, 1896; published on December 15, 1896.
Stage history:

Jan. 10, 1897	Swedish Theatre, Helsinki
Jan. 10, 1897	Finnish Theatre, Helsinki
Jan. 16, 1897	Frankfurt-am-Main
Jan. 17, 1897	Royal Theatre, Copenhagen, Emil Poulsen* as Borkman
Jan. 19, 1897	Drammen
Jan. 25, 1897	Christiania Theatre* (19 perfs.)
Jan. 25, 1897	Royal Theatre, Stockholm
Jan. 29, 1897	Deutsches Theater, Berlin, Hermann Nissen* as Borkman
Mar. 27, 1897	Residenz Theater, Munich
May 3, 1897	Strand Theater, London (5), W. H. Vernon* as Borkman
Nov. 9, 1897	Théâtre de l'Oeuvre
1897	Norwegian Theatre, Bergen* (1)
May 1898	Hoyt's Theatre, New York, pro. Criterion Independent Theatre*
Nov. 19, 1904	Maly Theatre, Moscow
Oct. 25, 1910	Court Theatre, London, Franklin Dyall as Borkman
Jan. 26, 1911	Court Theatre, London, James Hearn as Borkman
May. 1, 1912	Hoftheater, Braunschweig
Apr. 1, 1915	48th Street Theatre, New York (3), Emanuel Reicher* as Borkman
Mar. 14, 1917	Deutsches Theater, Berlin, dir. Max Reinhardt*
Dec. 6, 1921	Everyman Theatre, London, Franklin Dyall as Borkman
Jan. 29, 1926	Booth Theatre, New York (7), Eva Le Gallienne* as Ella
Nov. 9, 1926	Civic Repertory Theatre, New York (7), Eva Le Gallienne as Ella
Oct. 15, 1928	"Q" Theatre, London, Mrs. Patrick Campbell* as Ella
Oct. 21, 1935	Grafton Theatre, London, Clephan Bell as Borkman
Nov. 12, 1946	International Theatre, New York (21), Eva Le Gallienne as Ella
Mar. 1, 1950	Arts Theatre, London, Frederick Valk* as Borkman
Nov. 3, 1950	Schauspielhaus, Munich, Werner Krauss* as Borkman
Feb. 16, 1961	Mermaid Theatre, London, Bernard Miles as Borkman

Dec. 4, 1963	Duchess Theatre, London, Donald Wolfit* as Borkman
Jan. 28, 1975	Old Vic Theatre, London, Ralph Richardson* as Borkman
Jan. 19, 1977	Stage 1 Theatre, New York, Robert Pastene* as Borkman
Dec. 18, 1980	Circle in the Square Theatre, New York, E. G. Marshall* as Borkman.

Synopsis: Mrs. Gunhild Borkman sits knitting in her once-elegant drawing room in a house near Christiania. A maid announces the visit of Gunhild's twin sister Ella Rentheim. They are both elderly, but where Gunhild's face shows coldness, Ella's reveals suffering. Each waits for the other to speak first, and their initial words are awkward as if they are not used to communicating. Ella sits and observes that it has been eight years since they last met, a week before an unnamed man was set free. The remembrance causes pain to them both, but Gunhild is particularly frantic as she speaks of the disgrace to the family and of her own suffering; the child Erhart had to pay a price as well. Ella then asks how Borkman himself is bearing up. Gunhild claims to know nothing of her husband John Gabriel Borkman, who was jailed for five years; she swears that she will never see him again because at his trial he had claimed that her spendthrift habits had ruined him financially. Ella admits that Borkman too had squandered vast amounts of money in an effort to live up to his reputation. He had never bothered to tell Gunhild that they were spending money embezzled from the bank of which Borkman was president; then he was caught. Now, thirteen years later, Gunhild is determined to redeem her family's reputation and honor through her son Erhart. She believes that Ella had had similar plans for Erhart when she took him in after his father's arrest, an act of kindness that Gunhild still resents, largely because of jealousy. She also disdainfully notes that Ella managed to keep her fortune when the Borkmans were bankrupted. Gunhild demands to know why Ella gave Erhart such a good education; she will not believe that Ella's goal was to make the boy a happy person. In Gunhild's view, Erhart must achieve such a spectacular success that people will forget his father's crime. Ella cannot believe that Erhart shares this goal, but she expresses her happiness for Gunhild. Then she asks if she might speak with Erhart when he makes his nightly visit from town. Hearing footsteps in the room above, Ella incorrectly assumes that Erhart is already in the house; she is anguished to learn that it is Borkman who constantly paces his room.

For the past eight years he has remained upstairs while Gunhild has lived below, being continually reminded of her shame by the sound of his presence. They never meet because he never leaves his rooms. Occasionally, she has heard him walk halfway down the stairs and then retreat to his haven. Under Ella's questioning, Gunhild says that Borkman has no friends, no visitors except an old clerk, Vilhelm Foldal. Although the old man had lost all his money when the bank closed, he had refused to testify against Borkman. Now, says Gunhiild, Erhart has compensated Foldal's loss by helping his daughter Frida to an education so she can get a job. Erhart also provided the girl music lessons, and she sometimes plays for Borkman. Now the girl lives nearby with a rich widow, Mrs. Fanny Wilton. Gunhild seems fond of Mrs. Wilton because she clearly idolizes Erhart. Ella then asks Gunhild if she does not agree that she, Ella, has a claim on Erhart, not because of what she spent on him but because she loves him. Because of this love, she is alarmed because she sees both Gunhild and Mrs. Wilton as threats to Erhart. To secure Erhart's happiness Ella is prepared to fight Gunhild for him; this is not the first time they have vied for a human being, and Gunhild quickly notes that she won that first battle. Gunhild thinks that Ella can never establish her influence over Erhart because she has made him painfully aware that the family has depended on Ella for its livelihood and that she had stopped visiting because she was ashamed of them. Gunhild's dominant mood is shattered by Ella's announcement that she intends to remain in this house to the end of her life if necessary. Gunhild admits that she may do that because Ella owns the house; yet she, Gunhild, will never live under the same roof with Ella. At issue, then, is Erhart; they agree that he will chose between them.

The maid ushers in Mrs. Fanny Wilton. Before Ella can be introduced, Erhart bursts in, having stopped at Mrs. Wilton's to fetch Frida, who has gone up to play for Borkman. He is delighted to see his aunt. Mrs. Wilton says that she and Erhart are going to visit the Hinkels, but his mother advises him that the Hinkels are not suitable acquaintances for him. Somewhat embarrassed, Erhart capitulates to his mother's whim; Mrs. Wilton agrees to make his excuses. Laughingly, however, she says that en route she will telepathically order him to follow her to the party; Erhart agrees that in that circumstance, he would have to obey. Mrs. Wilton withdraws. Ella tells Erhart that she has come to consult a specialist because her health has been quite poor, and now she has decided to remain in this house. Erhart seems genuinely solicitous about his aunt's health, delighted that she will remain, and concerned that she should rest immediately. Gunhild sees his actions as preliminary to his leaving her to go to the party. Gunhild tells him to stay at home; Ella advises him to feel free. The women are in direct opposition, and Erhart picks up his hat to go. Upstairs Frida is playing "Danse Macabre"—the dance of death. As he leaves, Gunhild reminds him of his mission; Erhart responds that he was not meant to be a missionary. Gunhild concedes that Ella has momentarily won the skirmish for Erhart but will not be able to hold him because of Mrs. Wilton's influence. The sisters agree that Erhart has greater allegiance to Mrs. Wilton than to either of them. Ella retires, leaving Gunhild writhing on the floor crying that she cannot bear this life.

The scene of Act II is the great gallery of the Borkman house. John Gabriel Borkman, a distinguished-looking man in his sixties, stands listening to Frida Foldal playing the piano. He remarks that he first heard such tones when he was a boy in the mines. After a brief talk of his experiences as a miner's son, Frida excuses herself because she must go to play dance music at a party given by the Hinkels. Borkman is intrigued to learn that his son will be there; he is also interested to hear that Erhart has visited and talked to his mother and a strange woman. After Frida leaves, Borkman resumes his habitual pacing.

A knock on the door produces Vilhelm Foldal, a bent and tired old man, who has walked all the way rather than spend money on the tram. Foldal, who has not seen his daughter since she went to live with Mrs. Wilton, asks if she has been here. He admits to great loneliness since she moved out; his other five children do not understand him. Borkman concludes that exceptional men are never understood by mediocre people. Old Foldal, so miserable that he starts to cry, laments that his marriage of convenience was a mistake, but he had been so crushed at the time that a better match was not possible. Borkman interprets this outburst as an accusation that his embezzlement was the cause of Foldal's misery. Foldal denies this and explains that his children, more educated than their parents, expect more from life than he can offer; they are not impressed that he is a tragic poet. He produces a portfolio from which he draws a manuscript and eagerly shows Borkman some changes he has made. Borkman then says that when his power is restored, he will make things right for his old friend. The mere thought of his rise from ignominy produces an almost megalomaniacal description of Borkman the all-powerful. Foldal eagerly maintains that he believes the day of restitution will come. Each old man, then, has encouraged the other in his dreams of a better future. Not content to leave his dream of glory to come, Borkman discusses his vast plans for commerce, industry, banking, and power. Then he starts to relive his downfall and concludes that the worst sin is betraying confidences. At last it comes out that the person who had betrayed Borkman was Hinkel, who is now living a life of luxury while Borkman is an exile in his sister-in-law's house. The situation is even more ironic because Borkman's own son is at Hinkel's listening to Frida's music. Borkman further thinks that his son, because he was reared by his aunt and his mother, sides with Hinkel rather than his own father. He shouts that women are corruptors who prevent men from fulfilling their destinies. When Foldal states his belief that somewhere an ideal woman exists, Borkman turns on him and cites his inane poetic nature as the reason Foldal never amounted to anything. Foldal retaliates by saying that Borkman will never regain his power. Now the old men are bent on destroying dreams of a better future. They realize, as Borkman says, that friendship means deception; they have been deceiving each other for years. Borkman curtly dismisses Foldal, who sadly leaves. Borkman moves to summon his friend back but stops. Again he begins to pace. A knock at the door is heard.

Ella Rentheim has called. Borkman is dumbstruck at her appearance. After reminiscing about their romantic youth, they sit down and talk of their wasted lives. Borkman tells Ella that she could have been happy after he married Gunhild if she had only tried. Hinkel had repeatedly asked her to marry him, and when she refused, Hinkel thought that Borkman was responsible. To get even, Hinkel had used Borkman's letters to incriminate him and precipitate the bank's failure. In Borkman's estimation, Ella was the cause of his downfall. He feels particularly noble to think that when his financial world had toppled, he had refused to appropriate Ella's money as he had everyone else's. When she asks why he had spared her, Borkman replies that he could risk his life and position on a bold business venture but not what he held dearest. Yet, as Ella observes, he was able to spurn her love and marry Gunhild; Borkman reveals that such was the price of Hinkel's financial support. He had, in fact, sold Ella's love for control of the bank. She sees his monumental sin as the murder of her love, and in doing so, he killed his own soul. Borkman admits that his uncontrollable desire for power was stronger than his love. Although Borkman had robbed her of joy, Erhart was able to rekindle human emotions in her; if Ella could not have Borkman, she would become mother to his son. Now Ella is desolate because Gunhild has rewon Erhart's love. Or perhaps she has lost him to Mrs. Wilton. Now her illness has been diagnosed as incurable; she might live through the winter. Borkman gives his permission for her to try to recapture Erhart's love, since the son is not his any longer anyway. She then tells him that she plans to leave all her money to Erhart but that she wishes him to change his name to Rentheim. Borkman agrees to the scheme, but the door is cast open, revealing Gunhild who declares that Erhart will never bear that name. He will, she says, carry on his father's name, which will be restored to its former glory. He will, moreover, be his mother's child. Having said this, Gunhild exits. Ella tells Borkman that Gunhild's stance will wreck Erhart's life. The threat is so serious that both of them must go downstairs and confront her. The curtain falls.

Act III transpires in Mrs. Borkman's drawing room. When the maid enters, Gunhild chides her for being so slow to answer her summons. Then Gunhild sends her to the Hinkels' to tell Erhart to come home. The maid is surprised to hear that Erhart is at the Hinkels' rather than his accustomed haunt at Mrs. Wilton's. As the maid leaves, Ella and Borkman come into the room.

Borkman proposes to give an account of his motives to his wife, who does not care to hear anything from him. Borkman, oblivious to her wishes, commences his own vindication. After years of considering his case, he has acquitted himself because he had merely answered the inexorable call of the riches within the earth. What he cannot forgive is his decision to withdraw from the world when he was released from prison rather than facing reality and starting all over again. Gunhild predicts that the same thing would have happened again, and Borkman does not contradict her. The great loss of his life, he says, is that no one understood him enough to convince him that he had done anything that was irreparable. Gunhild asks why he never came to her for understanding; he responds that it would have done no good. When Borkman says that he sees a new life for himself, Gunhild counsels him to remain in his grave while she erects a monument in the guise of Erhart over his tomb. Gunhild is still confident that she will win the battle for Erhart, who at that moment returns from the party.

Gunhild rushes to him and confides that someone, meaning Ella, wants to take him away from his mother. Ella presses her claim by telling him of her approaching death. Erhart thanks her for everything she has done for him but says he cannot return to her. Gunhild's exultation is of short duration when he announces he cannot stay with her either. He says he cannot live a life of atonement, that he has discovered his own will. Borkman decides at last to speak to his son; he invites Erhart to join forces with him as he enters business again. Ella urges Erhart to do it while his mother tries to dissuade him. Erhart, however, says no to his father's offer. Ella despairingly asks him for only two months of his time; then his father and mother repeat their wishes for his allegiance. To all of them he replies negatively because he plans to find a new life of joy with Fanny Wilton, who has been waiting outside the door and now comes in.

Mrs. Wilton is decidedly uncomfortable in these circumstances, but she is quite capable of pointing out to the contending parties that her liaison with Erhart is the result of the exercise of the free will of both of them. Mrs. Wilton, Erhart, and Frida plan to leave for the South this very night. There had been no party at the Hinkels'; the trio had merely planned to meet there tonight and slip away. Erhart tries to say farewell to his mother, but she repulses him. Ella wishes him joy and happiness. The son merely bows to his father. Then they leave.

Borkman seeks his hat and coat because he has decided to go into the storm of life alone. Ella tries to restrain him, but he is adamant. She begs Gunhild to help her, but her sister is so full of self-pity that she cannot be budged. Gunhild calls Erhart's name and starts to run after him, but Ella stops her as the curtain falls.

Act IV has an out-of-doors setting—near the house. Borkman, Ella, and Gunhild are on the steps as Ella still tries to keep Gunhild from following Erhart. The sound of sleigh bells is heard, perhaps those of Mrs. Wilton's departing sled. As the tintinnabulation draws nearer, Ella urges Gunhild to call out to Erhart if she must, but by now the mother sternly decides to let her son go off in search of happiness. She goes into the house full of dire predictions about Erhart's life with Fanny.

Ella tries to convince Borkman to go inside the house, but he claims he will never enter it again. Vilhelm Foldal is seen struggling through the heavy snow. He is amazed to see Borkman outside; Foldal further reports that he has just been struck by a quickly departing sleigh. He has lost his glasses and injured his foot. Foldal has come to share the happy news that Frida left him a note saying that Mrs. Wilton has arranged for her to study music abroad. He is delighted at his daughter's good fortune but even more pleased that she took the trouble to write to him about it. Even so, he plans to keep her from going. Borkman tells the old man that Frida has already left, that she was in the covered sleigh that ran him down. Rather than being angry, Foldal is pleased that Frida has gone away with Fanny and Erhart in such fine fashion. Now he must return home to comfort his wife who will not be able to understand that Foldal's poetic gift has been reborn in Frida's music.

Ella again tries to get Borkman to enter the house, which he now sees as a prison. When the maid comes with Gunhild's instruction to lock the front door, he observes that they want to lock him away again. He is determined to fight his way back to life again and invites Ella to accompany him. She is worried about his health, but Borkman reminds her that Gunhild has pronounced him a dead man. Ella determines to follow him into the mountains.

The scenery dissolves into wooded slopes and escarpments. Borkman leads the way higher and higher up the mountain. They come out onto a flat place from which there is a spectacular view of the mountains and the fjord. Borkman walks to the edge of the precipice and exults in the vista that lies beneath. He speaks of steamships and factories that were a part of his kingdom when he died; now the mighty mountains are his kingdom. He launches into a frenzied paean to the veins of metal that lie imbedded in the mountain and the power and glory their mastery entails. Ella tells him that he will never inherit this Kingdom, Power, and Glory because his path to it involved the murder of her love. As she says this, Borkman staggers toward a bench as he clutches his heart. She takes off her cloak and covers him with it before starting off for help. Then she returns, feels his pulse, and sinks down into the snow in front of him. Moments later Gunhild appears, preceded by her maid with a lantern. Ella tells Gunhild that Borkman died when an icy metal hand clutched his heart. The sisters agree that the cold killed Borkman and made two shadows of them. They join hands over the corpse and watch over the dead man. Curtain.

Structural analysis: In this play Ibsen has draped complex psychological characterizations of Borkman, Gunhild, and Ella over a simple structural skeleton. Although the Plot is unified by action, this is a drama in which Character greatly overshadows Plot:

Borkman discovers that Ella wants to regain control of Erhart;

(as a result of which)

Borkman gives his permission for her to make the attempt;

(as a result of which)

Borkman discovers that Gunhild is adamantly opposed to the idea and intends to use Erhart for her own selfish purposes;

(as a result of which)

Borkman agrees that he and Ella should confront Gunhild;

(as a result of which)

Borkman discovers that Erhart intends to seek happiness by exercising his free will;

(as a result of which)

Borkman decides to do likewise, the first step of which is leaving the house;

(as a result of which)

Borkman discovers, as he dreams of the future, that he cannot inherit the Kingdom, Power, and Glory because he has murdered Ella's love;

(as a result of which)

Borkman dies.

The drama is rich in Ibsenian themes: the destructiveness of materialism, the necessity of personal freedom, the mystical attraction of mountains, the enervating effects of the North as contrasted with the promise of the South, and the sometimes numbing consequences of marriage.

References: Johnston, Brian. "The Tragic Farce of John Gabriel Borkman," *Edda*, 79, 2 (1979), 99-108; Leland, Charles. "Anagnorisis in *John Gabriel Borkman*," *Contemporary Approaches to Ibsen*, ed. David Haakonsen, IV (1979), 138-53; Röed, Arne. "The Utter Necessity," *Contemporary Approaches to Ibsen*, ed. Daniel Haakonsen, IV (1979), 154-68.

JOHNSTON, ALFRED (*The Lady from the Sea*): The American sailor once loved by Ellida Wangel.*

JOHNSTON, ANDREW: Under the pseudonymous initials B.S.S., Johnston published the first act of *Catiline** and summaries of the other acts as well as songs and poems from Ibsen's early plays: *Translations from the Norse*. Gloucester: J. Bellows, 1879.

JOHNSTON, MOFFAT (1886-1935): Johnston appeared in New York as Gregers Werle* (1925), Karsten Bernick* (1931), and Doctor Wangel* (1934) in support of Blanche Yurka,* Armina Marshall,* and Mary Hone,* respectively.

Reference: Who Was Who in the Theatre, III, 1309-10.

JONAS, EMIL JACOB (1824-1912): A Dane who spent much of his life in Germany, Emil Jonas made an unauthorized translation of *The Pillars of Society** in 1878. He received a stinging letter from Ibsen, largely because he abridged the action. Jonas' version achieved considerable currency in Germany because it was published in a cheap edition.

Reference: Dansk Biografisk Leksikon, XII, 66-67.

JONES, HENRY ARTHUR (1851-1929): One of England's most successful dramatists, Henry Arthur Jones first attracted attention by his melodrama *The Silver King* (1882). In the summer of that year, the actress Helena Modjeska* traveled in Europe, met Jones, and suggested that he make an adaptation of *A Doll's House**; her husband's version, *Thora,** was not presented until December 1883. Jones and his collaborator Henry Herman set to work, and *Breaking a Butterfly** was the result, a travesty which Jones later repudiated.

Saints and Sinners (1884) was Jones' next important drama, which prompted the first of a succession of critics to assert that Jones was an Ibsenite, an accusation which the author always hotly denied. In a typical response, Jones wrote, "I cannot remember when I first read *The Pillars of Society*,* and I am not sure whether I saw the play when it was done for a matinee in 1880. I am under the impression that I did see this single performance; but I think I may safely say that I was not indebted to Ibsen's *Pillars of Society* for the drift and bearing of *Saints and Sinners*. . . . I should not in the least mind acknowledging my indebtedness to Ibsen, if I thought I owed anything to him."

Jones was, in fact, too much of an idealist to respond warmly to Ibsen's social problem plays, and for a time, he was an articulate detractor. After praising Ibsen's insistence on dramatic truthfulness, Jones said, ". . . one cannot help regretting that Ibsen's colossal intellectual power should be employed in the research, not of beauty, and health, and strength, but of disease and moral deformity, of curious and exceptional depravity." (*The Era*, May 2, 1891).

When Jones' first book, *The Renascence of English Drama* (1895), first appeared, his attitude towards Ibsen could be summarized thus: "Lately a school has arisen amongst us which proclaims that the details of ugliness and disease are the chief importance for us to study, and that curious and distorted forms of vice and selfishness and human degradation are the essential elements to be preserved and treasured in our plays. I protest against this with all my might" (Jones, *Renascence*, p. 245). Years later, even Jones was converted to Ibsenism: "No glance at any corner of the modern drama can leave out of sight the ominous figure of Ibsen. . . . As there is no modern playwright who understands his craft that does not pay homage to Ibsen's technique, so there is no modern dramatist who has not been directly or indirectly influenced by him. . . . Like all good artists, he is greatest, not where he is most realistic, but when he is most imaginative" (Jones, *Foundations*, pp. 22-3).

References: Jones, Doris Arthur. *The Life and Letters of Henry Arthur Jones.* London: Victor Gollancz, 1930; Jones, Henry Arthur. *Foundations of a National Theatre.* Freeport, N.Y.: Books for Libraries Press, 1967 [1913]; Jones, Henry Arthur. *The Renascence of English Drama.* London: Macmillan, 1895.

JOSEPHSON, LUDVIG OSCAR (1832-99): Swedish director Ludvig Josephson was an important ally of Ibsen because he was a principal stager of Ibsen's dramas. He worked at the Christiania Theatre* from 1872 and inaugurated his regime with a production of *The Pretenders** (1873); he produced *Love's Comedy** the next year. *Lady Inger of Östraat** appeared under his direction in 1875 and *Catiline** in 1881. Josephson's staging was so meticulous that he may be viewed as a Scandinavian Georg II, Duke of Saxe-Meiningen.*

References: Josephson, Ludvig. *Ett och annat om Henrik Ibsen och Kristiania Teater.* Stockholm, n.p., 1898; *Norsk Biografisk Leksikon*, VII, 118-9.

JOSTEIN (*The Burial Mound*): A Viking standard-bearer.

JOVIAN (*Emperor and Galilean*): A Roman general.

JOYCE, JAMES (1882-1941): While a student at University College, Dublin, in early 1900, James Joyce read a paper praising Ibsen. On April 1, 1900, the *Fortnightly Review* published Joyce's review of *When We Dead Awaken*,* which was so complimentary that Ibsen thanked the young man through William Archer.* Believing Ibsen to be the "greatest man on earth," Joyce incorporated many allusions to Ibsen's plays in his *Finnegan's Wake* and *Ulysses*.

Reference: Ellmann, Richard. *James Joyce.* London: Oxford University Press, 1959.

JULIAN (*Emperor and Galilean*): Roman prince, half-brother of Gallus,* first Caesar, then Emperor of the Roman Empire. As the central figure in Ibsen's great world-drama, Julian is mainly a repository of ideas. When first seen, he is a nominal Christian but tainted by paganistic views; gradually, his growing paganism leads him to persecute Christians in his attempt to force a synthesis between Christianity and paganism that will end in the establishment of the Third Empire, over which he seeks to rule. He dies without ever seeing the real consequences of his apostasy.

K

KAARE THE PEASANT (*The Vikings in Helgeland*): A man of Helgeland who foments rebellion and precipitates a crisis for Gudmund.*

KACHALOV, VASILII I. (1875-1948): Russian-born V. I. Kachalov was "an actor of keen mind, fine imagination and impressive presence. . . ." (Sayler, p. 22). After 1900 Kachalov was a principal actor at the Moscow Art Theatre,* where he played Arnold Rubek* in 1900, Brand* in 1906, and Johannes Rosmer* in 1908.
Reference: Great Soviet Encyclopedia, XI, 329; Sayler, Oliver M. *The Russian Theatre*. New York: Brentano's, 1922.

KAHN, FLORENCE (1878-1951): Over a period of four years, American actress Florence Kahn appeared in four Ibsenian productions in New York. When she played Rebecca West* in 1904, the *New York Times* reported that she "has good looks and a sweetly modulated voice, precise, clear, and full of the color of passion, but she 'acted' always; not for a moment was she a live woman" (Mar. 29, 1904, p. 6, col. 1). Kahn played Irene de Satow* in 1905, Thea Elvsted* in 1907, and Rebecca West in 1908.
Reference: Who Was Who in the Theatre, III, 1323.

KARI (*Peer Gynt*): A cottager's wife who is Aase's* friend.

KASKET, HAROLD (1916-   ): According to *The Times* (London), Harold Kasket's sole excursion as Gregers Werle* into Ibsen's world was unfortunate: "Actors who fail to master Ibsen—that is, be equal to him—must expect to have all their inadequacies revealed. That is what happened here" (Nov. 1, 1947, p. 6, col. 4).

KEACH, STACY (1941-   ): American actor Stacy Keach's Peer Gynt* (New York, 1969) was greatly appreciated by most of the critics.

References: Hewes, Henry. "Romping Through Ibsen," *Saturday Review*, 52 (Aug. 2, 1969), 35-6; *Who's Who in the Theatre*, 16th ed., pp. 801-2.

KEJSER OG GALILAER: The Norwegian title of *Emperor and Galilean.**

KIELER, LAURA (1849-1932): Norwegian writer Laura Kieler thought herself to be the inspiration of Nora Helmer.* She was a friend of Ibsen, visiting him in Dresden in 1871 and Munich in 1876. Kieler wrote a book of biographical sketches called *Silhouetter* (1887) in which a chapter called "Henrik Ibsen in Copenhagen" appears.

References: Norsk Biografisk Leksikon, VII, 273-5; "The Real Doll's House," *Living Age*, 320 (1924), 415-6.

KIERKEGAARD, SÖREN AABYE (1813-55): Whether Ibsen was directly influenced by the writings of this Danish philosopher/theologian is a moot point; that Ibsen voiced many of Kierkegaard's premises is beyond question. Perhaps it will never be known whether Ibsen seriously studied Kierkegaard's works, for he was reluctant to admit a debt to anyone. When queried about the matter, Ibsen admitted that he had "read little of Kierkegaard and understood less" (Sprinchorn, p. 102), which is not to be doubted because Ibsen had little patience with theoretical literature.

On the other hand, as early as his days in Grimstad,* Ibsen perhaps was exposed to Kierkegaard through the good-will of a Scottish lady, Miss Georgiana Crawfurd,* who opened her library to him. Jens Crawfurd, her nephew, who often carried books to Ibsen, recalls that Kierkegaard's *Either/Or* was in his aunt's possession. Christoffer Lorentz Due,* more-over, one of Ibsen's friends, says that there was much talk of *Either/Or* and *The Works of Love* among himself, Ole Schulerud,* and Ibsen. It is also possible that Ibsen read Kierkegaard while at the University of Christiania, but there is no evidence of the fact. The Dane's influence, however, came closer to home in the person of Magdalene Thoresen,* Ibsen's mother-in-law, who was an avid advocate of Kierkegaard. Furthermore, Ibsen doubtless was exposed to Kierkegaard's thoughts by his clergyman-friend, Christopher Arnt Bruun.* Perhaps Kierkegaard was a topic of conversation in Ibsen's literary club, The Learned Hollanders.* In short, Ibsen could not have been wholly ignorant of Kierkegaardian ideas.

In a number of ways, Ibsen and Kierkegaard were remarkably similar: they were not handsome and suffered as a result; they were alienated by pietistic Christianity; and they were socially inept. In the intellectual realm also they were kindred. At the risk of being simplistic, Kierkegaard's major ideas must be stated as a means of showing Ibsen's utilization of them:

(1) Kierkegaard believed that knowledge comes to a person in a moment of enlightenment and wholly transforms the individual from ignorant to knowledgeable. At a decisive moment, the miracle may happen, unbidden and unexpected. Whatever is the vehicle of this enlightenment, Kierkegaard called "the god."

(2) Desperation is man's natural state, and the only deliverance is through faith that the miraculous transformation can and will come about.

(3) Since the individual cannot know any unwavering truth about the world of experience, the only alternatives are to remain in the darkness of despair or to take "the leap into absurdity," which is how he describes the faith that "the god" can intervene in human history. The risk of this leap is enormous because the enlightenment may not come, or it may not be recognized if it should transpire.

(4) There is an eternal conflict between a man's spiritual nature and his aesthetic, worldly dimension, but the spiritual is paramount and makes of the individual "the absolute last demand."

(5) If a person's choice of the spiritual be a valid option, he must have absolute freedom to choose between good and evil.

(6) Implicit in the individual's election of good is the supreme demand that he "be himself," that is, that he maintain his individuality at all costs.

Ibsen implemented these ideas particularly in *Brand** and *Peer Gynt.** They are also present in his apprentice dramas, especially *Catiline,** in his most cerebral work, *Emperor and Galilean,** and in his later dramas, notably *John Gabriel Borkman** and *When We Dead Awaken.**

Kierkegaard called his voluminous works "indirect discourse" to suggest that his task was not to supply answers but to ask questions. Ibsen said, "A dramatist's business is not to answer questions, but only to ask them." Again the congruity of their views is striking.

References: Kierkegaard, Sören. *Either/Or*, Vol. I. Trans. David F. Swenson and Lillian M. Swenson. Rev. H. A. Johnson. Princeton, N.J.: Princeton University Press, 1959; *Either/Or*, Vol. II. Trans. Walter Lowrie. Rev. H. A. Johnson. Princeton, N.J.: Princeton University Press, 1972; MacIntyre, Alasdair. "Kierkegaard," *The Encyclopedia of Philosophy* (New York: Macmillan, 1967), IV, 336-40; Sprinchorn, Evert, ed. *Ibsen: Letters and Speeches.* New York: Hill and Wang, 1964.

KIIL, MORTEN (*An Enemy of the People*): Kiil is the foster-father of Katherine Stockmann.* Kiil's tannery is the source of the pollution that taints the spa. He tries to blackmail Thomas Stockmann* to recant by tying Mrs. Stockmann's inheritance to Stockmann's actions.

A KITCHEN-MASTER (*Peer Gynt*): One of the ship's crew who drowns.

KJAEMPEHÖJEN: The Norwegian title of *The Burial Mound.**

KJAERLIGHEDENS KOMEDIE: The Norwegian title of *Love's Comedy.**

KLEIST, HEINRICH VON (1777-1811): German dramatist, author of *Kätchen von Heilbronn*, believed by some to be the plagiarized source of *The Feast at Solhoug.**

KLUNIS, TOM: Tom Klunis played Arnold Rubek* in a production of *When We Dead Awaken** in New York in 1982.
Reference: Theatre World (1965-66), Vol. 22. New York: Crown Publishers, 1966.

KNUD (*The Grouse in Justedal*): An old minstrel.

KNUDSEN, KNUD (1812-95): The son of Tormod Knudsen,* Knud Knudsen, a professor at the University of Christiania, was hired as "language teacher" at the Christiania Theatre* in 1852 when the Norwegian language was substituted for Dano-Norwegian. He may have inspired Huhu* in *Peer Gynt.**
Reference: Norsk Biografisk Leksikon, VII, 476-89.

KNUDSEN, TORMOD (1797-1868): A poet and politician from Telemark, Knudsen was rumored to be Ibsen's real father. Knudsen met Ibsen's mother in 1825 in Telemark. According to the story, the couple's affair continued after the lady became Fru Ibsen. Although Knudsen believed Ibsen to be his son, there was no family resemblance.
Reference: Norsk Biografisk Leksikon, VII, 489-90.

KNUDTZON, FREDERIK G. (1843-1917): Knudtzon was a Danish publisher who knew Ibsen in Italy in 1866 and later wrote his reminiscences of the days they spent together: *Ungdomsdage* [*Youthful Days*]. Copenhagen: Gyldendal, 1927.
Reference: Dansk Biografisk Lekikon, XIII, 2-3.

KNUT GJAESLING (*The Feast at Solhoug*): The king's sheriff, enamored of Signe.*

KOMMISARZHEVSKAYA, VERA (1864-1910): When she opened her own theatre in St. Petersburg on November 10, 1906, Vera Kommisarzhevskaya was already deemed one of Russia's most important actresses. She chose to inaugurate the venture with a production of *Hedda Gabler,** innovatively directed by Vsevelod Meyerhold.* Kommisarzhevskaya was what her brother Theodore* called a "synthetic actress," which is to say that she was uninterested in realistic details of characterization. "As an actress she was very economical and synthetic in her mode of expression and avoided outward typical details. She insisted that an actor's means of expression should be restricted to the simplest fundamentals in order to show the essential inner life of a character" (Kommisarzhevsky, p. 67). Under her brother's direction, she added Nora Helmer* and Hilde Wangel* to her repertory with great success.

When financial pressures threatened her theatre, Kommisarzhevskaya accepted an invitation to appear in *A Doll's House** and *The Master Builder** in New York, scheduled for March 2, 1908. Of her Nora, the *Dramatic Mirror* said, "It was a studied performance; not an inspired one. . . . A trick of passing her hands over her forehead or covering her face, to represent emotional stress, seemed old-fashioned and inexpressive. In short, she gave such a performance as might be expected of an intelligent and experienced stock company actress" (Mar. 14, 1908, p. 3, cols. 2-3). There is no evidence that *The Master Builder* was produced.

Kommisarzhevskaya's American tour was not a success. Her brother "was an impotent witness of a financial debacle, mainly because her managers were a couple of hopeless fools who knew about as much of theatrical conditions in America as of the life of the Tibetan Dalai Lama!" (Kommisarzhevsky, p. 81).

References: *Great Soviet Encyclopedia*, XII, 607; Kommisarzhevsky, Theodore. *Myself and the Theatre*. New York: E. P. Dutton, 1930.

KOMMISARZHEVSKY, THEODORE (1882-1954): One of the twentieth century's most influential directors because of his concept of "internal eclecticism," Theodore Kommisarzhevsky did his first important work in the theatre of his sister Vera* from 1906 to 1909. During that period he staged *A Doll's House** "produced in brown folded curtains hanging at an angle" (Kommisarzhevsky, p. 90) and *The Master Builder.** He attended his sister on her disastrous American tour of 1908. After her death in 1910, he managed several Russian theatres and production studios before emigrating to the West in 1919.

The Theatre Guild (New York) hired Kommisarzhevsky to direct Joseph Schildkraut* in *Peer Gynt** (February 5, 1923), which was an extremely successful production. Perhaps his most challenging association with an Ibsenian drama was his production of *The Pretenders,** which was staged in a vast outdoor theatre at Holyhead with Welsh amateurs (August 1927). Since all his company had weekday jobs, Kommisarzhevsky was forced to rehearse only on Saturday afternoons through the summer. Although progress was slow, it was nonetheless creditable, for Kommisarzhevsky noted "that the less 'experienced' [his] players were, i.e., the less they imitated professionals, the better were their performances." Undaunted by fierce seaside winds, audiences of thousands, and an unfamiliar text, Kommisarzhevsky's actors performed on a stylized platform dominated by the arms of Norway and so pleased the auditors that cries of "bis" ["again"] were heard.

Always interested in discovering and communicating the playwright's truth, Kommisarzhevsky through imaginative staging techniques sought to

delve beneath the surfaces of Ibsen's dramas in order to portray their essence. He did not subject Ibsen's plays to illusionistic staging.
References: Kommisarzhevsky, Theodore. *Myself and the Theatre.* New York: E. P. Dutton, 1930; "Reviving an Undramatic Masterpiece," *Literary Digest,* 76 (1923), 30-31.

KONGS-EMNERNE: The Norwegian title of *The Pretenders.**

KORSH, F. A. (1852-1921): From 1882 Korsh managed his own theatre, the largest private theatre in Moscow. Through his efforts, Muscovite audiences saw *A Doll's House** (1891) and *An Enemy of the People.**
Reference: "Korsh Theater," *Great Soviet Encyclopedia,* XIII, 423.

KRAP (*The Pillars of Society*): Karsten Bernick's* chief clerk.

KRAUSS, WERNER (1884-1959): Ibsenian roles stood at the beginning and the end of Werner Krauss' career. He played Peer Gynt* at Berlin's Deutsches Theater in 1913 and John Gabriel Borkman* in Munich in 1950.
Reference: Brockhaus Enzyklopaedie, X, 600-1.

KROGSTAD, NILS (*A Doll's House*): A felon at heart, Krogstad blackmails Nora Helmer* to use her influence with her husband to allow Krogstad to keep his position at the bank. His ability to respond to the friendly influence of Kristine Linde* is the only thing that keeps him from being utterly reprehensible.

KROLL (*Rosmersholm*): Professor Kroll is Beata Rosmer's * brother. He is a representative of the conservative element of local society and tempts Johannes Rosmer* with the editorship of a rightist newspaper. He is also the source of the implication that Rebecca West* has committed incest with her father.

KVIST, JÖRGEN (*St. John's Night*): A student, son of Mrs. Berg's first marriage.

KVIST, JULIANE (*St. John's Night*): Daughter of Mrs. Berg's* first marriage, Juliane is the principal romantic interest of the play. She is at first secretly engaged to Johannes Birk,* but she is eventually paired with Julian Poulsen.*

KYTRON (*Emperor and Galilean*): A philosopher.

L

LAADING, HERMAN (1813-94): A local schoolmaster in Bergen* since 1837, Herman Laading shared responsibilities with Ibsen in the direction of the Norwegian Theatre, Bergen.* After 1852 Laading was the role instructor while Ibsen served as stage instructor.
Reference: Paulsen, John. "En gammel bergenser," *Julehistorier.* Kjöbenhavn: Gyldendal, 1899.

LACKAYE, WILTON (1862-1932): In support of Olive Oliver,* Virginia-born Wilton Lackaye* played Karsten Bernick* for one performance in New York in 1904.
Reference: Who Was Who in the Theatre, III, 1395-7.

THE LADY FROM THE SEA: A five-act Realistic-Symbolistic serious drama.
Composition: Started on June 5, 1888; finished by September 25, 1888; published on November 28, 1888.
Stage history:

Feb. 12, 1889	Christiania Theatre* (27 perfs.), Johanne Dybwad* as Hilde
Feb. 12, 1889	Hoftheater, Weimar
Feb. 16, 1889	Royal Theatre, Copenhagen
Mar. 5, 1889	Schauspielhaus, Berlin, dir. Anton Anno*
Mar. 14, 1889	Hoftheater, Weimar
1889	Royal Theatre, Stockholm (5)
1889	Royal Theatre, Copenhagen (11)
1889	Swedish Theatre, Helsinki
May 11, 1891	Terry's Theatre, London (5), dir. Eleanor Marx*
Dec. 16, 1892	Théâtre Moderne, Paris, pro. Cercle des Echoliers, Aurélien-Marie Lugné-Poë* as Wangel

Mar. 1893	Royalty Theatre, London, Janet Achurch* as Ellida Wangel
Mar. 26, 1899	Residenz Theater, Munich
May 1899	Schiller Theater, Berlin
1899	Royal Theatre, Copenhagen (3)
1900	Royal Theatre, Stockholm (4)
Oct. 1, 1901	Hoftheater, Braunschweig
May 7, 1902	Royalty Theatre, London, Janet Achurch* as Ellida Wangel
Jan. 17, 1903	New Theatre, St. Petersburg, Lydia Yavorska* as Ellida Wangel
1904	Sens, Sarah Bernhardt* as Ellida Wangel
Sept. 1, 1904	Deutsches Theater, Berlin
Nov. 6, 1911	Lyric Theatre, New York (1), Hedwig Reicher* as Ellida Wangel
Dec. 15, 1917	Alexandrinsky Theatre, St. Petersburg, dir. Vsevelod Meyerhold*
May 5, 1921	Bilbo Theatre, Turin, Eleonora Duse* as Ellida Wangel
June 7, 1923	New Oxford Theatre, London, Eleonora Duse as Ellida Wangel
Nov. 29, 1923	Metropolitan Opera House (1), Eleonora Duse as Ellida Wangel
Feb. 2, 1925	Lyric Theatre, London, Lillebil Ibsen* as Ellida Wangel
Nov. 4, 1928	Apollo Theatre, London, Muriel Pratt as Ellida Wangel
Mar. 18, 1929	Bijou Theatre, New York (24), Blanche Yurka* as Ellida Wangel
May 1, 1934	Little Theatre, New York (15), Mary Hone* as Ellida Wangel
Mar. 13, 1946	Arts Theatre, London, Veronica Turleigh as Ellida Wangel
Dec. 6, 1949	Schauspielhaus, Munich, Paula Wessely as Ellida Wangel
Aug. 7, 1950	Fulton Theatre, New York (16), Luise Rainer* as Ellida Wangel
Dec. 4, 1956	Cherry Lane Theatre, New York, Christiane Feismann as Ellida Wangel
Mar. 15, 1961	Queen's Theatre, London, Andrew Cruickshank as Wangel
Apr. 29, 1971	Greenwich Theatre, London
Mar. 18, 1976	Circle in the Square Theatre, New York (77), Vanessa Redgrave* as Ellida Wangel
May 16, 1979	Round House Theatre, London, Vanessa Redgrave as Ellida Wangel

Synopsis: The outdoor action of the drama takes place in the vicinity of the house of Doctor Wangel, the district physician, near a fjord in northern Norway. An artistic-looking man by the name of Ballestad is discovered in the process of straightening the ropes of a flagpole when Bolette, the doctor's elder daughter, enters. Preparations are afoot to receive the visit of her former tutor, Professor Arnholm. Lyngstrand, a visitor to the area, walks along the road, sees Ballestad's artist's materials, and starts a conversation with Ballestad, who allows him to examine the landscape upon which he is working. The painting, it seems, will also depict a dying mermaid on the rocks, a poor creature who has strayed too far from the sea and now must die. Ellida Wangel, the doctor's wife, had suggested the theme, which, it happens, is a metaphor for her own life. Lyngstrand plans to be a sculptor. He also hopes to consult Doctor Wangel about his delicate physical condition. Although Lyngstrand is new to the area, Ballestad has been there for nearly two decades, having arrived with a theatrical company.

Bolette emerges from the house and is greeted by Lyngstrand, who has met the female members of the family at a band concert. Ballestad starts to collect his impedimenta and return to his hotel because he has noticed that the tourist-laden steamer has docked. The former scenepainter, now a landscape artist, is also a hairdresser, a dancing-master, and a bandleader; the tourists represent potential clients. He exits as Hilde Wangel, the younger daughter, emerges from the house carrying a footstool. Bolette brings flowers.

Lyngstrand remarks that he met Ellida this morning as she entered her bathhouse. Hilde's reaction to this news is enigmatic. In response to Lyngstrand's question as to the purpose of the decorations, Hilde bluntly says that they are celebrating their mother's birthday. She does not explain that Ellida is their stepmother. When Lyngstrand mentions that he is rooming with Mrs. Jensen, the midwife, Hilde reacts petulantly. Realizing he has said something inappropriate, Lyngstrand leaves with an apology.

Wangel comes in from making his professional calls and greets his daughters lovingly. He commends their decorations and inquires into the whereabouts of Ellida. He asks if Arnholm has yet appeared and understands that the girls intend to use the visit of Bolette's old teacher to disguise the fact that the celebration is really in honor of their mother's birthday. Wangel is uncomfortable with this arrangement because he fears that Ellida will feel slighted. Soon Arnholm makes his way down the road and enters the garden, causing great delight to his old friends whom he has not seen for eight or nine years. After exchanging pleasantries, the girls go into the house for refreshments as Wangel and Arnholm sit on the verandah to exchange mutual news. Wangel has to explain that his first wife had died soon after the birth of his daughters and that his second wife has made him very happy, although their baby boy died aged only five months. Arnholm wants to meet Ellida but learns that she is taking her daily swim, an invariable plunge regardless of the weather. Wangel says that she enjoys good general health but suffers from intermittent nervousness, which is ameliorated only by swimming in the fjord. Arnholm, who knew Ellida as a child, remarks that the sea had attracted her even then when her father had tended a lighthouse in a remote northern village. Now, Wangel says, the local folk know Ellida as "the Lady from the Sea."

This conversation is interrupted by the appearance of Ellida, her hair dripping wet, who greets Arnholm warmly and opines that she prefers the waters of the open sea to the unwholesome fjord. Wangel leaves Arnholm to be entertained by Ellida, who seats him in her summerhouse to converse. She notes that the verandah is largely the girls' domain, while the summerhouse is hers. Wangel divides his time between the two places. Arnholm reminisces about his acquaintance with Ellida ten years before when the village parson had called her "The Heathen" because she was named after a ship. It emerges that Arnholm had fallen in love with Ellida and had asked her to marry him. When she refused, he had gone away without knowing she loved someone else. Ellida is prepared to tell Arnholm the whole story, but she is hindered by the arrival of Lyngstrand, who has come to call.

He presents a bouquet to Ellida as a birthday memento without realizing that she is not the mother to whom Hilde had referred. Ellida is momentarily chagrined but soon rallies and pretends that her birthday was to have been kept a secret. As they chat, Lyngstrand tells how as a young sailor, he had been shipwrecked in the English Channel. A long period in the water had damaged his chest, which gave him a good excuse to avoid physical labor and become a sculptor. His artistic goal is to sculpt a grouping showing the troubled sleep of an unfaithful wife of a sailor who drowned and whose spirit, dripping water, watches over her. Since this work concerns the sea, Ellida most avidly wishes to discuss Lyngstrand's idea, which is based on a personal experience. It seems that as his ship had prepared to sail from Halifax, an American had joined the crew. He had pored over newspapers in an effort to learn Norwegian. One night during a violent storm, he was reading a Norwegian journal, alighted upon a particular line, roared wildly, and silently shredded the newspaper. Then he quietly muttered something about someone's marrying another man in his absence.

Ellida grows intensely interested when Lyngstrand first mentions an American seaman, but when he repeats the sailor's comments about a marriage, she becomes riveted and asks for more details. In perfect Norwegian the man had vowed to return to the woman even if he should be drowned in the meantime. He would rise up from the depths of the sea, beckon to her, and lead her away. Ellida clearly is unsettled by this narrative, but she asks what has become of the man. Lyngstrand believes he drowned when the ship broke up in the Channel. Ellida pointedly suggests that they adjourn to the house, but Lyngstrand takes his leave.

Seeing that she is upset, Arnholm asks the reason. He at first assumes that the birthday celebration has annoyed her, but Ellida asserts that she understands she must share her husband with the memories of his former wife, nor does she blame the children for continuing to love their mother. Then he suspects that she does not really love Wangel, but she protests that she has come to love him dearly. Pressed for an explanation, Ellida says that perhaps she will confide in him later. At that point Wangel and the girls appear, and the party starts to move indoors. Ellida goes back to collect her bouquet and remarks that they were a birthday present. The girls see that Ellida knows the real reason for the festivity, and Wangel with embarrassment tries to assuage Ellida's hurt. Ellida appears magnanimous, but Hilde believes that her acceptance of the celebration is only a means of humoring her husband. Arnholm is quizzical.

The locale of Act II is Prospect Park on the outskirts of town; a summer twilight envelops the scene. Ballestad enters conducting a party of German tourists and passes from view as Hilde appears followed by Bolette. Hilde is waspish because Lyngstrand's pace up the hill bores her; the fact that her father has pronounced him terminally ill does not make her more tolerant of his infirmities. An exhausted Lyngstrand, carrying Ellida's parasol, comes into view and explains that the rest of the party will join them later. When the subject of his illness is introduced, Lyngstrand passes it off as inconsequential, a tactic also employed by Hilde. When Lyngstrand goes off to guide the others to this spot, Hilde admits that her interest in him springs from his pose of planning a future as a sculptor while knowing that he is doomed. Then she turns her iconoclasm onto Arnholm, who she maintains is growing bald. Hilde suspects that his relationship with Ellida is not quite all it seems. She also thinks it likely that Ellida will go mad because her mother died a lunatic. Further speculations are abandoned at the entrance of Wangel, Ellida, Arnholm, and Lyngstrand. The girls conduct Arnholm and Lyngstrand to Pilot's Peaks some distance away.

Left alone with his wife, Wangel tells Ellida that they cannot continue as they are, that they must re-establish their former closeness, which Ellida says is impossible. Wangel thinks that she is still disturbed by the birthday party and that her obsession with competing with her predecessor has caused her to abandon his bed; he also knows that the environment—mountains, limited horizons, unbracing air—is stifling her. Ellida admits that she is homesick for the sea but is quite surprised to hear of Wangel's decision to move back to the sea to make her happy. She knows, however, that he would be sacrificing his own contentment by such a move. Although she tries to persuade Wangel to give up all thought of moving away, he insists that he is prepared to do so. His adamance impels her to tell him the truth about her disquietude.

Ellida asks Wangel to remember that when he proposed, she had honestly told him that she had been engaged to another man. He guesses that the fiancé was Arnholm, but she denies it. Ellida identifies her lover as Alfred Johnston, a sailor on an American ship who, rumor had it, had murdered his captain and fled. Together they had talked of the sea, storms, whales, porpoises, and other maritime matters. Because he had had a hypnotic effect on her, they became engaged because he said they must. When they parted, he had taken his ring and one of hers, put them together on a key-ring, and tossed them into the sea as a token of their marriage to the sea. Once he had departed, his mysterious hold over her was broken, and several times she wrote to tell him that their affair was over. He merely ignored her protestations and told her that one day he would come for her and she must follow him. Time passed, and then three years ago when she was pregnant with Wangel's child, Johnston's power over her reasserted itself. She lost the child when it was five months old, and she stopped being a wife to Wangel. When Wangel concludes that she still loves this man, Ellida hotly denies it and vows that he only fills her with terror. She seems on the verge of revealing something else when the girls and their guests appear and then pass off the stage.

Ellida summons Lyngstrand, gets him to talk of his shipwreck three years ago, and tells Wangel that the date coincides with the reappearance of her dread of Johnston. When the terror is the strongest, she sees him hovering at her side and wearing a blue-white pearl stickpin that looks like the eye of a dead fish. This outpouring convinces Wangel that Ellida is truly ill, to which she assents and begs him to help her before she is destroyed. Then she remembers their dead child's eyes that had changed color as the sea does when the weather changes; those eyes were Johnston's eyes. This, she says, is why she dare not be intimate with Wangel. Overcome by emotion and terror, Ellida rushes off down the hill only to be followed by Wangel.

The setting of Act III—an overgrown spot in Wangel's garden near a stagnant pond—reflects the mounting threat to Ellida's sanity. Hilde and Lyngstrand are fishing as Bolette sits on a stone and sews. The idyll is interrupted by the arrival of Arnholm, whose presence drives them away. Arnholm asks Bolette about Ellida's state of mind, but she pretends indifference. When Arnholm mentions the books at her side, Bolette admits that she enjoys reading but that her maintenance of the house leaves very little time for it. It seems that Bolette, not Ellida, is the housekeeper. Arnholm replies that she reads to breach the isolation of her life in this remote place. She says that her life's desire is to get away and pursue her studies. Arnholm recollects that Wangel used to speak of sending Bolette to college, but she responds that her father, who has not much strength of character, speaks of many things that do not come about. The old tutor encourages her to tell her father of her wishes, to which she says that she is like her father in having no strength of character. Besides, she says, Ellida so occupies Wangel's thoughts that he cares little for his children. Bolette realizes that someday she will have to leave, but she fears for her father because Ellida seems incapable of managing things, which may partly be due to the medicine he prescribes to bolster her spirits and prevent depression. Wangel, it seems, insists on a joyful household at any cost. Nevertheless, argues Arnholm, Bolette has a responsibility to insure her own happiness, toward which he has a suggestion. His advice must wait, however, because Ellida enters.

Ellida has returned from a walk and is about to go sailing with Wangel; hence, she is loath to join Bolette and Arnholm. She admits that now she feels safe and happy. At that moment she sees a ship at the quay and starts to rhapsodize about the joy of being aboard and taking a sea voyage, which she has never done. Arnholm observes that people are made for dry land, but Ellida strongly disagrees and suggests that people would be happier if they lived at sea, perhaps even in it. Arnholm does not dispute her but remarks that the wrong evolutionary choices were made eons ago and now it is too late to alter man's nature. Ellida believes that people realize that sad fact, which accounts for much anguish and melancholy. Arnholm rejoins that most people are basically happy, an opinion refuted by Ellida, who sees the bright happiness of summer marred by the realization that the dark wintry days must come. After this, Ellida tries to dispel this mood and sends

Arnholm to fetch Wangel as she can no longer see him. When Arnholm questions the statement, she says that when they are separated for any appreciable time, she forgets what he looks like. Arnholm starts to go, and Bolette insists on accompanying him because she suspects that Wangel has boarded the steamer in pursuit of old friends or drinks.

Left alone, Ellida peers into the stagnant pool and talks to herself. While she is thus occupied, the Stranger walks down the path, stares at her in silent delight, and finally speaks to her by name. Ellida wheels around as if she were expecting him and cries out that he has returned at last. Then she retreats as if she does not recognize him and asks who he is and whom he seeks. He answers that he came to see her. She then recognizes his remarkable eyes as those of Johnston. Although she threatens to summon help, Johnston assures her that he has no intention of harming her. He has arrived on the English steamer, coming to her as soon as he could. In anguish Ellida tells him to go away, reminding him that she had written and ended their affair. He seems not to hear her and continues to talk of his desire to return as soon as possible and take her away despite his knowledge of her marriage. Entirely distraught, Ellida buries her face in her hands as he asks if she does not wish to leave with him. She says that she does not, cannot, and dare not want to go away with him. Johnston appears to accept her decision, but he comes nearer as he confides that he has but one thing to say to her. Ellida is paralyzed by fear and screams that he must not look at her with his hypnotic eyes. Johnston's assurances that she has nothing to fear are interrupted by the entrance of Wangel, into whose arms Ellida rushes saying, "Save me! Save me—if you can!" In her frenzy Ellida cries that the man of her nightmares is here, Johnston is here. Wangel asks why he has come back since he must surely know that Ellida is now Mrs. Wangel. Johnston replies that he has known for more than three years when he saw an announcement of her marriage in a newspaper. He believes that the ceremony of the rings that he celebrated with Ellida was a valid marriage too. Ellida slumps in her anguish as Johnston simply says that he promised to return to her, and he has now done that. Ellida retorts that she never wants to see him again as Wangel asks what he intends to do about the situation. Johnston knows that it would be useless to take her away against her will, that she must go with him voluntarily. Now he must get back to his ship but will return the next night to learn her decision. He insists that she meet him alone, that she be ready to travel, and that their relationship will be forever ended if she does not accompany him tomorrow night.

Johnston departs as Wangel tries to comfort Elida, who is torn between her wish to be free of this man and her realization that he will never come again if she refuses him. Wangel threatens to have Johnston jailed for murder if he reappears, but Ellida insists that he must remain free, that he must never be caged as he belongs on the sea. She begs Wangel to save her from this man.

Lyngstrand and Hilde enter and report that they have just seen the

American sailor on the path, the same man with whom Lyngstrand had served aboard ship. Remembering the story of the sailor's vow to appear in a dream to his faithless lover, Lyngstrand tells the tale to Hilde while Ellida gazes at the steamer traveling up the fjord. She softly begs Wangel to save her from herself because she is bewitched by this man who is like the sea. Together they slowly exit through the garden.

At the beginning of Act IV, Bolette is discovered embroidering in the conservatory of the Wangel house. Within view are Lyngstrand, Ballestad, and Hilde. Lyngstrand introduces the subject of marriage and expounds his theory that a wife gradually becomes more and more like her husband as the union progresses. Bolette suggests that a husband might also become more like his wife, but this argument stymies the artist who believes that in the case of an artist, the wife could have no higher calling than to help her husband create art. Bolette haits this train of thought by calling Lyngstrand selfish, which makes him defensively refer to his illness. He is interested in Bolette's concern for him despite his health, which the artist believes may be restored because he is a lucky man. Her solicitous thoughts will aid him in the creation of his masterpiece. Arnholm's entrance interrupts this discussion, but as the teacher stops to chat upstage with Hilde and Ballestad, his failure to marry engages the comment of Bolette and Lyngstrand. Bolette surmises that Arnholm has remained a bachelor because he has taught nearly every young woman in the district; to marry one's tutor, she believes, simply is not done. By now Ballestad has collected his things and left the stage accompanied by Hilde. Arnholm joins Bolette and Lyngstrand.

Arnholm inquires about Ellida and hears from Bolette that she has locked herself in her room. The teacher is about to exit in search of Wangel, who appears in the garden room. The young people wander into the garden to keep Hilde company so that the doctor and Arnholm can continue their discussion of the previous night. Wangel asks if Arnholm has further advice on how to treat Ellida's illness, but the elder man defers to the physician. Although Ellida seems calm at the present, her moods change so capriciously that any alteration is possible. Wangel ascribes her morbidness to the fact that Ellida is a sea creature, one whose moods and thoughts are controlled by the restless sea. These people, he believes, cannot be transplanted; his mistake is having brought her inland. His love of Ellida has been so selfish that he never bothered to help her develop spiritually, and as her condition deteriorated, he saw his mistake and wrote to Arnholm for assistance in the belief that her one-time love of Arnholm lies at the foundation of her illness. As for Johnston, Wangel concludes that his effect on Ellida is beyond rational explanation. To Arnholm's query as to his belief of Ellida's assertion that their baby's eyes had changed colors like the sea, Wangel heatedly denies its truth. Wangel answers evasively when Arnholm asks if Wangel saw a resemblance between the baby's eyes and those of Johnston. Arnholm presses Wangel to admit that Ellida's sickness began three years ago when she heard that Johnston was en route to claim her, but Wangel ascribes her sickness to her pregnancy. Arnholm suggests moving away, but Wangel replies that Ellida has already concluded that no good could be served by doing so; moreover, he must consider the girls and the effect another move might have on their prospects of marriage. His grief is great as he expresses his torment at wishing to help his wife and provide for his children; his problem is that he sees no suitable way to do either. At this point Ellida enters.

Her first action is to ascertain that Wangel will remain at her side today. Arnholm greets her and then excuses himself to search for the girls. Nervously conscious of time, Ellida realizes that the steamer will return within twelve hours. Wangel asks her to describe Johnston's looks when he appeared in her dreams. When she says that he looked as he did yesterday, Wangel observes that she said that she had failed to recognize him yesterday, that his eyes sealed his identity. Then he notes that she had said that in her dreams he looked quite different and did not wear the scarfpin that looked like a fish's eye. Ellida admits that today she cannot remember how he looked on the day when they first parted. Wangel concludes that the reality of Johnston's appearance yesterday has erased the illusions she had held about him, which perhaps was a useful occurrence. Ellida then desires to share all her thoughts with Wangel, the first of which is that it was a great misfortune that they had married, as it must result in great unhappiness. Her view is that as a lonely widower with two children, Wangel had purchased her as a wife and mother without knowing if she would be suitable in either role. Deprived of her true lover, Ellida had agreed to Wangel's proposal for the sake of security but did so out of panic and not by free choice. Their marriage, consequently, has not been a true union; he must, therefore, allow her to leave him. His desolation only moves her to say that they should agree to "cancel the bargain." What will happen after that, she does not know, but Ellida begs Wangel to give her back her freedom of choice. When Johnston visits again, she must have the freedom to choose as she must. She admits that she is fascinated by the thought of committing herself to a sort of life she cannot imagine. In the face of her arguments, Wangel concludes that it is his right and duty to protect her from an unwise choice; he will not release her. Ellida responds that she is fascinated by Johnston and the life he offers and feels that she belongs with him. Wangel promises to release her tomorrow after Johnston has left, but that does not satisfy her. Then Arnholm, Bolette, and Hilde come into the room.

Wangel tells them that Ellida is going home to the sea tomorrow, the news of which causes Hilde to rush to Ellida in alarm. Ellida is surprised by this outburst of sentiment, and Bolette explains that all Hilde has ever wanted was a word of tenderness from her stepmother. Ellida is stunned as she considers that she may be needed in this house. Bolette announces dinner, and they adjourn to the dining room to drink a farewell toast to "the Lady from the Sea."

The stagnant pond at the end of the garden, upon which the girls, Arnholm, and Lyngstrand are punting, is the locale of Act V. Just as they push off, Ballestad enters carrying a French horn and music. He is bound for the quay where the band will play for the English steamer's last journey of the season. Ellida and Wangel appear and anxiously await the sight of the boat, after the sailing of which winter will soon set in and entrap them all in a prison of ice. After Lyngstrand leaves, Ellida nervously observes that only a half-hour remains until her encounter with Johnston which will determine whether she goes with him or returns to her home by the sea. Clearly, Ellida has not made her decision, nor have she and Wangel finished facing the truth of their lives together. They exit for a short walk before the steamer lands; meanwhile, the boaters reappear.

Arnholm and Bolette discuss the possibility of her going away to study, which will be possible with Arnholm's assistance. Delightedly Bolette accepts Arnholm's offer of help. Once he has established that she has broken her ties with her home, Arnholm asks her to marry him, which she emphatically refuses to do. He tells her that he had misread Wangel's letter of invitation to mean that Bolette had desired his presence. Although he now knows that Wangel had referred to Ellida, Arnholm cannot be responsible for his feelings toward Bolette. Once again he asks her to marry him, and when she again refuses, he offers to help her continue her studies in any case. Now, however, she feels that she cannot accept his help, but his arguments are tempting in view of the alternative of remaining at home. It is then that Bolette agrees to become his wife but asks him not to speak to the others of their engagement. They leave as Hilde and Lyngstrand enter.

Hilde surmises that Arnholm has been declaring his love of Bolette, but Lyngstrand is confident that she will not accept Arnholm since she has promised mentally to encourage Lyngstrand. The artist says that he is not interested in marrying Bolette but entertains the idea that several years hence Hilde will be precisely Bolette's current age and presumably just as attractive. While neither openly avows love, this certainly is a scene of courtship. Then the English steamer is sighted already docked at the pier. Wangel and Ellida return, see the ship, and send Hilde and Lyngstrand to the dock.

Ellida senses Johnston's proximity, and Wangel offers to meet him and send him away, but Ellida is determined to participate in the encounter. Johnston appears, stops outside the fence, and asks Ellida if she is prepared to make the journey. Wangel tries to answer for her, but Johnston ignores him and asks if she is ready to come of her own free will. The bell of the steamer rings a warning sound; Ellida must make her choice. The man exerts pressure to make her decide, so Wangel intervenes and tells Johnston to get out of the country before he is arrested for murder. Johnston's response is to produce a revolver with which he intends to guarantee his freedom from jail. Ellida tells Wangel that he can keep her body by force, but he can never keep her mind a prisoner, that mind that is attracted by the shadowy unknown. When Wangel sees that he is losing Ellida, he releases her to make her choice. She asks what prompted him to make this sacrifice, and he answers that it was his love of her. Now that she is absolutely free, Ellida sees that her situation has changed significantly. The second warning bell rings. She turns to Johnston and admits that she never could go with him now, that everything between them is over. His power to terrify and fascinate her is at an end. Realizing that he has lost, Johnston departs, leaving Wangel and Ellida to discuss their new relationship. He concludes that her longing for the unknown was a symbol of her growing determination to be emotionally and intellectually free. She is unable to assess the validity of this thought, but she willingly returns to Wangel's home as his wife and mother of *their* children.

The others enter and watch the steamer head for the ocean. Wangel announces that Ellida is remaining at home, which prompts Hilde tearfully to embrace Ellida. Ellida confides to Arnholm that it is difficult for a land creature to find its way back to the sea, to which Ballestad responds that a mermaid would perish then but people can acclimatize themselves to their environments. The play ends as the steamer skims the fjord.

Structural analysis: Ibsen constructed a complex plot unified by action, consisting of a major line of action (Ellida-Wangel-Johnston) and two minor ones (Bolette-Arnholm and Hilde-Lyngstrand). The incidents of the major line of action are unified causally:

Ellida discovers that Johnston has returned to claim her;

(as a result of which)

Ellida refuses to go away with him;

(as a result of which)

Ellida discovers that Johnston will return the next night to hear her irrevocable decision as to their future;

(as a result of which)

Ellida begs Wangel to give her her freedom;

(as a result of which)

Ellida discovers that Wangel is willing to send her back home to the sea but will not allow her to go with Johnston;

(as a result of which)

Ellida remains obdurate in her contention that she must have freedom of choice;

(as a result of which)

When Johnston returns, Ellida tells Wangel that he can imprison her body but never contain her mind;

(as a result of which)

Ellida discovers that Wangel has given her the freedom to choose her destiny [RE-VERSAL];

(as a result of which)

Ellida sends Johnston away and remains with Wangel as wife and mother.

An interesting feature of this plot is its late, third-act initiation. The incidents of the first two acts, for the most part, are merely expository and descriptive of character relationships. The denouement, when it finally comes, is notable for its swiftness and is not entirely devoid of moralizing. The Bolette-Arnholm line of action is fairly well developed, but Ibsen depends on implication to delineate the Hilde-Lyngstrand subplot. The final tableau of the three pairs of lovers is reminiscent of Augustin Eugène Scribe's* plays.

References: Barranger, M. S. *"The Lady from the Sea:* Ibsen in Transition," *Modern Drama*, 21 (1978), 393-403; Fjelde, Rolf. *"The Lady from the Sea:* Ibsen's Positive World-View in a Topographic Figure," *Modern Drama*, 21 (1978), 379-91.

LADY INGER OF ÖSTERAAD: A five-act Romantic serious drama.
Composition: Written in 1854; published in 1857; revised in 1874.
Stage history:

Jan. 2, 1855	Norwegian Theatre, Bergen* (2 perfs.)
1857	Trondhjem
Apr. 11, 1859	Norwegian Theatre, Christiania* (2)
Mar. 20, 1875	Christiania Theatre* (8), dir. Ludvig Oscar Josephson*
Nov. 17, 1876	Christiania Theatre (2)
1877	Stockholm
Nov. 29, 1878	Christiania* (4)
Dec. 1878	Berlin, dir. Georg II, Duke of Saxe-Meiningen*
Dec. 14, 1882	Christiania Theatre (4)
Sept. 1885	Norwegian Theatre, Bergen, Laura Svendsen Gundersen* as Lady Inger
1895	Dagmars Theatre, Copenhagen
Apr. 14, 1898	Royal Theatre, Stockholm
Jan. 22, 1902	National Theatre, Christiania,* Johanne Dybwad* as Eline
Jan. 28, 1906	Scala Theatre, London (2), Edyth Olive* as Lady Inger
Mar. 1931	National Theatre, Oslo, Johanne Dybwad as Lady Inger
Nov. 16, 1936	Prinzregenten Theater, Munich
Mar. 26, 1947	Gateway Theatre, London, Molly Veness as Lady Inger

Synopsis: It is night at Österaad Hall. The fire that crackles on the hearth does not dispel the gloom of the storm that rages outside. Two servants sit before the fire as they polish various bits of armor. Finn asks, "Who was

Knut Alfson" to which Björn answers, "Norway's last knight," who was killed by the Danes. As the scene progresses, Björn shows his impatience with Finn who is dissatisfied with the armed truce between Norway and Denmark, a situation in which there are no more knights and affairs are dictated by women such as Lady Inger, the mistress of the castle. Finn remarks her growing restlessness, pallor, and thinness. Eline, Inger's daughter, enters and in the shadows listens quietly to the servants' discussion. Finn tells Björn of an abusive song that is being sung about Lady Inger who is blamed for her people's thralldom to the king of Denmark. Eline slips away, and a horn announces the coming of a visitor.

Left alone, Björn speaks of his attempts to shield Lady Inger from innuendo, but the common feeling is that she has betrayed her people. Eline shows herself, and the two discuss her sister Lucia, who has been dead for six months. Björn asks for an explanation of Eline's wildly mercurial temperament, but Eline does not respond. Instead, she talks of her youth when Björn told her that she should be proud to be Inger of Gyldenlöve's daughter, implying that now there is no reason to be proud. She asks Björn to tell her a story as he did in her childhood. He starts to tell of a virile knight whose penetrating glance so inflamed women's hearts that they could never forget him; they could only waste away in grief when he went away. Eline recognizes the story as that of Nils Lykke, the foremost Danish knight. As Björn talks, Eline repeatedly listens intently as if she heard something, the steps of someone approaching. Eline and Björn withdraw into the shadows as a person in black is seen turning Knut Alfson's portrait to the wall. She is recognized as Lady Inger, who goes to the window, looks out toward the road, and then leaves the room.

Voices are heard outside, and Einar and other servants enter, followed by Lady Inger, whose permission is asked for Einar and his men to join the Swedes in an uprising against their king. Lady Inger protests that the Danish king would surely help the Swedish monarch and severely punish all who had joined the insurrection. Einar rejoins that the general upheaval is a godsend because in the confusion the Norwegians could throw off the Danish yoke. Lady Inger seems to be tempted to go along with the plan, especially when Einar reminds her that, once free, the Norwegians could elect a king of their own from the Sture family. Warning them again of the danger, she grants their request and allows them to strip the castle walls of the old armor. In the bellicose confusion that follows, Björn emotionally thanks Lady Inger for satisfying all those who had doubted her patriotism.

Finn enters with a letter for Lady Inger, the content of which visibly disturbs her. Half aloud, Lady Inger remarks that someone is coming to the castle this night, someone with whom she will have a battle of wits. This news prompts Lady Inger to prevent her retainers from embarking until she gives the word. They threaten to go anyway, but when Lady Inger picks up Knut Alfson's sword and dares anyone to defy her, it appears as if she has won this battle of wills. Lady Inger tells Björn to open the gate to any visitor who calls.

Inger detains Eline, who voices her disappointment that her mother has not proven more forceful in achieving her people's independence. Responding that children ought not to judge their parents, Inger tells Eline that she is expecting a guest whose presence and identity must remain a secret. Eline immediately sees this as evidence of a conspiracy, which reinstates her mother in her view. She thinks she knows who the mysterious visitor is, a member of the fugitive Norwegian nobility, but Lady Inger denies the truth of this. Inger says that the time is a crucial one because the Danes are planning the final subjugation of the Norwegians, who must play for time. The southern Norwegians are pro-Danish, but the sympathies of the northern people are unknown. Hence, the visitor is an envoy sent to sample local opinions. Eline immediately sees how seditious it might appear for Lady Inger to receive a Danish legate, but she is unconcerned. Recalling how unhappy Eline has been at Österaad, Lady Inger implies that she may be considering a dynastic marriage for her daughter, who receives the news with scorn. Eline speaks of her mother's guile in marrying her eldest daughter Lucia to a Danish knight in Bergen; then she bitterly describes how Lucia went to visit in Bergen, met and fell in love with a knight, but was forced to return home where she grieved herself to death. Inger responds that the knight was a dissembling Dane. As she relives these pathetic events, Eline vows that she will avenge the familial and Norwegian honor. Eline challenges Inger to make the ensuing interview count for something, and then she exits.

Lady Inger soliloquizes that this night will affect not only her child's life but also that of Norway itself. She vacillates as she considers the ethical ramifications of the paths that lie open to her; then she screams in agony as the phantoms of family members and national heroes close in on her. At that point Olaf Skaktavl enters.

Skaktavl, a Norwegian fugitive for the past twenty years, is intent upon revenge against the Danes who violated his home and killed his only son. Realizing that he is a fighter, not a strategist, he has come to Lady Inger for direction. Skaktavl rehearses his youthful impressions of Inger as a proud, fighting woman bent on securing Norwegian freedom. He has just come from Sweden to enlist her aid in the fight for independence. Skaktavl also knows that a stranger is expected to meet him at Österaad this very evening. The sounds of people on horseback are heard; it is the expected visitor, whose identity is unknown to Skaktavl. They retire for refreshment.

Nils Lykke, a Danish knight, and Jens Bjelke, a Danish commander, enter with Finn, who tells them that another visitor has already arrived. Bjelke rejoices that the capture of this individual is imminent. Finn withdraws. Then it emerges that the Danish knights are pursuing Nils Sture for fomenting rebellion and that they think he has taken refuge with Lady

Inger. Bjelke's inclination had been to storm the walls of Österaad and seize Sture, but Lykke has counseled guile instead and looks forward to matching his craftiness against Lady Inger's. Bjelke leaves to rejoin his men who are stationed some distance away. There follows a soliloquy by Lykke. First, he mentions Lucia's death following his seduction of her; she was merely a fool. His sense of humor turns macabre as he imagines Lucia turning in her coffin when he entered Österaad, climbing the stairs from the crypt even as he speaks and watching him from the shadows. He knows of Eline through Lucia but magnanimously decides not to add her to his list of conquests because she must be inexperienced. At last his fancy turns to imagining how Lady Inger will deal with him. At that point she enters.

Lykke is craftily insinuating in his attempt to exculpate himself from any blame in Lucia's misfortune, but Lady Inger keeps him at a distance, remaining unimpressed by his oily charm. The conversation devolves to the political situation. Lykke knows that she is poised between the necessity of satisfying her countrymen and giving token obeisance to the Danish throne; he, says Lykke, offers the means of extricating her from this difficulty: if she will hand over Nils Sture, the Swedish envoy, who Lykke believes may be a candidate for the Swedish throne if the incumbent be unseated, the Danish king will be willing to grant autonomy to Norway, even allowing it to choose its own king. She must merely produce her visitor whom the Danes will install on the Swedish throne, thereby winning political advantage to themselves. Lady Inger, mystified, goes off to fetch Olaf Skaktavl. Believing that he is about to capture Sture, Lykke gloats at having tricked Lady Inger into surrendering her charge, whom he intends to murder. He even considers spreading the rumor that Sture, son of a Norwegian chieftain, met his end with the collusion of Lady Inger. This, reasons Lykke, would destroy her credibility with the Norwegian people.

Lady Inger enters with Skaktavl. Lykke recoils in surprise that it is not Sture but recovers quickly enough to act normally, although the old man is unknown to him. Skaktavl has been apprised of Lykke's scheme and mentions the collusion of Peter Chancellor, a Swedish fugitive from the Danes, in his mission, a fact that greatly intrigues Lykke. When Skaktavl, thinking that Lykke is the emissary he was to meet, asks for papers from Chancellor, Lykke suggests talking business over a meal. Naturally, he knows nothing of the papers. Lady Inger says that she will have no part of their plans. She pours wine for each of them, and when they have drunk, she tells them that the goblets contained a welcome for her ally and death for her enemy. Both men are frantic, as Inger exults in her cleverness at discomfiting them so soundly. There was no poison.

Eline enters and is immediately fascinated by the sight of Lykke but scorns his advances. He, in turn, is mesmerized by the young woman.

Act III is set in the Great Hall following the banquet. Eline enters and soliloquizes about her hatred of Lykke, taking great pleasure in the feeling of hatred. Lykke enters, sees Eline, and starts a conversation by telling her that she can rejoice that he is leaving Österaad that night. Eline scorns him not only for seducing Lucia but also for mistreating scores of women just like her. In long, lyrical speeches Lykke justifies his behavior and breaks down Eline's defenses. It appears that she has fallen in love with him. After she leaves, Lykke congratulates himself for conquering Eline as he has vanquished all other women in his life. Although he is somewhat attracted to her, the sport of humiliating her is most compelling. Then he reveals his uncertainty about the political situation. How terrible would be his shame if he has been tricked by a mere woman, the redoubtable Lady Inger.

At that point Nils Stensson jumps through a window. Lykke surmises that this intruder must be Nils Sture. In an aside Stensson reveals that he is Peter Chancellor's emissary. Lykke tries to extract information from Stensson by plying him with wine. During the ironic conversation that ensues, both men talk at cross purposes and become mutually confused. Finally, Lykke accuses Stensson of being Count Sture, which the man denies, claiming that Sture is dead. Stensson, he says, had been impersonating Sture for some time as a means of keeping the insurrection alive. Lykke tells him that he will be arrested for fomenting rebellion, but Stensson believes that Lykke will protect him once he hands over a packet of papers from Peter Chancellor. Lykke greedily snaps them up and reads that Stensson is actually the son of Lady Inger, but this is merely implied. He accuses Stensson of being Sten Sture's son and confirms it by comparing the young man's features with those of the portrait with its face turned toward the wall. Then Lykke identifies himself as a Danish statesman, which confuses Stensson, regardless of which, they exit as collaborators.

At the beginning of Act IV, Lady Inger enters the Great Hall with Skaktavl and Björn, from whom she learns that Eline had talked with Lykke. She sends for the Danish knight. Despite Skaktavl's warning to the contrary, Lady Inger wishes to detain Lykke at the castle. To allay Skaktavl's mounting doubt of her patriotism, she admits that she had once sought Lykke's marriage to Eline as a means of reconciling warring factions, but she had abandoned the scheme. Professing her hatred of Lykke, she does not want Eline to fall in love with him and have a repetition of Lucia's experience. Rather, she wants him to fall in love with Eline so that Inger can chase him away humiliated and scorned. Lady Inger says that the day will come when her countrymen will have no reason to doubt her patriotism.

Lykke enters and confirms his intention of leaving that night. Skaktavl asks for the papers sent by Peter Chancellor, which Lykke, thanks to Stensson's appearance, is able to hand over, but he retains the letter that tells of Stensson's real identity. Lady Inger tries to persuade Lykke to remain longer at Österaad. When he remains adamant, she accuses him of leaving because he lost his game of craft with a mere woman, one upon whose support he cannot rely. Stung, Lykke responds that he has been the victor; Lady Inger wagers Österaad against his knee-buckles that this is not true, but he will not accept the wager because a mere two words will have her at his feeet. He knows that she is the mother of Sten Sture's illegitimate son. She falls in agony at his feet, begging for the release of her son, for which she will give anything. Lady Inger then tells the entire story of her clandestine involvement with Sture and her pain at being separated from their child. Her great fear has been that her countrymen would find out about her illicit liaison with a Swede. This story cements Skaktavl's allegiance to her. Lykke then tries to blackmail Lady Inger, promising the safety of her son in exchange for throwing the support of her countrymen to the side of the Swedish insurgents, thus placing Sture's illegitimate son Nils on the Swedish throne. Inger wavers, and Lykke accuses her of wishing to be a king's mother, which she denies. She wonders if Nils Sture is willing to go along with the plan, so Lykke tells her that young Count Sture is in the castle and can assure her of his compliance. So Lady Inger agrees to give her support. Lykke's plan is to tell the murderous Bjelke that Sture is not at Österaad and then transport the boy to Denmark. Inger suspects treachery, and while Lykke formulates his plan, she and Skaktavl whisper their own arrangements.

While Lady Inger writes a document pledging her support, Stensson, who has now been told that Inger is his mother, enters and summons Lykke. He is eager to greet his mother after years of separation, but Lykke tells him that she refuses to see him because he has become peasantlike. She greets him, however, as Sture's legitimate son.

The scene is interrupted by the noisy entrance of Skaktavl, Einar, and all the armed retainers who shout, "Long live Lady Inger Gyldenlöve!" She then releases them to fight in behalf of the Swedish insurgents and introduces Stensson as Count Sture, "King of Sweden and of Norway too, if God be willing." Lady Inger assures Lykke and Stensson that thousands of Norwegians will join them as they march through the country. She then insists that they leave at this moment, but Lykke knows that Bjelke's men lie in wait. Stensson's respect for his mother is so great that he insists on following her orders, even though it means disobeying Lykke. When Lykke starts to join Stensson and the warriors, Lady Inger restrains him and says that he will be a prisoner until the victory is won. She then sends Skaktavl to fetch her son, whose identity will be established by the possession of Sten Sture's ring. Meanwhile, Lykke sends Finn away to tell Bjelke that Count Sture is dead, that the young man at the head of the troops must not be harmed. Then Finn is sent to the dungeon before he can get away. Inger exits.

Lykke, left alone, considers that Lady Inger will be the cause of her son's death. How he wishes to escape! Then he hears music coming from Eline's room and resolves to use her in his desperate plight.

At the beginning of Act V, Lady Inger ponders alone in the Great Hall.

She congratulates herself for shrewdly saving her son, but is that all she wants? Would it not be good to be a king's mother? She decides that being reunited with her son is sufficient, but still the attraction of power haunts her as she leaves the room.

Lykke comes in with Eline, protesting his betrothal to her. She has given "all a woman can give to the man she loves." He claims that her love has reformed him, and he places his ring on her finger as a marriage vow. Eline intends to be reconciled with everyone she has hurt except the knight who ravaged Lucia. Hearing horses' hooves on the ground, Lykke prepares to leave and is shown a secret passageway through the vaults below the castle. Eline says, "Go straight ahead to the coffin with the death's head and the black cross; it is Lucia's." Lykke scampers down but quickly emerges wretching at the smell of death. A knock on the gate is heard.

Björn comes in telling of an ambush. Lady Inger rushes in saying that she knows everything about Lykke's plot to kill her son. She remembers that Lykke has the signed paper that can ruin her reputation, but he tears it up, saying that henceforward he will protect her but that he must now hurry away.

Seeing Eline, Lady Inger compliments her for ensnaring Lykke and preparing him for the ultimate degradation, since he was the cause of Lucia's death. Eline becomes frantic when she realizes that she is engaged to the seducer of her own sister. Numbed by the realization, she leaves her pitiable mother to brood on her treatment of all her children.

Stensson and Skaktavl run in and tell of the rout. Bjelke's men are at the castle gates. Stensson, completely nerveless, begs for a safe hiding place, in exchange for which he will tell the details of his arrangement with Lykke. Lady Inger hides him but decides that Stensson by talking will save his own life at the expense of her son's. She determines that Stensson must die because his revelations would endanger her child, so she dispatches Skaktavl to kill him. When it is done, he leaves for Sweden to fetch Lady Inger's son. The enemy soldiers enter in pursuit of Count Sture and learn from her that he has killed himself. She orders that the corpse be carried to Sweden in her own coffin.

In another soliloquy she determines that she will be a king's mother, that Sture's illegitimate son will be the Norwegian king. Even these grandiose dreams cannot rid her mind of the images of swords and blood. She orders many candles to be lighted and recoils at the stench of death in the air. She gradually becomes more demented as she confronts the pictures of her ancestors, the holy images of her religion. When Björn enters, he finds that she has ascended the throne and proclaims her son as king of all Scandinavia.

Lykke rushes in to tell her about Bjelke, but she is lost in her visions of the coronation of the king's mother. Lykke sees her distraction as divine judgment of his sin. The soldiers enter bearing the coffin, which snaps her back to a degree of reality. Bjelke comes in and is told that Count Sture committed suicide. He proclaims that the corpse is not Sture. A soldier produces a ring that Stensson wore around his neck, and Lady Inger snatches it from his hand, realizing that Stensson was indeed her real son. Lykke confirms the fact. Björn rushes in, sees his mistress, and asks if she wants anything. Draped across the coffin, she says, "Six feet of earth. A grave beside my child!" She collapses, and the scene ends in confusion.

Structural analysis: This early Ibsenian drama has all the earmarks of the well-made play,* featuring as it does intercepted letters, confused identities, and the appearance of causally related episodes. The causality of incident is deficient, however, and the unity is one of Character rather than of Plot. Ibsen thought that his work might be considered a tragedy, but in the Aristotelian sense it falls short because Inger's catastrophe, though by her own hand, comes about through an expedient rather than an ethical error of judgment. Her ending, while highly emotional, is merely pathetic, not tragic.

LADY INGER OF ÖSTRAAT: The revised version of Ibsen's earlier play was published in 1974. James W. McFarlane and Graham Orton list the major alterations effected by the dramatist (*The Oxford Ibsen*, I, 694-5)*:

1. The spelling of Lady Inger's hall is altered.

2. The *dramatis personae* gives more extensive titles to the characters.

3. Scene division is scrapped.

4. The number of asides is reduced.

5. Stage directions sometimes are more explicit.

6. Characters address one another more formally.

7. The diction is improved by making it less stilted, barring stylistic infelicities, and reducing long speeches.

8. References to the Danes are more circumspect.

9. Bjelke is identified as a Swede.

10. Numerous things are done to increase dramatic probability.

McFarlane and Orton cite other variations, but these sufficiently convey the sense of Ibsen's emendations.

LADY INGER OF GYLDENLÖVE (*Lady Inger of Österaad*): As the protagonist of the drama, Lady Inger is the center of dramatic interest. Her Norwegian retainers doubt her patriotism and suspect her of collusion with their Danish conquerors. She also shoulders the burden of having lost a daughter who was seduced by the antagonist of the drama, Nils Lykke.* Inger is by necessity a schemer, often a successful one, but her attempt to dupe Lykke, the Danish envoy, results in her unwittingly killing her illegitimate son, the heir of the Swedish throne and perhaps the putative ruler of the Norwegian realm. Her motives are essentially honorable, but ambition to be a king's mother is a factor in her actions.

LAIPSO (*Emperor and Galilean*): A subaltern.

LAIRD, JENNY (1917-   ): After essaying Nora Helmer* in London in 1945, Jenny Laird played Ella Rentheim* in *John Gabriel Borkman*￼* at Detroit's Meadowbrook Theatre in 1967.
Reference: Who's Who in the Theatre, 16th ed., pp. 829-30.

LAMMERS, GUSTAV ADOLPH (1802-78): Between 1848 and 1856 Gustav Lammers was pastor in Skien.* He was an evangelical firebrand and separated from the established church, but he was so charismatic that Ibsen's mother, sister, and younger brother fell under his spell. Lammers' influence precipitated numerous family quarrels and perhaps led to Ibsen's isolation from his family in 1850. Ibsen's unsympathetic treatment of clerics in his plays may stem from his stormy exposure to Lammers.
Reference: Norsk Biografisk Leksikon, VIII, 128-30.

LANDSMAAL: When Ibsen started writing, Norway had no linguistic unity. The country people spoke a dialect called *landsmaal*, which was derived from Old Norwegian. Language reform was a burning nationalistic issue during Ibsen's youth. Ivar Aasen (1813-96) advocated the creation of a dialect based on *landsmaal*, but that was not to happen until the Parliament, the Storthing, created *Nynorsk*, based on *landsmaal*, in 1929 and recognized it as the official language.

LARS (*When We Dead Awaken*): The servant of Ulfhejm.*

LASSEN, HARTVIG MARCUS (1824-97): Lassen left his native Bergen* and became a teacher at a girls' school in Christiania*; his academic specialty was literary history. Between 1872 and 1874 he was literary consultant to the Christiania Theatre* and expressed an interest in producing *Love's Comedy*,* but the production never materialized.
Reference: Norsk Biografisk Leksikon, VIII, 220-4.

LAWRENCE, WILLIAM MOORE [pseudonym Lawrence Moore] (1846-1910): Lawrence's name is known to history because of his translation of *A Doll's House*,* renamed *The Child Wife*￼* and presented in Milwaukee in 1882. As principal of the 4th District School in Milwaukee, Lawrence had been an amateur playwright prior to his introduction to Ibsen's works. In 1879 he composed a Civil War drama called *For Honor's Sake*. At some point thereafter, a friend told Lawrence of a production of *A Doll's House* that he had seen in Copenhagen. In 1881 Lawrence registered his translation of Ibsen's drama, entitled *Nora*, with the U.S. Copyright Office and approached young Minnie Maddern, a rising actress who became Mrs. Minnie Maddern Fiske,* about appearing in the drama. These negotiations came to nothing, perhaps because of the weakness of Lawrence's adaptation.

He returned to Milwaukee and produced another translation of *A Doll's House*, this time under the title of *The Child Wife*, which became the earliest English production of an Ibsenian play in the United States. Lawrence had consulted teacher/translator Rasmus Björn Anderson* about *The Child Wife*, and the more experienced translator reworked the script before they tried to organize its production by the Union Square Theatre Company in New York, then boasting of one of the two finest acting troupes in the metropolis. They hoped that Sarah Jewett would play the role of Nora Helmer,* but unhappily the production never occurred.

Meanwhile, Lawrence translated *The Pillars of Society** and *Ghosts,** asking Anderson to secure the American translating rights for him from Ibsen. The dramatist responded on September 14, 1882, that he would be pleased to legitimize Lawrence's translations to be made under Anderson's supervision. Yet the translations were never published for reasons that are not entirely clear. At one point Lawrence believed that his script of *The Pillars of Society* had been pirated by an unscrupulous manager, presumably A. M. Palmer of the Union Square Theatre, who in 1889 announced his intention of presenting the play. Under Palmer's management, English actor Edward S. Willard appeared as Karsten Bernick* in a single matinee performance in the winter of 1890-91.

Anderson's interests led him away from the Midwest, and as he got older, he lost interest in Ibsen's social problem plays. Perhaps Lawrence was frustrated by his dealings with Palmer and dispirited by Anderson's departure. At any rate, he turned from translating to writing original dramas. In 1883 he penned a melodrama called *The American Style*. In 1886 he moved to Chicago where he became successively headmaster of the Sheridan School and the Ray School. Lawrence's interest in the Civil War resurfaced in 1892 when he wrote *Libby Prison*, a four-act serious drama. His last known play was a melodrama entitled *Wyoming, or The Stone Cross* (1901). Lawrence died in 1910 without realizing the celebrity that history confers on the man who introduced Ibsen to Americans in their own tongue.

Reference: Haugen, Einar I. "Ibsen in America: A Forgotten Performance and an Unpublished Letter," *Journal of English and Germanic Philology*, 33 (1934), 396-420.

THE LEAGUE OF YOUTH: A five-act Romantic-Realistic comedy.
Composition: Started in October 1868; finished in May 1869; published on September 30, 1869.
Stage history:

Oct. 18, 1869   Christiania Theatre* (15 perfs.)
Dec. 11, 1869   Royal Theatre, Stockholm

Feb. 16, 1870	Royal Theatre, Copenhagen, dir. Johan Ludvig Heiberg*
Sept. 27, 1871	Christiania Theatre (8)
Feb. 14, 1874	Christiania Theatre (18)
1875	Royal Theatre, Stockholm
Feb. 25, 1877	Norwegian Theatre, Bergen*
Oct. 15, 1877	Christiania Theatre (2)
1878	Norwegian Theatre, Bergen
Apr. 20, 1879	Christiania Theatre (16)
Mar. 16, 1883	Christiania Theatre (3)
Apr. 24, 1885	Christiania Theatre (2)
June 4, 1886	Christiania Theatre (4)
Sept. 13, 1888	Christiania Theatre (11)
Mar. 29, 1890	Christiania Theatre (7)
Aug. 28, 1891	Christiania Theatre
Sept. 14, 1891	Christiania Theatre (100th performance)
Oct. 1891	Freie Volksbühne, Berlin
Jan. 6, 1895	Christiania Theatre (9), Johanne Dybwad* as Selma
Feb. 25, 1900	Vaudeville Theatre, London, pro. Incorporated Stage Society*
Sept. 1, 1900	Lessing Theater, Berlin
Nov. 8, 1900	Schauspielhaus, Munich
1900	Royal Theatre, Stockholm (6)
Jan. 11, 1907	New Theatre, Moscow
Oct. 23, 1907	New Theatre, St. Petersburg
Aug. 7, 1921	Theatre RSFSR I, Moscow, dir. Vsevelod Meyerhold*

Synopsis: A crowd of merrymaking local people has gathered on the estate of Chamberlain Brattsberg to celebrate the Seventeenth of May, Norway's Independence Day. The festive air is heightened by colored lights, decorations, and music for dancing. A local landowner named Lundestad leads the group in drinking a toast to freedom. Ringdal proposes a cheer for Lundestad as he descends from the speaker's dais; part of the audience cheers as another part hisses. The people then move away to various activities, leaving Monsen, his son Bastien, Aslaksen (a printer), and Steensgaard (a lawyer) to comment on the speeches that have just been made. Monsen and Aslaksen deprecate Lundestad's remarks as chronically repetitive, but Stensgaard worries that Ragna Monsen has been left alone. Bastien tells him that Ragna is not on her own but rather in the company of Helle, a young theological student. Monsen dismisses his daughter's situation and sits at a nearby table so that they can start to discuss the local situation in earnest. Ringdal intrudes to say that the table is reserved for Brattsberg's guests. Stensgaard, boldly taking a seat, replies that the guests can sit elsewhere. Lundestad comes up and repeats that the table is taken. Monsen rises and directs his group to a nearby table while sending Aslaksen to the refreshment tent for four bottles of champagne to be charged to Monsen.

Lundestad approaches Monsen's group to explain that the Committee has reserved the table for Brattsberg since he is the host of the entire celebration. Monsen and Stensgaard quickly dismiss the matter as inconsequential, and Lundestad withdraws to the background.

Aslaksen returns, preceding a waiter with the champagne. His remarks to Lundestad notwithstanding, Monsen is chafing because Brattsberg owns the local ironworks and has been honored by the King (the title "chamberlain" is roughly equivalent to a British knighthood with the title "Sir"). Since Stensgaard, a noted orator and politician, is new to the area, the situation must be explained to him. Lundestad is identified as Brattsberg's agent of repression, which surprises Stensgaard who thought the man was a Liberal. Monsen says that as a youthful politician, Lundestad had been liberal, but inheriting a seat in Parliament had made him a conservative pawn of the capitalists. Aslaksen invites Stensgaard to put a stop to all such abuses through his oratorical gifts and articles published in Aslaksen's newspaper. Monsen clearly is a candidate in the rapidly approaching election and boasts that the progressive younger generation will support him.

Daniel Hejre (literally "heron") enters and sits down with them for a glass of champagne. He is quite interested in meeting Stensgaard and is introduced to him as a capitalist. Hejre quickly says that he used to be a capitalist, but now he is a bankrupt because of some devious ploy of Brattsberg, upon whom Hejre is determined to be avenged. As Hejre launches upon a story of a high-living spree in London with a bevy of Norwegian youths, Aslaksen asks to be excused.

Hejre gloats that the printer is embarrassed for his associates to learn that he had been in Hejre's retinue and had been financed for a year in college by Hejre. Monsen directs the conversation back to the chamberlain, whose father, says Hejre, had in desperation sold a large parcel of land to Hejre's father. When the present Chamberlain Brattsberg succeeded to his father's estate, he claimed the lost land on the basis of a legal technicality. Monsen says that he too has felt the sting of Brattsberg's influence as he has been passed over for every important position in the town in favor of Brattsberg's toadies or even foreigners. Throughout the whole discourse, Hejre has interspersed his comments with barbs at everyone, particularly Bastien, who, he notes, has been trained for the university, as a painter, a civil engineer, and the builder of a bridge that collapsed. He implies that such dilettantism runs in families. Monsen enigmatically remarks that Stens-has the license to say what he pleases. Hejre waggishly remarks that Stensgaard must be Brattsberg's friend because he saw the lawyer visiting Brattsberg in a frock coat and yellow gloves. When Stensgaard protests that he has not spoken with any member of the Brattsberg family, Hejre coyly asks if he saw no one on his second visit either. Stensgaard insists that he had called only to deliver a letter from a friend in Christiania; Hejre knows, however, that Brattsberg had merely declined to meet the young lawyer whom he views as a demagogue and an adventurer. Stensgaard is naturally inflamed by this gossip. Hejre tries to calm him by saying that at tomorrow's dinner party, he can straighten out the whole misunderstanding; but Stensgaard has received no invitation. Monsen angrily storms off with Bastien in tow. When the confused Stensgaard asks for an explanation, Hejre feigns great compassion and leaves Stensgaard with a newly manufactured proverb: "Trustfulness is silver, experience is gold." Then he exits.

Chamberlain Brattsberg enters with his daughter Thora and with Fjeldbo, the resident doctor at Brattsberg's ironworks. Lundestad reassembles the crowd for Ringdal's speech, but Stensgaard demands to be heard. Ringdal, however, has mounted the rostrum and has started to praise Brattsberg for his hospitality and civic-mindedness. At the close of his brief encomium, the crowd presses around the chamberlain in great adulation. Again Stensgaard asks to speak and is granted permission. After announcing himself as a stranger but sympathetic to the people's aspirations, Stensgaard abolishes the local political committee for the sake of freedom of speech. The crowd cheers him. In impassioned utterance he refers to the hope of the future which is suppressed by the presence of personified evil; he appeals to the young men to crush the dragon of oppression. Throughout the speech, Brattsberg's mystification has prompted Fjeldbo (who sees that Stensgaard is referring to Brattsberg) to explain that the orator is calumniating Monsen and his friends. Stensgaard calls for the immediate formation of a young men's league to throw off the yoke of capitalism. A contingent of cheering youths carries him into the refreshment tent on their shoulders. Brattsberg, believing Stensgaard to have exposed Monsen, regrets not having received Stensgaard previously but determines to ask him to tomorrow's dinner party. He and Thora exit.

Fjeldbo is left alone for a second, but soon Aslaksen emerges from the tent and reports that about thirty-seven people have already signed the charter of the League of Youth. Fjeldbo observes to Lundestad that a struggle for power in the district has started; the old power broker is not disturbed by this but is interested sufficiently to enter the tent to observe the goings-on. Hejre comes out of the tent, and Fjeldbo asks what is his interest in the matter. He is told indirectly that Hejre hopes the two factions will destroy each other. A great cheer issues from the tent, out of which bursts a Bastien so emotional that he announces that he will go to the dance hall to fight a couple of fellows. Then Stensgaard emerges and sees Fjeldbo, whom he greets as an old friend and asks for a cessation of ridicule and irony. He is delighted that he has been elected head of the Young Men's League and becomes almost maudlin as he considers how ennobled he has become through the trust of all his supporters. Fjeldbo asks him what he intends to construct out of his mandate; he is told that first there is much to be torn down by him, the chosen instrument of God. Fjeldbo observes that his influence must be restricted to the district or the county and to achieve even that, he must resort to consorting with the likes of Monsen, Aslaksen, and Bastien. Fjeldbo urges Stensgaard to support Brattsberg who is an honorable man who would not stoop to manipulating him as Monsen has done. Stensgaard wishes to hear nothing detrimental about Monsen with whose daughter Ragna he is hopelessly in love. Fjeldbo advises him to pursue Ragna's interest if he is certain that he loves her. Stensgaard answers that his political activities are the best means of winning Ragna, an unworthy premise in Fjeldbo's view. Their talk is interrupted by another cheer from the tent.

Then Thora Brattsberg, Ragna Monsen, and Helle walk into view; Helle and Ragna say goodnight to Thora, who approaches Stensgaard with a letter from her father. She too departs.

Stensgaard reads the letter while making disparaging remarks about the chamberlain; he refuses, however, to divulge its contents to Fjeldbo. The exuberant young men leave the tent in search of their new president. Monsen mentions that a committee meeting has been arranged for tomorrow, but Stensgaard postpones it until the following day. Since the crew is eager to convey Stensgaard home, he is unable to finish his conversation with the doctor. The crowd calls for music, and Stensgaard leads the joyful procession from the stage. Fjeldbo remarks on the gallant cortege to Lundestad, who calls its leader gallant; then he goes home to bed, leaving a thoughtful Fjeldbo as the curtain falls.

The locale of Act II is the conservatory, sumptuously decorated, of Brattsberg's house. Aslaksen has called while the family is at dinner. As he waits, Fjeldbo enters, and rather than join the dinner party, he elects to remain with Aslaksen. The doctor inquires about the printer's tubercular wife and crippled son and observes that the son has been drinking heavily. Aslaksen blames others for the circumstances that make an inebriate of him: Hejre for taking him from the printshop and sending him to college; Brattsberg for ruining Hejre and sending him (Aslaksen) back to the printshop. He is embittered to think that once he had sat at Brattsberg's table and consumed the finest food and wine and now that world is denied to him. Now he is not of his own social caste but cannot rise above it.

By this time the dining party enters as Fjeldbo and Aslaksen stand back and watch; Stensgaard proudly has Thora on his arm as well as Selma Brattsberg; the trio exit to inspect the garden. Aslaksen especially wants to talk with Stensgaard. Hejre enters with Erik Brattsberg, the chamberlain's son; Hejre notes that his money has been spent on excellent sherry. Fjeldbo dispatches Aslaksen to wait in the anteroom until he can send Stensgaard to him.

Finally, Brattsberg, Lundestad, and Ringdal emerge from the dining room discussing Stensgaard's speech of yesterday. Brattsberg waspishly greets Fjeldbo but quickly becomes affable. Fjeldbo and Lundestad remain behind after the others have strolled into the garden. Lundestad is disturbed because the chamberlain thinks he had called Stensgaard an adventurer. Fjeldbo dismisses the concern as minor and also walks into the garden.

Lundestad and Ringdal discuss Stensgaard's appearance at this party, Lundestad concluding that the wily chamberlain invited the fiery lawyer in order to discuss his criticism. Eventually, they go into the garden as Stensgaard and Selma come inside.

Selma is on the verge of telling Stensgaard that the life of a wealthy matron (she is Erik's wife) is not entirely ideal, but her explanation is cut short by the entrance of her husband. Thora and the doctor enter, and Selma immediately assumes that Thora is ill since she has often consulted the doctor recently. Brattsberg enters to find his whole family gathered indoors and neglecting the other guests. Thora tells Fjeldbo to remain indoors while she goes out, as do Erik and Selma. Eventually, Fjeldbo is dispatched to attend to the guests while Brattsberg speaks with Stensgaard.

The lawyer expresses his confusion at seeing Hejre at the party in view of his opinions about Brattsberg; then he attributes his own rash comments yesterday to the fomentation of Hejre. Surprisingly, Brattsberg enjoins any disparagement of his guests. The chamberlain explains that Hejre is indirectly responsible for Erik's happy marriage, since he took care of Selma when she was orphaned and gave her a place in local society. So she was available when Erik sought a wife. Again Stensgaard apologizes for his speech, but Brattsberg merely asks to be warned when the young man proposes to make another such address. He is too old, he says, to be active in reforms, but Stensgaard is an ideal choice to do so. Their concord is interrupted by Hejre's entrance and report that Monsen's faction has joined the League of Youth. Brattsberg is agitated by this news and goes off in search of Lundestad.

Fjeldbo enters, and Hejre repeats his gossip, after which he goes out. Fjeldbo asks Stensgaard how he came to be here after his publicly expressed opinions of Brattsberg; the lawyer retorts that he attacks principles, not people. Besides, Thora is a lovely young woman. His present plan is to effect a reconciliation between the Brattsberg and Monsen parties. The subject of Ragna Monsen comes up, but she seems less attractive now that Stensgaard sees her as underbred. Now that he has seen and experienced the Brattsberg environment, he realizes how fetid is the atmosphere around Monsen. He has, in fact, come over to Brattsberg's side and will lead the League in that direction as well. His ultimate goal is a seat in Parliament, perhaps a ministry, and an advantageous marriage. Stensgaard is intoxicated by his brief introduction to aristocratic life. He rhapsodizes about the nobility of the chamberlain, his daughter-in-law, and, to a lesser degree, his daughter. Although he is attracted to Selma, he plans to fall in love with Thora. Fjeldbo tells him that that is out of the question, but Stensgaard remains obdurate, suggesting that perhaps Fjeldbo is also interested in Thora. The doctor denies it and tells the young man that neither Ragna nor Thora is to be had. Stensgaard warns him not to stand in his way because nothing will deter him from his plan. The discussion disintegrates into violent recrimination about the past and the future, leading Stensgaard to identify Fjeldbo as his only enemy. Rather than answer this, Fjeldbo summons Aslaksen and leaves the room.

The printer has come to get a statement about the League for the paper that goes to press soon. Stensgaard puts him off because he must change his comments about Brattsberg, which, he learns, have already been set in type. Then Aslaksen accuses Stensgaard of ruining him financially because the success of the paper depends on rabble-rousing tactics as advocated by Stensgaard; by muting his criticism of the chamberlain, Stensgaard is reducing the circulation of the newspaper. Aslaksen threatens to publish his report anyway, which prompts Stensgaard to insist that he will start a rival newspaper for the express purpose of driving Aslaksen out of business. The desperate printer rejoins that he will extort money from Brattsberg to keep Stensgaard's criticisms out of the paper. Stensgaard forbids him to approach Brattsberg by threatening to ruin him in less than a year. Finally, Aslaksen backs down and creeps out.

Lundestad comes in to have a chat with Stensgaard. His first concern is to deny that he ever disparaged Stensgaard, no matter what anyone might say. He further reveals that he is ready to retire from politics. Since Monsen is a questionable political risk, would Stensgaard consider running for his parliamentary seat if Lundestad could secure his support by the old landed gentry? Stensgaard avariciously assents to the plan. Lundestad explains that Stensgaard's candidacy as an elector, the first step to Parliament, will entail the dissolution of the Young Men's League because his election will make him one of the establishment. The young man readily agrees with this viewpoint. Finally, Lundestad suggests that marriage to a heiress will naturally follow upon this course of events since an office-holder must be a man of property.

At this point all the guests enter as servants light candles and hand around refreshments. Erik quietly asks Hejre about yesterday's events (at which he was not present) as he has heard from his father that Stensgaard openly broke with Monsen. Scenting further mischief, Hejre merely tells Erik to read the whole story in tomorrow's newspaper. They separate as the focus shifts to Brattsberg and Lundestad. At the news that Stensgaard is prepared to run for Lundestad's parliamentary seat, Brattsberg is surprised. Yet he talks of Stensgaard's attack on Monsen. Lundestad sees that Brattsberg has wrongly interpreted Stensgaard's remarks and that the words "money-bag," "griffin," and "basilisk" were used to describe him, not Monsen. The chamberlain is then dragged off to join a game of forfeits.

Having seen Lundestad in earnest conversation with Brattsberg, Stensgaard asks the old man how the chamberlain had reacted to his candidacy. Lundestad says that Stensgaard must apologize for his conduct of yesterday, which is in direct opposition to the advice Fjeldbo gave him yesterday. Declaring that he will seize the first opportunity, Stensgaard joins the game as Lundestad and Hejre start to talk.

Lundestad tells Hejre that Brattsberg believes that Stensgaard had attacked Monsen; of course, he knows that Hejre's vile tongue will make much of this news. Stensgaard has named Hejre judge of the forfeits game, and now the young lawyer has lost. It falls to Hejre to name his forfeit. He declares that Stensgaard must make a speech. Confident that his plan is afoot, Lundestad starts toward the door as Stensgaard begins his speech, an elaborate animal fable with the local people as characters. He ends by openly apologizing to the chamberlain, who is rendered speechless by the realization of his mistake. At last he collects himself sufficiently to ask Fjeldbo what he has done, since it was the doctor who convinced him that Stensgaard had spoken of Monsen. Stensgaard is radiantly pleased with himself, but no more so than Hejre. The curtain falls.

Act III takes place in the morning room of Brattsberg's house. Thora cries as her father paces angrily. She clearly blames Stensgaard for her father's embarrassment, but she sees Fjeldbo as the villain. Thora insists that it was he who told him that Monsen was the butt of yesterday's oratory. Fjeldbo bravely enters the room and greets its occupants. The physician seems on the verge of revealing something, but Thora surreptitiously signals him to remain quiet. Brattsberg laments that an honorable person such as himself should ever have sullied his family's name by associating with politicians like Lundestad. Fjeldbo reminds him that he was pleased as long as the mud-slinging was directed at Monsen; the mere mention of the name compounds Brattsberg's vexation. It seems that Monsen had convinced Erik to go into business instead of living as a gentleman on his inheritance from his mother. The chamberlain can never forgive Monsen for that.

Selma enters in search of Erik, who had said that he was coming here as a result of Monsen's visit this morning. The two women go into the drawing room to await Erik's appearance. Stensgaard comes in, much to Brattsberg's surprise and Fjeldbo's amazement.

He says he has not come to apologize since he knows he has insulted the chamberlain; instead, he has come to ask for Thora's hand in marriage. He expects Fjeldbo's support in this, but the doctor will not hear of it. Stensgaard forges on manfully, declaring that the Brattsberg bloodline will be strengthened by mingling with that of a man of will such as himself. The chamberlain insists that the lawyer leave, but Stensgaard warns him not to interfere in his career because he will pillory Brattsberg in the press and on the platform because he is God's instrument. He then challenges Brattsberg to allow Thora to decide for herself and warns the chamberlain that he must decide between Stensgaard's friendship and his enmity.

After Stensgaard exits, Brattsberg sees this ultimatum as only the first assault on his hereditary dignity. Fjeldbo swears to stand by him, but Brattsberg still sees him as the author of all his troubles. Despite his injured pride, Brattsberg cannot help admiring Stensgaard's openness.

Ringdal enters to announce that another visitor has come. Both Ringdal and Fjeldbo exit, and Monsen enters to offer to sell some property to

Brattsberg because he needs cash for a big business deal. Brattsberg feigns disinterest. Monsen offers to make Brattsberg part of the transaction, but still his adversary refuses. Desperately Monsen asks why Brattsberg is so adamantly opposed to him. Brattsberg gives two reasons: Monsen's bank has stolen the customers of Brattsberg's bank and Monsen has lured Erik into dangerous speculation. Brattsberg berates Monsen for trying to rise above his class through despicable business practices. Monsen says that the chamberlain's hands are not exactly stainless, as in the case of Daniel Hejre. The issue at stake is that of capitalist against capitalist, more precisely hereditary capitalist against self-made capitalist. Again Monsen asks for Brattsberg's aid, since Erik stands to make a lot of money from the deal. The refusal provokes a plea for Brattsberg to sign a surety note, which he disdains to do since he has never done so previously. Monsen says that he has seen such a note with Brattsberg's signature on it; Brattsberg labels it a forgery. Hotly angered, Brattsberg levels all his complaints against Monsen: his objectionable companions, his scandalous homelife, affairs with maidservants, and mistreatment of a wife who eventually went insane. That is why he has kept Monsen out of polite society. An enraged Monsen leaves threatening to bring down Brattsberg's decent society.

Brattsberg summons Ringdal and Fjeldbo, whom he sends to Lundestad, as director of both banks, to investigate the forged note. Ringdal says that Lundestad is nearby for a committee meeting, so Brattsberg summons him. Left alone, Brattsberg nervously paces before Erik comes in.

The son begs the father's help as he is heavily in debt to Monsen and will be ruined if he cannot pay what he owes. After a lecture on keeping bad companions, the chamberlain refuses to help his son. Hearing Erik's voice, Selma and Thora enter. Erik tells his wife that he is ruined and that they must bear the blow together. Selma, in a fit of restrained honesty, says that she will not now support him in his trouble because she has been kept out of his counsel at other times. When she had asked to share his woes, he had merely laughed and bought her a new dress as if he had been cosseting a doll. Now she will not suffer this final embarrassment; nothing remains but to leave him. She then dashes from the room to be followed by Thora. Erik also pursues his wife.

Ringdal enters to report that the bank never had a note signed by Brattsberg, and soon afterward, Fjeldbo and Lundestad come in to say that the only time Lundestad had seen Brattsberg's signature was on his son's note for two thousand specie-dollars. The savings bank held this note until it was redeemed by Monsen last week. The chamberlain is nearly prostrated by this news.

Then Daniel Hejre enters to repeat the gossip that Monsen's party plans to bribe Brattsberg for his support in the election. Although he does not know the implication of it, Hejre had seen Monsen hand to Stensgaard a note for two thousand specie-dollars. Brattsberg withdraws into a corner and a whispered conference with Hejre and Ringdal. Fjeldbo advises the chamberlain that he must save his son by acknowledging the signature on the note, but the old man will not besmirch his honor by condoning forgery. Erik must be left to the law. The chamberlain exits as the curtain falls.

Act IV is set in the bar of Madame Rundholmen's hotel where Stensgaard meets Aslaksen, who has brought copies of the newspaper and an extra edition dealing with Lundestad's retirement and Stensgaard's candidacy. Admonishing him not to start drinking, Stensgaard sends Aslaksen to the polls to convince waverers to vote in the proper manner. Madame Rundholmen enters and says that Monsen had awakened her quite early this morning to ask to borrow money. Hejre appears and engages Madame Rundholmen in banter about marriage. Fjeldbo enters to be asked if he knows the chamberlain's response to Stensgaard's recent letter reaffirming his intention to marry Thora and setting a time for a meeting on the next day. Fjeldbo advises him not to visit then because it is the chamberlain's birthday, for which a large crowd will be gathered. The lawyer admits that he has threatened Brattsberg, whose proxy he now holds in a sealed letter. The doctor knows that Brattsberg will not support Stensgaard but will propose a third party; he has done this because he knows that Lundestad will propose Stensgaard as his successor. Stensgaard is fully confident that Lundestad will work for him in order to break up the League and keep Monsen out of office. Fjeldbo reminds him that Lundestad now knows that Stensgaard does not enjoy the chamberlain's confidence; perhaps he will modify his actions. The young man sees no possibility that things will not fall out as he plans. Once again Fjeldbo tells Stensgaard to put Thora out of his plans, but the lawyer says that he cannot do so.

Then Lundestad enters and hears from Stensgaard of the chamberlain's vote. The old man is not at all disturbed by the news. Stensgaard's behavior prompts Fjeldbo to enter into some machinations of his own; he exits.

Stensgaard produces the two thousand dollar note and asks Lundestad if it is authentic. Before he can reply, however, Hejre re-enters agog with the news that confusion reigns because of whispers of an impending bankruptcy. Two strangers have been seen in town, so he must find out their business. Hejre exits as Lundestad says that the surety note does not look quite right because there are too many of them about. Lundestad allows Stensgaard to think that Brattsberg is about to become a bankrupt. He encourages Stensgaard to marry Thora despite her impending poverty, which the young man agrees to do. Lundestad then exits, and soon Bastien comes in declaring that he has come from the Nation.

He is, in fact, mouthing Stensgaard's clichés and imitating his manner and dress, for which he is severely chastised. Stensgaard learns from the son that the father will be in Christiania for about a week. Bastien asks Stensgaard's help in marrying Madame Rundholmen, whom he says he loves and who will also bring him fat contracts through her influence. Stensgaard renounces him as a hypocrite.

Fjeldbo comes in to report that Stensgaard seems to be getting all the

votes but that he cannot be elected because he is not propertied. The doctor
then departs.

Quickly changing his mind, Stensgaard decides to put in a good word for
Bastien if Bastien will be his partisan with Ragna. Bastien is happy to
comply. Young Monsen goes out to the polls as Madame Rundholmen
brings a report that the election is going in Stensgaard's favor. Stensgaard is
on the verge of proposing to the hotel-keeper when Ragna interrupts to ask
if her father has been seen.

When the barmaid goes out for drinks, Stensgaard asks Ragna why her
attitude toward him has changed since he is so much in love with her. She
puts him off by saying that he may speak to her of these things tomorrow.
Madame Rundholmen comes in with cakes and wine at the same time as
Helle enters, sees Ragna, and asks if she has seen her father. The two
strangers, it seems, have come to see him. Ragna and Helle pointedly leave
together.

Hejre comes in and suggests that Stensgaard could accept office if he
married Madame Rundholmen, a woman of property. Stensgaard produces
the Brattsberg note for Hejre's examination; his immediate verdict is that it
is a forgery. Even Erik Brattsberg's signature is not authentic. Hejre points
out that Monsen's ruin will precipitate Brattsberg's destruction as well, and
Stensgaard sees that both factions will be lost to him.

At that moment Aslaksen rushes in to announce that Stensgaard has been
elected with a majority of votes but that Lundestad has been returned as an
elector as well. Stensgaard is not cheered by this news as he sees his schemes
lying in ruins at his feet. Suddenly he has an idea! He asks Aslaksen if he
can arrange to publish his political testament in tomorrow's paper. Meanwhile, Bastien enters and admonishes Aslaksen to deliver a certain letter as
soon as possible. Stensgaard also asks Aslaksen to deliver a letter to
Madame Rundholmen tomorrow night. Bastien asks Stensgaard if he was
able to convince the barmaid to marry him, and when he learns that the
lawyer proved unsuccessful, Bastien decides to propose within the hour.
This convinces Stensgaard that he must work quickly, so he demands the
return of his letter from Aslaksen.

When Madame Rundholmen enters, Bastien approaches her, and in the
course of the conversation, he speaks of Stensgaard's intention of marrying
Ragna. Hearing talk about marriage, Lundestad volunteers that Brattsberg would not consider a lawyer a fit match for his daughter. This
information vexes Madame Rundholmen and Bastien. Stensgaard takes the
opportunity of handing his letter to the hoteliere with an admonition to read
it when she is alone. She exits immediately.

When Ringdal enters, Stensgaard cannot resist the urge to prophesy the
financial ruin of the chamberlain. Ringdal dismisses such rumors as the
devious scheme of someone who wishes to keep Stensgaard and Brattsberg
in opposition. The lawyer sees the truth of this contention and then realizes
that Madame Rundholmen is probably reading his letter at this moment. He

tells Ringdal to tell Brattsberg that he withdraws all his threats and will speak with him tomorrow and offer a complete explanation of his behavior. He then gives Ringdal the forged note, telling him to say to the chamberlain that this is how Stensgaard treats those who vote against him. Ringdal departs on this mission.

Stensgaard then charges Hejre with fomenting a lie against Brattsberg. Lundestad says that somehow Madame Rundholmen has been too closely involved with Monsen, that Monsen drove off before daylight, that Bastien had been trying to get his sister married. Hejre gleefully surmises that Monsen has hanged himself, but Monsen appears and orders champagne. He is jubilant because his business deal has netted him a hundred thousand dollars; he plans a luxurious dinner tomorrow night. After assuring his invitation, Stensgaard asks Hejre to defame him to Madame Rundholmen— merely as a joke, he says. Before he leaves, he asks Lundestad to meet at Brattsberg's tomorrow afternoon. Madame Rundholmen comes in asking for Stensgaard. Hejre says that he kissed the chambermaid and left. The curtain falls.

A large reception room in Brattsberg's house is the scene of Act V. Fjeldbo and Ringdal meet and gossip over the news that Monsen has absconded, that his jovial liberality yesterday had been merely a ruse. All his property has passed into receivership, and his daughters have come under Thora's protection.

Brattsberg enters, and when Fjeldbo wishes him happy birthday and calls him chamberlain, the old man asks him to dispense with the title because he is nothing but an ironmaster. He has renounced his post and his title because his honor has been tainted by recent events. Brattsberg is pleased to hear from Ringdal that Erik will be able to meet his creditors' demands but that nothing will be left over. Fjeldbo pleads for Erik's forgiveness, but the father will not relent. The doctor launches upon a stern moral lecture, the upshot of which is that the present experience should have taught the chamberlain to encourage his son's moral growth by setting a tolerant example. He then explains Stensgaard's poor behavior in terms of his home environment and genetic inheritance. The chamberlain says that the doctor has misjudged Stensgaard since he has returned the forged note and is now restored to Brattsberg's esteem. Fjeldbo urges him not to be taken in again, but the old man charges him with an unexplained transgression. The doctor replies that he will be making a greater sacrifice than Stensgaard by holding his tongue. This merely infuriates Brattsberg, who threatens to join the League of Youth.

Lundestad comes in and observes that yesterday's election went as he planned because Stensgaard would make a formidable enemy. His strength lies in the fact that he can sway the people and that liberalism comes easily to Stensgaard because he has nothing to lose by it. Lundestad's appreciation of Stensgaard's abilities is enhanced when Brattsberg shows him that the forged note has been surrendered.

At that point, the man in question enters and is greeted warmly by Brattsberg. Several others enter to wish him birthday felicitations. Thora also
comes in to thank Stensgaard for his generosity. He interprets her mood as
unspoken acceptance of his marriage proposal and is considerably
chagrined when Lundestad reports that Ragna has agreed to marry Stensgaard. Hejre joins the group and reports that Madame Rundholmen reacted
tearfully when he maledicted the lawyer, but today she was jubilant that she
was about to be married. Stensgaard's perplexity knows no bounds as he
thinks he is now engaged to three women. Hejre overhears Brattsberg and
Lundestad talking about the forged note, so the gossip admits that he had
pronounced both signatures forgeries merely to cause trouble. The old
chamberlain now sees that the return of the note was an empty gesture
because Stensgaard had believed it to be worthless. He is doubly enraged
because he has been doubly duped. The chamberlain asks Fjeldbo to turn
the adventurous Stensgaard out of his house in any way that seems feasible,
so the doctor requests silence for the announcement of his engagement to
Thora. General amazement follows, and no one is more affected than
Stensgaard, who is further stunned by Brattsberg's announcement that he
now joins the League of Youth. Lundestad starts to announce Ragna
Monsen's engagement, but Stensgaard, thinking he is to be named, interrupts. Thora produces Ragna and Helle and announces their betrothal.
Hejre also starts to proclaim an engagement, but before he can do so, Stens-
gaard, in the guise of public-spirited devotion, says that he will marry
Madame Rundholmen.

Aslaksen enters with an urgent appeal to report something to Stensgaard
but is silenced. Madame Rundholmen and Bastien come in and announce
their engagement. It seems that she was persuaded by a letter—Bastien's,
not Stensgaard's. The lawyer had been handed the wrong letter by Aslaksen
and had presented Bastien's suit to the barmaid. Now three pairs of lovers
are united, and Stensgaard asks to be excused because of a pressing
appointment. Nearly everything has been settled except the matter of Erik,
Selma, and the chamberlain. The young couple has been listening. Seeing
that Selma has forgiven his son, Brattsberg can do no less. After a scene of
reconciliation, the chamberlain pledges to work for the good of the district,
which prompts Lundestad to run again for Parliament and withdraw his
support from Stensgaard. The act ends as the curtain falls.

Structural analysis: Like many of Augustin Eugène Scribe's* dramas, *The
League of Youth* gives the appearance of being organically constructed. The
incidents, however, only *seem* at first glance to be linked causally:

Stensgaard discovers that local radical politicians desire his support against the
   hereditary propertied interests, namely Brattsberg;

(as a result of which)

Stensgaard makes a speech against Brattsberg which is understood by Brattsberg to be against Monsen;

(as a result of which)

Stensgaard discovers he is a welcome guest in the aristocratic home of Bratttsberg;

(as a result of which)

While there, Stensgaard accepts Lundestad's invitation to run for the electoral college as a prelude to standing for Parliament, a move that would require him to marry to acquire property;

(as a result of which)

Stensgaard discovers that he will win an elector's seat;

(as a result of which)

Stensgaard suggests marriage to Ragna, writes a proposal to Rundholmen, and later assumes that Thora wants to marry him;

(as a result of which)

Stensgaard discovers that all three women are in love with others than himself [RE-VERSAL];

(as a result of which)

Stensgaard stumps away defeated in "love" and politics.

This arrangement seems perfectly logical, but is not. In the first place, Lundestad's offering his political support to Stensgaard is not contingent upon their being in Brattsberg's home, although the deal was made there. In the second instance, the schematic does not take into account Stensgaard's political miscalculations in his handling of the forged note, which is instrumental in his political defeat but not germane to his romantic disappointment. Ibsen's debt to Scribe is also present in his use of the obligatory scene at the end, the confused letters, and the surreptitious amative alliances.

A LEAN PERSON (*Peer Gynt*): A character encountered by Peer Gynt* in Act V. The Lean Person describes Peer as a photographic negative rather than a positive.

THE LEARNED HOLLANDERS: In 1859 Ibsen became one of a group of scholars and writers who gravitated toward Paul Botten-Hansen* and called themselves The Learned Hollanders, a professorial group that was opposed to naive nationalism, *riksmaal*,* and Aasmund Olafsen Vinje's* *landsmaal*.* The Hollanders viewed Norwegian chauvinism with disdain, viewing Ludvig Holberg's* work in Danish literature as worthy of emulation.

LEFFLER, ANNE-CHARLOTTE (1849-92): Swedish dramatist, novelist, and feminist, Anne-Charlotte Leffler was a traveling companion of Ibsen in 1866. She described her experiences with him in her autobiographical work *En självbiografi* [*An Autobiography*] (1922).

LE GALLIENNE, EVA (1899-   ): Daughter of British poet Richard Le
Gallienne and Danish Julie Norregaard, Eva Le Gallienne became one of
Ibsen's major interpreters. After emigrating to the United States from
England in 1915, Le Gallienne was attracted by serious continental drama
and appeared as Hilde Wangel* in *The Master Builder** in 1924, a role to
which she returned in the following year and played for seventy-six performances. In 1926 she played Ella Rentheim* and Rita Allmers.*

Le Gallienne's desire to establish a workingmen's theatre in which to
present the world's classical dramas came to fruition in 1926 when she
opened the Civic Repertory Theatre (CRT) (costliest seat $1.50) in a derelict
playhouse in New York. Ibsen's works were the mainstay of the CRT's
repertory in the home theatre and on tour. In addition to playing Hilde and
Ella, Le Gallienne soon (March 26, 1928) added Hedda Gabler* to her list of
impersonations. A great artistic success, the CRT was not financially
viable; the doors of the theatre were closed in 1934, when the actress/
manager took her company on the road.

Le Gallienne derived great pleasure from performing the classics outside
of New York, and for her the classics included *A Doll's House,** *The
Master Builder*, and *Hedda Gabler,** the last of which she revived in New
York. On December 2, 1935, she staged *Rosmersholm** to uniformly bad
reviews. Abandoning Ibsen for a few years, Le Gallienne in 1946 formed the
American Repertory Theatre (ART) with Cheryl Crawford and Margaret
Webster, under the aegis of which she presented *John Gabriel Borkman**
(November 12, 1946). The ART, unfortunately, survived only one year
because of a $250,000 deficit. To recoup her losses, Le Gallienne turned to
*Ghosts** (February 27, 1948) and *Hedda Gabler*.

As an actress Le Gallienne deplored the stodgy Victorianism of William
Archer's* translations of Ibsen's dramas. Since she was linguistically gifted,
Le Gallienne had translated the ill-fated *Rosmersholm* of 1935. She then
turned to rendering *When We Dead Awaken,** a play that had always fascinated her, into speakable stage English. The actress continued to study and
translate Ibsen's dramas, and in 1951 Random House published her *Six
Plays by Henrik Ibsen* in the Modern Library series. A decade later, a
second volume was added. She had translated all the plays from *The Pillars
of Society** to *When We Dead Awaken*.

Eva Le Gallienne, together with Minnie Maddern Fiske* and Alla Nazimova* were Ibsen's principal champions in the United States during the
first third of the twentieth century.

References: Atkinson, Brooks, "The Play: Rosmersholm," *New York Times*, Dec.
    3, 1935, p. 32, cols. 5-6; Le Gallienne, Eva. *With a Quiet Heart: An Auto-
    biography*. New York: Viking Press, 1953.

LEHMANN, BEATRIX (1903-79): English actress Beatrix Lehmann's first
Ibsenian role was that of Hilde Wangel* in *The Master Builder* in London

in 1934, but she is remembered principally as an interpreter of Hedda Gabler,* first playing the role in 1943 and later in 1951. Of her earlier Helene Alving,* *The Times* (London) reviewer wrote: ". . . her playing is colorlessly correct and there is neither warmth in her regrets . . . nor passion in the apprehension with which she sees the past beginning to repeat itself. She is less a tragic heroine than the luckless heroine of a thriller." In 1970 Lehmann played Aase* at the Chichester Festival.

References: *The Times* (London), June 26, 1943, p. 2, col. 5; *Who's Who in the Theatre*, 16th ed., pp. 847-8.

LEITHNER, THERESE: This actress played Nora Helmer* in a German-language production of *A Doll's House* [*Ein Puppenheim*] in New York in 1889.

LENTULUS (*Catiline*): Lentulus is a dissipated malcontent who suggests Catiline* as captain of the conspirators against the Roman regime, does his best to enlist Catiline, but when he refuses, determines to become leader himself. When Catiline changes his mind, Lentulus' ambition is thwarted, and he becomes Catiline's enemy. He plans to assassinate Catiline to secure the leadership and later betrays Catiline to the Romans.

LEONTES (*Emperor and Galilean*): A quaestor.

LEWIS, FREDERICK G. (1873-1946): Frederick Lewis was associated with three early Ibsenian productions in New York. He was Ragnar Brovik* in 1900, Oswald Alving* in 1903, and Arnold Rubek* in 1905. A critic called the last production, the premiere of the play in America, "of little value for actors—an uninspired performance" (*New York Times*, Mar. 8, 1905, p. 9, col. 1).

Reference: Briscoe, Johnson. *The Actors' Birthday Book*, 2d ser. New York: Moffat, Yard, 1908.

LIAROVA, LUDMILLA N.: Russian actress Ludmilla N. Liarova came to the United States with the troupe of Paul Orlenev and played Helene Alving* in New York in 1912.

LIBANIUS (*Emperor and Galilean*): As an orator and philosopher, Libanius was an early idol of Julian.* He became chief magistrate of Antioch.

LIE, THEODOR J.: When Ibsen enrolled in Henrik A. S. Heltberg's* "crammer" in Christiania,* Theodor Lie became his tutor.

LILJEKRANS, LADY KIRSTEN (*Olaf Liljekrans*): As the strong-willed mother of Olaf Liljekrans* and a tribal leader as well, Lady Kirsten is determined to cement the dynastic marriage of her son. She is unscrupulous in the furtherance of her aims.

LILJEKRANS, OLAF (*Olaf Liljekrans*): Although pressed by his mother to marry Ingeborg* for the sake of political accommodation, Olaf becomes enchanted by a girl of the mountains, Alfhild.* At first he appears to be weak and easily dominated by his mother, but in the end Olaf marries Alfhild against all opposition.

LILLE EYOLF: The Norwegian title of *Little Eyolf.**

LIND (*Love's Comedy*): A divinity student as well as a lover, Lind is the fiancé of Anna Halm.*

LINDBERG, AUGUST (1846-1916): Swedish actor and director August Lindberg was closely associated with Ibsen's dramas near the end of the nineteenth century. While still an aspiring player, Lindberg was introduced to Ibsen by Ludvig O. Josephson* in 1880; three years later Lindberg staged the earliest European production of *Ghosts.** Later he produced *The Wild Duck** (1885), *Love's Comedy** (1889), *A Doll's House** (1889), *Hedda Gabler** (1891), *The Master Builder** (1893), and *John Gabriel Borkman** (1897).
Reference: Lindberg, Per. *August Lindberg.* Stockholm: Natur och Kultur, 1943.

LINDE, KRISTINE (*A Doll's House*): Kristine Linde's major function is to serve as confidante to Nora Helmer.* She is also instrumental in removing Nils Krogstad's* threat to Nora by entering into an alliance with him.

LION, LEON M. (1879-1947): Actor, manager, producer, and playwright, Leon M. Lion played Knut Brovik* in Granville Barker's production of *The Master Builder** (Little Theatre, London, March 28, 1911). Lion believed Ibsen's drama to be "the greatest since Macbeth" (Lion, p. 70), yet wholly incomprehensible to anyone under age forty. George Bernard Shaw* listened to many rehearsals, but Barker put the stars (Lillian McCarthy* and Norman McKinnel*) as well as Lion through their paces. When dismissing a Friday rehearsal, Barker announced that lines had to be memorized by the following Monday. On that day Lion struggled through his part with a minimum of prompting and afterwards sought the director's commendation: "You see, Mr. Barker, I've got my words today pretty well." "Yes, I noticed that, Lion," he replied. "Tomorrow, try to get a few more of the author's."

To Lion goes the credit for directing the first licensed production of *Ghosts** in England. On April 26, 1914, he staged the controversial drama at the Court Theatre for the New Constitutional Society for Women's Suffrage. The Lord Chamberlain allowed himself to be convinced that the play had lost its offensiveness, so Lion's production, starring Bessie Hatton and Fisher White, was moved to the Theatre Royal, Haymarket on July 14, 1914.

In 1936 Lion leased the Criterion Theatre in London and mounted a series of productions called "The Ibsen Cycle," which included *A Doll's House** (opened on March 2), *Hedda Gabler** (opened on March 9), and *The Master Builder* (opened on March 12). His stars were Lydia Lopokova* (Nora Helmer* and Hilde Wangel*), Jean Forbes-Robertson* (Hedda Gabler*), and D. A. Clarke Smith (Halvard Solness*).

References: "The Ibsen Cycle in London," *Theatre Arts Monthly*, XX 5 (May 1936), 398-9; Lion, Leon M. *The Surprise of My Life: The Lesser Half of an Autobiography.* London: Hutchinson, 1948.

LITTLE EYOLF: A three-act Realistic-Symbolistic serious drama.
Composition: Started on June 16, 1894; finished on October 13; published in December.

Stage history:

Jan. 12, 1895	Deutsches Theater, Berlin
Jan. 15, 1895	Christiania Theatre* (36 perfs.), Johanne Dybwad* as Asta
Jan. 21, 1895	Norwegian Theatre, Bergen*
Jan. 1895	Swedish Theatre, Helsinki
Jan. 1895	Finnish Theatre, Helsinki
Jan. 1895	Stadttheater, Gothenburg
Feb. 22, 1895	Milan
Feb. 27, 1895	Burgtheater, Vienna
Mar. 13, 1895	Royal Theatre, Copenhagen (7)
Mar. 14, 1895	Royal Theatre, Stockholm
Mar. 1895	Burgtheater, Vienna, Friedrich Mitterwurzer* as Alfred
Apr. 21, 1895	Hoftheater, Munich, Emil Messthaler* as Alfred
May 8, 1895	Théâtre de l'Oeuvre, Paris, Aurélien-Marie Lugné-Poë* as Alfred
1895	Chicago
Nov. 23, 1896	Avenue Theatre, London (5), Janet Achurch,* Elizabeth Robins,* and Mrs. Patrick Campbell* as Asta, Rita, and the Rat-Wife
1896	Royal Theatre, Copenhagen (6)
1897	Royal Theatre, Copenhagen (4)
Jul. 17, 1900	Schauspielhaus, Munich
Feb. 27, 1907	Residenz Theater, Munich
May 13, 1907	Carnegie Lyceum, New York
Oct. 12, 1907	Alexandra Theatre, St. Petersburg
Apr. 18, 1910	Nazimova Theatre, New York (48), Alla Nazimova* as Asta
Feb. 2, 1926	Guild Theatre, New York (8), Reginald Owen* as Alfred
Dec. 3, 1928	Everyman Theatre, London, Jean Forbes-Robertson* as Rita
Oct. 15, 1930	Arts Theatre, London
June 12, 1945	Embassy Theatre, London
Mar. 11, 1958	Lyric Theatre, Hammersmith (London), Robert Eddison as Alfred
Mar. 16, 1964	Actors' Playhouse, New York
June 28, 1979	Roundabout Theatre, New York (13)

Synopsis: Two women meet in a richly furnished garden room of a house near a fjord. They are Rita Allmers, a beautiful woman of thirty-three, and her somewhat younger sister-in-law Asta Allmers. Asta has come out from town to see her nephew Eyolf but is delighted to hear that her half-brother Alfred has returned unexpectedly from a trip for his health. Rita admits that she has been quite lonely with her husband away but says she quite understands that Asta's work as a teacher and her interest in a roadbuilder kept her from visiting very often during the six or seven weeks of Alfred's absence. Asking where Alfred is, Asta learns that he has long been with Eyolf in the schoolroom. Asta objects to Eyolf's being forced to study beyond his endurance. Rita is not happy with the situation but defers to Alfred's judgment. She concludes that Eyolf must do something since he is unable to go out and play with the other children.

Alfred, a serious-looking man, appears with Eyolf, an ethereal-looking boy who must walk with a crutch; his eyes are beautifully conspicuous. Brother and sister joyfully greet each other, and then Asta asks if Alfred has finished his book. He responds that he did not write a word but devoted his time entirely to thinking. Alfred states that someone will come who will write a much better book; as for himself, he plans to return to the tallest peaks of the mountains. Eyolf glowingly tells his father about how the engineer Borkhejm brought him a bow and arrows and will be asked to teach Eyolf to swim as the other boys do, but what he most desires is to be a soldier. Asta diverts Eyolf's thoughts by telling him that she has seen the Rat-Wife, whose presence in the district is confirmed by Alfred. This Miss Varg is called the Rat-Wife because she drives rats from the country. When Alfred sends Eyolf out to play, he declines the opportunity to play with the other boys because he is wearing a soldier's uniform and fears they will tease him.

A knock announces the entrance of the Rat-Wife, a wizened, old creature carrying a red umbrella and a black bag. Eyolf immediately recognizes her identity and is quite elated. She asks if there are any rats to be driven away but is told that there are no rats in the house. Sitting in a chair, the Rat-Wife says she is very tired because she has just dealt with the rats on the nearby island, where the rodents were eating everything in sight. Relishing the details of the macabre tale, the old woman describes the havoc caused by the rats, but her story is interrupted by a frightened shriek from Eyolf who has noticed that something is moving in her bag. A little dog with a black muzzle peers from the bag to the delight of its mistress and the loathing of the boy. His fear of the ugly canine is short-lived, however, for soon Eyolf approaches the bag and starts to pet the dog. The Rat-Wife says that the dog is tired too because he plays a large role in the extermination of rats. She leads the dog around the infested house three times while playing her pipes, which almost magically attract the rats from their dark hiding places. The Rat-Wife and the dog then walk to the water's edge, where she enters a row-boat that she oars with one hand, the other hand being used to continue her music. The dog swims out into the water after the boat, and the masses of rats swim after him and eventually drown. They are then swept into peaceful sleep and are hounded and abominated no more. Again she asks if any rats need exterminating, and being told no, she reminds them that she should be summoned when they hear nibbling and gnawing. Having said this, the Rat-Wife goes out, leaving an exuberant Eyolf, who has seen the Rat-Wife in person. Rita, unnerved by the encounter, goes onto the porch for some air while Eyolf also slips out.

Alfred notices a portfolio which Asta has brought; it contains family papers, including some letters to her mother. She wants him to see them, but she has forgotten to bring the key. Rita comes in, and the talk shifts to the visit of the Rat-Wife, which leads to Alfred's admission that he had an inner revelation in the mountains. He says that he escaped to the mountains not because of doctor's orders but because he no longer got satisfaction from his work. He had begun to feel that he could do something other than write books. Because of the money Rita had brought to the marriage, he had been able to devote all his time to a tome entitled *Human Responsibility*, but in the meantime, his interests have shifted to his responsibilities as a father. He wants to make Eyolf's deformity as easy to bear as possible, largely by causing him to achieve inner harmony by aspiring to the possible and forgetting the impossible. If he chooses, Eyolf can finish his father's book or write another one. He, Alfred, plans to devote his whole life to making the finest sort of man of Eyolf. The women are sorry that he will not finish his book, but Alfred answers that he will practice, not write about human responsibility. He claims that he will be able to accomplish this great goal with the help of both women, which fires Rita's jealousy of Asta. This difficult moment is saved by the entrance of Borkhejm, the rugged engineer.

After greeting each person, Borkhejm remarks that his road is at last finished, and he is about to go away to take up a new job building roads through the northern mountains. His conversation has been peppered with optimistic words about the future, all of which have been interpreted as signs of his interest in Asta, but when he asks her to take a walk with him, Asta refuses. At last she agrees to walk in the garden, so they exit.

Alfred too has sensed a growing romantic interest, about which he asks his wife. Rita is uncertain but does not hesitate to say that she hopes they will get married and go far away so she can have her husband to herself. She falls on him in a paroxysm of passion, but he fights free of her. She says that she hated sharing him with his book, and now she fears that Eyolf will separate them even further. She will not let the child come between them. Alfred insists that he must belong to both his wife and his child. If Eyolf had never lived, she asks, then what? Hearing that his loyalty would be undivided, Rita wishes that the child had never been born. She bore the boy, but she will not be a mother to him, nor will she be satisfied with Alfred's left-over tenderness. Rita reminds Alfred that when she heard that he was coming home, she made herself beautiful for him and arranged the house particularly nicely, but all he had wanted to do was talk about Eyolf. Her undressing before him did not prompt any loving regard; instead, he had asked about Eyolf's stomach and turned over and gone to sleep. Alfred, uncomfortable at the tenor of the discussion, tries to remain calm; it is then that Rita urges him not to take her for granted because she may be driven to find solace with someone else. She warns him that she will take revenge if he makes her share him with anyone else. She will cast herself into the embraces of the first man who comes along, perhaps even Borkhejm. Rita says that she would enjoy taking the engineer away from Asta as Eyolf has taken Alfred from her. Alfred sees that his wife is harboring wicked thoughts about their child.

A sad Borkhejm and Asta come in from the garden and announce that he is leaving alone. Rita surmises that the Evil-Eye has been cast on the road-builder, a particularly virulent spell when it takes the form of a child's eye. Agitated noise and great excitement are heard from the beach. Borkhejm calls out to the boys of the shore and learns that a child has drowned. Rita in horror fears that it is Eyolf. Borkhejm and Asta rush out to discover the identity of the victim as Rita stands on the verandah trying to make sense of the cries coming from the pier. She hears that a crutch is floating on the water. Alfred recoils at the suggestion and then recovers himself enough to dash out into the garden and toward the water. The curtain falls.

Act II is set in a wooded glade on the Allmers' estate; the water can be seen through the trees. Alfred stares vacantly over the fjord as Asta enters. After preliminary conversational sallies, Alfred expresses his inability to believe that Eyolf is gone; he surmises that the body has been swept out to sea. In agony he asks what sense there is in Eyolf's death. Asta thinks it is beyond understanding, but Alfred believes the loss may be purposeless. He is, moreover, convinced that Eyolf had seen the Rat-Wife rowing near the end of the pier. As he stared at her, he grew dizzy, fell into the water, and vanished. He cannot fathom the Rat-Wife's excuse for luring his son to his death, but he deduces that the Order of the Universe necessitated it. As he unburdens his heart to her, Asta sews ribbons of crepe on his hat and sleeve. She tells him that Borkhejm has returned and is walking in the garden with Rita. Alfred knows that Asta loves the engineer, but she refuses to discuss it. As she sews, they reminisce about their youthful days when death had left them with only each other; they were good times. Alfred remembers that Asta would have been named Eyolf if she had been a boy; she had even dressed as a boy when they were alone on his holidays from school. Alfred shudders because he had forgotten Eyolf in these moments of recollection of life before Eyolf's birth. Suddenly he starts toward the fjord declaring that he must be out there with his son. Asta deters him and persuades him to sit with his back to the water. Alfred thanks Asta for comforting him in a way that only a sister can. The sister responds that she owes literally everything to him. Their home life had not been particularly happy, and after a brief discussion of it, they drop the subject. Yet Alfred believes that the dead never let the living rest. Asta advises him to go to Rita, but Alfred insists that he is unable to do so.

Soon Rita and Borkhejm approach. Rita observes that their means of expressing grief are so different; whereas he sits quietly in one place, she is unable to settle anywhere. Asta and Borkhejm decide to take a walk, leaving the bereaved couple alone.

Rita tells Alfred that she had gotten Borkhejm to take her onto the pier to question the boys about Eyolf's death. At first, they said that the child vanished immediately, but now they say they saw him on the bottom of the fjord lying on his back with his eyes wide open. Alfred menacingly asks her if they were evil eyes; then he observes that things have turned out exactly as she had wished. Rita denies ever having wished Eyolf harm; she had only hoped that he would not come between her and her husband. Now she realizes that he has come between them more effectively than he ever could have in life. Alfred continues to taunt her about her remarks about Eyolf; Rita becomes quite frightened of him. Alfred says that sorrow brings out a person's evil nature. After a moment Alfred accuses Rita of never having loved their son. She says that she wanted to love Eyolf but that Asta had come between them. Then Rita turns the tables on Alfred by saying that he had never loved Eyolf either, at least not as much as his book. He responds that he had sacrificed his book for his son. She penetratingly says that the sacrifice was made because of self-doubt rather than love. Alfred admits that she is correct. They painfully agree that Eyolf had not belonged to either of them because they had not loved him. How, then, can they mourn the death of one who was little more than a stranger? Alfred rises to the attack as he claims it was Rita's fault that Eyolf was unable to swim and save himself. In the face of this charge, the details of Eyolf's earlier crippling accident emerge. Rita had left the sleeping infant on a table. Then Alfred had made amorous advances, and in the heat of passion, the child had been left unattended. He had fallen off the table and injured his leg. They now see Eyolf's death as punishment for having viewed his crutch and lameness as reminders of their negligence. They now agree that their present grief is nothing more than a manifestation of their guilty consciences. Rita then reproaches Alfred for dispelling her religious notions as superstitious nonsense because she now has no inner resources on which to draw. He asks her what she would do if she could be certain of joining Eyolf where he is now simply by giving up everything she now has. He presses her for an answer, which is that she would still have to remain here with Alfred. Then he demands to know what she would do if she could join both him and Eyolf on the other side. Still she says that she would be unable to commit suicide under any circumstances; Alfred admits the same conclusion. They wonder if they can ever be happy and forget their anguish. He dismisses the idea of moving and of surrounding themselves with people; he considers returning to his writing, but Rita remarks that to do so would only separate them even more. The spectre of a child's staring eyes will always remind them of their guilt, which has killed all physical passion in them. Their only bond is shared guilt. Alfred admits that he was first attracted by Rita's money, which he saw as a means of assuring Asta's future. Rita remembers that he used to call Asta by the name of Eyolf; he had in fact told her of this at the very moment of their lovemaking when Eyolf had been injured. Reminded of that scene, Alfred sees the present calamity as retribution.

Asta and Borkhejm enter, and Rita suggests that they all go back to the house. Alfred, however, remains behind with Asta, to whom he says that he can no longer live with Rita because they would destroy each other. He wants to live with Asta as they had done previously. Asta says that it is impossible not because of her interest in Borkhejm but because he would be doing Rita a great wrong. Alfred insists, which prompts Asta to tell him that they are not related as they had always thought; all the information is contained in her mother's letters. When Alfred says that does not matter, Asta concludes that it does matter because their relationship is now subject to the Law of Change. She makes a present to Alfred of some water lilies that she has gathered; she says they are from little Eyolf. In confusion he follows her up the path toward the house as the curtain falls.

Act III takes place on a high knoll above the fjord; it is dominated by a flagpole without a flag. Asta is discovered sitting on a bench by Borkhejm who has come to say goodbye. The engineer says that Rita has asked him to mount a flag at half-staff, which he does. Asta says that she is leaving by the steamer, and Borkhejm, by the train. Borkhejm laments that his lucky new job will bring no happiness because he has no one with whom to share it. Asta speaks of the happiness she had known when she and Alfred had lived together. Again he tries to convince her to go away with him as she is no longer needed here, but she says that at best she would be only half his. He would not settle for that, she thinks. Borkhejm has no recourse except to say farewell.

Alfred enters, sees that Borkhejm is leaving, and wonders if Asta is going with him. When he hears that she is not, he asks Asta to stay on with Rita and him. She says that she cannot do that but will go only as far as the town. He must not expect her to visit any time soon. When he says that he will see her in town, Asta tells him that he must not leave Rita at a time like this. Alfred turns to the engineer and surmises that perhaps it is best for him to be going alone.

Rita comes in and begs them not to leave her because she is haunted by the big staring eyes. Asta moves to comfort Rita as both Alfred and Rita implore her to stay. Rita asks Asta to remain and take Eyolf's place. Alfred asks her to linger and be his sister again. That convinces Asta, who asks Borkhejm what time the boat leaves. She has decided to go away with her roadbuilder.

Rita and Alfred are left alone. Alfred points out the approach of the steamer in the fjord, but Rita sees its lights as wide-open, staring eyes. After speaking of their mutual pain, they commence to carp at each other again, Alfred blaming Rita for letting whole days pass without even seeing her child. Then Rita complains of hearing the ringing of a death knell inside her head; it repeats the words "the—crutch—is—floating." Alfred says that he cannot hear anything. As the steamer pulls away from the pier, Alfred observes that Asta has really gone. Rita suspects that he will follow his sister, but he says that the years of their marriage bind him to Rita. Alfred opines that perhaps they are undergoing a new spiritual birth. Rita tells Alfred that now she would be willing to share him with his book just to keep him nearby. Then he suggests that parting might be better for both of them; perhaps he should go back to the mountains. He tells Rita of an experience he had on his mountain trek. He had gotten lost, and finding himself on a precipice, he had longed for the release of death. That experience was what convinced him that he must ennoble Eyolf's life. Now, he says, Eyolf has embraced death, and he is left. Rita again asks if they could not share what remains of existence, however bleak and pointless it may be. This discussion is interrupted by the sound of angry voices in the distance. Alfred decides that it is just the normal sounds of the villagers going about their usual sordid lives. Alfred speaks quite harshly of his fellow humans because he feels duty-bound to avenge Eyolf's death. He instructs her to raze the village after he has gone, but Rita surprises him by saying that then she will go to the village, make friends, and bring all the children home to live with her. They will be her children in Eyolf's place; this will be her attempt to fill her empty heart with something resembling love. Alfred sees that her doing that in the name of Eyolf would justify his birth and death. At Alfred's prodding, Rita admits that she would not be doing this out of altruism but as a means of atoning for her neglect of Eyolf. Alfred asks if he can help her do that. They agree to try to see if they can live together and make some sense out of their lives. Alfred goes to the flagpole and raises the flag to the top. They know that their lives will be busy, but in the quiet times they will remember both little Eyolf and big Eyolf and perhaps see them as they look toward the mountains, the peaks, and the great silence. Curtain.

Structural analysis: Ibsen's use of symbols in this play is extensive, particularly the mysterious juxtaposition of Eyolf's dead, staring eyes and the water lilies, the buds of which open and close like ocular pupils. As in so many of his previous dramas, Ibsen posits the mountains as the place of spiritual fulfillment as well as the source of existential paradox. The Rat-Wife is, of course, an appropriation of the Pied Piper of Hamelin tale.

The plot is unified by action, although the initiation of the action comes rather late:

Alfred discovers that he can no longer relate to Rita once Eyolf has died;

(as a result of which)

Alfred asks Asta to live with him as she did when they were younger;

(as a result of which)

Alfred discovers that Asta is not his sister and that their new relationship is subject to the Law of Change;

(as a result of which)

Alfred asks Asta to pretend to be a sister and live as a buffer between him and Rita;

(as a result of which)

Alfred discovers that Asta will go away with Borkhejm;

(as a result of which)

Alfred decides to return to the mountains;

(as a result of which)

Alfred discovers that Rita plans to nurture the village children as an act of atonement for her neglect of Eyolf;

(as a result of which)

Alfred decides to remain at home to try to share Rita's act of atonement.

Reference: MacFarlane, James. "The Structured World of Ibsen's Late Dramas," *Ibsen and the Theatre: The Dramatist in Production*, ed. Erroll Durbach (New York: New York University Press, 1980), pp. 131-40.

LOPOKOVA, LYDIA (1892-1981): As a dancer, Lydia Lopokova was associated with the Ballet Russe, and as an actress, with the Marinsky Theatre in St. Petersburg. She emigrated to England in the 1930s, where she twice appeared as Nora Helmer* (1934 and 1936) and as Hilde Wangel* in *The Master Builder.** The last two performances were part of the Ibsen Cycle as presented by Leon M. Lion.*

Reference: Who Was Who in the Theatre, III, 1528.

LORD, HENRIETTA FRANCES (1824-91): Frances Lord was the first English translator of *A Doll's House,** a first version of which was published in 1882 and a revision in 1890. In 1885 and 1888 she published translations of *Ghosts.** During 1878-79 Lord lived in Stockholm where she formed a curious linguistic notion: "Whatever is written in Swedish, Norwegian, or Danish can be read without a translator's help in Norway, Sweden, Denmark, and Finland." (Lord, p. 4). It is no surprise, then, that her translation is riddled with inaccuracies, which were detailed by William Archer* in the *Academy*. He also rebuked her for dividing the script into French scenes, which Ibsen had not done. Mrs. Lord quietly responded to Archer's criticisms by saying that her alterations had been for the sake of actors and English-speaking readers (*Academy*, XXIII [Jan. 13, 1883], 28). Each edition of her translation of *A Doll's House* is preceded by a lengthy essay on the play, although it masquerades as a "Life of Henrik Ibsen." Mrs. Lord, who made a living as a dressmaker in Birkenhead after her father's death, died in the spring of 1891 of bronchitis.

References: Archer, William. "Two Dramas by Ibsen," *Academy*, XXII (Jan. 6, 1883), 5-6; Ibsen, Henrik. *The [sic] Doll's House*. Trans. Henriettta Frances Lord. New York: D. Appleton, 1890.

LORIMER, WRIGHT (1874-1911): As Hjalmar Ekdal* in a production of *The Wild Duck* in Chicago in 1907, Wright Lorimer "played the photographer rationally, easily, and with numerous deft, artistic details that made the depiction as a whole very agreeable in the early acts" (*New York Dramatic Mirror*, Mar. 23, 1907, p. 10, col. 1).

LOVE'S COMEDY: A three-act Romantic comedy.
Composition: Started in the summer of 1862; published on December 31, 1862.

Stage history:

Nov. 24, 1873	Christiania Theatre* (12 perfs.), pro. Ludvig Oscar Josephson*
Feb. 11, 1874	Christiania Theatre (6)
Aug. 23, 1875	Christiania Theatre (2)
Mar. 2, 1877	Christiania Theatre (4)
1879	Norwegian Theatre, Bergen*
Mar. 5, 1880	Christiania Theatre (4)
Oct. 5, 1881	Christiania Theatre (7)
Jan. 12, 1882	Christiania Theatre (1)
Feb. 24, 1884	Christiania Theatre (5)
Mar. 1886	Royal Theatre, Copenhagen
Nov. 7, 1889	Stadttheater, Gothenburg, dir. August Lindberg*
1889	Royal Theatre, Stockholm
1890	Royal Theatre, Stockholm
Apr. 4, 1893	Christiania Theatre (28)
Jan. 13, 1894	Christiania Theatre (4)
Dec. 1895	Folk Theatre, Copenhagen
Dec. 5, 1896	Belle-Alliance Theater, Berlin
June 23, 1897	Théâtre de l'Oeuvre, Paris
Apr. 25, 1898	Christiania Theatre (4)
Sept. 15, 1900	Sezessionsbühne, Berlin
1906	Theatre Studio, Moscow, dir. Vsevelod Meyerhold*
Jan. 22, 1907	Kommisarshevskaya Theatre, St. Petersburg, dir. Vsevelod Meyerhold
Mar. 25, 1907	Kammerspiele, Berlin, dir. Max Reinhardt*
Mar. 23, 1908	Hudson Theatre, New York, Warner Oland as Falk
Feb. 22, 1909	Gaiety Theatre, Manchester
Jan. 21, 1915	Hoftheater, Braunschweig
Mar. 4, 1916	Residenz Theater, Munich

Synopsis: Act I is situated in the handsome garden of Mrs. Halm, the widow of a government official. In the summerhouse can be seen refreshments for a garden party. Mrs. Halm and her daughter Anna are sewing and conversing with Miss Skaere (literally ''Jay''), the fiancée of Styver, who is chatting with Falk, a writer, and Lind, a seminarian. Guldstad, a merchant, completes the group in the summerhouse. Svanhild, Mrs. Halm's other daughter, sits aside from the others. With the other men serving as chorus, Falk sings a bittersweet song in response to the ladies' request. The group notices that Svanhild is sitting abstractedly apart. The conversation turns to the poetical inadequacies of the song, faults that Styver, a law clerk, claims to have been able to correct in his youth. There is some surprise that Styver should have poetic gifts, but Miss Skaere quickly affirms that he is romantic by nature. Now, says Styver, he is engaged, which is preferable to being in love. Falk readily agrees. Styver recounts how he wrote poetry even during working hours, but once he fell in love with Miss Skaere, his muse fled. Guldstad steers the talk to Falk's lyrics, which, to him, are marred by the sentiment that the present must be enjoyed without any concern for the future. Falk responds that the present is everything, that the future merely limits happiness. He resents men's eternal striving to reach a subsequent stage; perhaps, he says, there is no rest from this pernicious urge even in the grave. Anna thoughtfully admits that Falk may be correct. Guldstad suggests that Falk as a poet must hold some creative idea in reserve lest he expend all his thought on one sonnet and the critics discover him bankrupt of matter. Falk concludes that the critics would not even recognize his deficiency.

Meanwhile, Lind has been riveted to the verandah, and jokingly Falk inquires if his study of the architecture there has been enthralling. Actually, Lind has been observing Anna, with whom he exchanges a secret glance while exclaiming that his position of happiness is at this moment replete. Miss Skaere supposes that Falk is writing much poetry in this idyllic environment, but Falk laughingly exclaims that he needs a romantic interest to inspire his creativity; yet before his happiness be consummated, Heaven must snatch away his treasure. Svanhild, having now joined the group, hopes that he can bear such deprivation manfully if it come. Falk retorts that he wonders if she has faith enough to carry matters through if her prayers for Falk's romance be answered. Svanhild warns him to wait until he is deprived of a lover to judge the efficacy of her prayers and the strength of her faith. As she joins the ladies on the verandah, Svanhild is chided by her mother for angering Falk. The poet himself wonders if Heaven may have such an experience in store for him. Guldstad advises that strenuous physical exercise is what Falk needs to rid him of his whimsies. Falk deliberates on the advisability of pandering to the flesh first or to the spirit. Mrs. Halm observes that it is past time for the visit of the pastor, a Mister Straamand (literally ''Strawman''), who also sits in the legislature. He is, it seems, coming to Christiania three or four days before the legislature convenes to give a holiday to his wife and children. Guldstad recalls that

Straamand was a rogue in his youth, but Miss Skaere, who will hear nothing adverse to her hero, recites Straamand's history. At college Straamand had been a good student, a stylish dresser, a successful amateur actor, an effective raconteur, and a poet. When Straamand had met Mary, his wife-to-be, on the stage, he composed a series of sonnets to her, wholly unimpressed, according to Miss Skaere, by the fact that Mary's father was a wealthy businessman. Mary's parent, however, had objected to the match, but the woman defied him and fled to Straamand, her lover, disowned by her family. They had lived on credit until Mary's father lost his money; then Straamand had accepted a pastorate in the north, leaving Mary with only his letters as solace. Falk sees this as the death of romance. Everyone except Falk and Lind go offstage to await the arrival of the Straamands.

Lind emotionally tells Falk that he is engaged, and the poet, assuming that Svanhild is involved, asks if he has considered the future. Lind responds that the present moment is everything. Lind then departs with the admonition that Falk tell no one his secret.

Svanhild comes out of the house and is arrested by Falk's stares. Falk suggests that she should change her name because, according to an old tale, it presages her death by being trampled by her own horse's hooves. They continue their badinage about the necessity of seizing what life offers without regard for the future. In the course of their conversation, Falk tells Svanhild that she has desolated him by becoming engaged to Lind; upon discovering that Anna is Lind's fiancée, he is immediately elated, but before he can explain himself, the rest of the party enters as twilight falls. Mrs. Halm sends Svanhild into the house to prepare refreshments for the Straamands.

Falk and Styver commence to talk about marriage, the poet comparing it with imprisonment, the clerk romanticizing it. As Miss Skaere takes Styver away, Lind discloses his growing impatience at keeping his engagement a secret, but Falk urges him to keep his pleasure to himself. Aside from the usual reasons for sharing his happiness, Lind thinks a public disclosure might forestall another suitor, namely, Guldstad. Anna shyly reassures Lind of her affection as Falk again suggests that the engagement should not be aired. Miss Skaere's watchful eyes send the lovers off in different directions. Guldstad seizes the opportunity of speaking alone with Falk, who alludes to the Lind situation in an extended metaphor of a drama. Guldstad suggests that he, too, has a secret and then asks if he might not be an apt hero of a drama of engagement and marriage. Falk tries unsuccessfully to discern the object of the older man's interest, but Guldstad merely withdraws enigmatically. As Lind passes Falk, the poet tells him that Guldstad may indeed be the source of his unhappiness, which convinces Lind to make his announcement soon. Guldstad, meanwhile, chats with Styver, whose gloomy expression also attracts Falk. Styver, soon to be a husband, needs financial assistance from the bank. Although Styver's plaint is directed toward Guldstad, the businessman makes no response, walking away to join the others who are congratulating Anna and Lind. Mrs. Halm is joyously tearful at Anna's engagement. In his elation Lind embraces Falk, who puts him off with the warning that engaged people join a temperance society of happiness.

Falk approaches Guldstad to compliment him on bravely bearing his disappointment about Anna, but Guldstad says that Svanhild is the object of his interest. Falk is shaken by the news but rallies sufficiently to respond with poetic rejoinders to Guldstad's comments about Svanhild's gaucherie. Lind steps forward, and Guldstad asks him how it feels to be newly engaged. Thinking still that the older man was his rival, Lind retorts tersely; he is surprised when Falk clarifies the situation.

Their conversation is abbreviated by the arrival of the Straamands and their eight children; four others remain at home. After accepting Mrs. Halm's assurance that their appearance is not intrusive, Straamand congratulates Anna on her engagement and launches into a flowery encomium of marriage. Miss Skaere prepares to depart to spread the news of the engagement as most of the party enters the house for refreshments.

Miss Skaere, romantically swayed by the moonlight, approaches Styver who is still gloomily concerned about the endorsement he needs from Guldstad. They walk off, and Falk is left alone to muse about the desolation of a world populated by couples. Svanhild comes out of the house, encounters Falk, and listens to his effusions about how married life has taken all the spirit from Straamand and his wife. Surprisingly, Svanhild agrees that social conventions are wretched. Emboldened by her mood, Falk suggests that they can defy tradition; Svanhild, however, believes that they would be crushed. Falk rhapsodizes about Svanhild's free spirit, her insistence on speaking her mind, and her inability to platitudinize. She can remember how she had been hurt by these traits. When she had tried to establish her independence by painting, she had lacked the talent, which drew her to the stage. The interference of family and friends ended those aspirations and forced her to become a governess. Falk recalls that he had always believed she was better than the society that surrounded her. He urges her not to allow the family and friends to shape her according to their mold. As his passions soar, Falk prods her to defy tradition and live fully with him now; when the spark of their ardor dims, then she can return to societal fetters. If she should help him now, he shall indeed be a true poet. Svanhild somewhat sadly chides him for having spoken as he has because the voicing of such sentiments dissipates true spiritual communion. Falk denies this conclusion, saying that he has shown her a goal that lies beyond the abyss of conformity; to achieve freedom, all she must do is take the leap across it. (See Kierkegaard, Sören Aabye*) Svanhild responds that she will never commit herself to him, knowing that she will be discarded when he is finished with her. After pouting a bit at this response, Falk says that he will make no further demands of her, but Svanhild dismisses his argument that she should be the breeze on which his falcon soars to the heights of freedom. She urges him to be a man of deeds, not merely a poet on paper. Then she goes back into the house.

As Falk stands alone, a boat becomes visible on the distant fjord, from which issues a song about daring everything for the sake of the attempt. Eventually, the music penetrates Falk's stunned consciousness, and when Guldstad leaves the house on his way home, Falk begs him to suggest a goal worthy of his life's effort. Guldstad tells him to try living, a suggestion that seems most apt to Falk, who concludes that from now on he will be a man of deeds, not of words. As he sees Svanhild in an upper window, Falk vows that by tomorrow they will be engaged. The chorus of music swells as the act ends.

Act II is opened by a choral tribute to romance and engagements. Anna, Miss Skaere, and several ladies chatter about Anna's betrothal. The atmosphere is festive as people laugh and converse in small groups; then all except Falk go indoors to tease Lind about his situation. The poet is angered by their foolish treatment of Lind, who manages to slip outdoors and elude his pursuers. The husband-to-be is appreciative of his friends' kindness but is totally exhausted by it; he, therefore, proposes to enjoy a quiet pipe in his room. No sooner has Lind exited than Miss Skaere and the other ladies emerge from the house in quest of him. Falk begs the women to give Lind some peace so he can begin to write a sermon in English as a first step in missionizing the new world. Miss Skaere takes him literally and summons her entire feminine contingent to deal with this problem.

Anna comes out of the house with the Straamands, her mother, Styver, Guldstad, and others; Miss Skaere immediately tells her of her fiancé's plan, to which Anna simply says that she intends to go with him. Falk suggests that Lind views his missionary call as a duty, but Miss Skaere asserts that a man's first duty is to his wife. Then she corners Anna, moves aside with her, and attempts to persuade her to make Lind remain in Christiania. Falk, meanwhile, starts to talk with Pastor Straamand, whose family remains at his side, urging him to intercede for Lind with the ladies. The minister replies that he felt that Lind was somewhat uncertain of his missionary vocation. Falk assures him that Lind's call is unmistakable, which Straamand interprets to mean a guaranteed salary. Falk is irritated by this conclusion and insists that he referred to Lind's purpose, not to his salary. Straamand concludes that money is necessary to missions in any case but admits that a single man is better suited to the mission field than a married one. Falk reminds him that Lind is prepared to make a substantial sacrifice to his calling, but again Straamand misunderstands by assuming that the sacrifice to which Falk refers is an offering made by Lind's putative flock. Falk once again sees that Straamand equates financial reward with ministry. Secure in his belief that Christian service ought to be comfortably rewarded, Straamand withdraws to speak with Anna.

Lind returns to report to Falk that their room is in tatters, but Falk admits to having destroyed the tools of his previous poet's trade as a symbol of his having become a man of action. Lind is not impressed by Falk's means of exhibiting his liberation from the past, especially since Falk has destroyed the lamp that Lind needs in order to cram for his examinations. Falk chides him for not forgetting the future and enjoying his present happiness. When Lind explains that as an engaged man, he has responsibilities to study hard, to establish himself professionally, and to meet his social obligations as a husband, Falk realizes that Lind has fallen prey to the sort of traditional values against which he has railed so exuberantly. Falk and Lind continue talking while Straamand addresses Anna.

Miss Skaere appears, determined to reconcile Lind and Anna; the young man does not realize that a breach exists. She tells Lind that Anna has been reduced to tears because of his American plan. Poor Lind is surrounded by Miss Skaere and her cronies as Straamand's conversation with Anna becomes clear. He tells her that all this stir is for nothing, that she should follow Lind wherever his duty calls him, that she should, in effect, model herself on Straamand and Mary. Mary, too, had been reluctant to leave the capital for a parish in the north, but when the twins came, she became reconciled. Leading Anna away, Straamand continues to exhort her. Miss Skaere emerges from the group and declares that Lind is now convinced, so the Straamands and the Skaeres like a Greek chorus are jubilant over reconciling the lovers. When Lind vows that he is willing to stay in Christiania while Anna agrees to go to the mission field, their joy is short-lived. Falk laughingly observes that both groups should be happy because they were able to manipulate the couple as they chose. The muddle is interrupted by the arrival of tea.

Falk and the ladies enter upon a discussion of what flower is the best metaphor for love. One suggests the rose; another, a snowdrop; a third, the dandelion. Lind proposes the bluebell, while Mrs. Halm counters with the evergreen tree. Then Iceland moss, horse-chestnut, and camellias are advocated. Straamand gathers his children around him and compares love with a pear tree with white blossoms in the spring and fruit in the summer, clearly implying that children are the "pears" of love. Falk dismisses all their suggestions and declares that tea is comparable with love. Then he enters upon a long discussion of their similarities in which he criticizes traditional marriage customs, ending with a farewell to Cupid. When taxed by the others that love is not dead, as their own company shows, Falk reiterates his belief that marriage is one thing and love another. He concludes that they are incompatible, which arouses the ire of everyone, particularly Straamand. When he posits his children as the natural result of love, Falk suggests that they are rather the product of matrimony. Falk then proposes to start a newspaper called *Cupid's Sporting News* in which he can air his anti-matrimonial views as well as Miss Skaere's romance about Straamand, Styver's love poetry, or Lind's "Saga of the Heart." All of these "authors" decline the honor. Wholly exasperated, Mrs. Halm requests that Falk move away from her home. By now Straamand has exited haughtily; Miss Skaere is about to faint; Styver and Lind terminate their friendship with Falk. All except Svanhild leave the stage.

The young woman tells Falk that she will be his ally in the battle for love, for she sees that he has changed since their conversation on the previous day. Falk excitedly asks Svanhild to be his companion both in the fight and in his life. To that end, he offers her a ring as she falls lovingly into his arms.

As Act III starts, a gay party in Mrs. Halm's house is in progress. Svanhild stands quietly on the verandah while Falk and his servant pack his belongings. The poet orders his portfolio to be burned; his books he gives away. After the servant leaves, Falk expatiates on his happiness in his new freedom as well as in Svanhild's decision to accompany him. Svanhild is rather melancholy about her sister's approaching marriage but quickly succumbs to Falk's rhapsody on their own blissful future. Svanhild wants to tell her mother about her engagement, but Falk counsels her to wait until tomorrow.

Mrs. Halm walks outside with Guldstad and is soon joined by Styver. They nervously converse about Falk's departure and his passionate stand against traditional values. Guldstad sees Falk and Svanhild in the shadows and immediately concludes that he knows Falk's intentions, which he proposes to reveal to Mrs. Halm as they walk through the trees. Styver, who has followed them, sees Falk and determines to talk sense to him, but his mission is interrupted by the arrival of Straamand. The pastor asks Styver to converse with Mrs. Straamand while he chats with Falk.

Falk answers in the negative when Straamand asks if he has changed his mind about taking his stand for freedom in love, but the poet admits that he never intended actually to publish his lovers' journal. Straamand is anxious, however, because he believes that the discussion of his youthful romance may have given Styver ammunition to use to force him to give legislative assent to an increase in salary for government employees. Falk, unsympathetic to the pastor's concern, merely attests his faith in Nemesis. Straamand extolls the virtues of family life, but he realizes that he has strengths unsuspected by Falk when it comes to defending his home and family. He admits that necessity had forced him to be avaricious of material things; he had married for money, grown bored by the arrangement, and been rejuvenated by the births of his children. He had found happiness, and Falk, by the exercise of logic and derision, had destroyed his halcyon existence. He begs Falk to deny his assertions so that his wife and family may be restored to their faith in him. Falk sternly refuses to do so as Straamand repeats prophetically Falk's own words about inexorable Nemesis.

Styver appears to call Straamand into the house; then he asks Falk to reconsider publishing his poems as it would be evidence of his shirking his duties by writing during office hours. Styver further reveals that any scandal must result in his resignation and the endangerment of the proposed raise for civil servants. Styver admits that if he were single and wealthy, he would join Falk in his poetic quest for freedom, but as things are, he must be cautious. Falk urges him to break his engagement, but Styver is too conventional even to consider doing so. He believes that happiness with Miss Skaere is possible. Having failed to convince Falk, Styver goes into the house.

Svanhild comes out of the house, sees Falk, and falls into his arms as he enlists her vow to keep their faith in love alive. She asks if they might move away, but since he believes that conditions are the same everywhere, Falk insists that they should remain in Norway to attest the truth of their beliefs. Again they agree to stand beside each other whatever adversities they encounter.

Meanwhile, Guldstad and Mrs. Halm have been watching Falk and Svanhild, who have retired into the shadows. Guldstad seems to have convinced Mrs. Halm that Falk and Svanhild are scheming, and she agrees to allow him to test his hypothesis. Guldstad approaches Falk and Svanhild and insists on a three-sided conversation before Falk departs in fifteen minutes. The older man reminds Falk that they had once been friendly enemies and that he, Guldstad, had also been young, so he is not entirely alienated from Falk's feelings. Guldstad declares his growing love of Svanhild and asks her to be his wife. When Falk objects, Guldstad suggests that by marrying Falk, she may be precipitating unhappiness for the three of them, for she would be desolated if she proved unable to remain true to Falk's ideal of free love when life became difficult. Guldstad says that he, too, was once idealistic about love, and yesterday he met his true love again, Mrs. Straamand, and discovered that no feeling for her was left. He had kept her young and beautiful in his thoughts, but romance died yesterday when reality showed her in her true form. Guldstad agrees that Svanhild may be the object of Falk's love, but is she a suitable wife for him? He reminds Falk that marriage imposes obligations that may be unrelated to love, that every couple must face the moment of decision when romance must give way to obligation. Even the Straamands, he says, were ideal lovers but destructive marriage partners. The older man further states that there are two bases of marriage—humbug and a sense of mutual responsibility. He offers the latter basis to Svanhild. Guldstad insists that Svanhild make a free choice between her two suitors. He then goes into the house.

Svanhild's confusion prompts her to ask if Falk can guarantee their continued happiness. He can only answer that it will last a long time. She comes to the decision that she must keep their love alive by refusing to marry him, realizing that she is not fitted to be his spouse. Seeing that he cannot dissuade her, Falk asks Svanhild to throw away his ring; she kisses it and throws it into the fjord, saying that she has lost him in this life but won him for eternity. He sees that they must go their separate ways and never meet nor indulge in self-pity. She will sacrifice her love to duty, and he will return to poetry. They kiss passionately and then tear themselves apart as the guests emerge from the house.

Styver and Straamand have resolved their conflict and walk arm in arm. The others notice that Falk and Svanhild are standing apart and draw the proper conclusions. Falk emotionally departs, paving the way for the resolution of all complications. Svanhild agrees to marry Guldstad on the condition that they move away. A troupe of singing students passes the house, pauses, and asks for Lind who has agreed to accompany them on their revels in the mountains. They are told that now that Lind is engaged, he will have time for no more such pastimes. Falk emerges from the wings clad in a student's cap and carrying a staff and knapsack; he proposes to go with the students and is joyfully accepted. Falk simply asks the company at Mrs. Halm's to forgive his shortcomings. He blesses Svanhild before he leaves. The students, with Falk, start off jubilantly as the party at Mrs. Halm's reaches a crescendo of traditional merrymaking.

Structural analysis: The unique feature of this drama, the first to precipitate censure of Ibsen's ideas, is its Diction. Although intended as contemporary idiom, the lines are written in rhymed verse, which helps to establish the idealized world of the play. The Plot is unified by action:

Falk discovers that Svanhild wants him to be a man of action;

(as a result of which)

Falk falls in love with her and vows to become engaged to her;

(as a result of which)

Falk, in an effort to impress Svanhild, alienates everyone by his views on love and marriage and his threat to publish *Cupid's Sporting News*;

(as a result of which)

Falk discovers that Svanhild shares his views and will stand by him;

(as a result of which)

Falk embraces Svanhild publicly, which prompts Guldstad to take action;

(as a result of which)

Falk discovers that Guldstad has put Svanhild in a position of having to choose between the two men;

(as a result of which)

Falk admits that he cannot guarantee Svanhild eternal happiness;

(as a result of which)

Falk discovers that Svanhild will marry Guldstad but continue to love him;

(as a result of which)

Falk resumes his poet's role and leaves for the mountains with a group of student revelers.

There are several biographical echoes in this drama. Ibsen had been married for several years when he wrote *Love's Comedy*, and in some ways it was an awkward arrangement. One is tempted to see his own unusual matrimonial existence as the genesis of Falk's views of love and marriage. Ibsen's two brothers had by this time emigrated to the United States, which is a theme that recurs in this and several other Ibsenian dramas. In this play Ibsen, through Svanhild, debates the advisability of leaving Norway to escape its conservative traditions, a move he himself was later to make.

Reference: Brown, Lorraine A. "Swan and Mermaid: *Love's Comedy* and *Lady from the Sea,*" *Scandinavian Studies,* 47 (1975), 352-63.

LUGNÉ-POË, AURÉLIEN-MARIE (1869-1940): As a youth Lugné-Poë was associated with Paul Fort's allegedly Symbolist Théâtre d'Art and André Antoine's Théâtre Libre.* After 1892 Lugné-Poë headed his own organization, the Théâtre de l'Oeuvre, the first phase of which ended in 1899. He thereafter periodically mounted productions under the name of the l'Oeuvre until 1929. Between 1893 and 1899 Lugné-Poë was responsible for fifty-one performances of forty-four programs; afterwards 103 separate entertainments were produced.

The actor/producer's goal was to acquaint audiences with the works of the great continental dramatists. Hence, it is not surprising that he embraced Ibsen and presented *The Lady from the Sea** (1892), *Rosmersholm** (1893), *An Enemy of the People** (1893, to the dress rehearsals of which the Parisian riot police were summoned), *The Master Builder** (1894), *Little Eyolf** (1895), *The Pillars of Society** (1896), *Peer Gynt** (1896), *Love's Comedy** (1897), and *John Gabriel Borkman** (1897). Unfortunately, Lugné-Poë staged Ibsen's Realistic dramas as if they were Symbolistic, and their "verbal décor" and fantastic settings caused Georg Morris Brandes* to remark that in France Ibsen was treated as a Symbolist in disguise (which is what he became). In the productions of 1897 and later (*A Doll's House,** *Hedda Gabler,** and *The Wild Duck**), however, the staging was more in line with Ibsen's wishes, perhaps because Hermann Joachim Bang,* Ibsen's emissary to Lugné-Poë, had been successful in his mission of eliciting Realistic performances from Lugné-Poë's troupe. Ibsen was so grateful for Lugné-Poë's interest that the Frenchman was appointed Ibsen's agent in France, replacing Count Moritz Prozor.*

Through the Théâtre de l'Oeuvre, Ibsen's dramas were seen in Holland, Belgium, Denmark, Norway, and England, as well as in France. In 1894 Lugné-Poë took his group to Christiania* to present *Rosmersholm* and *The Master Builder* at the Carl Johan Theatre, both of which productions Ibsen attended. The playwright was so pleased that he used his influence to have Lugné-Poë decorated by the French government. The actor/producer returned to Norway in the summer of 1897 when he introduced his wife, an actress, to Ibsen. The dramatist arranged for her to read scenes from *Peer Gynt* and *The Master Builder,* afterward pronouncing himself charmed by her understanding of his work. In the winter of 1906, Lugné-Poë traveled to Christiania with Eleonora Duse,* but Ibsen was near death and unable to receive them.

When Lugné-Poë reconstituted the Théâtre de l'Oeuvre in 1919, Ibsen's works were prominent in his repertory. As Ibsen's representative in France, the manager realized that Ibsen's acceptance must proceed from performances of his plays at the national theatre, the Comédie Française. When the state theatre finally agreed to stage *An Enemy of the People* in 1921, Lugné-Poë's influence was partially responsible. When the Comédie Française presented *Hedda Gabler* in 1925, the leading performer was Madame Piérat who had been in Lugné-Poë's production at the l'Oeuvre.

At the end of his life, Lugné-Poë heard of the German invasion of Norway in 1940 and exclaimed, "I'm suffering with my Norwegians!" The career of Lugné-Poë showed the depth of his attachment to Ibsen.

References: Jasper, Gertrude. *Adventure in the Theatre: Lugné-Poë and the Théâtre de l'Oeuvre to 1899.* New Brunswick, N.J.: Rutgers University Press, 1947; Lugné-Poë, Aurélien-Marie. *Ibsen.* Paris: n.p., 1936.

LUNDESTAD, ANDERS (*The League of Youth*): A landowner and wily politician, representative in Parliament of hereditary wealth.

LYKKE, NILS (*Lady Inger of Österaad*): A Danish knight, Nils Lykke is the major antagonist of Lady Inger of Gyldenlöve* since he represents the oppressive Danish king. Several years earlier he had seduced Lady Inger's eldest daughter and occasioned her death; he is, therefore, particularly odious in her sight. Lykke is cruel, insensitive, and very clever.

LYNGE, MRS. DOCTOR (*The Pillars of Society*): As one of the ladies who comprise Betty Bernick's* charitable group, Mrs. Doctor Lynge serves as a barometer of public opinion and acts (with others) almost as a Greek chorus.

LYNGSTRAND, HANS (*The Lady from the Sea*): Lyngstrand, a visitor to the locale of the play, is a sculptor who has come to consult Doctor Wangel* about his rapidly deteriorating physical condition. As a stranger, he is a useful dramatic device through which Ibsen provides exposition both about circumstances of the Wangel family and about Alfred Johnston,* Ellida Wangel's* lover. Although initially attracted by Bolette Wangel,* Lyngstrand falls in love with Hilde Wangel.*

LÖVBORG, EJLERT (*Hedda Gabler*): A dipsomaniacal scholar, Lövborg is a former lover of Hedda Gabler* and a professional rival of Jörgen Tesman.* He is also the beloved of Thea Elvsted.* Hedda in her boredom with middle-class life knows that Lövborg is an alcoholic and determines to manipulate his destiny. She starts him to drinking, and when he loses the precious manuscript of his book, she keeps it from him and agrees that his suicide is the only apt response to his having lost his "child." Ever the ineffectual person, Lövborg disappoints Hedda by not dying beautifully but by accidentally shooting himself in the groin.

M

MACK, WILLIAM B. (c. 1872-1955): Character actor William B. Mack achieved his first great success as Jörgen Tesman* to Minnie Maddern Fiske's* Hedda Gabler* in 1903 and 1904. In 1907 he repeated the role in support of Alla Nazimova* and played Doctor Rank* to her Nora Helmer.*
Reference: Briscoe, Johnson. *The Actors' Birthday Book*, 3d ser. New York: Moffat, Yard, 1909.

A MAIDSERVANT (*The League of Youth*): A domestic in the home of Chamberlain Brattsberg.*

MAKRINA (*Emperor and Galilean*): The sister of Basil of Caesarea,* Makrina tries to convince Julian* to recant his apostasy and is drafted into the army as a nurse for her pains.

MALCHUS (*Emperor and Galilean*): A tax-gatherer.

MALENE (*John Gabriel Borkman*): Gunhild Borkman's* maid.

MAMERTINUS (*Emperor and Galilean*): An orator.

A MAN AND WIFE (*Peer Gynt*): Newcomers to the district; parents of Solveig.*

MANDERS, PASTOR (*Ghosts*): As longtime adviser to the Alving* family, Pastor Manders is largely responsible for the misspent life of Helene Alving.* As her minister he had advised her to marry Captain Alving in full knowledge of his dissolution. When Helene fled from her home into the arms of Manders whom she truly loved, he merely read her a sermon on a wife's responsibilities and sent her back to her husband and a lifetime of regret. Years later he still cannot see that his advice was bankrupt and that Helene's life has been wasted.

MANDT, MIKKEL (1822-82): While still a teenager, Ibsen took intermittent art lessons from Norwegian painter Mikkel Mandt, who specialized in landscapes.
Reference: Norsk Biografisk Leksikon, IX, 59-60.

MANLIUS (*Catiline*): Manlius is a pensioned soldier who serves as Catiline's* second-in-command. The state's dispossession of his land pushes him into the arms of the conspirators.

MANNHEIM, LUCIE (1905-76): German actress Lucie Mannheim included the roles of Hedvig Ekdal,* Nora Helmer,* and Rebecca West* in her repertory in the 1940s.
Reference: Who Was Who in the Theatre, III, 1597-98.

MANSFIELD, RICHARD (1857-1907): Richard Mansfield, one of America's leading actors, rendered few but critical services to Ibsen. Mansfield presented his wife Beatrice Cameron* in *A Doll's House** in 1889, the first important production of the drama in the United States. His only appearance in an Ibsenian drama did not occur until a year before his death. His choice of a dramatic vehicle was not one of Ibsen's social problem plays but one of his most poetic, *Peer Gynt.** Mansfield's acting version, based on the William Archer* translation, consisted of eleven scenes. A moving panorama was used as a scenic background, and the music of Edvard Grieg* was employed. The production opened at the Grand Opera House (Chicago) on October 29, 1906. The dress rehearsal had gone badly, and the presence of 120 Norwegians in the opening night audience did little to cheer Mansfield. Little by little, however, he merited their attention, and Mansfield's Peer Gynt* ended as a triumph for both Ibsen and the actor/manager. Speaking of the physical difficulty of the role, Mansfield said, "I dig a spadeful of earth for my grave every time I play the part." The identical production reached New York on February 25, 1907, and achieved twenty-one performances.
Reference: Wilstach, Paul. *Richard Mansfield: The Man and the Actor*. New York: Charles Scribner's, 1909.

MARCH, FREDRIC (1897-1975): Although Fredric March's most notable performances were in films, his portrayal of Thomas Stockmann* in Arthur Miller's* version of *An Enemy of the People** in 1950 was extremely praiseworthy. The *New York Times* spoke of his "enormously rousing performance" and the "breadth and volume that are overwhelming" (Dec. 29, 1950, p. 1, col. 3).
Reference: Who Was Who in the Theatre, III, 1601-2.

MARGIT (*The Feast at Solhoug*): Margit is the bored wife of Bengt Gauteson,* a medieval knight. At twenty-three she is in love with an outlaw named Gudmund,* who coincidentally appears on the scene. Margit is prepared to sacrifice everything to go away with him and share his adventurous life, but Gudmund falls in love with Margit's younger sister Signe.* Margit decides to poison her husband but later fears that Signe has drunk the poison instead. When she learns that her husband has been killed in battle and that Signe and Gudmund are safe, she blesses them and retires into a convent. The role of Margit is one of great bravura but little depth.

MARGRETE (*The Pretenders*): The daughter of Earl Skule,* Margrete marries Haakon Haakonson* and becomes Queen of Norway. She proves unable to ameliorate the internecine rivalry between her father and her husband, and when Skule finally plunges the country into civil war, even Margrete accedes to his sacrifice in atonement for his insurrectionist activities.

MARIS (*Emperor and Galilean*): The Bishop of Chalcedon, Maris is brave enough to accuse Julian* of apostasy and call him to repentance, but to no avail.

MARSHALL, ARMINA (1900-   ): In addition to playing Kari* in the Theatre Guild's production of *Peer Gynt** in 1923, Armina Marshall essayed the role of Lona Hessel* in a production of *The Pillars of Society** in New York in 1931. Her Karsten Bernick* was Moffat Johnston.*
Reference: Who's Who in the Theatre, 16th ed., p. 908.

MARSHALL, E. G. (c. 1910-   ): E. G. Marshall starred with Irene Worth* in Austin Pendleton's production of *John Gabriel Borkman** at the Circle in the Square Theatre (New York) beginning on December 18, 1980. Perhaps to lighten the foreboding ambiance of the drama, Marshall portrayed the title role with moments of wry humor in the early parts, which unhappily disposed audiences to laugh at his brittle characterization toward the end. The *Christian Science Monitor* concluded that Marshall "misses the sense of vision which . . . possesses the magnate," but Clive Barnes of the *New York Post* called the production "the best English-speaking staging [of *John Gabriel Borkman*] since Peter Hall's version of the play with Ralph Richardson* at Britain's National Theatre."
References: New York Theatre Critics' Reviews, XLI, 21 (Dec. 31, 1980), 59-60; *Who's Who in the Theatre*, 17th ed., I, 460.

MARX, ELEANOR (1855-98): Karl Marx's daughter, Eleanor, espoused Ibsen because of what she viewed as his revolutionary ideas. With her lover Edward Aveling, she produced *The Lady from the Sea** in London on May 11, 1891; it lasted five performances. She was also instrumental in interesting Henry Havelock Ellis* in Ibsen, which eventuated in the publication of a cheap edition of some of Ibsen's plays. In 1901 Eleanor Marx published *The Prose Dramas of Henrik Ibsen.*

Reference: Tsuzuki, Chuschichi. *The Life of Eleanor Marx.* Oxford: Clarendon Press, 1967.

MASSEY, DANIEL (1933-): Canadian actor Daniel Massey played Johannes Rosmer* at London's Haymarket Theatre in October 1977 in support of Claire Bloom.* Although Massey met Ibsen's requirements, the production offered nothing new (*The Times* (London), Oct. 21, 1977, p. 17, cols. 3-5.

Reference: Who's Who in the Theatre, 17th ed., I, 465.

THE MASTER BUILDER: A three-act Realistic-Symbolistic serious drama.

Composition: Started in the summer of 1892; finished in September; published on December 12.

Stage history:

Jan. 19, 1893	Trondhjem, pro. William Petersen
Jan. 19, 1893	Lessing Theater, Berlin (3 perfs.), pro. Emanuel Reicher*
Feb. 1893	Chicago (in Norwegian)
Feb. 20, 1893	Trafalgar Square Theatre, London (3), Elizabeth Robins* as Hilde
Mar. 6, 1893	Vaudeville Theatre, London (21), Elizabeth Robins as Hilde
Mar. 8, 1893	Royal Theatre, Copenhagen (11
Mar. 8, 1893	Christiania Theatre* (15), Johanne Dybwad* as Hilde
Mar. 23, 1893	Stadttheater, Gothenburg
Apr. 5, 1893	Théâtre de l'Oeuvre, Paris
Apr. 19, 1893	Trondhjem, pro. William Petersen
June 2, 1893	Opera Comique, London (4), Lewis Waller* as Solness
Apr. 3, 1894	Théâtre de l'Oeuvre, Paris, Aurélien-Marie Lugné-Poë* as Solness
Oct. 1894	Théâtre de l'Oeuvre, Christiania
Mar. 1895	Opera Comique, London
Sept. 7, 1896	Christiania Theatre (13)
Mar. 2, 1898	Westendhalle, Munich, pro. Josef Ruederer
Mar. 21, 1898	Christiania Theatre (2)
Jan. 17, 1900	Carnegie Lyceum Theatre, New York (1), William Pascoe as Solness
Jan. 19, 1905	Schauspielhaus, Munich, Colla Jessen* as Solness
Apr. 7, 1905	Kommisarzhevskaya Theatre, St. Petersburg, Vera Kommisarzhevskaya* as Hilde
Apr. 30, 1905	Murray Hill Theatre, New York, J. H. Greene* as Solness
May 12, 1905	Madison Square Theatre, New York (1), Ida Jeffreys Goodfriend* as Hilde
Sept. 27, 1907	Bijou Theatre, New York (65), Walter Hampden* as Solness, Alla Nazimova* as Hilde
Mar. 1908	Daly's Theatre, New York, Vera Kommisarzhevskaya as Hilde

Mar. 12, 1908	Kharkov Theatre, St. Petersburg, dir. Vsevelod Meyerhold*
Mar. 21, 1908	Residenz Theater, Munich, Heinz Monnard as Solness
Mar. 16, 1909	Court Theatre, London
Mar. 30, 1909	King's Theatre, Hammersmith (London), (1)
Jan. 20, 1910	National Theatre, Christiania,* dir. Johanne Dybwad
Mar. 28, 1911	Little Theatre, London, dir. H. Granville-Barker, Lillah McCarthy* as Hilde
May 13, 1918	Court Theatre, London
Nov. 27, 1921	Chelsea Theatre, London
Nov. 10, 1925	Maxine Elliott's Theatre, New York (76), Eva Le Gallienne* as Hilde
Nov. 1, 1926	Civic Repertory Theatre, New York, Eva Le Gallienne as Hilde
June 11, 1928	"Q" Theatre, London
Oct. 4, 1928	Everyman Theatre, London, Charles Carson* as Solness
Nov. 19, 1931	Duchess Theatre, London, Donald Wolfit* as Solness
Apr. 15, 1933	Westminster Theatre, London, Donald Wolfit as Solness
Apr. 1933	Embassy Theatre, London, Donald Wolfit as Solness
Mar. 12, 1936	Criterion Theatre, London, Lydia Lopokova* as Hilde
Apr. 1943	Westminster Theatre, London, Donald Wolfit as Solness
June 29, 1943	Westminster Theatre, London
Jan. 1, 1947	Arts Theatre, London, Frederick Valk* as Solness
May 14, 1948	Westminster Theatre, London, Donald Wolfit as Solness
May 25, 1950	Cherry Lane Theatre, New York, William Scanlon as Solness
Mar. 1, 1955	Phoenix Theatre, New York (40), Oscar Homolka as Solness
June 9, 1964	Old Vic, London, pro. National Theatre of Great Britain, Michael Redgrave* as Solness, Maggie Smith* as Hilde
Nov. 17, 1964	Old Vic, London, pro. National Theatre of Britain, Laurence Olivier* as Solness, Maggie Smith as Hilde
Oct. 17, 1971	Roundabout Theatre, New York (64)
Oct. 12, 1983	Roundabout Theatre, New York

Synopsis: In the workroom in the house of Halvard Solness, a successful master builder, work Knut Brovik, an architect, and his son Ragnar, a draftsman. Old Brovik's niece Kaja Fosli serves as bookkeeper of the firm. In Solness' absence, an ailing Knut decides to broach an important matter to his employer, although the suggestion disturbs his son. When Solness' steps are heard outside, all three people rush back to their work tables and appear to be intent upon their tasks. Seeing Kaja bent over her ledger, Solness, a vigorous middle-aged man, comes near as if to study her accounts but actually flirts with her. He then asks Ragnar if anyone called in his absence and learns that a young couple who have hired him to design their first house had come in. Supremely confident in his worth, Solness almost contemptuously dismisses such a paltry commission. Knut asks to have a word in private with Solness. He tells the master builder that he gets weaker every day and that his chief desire before he dies is to see Ragnar and Kaja married. Solness is affronted by both suggestions because he fears being supplanted by the younger generation and he is infatuated by Kaja. Knut suggests that Ragnar be allowed to design the young couple's house since he has already prepared preliminary sketches that interested the clients. Solness sees all his fears about youthful replacement coming true. He cannot give way to Knut's request because such is his nature. Solness' dismissal of his request causes Knut to have a slight attack, so Ragnar is dispatched to take him home. Kâja remains behind because Solness wants to learn whether she wishes to marry Ragnar. She says that she once cared for the young man, but that was before she met Solness with whom she is in love. Solness advises her to convince Ragnar to keep his job with him; she can marry Ragnar if she likes because that would not interfere with her relationship with Solness. He kisses her hair as she falls to his feet in abject gratitude. This passionate interlude is broken up at the approach of Solness' sickly wife Aline, who sees Kaja and immediately assumes the worst.

Aline has come to ask if Solness can make the time to speak to old Doctor Herdal. He says that he will come presently, and so Aline departs.

Once again Solness urges Kaja to influence Ragnar because Solness needs him—quickly Solness amends his statement to express his need of Kaja. Before he sends Kaja home, he asks her to find Ragnar's drawings of the house. Then she leaves.

Aline ushers Herdal into Solness' office, clearly showing her disdain of Kaja and her distrust of Solness; the marital tension is undisguised. Aline then retires to the private portion of the house and leaves Solness free to ask if the doctor has noticed any change in Aline's condition. Herdal has not missed the evidence of Aline's jealousy of Kaja; he suggests that the girl might be replaced by a male clerk as a sop to Aline's weak constitution. Solness insists that there is nothing between them and that he cannot dismiss her. He explains to Herdal that he had hired Kaja to make Ragnar content to remain working for Solness. The strange thing was that he had merely thought of the plan, yet Kaja had read his thoughts and accepted the arrangement. Once she had started working in the office, however, she lost interest in Ragnar and centered her attention on Solness. Every day now he must keep up the pretense of being interested in Kaja merely to keep her there for Ragnar. The doctor asks why Solness had not explained the situation to his wife; the builder cryptically says that he has enjoyed the self-torture of knowing that his wife does not trust him. After a moment's pause, Solness' manner changes, and he accuses Herdal of smugly thinking he has drawn private confidences from him. He then says that he knows that Aline has convinced the doctor that he is losing his mind. Although the doctor denies it, Solness does not believe him. Then he expresses his fear of being supplanted by the younger generation. This conversation ends when a knock at the door is heard.

A young woman dressed in hiking clothes, Hilde Wangel, enters, greets the men, and waits to be acknowledged. She clearly expects Solness to recognize her, but it is Herdal who has met her in the mountains last summer. When Herdal calls her Miss Wangel, the name registers with Solness, who had met a Doctor Wangel when he built a new tower for the church in Lysanger. He had met young Hilde ten years earlier when she was twelve or thirteen. Hilde says that she had also met Mrs. Solness at the sanatorium in Lysanger; Aline had, in fact, invited Hilde to visit when she came to town again. Hilde announces that she plans to stay the night. Herdal goes to rejoin Aline as he remarks laughingly that the younger generation has indeed knocked at Solness' door.

Aline comes in, recognizes Hilde, agrees that she may stay, and departs to prepare her room, which is one of the three empty nurseries in the house. Solness makes small talk as Hilde examines the contents of the room. Finally, she asks if he does not remember what had happened when he was in Lysanger. She reminds him of the festive day when the church tower was completed and he had scaled the scaffolding to place a wreath around the weathervane. Hilde had been a small girl in the crowd who was impressed by the height of the tower and the brave builder who climbed it. As she had watched him at the top, she had heard the sound of harps in the air. Later when Solness went to the Wangels' for dinner, he had found Hilde alone, bent her head, and kissed her passionately many times, saying that ten years hence he would come and take his little princess away to a kingdom called Orangia. At first Solness denies it all, but Hilde's insistence on the truth of it convinces him. Solness is quite confused as to her intentions. Now that she is in town, Hilde says, she wants to travel around and see the things he has built. He remarks that he no longer builds churches but prefers to erect homes for human beings, one of which he has reared for himself, an edifice with a high tower. Hilde finally concludes that she means to have a more substantial kingdom than Orangia. Solness states that he has lived the past ten years with the knowledge that he had forgotten an experience he desperately wanted to recall. He then confides to her his fear of the younger generation and sees her as his hedge against youth. Aline comes in to announce supper. Quietly, Solness tells Hilde that she is just what he needs, and she remarks that she now has her kingdom. Then she says that she almost has it, as the curtain falls.

The locale of Act II is a small drawing room in Solness' house where he sits studying Ragnar's plans and Aline wordlessly waters her plants. From time to time Solness steals a look at his wife. Kaja comes in to report for work and to say that the ailing Knut cannot come to the office; then she returns to her room. As Aline prepares to take a walk, he asks if Hilde has yet arisen, which arouses Aline's jealousy. Solness tells her that their life will be more cheerful once they move into the new house, but he clearly means that Hilde's presence will make his own life happier. Aline maintains indifference to the house, but it brings back memories of her parents' house which had burned. She then alludes to something terrible which had happened after the fire and has tainted their lives afterward. Aline has become perfectly morbid, saying that neither this house nor the new one can ever be a home for them. He accuses her of looking for hidden meaning in everything he says, in fact, she is looking for proof that he is mad. Solness loudly maintains that he is not a lunatic whatever his wife and her doctor may think; his only problem is the tremendous debt of guilt he feels toward his wife. His despondency is immediately relieved, however, by the appearance of Hilde. As Hilde and Solness happily discuss dreams of falling, Aline prepares to leave to do some shopping. Although Hilde has changed from her hiking clothes, her appearance prompts Aline to remark that people may think her mad too. Solness identifies himself as the madman referred to by his wife. Then Aline leaves, and Hilde says that she wishes Aline would not talk so often of duty, a concept repugnant to the young woman.

As Hilde notices the books in the room and Ragnar's drawings, she remarks that reading is a waste of time as is teaching. Solness draws her to the window and points out the high tower of his new house that will also contain three nurseries that will never be used. At Hilde's urging, Solness reveals that he and Aline had twin boys who lived for only two weeks. When Hilde expresses interest, Solness says he is grateful he has found someone who is interested in his feelings. He volunteers to tell Hilde the whole story about the Solnesses' first residence, a house inherited from Aline's mother. Two weeks after the birth of the twins, the house had burned down, and Aline was so terrified by the experience that her milk was affected. Nonetheless, she insisted on nursing the boys because it was her duty, as a result of which the boys had died. Since that time Solness could not bear to erect churches but only tall-towered homes for people. He had subdivided the garden of the old house, built experimental houses there, and become a highly successful contractor. Yet, says Solness, the price he had to pay for his success, the price he paid for giving warm, sturdy homes to families, has been very great indeed. His contentment in his vocation forever destroyed his domestic bliss. When pressed by Hilde, Solness says that Aline can have no more children; yet he builds nurseries in his houses because he is mesmerized by the impossible. Hilde, delighted by this admission, says she feels the same way about the unattainable. Solness continues to bare his soul, confessing that his success has also thwarted Aline's great capacity for rearing children to be worthy adults. Now he is haunted by the fact that in some way he might have been responsible for the fire and its aftermath.

Ragnar enters, saying that his father is dying, and asks Solness to write an encouraging word on one of his drawings so that the old man's last moment may be cheered. Solness refuses to do so and advises Ragnar to continue working for him. Ragnar moves to take his portfolio, but Hilde asks him to leave it so that she may look at it. As Ragnar leaves, Solness begs him not to ask for things that are beyond Solness' power.

When they are alone, Hilde calls Solness' behavior ugly, cruel, and wicked. Solness replies that he alone should be allowed to build since he has paid the dear price of peace of mind for the right to do so. He then narrates how he had discovered a crack in the chimney of the old house and had delayed fixing it in the hope that the house would burn. As it happened, however, the fire started in a closet. He then asks Hilde if she believes there are people who can make things happen by willing them. She answers that someday they may find out if she is one of those. This problem, then, lies at the root of Solness' unease: was he responsible for Aline's unhappiness and the death of his sons? Had he called for the Helpers and the Servers to bring about his fondest wish? Hilde wonders if he were not born with a sickly conscience rather than a robust one as she possesses. She feels that something inside her made her leave home to go in search of Solness. First, Solness compares these uncontrollable inner urges with trolls, and then he speaks of good and bad devils. Next, they talk of the old Vikings whose robust consciences had countenanced their marauding behavior and the women who willingly had bowed to their demands. Hilde says that she would live of her own free will with a ruffian if she loved him and that the trolls and devils have already chosen her one and true love. She then suggests that Solness may have summoned her telepathically. He admits that he might have done so because she personifies the Youth that he so fears and yet desires. When Hilde tries to persuade him to write on Ragnar's drawings, Solness admits that if the young man ever gets his chance as a builder, he will ruin Solness. This pettiness horrifies Hilde who wants to see Solness as a great man. Completely in her power, Solness sits down and writes on a drawing. When Solness asks what she really wants from him, she simply says that she has come for her kingdom. Aline returns from shopping at about the same time as Hilde summons Kaja into the room. Solness tells Kaja that he has written on the drawings, that Ragnar can have his chance to build, and that the two of them may leave his employ to pursue their own lives. He then dismisses her with the order to take the drawings to Knut. Rather than being pleased that Kaja is now out of the house, the ever-miserable Aline implies that Hilde will take her place. Solness tells Hilde that he plans to hang a wreath on the tower of their new house, but Aline tries to dissuade him because he gets dizzy from heights, and she uses his obduracy as proof that he is indeed mad. She rushes out for the doctor. Hilde asks if her Master Builder "dare not, cannot climb as high as he builds." When he promises that he will climb the tower, Hilde is delighted.

Act III occurs on Solness' verandah from which in the distance can be seen the tower with its scaffolding. The time is sundown. Aline sits quietly in a chair as Hilde comes in from the garden. For a time they discuss Aline's disinclination to walk in the garden since so many strangers' houses now make it possible for people to stare at her. In a very sympathetic scene, Hilde speaks of Aline's suffering, drawing her out. Aline sees the death of her children as God's will but the loss of family portraits, lace, jewels, and dolls as the deprivations that break the heart. She had had nine dolls with which she had continued to live even after her marriage. Herdal enters in response to Aline's summons. Just before Solness appears, Aline asks if she and Hilde cannot be friends, which Hilde answers by an impetuous embrace. Aline and the doctor then go into the house.

Solness enters and greets Hilde, who says she feels as cold as if she had just risen from a tomb. As Solness tries to make conversation, Hilde remains unresponsive; after a pause she announces that she must go away. If she stays, she will hurt Aline, whom she now knows. She could hurt a stranger but not someone she knows. He says he cannot bear to live with a dead woman. Hilde asks what he will build next, and Solness responds that he probably will build very little. Together they agree that the optimum is to have the Viking spirit and a robust conscience. Then Hilde commands Solness to build the castle that will dominate her kingdom; he can then visit the princess in the tower. Afterward, the Master Builder and the princess will build only castles in the air, the loveliest thing in all the world. Ragnar comes out of the house carrying a large wreath of flowers and ribbons and reporting that Knut became unconscious before the drawings were delivered. Solness tries to send Ragnar home, but he insists on staying. Solness walks through the garden to take the wreath to the new house.

Hilde tells Ragnar that he ought to thank Solness, but the young man feels no gratitude because he knows Solness has kept him down merely to remain near Kaja. Kaja has admitted as much. Kaja has told Ragnar that Solness so completely possesses her that she can never leave him. Hilde, incensed upon learning Solness' real motives, insists that Ragnar's continued presence was Solness' true goal. Ragnar reluctantly believes Hilde's explanation but nevertheless calls Solness a coward who cannot even climb scaffolding. When Hilde tells about Solness' feat at the church tower, Ragnar scoffs that he could never do such a thing again.

Aline comes out, hears that Solness has taken the wreath to the new house, and dispatches Ragnar to talk him out of doing anything foolish. Aline wants to remain outside to see what Solness will do, but her duty compels her to go inside and act as hostess to a party of ladies who have come to call. She asks Hilde to make sure Solness does nothing dangerous.

Solness returns to the verandah expecting to find Aline and the doctor but is relieved to see only Hilde. She asks if he is afraid to climb and fall; Solness says he is afraid only of retribution. The master builder believes that the burning of the old house was a sign of God's displeasure with him; this thought occurred to him as he stood before the church tower at Lysanger. He had deduced that God wanted him to devote his life to building churches regardless of family ties or any other claim. Viewing such a vocation as a kind of slavery, he had done the impossible feat of climbing the tower and telling God that he would build Him no more churches, that he intended to be free. Now, however, Solness sees that building homes for people is disappointing too, since people cannot be happy in them. From now on he intends to build only castles in the air. Hilde tells him that the only thing that will make her believe wholly in his powers is to see him at the top of the tower; he must do the impossible again. He readily agrees to do so, and at the top, he will tell God that he plans to return to his princess whom he will love madly and with whom he will build castles in the air. Hilde is ecstatic because now he seems like the master builder of her youth.

A brass band is heard, guests are seen gathering for the dedication, and Ragnar tells Solness that the foreman is ready to place the wreath atop the tower. Aline has entered, hears this, and tries to convince Solness to remain with her during the ceremony. He insists, however, that he must be with his men. Since he gives evasive answers when Aline speaks of his climbing the tower, she thinks that Hilde has been successful in keeping him off the tower. Solness exits.

All eyes are on the tower. Ragnar tells Hilde that a group of students has come to laugh at Solness' inability to climb the tower, but Hilde boasts that they will be disappointed. A figure is seen climbing a ladder up the tower; first, it is believed that he is the foreman, and then he is clearly identified as Solness. Aline reacts with terror, Hilde with delight, and Ragnar with the certainty that Solness' dizziness will make him turn back. Now Solness is at the very top, and Hilde sees him as great and free again. Solness hangs the wreath around the weathervane. Then Hilde sees him striving with invisible contenders and hears a song in the air. Solness waves his hat in the air, and Hilde takes Aline's white shawl and flags a response as she cheers the master builder. The crowd joins in the cheer, which soon changes to a shriek of terror. Solness' body and loose planks are seen plummeting to the ground. Aline faints as Hilde stands petrified. Even Ragnar is affected. A voice from below announces that Solness is dead. Ragnar concludes that Solness could not climb the tower after all, but Hilde triumphantly says he made it to the top and caused the harps to play in the wind.

Structural analysis: The Master Builder is extremely rich in symbols—the harps in the wind, houses with towers, wreaths around weathervanes, and invisible forces. Certain questions such as why Solness should build three nurseries in his new house are left unanswered. Hilde Wangel is unique among Ibsen's creations because she appears in two dramas, *The Lady from the Sea** and *The Master Builder.** (There are two Aslaksens and several Ejnars, but Ibsen never specifies they are identical characters.) At first glance, the drama would seem to be unified by action as are most of Ibsen's later plays, but such is not the case; it is unified by character, as its actual title *Master Builder Solness* suggests. When Solness first appears, he is a petty, petulant, neurotic man. Youth, in the person of Hilde, comes into his life and causes him to make significant changes in his outlook. When Hilde sees that her plans for Solness will harm Aline and decides she must go, Solness despairs of his life's ever having any meaning. When Hilde prompts him to climb the tower and confront God as he had done in the past, Solness regains his control over his life; he dies fighting against his own private devils and seems to have experienced what Aristotle called anagnorisis, or recognition. Solness, therefore, is significantly different at the end than he was at the beginning; the intervening episodes illustrate that change.

References: Hinden, M. "Ibsen and Nietzsche: A Reading of *The Master Builder,*" *Modern Drama*, 15 (1973), 403-10; Kaufman, Michael W. "Nietzsche, Georg Brandes, and Ibsen's *The Master Builder,*" *Comparative Drama*, 6 (1972), 169-86; Sechmsdorf, Henning K. "Two Legends about St. Olaf, 'The Master Builder': A Clue to the Dramatic Structure of Henrik Ibsen's *Bygmester Solness,*" *Edda*, 54 (1967), 263-71.

MAURUS (*Emperor and Galilean*): A standard-bearer.

MAXIMUS (*Emperor and Galilean*): A mystic who exercises almost hypnotic influence over Julian,* Maximus is the vehicle of Julian's total lapse into paganism. He provides the same sort of destructive counsel to Julian as Nickolas Arnesson, Bishop of Oslo,* does in *The Pretenders.**

THE MAYOR (*Brand*): The Mayor is the focus of Brand's* anti-materialistic teaching. When Brand is a poor preacher, the Mayor is his enemy, but when Brand inherits his mother's fortune, the Mayor, as a true opportunist, becomes his ally in erecting the new church. At the end of the play, Brand and the Mayor strive for the people's loyalty, and Brand appears to win; but when Brand's path over the mountain becomes too strenuous for the fickle crowd, the Mayor is there to promise them something for nothing. He admits that he has lied to the people but excuses it on the grounds of expediency. In the end he leads the crowd back to the village for business as usual.

McCARTHY, LILLAH (1875-1960): Lillah McCarthy participated in the seminal seasons of Harley Granville-Barker (her husband) at London's Court Theatre in Sloane Square. On March 28, 1911, she opened as Hilde Wangel* in *The Master Builder** under Barker's direction.
Reference: McCarthy, Lillah. *Myself and My Friends.* London: T. Butterworth, 1932.

McGOOHAN, PATRICK (b. 1928): When Patrick McGoohan played Brand* in London in 1959, his performance was called "magnificent throughout in a part which is pitched on a single note" (*The Times* (London), Apr. 9, 1959, p. 3, cols. 3-5).
Reference: Who Was Who in the Theatre, III, 1659.

McGRATH, LEUEEN (1914-   ): In September 1961 Leueen McGrath appeared in New York as Helene Alving* in *Ghosts,** about which a critic wrote: "Mrs. Alving's growth in self-knowledge is as impressive and moving to us as it is painful to her. . . . Leueen McGrath's Mrs. Alving reveals with subtlety the frustrations of a life devoted to disagreeable duty and the gallantry with which she confronts her situation" (*New York Times*, Sept. 22, 1961, p. 29, cols. 1-3.
Reference: Who's Who in the Theatre, 16th ed., pp. 885-6.

McKELLEN, IAN (1939-   ): Ian McKellen played Karsten Bernick* in the Royal Shakespeare Company production of *The Pillars of Society** on August 1, 1977.
Reference: Who's Who in the Theatre, 17th ed., I, 446-7.

McKERN, LEO (1925-   ): Leo McKern appeared in Michael Elliott's production of *Peer Gynt** at London's Old Vic in September 1962. *The Times* (London) critic wrote of his performance: "Mr. McKern lacks the fantasy for Gynt's early escapades in the village; the magnetism which attracts Solveig has to be taken on trust. He came into his own as the bloated hedonist in Africa, uttering pious platitudes when his sexual powers decline and seeking domination instead" (Sept. 27, 1962, p. 16, cols. 6-7).
Reference: Who's Who in the Theatre, 16th ed., p. 892.

McKINNEL, NORMAN (1870-1932): Although known best for his Shakespearean roles, Norman McKinnel was Halvard Solness* in Harley Granville-Barker's production of *The Master Builder** at the Court Theatre in 1911.
Reference: The Green Room Book, 1906, ed. Bampton Hunt. New York: Frederick Warne, 1906.

McRAE, BRUCE (1867-1927): Ethel Barrymore* was Bruce McRae's Nora Helmer* in a production of *A Doll's House** in New York in 1905; Minnie Maddern Fiske* was his Rebecca West* in 1907. McRae played Torvald Helmer* and Johannes Rosmer.*
Reference: Who Was Who in the Theatre, III, 1666-7.

MEACHAM, ANNE (1925-   ): Anne Meacham received the Obie award for her performance as Hedda Gabler* in New York in 1960. Henry Hewes wrote of her performance, "Miss Meacham shows us an affected, completely selfish woman slowly driven mad by the boredom of being married to the kindly but inelegant and unexacting Tesman" ["Preferred Stock," *Saturday Review*, 44 (Jan. 28, 1961), 27]. This production had the longest run of any other Ibsenian drama—340 consecutive performances.
Reference: Who's Who in the Theatre, 16th ed., pp. 922-3.

MEDON (*Emperor and Galilean*): A corn-dealer.

MEMNON (*Emperor and Galilean*): The body-slave of Emperor Constantius.*

THE MEMNON STATUE (Peer Gynt): As Peer Gynt* soliloquizes before this ancient Egyptian monument, it begins to sing, a fact that Peer writes down.

MENCKEN, HENRY LOUIS (1880)1956): Literary critic H. L. Mencken advocated a commonsense approach to Ibsenian criticism after the initial furor over the subject matter of Ibsen's social problem plays had died down. He called Ibsen "a first-rate journeyman dramatist, perhaps the best." In 1935 Mencken published *Eleven Plays of Henrik Ibsen*.

Reference: Jansen, K. Edward. "Mencken on Ibsen: Even Mencken Nods," *Menckeniana*, 47 (1973), 13-18.

MERETA (*The Grouse in Justedal*): Foster-daughter and ward of Bengt of Bjerkehoug.*

MESSTHALER, EMIL (b. 1869): As producer of the Theater der Moderne, Emil Messthaler was devoted to popularizing the works of Realist playwrights, particularly Ibsen, Gerhart Hauptmann, and Hermann Sudermann. Among his numerous efforts in Ibsen's behalf, Messthaler played Alfred Allmers* in Munich in 1893 and Oswald Alving* in 1894.

MEYERHOLD, VSEVELOD (1874-1942): As an actor of the Moscow Art Theatre* from 1898 through 1902, Meyerhold encountered Ibsen's dramas but was dissatisfied with their Realistic productions. In 1905 Konstantin Stanislavsky* asked Meyerhold to head his experimental Theatre Studio and explore ways of producing Symbolist dramas; in this position Meyerhold directed *Love's Comedy** in 1905. When actress Vera Kommisarzhevskaya* opened her theatre in St. Petersburg, she asked Meyerhold, known by all to be innovative and thought by some to be controversial, to become her stage director. From that collaboration came one of Meyerhold's most notable productions, *Hedda Gabler*,* which opened the theatre on November 10, 1906. Meyerhold departed from traditional staging practices in a number of ways, but two examples suffice to indicate the novelty of his concept. Rather than mounting the drama in a setting ponderous with Victorian furniture and bric-a-brac and tenebrous with dark colors, Meyerhold conceived Hedda as "a goddess against a background of golden autumn" (Hoover, p. 33). The scenery and lighting were executed primarily in warm, golden hues with numerous white accents. In an effort to garner greater audience participation than was then usual, Meyerhold directed Hedda and Lövborg* at their first meeting to sit side by side and face forward. At no time were they to glance at each other or to move. The lines were delivered in a sing-song intonation with unnatural rhythmic cadences. He believed that such staging would encourage the audience to see behind the mere words to the strata of emotions that were not overtly expressed. The Kommisarshevskaya Theatre was also the scene of Meyerhold's *A Doll's House** (December 18, 1906) and *Love's Comedy* (January 22, 1907).

Between 1908 and 1918 Meyerhold was director of the imperial operatic and dramatic theatre in St. Petersburg, but this responsibility did not inhibit his experimental productions in other theatres. At the Kharkov Theatre he mounted *Hedda Gabler* (February 21, 1908) and *The Master Builder** (March 12, 1908). At the Alexandrinsky Theatre he staged *The Lady from the Sea** (December 15, 1917).

After joining the Communist party in 1918, Meyerhold produced *A Doll's House* in the theatre of the Workers' Club (Petrograd) on June 7, a production repeated at the Lenin Theatre, Novorossisk, on August 6, 1920. Nora Helmer's* solution to her domestic problems suited Meyerhold's political orientation, and on April 20, 1922, he staged his own adaptation of Ibsen's drama, now called *A Doll's House: or, How a Lady of Bourgeois Background Opted for Independence and a Job*, at the Actors' Theatre in Moscow.

Meyerhold was a teacher as well as a director and throughout his career developed a system of actor training known as biomechanics, which involved, among other things, physical training to enable actors to play certain set-roles, each of which was defined by physical traits. Ibsen's Oswald Alving,* for example, was a Second Lover (naive) type who could be played by a man of less-than-average height who carried no excess weight. Stensgaard* of *The League of Youth** was the first type of Mischief-Maker. He could not be above average height; his vocal range was unimportant; and he must have a slender figure. He should, moreover, have quite mobile facial muscles and expressive eyes. Lady Inger of Gyldenlöve* was the first type of Heroine, which meant that she must be tall, possess long legs, small head, almond-shaped eyes, and exceptionally communicative wrists.

In 1939 Meyerhold was arrested by Stalin's agents and mysteriously died in captivity. He was rehabilitated in 1955.

Reference: Hoover, Marjorie L. *Meyerhold: The Art of Conscious Theatre.* Amherst: University of Massachusetts Press, 1974.

MILLER, ARTHUR (1915-   ): In preparing his colloquial American version of *An Enemy of the People*,* in 1950, Arthur Miller stressed "the question of whether the democratic guarantees protecting political minorities ought to be set aside in times of crisis" or "whether one's vision of the truth ought to be a source of guilt at a time when the mass of men condemn it as a dangerous and devilish lie" (Miller, p. 8).

Rather than working from any of the standard translations, Miller employed a strict literal translation of Ibsen's words made by Lars Nordenson. Miller was then able to deduce the sense of each speech and express it in idiomatic American English. The adaptor also expunged any speeches the validity of which the passage of time had obviated. Reducing Ibsen's five acts to three, Miller eliminated transitions from scene to scene hoping to make each act a compact structural unit. Ibsen's fifth act, believed by Miller to be unnecessarily repetitive, was condensed by about one-half. Miller summarized his alterations: "Throughout the play I have tried to peel away its trappings of the moment, its relatively accidental details which ring the dull green tones of Victorianism, and to show that beneath them still lives the terrible wrath of Henrik Ibsen" (Miller, p. 12).

Lars Nordenson's production of Miller's Ibsen opened at the Broadhurst Theatre (New York) on December 28, 1950. The distinguished cast included

Fredric March,* Florence Eldridge, and Morris Carnovsky; the play ran only thirty-six performances.

References: Miller, Arthur, adapt. *An Enemy of the People by Henrik Ibsen.* New York: Viking Press, 1951; Murray, Edward. *Arthur Miller, Dramatist.* New York: F. Ungar, 1967.

MILTON, ERNEST (1890-   ): American actor Ernest Milton achieved his greatest success in his adoptive land, England. He often played Oswald Alving* in *Ghosts,** his initial representation of the role occurring when he replaced Basil Sydney in the production starring Letitia Darragh* at London's Kingsway Theatre (April 28, 1917). When the company went on a tour of the provinces, Milton remained as Oswald. He repeated the part of Oswald in the ill-fated People's Theatre* repertory in June 1923; in 1925 he played Oswald to Irene Rooke's* Helene Alving.* Earlier that year he was Lyngstrand* in *The Lady from the Sea,** and in October 1930 he essayed the part of Alfred Allmers* in *Little Eyolf** at the Arts Theatre. Often a member of the Old Vic Company, Milton was primarily a classical actor.

Reference: Who's Who in the Theatre, 11th ed. Ed. John Parker (New York: Pitman Publishing Company, 1952), pp. 1060-62.

MITCHELL, DODSON (1868-1939): Dodson Mitchell's Ibsenian career in the United States spanned twenty years during which he played the leading male roles in *A Doll's House** (1907), *Hedda Gabler** (1907), *The Master Builder** (1907), and *Ghosts** (1915) and Morten Kiil* in *An Enemy of the People** (1937).

Reference: Who Was Who in the Theatre, III, 1719-20.

MITTERWURZER, FRIEDRICH (1845-97): After establishing himself as one of the finest actors in his native Austria, Friedrich Mitterwurzer gained an international reputation by performing throughout Europe and America between 1886 and 1894. While performing in Chicago in 1887, Mitterwurzer introduced his English version of *Ghosts*, Phantoms, or The Sins of the Fathers.** In 1891 and 1895 in Vienna he added Hjalmar Ekdal* and Alfred Allmers* to his repertory of impersonations that included Mephisto, Macbeth, and Wallenstein.

Reference: Guglia, Eugen. *Friedrich Mitterwurzer.* Vienna: Carl Gerolds Sohn, 1896.

MODJESKA, HELENA (1840-1909): When already a leading actress in her native Poland, Helena Modrzejewska (as she was then called) emigrated to the United States in 1876, eventually settling near San Francisco. Soon thereafter, the actress adopted the more easily pronounced name of Modjeska. After a series of English lessons, Modjeska appeared at the Baldwin Theatre in San Francisco on August 13, 1877, in *Adrienne Lecouvreur.* In December she repeated the role in New York and assumed her position as an American star. Modjeska played frequently thereafter in America, the British Isles, and Poland.

Modjeska's connection with Ibsen, while slight, is important from a historical point of view. In 1882 she played Nora Helmer* in *A Doll's House** while in Poland—much to the dismay of her friends who thought her getting under a table and barking like a dog was "quaint," to say the least (Modjeska, p. 456). On December 7, 1883, she acted the same part in English in Louisville, Kentucky. The drama had been adapted from the Polish and German versions by her husband Karol Bozenta Chlapowski* and her secretary Louise Everson and appeared under the title of *Thora.** Since the public was not receptive to the play, it was taken off after one performance. It represents the earliest professional performance in English in the United States of any of Ibsen's dramas.

Shakespeare, not Ibsen, was Modjeska's métier. Rosalind, Viola, Beatrice—these were her celebrated roles.

References: Coleman, Marion M. *Fair Rosalind: The American Career of Helena Modjeska.* Cheshire, Conn.: Cherry Hill Books, 1969; Modjeska, Helena. *Memories and Impressions: An Autobiography.* New York: Benjamin Blom, 1969 [1910].

MOFFAT, DONALD (1930-   ): English actor. Donald Moffat played Hjalmar Ekdal* when *The Wild Duck* opened in London on January 11, 1967. He came to the role with twenty years' experience in classical roles performed at London's Old Vic and in the United States.

Reference: Who's Who in the Theatre, 16th ed., pp. 945-6.

MOGENS (*The Grouse in Justedal*): A priest.

MOISSI, ALEXANDER (1880-1935): Austria's Alexander Moissi was essentially a classical actor, but in 1911 he added Oswald Alving* in *Ghosts** to his list of impersonations. In February 1928 Moissi played in three performances of *Ghosts* in German in New York. Moissi's career was inextricably linked with that of Max Reinhardt.*

Reference: Enciclopedia della Spettacolo, VIII, cols. 682-4.

MOLVIK (*The Wild Duck*): A dipsomaniacal former theological student.

MONNARD, HEINZ (b. 1873): Munich's Residenz Theater was the scene of Heinz Monnard's appearance as Halvard Solness.* The date was 1908, and his Hilde Wangel* was Maja Reubke.

MONRAD, MARCUS JACOB (1816-97): As a professor of philosophy at the University of Christiania from 1845 to 1897, M. J. Monrad sought to unite the philosophies of Georg Wilhelm Friedrich Hegel* and Christianity. His ideas bore fruit with reference to Ibsen's *Emperor and Galilean,** but his initial influence on Ibsen eventuated through his encouragement of *Catiline** in 1850 in a journal of which Monrad was editor, *Norsk Tidsskrift for Videnskab og Litteratur* [*Norwegian Magazine for Science and Literature*].

MONRAD, S. C.: The brother of Marcus Jacob Monrad,* S. C. Monrad was a theological student with whom Ibsen read Greek and Latin in Grimstad.*

MONSEN, BASTIEN (*The League of Youth*): The bumbling, bungling son of Mons Monsen.* He is immediately taken in by the slickness of Stensgaard* and becomes his sycophant.

MONSEN, MONS (*The League of Youth*): Mons Monsen, a capitalist, is the chief opponent to the policies of Chamberlain Brattsberg* and the candidacy of his adherents for re-election to Parliament. His bank is a serious rival of that of Brattsberg, who detests Monsen because Monsen convinced Erik Brattsberg* to go into business rather than pursue the idleness of the rich. Monsen is instrumental in convincing Stensgaard* to enter local politics on an anti-Brattsberg platform.

MONSEN, RAGNA (*The League of Youth*): The daughter of Mons Monsen,* Ragna is one of the chief romantic interests in the play and becomes engaged to Helle.*

MOOR, BILL: Bill Moor got a cool reception for his Johannes Rosmer* in a production of *Rosmersholm** in New York in 1974.
Reference: New York Theatre Critics' Reviews, XXXV, 23 (Dec. 16, 1974), 122-3.

MOORE, STEPHEN (1937-   ): *The Wild Duck** was produced by the National Theatre of Great Britain in December 1979; English actor Stephen Moore was Hjalmar Ekdal.* He worked at the Old Vic before joining the National Theatre in 1977.
Reference: Who's Who in the Theatre, 17th ed., I, 490.

MOPSEMAN (*Little Eyolf*): The Rat-Wife's* dog.

MORGENSTERN, CHRISTIAN (1871-1914): Philosopher and art historian Christian Morgenstern was also a translator into German, both of August Strindberg* and Ibsen. The Ibsenian translations were *The Wild Duck* (1890), *The Pillars of Society** (1891), *An Enemy of the People** (1891), *Ghosts** (1893), *The Feast at Solhoug** (1898), *When We Dead Awaken** (1899), and *Catiline** (1903).
Reference: Bauer, Michael. *Christian Morgensterns Leben und Werk.* Munich: R. Piper, 1933.

MORISON, MARY: Mary Morison translated numerous Scandinavian works, including some of Georg Morris Brandes* and Björnstjerne Björnson,* into English. She worked on a translation of *The Feast at Solhoug** and published *The Correspondence of Henrik Ibsen.* London: Hodder and Stoughton, 1905.

MORRIS, WILLIAM (1861-1936): Apparently, the character of Johannes Rosmer* eluded William Morris when he played the role in New York in 1904, for the critic of the *New York Times* wrote that Morris "at once lacked the distinction of the aristocrat and the mentality of the man of elevated spirit" (Mar. 29, 1904, p. 6, col. 1). Morris never turned to Ibsen again.
Reference: Who Was Who in the Theatre, III, 1754-5.

MORTENSGAARD, PETER (*Rosmersholm*): The editor of a radical newspaper, Mortensgaard is eager to enlist Johannes Rosmer* on the side of liberalism, but he is shrewd enough to counsel Rosmer not to announce that he has abandoned the church.

MOSCOW ART THEATRE: The Moscow Art Theatre (MAT) was opened on October 14, 1898, by Vladimir Nemirovich-Danchenko* and Konstantin Stanislavsky,* both of whom wanted freedom to produce dramas and train actors as they wished. Both men directed productions, in some of which Stanislavsky acted; Nemirovich-Danchenko served as producer and literary consultant. Although the MAT produced numerous types of European classics, it was famous for its illusionistic productions of modern dramas, especially those of Chekhov.
    While still an acting teacher at the Moscow Philharmonic School, Nemirovich-Danchenko directed *A Doll's House** (1896). It was his insistence on Ibsen's merit that caused the MAT to present *Hedda Gabler** (1899), *An Enemy of the People** (1900), *When We Dead Awaken** (1900), *The Wild Duck** (1901), *The Pillars of Society** (1903), *Ghosts** (1905), *Brand** (1906), *Rosmersholm** (1908), and *Peer Gynt** (1912). One of Stanislavsky's most lauded roles was that of Karsten Bernick* in *An Enemy of the People*, but he remained puzzled by the symbolism of Ibsen's later dramas.
Reference: Sayler, Oliver M. *Inside the Moscow Art Theatre.* New York: Brentano's, 1925.

THE MOUNTAIN BIRD (1859): Originally called *Alfhild*, this Romantic opera was to have contained three acts, of which Ibsen sketched only one and the beginning of a second. He wrote to composer Martin Andreas Udbye* on July 18, 1861, about setting the music, but Ibsen did not complete the libretto. The story was used to some extent in *Olaf Liljekrans.**

MULHARE, EDWARD (1923-   ): Perhaps his failure in *The Wild Duck** in 1947 convinced Edward Mulhare to avoid Ibsen. *The Times* (London) critic wrote, "Actors who fail to master Ibsen—that is, be equal to him—must expect instead to have all their inadequacies revealed. That is what happened here" (Nov. 1, 1947, p. 6, col. 4).

MUNICH: The Bavarian capital where Ibsen lived between 1875 and 1878 and again between 1885 and 1891.

"THE MURDER OF ABRAHAM LINCOLN": One of Ibsen's most sensitive poems, "The Murder of Abraham Lincoln" was written soon after the event. W. H. Schofield's English translation is printed in *American Scandinavian Review*, 6 (1918), 104-6.

MYRRHA (*Emperor and Galilean*): The slave of Helena,* wife of Julian.*

N

NAAR VI DÖDE VAAGNER: The Norwegian title of *When We Dead Awaken.**

NANDRUP, J.: Ibsen negotiated a loan from Nandrup, a lawyer, in 1862. When Ibsen defaulted in 1866, Nandrup confiscated all of Ibsen's possessions.

NATIONAL THEATRE (Christiania): The National Theatre emerged from the ruins of the Christiania Theatre,* which was closed in 1899. Björn Björnson,* the son of Ibsen's friend and enemy Björnstjerne Björnson,* was its first director. The National Theatre gave the Norwegian premieres of *The Wild Duck** and *When We Dead Awaken.**
Reference: Wiers-Jensen, H. *Nationaltheatret gjennem 25 aar, 1899-1924.* Kristiania: Gyldendal, 1924.

NAZIMOVA, ALLA (1879-1945): Born in the Crimea, Nazimova studied to be a violinist before turning to the theatre. Her record at the Russian Academy of Art won her an apprenticeship to the Moscow Art Theatre,* where she remained for two years, eagerly absorbing the techniques of Konstantin Stanislavsky.* She then joined a theatrical troupe that performed in several European cities before going to New York where it played a varied repertory in Russian. In Russia Nazimova had appeared in *The Master Builder,* Hedda Gabler,** and *Little Eyolf,** roles which she reproduced in New York in 1905. When her actor/husband decided to return to Europe, Nazimova remained in the United States and set herself the task of learning English. In a mere five months she could speak English clearly enough for Henry Miller to present her as Hedda Gabler* on November 13, 1906.

Matinee audiences saw forty performances of Nazimova's Hedda, which received critical acclaim. Mrs. Thomas Whiffin, who played Aunt Juliane Tesman* in that production, recalls: "She was very eccentric at rehearsals and used to twist up the English language in a most amusing way. I remember she wanted me to wear full mourning in the play, but I argued that I would not have time to make the change and that it would make the character ridiculous. However, she insisted, but later, when the critics called attention to the error, she came to me and asked me to please 'wear open face.' I did not understand at first but soon learned from her wild gestures that she meant I was to wear no veil" (Whiffen, pp. 176-7). A small woman, Nazimova seemed to dominate the other characters in *Hedda Gabler*. When she later played Nora Helmer,* Nazimova seemed smaller than her normal five-feet-three. As Dame Edith Evans* later "assumed beauty," Nazimova said, "I make myself taller or shorter by thinking I am taller or shorter." Critic Arthur Ruhl described her Hedda as "a mermaid and a leopard."

On January 18, 1907, Nazimova played her first English-language Nora, and on September 23, 1907, she began a phenomenal run of sixty-five performances as Hilde Wangel* in *The Master Builder*, her study of which had consumed three years. On April 18, 1910, she opened the Nazimova Theatre as Rita Allmers* in *Little Eyolf*, which garnered an excellent forty-eight performances. The thirty-nine-year-old actress opened as Hedvig Ekdal* on March 11, 1918. Her Ibsenian repertory was now nearly complete, but she returned to these roles often during her career.

Nazimova left the stage between 1916 and the early 1920s, with a few exceptions, to devote herself to making films. Her own production company filmed *A Doll's House* in 1922. When she later returned to the stage, Nazimova appeared in *Ghosts** in 1935, and on November 16, 1936, she staged a bizarre production of *Hedda Gabler*. She updated Ibsen's script and throughout stressed youthfulness. She was a highstrung, neurotic Hedda married to a young graduate student. Lövborg* was a young and lusty poet, while Brack* was youngish and lustful. This production lasted thirty-two performances.

Between 1906 and 1936 Nazimova established herself as one of America's most distinguished exponents of Ibsen's heroines, second only to Minnie Maddern Fiske.*

References: McKerrow, Margaret. "A Descriptive Study of the Acting of Alla Nazimova." Unpublished doctoral dissertation, University of Michigan, 1974; "Nazimova Theatre Opened by Herself: *Little Eyolf*," *New York Times*, Apr. 19, 1910, p. 9, col. 1; Whiffen, Blanche. *Keeping off the Shelf*. New York: E. P. Dutton, 1928.

NEMIROVICH-DANCHENKO, VLADIMIR (1858-1943): Nobly born and well-educated in Russia, Nemirovich-Danchenko worked as a playwright and journalist before accepting in 1891 a position as acting coach at the school run by the Moscow Philharmonic Society. Nemirovich-Danchenko admired Ibsen's works and staged *A Doll's House** with his students in 1896, a few months before he discussed with Konstantin

Stanislavsky,* then a thirty-four-year-old actor and director, the desirability of forming a theatrical enterprise through which they could pursue their radical plans for the reformation of the Russian theatre. The Moscow Art Theatre* was the result of their determination.

As literary adviser of the new organization, Nemirovich-Danchenko strongly urged the presentation of Ibsen's plays, a task that was not always easy because Stanislavsky was lukewarm to Ibsen's merits. Nemirovich-Danchenko prevailed, however, and personally directed *An Enemy of the People** (1900), *When We Dead Awaken** (1900), *The Pillars of Society** (1903), *Brand** (1906), *Rosmersholm** (1908), and *Peer Gynt** (1912). With Stanislavsky he shared the direction of *Ghosts** (1905).
Reference: Nemirovich-Danchenko, V. I. *My Life in the Russian Theatre.* Trans. John Cournos. Boston: Little, Brown and Company, 1936.

NEVITA (*Emperor and Galilean*): A general.

NEY, MARIE (b. 1895): Marie Ney acted the role of Helene Alving* in *Ghosts** at London's Vaudeville Theatre on November 8, 1937.
Reference: Who Was Who in the Theatre, III, 1798-1800.

NIELSEN, LARS (c. 1825-65): When Lars Nielsen took over J. A. Reimann's* apothecary shop in 1847, he indirectly bettered Ibsen's living conditions. Nielsen was kind to Ibsen and encouraged him to enjoy a social life.

NIEMANN-RAABE, HEDWIG (1844-1905): Wishing to include *A Doll's House** in her touring repertory, the popular German actress Hedwig Niemann-Raabe strongly objected to the ending of Ibsen's drama on the irrelevant pretext that in similar circumstances, she would not desert her children. Wilhelm Lange, Ibsen's publisher and literary agent, told the dramatist that a happy ending of the play was demanded, and, rather than trust the skill of another writer, Ibsen himself composed a short alternative ending:

NORA: That our life together would be real wedlock. Good-bye. (*She is about to go.*)
HELMER: (*Takes her by the arm.*) Go, if you must, but see your children for the last time.
NORA: Let me go. I don't want to see them. I cannot.
HELMER: (*Draws her toward the door at the left.*) You must see them. (*Opens the door and says softly.*) Do you see,—there they sleep carefree and quietly. Tomorrow when they awaken and call for their mother, they will have none.
NORA: (*Trembling.*) No mother. . . .
HELMER: As you have had none.
NORA: No mother! (*Struggles within, lets her bag fall and says:*) Oh, I am sinning against myself, but I cannot leave them. (*She sinks down at the door.*)
HELMER: (*Happy, says softly:*) Nora!
    (*The curtain falls.*) [Eller, p. 39].

This is the version which Niemann-Raabe played despite Ibsen's calling it a "barbarous outrage" against his drama. Ibsen also made the altered ending available to Heinrich Laube of the Vienna Stadttheater but advised him not to use it.

References: Eisenberg, Ludwig. *Grosses Biographisches Lexikon der Deutschen Bühne in XIX. Jahrhundert* (Leipzig: Paul List, 1903), pp. 726-7; Eller, William H. *Ibsen in Germany 1870-1900.* Boston: Richard G. Badger, 1918.

NIETZSCHE, FRIEDRICH WILHELM (1844-1900): Toward the end of Ibsen's life, the notions of German philosopher Friedrich Nietzsche were coming into considerable currency. Nietzsche wrote of the earth-shaping influence of the superman whose exertions were so much more important than those of the mass of people. If humanity is to progress, he stipulated, it will be through the efforts of the superman rather than through the democratic process. Through his own energy, imagination, and bold deeds, the superman gives color and meaning to ordinary existence although he may break laws and flout conventions in his zeal for achievement. Clearly, Ibsen presaged the Nietzschean superman in Brand.* In *An Enemy of the People** Ibsen lamented that the majority is always wrong. John Gabriel Borkman* is a perverted superman whose dreams of a life of invigorating labor are hollow because they lack love. Halvard Solness* is another superman gone wrong. As a child Solness believed that his was to be a great destiny, and from the time of the burning of his house and the deaths of his children, Solness dedicated his life to the building of towers for the glory of God. Yet, he eventually yearned for independence even from the claims of the Ideal. With Hilde Wangel's* inspiration, Solness turns from building earthly houses to erecting castles in the air. Solness sacrifices his life in an affirmation of the absolute in human endeavor. Thus, there is considerable affinity between the thought of Ibsen and that of Nietzsche.

Reference: Kaufman, Michael W. "Nietzsche, Georg Brandes, and Ibsen's *The Master Builder,*" *Comparative Drama,* 6 (1972), 169-86.

NIKOLAS ARNESSON, BISHOP OF OSLO (*The Pretenders*): One of Ibsen's most intriguing characters, Bishop Nikolas is the incarnation of evil. During the strife between Haakon* and Skule* over the legitimate rule of Norway, Nikolas stands as an obstacle to rapprochement, which, to Nikolas, would represent a diminution of his influence. He is a tale-bearer and a false counselor, all for the sake of creating turmoil. Even on his deathbed, Nikolas dreams of a perpetual motion machine, a metaphor for continued dissension and strife. Late in the play, the ghost of Nikolas returns to spur Skule on to greater disaster.

NISSE: A goblin, as in *St. John's Night.** In Norse mythology, the nisse is usually short, gray-clad, and wears a red stocking cap. The nisse belongs to "a class of household spirits . . . he is both helpful in the house and barn, and annoyingly exacting. He is fed and fortified by the house-dwellers" (Leach, p. 794).

Reference: Leach, Maria, ed. *Standard Dictionary of Folklore, Mythology and Legend.* New York: Funk and Wagnalls, 1972.

NISSEN, HERMANN (1855-1914): Actor Hermann Nissen was the first John Gabriel Borkman* in Berlin (1897).
Reference: Brockhaus Enzyklopaedie (Wiesbaden, 1971), XIII, 487.

NORMA (1851): *Norma* is a one-act travesty on the Storthing, the Norwegian Parliament; it was never produced. The members of Parliament are represented by a chorus of Druids; the Government, by Adalgisa*; and the Opposition, by Norma.*
Reference: McLellan, Samuel G. ''Rhyme and Reason in Ibsen's *Norma*,'' *Comparative Drama*, 14 (1980-81), 321-31.

NORMA (*Norma*): Norma (the Government) has two children by Severus,* a politician. After chastising Severus for abandoning his children (votes of No Confidence), Norma asks the stage manager to drop the curtain on the perfidy of Severus.

NORREYS, ROSE (1862-1946): Rose Norreys played one performance as Nora Helmer* at London's Criterion Theatre in June 1891.
Reference: Reid, Erskine and Herbert Compton. *The Dramatic Peerage, 1891.* London: General Publishing Company, 1891.

NORWEGIAN SKIPPER (*Peer Gynt*): The captain of the vessel that takes Peer Gynt* home after his worldwide adventures.

THE NORWEGIAN SOCIETY: In 1859 Ibsen and Björnstjerne Björnson* formed the Norwegian Society to foster nationalistic programs, to encourage Norwegian actors, and to urge Norwegian actors not to perform in Danish theatres.

NORWEGIAN THEATRE (Bergen): Norway's first national theatre was opened on January 2, 1850, by Ole Bull,* the acclaimed violin virtuoso. Ibsen was hired by Bull, and on October 26, 1851, he assumed his duties as stage director of the new theatre. On November 6, Ibsen was confirmed as resident dramatic author. On October 6, 1852, he directed his first production. Subsequently, his plays *St. John's Night,* *The Burial Mound,* *Lady Inger of Österaad,* *The Feast at Solhoug,* and *Olaf Liljekrans** were performed in Bergen* under his direction. On August 4, 1857, he was officially separated from the Norwegian Theatre in Bergen.
Reference: Wiesener, A. M. ''Henrik Ibsen og Det norske Theater i Bergen 1851-57,'' *Bergens Historiske Forening,* 34 (1928), 5-52.

NORWEGIAN THEATRE (Christiania): The organization was founded in 1852 by Benedikt Klingenberg as a drama school; in 1854 it was renamed the

Norwegian Theatre (Christiania). On August 11, 1857, Ibsen joined the company as artistic director. Ibsen directed *The Vikings in Helgeland** there on November 24, 1858. In June 1862 the theatre was bankrupted, but the actors formed a corporation that enabled the doors to be kept open during the 1862-63 season. Since Ibsen was not part of the actors' arrangement, he became unemployed in June 1862.

Reference: Lund, Andhild. *Henrik Ibsen og Kristiania Norske Theater, 1857-63.* Oslo: n.p., 1925.

NUMA (*Emperor and Galilean*): A soothsayer.

O

OLAF LILJEKRANS: A three-act Romantic serious drama.

Composition: Started in summer 1856; finished in the autumn; published in 1902.

Stage history:

Jan. 2, 1857	Norwegian Theatre, Bergen* (2 perfs.)
June 18, 1911	Rehearsal Theatre, London

Synopsis: During Norway's Middle Ages, an old minstrel Thorgejr stands in the midst of mountainous terrain and listens to offstage choruses. The first chorus, sung by the household of Lady Kirsten Liljekrans, exhorts drowsing Christians to awaken from their enchantment. Arne of Guldvik's family, the second chorus, sings of its trek toward the wedding hall. Antiphonally, Lady Kirsten's group warns against the evil influences of the elves of the forest. Then Thorgejr disappears as the two groups of singers come nearer, Arne's full of joy, Kirsten's full of lamentation. Apostrophizing Olaf Liljekrans, they wonder why his sleep has been so chronic and deep.

The actual appearance of Arne and his kinsmen opens the second scene; their mien is decidedly festive. Arne's page, Hemming, enters and is asked by his master to point the way, for they are lost. Seeing a derelict bridge across the river, Hemming directs them to cross it. Once on the other side, Arne recognizes the river as the boundary between his property and that of Lady Kirsten to whose son he is marrying Ingeborg his daughter; they are now en route to the bridal house. Hemming expresses reservatons about the alliance because of Kirsten's noble birth, but Arne thinks his wealth is more than a match for her nobility. Upon learning from Hemming that the local people believe that Arne sacrificed his legal rights to arrange the match, Arne becomes angry and derides the lampoon at his expense that is currently being circulated. In order to save face with his followers, Arne exaggerates the esteem in which Lady Kirsten holds him and expects

Hemming to agree with his fantasies. At this point, the lady herself enters.

Lady Kirsten starts, for she had not expected to see Arne; when she recovers her composure, she is relieved that he is still unaware of something that makes her anxious. Arne thinks that Kirsten and her people have trekked out into the woods to welcome him and boorishly speaks of the gossip that the approaching wedding is one of convenience. Then he takes the opportunity to warn Lady Kirsten that Ingeborg is at times moody and fanciful. In an aside Kirsten implies that her son is also like that. This idea is not developed because Ingeborg comes riding up at the head of her retinue, but, Kirsten asks, where is Olaf? Ingeborg also notes and asks about Olaf's absence. Kirsten is forced to admit that Olaf is not with her because he has gone out hunting. She tries to evade Ingeborg's curiosity by suggesting that everyone adjourn to the banquet hall, but Arne will not be put off because he realizes that Kirsten is masking her true intentions. Under Arne's pressure, Kirsten declares that the wedding cannot occur tomorrow as planned. Arne's men excitedly draw their swords, which prompts reciprocal actions by Kirsten's retainers, but before they can start the fray, Kirsten interjects herself between the factions and begs Arne to listen to her explanation. He reluctantly agrees. The wedding has been postponed neither because of Kirsten's want of wealth nor because she has changed her mind. The simple fact is that Olaf has fled from home. Arne, remembering his family's long feud with Kirsten's angrily says that Kirsten must answer for her son. Hemming urges Arne to break the engagement, but Arne will not listen. Kirsten finally reveals that Olaf is troll-struck, that his condition dates from the engagement party three weeks earlier. After the celebration, he did not return home until morning; looking pale and withdrawn, he had lain abed all day and rushed off to the mountains at night. She is certain that Olaf, now missing for three days, is bewitched. Her search for her son accounts for her presence on the mountain.

Seeing Thorgejr, Arne decides to ask the minstrel if he has seen Olaf. Thorgejr answers that Olaf is with the elves and will not be harmed. As if in a trance, he sings a song about sleeping on the mountain and being bewitched by the elves who destroyed his memory. Recovering himself, Thorgejr says that he is going to Olaf's wedding in the mountain. He warns them about staying on the mountain at night and then withdraws saying he will greet Olaf in the elves' hall.

Ingeborg declares that she will not marry Olaf if he has been bewitched, which pleases Hemming. Arne sends his own and Lady Kirsten's people in search of Olaf, and he is led off by the woman. Only Hemming and Ingeborg remain.

She commands him to fasten her shoe buckles, and as he does so, Ingeborg taunts Hemming with her attraction to Olaf. He recalls another afternoon he had spent with her in pursuit of a lost goat; then she had been so kind to him that he had hoped that she might actually love him. Rather than continue the conversation, she sends Hemming in search of Olaf, but

before he leaves, Ingeborg calls him back and admits that she does care for
him. He vows to carry her off that very night, but she does not take him
seriously.

Ingeborg leaves, and while Hemming is admiring the bracelet she gave
him, Olaf emerges from the forest looking dazed and acting distrait.
Hemming talks to Olaf and discovers that he is addled from playing the
elfin game for three nights. Now he hears spirit music and sees visions of
maidens arising from the mist and knows that his bride's approach is
imminent. Olaf tells Hemming about his initial adventure with the elves
following his engagement celebration, as a result of which he will soon
marry an elfin maiden. Hemming goes out to tell Lady Kirsten.

Olaf wanders about in search of the loveliest flower, the petals of which he
has been instructed to pluck and scatter in the wind as a means of divining
happiness. While he is thus engaged, Alfhild, dressed in flowers, enters and
rushes toward him. As they talk, it is plain that Olaf thinks that Alfhild is
an elf, but she disclaims it. Olaf tells her how he had gotten lost in an
enchanted valley where, weary, he had fallen asleep. As he slumbered, the
elfin maidens had danced about him, and one of them, Alfhild, was so
beautiful that he was immediately besotted by her, the result of which was
an alienation from his home in the real world and an attraction to the elfin
kingdom. Still, Alfhild denies that she was ever involved. She tells him how
she had amused herself by dreaming of the lords and ladies of her father's
minstrel songs, the very songs Olaf had heard as he rode alongside the river.
The minstrel had sung of a handsome knight, a knight whom Alfhild now
recognizes as Olaf. She begs him to describe his home, family, and friends,
but Olaf is unable to do so because the elves have stolen his memory of
them. He barely remembers the location of his home, so together they travel
to a ledge by a waterfall from which they can look down on his former
world. Offstage are heard the voices of Lady Kirsten's men singing a
warning about the treacherous elves.

Hemming enters with Lady Kirsten, whom he has fetched to the place
where he left Olaf. Olaf was waiting for his bride, Hemming says, but not
for Ingeborg. As they look toward the horizon, Olaf and Alfhild are seen
gazing down upon the village; then they disappear. Kirsten sends Hemming
for Arne and his men; she intends to rescue Olaf. Left alone, Kirsten
wonders if Olaf has really been ensnared by elves, a view that seems
superstitious to her. She considers the possibility that Alfhild is a flesh and
blood enchantress. Then Kirsten hurriedly exits. The chorus of wedding
guests is heard offstage.

Olaf enters with Alfhild, who begs him to tell her more of his previous
life, but he is more interested in declaring his love to her. He passionately
takes leave of his former life and vows to make his marriage bed here in the
mountains. When Olaf embraces her, Alfhild draws back. Olaf's mind is
awhirl with undigested bits of memory. Was his intention to take her as his
bride back to the village? Had they been engaged three weeks ago? The

offstage chorus sings his name and says, "Why sleep you so long and so heavy?" Olaf starts at the sound, for he knows that it will summon him to his previous life below.

Unseen, Lady Kirsten enters and listens to the wild exultation of Olaf as he speaks of his magnificent wedding to Alfhild. Again the chorus is heard in the forest but much closer than before. Joyfully, Alfhild shouts that the wedding guests are coming as Kirsten rushes towards Olaf. She is unseen by Alfhild, who scans the forest for the approaching company. Kirsten tells Olaf that Arne is coming with Ingeborg, his wife, but Olaf will have none of it. He laments that her coming has awakened him from a beautiful dream.

Arne's men and Kirsten's retinue come onto the stage and see Olaf, who, as his mother explains, has been lost. Arne questions the presence of Alfhild, but Kirsten says that she is merely one of the people who have lived in the mountains since the time of the great plague. Arne wishes to continue the wedding ceremonies, but Olaf declines to leave Alfhild. Kirsten says that Alfhild must join them as she had faithfully nursed Olaf when he was lost; naturally, Ingeborg is not pleased by this decision. Kirsten solemnly swears that the wedding will take place on the next day. Hemming, still confident of Ingeborg's love of him, fondles the bracelet she gave him, but she sees him doing so and confiscates it, leaving Hemming amazed.

Everyone exits except Alfhild, who has stolidly watched the preceding events. As if waking from a dream, she realizes that she is to be the bride and must join the wedding party, but as she starts to go, Thorgejr enters and learns of her plan to join Olaf in the village. He tries to dissuade her but finally sends her off with his blessing and the warning that he will always watch over her. She jubilantly rushes out speaking of her wedding day while a troubled Thorgejr looks on thoughtfully.

Act II takes place in the courtyard of Lady Kirsten's estate where preparations for the wedding feast are afoot. Kirsten is busy directing servants and doing various chores herself. In the midst of her plans, she is still worried that something is amiss with Olaf, who enters mournfully in his festive clothes. He is still dejected over leaving the mountain and Alfhild. Kirsten tries to interest him in the events of the day, but Olaf simply remarks that the gathering storm is a sign that the gods do not approve of his marriage. He asks his mother how she would have reacted if he had married a poor man's daughter, only to learn that she would have cursed him and died of grief. Ingeborg's dowry is of great importance to her. Olaf seems so distracted that he cannot quite fathom that he is to marry Ingeborg, not Alfhild. Kirsten accuses him of being bewitched, to which Olaf agrees. Kirsten explains that she will be financially ruined if she cannot get her hands on Ingeborg's dowry, and that Olaf must, therefore, put Alfhild out of his mind and marry Ingeborg. She charges him to explain this to Alfhild and offer her money if she will leave quietly; then she exits.

Olaf broods about Alfhild's unhappiness when he tells her to go, but then he recalls his responsibilities to his family. As he considers his dilemma,

Alfhild enters from the church. She rushes into his arms, telling him of all the wondrous things she has seen in his home. Her joy in the discovery of these new things makes Olaf more miserable, but he knows that he must send her away. The scene is lengthened by Olaf's inability to deliver his blow as Alfhild rhapsodizes on her wedding day. Separation, he feels, would be death, a subject known to Alfhild only through romantic minstrel songs. A chorus of pallbearers brings a dead child to the graveyard. Still he cannot bring himself to cause Alfhild any distress, and when he sees his mother, Olaf rushes toward the house but is stopped by Kirsten. The lowering storm is about to break as the wind stirs the treetops and the sky is darkened by clouds. Olaf tells his mother that she must send Alfhild away, that he can never see her again.

Uncertain of how much Olaf has said to Alfhild, Kirsten speaks to her of Olaf's wedding, but Alfhild thinks she means Alfhild's nuptials as well. Misunderstanding Alfhild's responses, Kirsten concludes that Alfhild means to stay on after Olaf's wedding to tempt him. Kirsten promises her a wedding in the church that very night, but her intention is to marry Alfhild to another man. She sends Alfhild into the house to put on Kirsten's own wedding dress. Left alone, Kirsten is furious that Alfhild would marry the first man proposed by Kirsten. She can hardly wait to show Olaf the sort of woman he had loved, but the first task is to find a man to marry Alfhild. She settles on Hemming, who then enters.

Musing about Ingeborg's mercurial treatment of him, Hemming is greeted by Kirsten, who tells him that she knows he is enamored of a beautiful lady and she of him. Hemming, confused, thinks she means Ingeborg. When Kirsten says that she understands that he wishes to be the bridegroom at tonight's wedding, he admits that he has struggled against his growing love as has the lady in question. Kirsten believes he refers to Alfhild, which explains her readiness to marry. Telling Hemming that she will assist him in achieving his desire, Kirsten agrees to keep Olaf from interfering. When Hemming wonders what Arne's reaction will be, Kirsten volunteers to convince Arne and even to pay a suitable dowry since Hemming has no money. He promises to keep silent about these plans and to remain near Lady Kirsten. While she searches for Alfhild, Hemming rejoices in his good fortune but realizes that Kirsten, for some reason, wishes to break her agreement with Arne.

At that point Arne shouts offstage for Hemming, whom Kirsten sends to his master after telling him that everything will be arranged. The lady is left alone to consider the ramifications of her plan: Alfhild's duplicity in declaring her love of both Olaf and Hemming; Hemming's inexplicable belief that marrying Alfhild would separate him from Arne's service; Olaf's almost certain acceptance of the inevitable because Alfhild affronted his honor. Then she exits.

Hemming and Arne enter and drink ale surreptitiously while Arne speaks of his wish quickly to leave Kirsten's house, where he is subject to condescending jeers, foreign food, and sweet wine. He is further affronted because his gift of ale has been dispensed to the servants. Both Arne and his page reminisce about the sweetness of their former life with Ingeborg at home. Hemming is trying to shift the conversation toward his own interest in Ingeborg; then he says that Olaf is more interested in Alfhild than in Ingeborg. Arne derides him for his jealousy and refuses to believe Hemming, who even has dared to think that it was remotely possible that Ingeborg should care for him. This ironic confrontation is interrupted by the entrance of Lady Kirsten and the wedding guests who assemble in the courtyard.

Kirsten decides not to tell Olaf about Alfhild until after she is married to Hemming. Hemming meets Ingeborg and hints to her that Kirsten will arrange everything for their happiness, a revelation that mystifies the young woman. Olaf asks his mother about Alfhild and learns that she is happy and gay about the evening's events. Kirsten addresses Arne in joyous terms about the wedding and suggests that they seal their bond with a toast. Hemming is alarmed and fears that Kirsten has lied to him. Kirsten prompts Arne to promise again that the family feud is forever laid to rest as well as all demands for the restitution of property damaged in the past. The wedding party, partisans of Kirsten and Arne, congenially seals the pledge. Hemming in a whisper accuses Kirsten of betraying him, but she continues to win Arne's agreement that there will be no further boundary disputes. Finally, he vows to bestow upon the newly married couple a handsome dowry, after which Kirsten bids the bridal couple to attend the feast and then go to church. This display causes Arne to believe that Hemming's warning about Kirsten's duplicity was incorrect, but it makes Hemming despair and feel betrayed.

Kirsten, taking advantage of the happy moment, asks a favor of Arne: his consent to the marriage of Hemming and Alfhild. Ingeborg and Olaf are startled to hear this, and the guests are amazed. Olaf tells his mother that he will not allow her to bestow Alfhild, and Arne deduces from Olaf's agitated concern that Hemming was correct in saying that Olaf was more than passingly interested in Alfhild. Arne has penetrated Kirsten's plan, which she denies, but he concludes that he is justified in breaking the engagement. The two start to whisper animatedly while Ingeborg tells Hemming that he must make an open declaration. When he is unable to do so, she vows to do it herself, calling Alfhild "another man's wench." The guests are scandalized, and Olaf concludes that he is cursed and Alfhild disgraced. From Ingeborg's daring speech, Kirsten concludes that she loves Hemming, a situation that places Arne in forfeiture of his promise. It is now Kirsten who has the right to break the agreement. Since they are at a stalemate, Kirsten and Arne decide to keep the agreement in force, as Olaf will now, according to Kirsten, lose interest in a disgraced woman and pursue his marriage to Ingeborg.

Alfhild enters resplendent in a handsome wedding dress, and Kirsten

invites everyone to the feast. Both young women take Olaf by the hand as
the right of the bride. Kirsten tells Alfhild that Olaf is not her groom; then
she demands that Olaf tell her the same. After a period of inner struggle,
Olaf tells Alfhild that he will marry Ingeborg. The girl is dumbfounded and
then shattered as he tells her to leave, to return to the mountain. As he
offers her gold to leave, she strips off her bridal crown and jewels and lays
them at his feet, staring at him all the while. Alfhild sinks to the ground as
Olaf shouts his commitment to Ingeborg. He becomes more and more
frenzied, verbally abuses her, and invites any of the guests, particularly his
mother, to follow suit. By now Alfhild is supine. Lightning flashes and
thunder rolls as the whole scene darkens and the storm increases in fury. By
now Olaf vehemently urges the guests to drink, to celebrate, to light the
candles in the church, and to dance. The thunder answers his cries as he
dashes out. Kirsten is unmoved as she believes that Olaf's madness will soon
pass. Everyone withdraws except Hemming and Ingeborg, who tells the
young man that she will run away with him as she cannot marry Olaf
Liljekrans.

After their exit, Alfhild rises from the ground and laughs nervously
because of her grief. It has grown quite dark as she steals to the window of
the house, from which the sounds of reveling guests emanate. Unseen by
Alfhild, Hemming slips in to warn Ingeborg that the horses are saddled and
waiting. Standing in the wind and rain, Alfhild makes a pitiful spectacle in
comparison with the celebrants inside, but she says that her outer disarray is
nothing compared with her inner torment. She vows to remain with Olaf no
matter how he treats her. Servants enter on their way to the church to light
the bridal torches for the procession, and they cannot be stayed, although
Alfhild pleads with them to delay the ceremony until the next day. They
invite her to bear a torch as well; she assents in the belief, mocked by the
servants, that when Olaf sees her again, he will take her back. In her despair
Alfhild decides that she must die, as the heavens' fury increases. She then
hears organ music from the church, which increases her anxiety. In a rage of
unhappiness, she tosses her torch into the house and falls prostrate.
Hemming and Ingeborg appear as they make their escape; Hemming has
barred the doors of the house so that no one can prevent their departure to
Alfhild's valley. Alfhild meanwhile has rallied and gloats in her destructive
deed, saying, "The bride is burning on the bridegroom's arm!" Olaf is seen
at a hatch that he cannot open further. He offers her money to rescue him,
but Alfhild refuses and rushes off. Servants try their best to help as the roof
crashes in. Olaf, enveloped by flames, is the last sight as the curtain falls.

In Act III a roseate sunrise tints a mountain valley rife with flowers and
flowing water. Alfhild is discovered asleep near an overgrown hut. Olaf
enters, wearing a rough coat over his wedding clothes. He is searching for
Alfhild and is remembering his first encounters with her; he now intends to
confess his misdeeds against her. Thorgejr emerges from behind the hut and

greets Olaf. Thorgejr, it seems, is going below to the village. They talk cryptically and at cross-purposes about the events of last evening. Thorgejr intends to fetch his harp and sing at the wedding feast; with that in mind, he exits.

Left alone, Olaf deduces that Thorgejr is Alfhild's father. Then he sees Alfhild, who is in the throes of a terrible nightmare about last night's happenings. Waking, she sees Olaf and withdraws lest he do her further harm. He begs her forgiveness, but she thinks he is an imposter because her Olaf is dead by her hand. He tries to persuade her that, although the old Olaf is dead, he will stay by her side and bring her nothing but happiness, but Alfhild is irreconcilable in her sorrow. In her mind, she is already dead. She leaves Olaf to consider the full effect of what he has done. He too rushes off.

Ingeborg and Hemming enter in search of a place in which to live. The abandoned hut seems feasible, but Ingeborg is worried because she needs her clothes from home and servants to tend her. When she considers the hardships, she suggests that she should return to her father and that Hemming should be raised to knighthood because of valor in the wars. Then her father would agree to the match, but for the night they will remain here. Their idyll is interrupted by the sounds of an offstage chorus in pursuit of Alfhild. Frantically, they decide to hide in the hut. Hemming goes to fix the lock, and Ingeborg climbs the hill to keep watch.

Olaf enters without having found Alfhild as Ingeborg descends from the hill. They meet and are observed by Hemming. Olaf and Ingeborg argue about whom the search party is seeking and confess that neither really wanted to marry the other. They promise not to betray each other, and they part as good friends.

Kirsten, Arne, and their retainers enter in pursuit of Alfhild, whom Kirsten proposes summarily to punish on the spot where she will be discovered. She is incensed that Alfhild nearly killed the whole party, but Arne is more concerned that Ingeborg and Hemming might not have been able to escape the flames. Kirsten believes that the two eloped, but she does not tell this to Arne before everyone exits.

Alfhild enters, weary and distraught, bearing a bundle of her mother's belongings which she means to bury. While she soliloquizes, the sound of the elves' horn is heard several times. Her plan is to retreat to the icy heights of the mountain, but before she can go, Kirsten, Arne, and company enter and see her. Kirsten orders Alfhild to be bound while she accuses the girl of bewitching Olaf, then of blasphemy, and finally of holding Olaf prisoner after burning his house down. Alfhild's answers only further inflame Kirsten, who prepares to pass the death sentence on her when Olaf appears on a cliff unseen by anyone. Once he has realized what is in motion, he disappears. The girl is condemned to be cast off the cliff as a witch, and two men escort her to that place. Directly after Kirsten gives the order to push her over the edge, she decides to see if any poor man there will save Alfhild's life by swearing that she is innocent and marrying her. When given the chance to marry Alfhild, all the assembled men remain silent, but at the last moment, Olaf rushes in in his wedding clothes and proclaims he will marry her. Kirsten disowns Olaf for this disgraceful deed, but Alfhild is elated. When Kirsten sees how happy Olaf is, she relents and agrees to the marriage and even partially accepts Alfhild. Arne is still frantic at the loss of his daughter, but Olaf cheers him by saying that Ingeborg is alive and voluntarily dissolved her engagement to Olaf. Arne declares that any man to whom his daughter pledges her love will win his blessing and half his kingdom. Hearing this, Ingeborg and Hemming rush from the hut and claim their happiness.

Thorgejr with his harp in hand has already insinuated himself among the crowd and comes forth to sanction his daughter's marriage. Alfhild and Olaf vow to live on the mountain in perfect harmony until the time comes to ride to heaven on angels' arms.

Structural analysis: The unusual aspect of this drama is Ibsen's weaving the ballad into its structure. As a minstrel Thorgejr is an ideal character with which to render probable the use of the ballad form, but the numerous choruses contribute greatly to the plot as they provide exposition and advance the action. Ibsen's fascination with the mountains as a place of enchantment and potential harmony is clearly evident as well. Following his Scribean models, Ibsen constructed a plot unified by action:

Olaf meets Alfhild, falls in love, and takes her home with marriage in mind;

(as a result of which)

Olaf discovers that his mother's financial survival depends on her receipt of Ingeborg's dowry;

(as a result of which)

Olaf reluctantly agrees to marry Ingeborg but commissions Kirsten to break the news to Alfhild;

(as a result of which)

Olaf (falsely) discovers that Alfhild wants to marry Hemming;

(as a result of which)

Olaf sets the wedding rites in motion;

(as a result of which)

Olaf discovers through her elopement that Ingeborg loves Hemming;

(as a result of which)

Olaf goes in pursuit of Alfhild;

(as a result of which)

Olaf discovers he can save Alfhild's life by agreeing to marry her;

(as a result of which)

Olaf proclaims his love, wins his mother's approval, and covenants to live in harmony with Alfhild on the mountain.

OLAF TRYGGVASON: On October 15, 1849, Ibsen wrote to Ole Schulerud* that he had nearly finished the first act of a drama based on the deeds of Norse hero Olaf Tryggvason. For some reason he never completed the play.

OLD MAN OF THE DOVRË (*Peer Gynt*): The king of the trolls.* He is happy to wed his daughter to Peer Gynt,* provided the mortal agrees to view reality as a troll, but he becomes furious when Peer refuses to go that far. At the end of the play, the troll goes off to offer his services to the National Theatre.

OLD WOMAN WITH CORN-SACK: (*Peer Gynt*): Two such characters call for help to rescue Aase* from the roof.

OLIVE, EDYTH (c. 1872-1956): Cited as England's "only tragic queen," Edyth Olive's only foray into Ibsenian lands was the leading role in a production of *Lady Inger of Östraat** in London in 1906. *The Times* (London) critic noted that she performed the part "with just that combination of the heroic and the human that fits her so well for these parts" (Jan. 30, 1906, p. 7, col. 3). Olive often performed in Shakespearean dramas and Greek tragedies.
Reference: Who Was Who in the Theatre, III, 1840.

OLIVER, OLIVE (1871-1961): Olive Oliver was noted for her heavy, adventurous roles, some of which she played in support of Richard Mansfield.* For one performance in New York in 1904 she was Lona Hessel* to the Karsten Bernick* of Wilton Lackaye.*
Reference: Briscoe, Johnson. *The Actors' Birthday Book*, 2d ser. New York: Moffat, Yard, 1908.

OLIVIER, LAURENCE (1907-   ): It is unfortunate that Ibsen's works have not significantly attracted the interest of the century's finest actor, Laurence Olivier. When in 1944 Olivier and Ralph Richardson* inaugurated their distinguished management of the Old Vic (London), *Peer Gynt** was chosen as Richardson's primary vehicle, Olivier playing the small part of the Button-Molder.* After Olivier's performance as Titus Andronicus in 1955, Kenneth Tynan wrote, "All the grand unplayable parts, after this, are open to him: Skelton's Magnificence, Ibsen's Brand, Goethe's Faust—anything, so long as we can see those lion eyes search for solace, that great jaw sag" (Tynan, p. 105).

Olivier's first sortie into television drama was a controversial production of *John Gabriel Borkman** (November 19, 1958), which received one of the lowest ratings of the year. The star's performance was lauded in some critical quarters, but the drama's lack of humor depressed the television audience.

As director of the National Theatre of Great Britain, Olivier stepped into a production of *The Master Builder** on November 17, 1964, as a permanent replacement for Michael Redgrave.* His Solness* was praised for its truthful naturalness. During Olivier's tenure at the National, Ingmar Bergman's version of *Hedda Gabler** appeared with Maggie Smith* in the leading role.

In his autobiography Olivier writes of performing in Ibsen's plays: "Ibsen's dialogue on the surface gives the impression of honesty and candor, but underneath is a subtext of evil sexuality, elaborately wrapped in symbols" (Olivier, p. 269). It would appear that the prince of actors has been unable to escape the Freudian* tutelage of Ernest Jones whom he consulted about his epochal Prince of Denmark.

References: Cottrell, John. *Laurence Olivier.* Englewood Cliffs, N.J.: Prentice-Hall, 1975; Olivier, Laurence. *Confessions of an Actor.* New York: Simon and Schuster, 1983; Tynan, Kenneth. *Curtains.* New York: Atheneum, 1961.

OLLOVICO (*Catiline*): Envoy of the Allobroges to Rome.

O'NEIL, NANCE (1874-1965): In November 1905 Nance O'Neil performed the role of Hedda Gabler* four times in New York.

Reference: Browne, Walter, and E. D. Koch. *Who's Who on the Stage, 1908.* New York: B. W. Dodge, 1908.

ORANGIA: When Halvard Solness* and Hilde Wangel* spin their elaborate dreams of future happiness, Solness promises her a kingdom called Orangia, which sounds not very dissimilar from a fairy tale kingdom.

ORBECK, ANDERS (1891-1962): A Norwegian-American educator, Anders Orbeck published *Early Plays by Henrik Ibsen* in 1921. Donald Wolfit* used Orbeck's translation of *Catiline** in his production of 1936.

Reference: National Cyclopedia of American Biography (New York: James T. White, 1966), XLIX, 383.

ORDER OF VASA: A Swedish decoration, Ibsen's first, which was conferred upon him in 1869 by King Carl XV for his services to literature.

ORIBASES (*Emperor and Galilean*): A physician.

OTTMANN, VIKTOR (1869-1944): Viktor Ottmann, a writer of travel books, translated two of Ibsen's plays into German: *Hedda Gabler** (1891) and *The Master Builder** (1893).

Reference: Deutsches Literatur-Lexikon (Bern, 1956), III, 1964.

OUR LORD AND COMPANY: The original subtitle of *The League of Youth.** Ibsen omitted it at the suggestion of Frederik Hegel,* his publisher.

OVERSKOU, THOMAS (1798-1873): Danish actor and dramatist Thomas Overskou was chief instructor at the Royal Theatre, Copenhagen, in 1852 when Ibsen made his first continental journey. He hospitably demonstrated the inner workings of his theatre for the novice director.
Reference: Overskou, Thomas. *Af mit Liv og min Tid.* Copenhagen: n.p., 1868.

OWEN, REGINALD (1887-1972): A graduate of London's Academy of Dramatic Art, Reginald Owen had an active career on the stage before turning to films. In 1926 he played Alfred Allmers* in *Little Eyolf* in New York.
Reference: Who Was Who in the Theatre, III, 1860-61.

ÖRNULF OF THE FJORDS (*The Vikings in Helgeland*): An Icelandic chieftain, Örnulf is the father of Dagny* and the foster-father of Hjördis.* Örnulf has appeared in Helgeland to avenge himself on Gunnar* for abducting Hjördis. In doing so, he suffers the loss of his beloved son Thorolf* and his six brothers.

P

PAAL (*The Grouse in Justedal*): An old hunter.

A PAINTED WOMAN (*Emperor and Galilean*): One of the Roman crowd.

THE PALM TREE: Ibsen heard of a ship named *The Palm Tree* from Lars Nielsen,* his employer in Grimstad*; the apothecary's father had sailed in her. A ship by the same name figures in the action of *The Pillars of Society* * as the carrier of Dina Dorf* and Johan Tönnesen* to America.

A PARALYTIC MAN (*Emperor and Galilean*): One of the Roman crowd.

PARENTS OF THE BRIDEGROOM (*Peer Gynt*): Members of the wedding party.

A PARISH OFFICER (*Peer Gynt*): Local officer who threatens to arrest Peer Gynt* at the auction of his possessions.

PARKER, LOUIS NAPOLEON (1852-1944): Having missed the performances in London of *Quicksands* * (1880) and *Breaking a Butterfly* * (1884), Louis N. Parker, an English teacher and dramatist, discovered Ibsen in 1887 through occasional newspaper notices, presumably those of Edmund William Gosse* and William Archer.* He then studied Henrietta Frances Lord's* "very poor translation of *Ghosts* *" (Parker, p. 148) which "overwhelmed" him. Ibsen's latest drama *Rosmersholm* * had already been translated into German, once by Maria von Borch and another time by A. Zinck. Despite faulty German renderings, Parker considered *Rosmersholm* "the finest instance of modern stage technique" and "the only useful lesson in playwriting [he] ever had." Parker was so obsessed by the drama that he set about translating it into English, utilizing at first the

German versions, but when he sensed their inadequacies, he turned to the original and worked from that. As he later wrote, "I lived in and with *Rosmersholm* for a long time." His translation was brought out in 1889 "in a very limited edition" by Griffith, Farran and Company, thus becoming the earliest English version of the drama. It received "a kindly but puzzled welcome in the press" (Parker, p. 149).

After 1889 Parker became the author of numerous successful dramas such as *Disraeli* and *Pomander Walk* while retaining his position as director of music at the Sherborne School, Dorset, from 1873 to 1892. He was also an avid advocate of civic pageantry.

Reference: Parker, Louis N. *Several of My Lives.* London: Chapman and Hall, 1928.

PASSARGE, LUDWIG (1825-1912): After translating *Peer Gynt** and *Brand** into German in 1881 and 1882, respectively, Ludwig Passarge published *Henrik Ibsen.* Leipzig: Bernhard Schlicke, 1883.

Reference: Deutsches Literatur-Lexikon (Bern, 1956), III, 1984.

PASTENE, ROBERT: Robert Pastene's performance as John Gabriel Borkman* in New York in 1977 received tepid reviews.

Reference: New York Theatre Critics' Reviews, XXXVIII, 4 (Mar. 7, 1977), 353-5.

A PASTOR (*Peer Gynt*): The officiant at the funeral of the man who chopped off his finger to avoid military service.

PAULSEN, JOHN OLAF (1851-1924): J. O. Paulsen was a Danish writer who spent considerable time with Ibsen during his European exile. His accounts of the experience were published in 1906 and 1913 as *Samliv med Ibsen.* Paulsen later wrote a novel entitled *The Pehrsen Family* in which Ibsen saw his domestic life caricatured. The dramatist consequently severed his relationship with Paulsen.

Reference: Paulsen, John O. *Mine Erindringer* [*My Reminiscences*]. Copenhagen: Gyldendal, 1900.

PAXINOU, KATINA (1900-1973): Greek actress Katina Paxinou was an international performer in the 1930s. While appearing in London, Paxinou acted in Greek the leading roles in *John Gabriel Borkman** (1933) and *Ghosts** (1933) and the Green-Clad Woman* in *Peer Gynt** (1935). Once she learned English, Paxinou played Helene Alving* in London on May 30, 1940; she made her American debut in English as Hedda Gabler* in New York on January 29, 1942. Paxinou convinced audiences that she could rise to tragic heights, yet her dark, brooding appearance and her Greek accent when she spoke English destroyed the dramatic probability that she could be a Scandinavian. Her Hedda Gabler lasted only twelve performances. Paxinou had a distinguished film career in addition to her work on the stage.

References: New York Times, Jan. 30, 1942, p. 22, col. 2; *Who's Who in the Theatre,* 11th ed., p. 1146.

A PEASANT (*Brand*): With his son, the Peasant attempts to guide Brand* through a treacherous mountain defile but turns back when the danger seems too great.

PEER GYNT: A five-act Romantic serious drama in verse.

Composition: Started on June 14, 1867; finished on October 14, 1867; published on November 14, 1867.
Stage history:

Feb. 24, 1876	Christiania Theatre* (37 perfs.), pro. Ludvig Oscar Josephson*
1886	Dagmars Theatre, Copenhagen
Mar. 9, 1892	Christiania Theatre, Björn Björnson* as Peer
1892	Stadttheater, Gothenburg
1895	Norwegian Theatre, Bergen*
1895	Stockholm
1895	Trondhejm
Nov. 12, 1896	Théâtre de l'Oeuvre, Paris
1900	Royal Theatre, Stockholm (4)
1902	Deutsches Volkstheater, Paul Wiecke as Peer
Sept. 13, 1902	Schauspielhaus, Munich, Colla Jessen* as Peer
Nov. 30, 1905	Prinzregenten Theater, Munich, Paul Wiecke as Peer
Mar. 22, 1906	Hoftheater, Munich, Hans Salfner as Peer
Oct. 29, 1906	Grand Opera House, Chicago, Richard Mansfield* as Peer
Feb. 25, 1907	New Amsterdam Theatre, New York (22), Richard Mansfield as Peer
Feb. 26, 1911	Rehearsal Theatre, London, Pax Robertson as Peer
Apr. 30, 1911	Rehearsal Theatre, London, Pax Robertson as Peer
Oct. 9, 1912	Art Theatre, Moscow, dir. Vladimir Nemirovich-Danchenko*
Dec. 15, 1916	Residenz Theater, Munich, Albert Steinruech* as Peer
Mar. 6, 1922	Old Vic Theatre, London, Russell Thorndike* as Peer
Feb. 5, 1923	Garrick Theatre, New York (120), Joseph Schildkraut* as Peer
Sept. 23, 1935	Old Vic Theatre, London, William Devlin as Peer
Apr. 1936	National Theatre, Oslo, Johanne Dybwad* as Aase
May 4, 1936	Sadlers Wells Theatre, London, William Devlin as Peer
Aug. 31, 1944	New Theatre, London, pro. Old Vic Company, Ralph Richardson* as Peer
Jan. 28, 1951	ANTA Playhouse, New York (32), John Garfield* as Peer
Jan. 12, 1960	Phoenix Theatre, New York (32), Fritz Weaver* as Peer
Sept. 26, 1962	Old Vic Theatre, London, Leo McKern* as Peer
July 8, 1969	Delacorte Theatre, New York (19), Stacy Keach* as Peer
1970	Festival Theatre, Chichester, Roy Dotrice as Peer
Nov. 8, 1981	CSC Repertory Theatre, New York (47)

Synopsis: Act I, Scene 1. Peer Gynt, a hardy youth of twenty, and his mother Aase are engaging in a family quarrel as they walk through their wooded farm. Aase accuses Peer of lying, yet he maintains the veracity of his tale about his hunting a reindeer upon whose back he rode along a mountain ridge and into a lake. The tale is hair-raising and excites the mother's fear for her son until she remembers having heard of the identical exploit years ago. Peer has been spinning a tall tale, highly characteristic of him. Aase laments not only Peer's penchant for embroidering the truth but also their poverty, which is the result of her husband Jon Gynt's wastrel ways and Peer's inability to take life's responsibilities seriously. Even in the face of his mother's distress, Peer makes jokes. Aase's major complaint is that Peer's erratic behavior has kept him from marrying a rich farmer's daughter, Ingrid, who tomorrow will wed the village simpleton. Peer undertakes to go to Haegstag to woo Ingrid, and when Aase threatens to tell everyone the truth about him, he puts her on the roof of the millhouse to keep her at home. After Peer marches off, some passersby help Aase down, and she rushes off in pursuit of her carefree son.

Act I, Scene 2. Peer walks along the road to Haegstag and considers what will happen when he gets to Ingrid's house. His insecurities become clear as he imagines that people will speak unfavorably of him. To bolster his ego Peer constructs an elaborate daydream about being Emperor, but his reverie is interrupted by the appearance of his arch-enemy, Aslak the blacksmith, who bested Peer in a brawl some six weeks earlier. Aslak taunts Peer with his knowledge that Ingrid used to be interested in him. As he watches Aslak walk away, Peer becomes despondent at his rags, but the sound of music and dancing lures him to the wedding feast.

Act I, Scene 3. At the celebration Peer's spirits plunge because no one will talk to him unless it is to tease him. He tries to win acceptance from the guests by telling tall tales, but that only increases his isolation and unhappiness. Aslak decides to teach Peer a lesson by thrashing him, but he is thwarted by the entrance of Aase who is prepared to do battle for her son. Meanwhile, Peer has encountered Ingrid, and soon the Bridegroom shouts as he and the company watch Peer's abduction of the bride and their flight over the hillside.

Act II, Scene 1. Peer and Ingrid walk along a mountain path. He has already tired of her because his mind is still attracted to Solveig, a girl he had met at the wedding feast. He says he will remain irrevocably true to Solveig, so Peer and Ingrid part.

Act II, Scene 2. Aase walks past a lake lamenting the onslaught of a storm that may harm her son. Solveig tries to keep up with the woman, who tells her what comfort she used to derive from Peer's tall tales as they sat at home while Jon Gynt dissipated their meager income. Aase is less displeased with Peer than some mothers might be because she sees that by abducting Ingrid at least he has taken decisive action. Solveig's parents come in and are soon enlisted in the search for Peer. Aase is pleased to accede to Solveig's request to hear everything about Peer.

Act II, Scene 3. Peer runs high in the mountains as he tries to elude his pursuers. He encounters three female cowherds who are invoking the company of trolls because their lovers have deserted them. The ever-amorous Peer delightedly agrees to be their troll and dances away with them.

Act II, Scene 4. At sunset a dizzy and confused Peer staggers in the high mountains. His life lately has been rather hectic, and he dreams of flying high to attain purity of soul. He amuses himself by remembering the time when the Gynts were rich and powerful and dreaming of his future greatness. In his frenzy he dashes forward, hits his head on a rock, and falls senseless to the ground.

Act II, Scene 5. It is night, and a Green-Clad Woman passes through a densely wooded patch and is followed by a romantically capering Peer. They discover that they have much in common, specifically a contrary view of reality that sees black as white, ugly as beautiful, and dirty as clean. She is the Troll-Kings's [see Old Man of the Dovrë*] daughter, and confident of having found a suitable consort, she summons her bridal steed, a gigantic pig, upon whose back the pair rides off.

Act II, Scene 6. Great confusion reigns in the hall of the Troll-King because a Christian man has defiled the inner precincts. All sorts of creatures menace Peer, who is saved by the intervention of the Troll-King. The ruler is not averse from enlisting Peer as a troll because their numbers have dwindled. He outlines the rules of trolldom, and Peer easily adopts them, even agreeing to wear a tail. When he hears the chief maxim of the trolls, "Troll-King insists, however, that Peer's vision must be modified so that he will see reality in the troll way, he reneges. When he is told that his mere desire for the King's daughter has impregnated her and he must therefore marry her, Peer refuses. As a result, he is set upon by hordes of trolls and is saved only by the distant tolling of church bells, which scatters the trolls as the palace collapses and everything disappears.

Act II, Scene 7. In the dark Peer confronts an amorphous blob called the Boyg, which will not let him pass. The Boyg repeatedly tells Peer to take the roundabout way, which figuratively is Peer's usual behavior. He challenges the Boyg to battle, but the blob conquers without fighting. Invoking Solveig's love, Peer lashes into the monster but cannot harm it. Peer is about beaten when the sound of church bells dissolves the Boyg.

Act II, Scene 8. Near Aase's hut Peer sees Solveig's sister who tells him that Solveig is behind the hut. Eager to see her, Peer starts to go around, but Solveig threatens to run away. Peer, incapable of direct action, bribes Helga the sister with a silver button to represent him to her sister and ask her not to forget him. Helga runs off.

Act III, Scene 1. Peer chops down trees and dreams of owning a fine house with a tower and weathervane, but the difficulty of the work makes him settle for a simple hut. He spies a young man in the process of chopping off his finger to escape military service. Peer admires the man's ability to follow through decisively; he himself might conceive the idea and earnestly wish to do it, but there he would fail.

Act III, Scene 2. Aase and Kari, a peasant-farmer's wife, are sorting through her scant possessions and packing up things to be surrendered to Ingrid's father in recompense for Peer's abduction. Aase says she wishes to mend some of Peer's socks before taking to her sickbed.

Act III, Scene 3. Peer is discovered putting the finishing touches to the hut that he will share with Solveig, who then enters declaring her love of him regardless of his past actions. His joy is complete but short-lived, for an old woman enters with an ugly brat, who are eventually revealed as the Troll-King's daughter and her son by Peer. She threatens to make his life execrable if he marries Solveig, and true to his nature, Peer chooses the roundabout way of dealing with the situation. He flees rather than tell the truth to Solveig.

Act III, Scene 4. Aase lies abed near death. When Peer comes, she feels she can die in peace. Rather than face the reality of death, Peer spins an elaborate fantasy about their riding in a glittering sleigh to a banquet in St. Peter's castle. Aase enters into the spirit of the game and quietly dies. Peer tells Kari to see that his mother is suitably buried because he must wander far abroad.

Act IV, Scene 1. A middle-aged Peer talks with some acquaintances on the southwest coast of Morocco. Now Peer is a wealthy man, having made his fortune by slave-trading. He has also sold idols to the Chinese and then sent missionaries to convert them from idolatry. He launches into elaborate praise and then an explanation of "the Gyntish self," which he describes as wishes, appetites, desires, fancies, exigencies, and claims. His friends, a rather disreputable lot, are content to go along with his extravagances, but when he says that he plans to assist the Turks in their war against the Greeks, they desert him and steal his ship that is anchored in the bay.

Act IV, Scene 2. Peer runs along the coast exceedingly excited about the theft of his ship, which suddenly explodes before his eyes. It was carrying gunpowder. Peer sees this as God's deliverance of him, for if he had been aboard, he too might have been destroyed by the explosion.

Act IV, Scene 3. A troop of Moroccan soldiers says that the Emperor's white horse and sacred robes have been stolen.

Act IV, Scene 4. Peer, roosting in a tree, tries to fight off a band of monkeys as he fumes about the indignity of being in such a position.

Act IV, Scene 5. The thief of the Emperor's goods and a receiver of stolen property are frightened into abandoning their spoils. Peer enters, talking to himself about the multiplicity of creation, sees the tethered horse and the sacred robes, clothes himself, and rides off into the desert.

Act IV, Scene 6. Peer sits in Arabian splendor in a tent near an oasis. A somewhat fat and dirty Anitra and other girls dance for his delight in exchange for which Peer gives her an opal from his turban while misquoting Goethe by saying, "The eternal feminine draws us upward and onward" rather than "The eternal feminine attracts us."

Act IV, Scene 7. Coyly, Peer acts as a suitor to Anitra, who eventually falls asleep as he utters longwinded love speeches. In gratitude Peer showers the sleeping girl with jewels.

Act IV, Scene 8. Peer and Anitra gallop across the desert on his white steed. Anitra petulantly spurns his advances and tricks him into dismounting and giving her all his jewels. Then she rides boldly away, having duped the Emperor of the Desert.

Act IV, Scene 9. An hour later Peer can be philosophical about Anitra's trick. Now he will devote himself to the study of history and relive all the glorious chapters of man's progress.

Act IV, Scene 10. A middle-aged Solveig sits before Peer's hut and sings confidently of his return.

Act IV, Scene 11. Standing before Memnon's statue in Egypt, Peer says he has become an Egyptian but will journey through the ancient civilizations of the Middle East. The statue begins to sing, a fact Peer duly notes in his pocketbook.

Act IV, Scene 12. Peer appears next at Gizeh, where he gazes on the Sphinx and equates it with the Boyg. From behind the Sphinx, Peer hears the voice of Doctor Begriffenfeldt, who is fascinated by Peer's certainty that he is himself.

Act IV, Scene 13. Begriffenfeldt leads Peer into Cairo's Insane Asylum, locks the keepers in cages, and throws the key into a well. Peer meets a language reformer, whom he counsels to emigrate; a fellah (peasant), whom he advises to hang himself; and a man who thinks he is a pen, whom Peer urges to slit his throat. After this, Begriffenfeldt crowns Peer the Emperor of Self.

Act V, Scene 1. An elderly Peer is on a ship in the North Sea and homeward-bound. He decides to give presents to the sailors but becomes infuriated when he hears that they all have homes and families, of which Peer has none. Now all he will give them is enough brandy to kill their memories of home. A wrecked boat with three survivors is sighted, but the captain will not dare to save them because of the storm-tossed seas. Peer sees this as proof that Christianity does not exist. A mysterious stranger approaches Peer and expresses his delight that this storm will result in numerous corpses. He asks that he be allowed to study Peer's body if he should be killed because he wants to explore man's capacity for dreaming. Peer dismisses him as a blasphemer. At that point the ship goes aground and sinks.

Act V, Scene 2. As Peer swims in the wreckage, a small boat floats toward him. The ship's cook comes up on the other side of the boat, and they fight for possession of the craft. Peer magnanimously holds the man by his hair until he can finish his prayers; then he lets him slide beneath the water. Once in the boat, Peer sees the strange passenger swimming by; he is asked again for his body. Then they speak of dread (perhaps in the sense of conviction of sin) and the victory that may come through it. When Peer expresses his fear of death, the strange one says that he will not die in the middle of Act V. Then he glides away.

Act V, Scene 3. Peer passes a cemetery as a funeral is being conducted. The departed one is the man who chopped off his finger to avoid the draft; in his eulogy the Pastor commends him as a good husband and father, saying that his insignificance became significant because he was himself. As Peer listens, he thinks it a nice custom to praise the dead, but he does not apply the lesson to himself.

Act V, Scene 4. Peer attends the auction of the remains of his estate, so he decides to contribute his rubbish to the sale: a castle in the mountains, his horse, a dream of a silver-clasped book (Solveig's), a crown of straw (given to him by Begriffenfeldt), and the Prophet's beard. Now that he has the attention of the crowd, Peer tells a parable about the devil who hid a pig under his clothes so that he could produce a credible imitation of a pig's squeal. At the proper moment, the devil pinched the pig, which squealed obligingly. Afterward there was much discussion of the performance, the consensus being that the imitation was exaggerated. The moral, says Peer, is that the devil failed to analyze his audience. Having said this, Peer strolls off, leaving the people in amazement.

Act V, Scene 5. As Peer forages for food in the forest, he comes upon an onion patch. As he peels an onion layer by layer, he analogizes each with one of his careers; and just as the onion has no core, neither does his life. Peer looks around, spies Solveig's house, and hears her voice. This brings on the terror, the conviction, and the realization that "here was my Empire." He runs off into the woods.

Act V, Scene 6. As he stumbles through a field devastated by fire, Peer sees threadballs as the thoughts he never had, withered leaves as the watchwords he should have spoken, the whispering breeze as the songs he should have sung, and the dewdrops as his unshed tears. Broken straws are the deeds he never accomplished. Aase's voice says that he drove her to the wrong castle. Again he runs away.

Act V, Scene 7. Peer is menaced by a Button-Molder whose task it is to melt down the souls of people who have been only moderately good and tolerably bad and to remold them. Peer begs for a little more time, so a rendezvous is set for the next crossroads.

Act V, Scene 8. Peer meets an old, abandoned man who turns out to be the Troll-King. When Peer asks for the King's affidavit that Peer never officially adopted the troll life, he infuriates the old monarch. He reminds Peer that whether or not he embraced trolldom, he became rich and powerful because he had lived up to the troll motto: to thyself be enough. He is, therefore, a troll in deed if not in name. The King calls Peer a Prince of Trolls. The old man goes off to offer his talents to the National Theatre.

Act V, Scene 9. Again Peer meets the Button-Molder, whom he asks,

"What does it mean to be oneself?" The answer is "to slay oneself" or to fulfill the divine plan. Again Peer gains a stay of execution, this time to get a parson to vouch for him.

Act V, Scene 10. Peer approaches a thin man in priestly garb but discovers a cloven hoof beneath the cassock. Peer asks him for help and is told that he is not sinful enough to merit attention. The Thin One reveals that he is searching for someone named Peer Gynt who is like a photographic negative rather than a positive picture. Peer says he met the man in question around the Cape of Good Hope, to which the Thin One eagerly departs. Dispirited by his loneliness, isolation, and lack of satisfaction, Peer writes his own epitaph: "Here No One lies buried." As he comes to a crossroads, Peer meets the Button-Molder, who is growing impatient. They walk on, approach Solveig's hut, and hear her singing. There, says Peer, he can get a list of his sins. Reluctantly, the Button-Molder agrees to meet at a third crossroads and then retires. As Peer walks closer to the hut, he remembers his inclination to go the roundabout way but determines this time to face his fate directly. He sees Solveig, throws himself at her feet, asks her to catalogue his sins, and is abashed when she says he has not sinned. From behind the house, the Button-Molder prompts him to get the list. Peer asks Solveig to solve the riddle of where he has been for so long; she simply states that he has been in her faith, hope, and love. Peer's face lights up as he sees that in Solveig resides everything to which he has been fleeing, the love of a mother and a wife. As Peer is cradled in Solveig's arms, the Button-Molder is forced to postpone the third rendezvous. The curtain falls.

Structural analysis: Ibsen called this work a dramatic poem and never intended it for production on the stage. Today there is general agreement that it stands in the front ranks of Norwegian poetry. As a poem it is extremely diverse, incorporating rhymed verse of great variety. *Peer Gynt* may also be viewed as a drama, and in comparison with numerous contemporary plays, it does not seem unnecessarily diffuse or distractingly episodic. The play clearly is unified by character as it chronicles Peer's long passage from ignorance to recognition of the nature of real individualism.

References: Edwards, Lee R. "Structural Analysis of *Peer Gynt*," *Modern Drama*, 18 (May 1965), 28-38; Konner, L. "Psychiatric Study of Ibsen's *Peer Gynt*," *Journal of Abnormal Psychology*, 19 (Jan. 1925), 373-82.

THE PEOPLE'S HERALD (Also translated *MESSENGER* and *COURIER*): A newspaper edited by Hovstad* in *An Enemy of the People** to which Thomas Stockmann* contributes his essay on the polluted water.

PEOPLE'S THEATRE (London): A subscription theatre modeled on the European *Volksbühne* idea, the People's Theatre was the inspiraton of A. E. Filmer, a former director of the Birmingham Repertory Theatre, who in 1923 desired to establish a theatre for the working classes. He enlisted the aid of Jacob Thomas Grein,* who had founded the Independent Theatre,* and eventually acquired the Pavilion Theatre in the Whitechapel district of London's East End. Included in the first month's repertory was a production of *Ghosts,** which opened in June 1923 with Ernest Milton* as Oswald Alving* and Lillebil Ibsen* as his mother. There had been some concern that the intellectual level of Ibsen's play might not suit its audiences, but, according to Grein (pp. 84-5), he "heard nothing but a mass of people listening intently with bulging eyes, some with open mouths, many leaning forward holding the back of the seat." Even children and babies sustained a respectful silence. "Then the curtain descended, and applause endless and thunderous, shouts frenetic and prolonged, rent the air and seemed to overwhelm Ernest Milton . . . who had to come out again and again and yet once more, a dozen times." The People's Theatre proved that there was an audience in the East End for "high-brow" drama, but the continuance of the company depended on subsidies of affluent subscribers. By February 1924 the People's Theatre was a thing of the past.

Reference: Grein, J. T. *The New World of Theatre 1923-1924.* London: Martin Hopkinson, 1924.

A PERSIAN DESERTER (*Emperor and Galilean*): An enemy spy who persuades Julian* to burn his ships and mount an impossible siege, which results in the rout of the Emperor's forces.

PETER (*The Pretenders*): The illegitimate son of Earl Skule* by Ingeborg,* Peter becomes a fierce partisan in his father's struggle for the throne, even going as far as to commit sacrilege by seizing a shrine from a church. In the end he sacrifices himself to the mob alongside his father.

PETERSEN, CLEMENS (1834-1918): In 1862 Danish critic Clemens Petersen encouraged Ibsen by writing a long review of *Love's Comedy** in the journal *Faedrelandet,* but he broke with the dramatist over the philosophy of *Peer Gynt,** which he condemned as imaginatively and poetically deficient. As Denmark's most influential critic, Petersen invested Ibsen's works with importance merely by noticing them.

Reference: Petersen, Clemens. "Theatret i Christiania," *Nordisk tidskrift för politik, ekonomie och litteratur,* II (1867), 19-40.

PETERSEN, LAURA KIELER (1849-1932): See Kieler, Laura.

PETERSEN, MORTEN SMITH (d. 1872): Petersen retired to Grimstad* in the 1840s, ran his aged mother's business, and finally closed it. He also started a shipyard and ran an insurance company. The parallels with Karsten Bernick* are clear.

PETTERSEN (*The Wild Duck*): Servant of Haakon Werle.*

PHANTOMS, OR THE SINS OF THE FATHERS: When Austrian actor Friedrich Mitterwurzer* acted in America in 1886-87, he performed this version of *Ghosts,** which he had translated into English from the German.

PHOCION (*Emperor and Galilean*): A dyer.

THE PILLARS OF SOCIETY: A four-act Realistic serious drama.
Composition: Conceived in December 1869; started in January 1870; finished on June 15, 1877; published on October 11, 1877.

Stage history:

Nov. 14, 1877	Odense
Nov. 18, 1877	Royal Theatre, Copenhagen (21 perfs.)
Nov. 30, 1877	Norwegian Theatre, Bergen*
Jan. 25, 1878	Belle-Alliance Theater, Berlin
Feb. 2, 1878	Stadttheater, Berlin
Feb. 3, 1878	National Theater, Berlin
Feb. 5, 1878	Residenz Theater, Munich
Feb. 6, 1878	Ostend Theater, Berlin
Feb. 6, 1878	Reunion Theater, Berlin
Feb. 8, 1878	Residenz Theater, Munich
Feb. 22, 1878	Stadttheater Lauber, Vienna
Nov. 6, 1878	Möllergaden Theatre, Christiania (in Swedish)
1878	Norwegian Theatre, Bergen (8)
1878	Nya Theatre, Gothenburg
Feb. 2, 1879	Stadttheater, Milwaukee (in German)
Mar. 9, 1879	Christiania Theatre* (21)
1879	Stadttheater, Berlin
1879	Volkstheater, Berlin
1879	Norwegian Theatre, Bergen
Dec. 15, 1880	Gaiety Theatre, London, as *Quicksands**, W. H. Vernon* as Bernick
1888	Stadttheater, Cologne
1888	Residenz Theater, Munich
1888	Hoftheater, Munich
Mar. 20, 1888	Christiania Theatre (7)
1889	Stadttheater, Cologne
Apr. 20, 1889	Deutsches Theater, Berlin
July 17, 1889	Opera Comique, London, W. H. Vernon* as Bernick
Dec. 1889	Amberg's Theatre, New York (in German)
Apr. 1890	Deutsches Volkstheater, Vienna
Oct. 19, 1890	Ostend Theater, Berlin, pro. Freie Volksbühne
1890	National Theatre, Budapest
1890	Hoftheater, Munich
Mar. 6, 1891	Harlem Opera House, New York, J. B. Studley as Bernick
Mar. 6, 1891	Lyceum Theatre, New York (1), George Fawcett* as Bernick
1891	Hoftheater, Munich
1891	Deutsches Theater, Berlin

1891   Hoftheater, Mannheim (2)
Jan. 1893   Rome
1893   Hoftheater, Munich
Oct. 29, 1894   Burgtheater, Vienna, Friedrich Mitterwurzer* as Bernick
Nov. 21, 1894   Christiania Theatre, (14)
1894   Berliner Theater
1895   Burgtheater, Vienna
June 23, 1896   Théâtre de l'Oeuvre, Paris
1896   Lessing Theater, Berlin
1896   Deutsches Theater, Berlin
1896   Schiller Theater, Berlin
1896   Hoftheater, Dresden
1896   Deutsches Volkstheater, Vienna
Sept. 24, 1897   Michail Theatre, St. Petersburg, Fedor Gorev as Bernick
1897   Burgtheater, Vienna
1897   Hoftheater, Stuttgart
1897   Pollinis Theater, Hamburg
1898   Schauspielhaus, Berlin
June 15, 1899   Christiania Theatre (5), Lucie Wolf* as Lona
1900   Hoftheater, Mannheim
May 12, 1901   Strand Theatre, London (1), Oscar Asche as Bernick
May 15, 1901   Garrick Theatre, London (1), Oscar Asche as Bernick
Feb. 24, 1903   Art Theatre, Moscow,* dir. Vladimir Nemirovich-Danchenko,*
            Konstantin Stanislavsky* as Bernick
Nov. 2, 1903   Hoftheater, Braunschweig
Apr. 15, 1904   Lyric Theatre, New York (1), Wilton Lackaye* as Bernick
Oct. 6, 1905   New Theatre, St. Petersburg, Lydia Yavorska* as Lona
Mar. 28, 1910   Lyceum Theatre, New York (16), Minnie Maddern Fiske* as Lona
June 1, 1926   Kammerspiele, Munich, Albert Bassermann* as Bernick
July 13, 1926   Royalty Theatre, London, Charles Carson* as Bernick
Aug. 5, 1926   Royalty Theatre, London, Charles Carson as Bernick
Oct. 14, 1931   48th Street Theatre, New York (10), Moffat Johnston* as Bernick
Feb. 1951   Cherry Lane Theatre, New York, pro. Globe Repertory Players
Aug. 1, 1977   Aldwych Theatre, London, pro. Royal Shakespeare Company, Ian
            McKellen* as Bernick

Synopsis: The entire action takes place in the conservatory of the house of Karsten Bernick, a successful entrepreneur of a coastal town of Norway. Betty Bernick, his wife, is entertaining several friends at a sewing party for charity as schoolmaster Rörlund reads in the background and thirteen-year-old Olaf Bernick plays in the garden. Aune, the foreman of Bernick's shipyard enters, knocks at the door of Bernick's study, and meets Krap, Bernick's assistant, who is leaving the study. Aune has an appointment with Bernick, but Krap has been delegated to advise Aune to stop making speeches that inflame the workers. As head of the Workmen's Federation, Aune believes he is bettering society by calling for improvement of working conditions at the shipyard, but Krap tells him that Bernick insists that

Aune's loyalty should be to him. Aune deduces that Bernick has lost his patience because some American customers have complained about the slow progress of repairs on one of their ships. Both Aune and Krap leave the scene.

Rörlund by now has finished his reading aloud, and he and the ladies start to discuss the moral implications of the book as well as the moral climate of their society. Rörlund advocates keeping the town untainted by outside influences, such as the American seamen who are momentarily in their midst. Mrs. Bernick opines that her husband had saved the town from another corrupting influence when he kept the railway out last year. Karsten Bernick's sister Martha, a schoolteacher, expresses the view that she would like to see more of the world, but Rörlund says that she is better off here in the midst of an exemplary familial environment than she would be in the unprincipled world.

Betty's cousin Hilmar Tönnesen comes in and tells the group that the railroad issue is still very much alive and that Bernick is meeting now with local tycoons to discuss it. He picks up Rörlund's book and labels it nonsense: *Woman as the Servant of Society.* When young Olaf enters to greet his uncle, Tönnesen jokingly suggests that the boy should go to America on one of his father's ships to have a real adventure. The boy likes the idea because there he might meet his Uncle Johan and Aunt Lona.

Once the boy has left, Rörlund chides Tönnesen for filling his head with such impractical ideas; Rörlund then suggests that Tönnesen should emigrate to America, but Tönnesen claims that his health would not permit it nor would his commitment to keeping the banner of the ideal flying in his own home town. Loud sounds emerge from the study and give rise to speculation as to the content of the discussion. The group reminisces about former times in the town, and it comes out that Mrs. Rummel had played a lover in one of Tönnesen's plays that was presented by the local dramatic society. There were also professional actors who visited the town, but several of the women squelch that train of thought. Betty asks Dina Dorf, who lives with the Bernicks, to ask the servant to serve tea on the porch.

Once Dina has left, Mrs. Rummel scolds Mrs. Lynge for mentioning the actors in front of Dina, who, it turns out, is the result of an illicit liaison between Johan Tönnesen, Betty's brother, and Mrs. Dorf, a married actress whose tour brought her to town. Johan was caught and ran away to America; soon after his departure, it was discovered that funds had been embezzled from Bernick's company, the restitution of which had almost bankrupted old Mrs. Bernick, Karsten's mother. When Dorf discovered his wife's behavior, he deserted her and her child. Mrs. Dorf died within a year, and young Dina Dorf came to live with the Bernicks. As the gossip continues, the subject of Betty's half-sister Lona Hessel is brought up. She had followed Johan into exile in America but not before she had scandalized the town by wearing bobbed hair and men's boots. She had further raised eyebrows by striking Karsten Bernick when he was introduced to Betty Tönnesen's guardian as her fiancé. Lona continued to embarrass the upstanding Bernick by singing in a saloon, giving public lectures, and writing idiotic books. Dina returns with the coffee, forcing the praters to desist. All the ladies go outside for refreshments, but when Dina settles at the table to her sewing, she is joined by Rörlund, to whom she confides her impression that the ladies had discussed her in her absence.

Dina is hurt by the realization because she sees herself as a moral cripple, as was her mother. People here treat her so delicately and pityingly that she yearns to go far away, although that would mean being separated from Rörlund whose company she enjoys and with whom she is in love. His position as a moral leader of society keeps him from openly avowing his love of her, but the day will come when they will marry. This intimacy is interrupted by the emergence of Rummel, Sandstad, and Vigeland, all businessmen.

They announce that the railway plan is going forward. Bernick explains that last year's proposed coastal line would not have benefited the community, but now that an inland line is in the offing, he can support it wholeheartedly and use his influence to get the local government to assist as well. Only Rörlund, who fears contamination by the corrupt outside world, is not excited by the news. Bernick encourages Rörlund to continue to be a moral influence while he and the businessmen assure the town's prosperity and the women pursue their charitable activities. That way, nothing is to be feared from the external world. Bernick asks about Olaf, who, it seems, is playing by the water again; his father fears he will have an accident. Krap enters with a telegram from the American owners of the *Indian Girl,* the ship now docked in Bernick's yards. He says goodbye to his colleagues and turns to his telegram, in which he is told to send the ship to America as soon as it can sail as the owners are confident that the cargo will keep it afloat in case of emergency. Bernick is aghast at this cavalier attitude toward human life and maintains that no Norwegian shipowner would act in this callous manner.

Olaf enters greatly excited because a circus has come to town, but his uncle demeans this form of entertainment in favor of seeing real gauchos on the pampas. Through the windows they can see the steamer disgorging its passengers, among them the circus performers and the seamen of the *Indian Girl.* Rörlund and the women decide to close the curtains to deflect the immoral influences that abound outside. One of the traveling women whose appearance so disconcerted the Norwegian women boldly enters the room, much to the surprise of everyone. Then they see that she is Lona Hessel, who is not a member of the circus but had traveled in the same boat with it. She further astounds them by saying that she has brought Johan with her. Lona sweeps open the curtains and suggests that the charitable ladies take the day off from their sewing in celebration of her return. Rörlund, offended by Lona's presence, adjourns the meeting but convenes it for the next day. Lona promises to attend too—to bring fresh air to the Society for the Morally Disabled.

Act II is set in the garden room of the Bernicks; it is the next day. Betty sits sewing at the table when Bernick comes in. He notes the absence of the charitable ladies, attributing it to the appearance of Lona Hessel and Johan Tönnesen. When Betty starts to talk of the scandals of the past, Bernick dismisses them as idle gossip. He is greatly concerned that the return of Hessel and Tönnesen will prove to be injurious to his reputation at the precise time that his business interests require him to have the respect and trust of the populace. He complains of his lack of a confidant, and Betty tries to absolve herself of any connection with the untimely visit of her relatives. When she starts to cry tears of self-pity, Bernick tells her to stop it because people will think she is not happily married. Betty goes onto the terrace as Aune enters to be upbraided for the slow pace of repairs to the *Palm Tree* and the *Indian Girl*.

Aune promises that things are going as fast as proper methods will allow, but Bernick faults him for refusing to use modern equipment in favor of traditional tools. Aune admits that he fears that the machines will put men out of work. Bernick changes the subject, decreeing that both ships must be ready to sail on the day after tomorrow. He is particularly concerned that he is being blamed for the boisterous antics of the American sailors, which is deleterious to his public image. After Aune says that preparing the American ship within three days is impossible, Bernick threatens to fire him. Aune tries without avail to reason with Bernick, and in the end he agrees to clear the *Indian Girl* for sailing three days hence.

Aune exits, and Hilmar Tönnesen enters to report that the two Norwegian-Americans are traversing the town with Dina Dorf. He spurs Bernick's interest by saying that he thinks the local newspaper will have much to say about the return of the prodigals. Bernick glances up the street and sees the trio approaching the house with little Olaf. Bernick gives orders that everyone will treat Lona and Johan with the greatest courtesy.

They enter full of their observations of the park given to the town by Bernick, his new school, the gas works, and the water system. Lona goads him by saying she was unable to remind people that she is related to the town's principal benefactor. Lona then boasts of her accomplishment in forming Johan into a fine young man, which sends Hilmar to the terrace in a huff. Bernick, Betty, and Lona go out to view the garden, leaving Olaf and his uncle alone.

Hilmar rebukes the boy for being too dependent on his mother; Olaf vows that he will do something significant; then they too move into the garden.

Johan and Dina enter, and he asks if they can take a walk every morning. She is reluctant to agree because of her origins and turns the conversation to the fortunes to be made in America. Johan invites Dina to return to

America with them. She seems set on emigrating but says that she could not go with him. Bernick comes in to get Betty's shawl and sends Dina to accompany the women on their walk to the grotto. He wants to talk with Johan.

Once they are alone, Bernick fervently thanks Johan for making all his success possible. Johan indulgently agrees that one of them had to take the blame for the liaison with Mrs. Dorf. Since he was young, free, and adventurous, it was only apt that he should save Bernick from exposure. Their friendship more than compensated for the loss of his reputation. Johan says that he is eager to return to his American farm, that he only made the trip to humor Lona who was homesick. He reveals that at last he had told Lona the truth about his reasons for leaving Norway, but she and Johan have agreed not to speak a word of this truth while in Norway. Having disposed of this serious matter, Johan talks enthusiastically of Dina. Bernick says it was Martha's idea to open their home to Dina after her mother died. He also explains that once he went into the family business, he discovered that his mother's share had been dissipated, thus leaving Martha penniless at her mother's death. Bernick is fully satisfied to have Martha in the house to share the household responsibilities with Betty, but Betty regrets Martha's unenviable position of depending upon her brother for the necessities of life. Krap enters to tell Bernick that certain contracts are in order, the news of which prompts a pleased Bernick to go into his study with Krap.

Martha enters and seems eager to abbreviate her conversation with Johan. When he insists that she talk with him, she upbraids him for what he did to Mrs. Dorf and thereby to Dina. Johan is surprised to learn that Bernick has never come to his defense. Martha concludes that, for the sake of their friendship, she has tried to fulfill all his responsibilities both to the family and to Dina. Martha leaves when Lona and Betty come in from the garden.

Despite Betty's protestations, Lona is intent about mentioning something to someone; she sends Johan out to talk with Dina. Then Lona tells Betty that Dina would make a good wife for Johan and that Karsten can find some way out of the scandal that would be caused by the announcement.

Betty exits sobbing just before Bernick enters and discovers Lona, to whom he apologizes for his behavior with Mrs. Dorf and says that he truly loved her (Lona). He further reveals that he married Betty for her money so that he could save the endangered family business. Lona accuses him of living a triple lie: to her, to Betty, and to Johan. Bernick feels somewhat secure in that neither of the three will ask him to tell the truth, but Lona asks if something within him does not long for the truth. He sees it as a sacrificial revelation. Lona reminds Bernick that an ill-spoken word could ruin his ideal home, his ideal marriage, his ideal position in the community. Bernick asks why Lona has come home, but he mistrusts her response that she wants to help him plant his feet on solid ground.

Rummel comes in with Vigeland to remind Bernick that his presence is needed at a meeting with the Chamber of Commerce. Bernick is reluctant to leave Lona, but Rummel is insistent. Bernick is still wavering when Rörlund enters to complain about Dina's being seen in public with Johan. Bernick says he knows nothing about it and rushes toward the door. Hilmar and Betty come into view through the garden doors. Hilmar is also disturbed by Dina and Johan: he has heard Johan trying to tempt Dina to go to America with him. With everyone in an uproar, Bernick sends his associates to the meeting with the promise that he will soon follow. Johan rushes in to announce that Dina will accompany them to America. Rörlund is so scandalized by this announcement that he tells Dina that Johan is her father. Dina asks Johan if that is the truth; Johan calls on Bernick to answer, but the pillar of society refuses to speak of it today. Not yet satisfied by his pious interference, Rörlund then accuses Johan of stealing old Mrs. Bernick's money. Johan moves to strike Rörlund, but Lona restrains him. Rörlund says that he has told the truth as Bernick told it to the town. Johan quietly asks Bernick what he has done; Betty apologizes for bringing such shame upon his family's name; Sandstad calls for Bernick to hurry to the meeting as the railroad deal is in jeopardy. Lona tells him to go now and be a pillar of society. Johan says that he and Bernick will have a talk tomorrow. The act ends as a stunned Bernick leaves for the meeting.

At the beginning of Act III, Bernick rushes into the garden room after having spanked Olaf for slipping away on a fishing boat and threatening to run away when chastised for his misconduct. Krap interrupts his tirade by reporting that both the *Palm Tree* and the *Indian Girl* will sail tomorrow but that the American ship will not get far. He further says that Aune intends to let that ship sink with all hands on board because he has not done any repairs, just cosmetic effects. Bernick sends Krap to the yards to get definite proof of Aune's crime, as he intends to report it to the press in order to reveal his disinterested altrism to the public.

Krap leaves, and Tönnesen enters to congratulate Bernick on influencing the Chamber of Commerce to support the railroad deal. He also says that the newspaper editor plans to print a rumor that all the land along the new line has been bought, which will sour many of the local businessmen on the project. Bernick is distraught at this news, but Tönnesen changes the subject as through the window he sees Lona and Johan with the captain of the *Indian Girl*. He exits.

Lona comes in, and Bernick asks if she cannot see how any scandal would upset the precarious balance of his deal and his reputation. He further says that he was not guilty of robbing his mother because no robbery actually occurred; he had merely spread the rumor of the theft and Johan's part in it. By saddling Johan with a robbery, he had been able to get precious time from his creditors who were pressing for payment. Eventually, he had saved the company and paid everyone his due. Lona sees that his position in society is still based on a lie and urges him not to support a society that is based on lies and pretense. Bernick plans to make restitution to Johan by offering him money, but Lona knows that Johan will not accept it.

Johan enters and asks Bernick to tell the truth, not because he values his reputation but because he plans to marry Dina and stay in town to spite all his enemies. Bernick tries to dissuade him by appealing to his civic pride and family ties. He admits that he ruined many people by blocking the coastal railway so that he could profiteer later by supporting the inland railroad; now he has bought all the land along which the line will run. If the branch proceeds, he will be immensely wealthy, but if it fails, he will be a pauper. In either case he needs to maintain his reputation as a pillar of society. Even so, Johan sees his own future happiness as the central issue. Lona intercedes, asking Johan to keep quiet. Johan agrees to remain silent for the moment but promises to come back later and talk. Bernick offers him money, but Johan demands his reputation. In the meantime, he plans to sail on the *Indian Girl,* sell his farm, and return in two months to marry Dina. Then he will speak the truth. A desperate Bernick threatens to say that Johan is blackmailing him, but Johan has two letters that are explicit in their calumny of the writer, Bernick. For the present, Johan is thinking of his journey to America, from which he will return unless the ship sinks. At that moment Bernick's plan is born. At first, he implores Lona to keep Johan off that ship, but she claims to have lost all power over him. She then follows Johan out of the room.

Aune enters to ask if he would definitely be fired if the *Indian Girl* should not sail on the next day. At Bernick's affirmative answer, Aune declares that the ship will sail. Aune then leaves.

After a moment Krap enters to say he was unable to get any evidence against Aune because the ship was already being put in the water and was locked. Krap is still convinced that it is not seaworthy, but Bernick goes to great lengths to assure him that everything is as it should be. Vigeland enters to ask if the *Palm Tree* sails tomorrow because he is concerned about a gale warning. Vigeland concludes that both ships will be in the hands of God as they sail into the eye of the storm; then he leaves with Krap.

Rörlund comes in and is used by Bernick as a foil for his ethical deliberation as to whether the general good of all is worth the sacrifice of one individual. Rörlund's advice is to put the matter into the hands of Providence. Before Rörlund can leave, Johan enters and says that he intends to marry the girl Rörlund insulted yesterday. Betty, Lona, Martha, and Tönnesen come in as Rörlund plans to tell the truth to Johan. He then surprises everyone by announcing that Dina is his fiancée, which she admits. Rörlund then asks Betty to convey Dina from the room. Rörlund and Martha leave too. Lona exits to keep an eye on Rörlund. Johan tells Bernick that he plans to sail as planned and that he will return and take vengeance on everyone; then he exits.

Krap enters to be absolutely certain that the *Indian Girl* will sail tomorrow. Bernick states that it will sail and goes into the study. Krap goes off too. Hilmar Tönnesen has regarded this scene with great interest and is about to leave when Olaf runs in and says that his father will not have the chance to hit him again. He mentions Johan's sailing and says that tomorrow his uncle will be surprised by what happens. Both then exit.

Krap goes to the door of Bernick's study and reports that a terrible storm is growing. He wants to know if the ship will indeed sail tomorrow. Bernick's answer is "The *Indian Girl* still sails." The act ends.

It is late afternoon on the next day, a stormy one, as Act IV opens. Rummel in evening dress directs a servant in preparing the room for a surprise celebration. Bernick's unexpected entrance drives the servants out and forces Rummel to admit that a delegation is en route to honor Bernick, the town's most distinguished citizen. Bernick is not pleased by the news, but he becomes even less festive when he hears the sound of the *Indian Girl* en route to the pier. Rummel insists that he put a good face on the evening because it will mold public opinion in favor of the railroad scheme. Bernick's spirits fall as Rummel describes the speeches, toasts, and poses that will comprise the festivities. Bernick's mind, however, is really on the sea. Now he hears the claxon of the *Palm Tree* passing the buoy. Vigeland, Sandstad, and Krap come in with the news that the American crew is drunk. Lona comes in to say farewell for Johan and to report that he is on board the ship. Bernick learns from Lona that Johan's plan is unaltered. Rummel lowers the curtains so that they can be raised when the crowd gathers in the garden to reveal the pillar of society among his ideal family. Bernick and his associates go into the study.

Lona is surprised to see Johan enter dressed for the voyage; he has come to see Dina for the last time. Martha and Dina enter, and Dina also is dressed for traveling and carries a suitcase. She begs Johan to take her with him, exclaiming that she had never cared for Rörlund. Johan quickly agrees to take her to America, preferably as his wife. Dina decides to marry him. Martha quietly says farewell to Dina as Lona puts into her pockets some papers handed to her by Johan. The lovers quickly exit as Lona observes that she has lost Johan and Martha has lost Dina. They have a moment of tender sisterly feeling as both admit they have loved Johan more than anything.

Bernick leaves his office long enough to tell Martha to request everyone in the family, including Olaf, to dress up for the party. Lona says that Bernick must feel proud to receive his town's homage, but he suspects that she is merely taunting him. He admits that being a pillar of society is really being a puppet of society. Lona's answer is for him to turn his back on lies and deception, but Bernick's response is that his own actions will buy a good life for his son. In a burst of temper, Bernick exclaims that Lona will not crush him. Tönnesen enters searching for Betty; he merely passes into the next room. Lona tells Bernick that Johan has taken Dina away and that he will never come back. Bernick is horror-stricken to learn that both his brother-in-law and daughter are on the *Indian Girl,* but Lona says that they sailed on the *Palm Tree* because Johan did not trust the American crew. Seeing his plan ruined, Bernick shouts to Krap to stop the sailing of the *Indian Girl* but learns that the ship is already out to sea. Desolate, Bernick sees that the ship and its crew will be sacrificed for nothing. Lona then produces the incriminating letters that Johan had given her and tears them up in front of Bernick, all the while telling him that neither she nor Johan will now make him face the truth. If he is to be free of all his lies, he must take the responsibility. He says that his life has no meaning beyond Olaf.

Tönnesen rushes in to say that Olaf has stowed away on the *Indian Girl*. Bernick orders Krap to stop the ship, but that is impossible. His business associates try to reassure him that the boy is safely sailing on a ship readied by his own shipyard. Bernick's distraction and despair are interrupted by the approach of a crowd of townspeople. Betty is called, but she does not appear. The shades are raised and so Bernick can face the throng that proclaims his merit. He can think only of Olaf. Then Betty comes in and says she has brought Olaf home with her. Lona urges Bernick to win his son now that he is safe. Betty also reports that Aune delayed the sailing on his own initiative. Bernick is delirious with happiness.

The chorus of citizens swells, and after a long, eulogistic speech by Rörlund, Bernick addresses the townspeople. He repudiates Rörlund's comments and admits all his duplicitous dealings. He further surprises his colleagues by announcing that all the railway property will be owned as a public corporation from which anyone may benefit. Bernick further offers to manage the corporation if the people should deign to trust him; they enthusiastically agree. Then he announces Johan and Dina's marriage and admits that she is his daughter. Finally, he asks the people to think about his admissions and to determine later if he has lost or won by telling the truth. The crowd disperses; Tönnesen, Rörlund, and the businessmen are definitely angered by the previous events, but they all exit, leaving the family alone.

Betty is delighted because she had previously thought she had lost Bernick; she knows she had never had his love, but she is now determined to win it. He quickly tells her that she has won his love. Bernick quietly thanks Lona for helping him to see the truth, but he wants to know why she really came back. She merely says that she wished to see her childhood hero standing upright in truth and freedom. Olaf enters and has a joyous reunion with his newly reformed father. Seeing that Aune has brought Olaf, Bernick tells him that his job is saved; a delighted Aune promises to try to use the new machines. Bernick is now standing in a new relationship with his new family as the skies clear and the *Palm Tree* scuttles seaward in safety. Bernick concludes that women are the pillars of society. Lona corrects him: truth and freedom are the pillars of society.

Structural analysis: Augustin Eugène Scribe's* influence on Ibsen is nowhere stronger than in *The Pillars of Society*. The exposition is handled explicitly, and artistically; incriminating letters are central to the resolution of the plot. The play appears to be unified by action, but like some of Ibsen's Scribean models, that appearance is deceptive. The action may be schematized as follows:

Bernick discovers that Lona and Johan have returned;

(as a result of which)

Bernick does what? Orders that everyone be kind to them. There is no causal result of that. Bernick discovers that Johan intends to marry Dina and so the truth about him must be told;

(as a result of which)

Bernick plans to let Johan perish with the *Indian Girl*;

(as a result of which)

Bernick discovers that Johan is not on the ship but that his son is;

(as a result of which)

Bernick despairs that he is the agent of his son's death;

(as a result of which)

Bernick does what? There is nothing he can do.

Bernick discovers that Olaf is safe;

(as a result of which)

Bernick confesses his misdeeds, is forgiven by the town, and is reunited with his family.

The ending of the play *seems* to be the result of the beginning, but the line of causality is broken at two very important places. That, in addition to the numerous coincidences that lead to the denouement, have prompted critics to censure Ibsen's lack of craftmanship.

Reference: Jorgenson, Theodore. "The Pillars of Truth and Freedom," *Henrik Ibsen: A Study in Art and Personality* (Northfield, Minn.: St. Olaf College Press, 1945), pp. 309-25.

PLOWRIGHT, JOAN (1929-): English actress Joan Plowright's Rebecca West* was seen in London when *Rosmersholm** opened on May 17, 1973. Jeremy Brett* was her Johannes Rosmer.*

Reference: Who's Who in the Theatre, 16th ed., p. 1025.

POEMS: For those unable to read Norwegian, Ibsen's reputation as a dramatist has overshadowed his accomplishment as a poet. Yet he has been duly extolled for his poesy which was his earliest means of literary expression, dating from 1847-48. During his student days Ibsen expressed his revolutionary sentiments in poetry. His first publication was a poem entitled "In Autumn."* He was also a sonneteer. "On the Heights" (1859) is one of his best poems. In 1871 Ibsen collected and edited his poems, which were published in that same year.

POESTION, JOSEF CALASANZ (1853-1922): A writer of some note, J. C. Poestion translated *An Enemy of the People** into German in 1891.
Reference: Deutsches Literatur-Lexikon (Bern, 1956), III, 2078-9.

PORTER, ERIC (1928-   ): Eric Porter received the (London) *Evening Standard* award for Best Actor for his performance as Johannes Rosmer* in the production of *Rosmersholm** which opened on November 18, 1959. His Rebecca West* was Dame Peggy Ashcroft.*
Reference: Who's Who in the Theatre, 17th ed., I, 548-9.

POSSART, ERNST VON (1841-1921): Actor Ernst von Possart staged one of the twin German premieres of *A Doll's House** in Munich in 1880.
Reference: Brockhaus Enzyklopaedie, XV, 44-5.

POTAMON (*Emperor and Galilean*): A goldsmith.

POTOCKA, MARIA H. (1873-1944): Maria Potocka was a Polish actress who periodically performed for the large Polish audiences in Russia. She played Nora Helmer* in *A Doll's House** in Moscow in 1891 and in St. Petersburg in 1900.

POULSEN, EMIL (1842-1911): Danish actor Emil Poulsen was a major interpreter of Ibsenian characters, including Doctor Fjeldbo* (1870), Nikolas Arnesson, Bishop of Oslo* (1871), Sigurd the Strong* (1875), Karsten Bernick* (1877), Torvald Helmer* (1879), Hjalmar Ekdal* (1885), and John Gabriel Borkman* (1897).
Reference: Enciclopedia della Spettacolo, VIII, col. 395.

POULSEN, JULIAN (*St. John's Night*): One of Ibsen's most charming characters, Julian Poulsen is almost an archetypal Romantic hero. He falls in love easily and desperately, takes his own emotions too seriously, affects eccentric dress and manners, composes and quotes poetry, and nurtures an exaggerated melancholy. In the end all obstacles that stand in the way of his liaison with Juliane Kvist* are removed.

THE PRETENDERS: A five-act Romantic serious drama.

Composition: First considered in 1858; written in 1863; published in October 1863.
Stage history:

Jan. 17, 1864	Christiania Theatre* (7 perfs.), dir. Henrik Ibsen
Nov. 26, 1866	Christiania Theatre (3)
Dec. 14, 1869	Christiania Theatre (4)
Jan. 11, 1871	Royal Theatre, Copenhagen, dir. Johan Ludvig Heiberg*
Sept. 1, 1873	Christiania Theatre (6), dir. Ludvig Oscar Josephson*
1873	Koeniglisches Theater, Munich

Nov. 15, 1875   Hoftheater, Schwerin
June 3, 1876   Berlin, pro. Georg II, Duke of Saxe-Meiningen*
Nov. 1876   Hoftheater, Schwerin
Jan. 19, 1879   Nya Teatern, Stockholm, dir. Ludvig Oscar Josephson
1879   Norwegian Theatre, Bergen*
Nov. 12, 1880   Christiania Theatre (12)
Mar. 3, 1882   Christiania Theatre (6)
1886   Nya Teatern, Stockholm, dir. Ludvig Oscar Josephson
Feb. 26, 1888   Christiania Theatre (13)
Apr. 11, 1891   Burgtheater, Vienna (3)
May 10, 1891   Schauspielhaus, Berlin
May 31, 1891   Hofbühne, Berlin
Apr. 12, 1898   Vasa Theatre, Stockholm
Oct. 15, 1899   Royal Theatre, Copenhagen
1900   Royal Theatre, Stockholm (9)
1901   Schiller Theater, Berlin
Oct. 7, 1904   Neues Theater, Berlin, dir. Max Reinhardt*
Sept. 30, 1906 Maly Theatre, Moscow
Apr. 2, 1907   Waldorf Astoria, New York (2), Yale Dramatic Association
Sept. 23, 1907 Hoftheater, Munich, Emil Höfer* as Nikolas
Feb. 13, 1913   Haymarket Theatre, London, pro. Laurence Irving*
Nov. 14, 1926   Royal Theatre, Copenhagen, staged by Edward Gordon Craig*
Aug. 1927   National Festival Theatre, Holyhead (Wales), (in Welsh), dir.
                Theodore Kommisarzhevsky*
Apr. 23, 1928   Festival Theatre, Cambridge, dir. Terence Gray

Synopsis: Shakespearean in tone and scope, *The Pretenders* is set in the early
thirteenth century. Crowds of people wait expectantly in the yard of Christ
Church, Bergen. Some are clustered about Haakon Haakonson, the king-elect,
leader of the Birchbeiner (Birchleg) party, while others gravitate toward Earl
Skule, another pretender to the Norwegian throne. The atmosphere is charged
with tension magnified by the pealing of all the church bells in town. As the
chants of monks and nuns are heard, the great doors of the church open to
reveal Bishop Nikolas and his retinue, who announce that Inga of Varteig is at
that moment submitting to the ordeal of red-hot iron in support of Haakon's
claim to the throne. The clerics re-enter the church as Earl Skule nervously
awaits the outcome, while Haakon maintains his belief in God's assistance. As
the tension mounts, the doors swing open to the sight of Inga, the mother of
Haakon, extending her unburned hands that held the hot metal. Haakon
embraces Inga while some of the crowd jubilantly conclude that Haakon must
indeed be the son of the old king Haakon Sverresson, despite persistent rumors
of his illegitimacy and slights against his royal blood. Haakon says that he has
taken excessive pains to prove his claim to the throne for the sake of national
unity, even though his trusted friends counseled him to go to war for his
kingdom. Haakon further explains that he feels a sense of mission in assuming
the kingship at a perilous moment in Norway's history. Skule counters that
several of those present can rightly claim royal blood, Sigurd Ribbung for

example. Guthorm Ingesson is descended from Sverre but from the female side. Finally, Skule asserts his royal prerogative because he is the brother of a former king. Thus, although Haakon is king, his sway is disputed by several others, particularly Skule. Haakon intends to convene the Assembly for the purpose of confirming his election, but Skule and several others maintain that the ordeal did not make Haakon king; it merely established him as a legitimate pretender. Bishop Nikolas confirms Skule's rationale. Partisans on both sides quickly produce weapons to settle the issue, but Haakon persuades them not to resort to violence. After committing Inga to the care of one of his friends, Haakon releases the Birchlegs from their oaths of loyalty to him and proclaims that the Assembly shall choose the king from among the pretenders. He commands the Assembly to be convened, after which he exits to the blare of trumpets. Skule, impressed by Haakon's behavior, admits to a friend that he is satisfied as to Haakon's legitimate claim and that he will be content if either he or Haakon be named king. When Skule exits, Nikolas retains Dagfinn the Peasant and warns him to keep Skule and Haakon apart after the election. Then they leave the stage.

Inside the palace Skule's family anxiously awaits the outcome of the Assembly: Ragnhild, his wife; Margrete, his daughter; and Sigrid, his sister. From a convenient window they see a desperate Sigurd Ribbung concluding that no one supports his candidacy; they see a shame-faced Guthorm Ingesson skulking in the shadows. Then the women are shocked as they watch golden chairs being offered to Skule and Haakon, the partisans of each pretender trying to keep the rival claimants from sitting therein. In his fury Skule clambers toward the chair and tries to hold onto it. His wife is deeply embarrassed at his expression and behavior; she concludes that his soul will be damaged if he is not selected king. Shouts are heard as the choice is made. Out of the confusion of the Assembly, Margrete is able to discover that Haakon Haakonson is the rightful King of Norway. Suitable music announces the formation of a royal procession, and Sigrid leads a weeping Ragnhild from the room.

The great doors open, and King Haakon enters the room in state. He starts to talk to Margrete about their unfriendly childhood in the same household, and he then sits down to write as Dagfinn, Nikolas, Skule, and Vegard Vaeradal come in. Haakon tells Skule that he has written a note of thanks to his mother Inga along with his instructions that she is to live with royal honors at a place far removed from the palace. This precaution is ostensibly for her safety, but perhaps it is to remove her influence. Ivar Bodde, a courtier, suggests that Inga must be exhausted from her ordeal and should therefore postpone her departure until the next day. Nikolas quietly urges Haakon to take a further step, which he does resolutely: Haakon severs his connection with Kanga, whom he has long loved. This act of self-abnegation is calculated to win Skule's admiration, which it seems to do. Because it was Nikolas' idea, Haakon rewards him by offering to grant any request. As a result, Haakon appoints Vegard governor of Halogaland, although one of Skule's supporters is in the area and is a logical candidate. Haakon presents this move as an indication that their partisans must work in concert and forget old enmities. Then Haakon roundly surprises Skule by asking permission to marry Margrete and make her queen of Norway. She quietly agrees, so Skule shakes the king's hand, wishing him peace and friendship. Ivar and Dagfinn see this scene as a miraculous reconciliation, but Nikolas advises them to be on their guard. Haakon further seals his trust of Skule by allowing him to keep the royal seal. Throughout this scene, the role of Nikolas is unclear as he quietly counsels Haakon, Skule, and the other nobles; his asides suggest duplicity. After the bishop's exit, Haakon and Margrete plan their wedding to be solemnized the next summer; he tells her that he values her wisdom and advice. As Margrete leaves the hall, she meets her mother with whom she shares the news of her engagement; they exit together. Dagfinn announces that the archbishop of Nidaros, who had recently publicly humiliated Haakon, now expresses his homage, a gesture that convinces Haakon that now he is truly king. Haakon exits as Skule hides the royal seal in his clothing while observing that he still rules the kingdom.

The banqueting room of the palace at Bergen is the scene of Act II. Haakon sits in state while his retinue chats, drinks, listens to music, and plays chess. Although Haakon is king, he is being entertained to an engagement feast by Skule. As they talk among themselves, some of Skule's men indicate that their fealty is to the earl, not to the king. Bishop Nikolas goads Skule's people by suggesting that Haakon will force them to swear allegiance to himself. Some time has intervened since Act I, time enough for Haakon's hosts to quell insurrections in several parts of the country, largely fomented by the disappointed pretenders. A messenger enters and quietly tells Skule that a certain ship is prepared to sail; the earl produces a parchment bearing the king's seal and instructs his man to see that it leaves with the ship. This passage is closely observed by Nikolas, who comments that there is much for Skule to do. The king then rises and expresses pleasure at the state of the bishop's health, which for some time has been precarious. Nikolas states his hope that he may live long enough to accomplish all his plans. Haakon turns to Skule and remarks the absence of a number of his own supporters. Then Haakon is reminded that it is time for the tournament to begin. The king dedicates today to pleasure, tomorrow to dealing with insurgents.

After Haakon exits with Margrete on his arm, followed by most of the others, Nikolas asks Ivar Bodde some leading questions about Tamb, the sailor to whom Skule had entrusted his official document. Nikolas learns that Tamb is in the employ of the earl of Orkney, one of Haakon's vassals who has refused to pay his taxes. Nikolas says that he is unable to reveal the contents of the paper, but Bodde, loyal to the king, is greatly agitated by the news and rushes out to consult Dagfinn the Peasant. Nikolas then accosts

Gregorius Jonsson and tells him that Dagfinn intends to prevent Tamb's sailing. Jonsson hurries out to forestall Dagfinn, leaving Nikolas alone with Skule.

The earl is in a contemplative mood, and the bishop urges him to reveal his innermost feelings, especially those about wishing to be king. Skule bemoans the realization that he is so near to the throne yet so far from it. He has, in fact, suffered the kingship of three men, believing each time that he would be a better ruler. When his king-brother had died, Skule had believed that he was the logical successor. Yet Haakon had been chosen in his place. Nikolas chides him for always being unwilling to make the final desperate gambit that would result in his accession. Skule asks why Haakon is such a successful king; Nikolas' answer is simply that fortune favors his intuitions. Reviewing Haakon's career, Skule realizes that the king has indeed been preternaturally lucky. The bishop forces Skule to contemplate taking whatever action may be necessary to attain the kingship; the priest maintains that there is no such thing as good or evil, that everything must be sacrificed for sovereignty. He says that Haakon's protectors are heavenly and that Skule must be prepared to thwart even their designs; the bishop compares Skule with Satan himself. Skule is shocked by this advice and asks if Nikolas is "more or less than human." Nikolas maintains his innocence, which he defines as ignorance of good and evil. He tells Skule that he must act as if he were confident of his powers; then they will actually become potent. Then Nikolas plants the idea that Haakon is not the true son of old king Haakon Sverreson. Skule is stunned but asks for proof. The bishop says that Inga had borne a son after her kingly spouse's death and left it in the care of a priest for a whole year. The priest, not wishing to accept responsibility for an heir to the throne, petitioned his superior, one Father Nikolas, for advice. Following Nikolas' orders, he was to exchange the royal baby for a common one and present the commoner to Inga when she asked for her son. Neither Nikolas nor anyone else knows whether the priest obeyed his instructions, but Skule sees that such disputed origins could destroy Haakon's confidence in himself and weaken his reign. Nikolas urges Skule to act on this information, but while looking through the window, Skule sees Dagfinn approach the king amidst a crowd of courtiers; then he watches anger playing on Haakon's countenance. Nikolas, however, is not content to let matters rest. He tells Skule that the priest in question had written a letter about the royal child and had sworn to the truth of his statement. Nikolas maintains that he knows the location of the document, but before he can speak further, Haakon angrily rushes in and demands to know of Skule who is king in Norway.

Haakon has discovered that Skule has sent an official letter to the rebellious earl of Orkney, a letter the contents of which the king is ignorant. Skule explains that the king had been too busy with more pressing matters to deal with Orkney and that Skule was merely suing for a favorable reconciliation. To prove his honesty, Skule invites Haakon to read the letter, but Jonsson whispers to the earl that he had tossed the letter to the bottom of the fjord rather than allow it to fall into Dagfinn's hands. Skule, therefore, has no recourse but to defy the king and say that he will not produce the letter. In response to this defiance, Haakon orders Skule to surrender the royal seal to Bodde, and even Margrete's tears cannot cause him to relent. Skule then lashes out at Ivar Bodde as the author of the mistrust that has existed for years between him and the king, an accusation which the earl's men eagerly second. Bodde maintains his innocence and says that he does not wish to be in charge of the royal seal. Furthermore, he removes himself from the court, much against the king's wishes. Feeling himself bereft of close supporters, Haakon orders his friend Vegard Vaeradal to be summoned as an adviser, but Dagfinn reports that Vegard has been killed by a friend of Skule. Haakon commands Skule to execute his friend for the murder, but Skule objects, saying that he could kill for his country, but not this man. Yet he refuses to name his reason. (In Act IV, Scene 1, one learns that this man had married Ingeborg, whom Skule had deserted when she was pregnant.) Exasperated and puzzled, Haakon concludes that he himself will exact vengeance, but Skule warns him that blood will flow as a result. Nikolas intervenes and says that the person in question has become a crusader and is now out of the country. Haakon ends the marriage feast, announcing his intention to go west to Viken. Sigrid then petitions Haakon to have her named abbess of a convent at Rejn so that she will not have to go to Nidaros with Skule her brother. Sigrid, foreseeing a bloody time ahead for Norway, wants to be in a position to exercise spiritual influence over events to come. She goes out saying that she and her brother will meet again when he most needs her.

Haakon decides that all of Skule's men must take an oath of allegiance, which causes general confusion and dismay; but Haakon and the court exit, leaving only Nikolas and Skule. The bishop says that the priest's letter had been sent to him by a messenger as yet unknown to him. He promises to give it to Skule as soon as it arrives. Secure in the destructive power of the letter, Skule swears to do what he can internally to weaken Haakon's rule so that his power will topple when open warfare comes. By now Skule is so enamored of the royal sway that in a crescendoing litany he swears that he will pursue Haakon from town to town if Haakon is not the rightful king, that he will storm the holiest church, disregard the law of sanctuary, desecrate the high altar, and destroy the most sacred shrine to wrest the crown from Haakon's head. What will he do, asks Nikolas, if the crown is too tight to be snatched from Haakon's head? He will, says Skule, cut off Haakon's head. Saying this, he exits, leaving Nikolas to gloat over his successful manipulation of the earl.

Three years have passed. Paul Flida, one of Skule's men, appears at the bishop's palace in Oslo in Act III, Scene 1. He learns from the servant Sira Viljam that the aging prelate has already received the last rites of the church but is still lucid and asks for Skule, whom the king has created Norway's first duke. The scene is rich in the sights and sounds of monks and priests engaged in liturgical chant and ceremonial. Flida departs as the bustle of servants declares that Nikolas wishes to lie in this room.

The couch is prepared, and soon the old man, clad in almost full vestments, is led in and deposited on the bed. In his illness he says he is concerned with his sins, particularly those committed against the king, whose imminent arrival perhaps will bring absolution. Nikolas complains of the encroaching darkness, although the room is quite bright; his limbs grow cold. He calls for his miter and crozier, believing them effective armor against the Evil One. Then Nikolas sends away all the servants except Peter Skialdarband, son of the man who killed Vegard, to whom he gives a letter addressed to his mother and urges him immediately to ride north with it.

Left alone, Nikolas soliloquizes about the political situation. The incriminating letter about which he had told Skule still has not been given to him, and as long as Skule is kept in doubt about the truth of Haakon's parentage, he will keep the strife-ridden kingdom in turmoil. Neither Skule nor Haakon will be able to emerge as Norway's greatest hero. His evil gloating subsides as fear racks him. Now Nikolas realizes that his scheming lies behind all the factional bloodshed, but surely Haakon will forgive him. When he hears a knock at the door, the bishop presumes it announces Skule, but Inga of Varteig enters dressed in a black cloak and hood. She says that her brother Gunnulf has returned after a lengthy stay in England and has brought a letter to Nikolas from a particular priest. Dagfinn comes in to say that the king and court have just arrived in Oslo and will soon be at the bishop's house. Not wishing to embarrass her son for his shoddy treatment of her, Inga plans to pray for Haakon in church and later to observe him from the shadows before departing for her home.

After Inga and Dagfinn depart, Nikolas ruminates about the crucial letter that he now has in his hands. Is he bound by his promise to give it to Skule? May he not use it to his own greater advantage? Is it not his duty to reconcile Haakon and Skule, although it means razing the edifice of deceit that he has so systematically constructed? If he had not urged Vegard to convince the king to send Inga away from the court, she would not be nearby to deliver the letter. He concludes that he must force himself to live longer just to extricate himself from this quandary. Calling for his physician, Nikolas tries to strike a bargain for three more days of life, but Sigard sees that the end is near and goes to prepare a sedative that will be needed within an hour. This knowledge increases Nikolas' anxiety as he considers the merits of *perpetuum mobile,* a never-ending movement. If he could set in motion events that would continue for centuries, his lifetime would derive meaning and purpose. Enlivened by his schemes to cast further generations of Norwegians into bloody turmoil, Nikolas takes strength and calls for the prayers for the dead to be stopped. He plans to give the letter to Skule and also to cause Haakon to doubt his legitimacy; the resultant contention will ramify through the ages, and Nikolas will have attained immortality as the ruler of Norway's fate. At that point Skule enters.

The duke comes immediately to the point: where is the priest's letter? Nikolas defers discussion of the letter but says that when the king comes tonight, he will confess his part in switching the babies, thereby destroying Haakon's confidence in himself. Skule replies that such a course would be sinful if Haakon were the rightful heir. Since he will reveal the location of the letter to Skule, Nikolas observes that the duke will have the power to set Haakon's mind at rest if he is truly of the royal lineage. In exchange for the letter, Nikolas makes Skule swear to act against Nikolas' enemies, whose names are enumerated in a list. Before he can hand over the letter, however, Haakon and his company enter.

The king's initial comment is one of forgiveness of the bishop's obstreperousness, but he is quite annoyed to encounter Skule in Oslo and blames Nikolas for the affront. The old man claims that his illness had prevented his knowing that the king and the duke had not yet been reconciled. As Nikolas' strength commences to ebb, he tells of his boyhood ambition to rise to a position of ultimate power, but his cowardice had prevented his becoming a major pretender to the throne because eminence must be won on the battlefield. He has hated exceptional men for their acumen and beautiful women because of his own impotence. Even as a priest his only notable accomplishment had been singing the high notes designated for the *castrati* of the choir. He used to think that his failures were heavenly punishments, but now he sees them as heaven's sins against him. Now that he nears his end, Nikolas warns Haakon that he is opposing the man who controls Norway's destiny; he advises Haakon to divide the kingdom and share the rule with Skule. The king obdurately refuses to divest himself of any part of his right to rule. Skule's great concern is that the weakening bishop will die before revealing the location of the letter. Nikolas summons Skule to come closer and asks what he would do if he found that Haakon was the rightful ruler; the duke says that he would acknowledge the king. Telling him to reconsider, Nikolas gets the same answer, which convinces the bishop not to hand over the letter. Instead, he reintroduces the subject of the list of his enemies and magnanimously forgives them as Skule would do to Haakon. Nikolas tells Skule to cast the list into a nearby brazier. As he sees the paper burning, Nikolas is seized by his death throes. As Haakon shouts for help, the bishop triumphantly acknowledges that he has set into motion his *perpetuum mobile*. When the frantic Skule demands the location of the important letter, Nikolas tells him that he has just burned it. Then Bishop Nikolas dies. Frantic monks rush in forecasting great evil to come, saying prayers, and exclaiming about hearing wild laughter in a corner and voices shrieking, "We have him!" Haakon approaches Skule and orders him to surrender all his dignities in view of whatever evil he had been plotting with Nikolas; he further says that all issues that lie between them must be settled in tomorrow's Council. The king exits, and Skule decides that he must act tonight. The curtain falls.

In Scene 2, which takes place in a room of the palace, Queen Margrete watches over the infant Prince Haakon. She starts when Skule quietly enters the room but in her delight at seeing him expresses the wish that her husband and her father may settle their differences. The proud mother then displays her son to his grandfather. When Haakon's steps are heard on the stair, Margrete leaves Skule to guard the prince while she rushes to greet her husband. Skule soliloquizes that his heir might secure Haakon's throne even if the father were not the legitimate king. He considers telling Haakon the story about the switched babies but decides that since he himself does not really believe it, Haakon is not likely to be convinced. He further considers that if he should win the kingdom, his conscience would not be at rest because he would always worry that he had unseated the rightful king. Even so, he must force the issue between himself and Haakon. He seems to come to a decision and proclaims that God is responsible for what follows. First, he considers employing his larger army to defeat Haakon's troops, but even in that he wavers. He looks at the prince, realizing that the son would become king if Haakon should die, and old Skule would have to pay obeisance. Then he hatches the plan of abducting the infant as hostage for the kingdom but decides to delay until he speaks again to the king.

Margrete enters with Haakon and cautions Skule to be reasonable as her husband has sworn to do. She then retires. Skule prophesies that if no reconciliation follows their discussion, terror will invade the country, but Haakon is so confident of his power and so relieved that all his former opponents are dead or vanquished that he cannot see the logic of Skule's prediction. Skule admits that he may be the author of the strife, since absolute rule is the only thing that will satisfy him. All bitterness can be avoided if Haakon agrees to divide the kingdom, but the king will have none of that. Skule suggests that each rule alternately for three years, but Haakon will not agree to that either. As a last resort, Skule suggests man-to-man combat as a means of settling their differences. Haakon tries to explain that kingship is a state of mind reflected in kingly actions; it is not merely gold and purple privilege. Did Skule ever once, asks Haakon, do a kingly deed? Skule responds that quelling insurrections does not constitute that sort of kingship; in fact, royal power results from fear of the king or the need of his protection again stronger forces. This argument convinces Haakon that Skule could never be a true king because he cannot conceive of Norway as a nation. Under Skule it could be only a bellicose kingdom. In Haakon's opinion, nationhood must result from unity rather than disparity. The creation of such a nation requires greater strength than Skule could ever muster. Skule views nationhood as an impossibility. Since they are at an impasse, Haakon postpones his reckoning with Skule until tomorrow's Council, believing that Skule must not be entirely alienated because the nation has need of his abilities. Skule stalks out breathing imprecations.

Dagfinn enters to warn Haakon that Skule means some sort of mischief during the night; the duke's ships are ready to sail, and the Assembly has been told to meet aboard ship. Dagfinn is dispatched to get further information as Gregorius Jonsson enters to declare his new allegiance to the king and to whisper monumental news of Skule's doings. Haakon orders his troops to assemble. The king summons his wife after Jonsson has left. He tells her that Skule has nominated himself as king and is sailing to Nidaros for his coronation. Madly trying to plot a strategy to deal with this new development, Haakon asks Margrete if she knows a way in which he can have Skule killed before he is crowned. Naturally, she recoils at the idea, and so he relents. A knock on the door is heard, admitting Inga of Varteig, who saw Haakon as he left Nikolas' palace. His sadness would not permit her to depart without talking to him. The presence of his weeping wife and his wronged mother brings him to realize that God has brought him to this dangerous pass because of his unloving treatment of two women who have loved him without qualification. He makes his peace with his wife and mother and feels so attuned with God that even Dagfinn's report cannot dispel his confidence in the future.

At the opening of Act IV, a crowned Skule sits in state in the Great Hall of the palace at Oslo. Jatgeir the skald* commences to sing his ballad in praise of Skule's escapades. Through this expository song, one learns that Skule and his armed host trekked north to Nidaros, subduing all tribes in their wake. Finally, his armies met those of Haakon, and the slaughter was great. Skule emerged victorious, while Haakon went into hiding in peril of his life. Paul Flida corrects the ballad in one respect: it is known that Haakon is in Nidaros, having proclaimed his son the heir to the throne. Skule is not threatened by the thought that Haakon may take arms again, nor is he disturbed to think that the conquered tribes are only waiting for an opportunity to rise against him. The banquet is then resolved into a happy fantasy about the riches and honors that shall befall every man when Skule leads his troops to Nidaros to defeat Haakon once and for all. Finally, the courtiers depart, leaving a haggard Skule alone.

Far from the confident, smiling ruler of a few moments ago, he is a dispirited, weary man, not at all certain of his position or his eventual victory. In a bitter, resentful soliloquy, Skule bemoans his uncertain state, realizing that his chance of ruling successfully has been nonexistent since his conversation with Haakon about the nation of Norway. He even considers Haakon to be an exponent of God's will.

These reveries are interrupted by Paul Flida, who reports that many troops have rallied behind Haakon and perhaps will join battle with Skule before he had planned to attack. When they discuss possible allies, Skule's predicament becomes apparent: the Vikeners will not aid him because the Tronders, their enemies, are on his side. Flida exits while Skule continues to ponder Haakon's idea of a Norwegian nation. When Jatgeir comes in, Skule asks him if one woman can deeply love another woman's child. The bard's reply is that only childless women can do so. In this quiet moment, both king and skald speak openly and directly and discover a sense of kinship. Then Skule shakes off his pensiveness and decides to take action. Jatgeir reports rumors that Haakon is not really far off in the west where he is presumed to be. Then he exits.

Left alone, Skule compares himself with the barren woman who comes to love another woman's child, in this case, Haakon's brainchild of a united Norwegian nation. He wavers between conceding to Haakon and contesting the kingship merely to satisfy his ambition. He then summons Jatgeir again and asks him what he needs to be a king. The wise poet's answer is that he should have the gift of not doubting himself, for he is already a king. Skule starts to bemoan the fact that he has no son to whom to transfer his crown. He offers to make Jatgeir his heir if the bard will agree to compose no more poems, a price much too high for Jatgeir. When Skule angrily says he must have one person who believes absolutely in him, the poet counsels him to believe in himself to achieve salvation. Paul Flida enters with the news that Haakon's army is nearby. Skule is shocked almost into inanity. At last he resolves not to fight but to seek sanctuary in a church. Flida sees that Skule is not in control of himself and receives permission to act in the king's name. His first task is to destroy the bridges, but Skule stops him, thinking that he can parley with Haakon. Flida urges Skule to fight, but the king has so little faith in himself that he cannot decide what to do.

A woman and a priest are then brought before him. The woman is one whom Skule had once deeply loved and wronged—Ingeborg. Aside from harboring her love of him after Skule had deserted her for a richer woman, Ingeborg had married the man who murdered Vegard, who has since died. She had been pregnant when Skule left her, pregnant with his son. Now she believes she must return that son to the king. The knowledge that he now has an heir so fortifies Skule that he is transformed into an almost confident man. Ingeborg is willing in part with her boy if Skule will promise that young Peter's soul will not be tainted on the road to the throne. Having extracted his promise, Ingeborg urges him to kill Peter rather than imperil his soul. He also swears to that. Skule turns with delight to Peter, his son, the young priest. Peter swears to fight with all his strength for his father. Having accomplished her mission, Ingeborg leaves as Skule imparts to Peter "his" plan for creating a united Norway. The young man is overwhelmed by the enormity of the idea; he energetically swears that he believes wholeheartedly in Skule and his cause. Now Skule can face any opponent. News is brought that Haakon is at the gates, and Skule, Peter, and all the army rush out to do battle.

Scene 2 occurs on a street in Oslo before the church of St. Hallvard. Skule's trumpeter enters and signals that the battle is about to be joined. Various townspeople enter and utter excited comments about the situation; from time to time, soldiers of each faction rush across the stage. Haakon's men seem to be taking the day as Haakon himself enters. One of his soldiers staggers in, and as he collapses into death, he says that he will fight no more because he has just slain his brother who was fighting on the other side. Haakon laments the necessity of such internecine contention. Then Skule's men clamber over the walls of the churchyard and bring the combat even closer to Haakon. Skule enters on a magnificent white charger accompanied by Peter. To precipitate peace, Haakon offers to share the throne; Skule will not hear of it. Haakon says that his son will inherit the throne even if he should fall in battle. Skule orders his men to kill young Haakon wherever he may be found. That pronouncement steels Haakon to vow that he will kill Skule whenever he is seen on unconsecrated ground. By now the battle has moved offstage, where Skule's men have managed to retreat. Then Skule is observed to be fleeing. Haakon has won the day. Before Margrete comes ashore, Haakon makes his troops swear to protect the child without revealing to the queen that the prince is in danger. When she learns that Skule has not been killed, she rejoices, but then Haakon must tell her that he has settled on Skule's death. He says that he will agree to a separation if her loyalty to her father outweighs her allegiance to her king, but she remains as a faithful wife and subject.

The beginning of Act V sees Skule and his people ensconced in the palace at Nidaros. The sky is pierced by a portentous red light in the shape of a flaming sword, thought by one to signal the death of a great leader. Flida reports that Haakon's fleet is already in the fjord and may be expected in the town tonight. The outcome of the battle will be problematical because Skule has absented himself from his men ever since the retreat from Oslo. When Flida tries to communicate through Skule's door, the king professes to be ill. The news of Haakon's nearness only prompts him to order Flida to kill Haakon and his son. Peter brings news that the townspeople will go over to Haakon if Skule does not show himself and rally their spirits. The Tronders, too, threaten to desert. Only Peter's reminder that his kingdom will also be lost brings Skule, a graying, haggard man, from his retreat. When the shouts of the citizens draw him toward the window, Skule sees the sword in the sky and recoils in terror, but he forces himself to appear before the disgruntled people. They refuse to accept his kingship because he has not received homage at St. Olaf's shrine. Peter advises them to summon the Assembly and to fetch the shrine from the church, a task that he undertakes to do, although some of the elders consider it sacrilegious to tamper with the shrine. Peter's decisive action encourages Skule, who determines that the bridges must be destroyed to keep Haakon out of Nidaros; then he deploys his troops near the fjord. Next he appears before the crowd and promises them that he will fight and win, but his oration is interrupted by cries for his atonement. A priest dashes into the courtyard below, scourges himself, and tears his cowl to pieces, which the mob interprets as an evil omen. Skule is heartened to see that St. Olaf's shrine has been deposited in the courtyard and to hear the trumpet announcing the Assembly. Peter enters to receive his father's congratulations but reveals that he himself snatched the shrine from the altar after the monks excommunicated him and the archbishop fulminated. The assembled court flinches at the sacrilege. Peter says that the deed had to be done whatever the price. Even his father recognizes it as blasphemy; now he sees Peter as damned as he remembers his promise to Ingeborg. Flida enters to say that Skule's men have deserted and fled to the churches to atone for the sacrilege. The townsmen have also revolted, and Haakon is sailing unmolested up the river. Skule, terrified lest Peter should be killed with a mortal sin on his soul, agrees to retreat. The bridges, however, have been burned. The troop tries to swim the river to safety.

Once the room is cleared, an armed group of townspeople comes in to kill Skule, only to find that he has fled. Then a flurry of voices announces the appearance of King Haakon. The people tell Haakon that Skule has taken sanctuary in one of the churches. Rather than command that Skule be found and killed, Haakon sends Jonsson to find him and persuade him to leave the country. If he refuses to go, then he must die. He sends Dagfinn to escort the queen and prince to Elkslodge Convent, where Margrete's mother Ragnhild lives. Once Skule's men have been arrested and pardoned, he says, the country can enjoy peace again. A messenger enters and reports that Skule is also on his way to Elkslodge. The townsmen resolve to kill Skule in an effort to diminish Haakon's punishment for their having supported Skule.

The second scene is a copse high above Nidaros. Although the moon shines, the mountain mists create an eerie atmosphere. Skule and Peter enter at the head of a small band. The ill Skule must rest, and as they sit, the men consider ways of dealing with their situation. One suggests abducting Prince Haakon from the ship and using him to bargain for pardons. Peter seriously deems this a viable plan, but first he must get his father to safety. The kidnappers set out as Peter justifies any abominable action on the grounds that his father's vision of a Norwegian nation is more important than any single life. Voices are heard offstage; soon Skule learns that Margrete and the baby are in these woods en route to Elkslodge. At that moment some monks who remain faithful to Skule appear and offer monks' habits as disguises, a ploy quickly accepted by Skule who wishes to see his son and himself on holy ground. Peter confides Skule's care to Flida while he goes to intercept the kidnapping party.

Meanwhile, most of Skule's men silently desert him, leaving him to be tended by a solitary monk who has stood apart. The mists momentarily separate, allowing Skule to see a red comet in the sky. For the first time Skule takes notice of his monkish attendant, the palest man he has ever seen. The monk claims to be a friend, one who can lead him to the throne or to the high mountain to show him all the glories of the world. The monk identifies himself as an emissary of the oldest Pretender in the world. Then Skule recognizes him as the ghost of Bishop Nikolas, who admits in graceful verse that he was not admitted to heaven, so he took the other alternative. Now, Nikolas says, he has been assigned the territory of Norway to superintend for the Devil, who has decided that Haakon is no friend, that Skule is the man to rule Norway. Before arranging that, however, Nikolas insists that Skule must kill Prince Haakon at Elkslodge; then he will be king if he convenants that Peter will succeed him. Skule, seeing that Nikolas is bargaining for Peter's soul, sends him away and calls on God to help him in the hour of his need. Before withdrawing, Nikolas rejoices that his *perpetuum mobile* is now in place and tells future generations to see his hand in strife after bloody strife. Once he has disappeared into the mist, Skule sees that he must travel the road to Elkslodge alone. So he sets out.

The courtyard of Elkslodge Convent is the locale of Scene 3. Margrete and Ragnhild discuss the situation. Ragnhild offends one of the guards by suggesting that Skule ought to beg Haakon for his life. Ragnhild cannot believe that Haakon will actually execute Skule or that Margrete could love a man who swore to kill her father. This interchange is forestalled by a knocking at the well-fortified gate. It is Skule who signals, but Dagfinn refuses to open for an outlaw. Margrete intercedes, so Dagfinn admits Skule, who at last is safe on consecrated ground. Dagfinn posts guards at the bedside of the prince before embarking for Nidaros to tell Haakon that Skule is now confined. Embraced by his family, Skule is surprised when his sister Sigrid enters.

She reminds him that she promised to come to him in the hour of his greatest need. Skule is deeply moved by the outpouring of love that comes from his wife, daughter, and sister, each of whom has good reasons to despise him. Skule decides to ask for clemency when Haakon comes because his family has shown him that life is good. The sound of the townspeople knocking at the gate disturbs the reunion; they shout that they intend to kill Skule. Ragnhild and Margrete rush Skule into the church to claim the privilege of sanctuary. Before he gets inside, Skule hears the voice of Peter promising him victory. Then the wild-looking young man appears and asks where Prince Haakon is. He makes no attempt to disguise the fact that the desecrator of a shrine will have no scruples against killing a prince sleeping in a sacristy. Peter reminds Skule that he decreed that the child must be killed in his mother's arms if need be. While Skule wrestles with the present dilemma, the angry crowd outside the gates shouts its determination to kill both the desecrator and his father. Skule decides to surrender himself to save the others. Sigrid, alone, does not try to dissuade him because she sees that for the first time, Skule is doing a kingly deed. To Peter, Skule admits that he usurped the throne as well as the majestic idea of a Norwegian nation; he begs his son to renounce him in order to save his soul. Peter sinks down in agony as Skule prepares to sacrifice himself for Haakon's idea. Skule is strengthened in his resolution to let the Nidarians kill him because Margrete has said that she will leave Haakon if he executes her father. He looks up and sees that the bloody sword in the sky has paled. For the first time he realizes that he is doing God's will, a conclusion affirmed by Sigrid. At last Ragnhild and Margrete bow to the inevitable and accede to his sacrifice.

Skule tells Sigrid to convey to Haakon that he is certain that God intended Haakon to be king and to tell Ingeborg that he kept his promise about Peter. As the townspeople break open the gate, the hymns of Margrete and her mother are heard from the chapel as all the bells of Nidaros peal. Skule and Peter walk hand in hand to meet their fate outside the gates. The crowd cheers as Haakon rides up, but Skule's body blocks his path. Dagfinn advises that Haakon's program can succeed only over the body of Skule, so Haakon steps over the corpse. The reign of Haakon's noble idea has begun. *Structural analysis: The Pretenders* is composed of a large number of episodes illustrative of a significant change in Earl Skule, the protagonist; it is, therefore, unified by character. When Skule first appears, he has as legitimate claim to the throne of Norway as his antagonist, Haakon Haakonsson, but, when the council elects Haakon king, Skule initiates a series of machinations designed to unseat Haakon and place himself on the throne. Yet, two factors cause Skule to doubt his own suitability to reign: Haakon's imaginative concept of a united Norwegian people and Bishop Nikolas' evil interference. Even Skule sees that Haakon is a wise ruler, and Nikolas' attempts to discredit him seem dubious to Skule. Only after Skule has plunged the country into civil war and precipitated events that promise to damn his own son does the pretender realize that some values are more important than sovereignty. Skule then goes to his death with full recognition of the errors of his course of action. In terms of the magnitude of Ibsen's conception and the scope of the action, *The Pretenders* is the most Shakespearean of Ibsen's works.
Reference: Kittang, Atte. "*The Pretenders:* Historical Vision or Psychological Tragedy?" *Ibsen Aarboken,* 3 (1975-76), 78-88.

PRICE, NANCY (1880-1970): British actress Nancy Price played several Ibsenian roles, including Ella Rentheim* (1928), the Rat-Wife* (1928), Helene Alving* (1935), and Gunhild Borkman* (1944).
Reference: Oxford Companion to the Theatre, 3d. ed. Ed. Phyllis Hartnoll (London: Oxford University Press, 1967), p. 761.

AN OLD PRIEST OF CYBELE (*Emperor and Galilean*): In Act III, Scene 3 of Part II, Julian* sacrifices in the Temple of Cybele presided over by this priest.

PRISCUS (*Emperor and Galilean*): A philosopher.

THE PRISONER AT AKERSHUS: Ibsen projected a *nouvelle* by this name, but only a chapter was completed.

PROVOST or **DEAN** (*Brand*): As the immediate ecclesiastical superior of Pastor Brand,* the Provost appears in Gudbrandsdalen* for the dedication of Brand's new church. He is the epitome of the opportunistic, political, and insensitive churchman and naturally becomes Brand's adversary.

PROZOR, MORITZ, COUNT (b. (1849): Count Prozor, a Lithuanian married to a Swede, was a career diplomat. When he was stationed in Stockholm, he saw a production of *Ghosts** and immediately set himself to translating it into French. Numerous translations followed: *Ghosts* (1889), *A Doll's House** (1889), *Hedda Gabler** (1892), *The Wild Duck** (1893), *Rosmersholm** (1893), *The Master Builder** (1894), *Little Eyolf** (1895), *Brand** (1895), *Peer Gynt** (1897), *John Gabriel Borkman** (1897), and *When We Dead Awaken** (1900). Although his translations were said to be pedantic, Prozor sold his work to Aurélien-Marie Lugné-Poë* and was Ibsen's French agent until 1890.

PUBLIA (*Emperor and Galilean*): A Christian woman of Antioch who defies the Emperor Julian.*

Q

QUESNEL, MLLE. LÉO: Mlle. Léo Quesnel is the author of perhaps the earliest French notices of Ibsen's works. She published "Souvenirs du Danemark," *Revue Bleue,* May 31, 1873 and "Poésie Scandinave—Henri Ibsen," *Revue Bleue,* July 25, 1874.

QUICKSANDS, OR THE PILLARS OF SOCIETY: Quicksands is William Archer's* earliest version of *The Pillars of Society.* It is more an adaptation or abridgment than a translation. Unable to find a publisher, Archer decided to produce the play, and in actor W. H. Vernon* he found a willing collaborator. After many setbacks, the play was produced at London's Gaiety Theatre on December 15, 1880, thus being the first professional production of an Ibsenian work in London. Unhappily, the production was not good, and the critics were unappreciative.
Reference: "Quicksands," *Theatre,* III (Feb. 1, 1881), 105.

R

RAFF, HELENE (1865-1942): While at Gossensass in the summer of 1889, Ibsen met Helene Raff, who witnessed the beginning of his infatuation with Emilie Bardach.* When Bardach left for Vienna in the autumn, Ibsen returned to Munich. So did Raff, the young painter, who walked up and down Ibsen's street in order to stage a "chance" encounter. She was successful on October 19 and spent quite a lot of time with the dramatist in the days that followed. A week later she went to Ibsen's home, where they talked of many things, particularly of women who are disappointed because they wait in vain for men to bring excitement and beauty into their lives. On that day, as on others, Ibsen kissed her as they parted.

Raff often visited Ibsen at home and became friendly with Mrs. Ibsen; Ibsen called at Raff's studio and later arranged for his wife to accompany him there. As they spent increasingly more time together, Raff kept copious notes of Ibsen's opinions, a valuable source of information for his biographers. [Excerpts have been published in *The Oxford Ibsen,* VII, 562ff.] Ibsen doubtless was devoted to the young artist who perhaps was a major factor in his diminished interest in Emilie Bardach. Raff seemed content to be his flirtatious, companionable friend, but the relationship suffered when Ibsen moved back to Christiania* in 1891.

Ibsen wrote on March 30, 1892, to thank Raff for a birthday gift of a seascape. In this letter he fondly recalled their happiness in Munich and urged her to visit Norway. At the very least, he said, she should write more often. There is no evidence of any further contact between them.

Reference: Zucker, A. E. *Ibsen, the Master Builder.* London: Thornton Butterworth, 1929.

RAGNHILD (*The Pretenders*): Lady Ragnhild was the devoted wife of Skule* although he was less than an ideal husband. She is at his side when he makes the momentous decision to sacrifice himself to the crowd of angry Nidarians.

RAINER, LUISE (1912-): Although known primarily as a film star, Luise Rainer portrayed Ellida Wangel* in a production of *The Lady from the Sea** that was mounted in New York on August 7, 1950. It lasted only sixteen performances.
Reference: Who Was Who in the Theatre, IV, 1975-76.

RALEIGH, CECIL (1856-1914): Cecil Raleigh directed the Independent Theatre's* production of *Ghosts** in London in 1891.
Reference: Who Was Who in the Theatre, IV, 1977-78.

RAMLO, MARIE (1850-1921): Marie Ramlo, a German actress, played several of Ibsen's women—Nora Helmer* (1880), Lona Hessel,* Thea Elvsted,* and Aase* (1906).
Reference: Enciclopedia della Spettacolo, VIII, 724.

RANK, DOCTOR (*A Doll's House*): As a friend of the Helmers,* Doctor Rank is a frequent visitor in their home. Although his affection for Nora Helmer* has grown deeper than mere friendship would dictate, his death obviates the issue. He is something of a *raisonneur* and a confidant to Nora.

RANK, OTTO (1884-1939): Sigmund Freud* based his analysis of Rebecca West's* incest on the theories of Austrian psychoanalyst Otto Rank.
Reference: Rank, Otto. *Das Inzest-Motiv in Dichtung und Sage* (Wien: F. Deuticke, 1912), pp. 404-5.

RAPHAEL, CLARA (1830-72): Under her *nom de guerre* of Clara Raphael, Mathilde Lucie Fibiger was one of the first Norwegian champions of female emancipation. While at Grimstad,* Ibsen read her letters in the newspapers; they were published as *Breve til Clara Raphael* (1851).

THE RAT-WIFE (*Little Eyolf*): The Rat-Wife is Ibsen's version of the Pied Piper. She and her little dog Mopseman* rid towns of rats through a combination of music and drowning. Eyolf Allmers* is compared with a rat, and he meets his death by being lured into the fjord.

RAY, CATHERINE: The first Ibsenian drama to be rendered into English was *Emperor and Galilean,** translated and published in 1876 by Catherine Ray. Little is known of her beyond the fact that the next year she wrote a novel called *The Farm on the Fjord*.

A RECEIVER (*Peer Gynt*): A criminal who disposes of stolen property, in this case the royal robes and white stallion of the Emperor of Morocco.

REDGRAVE, MICHAEL (1908-): When the National Theatre of Great Britain staged *The Master Builder** in London in 1964, Michael Redgrave, one of the nation's leading actors, played Halvard Solness.* Although his

performance was critically acclaimed, he was unable to remain with the production and was replaced by Laurence Olivier.*
Reference: Who's Who in the Theatre, 16th ed., pp. 1052-3.

REDGRAVE, VANESSA (1937-): Great excitement attended the announcement that Vanessa Redgrave had chosen *The Lady from the Sea** for her debut in New York. When she opened as Ellida Wangel* at the Circle in the Square Theatre on March 18, 1976, with Pat Hingle as Doctor Wangel,* there was general agreement that she looked and sounded a perfect Ellida, despite a production that did not match her talent. Only Clive Barnes, an Ibsen enthusiast, saw merit in it: "What a lovely play this is! sea-green, passionate, but quiet!" Redgrave's Ellida was presumed to be pregnant. Audiences were sufficient to keep the production on for seventy-seven performances. Redgrave repeated the role in Manchester, England, in November 1978 and at the Round House Theatre (London) on May 16, 1979, with Graham Crowden as Doctor Wangel. As a young woman, Redgrave had played Bolette Wangel* in 1961.
References: New York Theatre Critics' Reviews, XXXVII (Mar. 15, 1976), 322-6;
    Who's Who in the Theatre, 16th ed., pp. 1053-4.

REICHER, EMANUEL (1849-1924): The name of Reicher the actor is inextricably linked with that of Ibsen the dramatist on both European and American stages. On January 9, 1887, Reicher played Pastor Manders* to Charlotte Frohn's* Helene Alving* in Anton Anno's* production of *Ghosts** at the Residenz Theater, a role to which he returned throughout his career. On May 5, 1887, the team of Reicher-Frohn-Anno staged *Rosmersholm** at the same theatre in Berlin. In 1887 Reicher commenced an association with Otto Brahm* that led him to the Freie Bühne* (of which he was a member of the governing board) and the Deutsches Theater; on April 3 Brahm directed Reicher as Hjalmar Ekdal* at the Residenz Theater.

On January 19, 1893, Reicher, playing Halvard Solness,* staged the German premiere of *The Master Builder** at the Lessing Theater (Berlin). Audiences in the German capital saw Reicher as Alfred Allmers* in the world premiere of *Little Eyolf** (Deutsches Theater, January 12, 1895). By 1900 he had added Arnold Rubek* to his repertory. In the new century the German theatres of the United States beckoned to Reicher, largely because his son Franz (d. 1965) was acting with E. H. Sothern's company. His daughter Hedwig Reicher* had come to America in 1907 and so pleased German-speaking audiences that she was offered a handsome contract to play in English-speaking theatres if she could master the language. By November 6, 1911, she was playing Ellida Wangel* in English under the direction of her father at New York's Lyric Theatre.

Emanuel Reicher was in New York during World War I, at which time (1915) he founded the Modern Stage Company, modeled on German repertory theatres of his youth, and the American People's Theatre, a transplanted *Volksbühne*. In 1916 he added a school for actors. Under the aegis of the Modern Stage, he presented Gerhart Hauptmann's *Elga* (1915), *John Gabriel Borkman** (1915), and *Rosmersholm* (1916). John Gabriel Borkman* was Reicher's debut in English and was called the "acting treat of the season." Alice Lewisohn Crowley of the Neighborhood Playhouse thought that Reicher's *Rosmersholm* demonstrated "the cleavage between his theatre world, now of the past, and ours, still in its infancy, yet demanding its own right to 'become' " (Crowley, p. 62). In 1919 Reicher signed on as a general director of the Theatre Guild, but after only one production, he returned to Germany where he died soon afterward.

References: Crowley, Alice L. *The Neighborhood Playhouse: Leaves from a Theatre Scrapbook.* New York: Theatre Arts Books, 1959; *Enciclopedia della Spettacolo,* VIII, 838-9.

REICHER, HEDWIG (1884-1971): The daughter of theatrical parents, Emanuel Reicher* and Lona Harf, Hedwig Reicher as a young girl visited with Ibsen in her parents' home in Berlin. She went on the professional stage in 1900 and spent the early years of the century studying and playing leading women's roles in her father's touring companies. Thus, she received considerable experience with Ibsen's heroines. In Germany her Nora Helmer* was particularly appreciated.

Hedwig's brother Franz (d. 1965) was at the same time a member of E. H. Sothern's company in the United States. At a hiatus between engagements, she traveled to New York in 1907 to visit her brother and was convinced to act in German at the Irving Place Theatre. She then performed at the New German Theatre. When producer Henry B. Harris saw her act in the spring of 1909, he offered her an American contract if she would learn English; six months later she opened in *On the Eve,* the first of several undistinguished productions in which she appeared. Reicher, therefore, readily joined the Drama Players of Chicago, which mounted a season in New York in 1911.

Her first two roles were negligible, but Reicher's considerable gifts were efficiently displayed as Ellida Wangel* when *The Lady from the Sea** opened on November 6, 1911, at the Lyric Theatre. The *New York Dramatic Mirror* (Nov. 15, 1911, p. 7, cols. 2-3) observed: "Ellida was wavering on the brink of insanity, and the chief merit of Hedwig Reicher's delineation owes its value to her realization and her expression of just that point. . . . The actress properly made her something less than human and something more than earthly. . . . Miss Reicher's methods are simple and direct and are decidedly interesting from start to finish." Reicher thereafter was closely identified with her father's projects in New York during World War I.

Reference: The American Stage of Today. Intro. William Winter. New York: P. F. Collier and Son, 1910.

REIGNOLDS-WINSLOW, CATHERINE MARY (1836-1911): At the time of her marriage to Boston merchant Erving Winslow in 1861, Kate Reignolds (as she was known in the theatre) was an actress at the Boston Museum. Soon she was a star. She tired of the stage but appeared occasionally as a public reader, in which capacity she introduced Ibsen to fashionable audiences. First in Boston and then in New York and Washington, D.C. (and perhaps other places), Winslow either rented public rooms or procured the use of drawing rooms of eminent citizens for her readings. Sitting at a low table and utilizing her communicative hands and expressive face, Winslow read from a marked script from which she had deleted very little.

Winslow's performances of Ibsen in New York were held in the second-floor ballroom of the Hotel Brunswick which easily accommodated the hundred ladies and few gentlemen who attended the reading of *The Pillars of Society** on March 10, 1890. Word-of-mouth advertisement as well as newspaper notices assured Winslow of larger audiences by the time she read *A Doll's House** on March 12, *An Enemy of the People** on March 14, and *The Lady from the Sea** on March 17. Indeed, the room was crowded for these presentations.

The nation's capital provided stiffer resistance than New York's cultured ladies had done. Winslow approached Mrs. John Wanamaker, the wife of the postmaster general, about making her house available for readings, but Mrs. Wanamaker, as well as Mrs. Levi P. Morton, the vice-president's wife, "gracefully excused" herself on the grounds of Ibsen's immorality. Mrs. Chief Justice Melville W. Fuller, according to one source, was "hoodwinked" into providing her parlor for the performance on March 30, which proved to be a "gratifying success."

New York producer A. M. Palmer had been amenable to presenting an Ibsenian drama at the Madison Square Theatre as early as the summer of 1889. He was, therefore, an ideal sponsor of Winslow's reading of *A Doll's House* on April 1, 1890. The response of the "surprisingly large" audience was on the whole positive, encouraging Winslow to project a longer tour of her Ibsenian cycle.

Word of Winslow's efforts in his behalf reached Ibsen, who penned the following chivalrous letter to the actress/reader:

6 April 1890

Very honored lady:

It was a great and deeply felt pleasure for me to learn some particulars of the readings you have already given of my dramatic works, as well as of the extended tour which you propose to undertake. For your active and unwearied endeavors to bring my writings before the public, in which you have already been so successful, I beg you to accept my warmest and heartiest thanks, whilst I wish you, at the same time, a great deal of good fortune in the artistic tour which you are planning. With the best and most courteous greetings, I have the honor to sign myself your very devoted

Henrik Ibsen

References: "The Lounger," *The Critic,* XVI, 327 (Apr. 5, 1890), 170; *New York Times,* Mar. 11, 1890, p. 5, col. 4; Mar. 12, 1890, p. 8, col. 4; Mar. 13, 1890, p. 4, col. 7; Mar. 15, 1890, p. 5, col. 3; Mar. 18, 1890, p. 4, col. 6; Mar. 30, 1890, p. 1, col. 3; Apr. 2, 1890, p. 4, col. 5; "Notes," *The Critic,* XVI, 330 (Apr. 26, 1890), 215; Reignolds-Winslow, Catherine. *Yesterdays with Actors.* Boston: Cupples and Hurd, 1887.

REIMANN, J. A.: Reimann was the apothecary in Grimstad* to whom Ibsen was apprenticed in his sixteenth year. For more than five years (1844-50), Reimann was Ibsen's master.

REINHARDT, MAX (1873-1943): Max Reinhardt, an Austrian, entered the theatre as an actor (one of his early roles was Jacob Engstrand*) but quickly established himself as one of the most important directors of his generation. Reinhardt was known for his eclectic approach to directing, which he applied to productions of Ibsen's plays during his tenure as head of Berlin's Deutsches Theater (1905-20 and 1924-32) and other theatres in Europe and America. His Ibsenian productions included

*The Pretenders,**	Neues Theater, Berlin, October 7, 1904
*Rosmersholm,**	Kleines Theater, Berlin, April 28, 1905
*Ghosts,**	Kammerspiele, Berlin, November 8, 1906
*Hedda Gabler,**	Kammerspiele, Berlin, March 11, 1907
*Love's Comedy,**	Kammerspiele, Berlin, March 25, 1907
Ghosts,	Budapest, May 1910
Ghosts,	Dresden, September 1913
Ghosts,	Budapest, May 1914
Ghosts,	Amsterdam, April-May 1916 (in repertory)
*John Gabriel Borkman,**	Deutsches Theater, Berlin, March 14, 1917
*A Doll's House,**	Kammerspiele, Berlin, November 23, 1917

When Reinhardt first produced *Ghosts,* he commissioned Edvard Munch, the Norwegian painter, to collaborate with him on the scenery in which "the combinations of colors and the shape of the furniture breathed a spirit of oppressiveness, of grief, and of the sense of destiny. . . . " (Sayler, p. 26). Munch and Reinhardt had, in fact, created an Expressionistic setting for a Realistic play, which in 1906 was a novel undertaking.

References: Carter, Huntley. *The Theatre of Max Reinhardt.* New York: M. Kinnerley, 1914; Sayler, Oliver M. *Max Reinhardt and His Theatre.* New York: Benjamin Blom, 1968 [1929].

RÉJANE, GABRIELLE (1857-1920): Recipient of an acting scholarship to the prestigious Conservatory of Paris, Réjane joined the troupe of the Vaudeville Theatre in 1875, a position she held for eight years. After achieving considerable acclaim in several other theatres, Réjane returned to the Vaudeville where she appeared as Nora Helmer* in *La Maison de Poupée, the French version of A Doll's House,* on April 20, 1894. Audiences and critics responded enthusiastically to the production, the adviser on which had been Ibsen's representative, Hermann Joachim Bang.*

Réjane's talents lay in playing comedy, but her Nora "showed her in a new and more serious light, demonstrating at once her genuine versatility and her considerable emotional power." (Izard, p. 163.) The play was not in her repertory when she visited London in 1894, but audiences in New York saw it in 1895. American critics generally recognized Réjane's comedic powers, but for most of them the language barrier was insuperable. Both of her American tours (1895 and 1904) were financially unsuccessful. *La Maison de Poupée* was finally seen in London in June 1903.

A truly international star, Réjane was seen in many places before she opened her own Théâtre Réjane in Paris in 1906, a house dedicated to comedy. She retired in 1915.

References: Antona-Traversi, C. *Réjane.* Paris: Editions le Calame, 1931; Izard, Forrest. *Heroines of the Modern Stage.* New York: Sturgis and Walton, 1915.

RELLING, DOCTOR (*The Wild Duck*): As the *raisonneur,* Relling makes the point that people need their illusions in order to sustain life. Believing this, he is the fierce opponent of Gregers Werle.*

RENTHEIM, ELLA (*John Gabriel Borkman*): The twin sister of Gunhild Borkman,* Ella Rentheim had once loved John Gabriel Borkman* and had vied with Gunhild for the love of the Borkman son. Her appearance and renewal of the contest for the boy's love precipitate the action of the play. It is Ella who convinces Borkman to leave his self-imposed exile, and it is she who is at his side when he dies. Ella herself is dying of a fatal disease.

"RESURRECTION DAY": Arnold Rubek's* masterpiece of sculpture in *When We Dead Awaken.**

RICHARDSON, RALPH (1902-1983): Ralph Richardson, who until his death was the oldest of the trio of England's most distinguished contemporary actors that included John Gielgud* and Laurence Olivier,* was ideally suited by temperament and method to portray Ibsenian roles. Happily, he had extensive experience in the plays of Ibsen. When Richardson and Olivier assumed the management of London's Old Vic Theatre near the end of World War II, Peer Gynt* was chosen as Richardson's first major role; previously, he had read the part of Peer in a

BBC radio production. Richardson's Peer, lauded by the critics, was "an unfixed wide-ranging being whose very centre reveals an enigmatic lack of substance" (O'Connor, p. 116). Richardson's ability to alter his voice to suggest different stages in Peer's development was noted favorably. When the London engagement of the production ended, the Old Vic Company toured Europe with Richardson's Peer Gynt as a staple of the repertory. In 1945 the king of Norway decorated Richardson with the Star of St. Olaf for his service to Norwegian culture.

In 1952 Richardson played the title role in a BBC radio version of *Brand** but in 1963 declined to play Doctor Wangel* to Margaret Leighton's Ellida Wangel.* He returned to Ibsen in 1972 when he portrayed Judge Brack* in a film of *Hedda Gabler.**

Richardson's John Gabriel Borkman* (January 1975) provided a high-water mark for his career, as Peer Gynt had done thirty years earlier. In rehearsal Richardson remarked, "I've got the John, I've got the Borkman, I'm still looking for the Gabriel." Writing of Richardson, Harold Hobson observed, "He can be simultaneously the totally ordinary embodiment of kindly domestic commonsense and a man whom the chaos of the universe has driven out of his mind." John Gielgud added, "I shall never forget the noise he made when Borkman died. As if a bird had flown out of his heart" (O'Connor, pp. 209, 210, 211). Richardson's last Ibsenian character was Old Ekdal* in *The Wild Duck** of the National Theatre of Great Britain (December 1979).

References: Hobson, Harold. *Ralph Richardson.* London: Rockliff, 1958; O'Connor, Garry. *Ralph Richardson: An Actor's Life.* New York: Atheneum, 1982.

RIKSMAAL: In Ibsen's day the written Norwegian language was called *riksmaal* and was nearly indistinguishable from written Danish. In 1907 *riksmaal* was given a different orthography, and in 1917 Danish words in the language were respelled as Norwegian, and a purely Norwegian pronunciation and grammar were added. *riksmaal* is now called *bokmaal.*

RINGDAL (*The League of Youth*): Manager of Chamberlain Brattsberg's* ironworks.

ROBERTS, FLORENCE (1871-1927): American actress Florence Roberts played Nora Helmer* on the Pacific coast of the United States during the 1903-4 season.

Reference: Briscoe, Johnson. *Actors' Birthday Book*, Ser. 3. New York: Moffat, Yard, 1907.

ROBERTS, RICHARD ELLIS (1879-1953): R. E. Roberts translated *Peer Gynt** into English in 1912 and again in 1936. These were the standard versions for production.

ROBINS, ELIZABETH (1862-1940): After proving herself as an actress with the Boston Museum company, James O'Neill's troupe, and the distinguished Edwin Booth-Lawrence Barrett combination, Elizabeth Robins went to England in 1888 and almost immediately established herself as one of Ibsen's foremost interpreters. Her first Ibsenian role was that of Martha Bernick* in *The Pillars of Society** (July 17, 1889) with W. H. Vernon* and Genevieve Ward in the leading roles.

Mrs. Edvard Bull, one of the original company at the Norwegian Theatre, Bergen,* whetted Robins' interest in Ibsen. In 1890 she conceived the idea of presenting *Ghosts** with herself as Helene Alving.* She approached Herbert Beerbohm Tree* about making the Haymarket Theatre available for matinee performances. Tree agreed—if he were to be allowed to play Oswald Alving.* Robins had settled on Fred Terry for the role, but he was dissuaded by Tree himself. These discussions reached an impasse, Robins had to rehearse another production, and *Ghosts* was postponed indefinitely.

Her zeal for Ibsen undaunted, Robins eventually appeared as Hedda Gabler* (April 20, 1891, March 30, 1898), Kristine Linde* (January 27, 1891), Rebecca West* (May 31, 1893), Hilde Wangel* in *The Master Builder** (February 20, 1893), Agnes* in Act IV of *Brand** (February 20, 1893), Rita Allmers* (November 23, 1896), and Ella Rentheim* (May 3, 1897).

As an actress and a producer, Robins was celebrated; as a proponent of Ibsen, she was incalculably important. In her sixties Robins reviewed her exertions in Ibsen's behalf, the result of which was a speech and a book based on it, *Ibsen and the Actress* (1928).

References: Cima, Gay Gibson. "Elizabeth Robins: The Genesis of an Independent Manageress," *Theatre Survey,* XXI, 2 (Nov. 1980), 145-63; Robins, Elizabeth. *Both Sides of the Curtain.* London: William Heinemann, 1940.

ROBSON, FLORA (1902-): Dame Flora Robson played Helene Alving* in *Ghosts** in London at the Old Vic in 1958 and 1959 to great acclaim.
Reference: Dunbar, Janet. *Flora Robson.* London: Harrap, 1960.

RODERIK (*The Burial Mound*): An old recluse who is really a Viking chieftain.

ROOKE, IRENE (1878-1958): The tiny Everyman Theatre in London was the scene of Irene Rooke's venture as Helene Alving* in *Ghosts.** The year was 1925. In general, critics were kind to the production, but it was noted that Rooke's technique, though good, was too obvious (*The Times* [London], Oct. 14, 1925, p. 14, col. 4).
Reference: Oxford Companion to the Theatre, 3d ed. Ed. Phyllis Hartnoll (London: Oxford University Press, 1967), p. 809.

ROSMER, BEATA (*Rosmersholm*): Although Beata does not appear in the drama, her presence is nonetheless real. As the invalid wife of Johannes Rosmer,* Beata was encouraged to think that Rebecca West* was pregnant by Johannes and that the only way to save his reputation was by freeing him to marry Rebecca. Consequently, Beata committed suicide.

ROSMER, JOHANNES (*Rosmersholm*): The master of Rosmersholm,* Johannes Rosmer comes from a long line of conservative landowners and professional men. When his father secured him a pastorate, Johannes discovered that he lacked the application to succeed in such a calling. He is, in fact, painfully tractable, as Rebecca West* discovers. She converts him to radicalism, convinces him that he can make a difference to mankind, and plans to desert him when even he admits his ineffectuality. Rosmer asks Rebecca to demonstrate her love by dying for him, and when she agrees, the sacrifice is so attractive that he joins her in death.

ROSMERSHOLM: The ancestral home of the Rosmer family was called "Rosmersholm," the literal meaning of which is "Rosmer's island." Clearly this is an apt name for the arena in which the action of *Rosmersholm** occurs because Johannes Rosmer's* estate is similar to a small island surrounded by a hostile sea of inimical forces. Rosmer himself is isolated on that island with only Rebecca West* and the pictures of his ancestors as company. By placing the dramatic action in such isolation, Ibsen achieved a concentration of dramatic effect that is quite potent.

ROSMERSHOLM: A four-act Realistic-Symbolistic serious drama.

Composition: First draft written in February 1886; third draft completed on September 27, 1886; published on November 23, 1886.

Stage history:

Jan. 17, 1887	Norwegian Theatre, Bergen*
Mar. 1887	Stadttheater, Gothenburg
Apr. 12, 1887	Christiania Theatre* (13 perfs.)
Apr. 16, 1887	Augsburg
Apr. 1887	Stockholm
May 5, 1887	Residenz Theater, Berlin (23), Emanuel Reicher* as Rosmer
1887	Berlin
1888	Zürich
Apr. 1, 1889	Thalia Theater, Hamburg
Feb. 23, 1891	Vaudeville Theatre, London (2), Frank R. Benson* as Rosmer
May 4, 1893	Deutsches Volkstheater, Vienna
May 31, 1893	Opera Comique, London (4), Lewis Waller* as Rosmer
Oct. 6, 1893	Salle des Bouffes du Nord, Paris, pro. Théâtre de l'Oeuvre, Aurélien-Marie Lugné-Poë* as Rosmer

July 2, 1894	Orpheus Theater, Munich, pro. Alfred von Wolzogen*
Mar. 25, 1895	Opera Comique, London, Aurélien-Marie Lugné-Poë as Rosmer
Apr. 21, 1895	Westendhalle, Munich, Emil Messthaler* as Rosmer
Nov. 17, 1897	Schauspielhaus, Munich
1899	Dagmars Theatre, Copenhagen
1901	Schiller Theater, Berlin
Mar. 28, 1904	Princess Theatre, New York (8), Florence Kahn* as Rebecca
Apr. 28, 1905	Kleines Theater, Berlin, dir. Max Reinhardt*
Oct. 21, 1905	Hoftheater, Braunschweig
Nov. 7, 1905	Kommisarzhevsky Theatre, St. Petersburg
Nov. 15, 1905	National Theatre, Christiania,* Johanne Dybwad* as Rebecca
Dec. 5, 1905	Pergola Theatre, Florence, Eleonora Duse* as Rebecca
Oct. 15, 1907	Residenz Theater, Munich
Dec. 30, 1907	Lyric Theatre, New York (30, followed by 169 on tour), Minnie Maddern Fiske* as Rebecca
Feb. 10, 1908	Terry's Theatre, London, Florence Kahn as Rebecca
Mar. 5, 1908	Art Theatre, Moscow,* dir. Vladimir Nemirovich- Danchenko*
June 11, 1909	Residenz Theater, Munich
May 28, 1912	Little Theatre, London, Leigh Lovel as Rosmer
Mar. 5, 1915	Hoftheater, Braunschweig
June 5, 1917	St. Martin's Theatre, London
Apr. 23, 1918	1st Studio, Moscow, dir. E. Vakhtangov
May 5, 1925	52d Street Theatre, New York (30), Margaret Wycherly* as Rebecca
Sept. 30, 1926	Kingsway Theatre, London, Edith Evans* as Rebecca
Dec. 2, 1935	Shubert Theatre, New York (8), Eva Le Gallienne* as Rebecca
Mar. 5, 1936	Criterion Theatre, London
Aug. 18, 1945	Torch Theatre, London, David Markham as Rosmer
July 8, 1948	Arts Theatre, London, Jean Forbes-Robertson* as Rebecca
Aug. 22, 1950	St. Martin's Theatre, London, Signe Hasso* as Rebecca
Jan. 1951	Arts Theatre, London, Jean Forbes-Robertson as Rebecca
Nov. 18, 1959	Royal Court Theatre, London, Peggy Ashcroft* as Rebecca
Jan. 5, 1960	Comedy Theatre, London, Peggy Ashcroft as Rebecca
Apr. 11, 1962	4th Street Theatre, New York (58), Nancy Wickwire* as Rebecca
May 17, 1973	Greenwich Theatre, London, Joan Plowright* as Rebecca
Dec. 15, 1974	Roundabout Stage 2, New York, Jane White* as Rebecca
Oct. 19, 1977	Haymarket Theatre, London, Claire Bloom* as Rebecca

Synopsis: In the sitting room of Rosmersholm (literally "Rosmer's Island") presided over by numerous portraits of illustrious Rosmers of successive generations, Rebecca West, companion of the late mistress of the house, is discussing dinner arrangements with Mrs. Helseth the housekeeper, when they notice that Johannes Rosmer is walking again on the path that skirts the mill but avoiding the footbridge. In an interchange designed to engender suspense, Rebecca and Mrs. Helseth, who is a vociferously superstitious woman of the people, allude to the unnatural influences of the dead upon the inhabitants of Rosmersholm. At this point Mrs. Helseth makes a veiled reference to the White Horse that mysteriously appears when the death of a Rosmer is imminent.

These ruminations and the eerie mood are interrupted by the appearance of Professor Kroll, the brother of the late Mrs. Beata (literally "blessed") Rosmer. His visit is remarkable because he has avoided Rosmersholm since the death of his sister months earlier. Kroll notes the cheerful flowers that adorn the parlor and recalls their asphyxiating effect on Beata. The flowers, then, are emblematic of the passing of the old feminine regime and the ascent of the new.

Mrs. Helseth leaves, and the conversation turns to Kroll's recent political activities on the side of extreme conservatism. When he brings up the matter of the way in which the radical newspapers have abused him, Rebecca hints that she is fully conscious of their content, which foreshadows her espousal of free thought. Kroll and Rebecca next turn to a consideration of her place at Rosmersholm now that Beata is gone. She plans to stay as long as Rosmer needs her, presumably until he adjusts to the life of a widower or remarries.

Exposition is skillfully woven into this scene as the pair talk about Doctor West, Rebecca's father, who was half-paralyzed but became a burden only after they moved south from Finmark. In the north he bore his affliction stoically, but in the south his emotions surged to the surface. (This geographical dichotomy appears in most of Iben's plays.) After her father's death, Rebecca came to Rosmersholm as the companion of another invalid, Beata. Kroll surprises Rebecca by saying that he did not nor does he now resent Rebecca's presiding over the household affairs; indeed, he would be pleased to see her become Mrs. Johannes Rosmer. Rebecca's response to the suggestion is veiled, and the discussion is then interrupted by the entrance of Rosmer.

When Rosmer and Kroll begin to talk about Beata, Rebecca makes a point of lighting the lamp as if to dispel Beata's shade. Rebecca has carefully addressed Rosmer as "Mister," but Rosmer tellingly slips and calls her by her Christian name, then he corrects himself. Since a considerable time has elapsed without their meeting, Kroll begins to tell Rosmer about his political concerns and his belief that the radicals have infiltrated even into his own school and turned the most gifted students against him. Mortensgaard, the editor of *The Beacon,* is the chief culprit, and even Kroll's own children have embraced the radical cause with their mother's support. While Kroll laments the disruption of his own home, Rebecca demands that Rosmer tell Kroll something immediately, but Rosmer resists. Rebecca immediately senses that Kroll is trying to enlist Rosmer, as the most influential man in the district, to join the conservative ranks. She suggests to Kroll that Rosmer has taken a wider view of life than he formerly held. Kroll offers Rosmer the editorship of the *County News,* the conservative newspaper, but Rosmer refuses on the grounds that he is unsuited to the task. It then comes out that his father had gotten him appointed minister of the local church, but Rosmer had believed himself incapable and resigned. When he realizes that Rosmer is obdurate, Kroll asks at least for his moral support and, referring to the array of ancestral portraits, calls upon the previous two centuries of conservative Rosmers as allies. Rosmer weakly wavers while Rebecca, incensed, is about to tell Kroll something against Rosmer's wishes when Mrs. Helseth enters with the news that a caller is at the kitchen door.

The tension of the previous scene is mitigated by the word that Ulrik Brendel, remembered variously as a scoundrel, writer, actor, pauper, and revolutionary, has come to call. Brendel is fondly recollected by Rosmer, his former pupil, because Brendel had been abused by Rosmer's father, whose behavior as a martinet is painfully remembered by his son. This vagabond philosopher has returned for the purpose of renting a hall and inaugurating a series of lectures on his personal abstract views of life, which he hopes will change the nature of human existence. Throughout the entire interchange, Brendel provides an almost comical contrast with his sober auditors. Despite penury, which forces him to borrow a clean shirt from Rosmer, Brendel is grandiloquent, sanguine, and utterly convinced of his mission. At his dramatic departure, Rosmer plaintively observes that ''at least he'd had the courage to live life in his own way.''

The encounter with Brendel gives Rosmer the resolution he needs to confess to Kroll that he agrees with the Kroll children and the radical cause. He says that he plans to work for Freedom and the creation of a true democracy, in pursuit of which he has thrown over his former religious faith in preference to a more basic platform. Rosmer invites Kroll to join him in the attempt to reconcile the warring factions. The professor heartily declines and declares their friendship at an end. Rosmer maintains that he can persevere because Rebecca stands with him, which prompts Kroll to remark that Beata had implied that Rosmer and Rebecca were closer than they ought to have been.

After Kroll storms out, Rosmer affirms that together he and Rebecca can face the world, but instead of remaining with her to celebrate his open declaration of liberation, he goes to bed, leaving Rebecca alone. Rebecca instructs Mrs. Helseth to clear up the dinner things as no one intended to eat the meal. She jokingly remarks that she hopes Kroll does not meet the White Horse in his rage, as she thinks that the ghosts of the past will be active for quite a while.

As if to indicate the increasingly intimate nature of Rosmer and Rebecca's friendship, the second act takes place in Rosmer's study. Whereas the ponderous events of the first act occurred in the early evening, the present act takes place in the morning. When Rebecca enters in a dressing gown, Rosmer asks if his ''dear'' wants anything in particular. They jointly rejoice in the declaration of independence uttered by Rosmer on the previous night, which encourages Rebecca to admit that she passed a note to

Mortensgaard requesting him to oblige Rosmer by assisting Brendel in any way possible. Rosmer correctly interprets the gesture as an appeal for the radical editor's friendship and is not pleased. At the precise moment when Rebecca predicts that Kroll has been irretrievably alienated, Mrs. Helseth brings word that the professor has called again. Rebecca leaves the room as Kroll enters.

Aside from being scandalized by meeting Rebecca in her negligee, Kroll brings news of Brendel's taking up with disreputable companions, his drinking and brawling, and his eventual rescue by none other than Mortensgaard. Kroll tells Rosmer that Rebecca has been corresponding with Mortensgaard and is discomfited to learn that Rosmer knows and approves of it. Undaunted, Kroll embarks upon a Socratic dialogue through which he hopes to convince Rosmer of his apostasy. First, he asks if Rosmer knows the reasons for Beata's suicide. When Rosmer attributes the death to dementia, Kroll remarks that the doctors did not verify the diagnosis. Rosmer, however, is convinced that Beata's morbidity and self-loathing were ample evidence of her madness, which derived from her inability to produce children. Kroll then asks if any modern books on marital relations ever found their way into Beata's hands. Rosmer answers that such a book inherited from Doctor West's library was about the house but denies that it was ever given to Beata. Kroll's clear implication is that Rebecca deliberately pressed the book onto Beata in order to aggravate her mental condition. In her despair Beata had gone to her brother and spoken with anguish about her fears that Rosmer was about to break with the church, but Kroll could not believe that the heir of the Rosmers could ever consider such a course of action. Surely, he thought, Beata was mad. A month later when he talked again to Beata, Kroll believed she was resigned to whatever the future held. She predicted the imminent appearance of the White Horse at Rosmersholm. Two days later she hurled herself into the millrace. Before Beata died, according to Kroll, she had said that Johannes *must* marry Rebecca at once, and now Kroll brazenly asks if Beata's accusation has any foundation. Rosmer heatedly denies that his conduct has been impure, which goads Kroll into saying that he sees very little difference between freethinking and free-loving. This interchange is interrupted by Mrs. Helseth, who has come with a message for Rebecca. She learns that Rebecca is upstairs; the intrusion heightens the emotional level of the scene.

When the argument is resumed, Kroll urges Rosmer to think whatever he pleases but to keep his opinions to himself, thus preserving the appearance of orthodoxy. Then he appeals again to Rosmer's family tradition and his genetic inheritance to protect "the Rosmer Way of Life," all of which Rosmer refuses. Mrs. Helseth comes in again to say that Mortensgaard is downstairs and that Mrs. West has said he might come up for an interview. The incursion of his sworn enemy in Rosmer's house more fully alienates Kroll and sends him from the room in rage. As he passes Mortensgaard,

Kroll tauntingly scores him for violating the seventh commandment against adultery, perhaps a reference to Rebecca.

Left alone with Rosmer, Mortensgaard asks if he might announce in *The Beacon* that Rosmer has embraced the radical position, to which Rosmer assents. The editor learns to his great chagrin that Rosmer has also turned away from the church, which makes the former clergyman a less desirable ally. Mortensgaard urges Rosmer not to make public his defection from the church. Then the editor introduces the subject of a letter he had received from Beata in which irregular conduct at Rosmersholm was suggested. After urging Rosmer to be discreet, he departs with a promise to print an item about Rosmer's adoption of the radical cause but to remain silent about his heterodoxy.

Once Rosmer is alone, Rebecca draws the curtains from the doorway in which she had hidden during the discussions with Kroll and Mortensgaard. Rosmer is relieved that Rebecca knows everything that has passed, but he continues to be disturbed that Beata would have thought that there was anything untoward in his relationship with Rebecca. As he imagines the tortures to which his behavior subjected Beata, Rosmer becomes increasingly agitated and finally collapses in despair. At this moment Rebecca senses that she has lost him. She begins to reminisce about their former happiness while Rosmer reconstructs Beata's misery. He concludes that he will never escape his fixation on the dead past even if it means giving up "being alive in life." The alternative as seen by Rebecca is to be dead in life, the very fate from which she had rescued him. Rosmer then seems to rally and to declare that he must be free of the dead by the only effective means: the creation of new life. To that end, he asks Rebecca to marry him. Rebecca recoils and says that she can never be his wife and that he must not mention the proposal again. When pressed for her reasons, Rebecca says that marriage is impossible for both their sakes but refuses to be more specific. As a response to Rosmer's insistent questions, she vows that their relationship has ended, that she will leave Rosmersholm by the same route Beata traveled. With that grim announcement, Rosmer is left alone to ponder her meaning.

Act III occurs on a sunny morning when Mrs. Helseth and Rebecca are cleaning the sitting room while talking about local affairs. Mrs. Helseth repeats the rumors that Mortensgaard fathered a child with a married woman whose husband had abandoned her. Then Mrs. Helseth reveals that she once carried a letter from Beata to Mortensgaard, and upon Rebecca's prompting, says that Mrs. Kroll encouraged Beata to think the worst of Rosmer and Rebecca. When the subject of Beata's childlessness arises, Mrs. Helseth opines that Rosmersholm is an unwholesome environment for children, for it is a place in which children never cry and adults never laugh, an aberration that emanates from the house and spreads like a contagion throughout the countryside.

Rosmer enters and is greeted by Rebecca, who has now begun to call him "dear." The *County News* has arrived, and Rosmer learns that Kroll has soundly excoriated him for godlessness and immorality, although the name of Rosmer is not specifically mentioned. This terrible news increases Rosmer's desire to do something that will make all the factions come to their senses, a wish in which he is encouraged by Rebecca. His reformer's zeal is soon dampened by his belief that because of his guilt he can never be the agent of good. At that point Mrs. Helseth slips in and whispers something to Rebecca. As his mind rambles through the past, Rosmer admits that he has long loved Rebecca, that what he had viewed as friendship was actually spiritual marriage. Rebecca maintains that all his doubts and fears are but ancestral relics come to haunt him, but Rosmer continues to think that only a happy and blameless man can be mankind's benefactor. When chided by Rebecca that he cannot be happy because he does not know how to laugh, Rosmer retorts that nevertheless he has a great capacity for happiness. Then he goes outside for a walk.

With Rosmer out of the way, Kroll is brought into the sitting room. The professor has come to say that he thinks Rebecca is the cause of Rosmer's altered outlook. She hints that there had been a time when the warmth of her relationship with Kroll was equally persuasive. Kroll says that she merely used him as a means of insinuating herself into Rosmersholm when she reduced both Beata and Rosmer to a state of idolatry of herself. When Kroll accuses Rebecca of destroying Rosmer's happiness, she rejoins that the professor actually did that by convincing Rosmer of his guilt in Beata's death. A discussion of Rosmer's heredity leads to an acidulous exposition of Rebecca's heritage, which, according to Kroll, accounts for her behavior. He maintains that the Doctor West who had adopted her had been her natural father and that Rebecca had been conceived in an adulterous liaison. Her only legacy from him was her behavioral proclivities and a trunk full of books. This conclusion rattles Rebecca, for she cannot refute Kroll's alleged facts. The professor points out that her free-thinking has been only skin deep: when confronted with the likelihood of her own illegitimacy, Rebecca shrinks in traditional revulsion. If she cannot accommodate this discovery about herself, how can Rosmer be expected to flout all his family traditions with impunity? The only recourse, Kroll adds, is to repudiate Rosmer's apostasy and marry Rebecca to squelch the gossip. At that point Rosmer returns, and Rebecca begs Kroll as the last favor she will ever ask of him to remain and hear what is to follow.

Faced with an impossibly uncomfortable confrontation, Rebecca greets Rosmer by calling him "dearest," which shocks Kroll. With the calm of one who has made a difficult decision, Rebecca sets out to tell Rosmer the truth about everything. She proposes to restore Rosmer's sense of innocence by describing her decision to take up Rosmer's education in modern ideas where Brendel had left off. Since the unhappy marriage to Beata lay in the way of her plans for Rosmer, Rebecca had cunningly led Beata along the path to madness and suicide by insinuating that he had lost his faith and that a romantic affair between herself and Rosmer was inescapable. At Kroll's instigation, Rebecca confesses that she might also have led Beata to believe that Rebecca's pregnancy necessitated her hypothetically imminent departure. The almost inevitable result was Beata's seeing the necessity of removing herself from the scene.

When Rosmer asks her how she could contemplate such a scheme, Rebecca answers that she had to choose between Rosmer's life and Beata's but that she never fully believed that the plan could work although she ardently desired its success. Bit by bit, the pieces fitted together, and before she knew it, Beata was dead. If she feels remorse at her conduct, she does not reveal it. Kroll, gloating in his victory, takes a willing Rosmer back to town with him while Rebecca orders Mrs. Helseth to bring her trunk down from the attic. Rebecca contemplates leaving Rosmersholm and going on a long journey. To the faithful housekeeper, Rebecca admits that she too has seen the White Horses—note the plural—of Rosmersholm.

It is night again when Act IV resumes, and Rebecca is packing a bag in the sitting room. She remarks to Mrs. Helseth that the coachman will be required at eleven o'clock because the steamer sails at midnight. Mrs. Helseth is angry because she believes that Rebecca is pregnant and is leaving because Rosmer will not accept his responsibility for her condition.

At that moment Rosmer enters and discovers that Rebecca plans to return to the north whence she came. Rosmer tells her that his old friends have returned to him and convinced him that he is not the person to accomplish the rehabilitation of mankind. In a last effort to make Rosmer understand her actions, Rebecca admits that she had schemed to gain admittance to Rosmersholm and to win ascendancy over Rosmer, but all her plans became secondary to her growing, uncontrollable passion for him. That passion, in effect, caused her to kill Beata, for she knew she could never possess Rosmer until he was free of Beata. When he reminds her that he offered her marriage, she says that she was unable to accept because by then Rosmersholm had crippled and warped her spirit, robbed her of her power of action. The environment and its traditions were capable of killing happiness.

When Rosmer again suggests marriage, Rebecca rejects it ostensibly because of the taint of her illegitimacy, which Rosmer is willing to overlook. Then the conversation turns to the possibility of a person's being ennobled by pure, unselfish love, an idea that is attractive to them both, but Rosmer cannot fully believe that Rebecca loves him. He has lost all faith and sees nothing in life worth living for. In a restless maneuver Rosmer demands that Rebecca restore his faith in love. She must give him a proof of her love.

The discussion ceases as Ulrik Brendel enters and says that he is now going downhill toward the great Nothingness (one of Sören Aabye

Kierkegaard's* concepts), having arrived at his present state of despair when he discovered that the secret of life is to have no ideals. Brendel foresees victory for Rosmer through the sacrifices of the woman who loves him. On this enigmatic note, he withdraws, leaving Rebecca gasping for breath.

For the first time in the drama, she *opens* rather than closes a window. The lovers are now agreed that Rebecca must go away but need not fear for her financial security, for which Rosmer has made provision. She hints that her future is already accounted for, but Rosmer continues talking about suicide as an antidote to his many failures. Rebecca tries to encourage him to fight for the good of mankind, but Rosmer believes the loss of his faith to be enervating. When Rebecca insists that he has changed her life and asks what she can do to prove her sincerity, Rosmer asks if she has the courage to follow Beata into the millrace. That, he avers, would restore his faith in his ability to affect someone else. She calmly observes that he will then have his faith again. Seeing what he has done, Rosmer becomes morbidly excited at the prospect of Rebecca's sacrifice. Rebecca is resigned to death because it will pay the penalty for her sin (an incestuous relationship with Doctor West), but Rosmer, the new free-thinker, says that each individual must judge his own actions, that there is no higher power. Fascinated by Rebecca's growing fondness of the idea, Rosmer decides to join her in the great adventure but not until he solemnizes their spiritual marriage. Then they go hand in hand to the bridge. Mrs. Helseth enters, looks out the window, first sees a figure in white (Rebecca's shawl), then discerns two silhouettes, and in anguish watches them hurl themselves into the torrent. "The dead wife has taken them," she mutters.

Structural analysis: Ibsen formulated his plot in such a way as to give the appearance of causally related incidents stemming from Rosmer's revelation to Kroll that he has abandoned his faith and intends to rehabilitate mankind (Act I). A cursory glance at the plot suggests that the double suicide of Rosmer and Rebecca is the direct result of this admission, but the causality is defective, as the following schematic shows:

Rosmer admits his apostasy to Kroll;

(as a result of which)
Rosmer discovers through Kroll his own implication in Beata's death;

(as a result of which)
Rosmer proposes marriage to Rebecca to expunge the past by the creation of a new life;

(as a result of which)
Rosmer discovers that Rebecca will not marry him;

(as a result of which)
Rosmer concludes that his guilt will exclude him from ever being the agent of good for mankind.

Thus far there is no structural flaw in the causality. Rosmer's conclusion, however, is not the cause of the next discovery, which initiates the subsequent events that lead to the denouement.

Rosmer discovers that he was merely Rebecca's pawn as she engineered Beata's death;
(as a result of which)
Rosmer deserts Rebecca and goes off once again allied to Kroll;
(as a result of which)
Rosmer discovers upon his return that Rebecca is planning to leave;
(as a result of which)
Rosmer questions Rebecca better to understand her motivations;
(as a result of which)
Rosmer discovers that Rebecca's passion for him led her to push Beata toward suicide;
(as a result of which)
Rosmer demands that Rebecca prove her love of him;
(as a result of which)
Rosmer discovers through Brendel that he can achieve victory through the sacrifice of a woman who loves him;
(as a result of which)
Rosmer taunts Rebecca with the idea that her death would prove her love;
(as a result of which)
Rosmer discovers that Rebecca is willing to die;
(as a result of which)
Rosmer becomes fascinated with the idea of death as an atonement;
(as a result of which)
Rosmer, with Rebecca, commits suicide.

The drama, then, is constructed in such a way as to suggest organic unity, with Rosmer's admission as the beginning of the action and the double suicide as the ending. The structural problem lies in the fact that a hiatus interrupts the causal linkage of incidents. Nevertheless, Ibsen maintains the illusion of causality, and in this respect his grounding in the principles of the well-made play* is obvious.

References: Carlson, Marvin. "Patterns of Structure and Character in Ibsen's *Rosmersholm*," *Modern Drama*, 17 (1974), 267-75; Van Laan, Thomas F. "Art and Structure in *Rosmersholm*," *Modern Drama*, 6 (1963), 150-63.

RUBEK, ARNOLD (*When We Dead Awaken*): As an internationally known sculptor, Arnold Rubek is disillusioned with life. When he meets Irene de Satow,* his former model and lover, at a tourist retreat, Rubek discovers that existence can still be piquant. Rubek deserts his fatuous wife Maja* and goes off to the summit of the mountain with Irene in an attempt to recapture the youthful vitality they had once shared. As they approach the pinnacle, an avalanche buries them both.

RUBEK, MAJA (*When We Dead Awaken*): A young wife married to an older, famous husband, Maja likes the trappings of renown but not the boredom of being married to a man whose work has always come first. When she meets Ulfhejm* the mountaineer, Maja eagerly seizes the opportunity for adventure with him by encouraging Arnold* her husband to amuse himself with Irene de Satow.*

RUMMEL (*The Pillars of Society*): A merchant; business associate of Karsten Bernick.*

RUMMEL, HILDA (*The Pillars of Society*): A youthful member of Betty Bernick's* circle of charitable ladies.

RUMMEL, MRS. (*The Pillars of Society*): One of Betty Bernick's* charitable group who serves as part of the chorus of public opinion.

RUNDHOLMEN, MADAME (*The League of Youth*): As the widow of a storekeeper and publican, Madame Rundholmen is the confidante of several of the characters, and as a successful businesswoman, her money makes her a goal of the conniving Stensgaard.*

RYPEN I JUSTEDAL: The Norwegian title of *The Grouse in Justedal.**

RÖRLUND, DOCTOR (*The Pillars of Society*): The schoolmaster and self-appointed keeper of public morals. He claims to wish to marry Dina Dorf.*

S

ST. JOHN'S NIGHT: A three-act Romantic comedy.

Composition: Started in the spring and finished in the summer of 1852; not published until 1909 because Ibsen forbade its circulation.
Stage history:
Jan. 2, 1853   Norwegian Theatre, Bergen* (2 perfs.)
May 1, 1921   Pax Robertson Salon, London

Synopsis: The setting is a garden in Telemark, with a handsome modern house on one side and an old-fashioned cabin on the other. Anne, a young girl, is singing a folk song as she places a birch twig above the door of the log house. Mrs. Berg and her daughter Juliane enter to urge Anne to dress in anticipation of the arrival of visitors. Anne, continuing her task and her song, refuses to change clothes or to do anything else. Mrs. Berg's tone suggests that Anne's intractability has been a chronic problem. Juliane advises her mother that kindness to Anne is apt to be more persuasive than force. When Mrs. Berg asks Anne to cooperate, she immediately does so. Juliane, with her mother's agreement, blames Anne's odd behavior on her grandfather who tells her tales of elves and goblins. His influence is likely to be of some duration, for his son promised him the log house for the rest of his life. Mrs. Berg criticizes the house, but Juliane thinks it a charming relic of the past, so picturesque, in fact, that it might be haunted by a goblin. Juliane goes in to dress, leaving Mrs. Berg to soliloquize about the parlous state of her finances, her ambition to marry Juliane to a rich husband, and the possible existence of some papers, perhaps hidden in a jackdaw's nest in the old house, the discovery of which could have disastrous results. As she speaks, Anne crosses toward her grandfather's house.
Old Berg, emerging from his cabin, calls out to Anne, who joins him with

a bowl of strawberries. As they chat, the fact that Jörgen is coming home from school and bringing a visitor, someone who is secretly engaged to Juliane, is stressed. There is a moving bond of attachment between the old man and the young girl that cannot be penetrated by Mrs. Berg and her children, since they are outsiders. (Juliane and Jörgen are children of Kvist, Mrs. Berg's former husband.) They speak matter-of-factly about the goblin who lives in the loft. Anne tells her grandfather that Juliane and her new husband will live on the farm at Birkedal, a place won by her father in a lawsuit. The old man excitedly declares that this must not occur, but he will not reveal his reason. Mrs. Berg shouts for Anne, so she takes Berg into the house and walks toward her stepmother and Juliane. As Anne lays the table, Juliane and her mother speak of her engagement to Johannes Birk, whom she met in Christiania. Juliane fears that he will embrace her in public before the announcement of their engagement is made, thus revealing the secret. Mrs. Berg consoles her by saying that Birk is neither demonstrative nor passionate. Juliane wishes that the engagement would not be announced so soon since she still recalls an infatuation from her days at the Academy, but her mother is firm.

Two young men, Birk and Jörgen, approach the house, and, to Juliane's relief, Birk merely shakes her hand in lieu of an embrace. During this encounter, Anne stares quizzically at Birk, who refers to his friend Julian Poulsen, a newspaper critic and founder of the Society for the Restitution of Old Norse. Anne identifies herself to Birk, who is told by Mrs. Berg that she is not "quite all there." The talk returns to Poulsen, who is also an unpublished poet and ardent nationalist. They all go inside to eat, and then Julian Poulsen enters.

The poet is somewhat exercised by having seen the young pair holding hands as they went indoors, for he does not know of their engagement. A true Byronic poet, Poulsen soliloquizes about primitivism, self-obsession, and fatalism. Anne enters carrying a tea urn and singing a folk song about an isolated singer, which reminds Poulsen of himself. Anne tells him to join the others, which causes Poulsen some agitation as he ponders what they will say when they see him: "Is that him . . . is that him? Intelligent face! Clever look . . . bit melancholy . . . but interesting . . . damnably interesting . . . you can see immediately." His self-conscious ruminations are interrupted by the entrance of the house party. As tea is served, Poulsen rhapsodizes about being in the midst of untamed nature where he can recapture his primitive self. When reminded that it is only a garden, Poulsen is unmoved. Although he has not yet spoken in the old dialect that no one can understand, Poulsen remarks that midsummer night in the country is the ideal time and place for the primitive national spirit to express itself unrestrainedly. Jörgen tells him that everyone will spend the night on the mountain celebrating midsummer night. Others try to talk as Poulsen monopolizes the conversation, which causes him to lose his train of thought. "Now what was it I wanted to talk about?" he asks. "About yourself, of course" is the answer. As Poulsen mentions his interest in superstition, the goblin looks out the window of the log house. Poulsen continues, "What is the point of fairy tales and legends if we who are endowed with poetic insight don't invest them with significance and philosophical value," which causes the goblin to guffaw loudly. As they joke about goblins and superstitions, Anne reacts strongly, telling them not to ridicule such things, especially the old house. She goes inside, and the conversation turns to the preparation of punch and the trek up Midsummer Hill. Birk and Poulsen are left alone to muse about Anne's reaction and Poulsen's attraction to Juliane. Birk becomes quite short-tempered with Poulsen and stalks off. As Poulsen goes into the house, Anne sets a bowl of punch on the table and says that she feels very peculiar. As Anne goes in to see to her grandfather, the goblin climbs down, brushes himself off, and speaks.

He says that goblins celebrate midsummer night as well as people. After a year of attending to goblin duties, he is free to enjoy himself on this special night by dressing up and visiting his friends on the hill and watching the mortals disport themselves around the bonfire. As he starts to leave, the goblin sees the punch bowl, which gives him an idea. He produces a magical flower that enables the sensitive to be unduly perceptive and the dull merely to sleep. After squeezing the sap into the punch, he disappears into the ground.

The mortals return, and all except Mrs. Berg sample the punch. After their potation, Jörgen, Juliane, and Poulsen, the latter two arm-in-arm, start promenading when they meet Birk. Poulsen warns him that it is every man for himself. Birk helps himself to a glass of punch and starts talking to Anne, who is quite receptive to his mood. When he apologizes for laughing at the old house and customs, Anne says that she was particularly hurt that he would have joined in; the others did not matter. Birk is obviously entertaining doubts about his engagement which will be formalized tomorrow, but he is eager for Anne to take him by the hand, lead him onto the mountain, and initiate him into the midsummer mysteries. She agrees to be his escort after midnight, but now she must see her grandfather. As Birk realizes that Juliane has little attraction for him, he drinks several more glasses of punch and then falls asleep as a fiddler and a group of revelers dance up the mountain.

Poulsen and Juliane appear talking animatedly and at cross-purposes. She thinks him well-mannered, but he wants to think that she sees him as wild and neurotic. Then Poulsen reveals his innermost secret: once he fell in love with a wood nymph, a hulder,* but was repelled when he learned that she had a tail. This awful situation brought his national, primitive soul into conflict with his aesthetic self, which accounts for his melancholy. Joined by the experience of unfortunate attachments, they adjourn to the mountain.

Jörgen comes outside and starts to follow them up the hill. Anne then steals out of the log house, rouses Birk from sleep, and beckons him to follow her to the festivities. Birk, his head spinning, follows her as the goblin suddenly materializes and descants on the fun he is about to have at the mortals' expense.

The second act opens in the forest which is illuminated by periodic flare-ups of the bonfire and by moonlight. Violin music and singing set the magical mood before the goblin appears to announce that the revels of the spirit world are about to begin. A band of invisible elves summons the spirits to the celebration. Poulsen and Juliane momentarily appear and then proceed along the path. They are followed by Jörgen, who is excited because he saw his engaged sister embracing the poet; he pursues them and passes out of sight. As the goblin rubs his hands and chortles, Poulsen and Juliane emerge from the forest. He spreads a handkerchief for her to sit upon while again he expresses his discomfiture: his national self says to him, "You are a man of the people, you wear a sheath knife at your belt and write all your nouns with a small initial letter, how can you possibly admit to renouncing a creature which our national poets cling so fast to." His peroration is interrupted by the entrance of Birk and Anne en route to Midsummer Hill. On the way Anne picks three cowslips apiece and warns Birk to keep them. During her explanation, music intrudes as the hill opens up revealing a dazzling throne room where the mountain king sits in state viewing fairy entertainment. Birk is astonished because he sees the apparition, but Poulsen merely thinks he sees the bonfire. The goblin's punch has produced its effects. In the mountain hall the king descends from his throne to receive a maiden who is led toward him. Anne tells Birk that she is Karin who folk tradition says will be the king's bride. Juliane and Poulsen can now see the scene but cannot interpret its significance, believing the elves to be real people. The king offers various costly gifts, but Karin spurns them all until he pours her a quaff of red gold; then she falls into his arms. Then, Anne explains, the story of Eric and Swanwhite is enacted. During this dumbshow, Juliane recalls her unhappy romance that started at Madame Olsen's Academy, the mere mention of which startles Poulsen. At a dance at Harmony Hall, she had met an ashen boy with dreamy eyes who had asked her to dance, but he stepped on her white shoes, she screamed, and he disappeared in embarrassment. Poulsen confesses that the dreamy-eyed young man was himself. In a fit of romantic zeal, he kneels on a handkerchief before Juliane, but before he can speak, a bush opens up to expose the laughing goblin; then it closes. Frightened, the lovers dash off, leaving Birk and Anne, who recognize each other as the childhood friends who had been separated by circumstance. As they embrace, the goblin jubilantly announces that this year's festivities have ended.

Now (Act III) it is early morning in the Bergs' garden. Anne and old Berg converse while Poulsen sleeps on the steps of the new house. Berg is still trying to remember something his son told him to do just before he died, something concerning the deeds of the estate. Anne talks of the night's experiences as if they had been a dream and produces a key, the origin of which she does not know. The old man immediately recognizes it as the key to a chest, and they quickly go inside to investigate.

Birk comes in recalling his time on the mountain and regretting that he has to give Anne up after rediscovering her. Jörgen enters and expresses relief at finding everyone safely at home. At first Jörgen fears that Poulsen has told of his indiscretion with Juliane, but he becomes more concerned about Birk who speaks strangely of elves, mountain halls, and childhood memories; then he goes into the garden. Jörgen wakens Poulsen and chides him about his behavior with his sister. Unfortunately, the poet recalls things rather unclearly. Poulsen tells Jörgen that he plans to marry Juliane if she will accept him, which forces Jörgen to tell him of her engagement to Birk. Poulsen, distracted, goes out in search of Birk, followed by an anxious Jörgen.

Anne enters with Birk, and as they tell each other about their lives, Birk reveals that Anne's father had supported him after his own father had died. As time passed, he found himself engaged to Juliane almost as a matter of course but without personal commitment. Birk, of course, is indirectly trying to tell Anne of his love of her, but she still seems to see the relationship as that of playmates. Birk views her attitude as one of arrested development, but still he says outright that he loves her, and Anne answers that she loves him too. For Anne's sake, Birk affects sincere attachment to Juliane, which breaks Anne's heart. After she retreats into her grandfather's house, Birk considers breaking off his engagement but decides that he must go through with it.

Mrs. Berg enters and takes Birk to one side to discuss business. Juliane enters and says that she must explain things to Poulsen or risk breaking his heart. She would like to break off the engagement, but duty requires her compliance. Jörgen rushes in in search of Poulsen and tells Juliane of the poet's love. When Anne and Berg come outside, Birk recognizes the old man, who asks Mrs. Berg if she intends to give the Birkedal estate to the engaged couple, a notion that surprises Birk. Berg then produces the deed to Birkedal which his son had told him to give to the son of the previous owner—Johannes Birk. Mrs. Berg's husband—a lawyer—had argued the case against the senior Birk knowing that a claim against Birkedal was spurious. For that reason he had supported Birk when his father died. Mrs. Berg fears that Birk will use the papers to ruin her, but he tears them up and breaks the engagement to Juliane. Poulsen enters still under the impression that Juliane is engaged and confronts Birk. In an obligatory scene, Poulsen is set straight, and both pairs of lovers are free to marry.

Structural analysis: Although Ibsen repudiated this youthful drama, it is not without charm. Its debt to Shakespeare's *A Midsummer Night's Dream* is obvious as is its Scribean quality. The play is worthwhile for the characterization of Julian Poulsen if for no other reason. It is remarkable that Ibsen could take such delight in a character some of whose traits were present in the author and his friends. Despite its one excellent character and its interesting spectacular requirements, the plot is conventional: the young people drink the magical punch, discover they are in love but cannot get together for various reasons, and eventually unite because all the obstacles have been removed. All this is accomplished not by their own doing but by that of the goblin and old Berg.

SALLUST OF PERUSIA (*Emperor and Galilean*): A member of Libanius'* entourage; servant of Julian.*

SAMFUNDETS STÖTTER: The Norwegian title of *The Pillars of Society.**

SAMFUNDSBLADET [*The Union Newspaper*]: The Students' Union at the University of Christiania published this handwritten newspaper to which Ibsen submitted articles. In 1851 he became one of its editors.

SANCTHANSNATTEN: The Norwegian title of *Saint John's Night.**

SANDSTAD (*The Pillars of Society*): A merchant; a business associate of Karsten Bernick.*

SATOW, IRENE DE (*When We Dead Awaken*): Although she was Arnold Rubek's* model and lover, Irene de Satow was unable to share him with his art. She felt her life ended when they separated, and she thinks herself already dead when she meets him again. Irene still has the power to besot Rubek and with him she scales the mountain, only to be swallowed by an avalanche.

SAVINA, MARIA G. (1854-1915): By friends and foes alike, Maria G. Savina was known as "Maria the Warrior." Savina the actress was renowned for her classically lucid style; Savina, the motive force behind the Alexandrinsky Theatre (St. Petersburg) from 1874, was a temperamental martinet who demanded her actors' best at all times. Her Nora Helmer* was first seen on February 8, 1884. She appeared as Hjördis* in 1895 and as Helene Alving* in 1897.
Reference: Greater Soviet Encyclopedia, 3d ed. (New York: Macmillan, 1976), XXII, 657.

SAXE-MEININGEN, GEORG II, DUKE OF (1826-1914): Prince Georg, as he was styled prior to 1866, learned to love art as a child, and when he entered the University of Bonn, he studied art, traveled to several European capitals, and fraternized with cultured people. The revolutionary events of 1848 necessitated his return to Meiningen, where two years later he married the first of three successive wives. After becoming a widower in 1855, Georg remained unmarried until 1858. Eight years later he succeeded by fiat to the ducal throne. In 1872, again a widower, he married a young actress, Ellen Franz. By then he had already established himself as a pioneering director of the Meiningen Court Theatre.

Known to history as the first modern stage director, Duke Georg brought a strong pictorial sense to his stage groupings, designed illusionistic settings, demanded historically accurate costumes and properties, trained his actors to achieve an ensemble effect, and exercised firm control over every aspect of production. Too much attention has been paid to his rigidly choreographed crowd scenes, but this too was one of his contributions to stagecraft. Other facets of his method were novel as well: his disinclination to commit his plans to a promptbook, his insistence that all scenery and properties be available at the first rehearsal, his requirement that actors rehearse at performance intensity, his refusal to open a production until it was ready regardless of how many rehearsals were required, and his practice of changing details even after the production had been presented to the public. While his directorial practices were unique, his repertory was merely traditional, featuring the works of Schiller and Shakespeare and giving Heinrich von Kleist an important showcase. Modern Realistic drama had little attraction for Duke Georg, who presented *The Pretenders** in 1876, *A Doll's House** in 1884, *Ghosts** in 1886, and *An Enemy of the People** in 1888.

Ibsen witnessed *The Pretenders* in Berlin, and it is not impossible that Duke Georg's attention to detail encouraged Ibsen to strive toward illusionism in *The Pillars of Society** upon which he was then working.

References: De Hart, Staven. *The Meininger Theatre: 1776-1926.* Ann Arbor, Mich.: UMI Research Press, 1982; Grube, Max. *The Story of the Meininger.* Coral Gables, Fla.: University of Miami Press, 1963.

SCAIFE, GILLIAN (d. 1976): Turkish actress Gillian Scaife essayed Nora Helmer* in London in 1928, playing at the Kingsway Theatre.
Reference: *Who Was Who in the Theatre,* IV, 2125.

SCHILDKRAUT, JOSEPH (1896-1964): The son of Austrian actor Rudolf Schildkraut, Joseph Schildkraut studied at the American Academy of Dramatic Art and performed in *The Pillars of Society** as one of his examination pieces in 1913. He was engaged in Berlin between 1913 and 1917 by Max Reinhardt.* There Schildkraut appeared with Albert Bassermann* in *The Master Builder** and in Franz Werfel's adaptation of *Emperor and Galilean,** which took six hours to perform, although the two parts were condensed into one. After World War I, Schildkraut acted with

Bassermann in *A Doll's House** and *The Wild Duck** at Vienna's Deutsches Volkstheater.

Returning to New York in 1920, Schildkraut played in Ferenc Molnar's *Liliom* (1921) with Eva Le Gallienne*; then in the autumn of 1922 he began rehearsals for *Peer Gynt*.* This enterprise, with Schildkraut in the title role, Dudley Digges* as the Troll-King, and Edward G. Robinson as the Button-Molder,* was directed by the Russian genius, Theodore Kommisarzhevsky* and was admired by Konstantin Stanislavsky,* who was performing in New York with his Moscow Art Theatre.* The production, which ran for 120 performances, had to be moved to a larger theatre to accommodate the audiences; it had opened on February 5, 1923, at the Garrick Theatre and was transferred to the Shubert.

References: Schildkraut, Joseph. *My Father and I.* New York: Viking Press, 1959; *Who Was Who in the Theatre,* IV, 2127-8.

SCHLENTHER, PAUL (1854-1916): Germany writer Paul Schlenther accompanied Otto Brahm* to several Ibsenian productions and came away a proponent of the Norwegian's dramas. He was connected with the Freie Bühne* and edited Ibsen's *Complete Works* in German.

Reference: Enciclopedia della Spettacolo, VIII, cols. 1680-1.

SCHOOLMASTER (*Brand*): One of the most vocal of Brand's* followers and then one of his most stringent detractors.

SCHRÖDER, HANS (1836-1902): Between 1879 and 1899 Hans Schröder was director of the Christiania Theatre.* In 1897 he staged *The Feast at Solhaug.**

Reference: Just, Carl. *Schröder og Christiania Theater.* Oslo: A. Cammermeyer, 1948.

SCHULERUD, JOHAN: Johan Schulerud shared a room in Christiania* with his brother Ole* and Ibsen: the year was 1850. He published his reminiscences of these days in *Verdens Gang,* June 23-24, 1910.

SCHULERUD, OLE (1827-59): Ibsen did not have many friends in Grimstad,* but in Ole Schulerud, who worked at the customshouse, he met a kindred spirit. It was Schulerud who went to Christiania* to try to arrange a production of *Catiline** and who paid for the publication of the play from his own funds.

SCOTT, CLEMENT WILLIAM (1841-1904): As dramatic critic of the *Daily Telegraph* (London) and editor of *The Theatre* from 1880 to 1889, Clement Scott was Ibsen's most powerful adversary in England. In 1899, when his own and Ibsen's lives had nearly ended, Scott still excoriated the

Norwegian dramatist: "The public voice sent Ibsen to the wall, but the trail of the Ibsen serpent has been left on the stage and our cleverest and most literary dramatists have been ensnared by it" (Scott, p. 269). Naturally, this passionate critic's ire was particularly stimulated by *Ghosts,** about which he wrote, "I absolutely deny that the subject of Ibsen's *Ghosts* is fit for any dinner-table, unless, indeed, we are so advanced that we can discuss hereditary diseases with our soup, and over the *entrée* enlist the conversation of a pretty woman as to the ravages derived from sensuality, and the sins of the fathers inherited by the children" (Scott, p. 269).

As a writer himself, Scott's antipathy to Ibsen is all the more remarkable, but the critic had what seemed to him to be sound reasons for his opposition to Ibsenism. His perpetual plea in behalf of the theatre was "Give me pleasure houses for the people, not morgues, or dissecting rooms, or doctors' laboratories, or places where unhealthy, morbid subjects are introduced, or hereditary disease is openly discussed, and all that is lovely in form, colour, art, and expression is distorted. Give me pleasure houses for the people to enjoy good, wholesome, human plays, and fine, stirring dramas" (Scott, p. 7). It is clear from this statement and his many critical articles that the conservative Scott favored a prolongation of a highly romanticized theatre.

Reference: Scott, Margaret Clement. *Old Bohemian Days in London: Recollections of Clement Scott.* New York: Frederick A. Stokes, 1919.

SCRIBE, AUGUSTIN EUGÈNE (1791-1861): Long believed to be a major influence on Ibsen's development, Scribe was France's most popular nineteenth-century playwright, creating 374 dramas of several types, including the *pièce bien faite,* the well-made play.* Ibsen certainly had numerous opportunities to see Scribe's dramas. When he was a student at Christiania,* for example, the Christiania Theatre* presented fifteen works by Scribe alone or in collaboration.

While on his European study tour, Ibsen saw productions of Scribe's works, and while at the Norwegian Theatre in Bergen,* he directed twenty-seven of Scribe's plays. Neither seeing nor directing Scribe's dramas would necessarily have made a disciple of Ibsen, but he may have absorbed something of the mechanics of playwriting from the dramatist whom he dismissed as trivial as early as 1851.

Reference: Arvin, Neil Cole. *Eugène Scribe and the French Theatre, 1815-1860.* Cambridge: Harvard University Press, 1924.

SEVERUS (*Emperor and Galilean*): One of the treasonous, flattering generals of Julian.*

SEVERUS (*Norma*): The politician who courts both Adalgisa* and Norma.*

SEXTON (*Brand*): The character who with the Schoolmaster* provides the exposition about Brand's* actions between the death of Agnes* and the opening of his new church.

"SHAKESPEARE AND HIS INFLUENCE UPON SCANDINAVIAN LITERATURE": An address Ibsen delivered before the December 22 Society. The content of the talk is unknown.

SHARP, ROBERT FARQUHARSON (1864-1945): Between 1911 and 1915, R. Farquharson Sharp translated most of Ibsen's dramas into English. They were somewhat more colloquial than the translations of William Archer* and therefore won a degree of acceptance.

SHAW, GEORGE BERNARD (1856-1950): Seldom has a playwright had a more articulate champion than Ibsen had in the Irish critic-novelist-playwright-reformer Bernard Shaw. Seldom, too, has a playwright's work been more grossly misrepresented. William Archer* met Shaw in the Reading Room of the British Museum late in 1881, and soon he was sharing his enthusiasm for Ibsen with the young man who was then a struggling novelist. Through Archer's influence, Shaw found work as a book reviewer, then as an art critic, and later as a music critic for several important periodicals. Meanwhile, Archer continued to boast of Ibsen to Shaw.
    Then on January 15, 1886, Shaw played Nils Krogstad* in Eleanor Marx's* reading of *A Doll's House.** By this time Shaw was an ardent Ibsenite and a committed Fabian socialist. When on July 18, 1889, Shaw lectured on Ibsen to the assembled Fabians, he joined Edmund William Gosse* and William Archer in the front ranks of Ibsen's British yeomanry. This lecture, which was concerned principally with *A Doll's House,* precipitated such controversy that Shaw expanded it and eventually published his thoughts on Ibsen as *The Quintessence of Ibsenism* (1891). Although a delightful book, its publication had several unfortunate ramifications. First, as so many have observed, a more appropriate title would be *The Quintessence of Shavianism,* for the book is more reflective of Shaw's views than of Ibsen's. Second, Shaw painted Ibsen primarily as a social reformer, an appellation that particularly incensed Ibsen. Third, as a socialist, Shaw concentrated on Ibsen's social problem plays, thus creating the opinion that only this group of Ibsen's dramas is worthy of consideration, an idea that deserves a merciless death. Regardless of these negative results, Shaw spoke in Ibsen's defense whenever he could. His newspaper criticisms and letters reveal a much greater understanding of Ibsen's dramas than does *The Quintessence of Ibsenism.*
    Shaw was a loyal supporter of the Independent Theatre* and the Incorporated Stage Society,* both producers of the Ibsenian corpus as

well as Shaw's early dramas, the first of which, *Widowers' Houses*, was presented in 1892. Shaw's desire to promote Ibsen and to advertise himself grew into his anti-Shakespeare pose and his campaign against England's most respected actor, Henry Irving. As actor/manager of the Lyceum Theatre, Irving was renowned for his magnificent productions of Shakespearean and other poetic dramas. Although quite mannered, Irving was undeniably an able theatrical craftsman, and Shaw was irked that Irving could not be convinced to act an Ibsenian role. So, as Shaw's biographer paraphrases Shaw's argument, "if Ibsen was as wonderful as Shaw thought him, then Shakespeare was not as wonderful as other people thought him, and Irving, by neglecting Ibsen and producing episodes from Shakespeare's plays, was not only an enemy to the modern movement but a bardolater by false pretenses" (Pearson, p. 135).

References: Pearson, Hesketh. *G.B.S.: A Full Length Portrait*. Garden City, N.Y.: Garden City Publishing Company, 1946; Shaw, G. B. *Shaw's Dramatic Criticism*, ed. John F. Matthews. New York: Hill and Wang, 1959.

SHAW, MARY (1854-1929): Mary Shaw was a distinguished (at least one critic thinks the best) American interpreter of Ibsen's women. In New York and on tour, she played Helene Alving* (1899, 1917, 1922) and Hedda Gabler* (1904).

Reference: Who Was Who in the Theatre, IV, 2161-2.

A SHORT-SIGHTED GENTLEMAN (*The Wild Duck*): One of the aristocratic houseguests of Haakon Werle* who managed to make Hjalmar Ekdal* feel out of place.

SIEBOLD, P. F.: A traveling salesman from Kassel, P. F. Siebold translated *Brand** into German in 1872. This marked the first publication of an Ibsenian drama in a non-Scandinavian language.

SIGARD OF BRABANT (*The Pretenders*): A physician.

SIGNE (*The Feast at Solhoug*): The younger sister of Margit*; the beloved of Gudmund.*

SIGRID (*The Pretenders*): The sister of Earl Skule,* Sigrid becomes abbess of the convent of Elkslodge and counsels Skule to die while doing a kingly deed.

SIGURD RIBBUNG (*The Pretenders*): One of the several pretenders to the Norwegian throne, Sigurd Ribbung is disappointed when Haakon* is elected.

SIGURD THE STRONG (*The Vikings in Helgeland*): As head of a Viking band, Sigurd, a bold warrior, encounters his father-in-law Örnulf* in Helgeland whither he has gone to avenge the seizure of Örnulf's stepdaughter Hjördis* by Gunnar.* Although married to Dagny,* Sigurd arouses the passions of Hjördis who causes his death after inviting his joint suicide with her.

SINTULA (*Emperor and Galilean*): Julian's* master of the horse.

SIRA VILJAM (*The Pretenders*): The chaplain of Nikolas Arnesson, Bishop of Oslo.*

SKAKTAVL, OLAF (*Lady Inger of Österaad*): An outlawed Norwegian who casts his lot with Lady Inger of Gyldenlöve.*

SKALD: A court poet who sang of mighty deeds in old Norse times.

SKIEN: Ibsen's birthplace in Norway.
Reference: Mosfjeld, Oskar. *Henrik Ibsen og Skien.* Oslo: Gyldendal, 1949.

SKULE, EARL (*The Pretenders*): A pretender to the throne of Norway, Skule is the protagonist of the drama. He wants the throne because he feels if is his due; he will do nearly anything to attain it, even plunging the country into a bloody civil war. Skule's defeat eventually comes through an idea, Haakon's* vision of a truly united Norwegian nation. Skule finally realizes that love and family are the important constituents of life and that he does not have the vision to be a good king. He achieves a bit of nobility by sacrificing himself to the very people he aroused into rebellion against the rightful king.

SKYTTE, KNUT (*The Mountain Bird*): A young farmer.

SKAERE, MISS (*Love's Comedy*): Miss Skaere ("Jay") is the embodiment of a prim spinster with traditional Norwegian bourgeois values. Although she is engaged to Styver,* there is little of the romantic about her. She serves as the leader of a chorus that rises in opposition to the radical ideas about love and marriage espoused by Falk.*

SMITH, MAGGIE (1934-): One of England's finest actresses, Maggie Smith was a notable Hilde Wangel* in an Old Vic production of *The Master Builder*￼ in 1964 and a memorable Hedda Gabler* in Ingmar Bergman's presentation at the National Theatre of Great Britain in 1970.
Reference: Who's Who in the Theatre, 16th ed., p. 1138.

SNOILSKY, CARL (1841-1903): Ibsen based his portrait of Johannes Rosmer* on Carl Snoilsky, a Swedish poet. In 1879 Snoilsky antagonized his family, abandoned his diplomatic post, divorced his wife, remarried, and left Sweden. In 1885 he returned to his native land and was treated as an outcast.

SOLNESS, ALINE (*The Master Builder*): Aline's marriage to Halvard Solness* is not a happy one. She suspects him of constant philandering, which aggravates her mental anguish over the loss of their children in a fire. She is unable to bear more children, so her life is a hell in a house with three empty nurseries.

SOLNESS, HALVARD (*The Master Builder*): Halvard Solness, a building contractor, is married to Aline Solness.* His prime motivation is his fear of youth, which makes him particularly vulnerable when Hilde Wangel* appears and treats him sympathetically. Solness has switched from building churches as habitations of God to erecting houses as dwellings for people; yet all his houses have soaring spires. He builds a new house for himself and meets his death while crowning the tower with a wreath in order to impress Hilde. Aloft, he challenges God, struggles with invisible powers, and falls to the ground.

SOLVEIG (*Peer Gynt*): A newcomer to the district, Solveig sees Peer Gynt,* falls in love with him, and waits many years for his return to his native land. It is she who teaches him that love, family, and home are the rightful bases upon which to build a meaningful life.

SONDERGAARD, GALE (1901-): Actress Gale Sondergaard appeared as Gunhild Borkman* in New York in 1976 and as Ella Rentheim* in 1977. Of the latter performance a reviewer noted that she "speaks in ice cubes."
Reference: New York Theatre Critics' Reviews, XXXVIII, 4 (Mar. 7, 1977), 353-5.

SONTUM, HELENE: Helene Sontum was Ibsen's landlady in Bergen* and grandmother of Hildur Andersen.* Sontum also introduced Ibsen to Rikke Holst.

SORMA, AGNES (1865-1927): Agnes Sorma played Regine Engstrand* in the Freie Bühne* production of *Ghosts** in 1889. She also played Nora Helmer* in 1892 and Rita Allmers* in the world premiere of *Little Eyolf** in 1895. Sorma added Helene Alving* to her repertory in 1906. In 1897 she performed Nora in German in New York.
Reference: Bab, Julius. *Agnes Sorma: Ein Gedenkbuch.* Heidelberg: N. Kampmann, 1927.

THE SPHINX AT GIZEH (*Peer Gynt*): A mute character addressed by Peer Gynt* in Act IV.

STANISLAVSKY, KONSTANTIN (1863-1938): Both as actor and director, Stanislavsky encountered Ibsen's works at the Moscow Art Theatre (MAT),* and with the exception of *An Enemy of the People,** he was decidedly reserved in his judgment of Ibsen's accomplishments. Believing that the most popular Ibsenian plays were too symbolic to lend themselves to Realistic acting techniques, he nevertheless achieved personal success in his portrayal of Ejlert Lövborg* in *Hedda Gabler** (which opened on February 19, 1899), but the production closed after only eleven performances. One observer noted, "His [Lövborg] was both a profligate genius and a genius in profligacy" (Magarshack, p. 188).

Stanislavsky's favorite role, Thomas Stockmann,* provided one of his most distinguished triumphs as an actor. The drama entered the repertory of the MAT on October 24, 1900, and was often revived. He seemed to identify immediately with the outcast reformer and thus was able to dispense with his usual agonized search for a characterization. The production was repeated in St. Petersburg in 1905 on the very day of the massacre in Kazansky Square. *An Enemy of the People* appealed especially to the budding revolutionists, who attended in great numbers. The audience also included state censors who were there to insure that Stanislavsky did not deviate from the censored text. The response to the play was vocal and frequent, and when in the last act, Stockmann speaks of new coats and freedom, the seething revolutionary crowd surged up to the stage to shake the hand of Doctor Stockmann (Stanislavsky, pp. 378-9).

Stanislavsky's production of *The Wild Duck** (1901) and his appearance as Karsten Bernick* in *The Pillars of Society** (1903) were both failures. The latter production was directed by Stanislavsky's partner Vladimir Nemirovich-Danchenko,* who was much more sympathetic to Ibsen than was Stanislavsky. With his partner, Stanislavsky shared the direction of *Ghosts** (March 31, 1905).

References: Magarshack, David. *Stanislavsky: A Life.* New York: Chanticleer Press, 1951; Stanislavsky, Konstantin. *My Life in Art.* Trans. J. J. Robbins. New York: Theatre Arts Books, 1924.

STATILIUS (*Catiline*): One of the young, noble traitors who lure Catiline* into conspiracy against Rome.

STEENSBALLE, P. F.: Steensballe was the bookseller in Christiania* who published *Catiline.** He also contracted to publish *The Burial Mound,** but it never appeared.

STENSGAARD (*The League of Youth*): The opportunist Stensgaard forms the League of Youth against the interests of Chamberlain Brattsberg,* but he is seduced by the opportunity to be accepted by the aristocracy. He is maneuvered into running as a local elector and eventually for Parliament and in so doing becomes the pawn of several unscrupulous politicians. At the end he is left with nothing except chastisement.

STENSSON, NILS (*Lady Inger of Österaad*): Lady Inger of Gyldenlöve's* illegitimate son, but unknown to her. Thinking him to be the heir to the throne, Inger has Stensson killed, only to discover that he was her son and not even in line for the throne.

STEVENS, EMILY (1882-1928): As the niece of Minnie Maddern Fiske,* Emily Stevens spent her early career in support of her distinguished relative, first appearing on the American stage in 1900. She played Berte* in her aunt's production of *Hedda Gabler* in 1903.
Reference: Who Was Who in the Theatre, IV, 2259-60.

STJERNSTRÖM, EDVARD (1816-77): Stjernström opened the New Theatre in Stockholm in January 1875. On November 3, 1875, he presented *The Vikings in Helgeland.**
Reference: Svenskt Biografiskt Handlexikon, ed. Herman Hofberg (Stockholm: Albert Bonniers, 1906), II, 536.

STOCKFLETH, W. F.: Stockfleth, a teacher with a theological degree, ran a school in Skien* which Ibsen entered in 1841. He remained under Stockfleth's tutelage for two years.

STOCKMANN, EJLIF (*An Enemy of the People*): The Stockmanns'* thirteen-year-old son.

STOCKMANN, KATHERINE (*An Enemy of the People*): As the wife of a man who frequently embraces causes, Katherine Stockmann is supportive of her husband Thomas'* movement to clean the municipal baths, but when it appears that he will be unpopular for doing so, she counsels moderation for the sake of the children. Once her husband has fully committed himself to standing up to the mob, however, Katherine stands at his side.

STOCKMANN, MORTEN (*An Enemy of the People*): The Stockmanns' ten-year-old son.

STOCKMANN, PETER (*An Enemy of the People*): Thomas Stockmann's* older brother: Mayor, Chief of Police, Chairman of the Board of the Municipal Baths. Peter is a bourgeois politician whose greed impels him to persecute his brother and suppress his report on the polluted water.

STOCKMANN, PETRA (*An Enemy of the People*): The eldest child of the Stockmanns,* Petra is a schoolteacher and old enough to appreciate the ethical implications of her father's stand. She is, therefore, bold and committed to his course of action.

STOCKMANN, THOMAS (*An Enemy of the People*): As physician-in-residence of the Municipal Baths, Doctor Stockmann discovers that the spa is unsafe. Although a champion of many causes, Stockmann has never stood high in his townsmen's estimation. He sees the issue of the water as the means of making himself a hero in the eyes of the townspeople; he is completely unnerved when he is branded an enemy of the people. Yet the more they try to muffle his voice, the more certain he is that he must speak, whatever the consequences. When the situation seems too grim, he considers emigration to America, but when it worsens, he decides to stay and fight the majority.

STOCKMANNSGAARDEN [Stockmann House]: The building in Skien* where Ibsen was born. It stood on one side of the square, the town pillory to the right, the madhouse and jail at the left. The Latin and grammar schools stood opposite, with the church in the center of the square. The house was destroyed in a fire in 1886.

STRAAMAND (*Love's Comedy*): Straamand (literally "straw man") is but the first of Ibsen's unflattering portraits of clergymen. Straamand is the epitome of middle-class sanctity and virtue—pompous, fecund (ten children), money-grubbing. Straamand and all his values stand in opposition to Falk and his beliefs about love and marriage.

STRAAMAND, MRS. MARY (*Love's Comedy*): The archetypal mother and wife of a country clergyman.

STRAIGHT, BEATRICE (1918-): American actress Beatrice Straight received her training from Michael Chekhov and entered the theatre in 1935. Her performance as Helene Alving* extended the run of *Ghosts** in New York in 1973 to eighty-nine performances, an enviable record for a first attempt at playing an Ibsenian role.
Reference: Who's Who in the Theatre, 16th ed., p. 1161.

A STRANGE PASSENGER (*Peer Gynt*): When Peer Gynt* sails back to Norway in the beginning of Act V, he encounters a Strange Passenger, a man who is unnaturally focused on death. Twice he asks if he might have Peer's body for dissection if Peer should die.

A STRANGER (*The Lady from the Sea*): The Stranger used the name Alfred Johnston.* He had fallen in love with Ellida Wangel* and entered into a spiritual marriage with her, but when he was in danger of being falsely arrested for murder, he fled, vowing that he would return for her. Once he was out of her life, Ellida saw that Johnston had exercised a type of mind control over her, and she tried to sever her relationship with him. The crisis of the play comes when he returns to take Ellida with him.

STRINDBERG, AUGUST (1849-1912): Swedish dramatist August Strindberg's youthful adulation of Ibsen degenerated into a psychotic hatred. Between 1869 when he first read *Brand** and the year of his death, Strindberg wrote sixty-two plays, almost a dozen novels, nearly eightscore stories, three books of poetry, and numerous critical essays and letters. Strindberg's second play, *The Freethinker* (1870) is not unlike *Brand,* which ignited Strindberg's creative fires. His prose version of *Master Olof* (1871) also deals with a larger-than-life, uncompromising hero of the Brand type.

In 1877 Strindberg contracted the first of three depressing marriages that resulted in separation and the loss of his children. His own childhood observations of marriage were bleakly colored by the fact that his father had married beneath his social class and caused his progeny to suffer for his lack of foresight. Perhaps because of these traumatic experiences, Strindberg developed an exalted but exaggerated concept of the traditional female role. It is not surprising, then, that when he first saw *A Doll's House,** he should view it as an affront to his own belief in motherhood as woman's highest calling. In Strindberg's eyes, Ibsen had become the tool of the hated feminists. His repugnance at *A Doll's House* was manifested in a collection of short stories called *Marriage* (1884), including a tale called "A Doll's House," which describes the break-up of a marriage because of Ibsen's play.

Strindberg was rather attracted to *Ghosts** and *Rosmersholm,** but in general his acerbity towards Ibsen increased in proportion to his own marital troubles, his alienation from Sweden (in 1883 he became a self-exile), and his worsening mental state. Later, in the years 1894-96 he would experience five mental breakdowns. Ibsen's particular crimes, as Strindberg saw them, included allying himself with the feminists and toadying to the aristocrats; the Swede also came to blame the Norwegian for having influenced him. Ibsen's effect on Strindberg is clear, not only in the previously mentioned works, but also in the dramas *The Outlaw* (1871) and *Herr Bingt's Wife* (1881-82) and in the collection of poems *Somnambulist Nights in Broad Daylight* (1884), to name but a few. To his catalogue of reasons for his growing contempt of Ibsen, Strindberg added his belief that Ibsen plagiarized *The Secret of the Guild* (1880) in his creation of *The Master Builder**; he also felt that Ibsen ridiculed him by the characterizations of Hjalmar Ekdal* and Ejlert Lövborg.*

Like Ibsen, Strindberg was fascinated by hypnotism and the idea that one could gain absolute mental dominance over another. He dealt with this subject in an essay entitled "Psychic Murder" (1887). Rebecca West's* psychic murder of Beata Rosmer* is the focal point of this study. Strindberg wrote, "We never learn in *Rosmersholm* how Rebecca committed her murder; this in itself might have constituted the entire action in the play, which presently develops in a different direction. She presumably used the old familiar method of persuading the weaker brain that it was sick and then 'proving' to her or making her believe that death was a blessing" (Lamm, p. 205).

The Father (1887), one of Strindberg's best efforts, was in some ways the Swede'e angry retort to *Ghosts*. He sensed that Ibsen intended to show the devastating effects of a woman's sacrifice to a man for the sake of propriety. Strindberg, ever distrustful of women's motives, causes the Doctor to say (II, 4), "Do you know, when I sat in the theatre the other evening and heard Mrs. Alving orating over her dead husband, I thought to myself: 'What a damned shame the fellow's dead and can't defend himself' " (Michael Meyer's translation). *The Father* is to some extent a vindication of Captain Alving's behavior. Later, Strindberg would claim that *Hedda Gabler** was derived from *The Father*.

For his part, Ibsen had guarded respect for Strindberg. In addition to reading his plays with great interest, Ibsen bought Christian Krohg's immense portrait of the Swede and kept it hanging in his study, drawing inspiration from the madman's eyes. The two dramatists never met; once en route to visit Ibsen, Strindberg turned back because the weather was not to his liking. In a letter to Aurélien-Marie Lugné-Poë* (December 16, 1894), Strindberg encapsulated his long attachment to Ibsen: "J'ai été sa victime depuis dix ans." ["I have been his victim for ten years."]

References: *August Strindbergs brev,* ed. Torsten Eklund (Stockholm: Albert Bonniers, 1948-69), X, 332; Lamm, Martin. *August Strindberg.* Trans. and ed. Harry G. Carlson. New York: Benjamin Blom, 1971 [1948].

STRODTMANN, ADOLF (1829-79): Strodtmann was a German critic, biographer, and anthologizer. He wrote favorable articles about Ibsen in the *Hamburg Correspondent* and translated *The League of Youth** (1862) and *The Pretenders** (1872).

Reference: Kosch, Wilhelm. *Deutsches Literatur-Lexikon* (Bern: A. Francke, 1958), IV, 2110.

STUB, POUL JANSENIUS (fl. 1850-65): In 1850 while in Grimstad,* Ibsen prepared for the matriculation examination of the University of Oslo by taking a correspondence course in writing from invalid schoolmaster Poul Stub, who resided in Bergen.* Apparently Stub's instruction was worthless because Ibsen received only a moderate score when he later took his university examination in Norwegian composition.

Ibsen again encountered Stub in 1851. Ibsen was incensed by Stub's unfair criticism of the performances and policies of the Norwegian Theatre,

Bergen.* Stub, as a writer for one of the local newspapers, had received no complimentary tickets for the theatre since its inauguration because all the seats had been filled by the paying public. He was, therefore, unnecessarily caustic in his published remarks about the organization. Ibsen responded to Stub's barbs in four well-written articles in the rival newspaper.

Stub's path crossed Ibsen's for the last time around 1875 in Munich.* By then Ibsen was rich and famous; Stub had fallen on hard times and was eking out a seedy subsistence in Germany where the cost of living was less than in Norway. Ibsen merely watched the old teacher walk down the street. There is no record of any attempt on Ibsen's part to ameliorate Stub's condition.

STYVER (*Love's Comedy*): An impecunious law clerk; fiancé of Miss Skaere.*

SUZMAN, JANET (1939-): This South African actress joined England's Royal Shakespeare Company in 1962 and frequently appeared in roles from the classical repertory. Her only professional involvement with Ibsen's plays occurred in 1977 when she played Hedda Gabler* in both London and Edinburgh. In a translation of Ibsen's play by David Essinger and Vicky Caristrand, Suzman portrayed Hedda as "a coward pure and simple" rather than a masked coward. Her Hedda was "a glum, statuesque figure, armour-plated in quilted satins . . . and discharging much of the text in a cryptic undertone." The translators assumed that Hedda was indeed pregnant, so their version gave Suzman clear opportunities of exploiting that idea. Nevertheless, the critic of *The Times* (London) thought the dramatic battle was lost before the curtain rose (June 16, 1977, p. 12, cols. 4-6). Suzman again acted Hedda in a television production in 1977.
Reference: Who's Who in the Theatre, 17th ed., I, 648.

SVANHILD: Svanhild is a fragment of a prose version of *Love's Comedy*.* It consists of only one act divided into four scenes.

SVEND (*The Mountain Bird*): A servant.

SVENNBERG, TORE (b. 1852): The part of Skule* was enacted by Tore Svennberg, a Swedish actor, in Stockholm in 1898. He toured with Julia Haakonsson* in 1898-99, 1902-5, and 1905-7 and performed in her Ibsenian repertory. Svennberg's best-known roles were Karsten Bernick* and Aslaksen* in *The League of Youth.*

SAETER GIRLS (*Peer Gynt*): Cowherds who summon the spirits of the mountain for Peer Gynt.*

SÖRBY, BERTA (*The Wild Duck*): Berta Sörby is the friend and former housekeeper of Haakon Werle.* She boasts that she and Werle have an honest relationship, one that results in their marriage.

T

TERRY, ELLEN (1847-1928): Between 1878 and 1892 Ellen Terry attained the heights of her profession as her alliance with Henry Irving made the Lyceum Theatre the most fashionable place of entertainment in London. Primarily identified with Shakespearean and Romantic heroines, Terry was the object of one of George Bernard Shaw's* epistolary romances, and through him she became interested in Ibsen's works. Since Irving, the first actor to be knighted, was the leader of his profession, Ibsenites earnestly wanted him to appear in one of the Norwegian's works. Terry tried to interest the actor in *John Gabriel Borkman** when it was published in 1897, but Irving demurred.

Terry leased the Imperial Theatre and went into management in 1903, largely to enable her son Edward Gordon Craig* to have an opportunity to exhibit his then-experimental stagecraft. Opting to present *The Vikings in Helgeland,** Terry herself appeared as Hjördis* because the actress felt that she could invest the role with a kind of brilliance that would diminish its ponderosity. Her daughter Edith Craig provided the costumes, and her son created the monumental, evocative settings for which he later became renowned.

As Gordon Craig later wrote, the production was "an artistic success but a financial failure." He attributed the difficulties to "unruly" actors who "did their best to ruin its prospects." Craig also believed that the out-of-the-way location of the Imperial Theatre limited the run of the play to a single week in April. Terry took the financial loss stoically and embarked on a provincial tour to recoup.

References: Craig, Edward G. *On Art of the Theatre.* Chicago: Browne's Bookstore, 1911; Terry, Ellen. *The Story of My Life.* London: Hutchinson, 1909.

TESMAN, HEDDA GABLER. See Gabler, Hedda.

TESMAN, JÖRGEN (*Hedda Gabler*): Jörgen is the Norwegian equivalent of George, which in its Latin form means "good husband" or "husbandman." When he asks why his wife does not call him by his Christian name, Hedda replies that he would require a different name from the one he was given. In other words, he is not capable of being a good husband to Hedda Gabler.* Tesman is a scholar, rather dull and plodding, but good-hearted and kind. He has been pampered by his maiden aunts; Hedda has led him into a life with which he is wholly incompatible.

TESMAN, JULIANE (*Hedda Gabler*): Jörgen Tesman's* maiden aunt who cossets him and sacrifices for him. She is a plain woman who rejoices in her nephew's good fortune in marrying such a woman as Hedda Gabler.* Her motivation is the need to care for someone.

TESMAN, RINA (*Hedda Gabler*): Although she does not appear at all and dies in the course of the action of the play, Jörgen Tesman's* other maiden aunt has an important role: she mortgages her pension to buy a house beyond his means.

THÉÂTRE LIBRE [FREE THEATRE]: The Théâtre Libre was founded in Paris in 1887 by André Antoine* in order to produce new works which the state censor did not allow to be shown commercially. Since the audience was comprised of subscribers, members of the organization, the Théâtre Libre did not qualify as a commercial organization. On May 29, 1890, Antoine staged *Ghosts** and appeared as Oswald Alving.* Much controversy was engendered, and as a result, *Ghosts* was seen throughout France in about two hundred performances. In 1890-91 the group presented *The Wild Duck,** which also caused something of a scandal. These performances are important because they mark the introduction of Ibsen to France; the organization served as the model of the Independent Theatre,* the Freie Bühne,* the Moscow Art Theatre,* and numerous other producing organizations that brought Ibsen's works to continental stages.

THEMISTIUS (*Emperor and Galilean*): An orator.

A THIEF (*Peer Gynt*): Peer Gynt* takes up the Emperor's robe and white stallion abandoned by the Thief* and the Receiver.*

THIMIG, HELENE (1889-1974): Actress Helene Thimig was involved with Ibsen throughout her long career. She played Thea Elvsted* in Meiningen and quickly added Eline* of *Lady Inger of Östraat** to her repertory. In

1950 she played Ella Rentheim* and Helene Alving* in Munich with the support of Alfred Bassermann.*
References: *Brockhaus Enzyklopaedie,* XVIII, 646; *Enciclopedia della Spettacolo,* IX, 885.

THORA: A translation from Polish and Russian versions of *A Doll's House** by Karol Bozenta Chlapowski* and Louise Everson, husband and secretary of Helena Modjeska,* respectively. *Thora* was performed once in Louisville, Kentucky, on December 7, 1883.

THORESEN, MAGDALENE (1819-1903): Ibsen's mother-in-law was a Danish author of novels and short stories. In addition to being married to the Dean of Bergen, Thoresen both translated plays from the French and wrote original dramas, some of which were produced by the Norwegian Theatre, Bergen.*
Reference: *Breve fra Magdalene Thoresen, 1855-1901.* Eds. J. Clausen and P. F. Rist. Copenhagen: Gyldendal, 1919.

THORGEJR (*The Mountain Bird*): An old minstrel.

THORGEJR (*Olaf Liljekrans*): An old minstrel; the father of Alfhild.*

THORNDIKE, RUSSELL (1885-1972): Russell Thorndike received good notices for his performance as Peer Gynt* in the Old Vic (London) production of *Peer Gynt** in March 1922.
Reference: *Who Was Who in the Theatre,* IV, 2362-4.

THORNDIKE, SYBIL (1882-1976): When noting that she had appeared in only two of Ibsen's dramas, Dame Sybil Thorndike lamented, "There just hasn't been time" (Sprigge, p. 250). The theatre is poorer as a result because in Dame Sybil lay the sensibility and technique to enliven Ibsen's heroines such as Hjördis,* Lady Inger of Gyldenlöve,* Hedda Gabler,* and Gunhild Borkman.*

    When she first appeared as Helene Alving* in *Ghosts** on April 19, 1930, Thorndike was deeply moved by the role in which she saw similarities to Greek tragedy. In her numerous international tours, the actress refined her characterization about which her son Christopher Casson said, "Ibsen did not accept the darkness. Neither does my mother. The unopened bottle of champagne symbolizes light and joy bottled up. The open bottle is Oswald's life as an artist. . . . At the end Mrs. Alving accepts absolute truth—and will not kill. My mother and father shared this deep belief in a life force" (Sprigge, p. 207).

    When the Old Vic Company presented *Peer Gynt** on August 31, 1944, Thorndike's Aase* appeared "big, like Hecuba." Critic J. C. Trewin wrote that "Aase's dying voice would have melted marble." (Sprigge, p. 249). Such a lofty conception might have overwhelmed the ordinary actor, but Thorndike was playing against Ralph Richardson* as Peer Gynt* and Laurence Olivier* as the Button-Molder.*

Reference: Sprigge, Elizabeth. *Sybil Thorndike Casson.* London: Victor Gollancz, 1971.

THOROLF (*The Vikings in Helgeland*): The youngest son of Örnulf.*

THRANE, MARCUS MÖLLER (1817-90): When socialist Marcus Thrane organized the workers in Drammen in 1848, he was imprisoned and sentenced to three years' detention. He had edited the *Workers' Union News* to which Ibsen occasionally contributed and founded a worker's organization to which Ibsen's friend Theodor Abildgaard* belonged. Thrane was, therefore, a central figure in Ibsen's youthful social consciousness. In 1863 he emigrated to the United States where he became a journalist. In Chicago he helped found the Norsk Theatre in Chicago and wrote several plays.

Reference: Wilt, Napier, and H.C.K. Naeseth. "Two Early Norwegian Dramatic Societies in Chicago," *Norwegian-American Studies and Records,* X (1938), 44-75.

TITHERADGE, MADGE (1887-1961): The production of *A Doll's House** at London's Playhouse Theatre in November 1925 starred Australian actress Madge Titheradge as Nora Helmer.* Prior to this engagement, Titheradge had appeared in romantic plays, pantomimes, and an occasional foray into Shakespeare's dramas.

Reference: Who Was Who in the Theatre, IV, 2373-4.

TREE, HERBERT BEERBOHM (1853-1917): History has reserved a place for Beerbohm Tree because of his accomplishments as actor/manager of London's Theatre Royal, Haymarket (1887-96) and Her (His) Majesty's Theatre (from 1897 until his death), but his connection with Ibsen is also worthy of remembrance. Entering the professional theatre in 1878, he was a rather unseasoned player when he appeared in the ludicrous *Breaking a Butterfly** (1884).

By the time he played Thomas Stockmann* in *An Enemy of the People,** starting on June 14, 1893, Tree's somewhat limited powers as an actor had been highly developed. Steeped in the Romantic stage tradition, yet fascinated by the demands of Realism, Tree at first played his role for comic effect. Discussions with friends led him somewhat to abandon this approach and take the character seriously; as a result, the role was viewed as one of his most representative impersonations. Desmond MacCarthy chronicled Tree's approach to Stockmann.

Since Tree was quite a large man, he engaged a very small actor as Peter Stockmann,* "the representative of the compact majority," for the sake of contrast. The mayor's hat, moreover, was the subject of a running joke. Despite these directorial touches, MacCarthy called Tree's own performance "masterly and subtle." During Stockmann's thunderous speech about domestic pettiness, the actor briefly put his hand on Mrs. Stockmann's shoulder as if to reassure her that he was not referring to their home. MacCarthy saw this as evidence of how entirely Tree understood his character.

Over the years Tree returned numerous times to *An Enemy of the People*, presenting it both in England and the United States. Lady Maud Tree recalls that her husband passionately admired Ibsen's dramas, including *A Doll's House** and *The Master Builder.** He even dreamed of staging *Peer Gynt.** Tree's prestige as a theatrical knight and gentleman of the theatre perhaps hastened Ibsen's acceptance in England.

References: MacCarthy and Lady Tree's comments are found in *Herbert Beerbohm Tree: Some Memories of Him and His Art,* ed. Max Beerbohm. New York: E. P. Dutton, n.d.; Pearson, Hesketh. *Beerbohm Tree: His Life and Laughter.* New York: Harper and Brothers, 1956.

TROLLS: Trolls and their traits are prominent in several of Ibsen's plays but most notably in *Peer Gynt.** According to folk tradition, when Lucifer's angels fell from heaven into the woods, they became trolls, dwarfish people who inhabited hills and caves. As fallen angels, trolls are evil and have the power of dominating human souls and controlling behavior. Through their influence, man's deepest, most animalistic nature rises to the surface.

References: Anderson, Marilyn A. "Norse Trolls and Ghosts in Ibsen," *Journal of Popular Culture*, V, 2 (1971), 349-66; Leach, Maria, ed. *Standard Dictionary of Folklore, Myth and Legend.* New York: Funk and Wagnalls, 1972.

TRUMPETERSTRAALE, HERR (*Peer Gynt*): One of the traveling gentlemen encountered by Peer Gynt* in Africa.

TÖNNESEN, HILMAR (*The Pillars of Society*): Betty Bernick's* cousin; a local gadfly.

TÖNNESEN, JOHAN (*The Pillars of Society*): Betty Bernick's* younger brother Johan has been content to accept the blame for Karsten Bernick's* financial duplicity and Dina Dorf's* illegitimacy, but when he comes home from America and falls in love with Dina, he insists that the truth be told. By so doing, Johan may ruin Bernick's position as a pillar of society. When Dina asks to go to America with Johan as his wife, however, Johan sails away without precipitating the crisis.

TÖNSBERG, CHRISTIAN (1813-97): A Norwegian publisher, Tönsberg brought out *The Feast at Solhoug** on March 19, 1856. It took him fifteen years to recover his investment.

Reference: Norsk Biografisk Leksikon, XVII, 253-61.

U

UDBYE, MARTIN ANDREAS (1820-89): Udbye wrote the first Norwegian opera, *Fredkulla* (1858). In 1861 Ibsen approached him about composing an opera with *Olaf Liljekrans** as the libretto. Udbye expressed an interest, but two years later he still had not received the libretto from Ibsen. The idea came to nothing.
Reference: Michelsen, Kari. "Udbye, M. A.," *New Grove's Dictionary of Music and Musicians* (London: Macmillan, 1980), XIX, 308.

AN UGLY BRAT (*Peer Gynt*): This unfortunate child had Peer Gynt* as a father and the Troll-King's daughter as a mother.

ULF (*Brand*): The child of Brand* and Agnes*; he eventually dies because of the unwholesome, sunless atmosphere of Gudbrandsdalen.*

ULFHEJM (*When We Dead Awaken*): A landed proprietor who successfully diverts Maja Rubek.*

ULLMAN, LIV (1938-): Primarily a film actress, Norwegian Liv Ullman has been involved with the role of Nora Helmer* in a stage production in Oslo, a Norwegian radio adaptation, and finally the English version staged by the New York Shakespeare Festival starting on March 5, 1975. Ullman's sixty-six performances in the New York production won her the New York Drama Critics' Award for best actress of 1975. Since her first two Noras were played in Norwegian, Ullman had considerable difficulty in rethinking the role in English. Dissatisfied with the translation, she altered her part to strengthen Ibsen's nuances. Ullman viewed Nora as a dancing doll. "It is a little girl," she wrote, "who slams the door behind her. A little girl in the process of growing up." (Ullman, p. 210). The critics praised her but damned the production.

In 1982 Ullman mistakenly agreed to appear in *Ghosts** in New York thinking it to be *When We Dead Awaken** because the Norwegian title of *Ghosts, Gengangere,** literally means something like awakened spirits. Not surprisingly, then, Waltger Kerr found her performance as Helene Alving* to be "light and uncommitted."

References: Kerr, Walter. "A 'Ghosts' That Grows Evermore Lightweight," *New York Times,* Sept. 5, 1982, Sect. H, p. 3, cols. 1-4; *New York Theatre Critics' Reviews,* XXXVI, 6 (Mar. 17, 1975), 318-23; Ullman, Liv. *Changing.* New York: Alfred A. Knopf, 1977.

DE UNGES FORBUND: The Norwegian title of *The League of Youth.**

URSULUS (*Emperor and Galilean*): The royal treasurer.

V

VALK, FREDERICK (1895-1956): Frederick Valk, a Czechoslovak, established himself as one of the midtwentieth-century's busiest Ibsenian actors. He played John Gabriel Borkman* in 1944 and again in 1950, Halvard Solness* in 1947, and Alfred Allmers* in 1950. Valk made his English debut in 1939 and played numerous Shakespearean roles at the Old Vic.
Reference: Who Was Who in the Theatre, IV, 2428-9.

VARG, MISS (*Little Eyolf*): The real name of the Rat-Wife*; it means "wolf."

VARRO (*Emperor and Galilean*): A subaltern.

VASENIUS, VALFRID (b. 1848): While still a graduate student in Finland, Valfrid Vasenius wrote a doctoral dissertation in 1880 that became the second full-length book about Ibsen's plays to be published. Two years later he published *Henrik Ibsen, ett skaldeportratt* [*Henrik Ibsen, A Bard's Portrait*].
Reference: Finsk Biografisk Handbok (Helsingfors: G. W. Edlund, 1903), II, 2350-1.

VEGARD VAERADAL (*The Pretenders*): One of Haakon's* guard who is eventually murdered by Skule's* man.

VENSTÖP: When the Ibsen family suffered serious financial reversals, it was forced to move to this broken-down farmhouse on the outskirts of Skien.* It had been owned by a sea captain, who left a number of books including Harrison's *History of London.**

VERNON, W. H. (1844-1905): Actor W. H. Vernon paid William Archer* twenty to twenty-five pounds for his translation of *The Pillars of Society*,* which was produced as *Quicksands** (1880). Vernon played Karsten Bernick* in this apprentice piece and returned to the role in 1889.
Reference: Who's Who in the Theatre, London: Pitman, 1907.

VIBE, FREDERIK LUDVIG (1803-81): F. L. Vibe was on the classical philology staff of the University of Christiania in 1850 when he reviewed *Catiline** in the *Christiania Post* (May 16, 1850). He criticized Ibsen for tampering with historical facts and indulging in forced emotion but praised him for his tragic power and purity of expression.
Reference: Norsk Biografisk Leksikon, XVII, 545-51.

VIGELAND (*The Pillars of Society*): A merchant; one of Karsten Bernick's* business associates.

THE VIKINGS IN HELGELAND: A four-act Romantic serious drama.
Composition: Started in the spring and completed in the autumn of 1857; published on April 25, 1858.

Stage history:

Nov. 24, 1858	Norwegian Theatre, Christiania* (5 perfs.), dir. Henrik Ibsen
Feb. 10, 1859	Trondhjem
Mar. 4, 1859	Norwegian Theatre, Bergen,* dir. Börnstjerne Björnson*
Apr. 11, 1861	Christiania Theatre* (6)
Sept. 29, 1867	Christiania Theatre (4)
Nov. 28, 1870	Christiania Theatre (2)
Feb. 19, 1875	Royal Theatre, Copenhagen
Nov. 3, 1875	New Theatre, Stockholm, dir. Edvard Stjernström*
Apr. 10, 1876	Hoftheater, Munich
Oct. 26, 1876	Burgtheater, Vienna, Charlotte Wolter* as Hjördis
Oct. 27, 1876	Hoftheater, Dresden
Nov. 24, 1876	Hoftheater, Munich
Nov. 1876	Royal Theatre, Stockholm
1876	Norwegian Theatre, Bergen
1876	Royal Theatre, Copenhagen
1876	Stadtheater, Leipzig
1877	Hoftheater, Munich
Apr. 13, 1877	Christiania Theatre (13), dir. Ludvig Oscar Josephson*
1877	Royal Theatre, Stockholm (1)
1878	Trondhjem
Nov. 21, 1879	Christiania Theatre (6)
Mar. 12, 1880	Christiania Theatre (2)
1880	Nya Teatern, Stockholm, dir. Ludvig Oscar Josephson

Jan. 28, 1881	Christiania Theatre (3)
Feb. 13, 1882	Christiania Theatre (6)
Aug. 24, 1883	Christiania Theatre (2)
Mar. 5, 1884	Christiania Theatre (5)
1884	Oldenburg
Dec. 10, 1885	Christiania Theatre (4)
Feb. 2, 1886	Christiania Theatre (2)
Feb. 16, 1887	Christiania Theatre (4)
1889	Darmstadt (2)
Jan. 17, 1890	Christiania Theatre (15)
Feb. 12, 1890	Deutsches Theater, Berlin
June 1891	Residenz Theater, Munich
Sept. 22, 1891	Christiania Theatre (7)
1891	Hoftheater, Munich
1891	Stadttheater, Gothenburg, Julia Haakonsson* as Hjördis
Jan. 14, 1892	Maly Theatre, Moscow, Glikerija Fedotova as Hjördis
Dec. 28, 1893	Christiania Theatre (1)
Jan. 3, 1894	Christiania Theatre (6)
Aug. 30, 1895	Christiania Theatre (10)
1895	Maly Theatre, Moscow
Mar. 20, 1896	Christiania Theatre (1)
Apr. 15, 1903	Imperial Theatre, London (8), Ellen Terry* as Hjördis
Mar. 22, 1907	Empire Theatre, New York (1), pro. American Academy of Dramatic Art
Apr. 29, 1911	Hoftheater, Braunschweig
Jan. 18, 1912	Mikailov Theatre, St. Petersburg
Nov. 3, 1923	Great Dramatic Theatre, Leningrad
Mar. 26, 1927	National Theatre, Christiania,* Johanne Dybwad* as Hjördis
May 12, 1930	New Yorker Theatre, New York (8), Blanche Yurka* as Hjördis

Synopsis: On a craggy coast of the island of Helgeland in the tenth century, a Viking king named Sigurd appears, spies a boatshed, and proceeds to break it open, but before he can succeed, he is interrupted by Örnulf, an Icelandic chieftain, who is fully armed. Both have chosen the shed as shelter for their dependents, Örnulf for his men, Sigurd for a woman; their dispute over the shed results in a passage of arms, and as they fight, Dagny and Sigurd's friends appear on one side. On the other side, the six sons of Örnulf come into view. Before the factions come to the aid of their principals, Sigurd wounds Örnulf in the arm. Despite his wounds, Örnulf appreciates the skill requisite to inflicting it and repeats a bardic stanza about Sigurd the Strong. At that point Örnulf's sons realize that Sigurd himself stands before them. Ornulf pulls back his hood, revealing himself as the father of Dagny whom Sigurd has taken for his wife. In a tense moment, both groups prepare to enter the fray, but Örnulf stops them by suing for peace with Sigurd. He speaks of the day five years ago when Sigurd stole Dagny from him, a misdeed that can be propitiated by the payment of a sum of money; he also tells how at the same time Gunnar Headman of Helgeland carried away Hjördis, his foster-daughter. Then Örnulf's motives are made plain: he wants Sigurd to help him punish Gunnar, since the gods fortuitously arranged for them to come to Helgeland at the same time. It has become a matter of honor to Örnulf to come to terms with Gunnar because he swore before his kinsmen to recapture his honor before setting foot in Iceland again.

Kaare, a peasant, enters and asks for their protection because he has slain one of Gunnar's men in an argument over a stolen ox, spurred on by the vengeful Hjördis. A band of wayfarers approaches, at the head of whom rides Gunnar. Örnulf volunteers to speak to Gunnar in Kaare's behalf.

Gunnar warily greets his father-in-law and brother-in-law but quickly agrees to make the proper atonement for abducting Hjördis; he further consents to pardon Kaare's crime. All the rival groups, then, are assuaged when the serenity of their resolution is marred by the entrance of Hjördis at the head of an armed troop. She is somewhat non-plussed by the identities of the assembled company. She greets Dagny coolly; Kaare arouses her vindictiveness, which is tauntingly directed toward Gunnar when she hears that he has excused the peasant; at the sight of Sigurd, she tenses slightly. Then she derides Gunnar's bravery for sending their youngest son Egil to the south when he had seen the masts of Örnulf's ships. Hjördis brings up the matter of Gunnar's having slain a fierce white bear that had guarded her quarters in Iceland, a deed that had made Gunnar the bravest of the brave. By her reasoning, Gunnar's honor would be compromised by making a pact of atonement with Örnulf. The confrontation degenerates into a legalistic argument in which Hjördis claims that Örnulf must atone for slaying her father, to which he replies that he was dishonestly duped into adopting the daughter of a man whom he had killed in a fair fight. Then Hjördis argues that Gunnar cannot make amends to Örnulf for eloping with her because Gunnar must be the instrument of vengeance for the slaying of her father. Örnulf's response is that Hjördis is not legally married since she was taken by force. This declaration reduces Hjördis to concubinage, for which she swears eternal revenge; she then storms out, exhorting Gunnar to erase her shame on the battlefield. Before he withdraws, Gunnar asks Sigurd to speak with him before leaving Helgeland.

Örnulf fumes about his encounter with Hjördis and vows that Gunnar will pay dearly for her behavior. Sigurd says that he will see that Örnulf does not bear arms against Gunnar; he explains that Gunnar is his close friend and begs Örnulf not to hold him responsible for Hjördis' deeds. In recompense, Sigurd offers Örnulf one of his treasure-laden ships to salve his conscience. When Örnulf hesitates, Sigurd offers both ships; but Örnulf is considering the claims of honor, not of fortune. Having heard this interchange, Kaare, now branded an outlaw by Hjördis, suggests that Örnulf might be placated if Kaare burns Hjördis' hall and all its inhabitants. Both Örnulf and Sigurd upbraid Kaare for his base scheme and drive him off, but not before he mutters that he has a plan for dealing with Hjördis. Örnulf thinks that no punishment of Hjördis would be excessive in view of all the trouble she has caused. He recalls her father's dying prophecy that misfortune would follow the man who adopted her, a child said to have unnatural ferocity as a result of ingesting a wolf's heart. These recollections are cut short by the entrance of Gunnar who has returned to invite all the strangers to his hall for refreshment. He offers a pact of peace, to which Hjördis has come to agree. Although Sigurd is somewhat apprehensive about Hjördis' intentions, he says he will attend the feast; but Örnulf postpones his decision until he has had time to weigh it. Dagny and Sigurd exit to collect gifts to take to Gunnar as host.

Thorolf, Örnulf's youngest son, enters and tells his father that a man calling himself Kaare passed him on the shore and said he intended to journey with a band of twenty outlaws to the southern sanctuary of Gunnar's son Egil, whom they will kill. This news pleases Örnulf, who sends Thorolf to Hjördis' banquet and then retreats with his troop in the direction of his ships. Before leaving, he warns Thorolf to say nothing of his father's whereabouts.

Left alone, Thorolf is soon joined by Sigurd and Dagny on their way to Gunnar's hall. After Thorolf joins Sigurd's men in mooring the ships, Sigurd tells Dagny of his premonition of danger. He asks her to cast into the sea a golden armband that might prove to be a source of great strife at Hjördis' house. Then he explains his cryptic request to his wife.

Years earlier when Gunnar and Sigurd, as marauding Vikings, swore to carry off two Icelandic maidens, Hjördis remained with the roistering men in the banquet hall, drank too much, and boasted that no man would seize her except one who could slay the mighty white bear that guarded her. Although Gunnar had claimed credit for the feat, it had actually been accomplished by Sigurd. Gunnar had fallen in love with Hjördis but feared the bear; therefore Sigurd secretly put on Gunnar's armor, slew the bear, entered Hjördis' bedroom, and slept the night in the woman's bed. Hjördis believed that Gunnar had wooed and won her. In the morning he had put the stuporous Hjördis on Gunnar's ship and then proceeded to take Dagny. While in Hjördis' arms, Sigurd was given the golden circlet now worn by Dagny, and the very sight of it would immediately arouse Hjördis' suspicions. Dagny, however, is so attached to it that, rather than throwing it into the sea, she swears to keep it hidden from Hjördis. Then Thorolf enters, and the three of them go to Hjördis' feast with the words of Sigurd's warning ringing in their ears.

Act II takes place in Gunnar's lodge, where Hjördis enters with Dagny after having shown her the house. Suitably impressed by her foster-sister's material possessions, Dagny wonders why Hjördis is not content. Hjördis feels captive in Gunnar's house, a condition that is not ameliorated by the presence of her son Egil, whose existence is dishonored because he was born of a concubine. Although Dagny attempts to convince her that Örnulf's accusation was meaningless since it was uttered in anger, Hjördis remains implacable, referring to Egil's innate weakness. She speaks of sewing Egil's clothes to his skin to show that his tortured response would not be worthy of a king's grandson. Hjördis passes this comment off as a jest but admits that at times such behavior is attractive because she is a descendant of Scandinavian giants. Having introduced the idea that she is not a typical woman, Hjördis speaks ardently of the thrill of entering into battle alongside the men. Then she asks Dagny about her feelings when loved by a virile man, a feeling she has not had since the night Gunnar stole her from her chamber. Dagny is at first rattled because she knows the truth of that night, but she collects her wits as Hjördis starts to rhapsodize about the thrill of being a bloodthirsty Viking and then to bemoan the fact that she must merely wait at home listening to the wail of the draugen and anticipating the hoofbeats of the dead warriors as they ride to Valhalla. Her ecstasy is so frenetic that Dagny is frightened, but the scene is interrupted by the appearance of Gunnar, Sigurd, and Thorolf.

Gunnar happily speaks of being reunited with his old friend, of entertaining Thorolf, and of his anticipation of being joined by Örnulf. The subject of Egil comes up, and once again Hjördis charges Gunnar with dishonor for sending Egil away for his protection, but Gunnar refuses to become exercised by her taunts. In a quiet moment, Dagny begs Sigurd to leave Hjördis' house because her raving is disquieting. It is too late, however. The house is filled by guests, and the feast begins.

After placing Sigurd and Thorolf in seats of honor, Hjördis proposes that they entertain one another by reciting tales of their individual bravery, but Gunnar warns that to do so could end badly. Sigurd asks Gunnar to tell of his perilous journey to Bjarmeland, but Hjördis will not be appeased. She demands that Sigurd tell of his mightiest deed, so he obliges with a modest, brief tale. Hjördis next calls upon Gunnar, who with embarrassment narrates a similarly humble occurrence. Hjördis in a rage pointedly tells the episode of Gunnar's encounter with the bear that guarded her bedroom. Although Sigurd and Gunnar urge her to be silent, she insists that the assembled company decide whether Gunnar or Sigurd is the mightier. On the face of the evidence, the guests declare Gunnar victor and Sigurd second, a judgment concurred with by Sigurd who vows eternal friendship with Gunnar. Seeing that she cannot rile Sigurd and Gunnar, Hjördis turns her attention to Thorolf, whom she insults by saying that his absent father could have the third highest seat of honor. Thorolf immediately rejoins by disparaging Hjördis' father, who was slain by Örnulf; this precipitates rising indignation among the party. Hjördis accuses Örnulf of magnifying his bravery without justification. When Thorolf interprets this remark as a challenge, Hjördis invites him to defend his father's honor, but not before they trade insults. Despite the efforts of Dagny, Sigurd, and Gunnar to check the mounting fury on both sides, Hjördis accuses Örnulf of practicing sorcery in women's clothes. This remark goads the adolescent Thorolf into blurting out that Örnulf and his sons have now gone southward and slain the innocent Egil. Both Gunnar and Hjördis are agonized by this announcement. When Thorolf exits in a rage, Hjördis impels the stricken Gunnar to avenge his son's murder; he takes up an axe and rushes out in pursuit of Thorolf. A cry from the crowd that has flooded outside to watch Gunnar's terrible vengeance tells that Thorolf is slain, which is confirmed by the returning Gunnar. Hjördis is jubilant because she knows that the deed will bring bloody strife in which she plans to take an active part; Gunnar for his part realizes that he will never be able to rid his mind of the event. Not content to let matters be, Hjördis starts to inflame Gunnar by reminding him that Örnulf still has six sons while he has none, but she is interrupted by the news of Örnulf's approach.

Örnulf enters with Egil, alive, in his arms. The realization of the magnitude of his deed strikes Gunnar with paralyzing force. He becomes more distraught as Örnulf tells of rescuing Egil from the evil Kaare and his murderous band, a feat of valor that cost Örnulf the lives of his six sons. Though greatly bereaved, Örnulf takes comfort in the fact that he still has Thorolf, whom he asks to see. When all look distracted and no one summons his son, Örnulf becomes suspicious. Gunnar finally tells him that he will see Thorolf no more. Hjördis interrupts by saying that Thorolf had behaved quite badly at the feast, that he had spoken of Egil's death, and that he deserved death at Gunnar's hand. Örnulf exits to take charge of Thorolf's body and will allow no one to accompany him; he leaves the room with dignity and quiet resolution.

Once Örnulf has gone, Hjördis starts to mock him, to the dismay of Dagny and Sigurd. Dagny is so incensed that she tells Hjördis the truth about her abduction by Sigurd, the truth of which she attests by displaying the golden armband to a stupefied Hjördis. Gunnar admits the truth but maintains that he is not a coward, to which Sigurd warmly agrees. Dagny and Sigurd leave with their retainers, and Hjördis declares that the only result of the evening's strife can be the death of Sigurd or of herself.

Hjördis is seen in the great hall at the beginning of Act III. As she rehearses her hatred of Sigurd, she prepares a bow and arrow for the confrontation. Gunnar enters, still depressed by the events of the previous day, and notices what she is doing. He observes that she has woven a bowstring from her own hair. He tells Hjördis that in the dead of night he saw her making arrowheads before the fire and chanting magical incantations over them. Gunnar knows that she intends them to kill Sigurd but vows to keep peace with his friend whatever Hjördis may do. She is confident that Gunnar will change his mind, however. Hjördis is surprised to hear that Gunnar intends to return to the sea as a means of regaining his honor. In a moment of clear insight, Gunnar realizes that Sigurd should have married Hjördis, for only he could have guaranteed her happiness. The thought momentarily tantalizes Hjördis, but in a moment of frenzied passion, she implores Gunnar to kill Sigurd. If he would but help her slay Dagny and Sigurd, who are jeering behind their backs, she would love him passionately and atone for her five years of amatory coldness. She paints such a glowing picture of their future marital happiness that Gunnar is almost swayed, but their discussion is interrupted by the appearance of Dagny.

Dagny has come to warn Gunnar to arm himself because Kaare and a band of bellicose warriors are fast approaching and mean to do him and Hjördis grievous harm. Sigurd plans to face them but may not be able to contain the threat. This news of Sigurd's faithfulness banishes all of Hjördis' blandishments from his mind. Before summoning his men, Gunnar asks Dagny about Örnulf, who had carried Thorolf's corpse to his ship and erected a burial mound for his fallen sons on the shore. Then Dagny and Hjördis are left alone.

Dagny asks Hjördis' forgiveness for her cruelty at the feast, a moral lapse from which she will never recover. Hjördis recalls the first time they ever saw Sigurd and Gunnar in Örnulf's hall. Then Sigurd had said that his happiness depended upon having a warlike wife who would spur him on in battle. Now Hjördis wonders if Sigurd ever was happy with the docile Dagny. Dagny, reduced to tears, begins to doubt her husband's contentment. She vows no longer to be an encumbrance to Sigurd, whose approach is announced by a servant. Dagny leaves because she cannot bear to face Sigurd to whom she has been the unwitting cause of unhappiness. Hjördis rejoices in the damage she has inflicted and wonders if she has not injured Sigurd more than if she had merely killed him. Now Hjördis has hatched some secret plan by which she will take revenge on Sigurd and Gunnar while besting even the Norns, the fates.

When Sigurd comes in, she speaks indirectly of this scheme but does not divulge it. As they face each other, it is clear that they are mutually attracted. Sigurd attempts to explain his feelings by telling a story of how two young Vikings found themselves at the court of Örnulf. They were both attracted by the bold foster-daughter of the chieftain. Hjördis can barely believe the news. Sigurd continues: he had intended to slay the bear and win Hjördis for himself, but when his friend expressed such ardent love of her, he, Sigurd, had sublimated his own desires and captured her for Gunnar. Although Sigurd had married another, he only prized her, never loved her. Hjördis thus learns that her evil imaginings were absolutely true. Now Sigurd plans to say farewell and never see her again. Hjördis is crazed but manages to say that she has always loved him. Ever honorable, Sigurd sees that their love must remain unrequited, but Hjördis urges him to wreck the lives of Gunnar and Dagny by taking to the seas with her at his side. Sigurd cannot do this, but Hjördis continues to excite him with images of the glory and fame, even a throne, that might be his if he merely acquiesces to her scheme. After Sigurd still demurs, Hjördis threatens to tell all to Dagny and Gunnar. Sigurd asks how she would react if he slew Gunnar on the field of battle; her response is that she would keep quiet and avenge Gunnar's death for honor's sake. Sigurd then pronounces the death sentence on Gunnar and himself.

Gunnar enters and says that he has been unable to assemble enough fighting men to repel Kaare and his troop because Gunnar's name has been dishonored. Sigurd promises that the night will bring sufficient help, but once Kaare has been repulsed, Gunnar must defend his honor for killing Sigurd's kinsman. Gunnar is unable to believe that Sigurd is serious, but he soon deduces that Hjördis is at the bottom of Sigurd's resolution. Sigurd gives orders to the servants to summon the fighting men to ally themselves with Sigurd the Strong against Kaare the Peasant. Gunnar now understands that Sigurd has challenged him to reestablish Gunnar's honor, and so he thanks him profusely. Sigurd admits that Hjördis is the reason for his action. They clasp hands, and both exit, Sigurd stealing a glance at Hjördis, who is left alone to wonder which man will fall in mortal combat. She resolves that she and Sigurd will be together no matter what the outcome of the fight.

Act IV depicts the coastline occasionally illuminated by moonlight that breaks through storm clouds. A grave mound is seen upstage. Örnulf watches his men making the funeral preparations. Sigurd and Dagny speak of Örnulf's debilitation since Thorolf's death. Dagny wants to be reassured that Hjördis was lying when she said that Dagny had made Sigurd's life miserable; Sigurd says that he plans to buy land, settle down, and end the Viking life, but never again must Dagny mention Hjördis' name. When the burial mound is finished, Dagny speaks to Örnulf, urging food and warm clothes upon him, but he says that he intends to sit exposed to the elements until death overtakes him. Dagny, in a ploy to restore his interest in life, reminds Örnulf that he is a skald* whose sacred responsibility is to compose a song extolling the deeds of his sons. He sees that she speaks the truth and starts to sing of his sons with rising enthusiasm until the deed works its therapeutic effect and restores his vigor. He goes into the boathouse to eat, leaving Sigurd and Dagny to ruminate over the activities of the coming day.

Along with the rumblings of the approaching storm, Kaare enters boasting that Gunnar will be an unworthy opponent to Sigurd once he has finished with him. Sigurd enlists Örnulf's aid in keeping Kaare from robbing them both of honorable redress against Gunnar. Reluctant at first, Örnulf leads his men toward Gunnar's hall; Sigurd dispatches Dagny to insure that no harm comes to Hjördis from either Kaare or Örnulf.

Left alone, Sigurd listens to the sounds of the battle but is astonished to see Hjördis approaching, fully armored and carrying the bow strung with her own hair. With great alarm she rushes up to Sigurd and speaks of a red-eyed, wolf-like creature, the fylgie, the incarnation of her moral nature, that is pursuing her. Its appearance means that she must die in this night. Despite his attempts to calm her, Hjördis pleads that he should take her into his arms and journey to the world of the dead with her. She offers her enchanted bow-string as his means of entering the world of fallen heroes. While Hjördis raves passionately, the flames of Gunnar's burning hall light the skies. Hjördis takes no notice of the probable deaths of Egil and Gunnar. The thunderstorm at last bursts onto the scene, and in its billows, Hjördis sees the dead men on their sooty steeds making their way to Valhalla. She draws her bow and transfixes Sigurd with an arrow. Her rejoicing is cut short when he reveals that he is a Christian and will not be her consort in Valhalla. Stunned, Hjördis drops her bow to the ground, and thinking that the black, pagan gods are jeering at her, runs to the edge of the cliff and throws herself into the sea.

The battle is over, and Örnulf, Dagny, Egil, and Gunnar enter. Örnulf is at peace because he has avenged his sons' deaths; Gunnar asks shelter for himself and Egil. Then Dagny notices the fallen Sigurd and rushes to him. Gunnar sees in the scene the hand of Hjördis, and Dagny recognizes her bow. Gunnar believes that Hjördis killed Sigurd before he had a chance to harm Gunnar; thus, he is convinced, she really loved him. All such thoughts are placed in abeyance when the skies are rent by the sight and sound of the ride of the fallen warriors to Valhalla. Egil sees Hjördis in their number. Then the apparition fades, the clouds are dissipated, and the moon brightens the scene. Gunnar realizes that Hjördis is dead. Örnulf's honor is satisfied, and he offers the hand of friendship to Gunnar, who decides to sail with him to Iceland.

Structural analysis: Although the structural machinery of this play creaks, it has moments of undeniable power, such as the ironic scene when Örnulf appears with an unharmed Egil and the spectacular procession of fallen heroes toward Valhalla. The unity of the plot, however, is defective:

Hjördis goads Thorolf into boasting of his father's supposed murder of Egil;

(as a result of which)
Hjördis (falsely) discovers that her son is dead;

(as a result of which)
Hjördis insists that Gunnar take vengeance by killing Thorolf.

If the play were truly unified by action, the next incident would be the result of Thorolf's murder. It is not.

Hjördis discovers that Egil is alive;

(as a result of which)
Hjördis jeers at Örnulf, thus angering Dagny;

(as a result of which)
Hjördis discovers that Sigurd rather than Gunnar had taken her in her bedroom;

(as a result of which)
Hjördis decides that she must have Sigurd whatever the cost;

(as a result of which)
Hjördis discovers that Sigurd will remain with Dagny;

(as a result of which)
Hjördis kills Sigurd so they can be together in Valhalla;

(as a result of which)
Hjördis discovers that Sigurd is a Christian and will not go to Valhalla;

(as a result of which)
Hjördis plunges into the sea.

VILDANDEN: The Norwegian title of *The Wild Duck.* *

VINJE, AASMUND OLAFSEN (1818-70): Vinje, a poet, journalist, and language reformer, was typical of the sort of friend courted by Student Ibsen in Christiania.* Vinje was also the co-founder with Ibsen and Paul Botten-Hansen* of *Andhrimner,* * a political newspaper.
Reference: Norsk Biografisk Leksikon, XVIII, 73-110.

W

WALBROOK, ANTON (1900-66): Viennese actor Anton Walbrook was on the stage for nineteen years before he first appeared in London in 1939. His involvement with Ibsen's work was brief but significant, being limited to a production of *The Wild Duck** which opened at the St. Martin's Theatre (London) on November 3, 1948, and ran for 164 performances. Walbrook acted Hjalmar Ekdal* to the Gina Ekdal* of Fay Compton.*
Reference: Who Was Who in the Theater, IV, 2469.

WALLER, LEWIS (1860-1915): Matinee idol Lewis Waller was pleased to exchange his swashbuckling roles for sorties into Ibsen's world. On January 26, 1893, Waller was Oswald Alving* to Mrs. Patrick Campbell's* Helene Alving* in the Independent Theatre's* production of *Ghosts.** In May and June of 1893, he joined Elizabeth Robins* at the Opera Comique (London) as Ejlert Lövborg,* Johannes Rosmer,* and Halvard Solness*; each production was given four performances. Evidently, Waller's playing surprised the critics. Of his Rosmer, one reviewer wrote, "The intense feeling infused into their long scenes lent the new guilty couple an absorbing interest" (Franc, p. 94). Waller's Solness "revealed Mr. Waller in a new light. As Solness he looked beneath the surface of the part, abandoned the hero's claim to be heroic, and played not like a leading actor, but the unhinged architect of Ibsen's puzzling pages" (Franc, p. 94). Unfortunately Waller's audiences demanded a certain type of characterization, so he had to desert Ibsen.
References: Franc, Miriam A. *Ibsen in England.* Boston: Four Seas Company, 1919; *Who Was Who in the Theatre,* IV, 2479-83.

WANGEL, BOLETTE (*The Lady from the Sea*): As Doctor Wangel's* eldest daughter, Bolette is dissatisfied with her life with her new mother,

Ellida.* She dreams of going away and creating a new lifestyle for herself. When her old teacher, Professor Arnholm,* proposes marriage, Bolette eventually accepts.

WANGEL, DOCTOR (*The Lady from the Sea*): Wangel, the father of two girls, is the district physician in an inland Norwegian town. He is married to Ellida,* his second wife, who carries with her an aura of mystery and an unnatural devotion to the sea. Wangel steers an even course between his new wife and the children of a former marriage. He loves Ellida but is frustrated because they have had no physical intimacy since their baby died. When Alfred Johnston* returns and forces Ellida to choose between them, Wangel shows his strength of character by setting Ellida free to make her choice.

WANGEL, ELLIDA (*The Lady from the Sea*): Ellida Wangel comes from the north of Norway where she was known as "The Lady from the Sea" because of her fascination with the ocean. She had once loved a sailor, Alfred Johnston,* who had quickly departed because of a brush with the law; once he was out of sight, Ellida saw that he had exercised some sort of mind control over her and that she really did not love him. Ellida married Doctor Wangel* for the sake of convenience and as a means of protecting herself against the sailor's eventual return to claim her. Now that her husband works in an inland town, Ellida pines for the sea in an obsessive way. Johnston appears, forces Ellida to choose between him and Wangel, and disappears when she elects to remain with the doctor. She sees that she can adapt to a normal life with Wangel once he grants her freedom of will.

WANGEL, HILDE (*The Lady from the Sea*): Hilde is Doctor Wangel's* younger daughter. Under a guise of not caring for Ellida,* Hilde masks a poignant need to be noticed and loved by her foster-mother.

WANGEL, HILDE (*The Master Builder*): This is the same Hilde Wangel of *The Lady from the Sea** grown ten years older. Once Halvard Solness* had impressed her by climbing the tower of a church he built in her town; later he had promised to give her a kingdom when she grew up. In this play, Hilde has come to claim that promise. She is bold, flirtatious, scheming, highly idealistic, and, in the end, compassionate. Hilde is capable of taking Solness away from his wife, Aline Solness,* but once Hilde meets her, she is powerless to harm Aline. Hilde urges Solness to climb one of his towers, although she knows he suffers from vertigo and might fall to his death; yet she presses him, believing that death resulting from the pursuit of ideals is better than a life with no prospects.

WARRINGTON, ANN (fl. 1895-1909): Ann Warrington's only excursion into Ibsen's world was not a particularly effective one. She played Ella

Rentheim* in a production of *John Gabriel Borkman** staged in New York on November 18, 1897, by the Criterion Independent Theatre.* According to some press reports, the audience was large and receptive but uncritical because many had received free admission. A backstage fire diverted attention from the drama, which was damned by the anti-Ibsenites and praised by the modernists. Warrington's Ella was deemed "a particularly able and sympathetic portrayal" (Briscoe, p. 216).

References: Briscoe, Johnson. *The Actors' Birthday Book,* 2d ser. New York: Moffat, Yard, 1908; *New York Dramatic Mirror,* Nov. 27, 1897, p. 16, col. 1; *New York Times,* Nov. 19, 1897, p. 7, col. 5.

THE WARRIOR'S BARROW: See *The Burial Mound.**

WEAVER, FRITZ (1926-): American actor Fritz Weaver's Peer Gynt* was generally appreciated by the critics when it was seen in New York in January 1960, but audiences supported it for only thirty-two performances.

Reference: Who's Who in the Theatre, 16th ed., pp. 1233-4.

WEBER, T.: As headmaster of an academy in Copenhagen, Weber, ostensibly armed only with an English dictionary and a grammar, published a translation of *A Doll's House** in 1880 which he called *Nora* and dedicated to the Danish-born Alexandra, Princess of Wales. As a reflection of Ibsen's artistry, Weber's translation is worthless, but as unintentional comedy, it is priceless, as a few examples demonstrate:

Weber: NORA: But, Thorvald, we must enjoy ourselves a little. It is the first Christmas we need not to spare.
  HELMER: Know that we cannot dissipate.
Archer: NORA: Why Torvald, surely we can afford to launch out a little now! It's the first Christmas we haven't had to pinch.
  HELMER: Come, come; we can't afford to squander money.

* * * *

Weber: NORA: It is charming to have excessively much money and need not to give one's self any concerns, is it not?
Archer: NORA: It's splendid to have lots of money, and not need to worry about things, isn't it?

* * * *

Weber: NORA: But, Kristine, such work is so extremely fatiguing; and already now you look so exertly.
Archer: NORA: But, Christina, that's so tiring, and you look worn out already.

* * * * *

Weber: RANK: Thus you have come to town in order to recreate during all banquets?
Archer: RANK: Then you have come to town to find rest in a round of dissipation?

* * * *

Weber: HELMER: You are first of all a wife and mother.
  NORA: I no longer believe in that. I believe that I am first of all a man, I as well as you,—or, at all events, that I am to try to become a man.

Archer: HELMER: Before all else you are a wife and mother.
  NORA: That I no longer believe. I think that before all else I am a human being,
    just as much as you are—or, at least, I will try to become one.
                                    * * * *
Weber: HELMER: Change yourself in such a manner that—
  NORA:—that cohabitation between you and me might become a matrimony.
    Goodbye.
Archer: HELMER: We must so change that—?
  NORA: That communion between us shall be a marriage. Good-by.
                                    * * * *

Weber's translation was read in England two years before that of Henrietta
Frances Lord,* but its ineptitude prompted Harley Granville Barker to
remark (with reference to the last example) that he was "not indisposed to
offer a prize at the Royal Academy of Dramatic Art to the student who
could manage to speak [it] without making the audience laugh" (Barker,
p. 196).

References: Archer, William. "Ibsen as He is Translated," *Time*, N.S. 1 (Jan.
    1890), n.p.; Barker, Harley Granville. "The Coming of Ibsen," *The Eighteen-
    Eighties*, ed. Walter de la Mare. Cambridge: Cambridge University Press,
    1930; Ibsen, Henrik. *Nora: A Play in Three Acts*. Trans. T. Weber.
    Copenhagen: Weber's Academy, 1880.

WELL-MADE PLAY: There is a fundamental difference between a well-
constructed play such as *Hamlet* and a well-made play, the acknowledged
master of which was Augustin Eugène Scribe.* Early critics of Ibsen's
dramas concluded that the Norwegian adopted and improved the Scribean
technique in the creation of his dramas. Later writers such as Michael
Meyer insist that Ibsen held Scribe's plays in such disdain that he could not
possibly have learned anything from them.

The confusion rests, of course, with the definition of the well-made play.
In his introduction (pp. xii-xiii) to *Camille and Other Plays*, Stephen S.
Stanton lists traits of the well-made play as commonly understood: "(1) a
plot based on a secret known to the audience but withheld from certain
characters. . . ; (2) a pattern of increasingly intense action and suspense,
prepared by exposition . . . ; (3) a series of ups and downs in the hero's
fortunes, caused by his conflict with an adversary; (4) the counterpunch of
peripateia and *scène à faire* [obligatory scene] . . . ; (5) a central
misunderstanding or *quiproquo*, made obvious to the spectator but
withheld from the participants; (6) a logical and credible denouement; (7)
the reproduction of the overall action pattern in the individual acts." Patti
P. Gillespie (pp. 21-31) has shown that Stanton's definition (as well as
several others) is deficient because it is imprecise, does not discriminate
between well-made and well-constructed plays, and was formulated without
consideration of the majority of Scribe's plays.

Gillespie analyzes all of Scribe's plays that have been called well-made in order to formulate a workable definition. She concludes that the quality of being well-made is not as much a matter of form as of the employment of certain techniques and devices, especially in the area of dramatic preparation. Scribe often introduced discoveries in order to establish probability rather than to prepare for subsequent, related discoveries. A certain character, for example, is introduced as an amateur chemist not because that avocation is central to his character but because he needed access to poison.

Another device Scribe favored is the use of one common property to suggest a relationship among otherwise unrelated entities. An obvious example is Scribe's *A Scrap of Paper*, as are Arthur Schnitzler's *La Ronde* and Thornton Wilder's* *The Long Christmas Dinner*. Ibsen used the orphanage in *Ghosts** in exactly the same manner.

A third technique of the well-made play is the logical manner of introducing exposition. Often a stranger asks for information, or a traveler must be apprised of what has happened in his absence. Berte* in *Hedda Gabler** provides information to Aunt Juliane Tesman* just as Thea Elvsted* instructs Hedda Gabler* about Ejlert Lövborg's* life with her. A fourth characteristic is clearly explained entrances and exits.

Gillespie concludes that "Scribe developed techniques for implying unity where none existed and for suggesting probability where even credibility could be questioned" (p. 263). These, then, are the actual distinguishing traits of Scribe's dramaturgy, characteristics which Ibsen did not wholly eschew even in his later plays.

References: Gillespie, Patti P. "Plays: Well-Constructed and Well-Made," *Quarterly Journal of Speech,* 58, 3 (Oct. 1972), 313-21; Gillespie, Patti P. "The Well-Made Plays of Eugène Scribe." Unpublished doctoral dissertation, Indiana University, 1970.

WERGMANN, P. F.: Called the first national scene-painter of Norway, Wergmann designed the first production of *The Pretenders** (January 17, 1864), directed by Ibsen at the Christiania Theatre.*

WERLE, GREGERS (*The Wild Duck*): Gregers Werle is a young man driven by "the claim of the ideal" to embark upon a mission of forcing his acquaintances to face the truth about themselves, no matter how destructive that truth may be. His fanatical devotion to his mission causes him to precipitate the death of Hedvig Ekdal* and the destruction of the marriage of her parents. Unfortunately, Gregers learns nothing from the experience; he intends to continue pressing "the claim of the ideal."

WERLE, HAAKON (*The Wild Duck*): The father of Gregers Werle,* Haakon Werle is a wealthy wholesale merchant and manufacturer. In his declining years Werle wishes merely to put his youthful indiscretions and parental failures behind him. As his eyesight fails and blindness is imminent, Werle desires to see his son settled before the father retires with his friend Berta Sörby.*

WEST, REBECCA (*Rosmersholm*): Before going to Rosmersholm* as companion to the invalid Beata Rosmer,* Rebecca West had learned to be a free-thinker and radical politician from Doctor Haakon West, who she believed was her foster-father. Rebecca decided to become mistress of Rosmersholm and to convert Johannes Rosmer* to her own radical principles. She insinuated herself into Beata's confidence, allowed her to think that her husband had impregnated Rebecca, and drove her to suicide. Just when the success of her plan seemed secure, Rebecca discovered that Doctor West was her real father. Ibsen implies that Rebecca had had an incestuous relationship with him. Rebecca is unable to accept Rosmer's marriage proposal, and to prove her love of him, she agrees to kill herself.

WESTPHALER, GERT: The name of the talkative barber in Ludvig Holberg's* play of the same title, Westphaler discovered that he had drunk to friendship with the public hangman. Ibsen's associates of The Learned Hollanders* christened him Gert Westphaler.

WHEN WE DEAD AWAKEN: A three-act Realistic-Symbolistic serious drama.
Composition: Started in February 1899; finished on September 21, 1899; published on December 22, 1899.

Stage history:

Jan. 15, 1900	National Theatre, Christiania*
Jan. 26, 1900	Hoftheater, Stuttgart
Jan. 1900	Copenhagen
1900	Helsinki
1900	Stockholm
Feb. 6, 1900	National Theatre, Christiania, Johanne Dybwad* as Maja
Feb. 1900	Chicago (in Danish)
Mar. 5, 1900	Gärtner Theater, Munich, August Ellmenreich* as Rubek
Apr. 17, 1900	Deutsches Theater, Berlin
Nov. 28, 1900	Art Theatre, Moscow, Vasilii Kachalov* as Rubek
Nov. 2, 1901	New Theatre, St. Petersburg, Lydia Yavorska* as Irene
Jan. 25, 1903	Imperial Theatre, London (2 perfs.), pro. Incorporated Stage Society,* G. S. Titheradge as Rubek
Mar. 30, 1904	Schauspielhaus, Munich
Mar. 7, 1905	Knickerbocker Theatre, New York (27), Florence Kahn* as Irene
Dec. 2, 1913	Cosmopolis Theatre, London, Rathmell Wilson as Rubek
May 17, 1926	Central Park Theatre, New York, R. Matthews as Rubek
Nov. 18, 1938	Torch Theatre, London
Mar. 17, 1945	Chanticleer Theatre, London
Apr. 18, 1966	Masque Theatre, New York (8), pro. Gregory Reardon

Apr. 15, 1973   Circle Theatre, New York, Maurice Blanc as Rubek
Jan. 11, 1982   Open Space Theatre, New York, Tom Klunis* as Rubek

Synopsis: At a hotel in a Norwegian spa, the elderly but noted sculptor Arnold Rubek sits outdoors with his young wife Maja. They have finished their breakfast, and Rubek is occupied with a newspaper. Maja notes the almost audible silence, which she ascribes to their home land. Both have spent a considerable time out of the country, which makes Rubek feel alien to his native land. Maja urges him to commence traveling again, perhaps to their new house. When Rubek gently suggests that she meant to say "home," she rather curtly sticks to "house." Rubek reminds Maja that she has been away from Norway for four years, which coincides with the length of their marriage. When she remarks how Norway has changed during that time, Rubek observes that her life as wife of a distinguished artist with a spacious house and plenty of money is far different from what she had known in her youth. Yet even Rubek concedes that Norway's changes have not necessarily been improvements. At least, he says, their malaise may be treated by a boat-trip to the Arctic Circle. Rubek bristles when Maja agrees that the trip would be good for him, although he admits that he has grown increasingly restless and shy of people. Even worse, his interest in his work has also diminished, which dates from the completion of his masterpiece "The Resurrection Day." Rubek cryptically says that at first it was a masterpiece and now it is not, although it has received worldwide acclaim. He is discouraged because the masses have not seen his real meaning but have persisted in reading false significance into it. Maja believes that sort of work more worthwhile than the portrait busts with which he has occupied himself for the past several years. Rubek becomes exercised at the implication that his latest works have been mere portraits; he insists that they are filled with covert satire and irony. His pleasure comes from making artistic comments on "fatuous, self-satisfied asses, pompous, self-righteous horses, cringing curs, greedy swine, and ruthless, brutal bulls" (Le Gallienne* translation). How wonderful, Rubek thinks, to be paid handsome commissions for depicting his clients as the animals they are. The couple agrees that a certain amount of happiness is to be derived from material wealth, but for Maja it is not enough. She reminds Rubek that at their marriage, he had promised to take her to the mountain heights and unfold the glory of the world to her. His immediate reaction is to wonder if he had promised Maja that too, clearly implying that she was not the first. When she presses him for an explanation, he merely says that it is a metaphor that he has employed since boyhood. Maja then accuses him of never taking her to that mountain, to which Rubek responds that he had concluded that she was unsuitable for mountain climbing. He confesses that periodically the four or five years of their marriage seem like a long time. Piqued, Maja picks up her newspaper and says that she will not bore him any more.

Rubek tries to tease her into good humor, but she remains cool to the attempt.

As the Rubeks sit in silence, the life of the spa goes on around them. As guests and functionaries come and go, the inspector of the spa stops to greet the sculptor and his wife. To the inspector's query, Rubek answers that he was unable to sleep much last night, a chronic complaint these days. Rubek asks if any of the guests take midnight baths and then if any of them walk in the park at midnight. To both questions, the inspector says no. It seems that during the night Rubek had seen a figure, probably female, followed by a dark figure like a shadow. The inspector says that he can identify the apparition, but before he is able to do so, a remarkable figure of a woman crosses the park. Clad in flowing cashmere robes with a silver pectoral cross, the woman is followed by a deaconess attired in religious black; they disappear into the pavilion. Rubek asks her identity and learns from the inspector that she is a stranger registered as Mme. de Satow. The artist muses over the name and asks what nationality she is. Although madame speaks Norwegian like a native, the inspector answers, she talks in an unknown tongue to her companion. When pressed, the inspector guesses that she speaks a northern Norwegian dialect, which seems to intrigue Rubek. Sensing Rubek's latent excitement, Maja asks if the lady can be one of Rubek's former models, the number of which she believes to be considerable. Rubek responds that he used only one model for all his work. The inspector prepares to leave because he does not wish to meet a certain bear-hunter named Ulfhejm, who has just appeared. Rubek says that he had once known this man slightly. Meanwhile, the inspector hurries off but not before he is spotted by Ulfhejm, who calls out to him.

The bear-hunter is a rough-clad man, dressed for hunting and accompanied by a servant and a brace of hunting dogs. Hailing the inspector, Ulfhejm gruffly dismisses his man. He rudely instructs the inspector to have a hamper of food prepared for him and finds himself alone with the Rubeks when the inspector exits. After staring for a moment, he greets Rubek by name and recalls that they had met years ago when Rubek still lived in Norway. Maja is definitely interested in this man who contrasts so markedly with her husband. She asks if he hunts only bears, to which he answers that he hunts anything warm, fresh, and full-blooded. Then he compares his work as a bear-killer with that of Rubek, both of whom approach, conquer, and vanquish the resistant materials of their respective métiers. Rubek admits the validity of the comparison, and Maja asks if Ulfhejm hunts in the forests. No, responds Ulfhejm, in the mountains. He asks Maja if she has ever been in the mountains, and she pointedly replies negatively. The hunter magnanimously offers to take them both to the mountains, but they tell him of their plan for a sea voyage. He begins to rhapsodize about the preferability of the mountains but is interrupted by the appearance of the deaconess, who enters the hotel. The nun reminds the hunter of sickness and death. Ulfhejm says that he has always shot and buried his sick companions. Maja is relieved to hear that he means his dogs, not people. The deaconess comes back with a tray of bread and milk which she places on a table outside the pavilion. Ulfhejm derides this sort of food and takes Maja off to see him feeding his dogs dripping, bloody meat, which they will eat, vomit, and eat again.

Left alone, Rubek watches Mme. de Satow come out of the pavilion, sit at her table, and start to eat her meager repast. He stares intently at her, then walks across to her, and addresses her by the name "Irene." She seems surprised that he recognizes her, although she knows him at once; at least he, she says, is still alive. Irene asks if Maja is Rubek's wife and, finding that she is, dismisses her from her thoughts, since Maja came to Rubek after Irene had ceased to be. When Rubek questions her use of such an odd expression, Irene ignores the question and speaks of the child they created, meaning, of course, the sculpture. Rubek says that he owes his present fame to her, but Irene says that she should have killed the child before she left him, a deed she has done many times in her heart. Rubek presses her to say why she left him without an explanation. She cryptically replies that he no longer cared for her, that she was of no further use to him. None of that matters now because she lives on another plane of existence. Irene tells Rubek that she has traveled over the world as a music-hall performer and loved many men, one of whom, a South American diplomat, she married. She had derived immense pleasure from driving him first insane and then to his grave as a suicide. De Satow was her second husband, who is now dead in his Russian gold fields, presumably killed by her, as are all her children whom she slew before they were born. Now she sees herself as dead. Rubek remonstrates that she is still alive and suffering from injurious delusions. Irene tells of her death, burial, and recent incipient resurrection. Rubek is to blame for her whole pathetic experience. After this recital, she grows calmer and invites Rubek to sit with her as they talk.

Irene then recalls how she had served him with every aspect of her young body, although he had never once come near her. He says that his intoxication by her body had kept them apart, and she says that she would have killed him if he had ever made physical advances, yet he could have shown some interest. Rubek maintains that he was interested as an artist. His masterpiece was to be a portrait of the Ideal Woman rising from death; in her he found the perfect model who was willing to help him achieve his goal. Irene had left her home and friends and followed Rubek, who adored her from a distance but feared to react physically to her lest his inspiration for the sculpture should fade. She scorns him for being more devoted to art than to people. At any rate, Irene says, he was victorious in his goal of creating a masterpiece; then he discarded her for other models. Rubek answers that he had found no other models because she had been his inspiration, not merely his model. They then talk of his impending sea voyage, and Irene advises him to go to the mountains instead. He wonders if she will be there if he visits the mountains. He wonders if she will be there if he goes to the heights. Irene seductively taunts him to join her on the mountain.

Meanwhile, Maja appears, flushed with the excitement of her visit with Ulfhejm. Seeing that Rubek is talking with Irene, Maja reports that she cannot go to the sea with him, that she earnestly wants to go to the mountains with the bear-hunter. Rubek indulgently allows her to accompany her new friend as he himself may be scaling the peaks too. Elated, Maja rushes off to tell Ulfhejm. Rubek and Irene reaffirm their intention to meet since Irene has been searching for him for years. When asked when she commenced her search, Irene responds that it was as soon as she realized that she had given him what she should never have surrendered—her soul. Once she had given him that, she was dead. The deaconess opens the door of the pavilion, and Irene goes in, leaving Rubek staring after her and whispering her name, which, after all, means "peace."

The action of Act II takes place near a health resort in the high mountains. As the happy sound of frolicking children punctuates the scene, Rubek, sitting on a bench, sees Maja approach in full mountain regalia. She walks up and says that she has been looking for Rubek, who observes that she had not eaten lunch in the hotel. Maja has taken her meal in the open with the bear-hunter, who has invited her to stalk a bear with him. In fact, she plans to embark this evening. Rubek professes to be disinterested in her plans but invites Maja to sit down and rest because she looks tired After a moment's silence, Maja chides him for sitting within range of the children's voices, which she finds silly. Ever the artist, Rubek sees grace and harmony in their movements. Maja observes that Ulfhejm is not a bit artistic but that he shares ugliness with Rubek. His ugliness, she believes, is not caused by age but by his weariness and resignation; in his eyes Maja has seen the growth of evil, as if Rubek were scheming against her. Rubek asks if she knows why he has brought her to the mountains, and she guesses that Irene was his reason. Rubek claims that she was only his model who was discarded after she fulfilled her function, but Maja thinks it would be difficult to forget a woman who had posed naked for him. Not to be swayed from his subject, again Rubek introduces his reason for coming to the mountains. What is the cause of his restlessness, he asks. Maja quickly sees that her company bores him because she cares nothing for art, which leaves only her interests as a conversational topic. Rubek is not stimulated by such talk, which serves to fill the time but has no other purpose. He admits that he cannot continue much longer in this manner, to which Maja immediately suggests that he can easily get rid of her. Parting, however, is not his solution. His plan is to rekindle his relationship with Irene and allow Maja the same freedom with Ulfhejm. Rubek recollects that after Irene left and he realized that his sense of a sacred artistic vocation was meaningless, he had desired to partake of life, which at first he had identified with material possessions. His years with Maja demonstrated that luxury did not necessarily constitute life. He must create, and Irene holds the key to his creativity. Maja is not at all scandalized by this admission and suggests that Rubek and Irene could live in the townhouse and she could inhabit the villa, or the three of them could cohabit in the city. Rubek is concerned about what would happen if this arrangement should not work out, but Maja says simply that they would separate. She would, in fact, be free. At that point Maja sees Irene striding toward them, and in the sight Rubek sees "The Resurrection" walking. He mutters something about his foolishness in altering the sculpture but refuses to be specific.

Irene approaches the children and immediately establishes rapport with them. At her bidding they all leave the plain and head toward the hotel. Maja urges Rubek to go down and talk with Irene while she finds something to amuse herself. She walks towards Irene and tells her that Rubek wants her to help him open a box, the metaphor Rubek had used to describe his creativity. Maja earnestly bids her to join Rubek and then strolls toward the hotel. Irene and Rubek are left to converse with a small stream separating them. Rubek admits that he has been waiting for her for years, but Irene replies that she was unable to join him because she was in the tomb. When he talks of a new life ahead for them, Irene urges him not to expect too much. Rubek then crosses over to her and wonders how she has spent the day. Since she was on the distant moor, Rubek thinks she escaped the scrutiny of the deaconess, but Irene contends that she is always observed. One day she will have to kill the nun, whom she calls a practitioner of black magic who actually transformed herself into Irene's shadow. Rubek sits on a rock and averts his eyes, which causes Irene to ask why he does not look at her. His troubled conscience is the reason. Irene unexpectedly ejaculates, "At last!" and appears delivered of some heavy burden. She says that "they" have momentarily released her, so it is briefly possible to converse as they had done in the past.

To Irene's assertion that she has returned to him over a great distance, Rubek likens it to an endless journey. He inquires if she had not given him up for someone else, but Irene claims that it was for his sake. He knew that he would be unable to create in separation from her; she wanted their "child" to be central and solitary. Did she do it because of jealousy, he asks. No, she responds; she was driven by hatred of his artistry which prompted him to use a woman's soul for the sake of formulating a mere work of art. Rubek cannot believe that she was not as devoted to art as he was, but Irene claims to have disliked art before she met him and hated it afterwards. Nor had she admired the artist in him; she had, in fact, hated him for remaining unmoved every time she disrobed. As the statue had taken shape, however, she grew to love it and to consider it as their child. Then she admits that she has made this journey for the sake of this child, but Rubek cautions her that she must never see the statue, for it is not the same as it was when she last saw it. He had enlarged the base on which her likeness had stood so that it would accommodate images of things he had seen in the world once he had grown worldly. Now "The Resurrection Day" includes a section of a terrestrial sphere out of which creep humans with subtle animalistic features. The virginal maiden modeled on Irene is no longer the focal point of the work. At this shocking news, Irene draws a knife and tells Rubek that he has just signed his own warrant of execution. When he turns to look at her, she hides the knife as he admits that he has portrayed himself beside a stream vainly trying to wash his hands. The Rubek-figure knows that he will never be resurrected, that he must remain forever in hell.

Irene scoffs that he expects absolution for the murder of her soul simply because he depicts himself as a penitent. She calls him a poet rather than an artist, since the word "poet" is an apologetic word and covers a multitude of human frailties. She will never be able to atone for the suicide of her soul in his behalf. As she picks flowers, Irene observes that she was meant to bear real children. Does he remember, she asks, what he had dubbed their relationship. He does not recall that when he had called it an "episode," she left him. They agree to try to escape from the painful, sad events of the past. They talk of birds, and imaginary ships, and summers beside a favorite lake, but the conversation returns to "episodes" and the fact that he and Maja now live beside the lake where once Irene and Rubek had communed. They had been happy but had let that happiness go. Rubek wonders if it is too late for repentance. Irene exults in the glorious sunset and recalls a time when she and Rubek had witnessed a sunset in the mountains. He had promised to take her up the mountain and show her the glory of the world. When they had reached the heights, she fell to her knees and worshiped him. Then she saw the sunrise. Rubek changes the subject by asking if she would like to live with them in the lakeside villa. Irene seems scornful of the suggestion that she should live with Maja, but Rubek assures her that she would live with him and unleash the flow of his artistry again. Irene, however, concludes that she no longer has the power to do so; there can be no resurrection of their old relationship. With Irene's assent, Rubek concludes that they had better continue playing then.

Maja, Ulfhejm, Lars, and the dogs can be seen coming up the slope of the mountain. Rubek is resigned to the fact that his wife is perhaps now attached to the bear-killer. Maja calls out that she is in pursuit of adventure and invites him to dream of her, since she is choosing life now. She joyfully sings about being free. When Rubek bids her goodnight and good luck, Ulfhejm keeps him from speaking of good luck as they are going shooting. Maja laughingly says that she will put a bullet through the wing of a bird of prey and bring it back to Rubek to use as a model. Falling in with Ulfhejm's hunter's superstition, Rubek bids them goodnight and bad luck, at which

Ulfhejm laughs goodnaturedly. The adventurers pass from sight, and Irene asks Rubek to spend the night on the moor with her, to which he enthusiastically accedes. Irene cautions that it will be only an "episode" and then tenses as she realizes that the deaconess is watching her from the bushes. She pretends to say goodnight but intends to meet Rubek on the moor. Rubek gloriously imagines the life they might have had together, but Irene observes that they will come to realize what they have lost only "when we dead awaken." Then they see that they have never lived. Irene and the deaconess walk down the path while Rubek sits beside the stream and Maja's voice is heard singing her song of freedom.

A misty dawn covers the rugged escarpment of Act III. Maja and Ulfhejm enter angrily and approach a dilapidated hut that Ulfhejm invites her to enter. Obviously, the hunter thinks it a suitable haven, but the materialistic woman is repelled by its crudeness. She is set on returning to the hotel, but Ulfhejm knows that she cannot descend without his help. He teases her about carrying her down but lapses into a recollection of another girl he had once picked up from a gutter and learned to love. His reward was to be cuckolded. Maja in turn tells the story of a poor girl who was swept away by a powerful man who offered to take her to the highest mountain and show her the world's glory. Instead of a mountain, he showed her a cage. Seeing that they have so much in common, Ulfhejm asks if they might not be able to have a life together. Maja laughs at the suggestion, but the hunter refuses to accept her refusal. When she says that she is restrained by a tame bird of prey, Ulfhejm threatens to put a bullet through its wing. Emboldened by his resolution, Maja falls into his arms and casts her lot with him. Maja then wanders to the edge of the precipice and dizzily reels backwards. Ulfhejm looks down and sees Rubek and Irene making the ascent; he identifies Rubek as Maja's bird of prey. They decide to face Rubek in this wild place and declare her independence from him.

Then the four come face to face. When Rubek says that he and Irene have agreed to walk the same precipitous path, Ulfhejm oracularly warns them against becoming mountain-bound and being able neither to advance nor retreat. Then a storm quickly arises; Ulfhejm predicts it will cover them like a shroud. Knowing the danger, Ulfhejm advises Irene and Rubek to wait in the hut for help while he and Maja descend.

Irene seems unnaturally afraid that a lot of men will be sent to fetch her; the nun will come also to put her in a strait-jacket. Irene brandishes her knife as a means of preventing that. When Rubek tries to take it away from her, Irene says that it was meant for him, that she had nearly stabbed him yesterday during the conversation about "episodes." She had relented only when she realized that he was already dead. They were two corpses playing beside a stream. Rubek insists that their love is not dead, but all earthly love, she says, is dead for her. Rubek maintains that his love is not dead. Irene feels sullied because she had posed nude in a music-hall tableau and was lusted after by many men, but Rubek admits that he was to blame for that. They agree that nothing that has happened has lowered her worth, which means to Rubek that they are free from the past. Irene in her resurrected state had searched for Rubek only to find that both he and life are dead. Rubek embraces her passionately and suggests that, if they are dead, they should live gloriously before they go to their graves. She ecstatically assents, and Rubek concludes that a misty mountainside is not the proper setting for their joy. Irene urges that they climb to the very summit where, says Rubek, they will celebrate their marriage. The very sun will be the nuptial witness. Rubek asks if his bride will follow him through the mist. She agrees to go with him through the haze to the top of the glittering tower.

The scene becomes enveloped by clouds as they climb up the snowy slopes toward the crest of the mountain. The wind laments wildly as the deaconess enters and searches for her charge. Maja's freedom song echoes throughout the range. A thunderous sound is heard heralding an avalanche, through the heavy fold of which can be slightly seen the figures of Rubek and Irene, who are buried together. The deaconess cries, "Irene!" She then makes the sign of the cross and says "Pax vobiscum." Maja's song is heard from farther away.

Structural analysis: Ibsen's last play is rife with echoes of his earlier work; it is, in fact, an epilogue, as he named it. Rubek's death is similar to that of Brand*; his being reunited with his lover after many years is reminiscent of John Gabriel Borkman* and Ella Rentheim*; Irene's conception of the sculpture as their child repeats Thea Elvsted's* notion; Irene's urging Rubek to climb the tower is suggestive of the final scene of *The Master Builder*; Ulfhejm's addiction to bear-hunting calls Sigurd* the Strong and the white bear to mind. There are numerous other allusions to Ibsen's previous dramas.

The play also has a rich inheritance from the Symbolists, particularly the mysterious atmosphere, the mists, the enveloping clouds, and the almost sinister, brooding presence of the deaconess. As the wild duck, one of Ibsen's notable symbols, had been shot in the wing, so both Maja and Ulfhejm speak of winging a tame bird of prey, Rubek. Water is also an important symbol in this play.

The plot, unified by action, is straightforward:

Rubek discovers that he has found Irene again;

(as a result of which)

Rubek agrees to take Maja to the mountains as a pretext for further commerce with Irene;

(as a result of which)

Rubek discovers that Maja will not interfere with his liaison with Irene;

(as a result of which)

Rubek asks Irene to continue seeing him;

(as a result of which)
Rubek discovers that Irene wants him to spend the night with her;

(as a result of which)
Rubek and Irene decide to scale the heights of the mountain;

(as a result of which)
Rubek discovers because of the storm that their love is not dead;

(as a result of which)
Rubek suggests that they live gloriously before going to their graves;

(as a result of which)
Rubek discovers that Irene will accompany him to the peak;

(as a result of which)
Rubek, with Irene, meets his death.

References: Barranger, M. S. "Ibsen's *Endgame*: A Reconsideration of *When We Dead Awaken*," *Modern Drama*, 17 (1974), 289-99; Northam, John. "Ibsen's Use of Language in *When We Dead Awaken*," *Ibsen and the Theatre: The Dramatist in Production* (New York: New York University Press, 1980), pp. 105-17.

WHITE, JANE (1922-): Jane White's first professional Ibsenian role was The Green-Clad Woman* in *Peer Gynt** in 1947; her appearance as Rebecca West* at New York's Roundabout Stage lasted only two performances. Critics were decidedly cool to the production that opened on December 15, 1974.
Reference: New York Theatre Critics' Reviews, XXXV, 23 (Dec. 16, 1974), 122-3.

WICKWIRE, NANCY (1925-74): American actress Nancy Wickwire had a varied career in the theatre and television before playing her first Ibsenian role. When Wickwire appeared in New York in 1962 as Rebecca West,* her performance was lauded. For it she received the Lola D'Annunzio Award. The production lasted fifty-eight performances.
Reference: Who's Who in the Theatre, 16th ed., p. 1250.

THE WILD DUCK: A five-act Realistic-Symbolistic serious drama. *Composition:* Started on April 20, 1884; finished around August 30, 1884; published in November 1884.

Stage history:

Jan. 9, 1885	Norwegian Theatre, Bergen* (22 perfs.)
Jan. 11, 1885	Christiania Theatre*
Jan. 1885	Helsinki
Jan. 30, 1885	Royal Theatre, Stockholm
Feb. 1885	Royal Theatre, Copenhagen (9)
1885	Stadttheater, Gothenburg
1886	Royal Theatre, Copenhagen (3)
Mar. 4, 1887	Residenz Theater, Berlin

Apr. 3, 1887	Residenz Theater, Berlin, pro. Otto Brahm*
1888	Berlin
Mar. 6, 1889	Residenz Theater, Berlin
1889	Royal Theatre, Stockholm (3)
1889	Breslau (7)
1889	Bern
1889	Dresden
Nov. 14, 1889	Christiania Theatre (7), Johanne Dybwad* as Hedvig
Feb. 1891	Deutsches Volkstheater, Vienna, Friedrich Mitterwurzer* as Hjalmar
Apr. 16, 1891	Deutsches Volkstheater, Vienna (3), Friedrich Mitterwurzer as Hjalmar
Apr. 17, 1891	Burgtheater, Vienna
Apr. 28, 1891	Théâtre des Menus Plaisirs, Paris, pro. Théâtre Libre,* André Antoine* as Hjalmar
1892	Royal Theatre, Copenhagen (8)
Mar. 8, 1893	Christiania Theatre, Johanne Dybwad as Hedvig
June 2, 1893	Christiania Theatre (7)
May 4, 1894	Royalty Theatre, London (5), pro. Independent Theatre,* Charles J. Fulton* as Gregers
June 15, 1895	Orpheum Theater, Munich, pro. Alfred von Wolzogen*
1895	Royal Theatre, Copenhagen (7)
Jan. 16, 1897	Burgtheater, Vienna
May 17, 1897	Globe Theatre, London (5), Courtenay Thorpe as Gregers
Sept. 19, 1901	Art Theatre, Moscow (2), dir. Konstantin Stanislavsky*
Apr. 22, 1903	Hoftheater, Braunschweig
Nov. 21, 1903	Residenz Theater, Munich
Mar. 16, 1904	National Theatre, Christiania,* Johanne Dybwad as Hedvig
Mar. 8, 1905	Gt. Queen Street Theatre, London (as *Die Wildente*)
Oct. 17, 1905	Court Theatre, London, Granville Barker as Hjalmar
Mar. 12, 1907	McVicker's Theatre, Chicago (2), Wm. C. Mason as Hjalmar
Sept. 27, 1907	Théâtre de l'Odéon, Paris (1 mo.), pro. André Antoine
Dec. 1, 1913	St. James Theatre, London (3), Harcourt Williams as Gregers
Mar. 11, 1918	Plymouth Theatre, New York (32), Alla Nazimova* as Hedvig
Feb. 24, 1925	48th Street Theatre, New York (105), Blanche Yurka* as Hedvig
June 30, 1925	Everyman Theatre, London
Nov. 18, 1928	49th Street Theatre, New York (80), Blanche Yurka as Hedvig
May 6, 1929	Shubert-Belasco Theatre, New York, Blanche Yurka as Hedvig
Oct. 9, 1930	Everyman Theatre, London
Nov. 3, 1936	Westminster Theatre, London, Alan Napier as Hjalmar
Apr. 16, 1938	49th Street Theatre, New York (5), Eric Franson as Hjalmar
Oct. 31, 1947	Torch Theatre, London, Edward Mulhare* as Hjalmar
Nov. 3, 1948	St. Martin's Theatre, London (164), Anton Walbrook* as Hjalmar
Dec. 26, 1951	City Center Theatre, New York (15), Maurice Evans* as Hjalmar
Dec. 21, 1955	Saville Theatre, London, Emlyn Williams* as Hjalmar
Jan. 11, 1967	Lyceum Theatre, London, Donald Woods as Hjalmar

Dec. 13, 1979   Olivier Theatre, London, pro. National Theatre of Great
                  Britain, Michael Bryant* as Gregers.

Synopsis: As the play opens, a party is in progress in the home of Haakon
Werle, a wealthy businessman. The guests of honor are a group of
chamberlains, local court dignitaries, and Gregers Werle, Haakon's son
who has just returned after years of managing the family concerns in the
northern city of Hoidal. The party is still in the dining room, but the
animated chatter can be heard by Pettersen, a servant, and Jensen, a hired
waiter, as they prepare the study to receive Werle's guests. Since Jensen is
not a regular member of the menage, he can legitimately ask questions
about Mrs. Sörby, Werle's housekeeper and hostess, and Gregers, thus
providing the necessary exposition of preceding events. As they talk, a
number of facts emerge: gossip romantically links Haakon and Mrs. Sörby;
Haakon has a reputation with the ladies; Gregers has not visited his father's
home for many years. Their exchange is interrupted by the furtive
appearance of old Ekdal, who is dressed shabbily and sports a red wig. The
old man wishes to use the private entrance to Werle's office, the public door
being locked since it is after hours. Petterson admits Ekdal to the office and
then explains to Jensen that the old fellow worked for Werle as an outside
copyist, largely as an acknowledgement of his former association with
Werle. Years ago Werle and Ekdal had managed the works at Hoidal; then
a shady lumber deal had precipitated Ekdal into jail.

Mrs. Sörby then leads the guests from the dining room to the study with
Gregers Werle and Hjalmar Ekdal bringing up the rear. As the party passes
into the adjacent music room for coffee, Haakon alerts Gregers to the fact
that they were thirteen at table; Hjalmar clearly is the unexpected guest. As
Haakon leads the remainder of the group toward the music room, Hjalmar
apologizes to Gregers for annoying his father by his presence, as he is not
accustomed to calling on old Werle. Gregers thinks it natural that he should
invite his boyhood friend whom he has not seen for seventeen years. Despite
having gained weight, Hjalmar explains, his life in the interim has not been
what he would wish, especially in view of old Ekdal's condition after his
release from prison. Hjalmar asks how Gregers found life in the north,
which, he learns, provided the opportunity to think deeply about many
things. Hjalmar expresses his relief that Gregers seems to bear him no ill will
over the upset that might have landed Haakon into jail along with old
Ekdal. Gregers denied ever having blamed Hjalmar and is abashed that old
Werle has told Hjalmar that he actually bore him a grudge. Thus, the two
had not communicated for seventeen years, in which time Hjalmar had
become a photographer rather than continuing his education and leading
the sort of life for which his former station in life had groomed him.
Hjalmar had desired to pay his father's debts, most of which were owed to
old Werle, who had urged Hjalmar to sever all his connections with his

previous life and had provided the financial support to set him up as a photographer. In addition, old Werle had made it possible for Hjalmar to marry Gina Hansen, formerly Werle's housekeeper, described by Hjalmar as capable and cultured. When pressed by Gregers for details, Hjalmar relates how Gina quit service the year before Mrs. Werle died, lived at home with her mother, and met and fell in love with Hjalmar, who rented a small room in the Hansen house at Werle's suggestion. Since Gina had already learned how to retouch photographs, the young couple agreed with Werle that they should go into the business of photography. As Hjalmar extols Werle's kindness, Mrs. Sörby enters with Werle telling him that the bright lights in the music room are bad for his weakened eyesight. The other guests follow.

The next moments are extremely embarrassing for Hjalmar as the chamberlains condescendingly try to draw him into the conversation by asking if he brought samples of his pictures for their entertainment. Then the talk turns to Tokay wine, about which Hjalmar knows nothing; but he notes how the guests speak of it. Meanwhile Mrs. Sörby functions as an apt and affable hostess, flirting casually with the guests of honor. The banter momentarily ceases as the bookkeeper Graaberg asks if he and Ekdal may leave the office through the house as the outside door is locked. As old Ekdal stumbles through the room mouthing apologies, Haakon mutters curses and Hjalmar averts his head in an effort not to see his father. When questioned by a chamberlain, Hjalmar denies his knowledge of the old man's identity. Mrs. Sörby quietly instructs a servant to give something to old Ekdal on the outside, as Gregers chides Hjalmar for denying his father. The noise of the party increases as everyone talks more loudly in an effort to cover an embarrassing situation. Hjalmar's already deep discomfiture is exacerbated when a chamberlain asks if he cannot recite a poem for their amusement. Dismissing the suggestion, Hjalmar stammers to Gregers his intention of going home. When Gregers says that he might visit him there, Hjalmar insists that his home is a sad place, wholly inappropriate to their meeting. Then Hjalmar exits unobtrusively.

Mrs. Sörby corners the servant and asks what he gave to old Ekdal; she learns that Ekdal received his favorite gift—cognac. Mrs. Sörby leads the guests into the music room, leaving Gregers and his father alone.

As they talk, the sound of the piano is heard from the other room. Gregers asks how his father could have witnessed the dissolution of his old friend's family, meaning old Ekdal. When Werle brings up the illegality at Hoidal, Gregers suggests that his father might have been equally guilty of the crime of which Ekdal was convicted. While not denying this, Werle insists that he was acquitted of any wrongdoing and that he has subsidized old Ekdal by giving him the copyist's job. Gregers asks what it had cost to set up Hjalmar in the photographer's trade. Gregers continues his assault by demanding to know why he had not been told that Hjalmar had married

Werle's former housekeeper, for whom the father had held a deep attachment. Although Werle denies this, Gregers firmly believes it happened because his mother had told him on her deathbed. Werle descends to a vituperative account of his highstrung wife and her unfounded suspicions; then he counterattacks by asking why Gregers continues to slave as a mere clerk at Hoidal rather than coming into the firm as a partner. Werle's plan is for Gregers to manage the office in town while Werle moves to Hoidal to superintend the operation there. Ever suspicious, Gregers doubts his father's motive for making such an offer. He is correct in this assumption, because Werle wishes to scotch the gossip about Mrs. Sörby's position in the household by presenting the appearance of a unified family. Gregers' return would legitimize her position, and his sanction of their marriage would erase any suspicions of irregularity. Gregers refuses to be part of such a deception, partly because he sees how empty Hjalmar's life is since it is built on a lie. At that point, Gregers sees his mission in life (the initiation of the action) and expresses his intention of leaving his father's house and setting to work. Gregers leaves the room as his father, uncomprehending, notes that he is highstrung as was his mother.

Act II and the remainder of the drama take place in the studio of Hjalmar Ekdal, an unpretentious room that serves both as living and working space. As Gina sits sewing, she notes fourteen-year-old Hedvig reading a book and shading her eyes. The mother cautions the girl against reading by poor light in the evening. Gina then picks up her account book, entering her expenditures on groceries and her earnings as a photographer. Hedvig is excited that her father is at Werle's sumptuous house, especially since he promised to bring her an edible treat. She is hungry because Gina economized on food since Hjalmar was away. Old Ekdal enters, shows his stack of new copying work, draws open a double door, peers into the room, and observes that "they" are sleeping soundly. He seems particularly pleased that "she" is asleep in a basket. In discussing Hjalmar, Hedvig supposes that the party will put him in a good mood, but Gina notes that he would be even more pleased to learn that she had rented the spare room. Both females seem inordinately eager to insure Hjalmar's good spirits. Ekdal, in the meantime, has boiled water in the kitchen for a surreptitious hot toddy; he retreats to his own room to drink in private.

Hjalmar comes in, and when Hedvig remarks that he has returned early, he lies by saying that the party had already broken up. He adds another half-lie by saying that there had been twelve or fourteen people in attendance. Old Ekdal enters to ask if Hjalmar saw him at Werle's; Hjalmar denies that he did. As his family questions him about the party, Hjalmar exaggerates his own importance by suggesting that he was the center of conversation, that he could not condescend to recite a poem; he then astounds his little audience by his knowledge of Tokay, repeating every cliché he had heard an hour previously. Then Hjalmar takes off his dinner coat that was borrowed from Molvik, one of his friends. Hedvig finally asks for the treat he promised to bring, but he has obviously forgotten. After a pause, Hjalmar produces the evening's menu and plans to tell how each dish tasted as Hedvig reads its name. Hedvig, in tears, is desolated, which is Hjalmar's cue for a show of righteous indignation. He turns to his father and inquires about the inhabitant of the garret room. The old man says that some improvements must be made in the arrangements, a subject that Hjalmar finds more comfortable than his neglect of Hedvig. Then he blames Gina for not acquiring more photographic business and for not renting the spare room. Seeing how his disposition has deteriorated, Gina abases herself and apologizes, and Hedvig tries to get him to play his flute. Not to be mollified, Hjalmar resigns himself melodramatically to unremitting work and selflessness. When Hedvig offers a bottle of beer, however, his mood changes; he embraces her and apologizes for forgetting her treat but exonerates his oversight because he had so many pressing cares to distract him. He then takes up his flute, plays for a short time, and concludes that, despite financial need, his home is everything. A knock at the door is heard; it is Gregers who announces that he has left party and home.

Commenting on the studio, Gregers learns that Hjalmar has a room to rent. As Hedvig goes to the kitchen to fetch beer, Hjalmar tells Gregers that Hedvig is in danger of losing her eyesight, the result of an hereditary weakness. Gina immediately remarks that Hjalmar's mother had poor eyesight. After an impassioned outburst about Hedvig's condition, Hjalmar exclaims how pitiful his situation is. In response to his question, Gregers learns from Gina that Hedvig will be fourteen in two days. He then hears from Gina that they have been married for fifteen years. Old Ekdal returns from his room, this time rather inebriated. He starts when he sees Gregers, who puts him at ease by referring to the days when the old man was a noted hunter. Gregers wonders how an outdoorsman like Ekdal can now live in a cramped city, which inspires Ekdal to show Gregers what lies behind the closed doors. As they open the doors, a loft is revealed. Gregers sees roosting hens and pigeons and rabbits, and oddest of all, a wild duck asleep in a basket. It seems that Haakon Werle was out in his boat, shot and wounded the wild duck, which dived toward the bottom of the lake but was rescued by Werle's dog. Since the wounded fowl had fared poorly at Werle's house, a servant had been ordered to kill it. Old Ekdal had rescued the duck from certain death, and now she is thriving in captivity. Gregers warns them not to let the duck see the sea and sky again because that would remind her of her old life. Then he asks to be allowed to rent the spare room, which delights Hjalmar and agitates Gina. She claims that the current roomers, Molvik and Relling, would disturb him by their drinking. Gregers, however, is not to be put off. When Hjalmar asks him what he wishes to be in life, Gregers answers by saying that he would like to be a really good hunting dog which could rescue wild ducks that get mired at the bottom of the lake. Then he says goodnight and makes plans to move in the next day.

Gina is puzzled by Gregers' comment about the dog, but Hedvig sees that he meant something entirely different from its literal content. Hjalmar returns from seeing Gregers out and boasts of his own efficiency in renting the room. Gina is still disturbed that Gregers will live under the same roof as they. Hjalmar, however, views the coming of Gregers as a sign of better times that will allow him to realize his mission in life, the rehabilitation of his father's reputation. Old Ekdal has long since fallen asleep by the fire. Hjalmar and Gina lift him from his chair to take him to bed as the curtain falls.

As Act III begins, it is the next morning. As Hjalmar retouches a picture, Gina tells him how Gregers created havoc as soon as he moved in by closing the damper of his stove, filling the room with smoke, and pouring a pitcher of water into the stove. Hjalmar has invited Gregers to lunch as well as Molvik and Relling, but it is Gina who must cope with the preparations and the expense. Old Ekdal comes in to amuse himself in the loft with the birds. When Hedvig enters to inquire about his work, once again Hjalmar magnifies his efforts by suggesting that work is injurious to his health. Hedvig offers to finish the retouching, despite her failing eyesight, so that Hjalmar can join his father in the loft. As the men busy themselves rearranging the birds' accommodations, Hedvig admits Gregers who says he is content to watch her work.

Gregers makes small talk about the wild duck and learns that Hjalmar keeps her from school because of her eyes. Yet, says Hedvig, there are many educational things in the loft, such as a great picture book called Harrison's *History of London*.* Hedvig, Gregers learns, has no desire to see the world for herself; she is pleased to live in the studio apartment and help her parents. Then the conversation returns to the wild duck.

When Gina starts to bring in the luncheon things, Hedvig clears the table and starts to help her mother. As Gregers and Gina talk about her contributions to the family business, they are startled by a gunshot. Hedvig explains that the men are hunting in the loft. Hjalmar emerges and shows his double-barreled pistol to Gregers before placing it on the bookshelf and warning Hedvig not to touch it because one barrel is still loaded. Gina and Hedvig go into the kitchen as Hjalmar shuts the double doors to the loft, observing that Gina does not approve of animals in the studio. In response to Gregers' question about their division of labor, Hjalmar says that Gina does all the routine work while he sits in solitary state to consider more important things, such as his phenomenal invention, the details of which must be kept secret. The success of the invention will enable Hjalmar to realize his life's mission, saving his father's reputation and self-respect. Old Ekdal, he says, was so shamed by his conviction that he had considered suicide with the very pistol that lies on the bookshelf, but his cowardice had prevented it. While the old man was in prison, Hjalmar too had toyed with ending his life with that firearm, but he too "chose life" instead of death. That is why the completion of his invention is necessary to restoring the honor of the family. When pressed for details of the invention, Hjalmar avoids the issue, clearly implying that little or nothing had been done. Gregers concludes that, like the wild duck, Hjalmar has plunged to the bottom of the pond, but that he, Gregers, also has a mission in life. Gina returns with drinks as the other guests arrive.

Gregers is introduced to Molvik, but he already knows Doctor Relling from Hoidal. The men sit down and start to eat while the women serve them. Speaking of Molvik's drunkenness last night, Relling explains that the theological student is demonic, which accounts for his aberrations from the narrow path of virtue. Relling then remembers that at Hoidal, Gregers had gone from cottage to cottage exhorting the villagers to answer the "Summons to the Ideal," a bit of idealism that failed. Gregers maintains that he has not lost his faith in that premise. Relling congratulates Hjalmar for having his mission to give savor to his life; he further says that Hjalmar is fortunate to have a good wife and dutiful daughter, to which Hjalmar assents. Of Gregers, Relling inquires if it is not good to bask among a happy family, but Gregers compares the atmosphere with marsh gas. Relling warns Gregers not to try to deliver his "Summons to the Ideal" in the Ekdal house on pain of being tossed down the stairs. A knock announces the arrival of Haakon Werle, who wishes to speak to Gregers alone; the others withdraw.

Werle wants to know what Gregers intends to do to spite his father; the son answers that his intention is to make Hjalmar see the truth of his situation, which is his mission in life. Gregers accuses his father of suffering attacks of conscience ever since old Ekdal was wrongly convicted of crime. At least, he reasons, he can give the gift of truth to Hjalmar. Werle does not believe that Hjalmar will appreciate the gift; then he establishes that Gregers will not come back home, that he will not share the business, and that he will not continue working at Hoidal. Gregers maintains that his scant funds will last as long as he will. Father and son part as the others return to the studio. Gregers invites Hjalmar to take a long walk with him, to which Hjalmar assents, even though Gina begs him not to go. Relling also urges him not to go. After Hjalmar leaves, Relling concludes that Gregers suffers from "an acute case of moralistic fever." Then Relling leaves as the act ends.

Act IV resumes later the same day. Gina and Hedvig are anxious because Hjalmar has not returned in time for dinner, but soon he appears. Seeming distracted, Hjalmar announces that tomorrow he will start to work assiduously, which he amends to the next day upon being reminded of Hedvig's birthday. He further asserts that he will never again set foot in the loft unless it be to wring the wild duck's neck. In view of Hedvig's attachment to the duck, Hjalmar promises not to harm it. He then sends Hedvig outside for a walk, deducing that the air inside the house is unwholesome for her eyes.

Once Hedvig has gone, Hjalmar tells Gina that he intends to start keeping the household accounts so that he can satisfy his suspicion that their money lasts far longer than it ought. He seeks financial information from her and learns that Ekdal's salary for copying covers his expenses as well as some spending money. Hjalmar is infuriated to learn that Werle is providing the old man's keep. Then he asks Gina if there had been some sort of attachment between her and Werle, to which she answers that she was blameless, although Haakon had pursued her and his wife believed that he had been unfaithful with Gina. She had quit her job, but Werle's adamancy coupled with her mother's advice eventually caused her to give in to him. Hjalmar's greatest anger is that his wife was not a virgin when they married. He asks if she is not sickened by her web of deception, but Gina answers that she has been so busy that she seldom thinks of it. Gina, however, reminds him that he did not come to the marriage as a blameless youth but that they both settled down once they were united. At last comes Hjalmar's greatest threat: Gina's past may make it impossible for him to finish his great invention. Now, says Hjalmar, everthing he ever dreamed of is over.

Gregers gingerly enters, and Hjalmar tells him that he has faced Gina with the truth, "the bitterest hour" of his life. Gregers thinks that Hjalmar should feel exalted rather than depressed. He had expected to see them both transfigured by the truth and expectant of their future life together.

Relling enters and soon senses the import of what has happened, for which he curses Gregers. Gregers responds that he wants to substitute a true marriage for a merely good one. Relling presses him to admit that he has never seen a true marriage, but he cautions Gregers not to accost Hedvig with his idealistic notions because in her preadolescence, she may harm herself or someone else if overly excited.

Mrs. Sörby comes in to tell the Ekdals that Werle has already left for Hoidal, and she will depart the next day. Gregers blurts out that Mrs. Sörby and Relling were once intimately related, which she admits; he hints that he may tell his father, but she has already done so. She claims to have told him everything about herself and to have heard all his secrets. Mrs. Sörby says that she will be a good wife to Werle, particularly as he grows more helpless as a result of blindness. Gregers urges her not to speak of blindness in front of the Ekdals. When Mrs. Sörby tells Hjalmar to apply to Werle's book-keeper should he need any financial assistance, Hjalmar instructs her to tell Werle that he requires a complete accounting of Werle's expenditures on the Ekdals because he intends to repay this "debt of honor." Mrs. Sörby, realizing that something important has happened in this house, exits.

Hjalmar feels quite proud of his stand and quickly agrees with Gregers that it was a good thing he urged the summons to the ideal. Yet Hjalmar is somewhat uneasy to realize that Werle, after all, is going to have a true marriage; where, he asks, is universal justice in that? Gregers observes that Werle's blindness is the hand of justice.

Hedvig returns from her stroll and tells them that she met Mrs. Sörby who gave her a letter to be read in bed on her birthday morning. Since it is from Werle, Hjalmar wants to read it at once. After poring over the document, Hjalmar turns pale and hands it to Hedvig, who carries it to the lamp and squints in order to read it. Werle has arranged that henceforth Old Ekdal can draw one hundred crowns per month from his account, but all Hjalmar can think of is the "coincidence" that both Werle and Hedvig should be going blind. And how to explain Werle's gift, which after the old man's death will pass to Hedvig? The girl is naturally excited and embraces Hjalmar, who pushes her away. Gregers sees Werle's action as an attempt to entrap Hjalmar, who wildly seizes the letter and shreds it. Gregers is delighted that his influence has been so strong. Hjalmar now asks Gina the ultimate question: is Hedvig his daughter? She answers that she does not know, which goads Hjalmar to prepare to leave the house believing that he has no child. Gregers is alarmed that he will run away rather than face the truth and build a new relationship on it. Hedvig rushes to Hjalmar, but he pushes her away, exclaiming that he cannot bear the sight of her. He dashes through the door, leaving Hedvig in desperation that he will never return. Hedvig supposes that she will die from everything that has happened. Gina exits to search for Hjalmar, leaving Hedvig and Gregers alone.

Gregers is startled when Hedvig suggests that Hjalmar is upset because she is not really his child; then she explains by suggesting that she is a foundling. Gregers turns the talk to the wild duck, suggesting that she could win her father's love by sacrificing the duck for his sake. Hedvig agrees to the deed, planning to do it early on her birthday morning. Gina returns without having found Hjalmar. Gregers leaves; Hedvig falls sobbing into her mother's arms as the curtain falls.

In Act V it is the next morning. Hjalmar still has not returned, but Hedvig has heard that he is at Relling's. Gregers enters, hears this, and is disappointed that Hjalmar went on a binge when he needed solitude in which to ponder his new life. Relling comes in to say that Hjalmar is sleeping peacefully on his couch. Gina and Hedvig exit to do the housecleaning while Relling faces Gregers, who expects that a great spiritual rebirth has taken place.

Relling merely says that Hjalmar's hereditary traits and the environment of his hysterical aunts who reared him made him nothing more than an ineffectual plodder. Gregers hates to hear this opinion because, as Relling rightly thinks, he needs a hero to worship. Relling, as a doctor, has tried to maintain the life-lie, the Kierkegaardian illusion of significance, in the lives of his associates. He has convinced Molvik, for example, that he is demonic and therefore not responsible for his alcoholism. Ekdal has discovered his own life-lie by playing the intrepid hunter in the loft with his caged quarry. For Relling, the maintenance of the life-lie is necessary to happiness, but Gregers vows to get Hjalmar out of his clutches. Hedvig enters as the doctor leaves.

Gregers deduces that Hedvig has not killed the wild duck, which she admits. She thinks that such a sacrifice is not as beautiful as she had imagined on the previous night. He leaves maintaining his faith that she will do what is right.

When Old Ekdal comes into the studio from the loft, Hedvig asks him how he would go about shooting a wild duck. He answers that it should be done in the breast and against the feathers. He then departs.

Hedvig thinks for a moment before going to the bookcase and picking up the loaded pistol. When Gina unexpectedly enters, Hedvig puts down the pistol. The mother sends the girl to the kitchen to check on the coffee.

A bedraggled Hjalmar enters just as Hedvig comes back into the studio. She rushes toward him, but he pushes her away and shouts angrily at her. Gina quietly sends Hedvig from the room.

Hjalmar, it seems, has returned for his books. As he rummages through the table drawer, Gina fetches some food and drink for him. Hjalmar opens the door and sees Hedvig in the living room. He insists that she stay away from him, which reduces the child to tears. As she sees how distraught he is, Hedvig decides to sacrifice the wild duck. She slips in, steals the pistol, and disappears into the loft. Meanwhile, Gina and Hjalmar rush from room to room packing his things. He wants his pistol, but when they discover it is missing, they conclude that Ekdal has it in the loft with him. Hjalmar then starts to eat the food Gina has prepared and considers her suggestion that he might postpone his search for new accommodations for himself and his father. He then sees Werle's torn letter and advises Gina not to lose the pieces as his father may decide to use it. Then he proposes to paste it together himself.

Gregers comes in and asks Hjalmar's plans. When Hjalmar answers that he intends to leave, his friend asks if that is really necessary. There is, after all, his invention to consider. For the first time Hjalmar realizes that Relling had convinced him that he might invent something and that he had maintained the fiction because Hedvig had said she believed in it. His difficulty is that he can no longer believe that Hedvig ever loved him. Gregers suggests that she might give him cogent proof of her love. Soon a shot is heard, which delights Gregers because he sees it as proof of her love of Hjalmar. He then tells Hjalmar that Hedvig had her grandfather shoot the wild duck as a sacrifice. Hjalmar immediately melts toward Hedvig, who cannot be found. Since they have assumed that Old Ekdal fired the pistol in the loft, they are surprised to see him in the doorway of his room. He disclaims having fired a shot. Gregers concludes that Hedvig herself shot the duck.

Hjalmar rushes to the doors to the loft, looks in, and sees Hedvig lying on the floor. Gregers is aghast. Hedvig is dragged into the studio, the pistol still clutched in her hand. Relling is summoned to tend to her; Relling discovers that she has been wounded in the breast and is already dead. Hjalmar is plunged into a frenzy of grief and self-accusation, finally blaming God himself. Gina and Hjalmar carry Hedvig toward her bedroom intending to allow the pistol to remain in her hand. Gina observes that in death, Hedvig belongs to them both. Relling knows that Hedvig was a suicide but is curious as to her motivation. Gregers sees the death as the justification of his philosophy: Gina and Hjalmar are now united by their grief and can start their true marriage. Relling concludes that neither Hjalmar's grief nor his newly found strength will last a year. Gregers answers that life will not be worth living if that be true; nevertheless, he is glad that his destiny is to be the thirteenth man at the table. The curtain falls as Relling tells him to go to hell.

Structural analysis: The line of causal action is quite clear, although some of the symbolism is opaque:

Gregers discovers that his mission is to reveal the truth;

(as a result of which)
Gregers leaves his father's house where truth is a stranger;

(as a result of which)
Gregers discovers that the Ekdals want to let a spare room;

(as a result of which)
Gregers rents the room and starts to associate with the family;

(as a result of which)
Gregers discovers the extent to which the Ekdals' lives are based on lies and deception;

(as a result of which)
Gregers tells Hjalmar the truth about Werle and Ekdal and Gina;

(as a result of which)
Gregers discovers that the truth has not liberated Hjalmar;

(as a result of which)
Gregers convinces Hedvig to sacrifice the wild duck to prove her love of Hjalmar;

(as a result of which)
Gregers discovers that Hedvig has killed herself;

(as a result of which)
Gregers concludes that his mission has been successful because death seems to have reunited Gina and Hjalmar.

Despite the compactness of the plot-line, some important questions remain unanswered: (1) Is it possible that Hedvig inherited her eye problems from her paternal grandmother rather than Werle? (2) Is it possible that Hedvig died by accident rather than suicide? (3) Is suicide part of Gregers' plans for himself as he twice implies? (4) Has this experience taught Gregers anything, or will he merely repeat his actions and ruin another life? Such questions may appear merely academic, but their answers are quite germane to the performances of actors in these roles.

References: Reinart, O. "Sight Imagery in *The Wild Duck*," *Journal of English and Germanic Philology,* LV (1956), 457-62; Watts, C. T. "The Unseen Catastrophe in Ibsen's *Vildanden*," *Scandinavia,* XII (1973), 137-41.

WILDER, THORNTON (1897-1975): When actress Ruth Gordon* asked dramatist Thornton Wilder to adapt *A Doll's House** in response to his advice that she should appear in a classic play, he refused. When she later told him that Noël Coward, S. N. Behrman, and Lillian Hellman refused her as well and that producer Jed Harris had insisted on a contemporary adaptation before he would consider mounting a production, Wilder laid aside his current work, *Our Town,* and turned to Ibsen.

Wilder made minimal alterations to Ibsen's text, consisting mostly of the elimination of Victorianisms and uncolloquial diction. His version was tried out at the Central City (Colorado) Drama Festival before it was put into Gordon's hand in 1937, when it lasted 144 performances and became one of history's longest running Ibsenian productions.

References: Gordon, Ruth. *Myself Among Others.* New York: Dell Publishing Company, 1972; Haberman, Donald. *The Plays of Thornton Wilder: A Critical Study.* Middletown, Conn.: Wesleyan University Press, 1967.

WILLIAM, WARREN (1894-1948): Warren William supported Margaret Wycherly* in *Rosmersholm** in New York in 1925 and Blanche Yurka* in *The Vikings in Helgeland** in 1930.

Reference: Who Was Who in the Theatre, IV, 2575.

WILLIAMS, EMLYN (1905-): Welsh actor Emlyn Williams appeared as Hjalmar Ekdal* in a production of *The Wild Duck** in London in 1955 and published a version of *The Master Builder** in 1967.

Reference: Who's Who in the Theatre, 11th ed., pp. 1462-3.

WILSON, WILLIAM: English translator of *Brand** (1891, 1894, 1906).

WILTON, MRS. FANNY (*John Gabriel Borkman*): Fanny Wilton is an American widow, wealthy and fun-loving. She takes Erhart Borkman* out of the cloying environment of his mother's house.

WINTER-HJELM, HEDVIG CHARLOTTE (b. 1838): In her youth Swedish actress Charlotte Winter-Hjelm played a number of Ibsen's women, including Lady Inger of Gyldenlöve.* She was persuaded to come out of retirement to play Helene Alving* in August Lindberg's* production of *Ghosts** in 1883.

WOLF, LUCIE (1833-1902): Norwegian actress Lucie Wolf worked with Ibsen in both Bergen* and Christiania.* She was the recipient of correspondence from him, and in 1898 Wolf wrote of Ibsen in her reminiscences.

Reference: Wolf, Lucie. *Mine livserindringer* [*My Reminiscences*]. Christiania: A. Cammermeyer, 1898.

WOLF, NICHOLAI BRATSBERG (1824-75): Nicholai Wolf played Nikolas Arnesson, Bishop of Oslo* when *The Pretenders** was presented in Christiania* in 1864.

Reference: *Dansk Biografisk Leksikon*, XXVI, 234.

WOLFIT, DONALD (1902-68): While at the Sheffield Repertory Theatre in 1927, Donald Wolfit, still a supporting player in provincial companies, played Torvald Helmer* and Jörgen Tesman.* By the time he attempted Halvard Solness* in *The Master Builder** for the Croyden Repertory Theatre (1931), he was a leading actor; in 1933 he repeated the same role in London. Solness remained one of Wolfit's favorite parts, one to which he returned in April 1943 and May 1948 (London), 1955 (Salisbury), and 1963 (South Africa).

In the meantime Wolfit introduced the seldom-performed *Catiline** at the Croyden Repertory on January 27, 1936. He had met Norwegian director Stein Bugge, who convinced Baxter Summerville, head of the Croyden group, to produce the play with Wolfit in the leading role. During *Catiline*'s brief run in Croyden, a metropolitan producer saw the production and offered to present it at London's Royalty Theatre. This event marked Wolfit's emergence as a star in London. Critics received the production warmly, seeing in Catiline* an embryonic Peer Gynt.*

During World War II, Wolfit was indefatigable in bringing theatre to a bomb-beleaguered capital. One of his most notable achievements was his wartime production of *The Master Builder*. As Wolfit said, "By now I had the measure of Solness and saw reasonably well where Ibsen left the earth plane and soared into the realm of metaphysics and out into the spiritual world" (Wolfit, p. 216). Wolfit's biographer speculates that the actor's great success with Solness emanated from his realization of the parallels between his life and that of Solness.

In 1959 Wolfit had the opportunity to play a role especially suited to his talents, Pastor Manders* in the Old Vic production of *Ghosts,** with Flora Robson* as Helene Alving.* On December 4, 1963, he opened at the Duchess Theatre in the title role of *John Gabriel Borkman.**

References: Harwood, Ronald. *Sir Donald Wolfit: His Life and Work in the Unfashionable Theatre.* New York: St. Martin's Press, 1971; Wolfit, Donald. *First Interval.* London: Odhams Press, 1954.

WOLTER, CHARLOTTE (1834-97): When *The Vikings in Helgeland** was produced in Vienna in 1876, Charlotte Wolter played Hjördis.*
Reference: Brockhaus Enzyklopaedie (Wiesbaden, 1974), XX, 478.

WOLZOGEN, ALFRED VON (1823-83): Theatre artist, dramatist, and biographer Alfred von Wolzogen translated *Brand** into German in 1876.
Reference: Wolzogen, Hans Paul von. *Karl August Alfred von Wolzogen.* Berlin: Rostock und Ludwigslust, 1883.

WOMAN AS THE SERVANT OF SOCIETY: The book read by Doctor Rörlund* while the ladies of *The Pillars of Society** did their charitable sewing.

WOMAN FROM THE HEADLAND (*Brand*): When this woman runs into Gudbrandsdalen* with a frantic plea for help for her dying husband, Brand* braves a storm and goes to him, a deed that commends him to the people.

WORTH, IRENE (1916-): Irene Worth's services to Ibsen occurred in three countries. Her Hedda Gabler* was seen in Stratford, Ontario, in June 1970; her Helene Alving,* in London in January 1974; and her Ella Rentheim,* in New York in December 1980. Of this last performance, Clive Barnes wrote that Worth's Ella moved "like a tortured black swan."
References: New York Theatre Critics' Reviews, XLI, 21 (Dec. 31, 1980), 60; *Who's Who in the Theatre,* 16th ed., pp. 1272-3.

WRIGHT, ALICE AUSTIN (d. 1922): Alice Austin, better known as Mrs. Theodore Wright, retired from the stage after her marriage but was persuaded to appear as Helene Alving* in the Independent Theatre Society's* production of *Ghosts** (March 1891). This performance brought her a degree of prominence, and Mrs. Wright had the opportunity to repeat the role in 1897. Thereafter she acted in a number of Realistic plays, as she came to be identified with the "modern" movement. In April 1909 she appeared at His Majesty's Theatre as Katherine Stockmann* in *An Enemy of the People.**
Reference: Who Was Who in the Theatre, IV, 2632.

WYCHERLY, MARGARET (1884-1956): Actress Margaret Wycherly had two adventures in the world of Ibsen's plays: Rebecca West* in 1925 and Juliane Tesman* in 1942.
Reference: Who Was Who in the Theatre, IV, 2634-5.

Y

YAVORSKA, LYDIA (1874-1921): In her native Russia, Lydia Yavorska ran her own theatre in St. Petersburg, where she played Nora Helmer,* Hedda Gabler,* Rebecca West,* and Ellida Wangel.* Emigrating to London in 1909, Yavorska appeared as Hedda at His Majesty's Theatre on February 14, 1911, and again as Hedda at the Kingsway Theatre on May 27, 1911. Her performances were marked by an oriental exoticism, yet she was among the most successful alien interpreters of Ibsen on the English stage, largely because she spoke English rather well and surrounded herself with competent companies. Some critics dismissed Yavorska's Hedda as overly dramatic, but her feverish passion and energetic movements as Nora caused a sensation (*The Academy*, March 11, June 3, 1911).
Reference: *Who Was Who in the Theatre*, IV, 2651-2.

YURKA, BLANCHE (1887-1974): Although Ibsen's reputation as a major dramatist was established before Yurka discovered him, her exertions helped to prove the commercial viability of his works. As one of the directors of the Actors' Theatre, Yurka proposed a production of *The Wild Duck*,* which subsequently opened on February 24, 1925, under the joint direction of Dudley Digges* and Clara Eames.* As Gina Ekdal,* Yurka deviated markedly from the standard interpretations of the role. Rather than a stumbling, ignorant housewife, Yurka's Gina was "a queenly humble person, comely in appearance and often elegant in manner. She is majestic and well-dressed, to a degree, sane, practical, sympathetic and dominant." Audiences and critics responded so warmly to the production that it ran for 103 performances, and Gina remained among Yurka's favorite roles. She played it again in New York on November 18, 1928, and May 6, 1929.

Hedda Gabler* was Yurka's next Ibsenian role, a character whose evil grows slowly rather than being obvious at first. A piece of stage business in Act III was particularly apt. Ejlert Lövborg* tells Hedda that he has lost his precious manuscript, and as he grows increasingly hysterical, Hedda stretches her hand out toward a wooden box on a nearby table in which she has placed the book. Smiling condescendingly, she seems on the verge of restoring the manuscript to the wretched man, but when he says, "Thea's pure soul was in that book," Hedda lets the lid of the box fall. Critic John Anderson noted that the sound "was like the closing of a coffin lid." This production, which opened on February 2, 1929, lasted twenty-five performances, and during its run, Yurka started work on Ellida Wangel.*

Yurka saw *The Lady from the Sea** in terms of pre-Freudian psycho-analysis of sexual frustration and suppressed desire; yet, to her own satisfaction, she was never able to make the last act credible, believing Ellida's decision to be improbable. The production opened on March 18, 1929, and ran for twenty-four performances, after which Yurka toured with *The Wild Duck* and *The Lady from the Sea*. A young actress named Bette Davis was hired to play Hedvig Ekdal* on tour.

Although she excelled in portraying Realistic characters, Yurka adventurously appeared in dramas such as *Hamlet* and *Electra*. Hence, her decision to play Hjördis* in *The Vikings in Helgeland** was fully in character. Staged at the New Yorker Theatre, *The Vikings* lasted eight performances, equaling the run of Ellen Terry's* production.

References: Who Was Who in the Theatre, IV, 2657-9; Yurka, Blanche. *Bohemian Girl: Blanche Yurka's Theatrical Life.* Athens: Ohio University Press, 1970.

Z

ZAPOLSKA, GABRIELA (1857-1921): Polish actress Gabriela Zapolska portrayed Nora Helmer* in the year of its appearance (1879). Ibsen's heroines remained in her repertory throughout her career. As a member of the Posen Theatre, Zapolska acted Nora on January 25, 1883, in St. Petersburg, perhaps the first performance of *A Doll's House** in Russia. After becoming a member of the troupe at Warsaw's Imperial Theatre, Zapolska revived her Nora occasionally (September 27, 1887; April 13-16, 1889). In 1896 she journeyed to Paris to act the Rat-Wife* in Aurélien-Marie Lugné-Poë's* production of *Little Eyolf,** which commenced on May 8. A confirmed Naturalist, Zapolska frequently wrote and spoke against the evils of modern industrial society.
Reference: Great Soviet Encyclopedia, 3d ed. (New York: Macmillan, 1976), IX, 583.

ZETTERLING, MAI (1925-): As an apprentice at Sweden's Royal Theatre, Mai Zetterling encountered Ibsen's dramas; during her tenure as a full member of that company (1942-47), Ibsen's works were periodically revived. Her debut on the London stage was as Hedvig Ekdal* in *The Wild Duck,** which opened on November 3, 1948, with Anton Walbrook* and Fay Compton* in the principal roles. A few years later, on September 18, 1953, she began a brief engagement as Nora Helmer* at the Lyric Theatre, Hammersmith (London).
Reference: Who's Who in the Theatre, 11th ed., p. 1499.

Appendix: Early Translators of Ibsen's Works

ENGLISH TRANSLATORS

THE FEAST AT SOLHAUG
   William Archer* and Mary Morison* (1906)
THE VIKINGS IN HELGELAND
   William Archer* (1890)
   Robert Farquharson Sharp* (1911)
LOVE'S COMEDY
   Charles Harold Herford* (1900, 1912)
   Robert Farquharson Sharp* (1915)
THE PRETENDERS
   William Archer* (1890, 1913)
   Robert Farquharson Sharp* (1913)
BRAND
   William Wilson* (1891, 1904, 1906)
   Fydell Edmund Garrett* (1894)
   Charles Harold Herford* (1894, 1901)
   J. M. Olberman (1912)
PEER GYNT
   William Archer* and Charles Archer* (1892, 1907)
   Fydell Edmund Garrett* (1904)
   Isabelle M. Pagan (1909)
   Richard Ellis Roberts* (1912)
THE LEAGUE OF YOUTH
   William Archer* (1890, 1901)
   Henry Carstarphen (1900)
   Robert Farquharson Sharp* (1915)
EMPEROR AND GALILEAN
   Catherine Ray* (1876)
   William Archer* (1890)
THE PILLARS OF SOCIETY
   William Archer* (1888, 1890, 1900)

Robert Farquharson Sharp* (1913)

A DOLL'S HOUSE
T. Weber* (1880)
Henrietta Frances Lord* (1882, 1889, 1890, 1893)
William Moore Lawrence* (1882)
Marion Booth Douglas* (1882)
Karol Bozenta Chlapowski* and Louise Everson (1883)
Henry Arthur Jones* and Henry Herman (1885)
William Archer* (1889, 1892, 1897, 1900, 1914)
Henry L. Mencken* (1909)

GHOSTS
Henrietta Frances Lord* (1885, 1888, 1890, 1891)
William Archer* (1890, 1891, 1897, 1900)
Robert Farquharson Sharp* (1911)

AN ENEMY OF THE PEOPLE
William Archer* (1890, 1902)
Eleanor Marx* (1890, 1898, 1914)
Robert Farquharson Sharp* (1911)

THE WILD DUCK
Frances Elizabeth Archer* (1890, 1897)
Eleanor Marx* (1900)

ROSMERSHOLM
Louis Napoleon Parker* (1889)
Charles Archer* (1891, 1906)
M. Carmichael (1900)
Robert Farquharson Sharp* (1913)

THE LADY FROM THE SEA
Clara Bell (1890, 1900)
Eleanor Marx* (1890, 1891)
Frances Elizabeth Archer* (1891, 1897)

HEDDA GABLER
William Archer* (1891)
Edmund William Gosse* (1891, 1901, 1903, 1912)

THE MASTER BUILDER
John William Arctander* (1893)
Wiliam Archer* and Edmund William Gosse* (1893, 1895, 1900, 1901)

LITTLE EYOLF
William Archer* (1897, 1905)
Henry L. Mencken* (1909)

JOHN GABRIEL BORKMAN
William Archer* (1897, 1906)

WHEN WE DEAD AWAKEN
William Archer* (1900, 1906)

EUROPEAN TRANSLATORS

CATILINE
Russian: A. and P. Ganzen (1906)

French: Ludovic de Colleville* and Fritz Zépelin* (1902, 1903, 1908)
German: Hugo Greinz*

LADY INGER OF ÖSTRAAT

French: Ludovic de Colleville* and Fritz Zépelin* (1902, 1903)
Italian: Paolo Rindler and Enrico Minneci (1900)
Spanish: Pedro Pellicena (n.d.)
German: Emma Klingenfeld (1877); Maria von Borch (1891); Wilhelm Lange (1906)
Finnish: Joel Lehtonen (1919)

THE FEAST AT SOLHAUG

Swedish: Hjalmar Procopé (1916)
French: Ludovic de Colleville* and Fritz Zépelin (1903)
German: Emma Klingenfeld (1888)

OLAF LILJEKRANS

French: Ludovic de Colleville* and Fritz Zépelin (1903)

THE VIKINGS IN HELGELAND

Swedish: William Aabjörnson (1876)
Italian: Paolo Rindler (1900)
German: Emma Klingenfeld (1876, 1910); Maria von Borch (1890)
Finnish: Edvard Törmanen (1878)

LOVE'S COMEDY

Russian: A. and P. Ganzen (1904)
Swedish: Harold Molander (1888)
French: Ludovic de Colleville* and Fritz Zépelin (1896, 1903)
Dutch: J. Clant van der Mijll-Piepers (1908)
German: Maria von Borch (1889); Phillip Schweitzer (1890)
Finnish: Aarni Kouta (1905)

THE PRETENDERS

Russian: A. and P. Ganzen (1904)
French: Jacques Trigant-Geneste (1893, 1902)
Dutch: Marg. Meijboom (1910)
Italian: A. G. Amato (1895)
German: Adolf Strodtmann* (1872, 1889); Maria von Borch (1890)
Czechoslovakian: Jaroslav Vrchlicky (189?)
Finnish: Eliel Aspelin (1884)

BRAND

Swedish: M. H. Elmblad (1870); Sigrid Elmblad (1920)
French: Moritz Prozor* (1903, 1907, 1911)
Italian: Tyra Kleen and Arnaldo Cervesato (1910)
Spanish: Pedro Pellicena (1903)
German: P. F. Siebold* (1872, 1880); Julie Ruhkopf (1874, 1885); Alfred von
    Wolzogen* (1877); Ludwig Passarge* (1882)
Dutch: R. van Drooge (1893); W.J.W. van Groningen (1904); J. Clant van der
    Mijll-Piepers (1908, 1915)
Finnish: Kasimir Leino (1896)

PEER GYNT

Russian: A. and P. Ganzen (1905)
French: Moritz Prozor* (1899, 1903, 1907, 1912)
Italian: B. Villamova d'Ardenghi (1909)

German: Ludwig Passarge* (1881, 1887); Ludwig Fulda (1916); Dietrich Eckhardt
   (1917)
Dutch: J. Clant van der Mijll-Piepers (1908)
Finnish: O. Manninen (1911, 1916)
Polish: Marya Kreczowska (1910)
THE LEAGUE OF YOUTH
Russian: A. and P. Ganzen (1905)
French: Pierre Bertrand (1893)
Spanish: A. Palau y Dulcet (1903)
Italian: Maria G. Savina* (1894)
German: Adolf Strodtmann* (1872, 1890), Wilhelm Lange (1881)
Czechoslovakian: Alois Lucek (1891)
EMPEROR AND GALILEAN
French: Christian de Bigault de Casanove (1895, 1902)
Spanish: Eusebio Heras (1903)
Italian: Mario Buzzi (1902)
German: Paul Herrmann* (1888); Ernst Brausewetter* (1888)
THE PILLARS OF SOCIETY
French: Pierre Bertrand and Edmond de Nevers (1893, 1902)
Spanish: José Farran y Mayoral (1903)
Italian: Paolo Rindler and E. P. Santarnecchi (1892); Bice Savini (1897)
German: Wilhelm Lange (1878, 1907); Emil J. Jonas (1878); Emma Klingenfeld
   (1878, 1890); Christian Morgenstern* (1891); Helmine Fick (1897)
Dutch: F. Kapteijn (1893, 1905); J. Clant van der Mijll-Piepers (1906)
Finnish: Joel Lehtonen (1916)
A DOLL'S HOUSE
Russian: P. V. Garvina (1883)
French: Albert Savine (1906)
Spanish: Ludwig Passarge* (1894)
Italian: Luigi Capuana* (1892); Pietro Galletti (1894, 1906)
German: Wilhelm Lange (1880, 1907); Maria von Borch (1890); Charles Kirschen-
   stein (1891); J. Engeroff (1892); Marie Lie (1904)
Dutch: S. J. Warren (1887); Henrica Tweede (1893); Marg. Meijboom (1908)
Polish: Cyryla Danielewskiego (1882)
Finnish: Maila Tallvio (1913)
GHOSTS
Russian: N. Limonova (1891)
French: Moritz Prozor* (1888, 1889, 1892, 1896, 1904, 1906, 1908, 1912);
   Rodolphe Darzens* (1890, 1903)
Spanish: Pompeyo Gener (1903); Antonio de Vilasalba (1904); A. Lopez White (1903)
Italian: Paolo Rindler and E. P. Santarnecchi (1892)
German: Maria von Borch (1890); Fritz Albert (1890); Christian Morgenstern*
   (1893); Wilhelm Lange (1899, 1906)
Dutch: J. Clant van der Mijll-Piepers (1906)
Czechoslovakian: Alois Lucek (1891)
Bulgarian: A. Jaranov and S. M. Kotljarevski (1902)
AN ENEMY OF THE PEOPLE
Russian: N. Nirovich (1891); Jurij Kmit (1899)

French: Moritz Prozor* (1905, 1913); Chenevière and Johansen (1893)

Spanish: C. Costa and J. M. Jorda (1903)

German: Wilhelm Lange (1883, 1907, 1913); Maria von Borch (1890); Josef Calasanz Poestion* (1891); Christian Morgenstern* (1891)

THE WILD DUCK

French: Moritz Prozor* (1891, 1893, 1900, 1907, 1909); Albert Savine (1908)

Spanish: Manuel M. Blanquè y Puig (1903)

Italian: Paolo Rindler and E. P. Santarnecchi (1894, 1900)

German: Ernst Brausewetter* (1887); Maria von Borch (1887, 1889); J. Engeroff (1894); Wilhelm Lange (1907)

ROSMERSHOLM

Russian: A. and P. Ganzen (1904)

Spanish: A. de Vilasalba (1905)

Italian: Paolo Rindler and E. P. Santarnecchi (1894, 1898)

German: A. Zinck (1887): Maria von Borch (1887, 1890); Ernst Brausewetter* (1890); J. Engeroff (1893); Wilhelm Lange (1899, 1906)

Dutch: E. Kapteijn (1892)

Czechoslovakian: Karel Kucera (1898)

THE LADY FROM THE SEA

Russian: E. E. Matterna and A. P. Vorotnikova (1901)

French: Moritz Prozor* (1908); Chenevière and Johansen (1892, 1899, 1905)

Spanish: A. de Vilasalba (1904)

Italian: Paolo Rindler and E. P. Santarnecchi (1894, 1906)

German: Maria von Borch (1889); Julius Hoffory* (1889); Fritz Schulze (1894); Wilhelm Lange (1907)

Finnish: Yrjö Koskelainen (1910)

HEDDA GABLER

Russian: S. L. Stepanovoj (1891)

French: Moritz Prozor* (1891, 1892, 1900, 1909)

Spanish: C. Costa and J. M. Jorda (1903)

Italian: Paolo Rindler and E. P. Santarnecchi (1893, 1899)

German: Maria von Borch (1891); Victor Ottmann (1891); Emma Klingenfeld (1891, 1900); Wilhelm Lange (1906)

THE MASTER BUILDER

Russian: P. Ganzena (1893, 1904)

French: Moritz Prozor* (1893, 1895, 1899, 1909)

Italian: Paolo Rindler and E. P. Santarnecchi (1893, 1898)

German: Sigurd Ibsen* (1893); Victor Ottmann (1893); Paul Herrmann* (1893); Wilhelm Lange (1907)

Czechoslovakian: Karel Kucera (1905)

Finnish: Joel Lehtonen (1918)

Polish: Jan Sliwon (n.d.)

LITTLE EYOLF

French: Moritz Prozor* (1895, 1908)

Spanish: José Farran y Mayoral (1905)

Italian: Ernesto Gagliardi (1897)

Finnish: Teuvo Pakkala (1895)

Rumanian: T. Maiorescu (1895)

JOHN GABRIEL BORKMAN
  French: Moritz Prozor* (1897, 1903)
  Italian: Mario Buzzi (1900)
  Dutch: J. H. Rössing (1897)
WHEN WE DEAD AWAKEN
  Russian: Ju. Baltrusajtisa and S. Poljakova (1900); A. and P. Ganzen (1904);
    Ant. Kruselnecky (1900)
  French: Moritz Prozor* (1900, 1909)

Selected Bibliography

Editions of Ibsen's Works

The Collected Works of Henrik Ibsen, 12 vols. Ed. William Archer. London: William Heinemann, 1906-12.

The Oxford Ibsen, 8 vols. Eds. James McFarlane and Graham Orton. London: Oxford University Press, 1960-70.

Samlede Verker: Hundreaarsutgave, 21 vols. Eds. Francis Bull, Halvdan Koht, and Didrik Arup Seip. Oslo: Gyldendal, 1928-57.

Speeches and Letters

Breve fra Henrik Ibsen. Eds. Halvdan Koht and Julius Elias. Copenhagen: Gyldendal, 1904.

The Correspondence of Henrik Ibsen. Ed. Mary Morison. London: Hodder and Stoughton, 1905.

Ibsen: Letters and Speeches. Ed. Evert Sprinchorn. New York: Hill and Wang, 1964.

Bibliographies

Breed, Paul F. and Florence M. Sniderman. *Dramatic Criticism Index*. Detroit: Gale Research Corporation, 1972.

Firkins, Ina T.E. *Henrik Ibsen: A Bibliography of Criticism and Biography*. New York: H. W. Wilson Company, 1921.

Palmer, Helen H. *European Drama Criticism, 1900-1975*, 2d. ed. Hamden, Conn.: Shoe String Press, 1977.

Tedford, Ingrid. *Ibsen Bibliography, 1928-1951*. Oslo: Oslo University Press, 1961.

Biographies

Bull, Francis. *Ibsen: The Man and the Dramatist*. Oxford: Clarendon Press, 1954.

Gosse, Edmund. *Ibsen*. London: Hodder and Stoughton, 1907.

Heiberg, Hans. *Ibsen: A Portrait of the Artist*. Trans. Joan Tate. Coral Gables, Fla.: University of Miami Press, 1969.

Ibsen, Bergliot. *The Three Ibsens: Memories of Henrik, Suzannah and Sigurd Ibsen*. Trans. G. Schjelderup. London: Hutchinson, 1951.

Jaeger, Henrik. *Henrik Ibsen: A Critical Biography*, 2d ed. Trans. William M. Payne. Chicago: A. C. McClurg, 1901.

Jorgenson, Theodore. *Henrik Ibsen: A Study in Art and Personality*. Northfield, Minn.: St. Olaf College Press, 1945.

Koht, Halvdan. *The Life of Ibsen*. Trans. Clara Bell. London: William Heinemann, 1890.

Meyer, Michael. *Henrik Ibsen: The Making of a Dramatist, 1828-1864*. London: Rupert Hart-Davis, 1967.

_____. *Ibsen: A Biography*. Garden City, N.Y.: Doubleday, 1971.

Moses, Montrose J. *Henrik Ibsen: The Man and His Plays*. New York: M. Kennedy, 1908.

Criticism

Anderson, Rasmus B. "Henrik Ibsen," *American*, IV (Apr. 15, 1882), 8-9.

Anstensen, Ansten. *The Proverb in Ibsen*. New York: Columbia University Press, 1936.

Balmforth, Ramsden. *The Problem Play and Its Influence on Modern Thought and Life*. New York: Henry Holt, 1928.

Bermel, Albert. *Contradictory Characters: An Interpretation of Modern Drama*. New York: E. P. Dutton, 1973.

Boyesen, Hjalmar H. *A Commentary on the Works of Henrik Ibsen*. London: William Heinemann, 1894.

Bradbrook, Muriel C. *Ibsen, the Norwegian: A Reevaluation*. London: Chatto and Windus, 1946.

Brandes, Georg. *Eminent Authors of the Nineteenth Century*. New York: Crowell, 1886.

Contemporary Approaches to Ibsen. Eds. Harald Noreng, et al. Oslo: Universitetsforlaget, 1977.

Doumic, René. *De Scribe à Ibsen: Causeries sur le Théâtre Contemporain*. Paris: Perrin, 1896.

Downs, Brian W. *Ibsen: The Intellectual Background*. Cambridge: Cambridge University Press, 1946.

_____. *A Study of Six Plays by Ibsen*. Cambridge: Cambridge University Press, 1950.

Fjelde, Rolf, ed. *Ibsen: A Collection of Critical Essays.* Englewood Cliffs, N.J.: Prentice-Hall, 1965.

Freedman, Morris. *The Moral Impulse: Modern Drama from Ibsen to the Present.* Carbondale: Southern Illinois University Press, 1967.

Gaskell, Ronald. *Drama and Reality: The European Theatre since Ibsen.* London: Routledge and Kegan Paul, 1972.

George, David E. R. *Henrik Ibsen in Deutschland.* Goettingen: Vandenhoeck and Ruprecht, 1968.

Grene, David. *Reality and the Heroic Pattern: Last Plays of Ibsen, Shakespeare, and Sophocles.* Chicago: University of Chicago Press, 1967.

Heller, Otto. *Henrik Ibsen: Plays and Problems.* New York: Houghton and Mifflin, 1912.

Holtan, Orley I. *Mythic Patterns in Ibsen's Last Plays.* Minneapolis: University of Minnesota Press, 1970.

Hornby, Richard. *Patterns in Ibsen's Middle Plays.* Lewisburg, Penn.: Bucknell University Press, 1981.

Hurt, James. *Catiline's Dream: An Essay on Ibsen's Plays.* Urbana: University of Illinois Press, 1972.

Knight, G. Wilson. *Ibsen.* London: Oliver and Boyd, 1962.

Lee, Jeanette. *The Ibsen Secret: A Key to the Prose Dramas of Henrik Ibsen.* New York: G. P. Putnam, 1907.

Lyons, Charles R. *Henrik Ibsen: The Divided Consciousness.* Carbondale: Southern Illinois University Press, 1972.

McFarlane, James, ed. *Discussions of Henrik Ibsen.* Boston: D. C. Heath, 1962.

Northam, John. *Ibsen: A Critical Study.* Cambridge: Cambridge University Press, 1973.

Serum, Robert W. "The Evolution of the Chorus in the Plays of Henrik Ibsen." Unpublished doctoral dissertation, University of Alabama, 1975.

Setterquist, Jan. *Ibsen and the Beginnings of Anglo-Irish Drama.* 2 vols. Cambridge: Harvard University Press, 1951-60.

Shatzky, Joel. "Heredity as Metaphor in Ibsen's Plays," *Edda,* 74, 4 (1974), 227-34.

Tennant, P.F.D. *Ibsen's Dramatic Technique.* Cambridge: Cambridge University Press, 1948.

Thune, Ensaf Z. "Main Currents of Ibsen Interpretation in England and America." Unpublished doctoral dissertaton, University of Washington, 1962.

Twetley, A. Corine. "Ibsen the Playwright: A Study of His Theatrical Apprenticeship and the Influence on the Construction of His Plays." Unpublished doctoral dissertation, Yale University, 1945.

Williams, Raymond. *Drama from Ibsen to Brecht.* New York: Oxford University Press, 1968.

_____. *Modern Tragedy.* Stanford, Calif.: Stanford University Press, 1966.

Theatrical Works

Anker, Öyvind. *Christiania Theaters Repertoire, 1827-1899.* Oslo: Gyldendal, 1956.

Bahr, Hermann. *Wiener Theater, 1892-1898.* Berlin: S. Fischer, 1899.

Bull, Marie. *Minder fra Bergens förste nationale scene.* Bergen: n.p., 1905.

Robins, Elizabeth. *Ibsen and the Actress.* London: Hogarth Press, 1928.

Wagner, Hans. *200 Jahre Münchner Theaterchronik, 1750-1950.* München: Robert Lerche, 1958.

Wais, Kurt K. *Henrik Ibsens Wirkung in Spanien, Frankreich, Italien.* Braunschweig: Georg Westermann, 1933.

Wisener, A.M. *Henrik Ibsen og det Norske Theater i Bergen, 1851-1857.* Bergen: n.p., 1928.

Biography: General and Theatrical

Dansk Biografisk Leksikon, 19 vols. Köbenhavn: Gyldendal, 1934.

Eisenberg, Ludwig J. *Grosses biographisches Lexikon der deutschen Bühne im XIX. Jahrhundert.* Leipzig: Paul List, 1903.

Enciclopedia della Spettacolo, 10 vols. Roma: Casa Editrice le Maschere, 1954-1966.

Kosch, Wilhelm. *Deutsches Theater-Lexikon,* Vol. I. Klagenfurt: Ferd. Kleinmayr, 1953.

Nordensvan, Georg. *Svensk teater och svenska skaadespelare,* 2 vols. Stockholm: Bonniers, 1918.

Norsk Biografisk Leksikon, 12 vols. Oslo: Aschehoug, 1923.

Who's Who in the Theatre. 2 vols. Ed. Ian Herbert, et al. 17th ed. Detroit: Gale Research Company, 1981.

Who's Who in the Theatre: A Biographical Record of the Contemporary Stage. Ed. John Parker. 11th ed. London: Pitman, 1952.

Who's Who in the Theatre: A Biographical Record of the Contemporary Stage. Ed. Ian Herbert. 16th ed. London: Pitman, 1977.

Who Was Who in the Theatre, 1912-1976, 4 vols. Detroit: Gale Research Corporation, 1978.

Ibsen's Works on the Stage

Andersen, Annette. "Ibsen in America," *Scandinavian Studies and Notes,* XIV, 5 (Feb. 1937), 65-109; XIV, 6 (May 1937), 115-55.

Arestad, Sverre. "Ibsen in Seattle," *Norwegian-American Studies,* XXV (1972), 167-85.

Dannenburg, Joseph P. "Playing Ibsen in the Badlands," *Theatre,* VI (Aug. 1906), 219-21.

Egan, Michael, ed. *Ibsen: The Critical Heritage.* London: Routledge and Kegan Paul, 1972.

Eller, William H. *Ibsen and Germany, 1870-1900.* Boston: Richard G. Badger, 1918.

Franc, Miriam A. *Ibsen in England.* Boston: Four Seas Company, 1919.

Gregersen, Halfdan. *Ibsen and Spain: A Study in Comparative Drama.* Cambridge: Harvard University Press, 1936.

Krog, Erik. "Ibsen i Russland," *Edda,* 28 (1928), 72-95.

Lundeberg, Olav K. "Ibsen in France: A Study of the Ibsen Drama, Its Introduction, Vogue, and Influence on the French Stage," *Scandinavian Studies,* VIII (1924), 93-107.

Marker, Frederick J., and Lise-Lone Marker. *Edward Gordon Craig and The Pretenders, A Production Revisited.* Carbondale: Southern Illinois University Press, 1981.

Meuleman, B. A. *Ibsen en Nederland.* The Hague: n.p., 1931.

Nilsson, Nils A. *Ibsen in Russland.* Stockholm: Almqvist and Wiksell, 1958.

Pasche, Wolfgang. *Scandinavische Dramatik in Deutschland.* Basel: Helbing und Lichtenhahn, 1979.

Paulus, Gretchen. "Ibsen and the English Stage, 1889-1903." Unpublished doctoral dissertation, Radcliffe College, 1959.

Soller, Larry Steven. "Critical Reactions to Productions of Henrik Ibsen's *A Doll's House* on the New York Stage." Unpublished doctoral dissertation, University of Georgia, 1973.

Stein, Philipp. *Henrik Ibsen, zur Bühnengeschichte seiner Dichtungen.* Berlin: Otto Elsner, 1901.

Index

Names of characters in Ibsen's plays are followed by the name of the play in parenthesis. Titles of Ibsen's plays appear in italics in all capital letters. Entries appear on pages listed in italics.

428

About the Author

GEORGE B. BRYAN is Associate Professor of Theatre at the University of Vermont. His earlier works include *Ethelwold and Medieval Music-Drama at Winchester* and contributions to *American Theatrical Companies: A Historical Encyclopedia* (forthcoming from Greenwood Press), *Theatre Survey*, *Educational Theatre Journal*, *Shakespeare Survey*, and *New England Quarterly*.